OXFORD DATA PROTECTION AND PRIVACY LAW

Series Editors

CHRISTOPHER KUNER

Affiliated Professor of Law, University of Copenhagen

GRAHAM GREENLEAF

Professor of Law and Information Systems, University of New South Wales

Governing Cross-Border Data Flows

OXFORD DATA PROTECTION AND PRIVACY LAW

Series Editors

Christopher Kuner, Affiliated Professor of Law, University of Copenhagen
Graham Greenleaf, Professor of Law and Information Systems, University of New South Wales

The aim of this series is to publish important and original books on legal issues of data protection and privacy. This includes many different areas of law, including comparative law, EU law, human rights law, international law, privacy on the Internet, and others.

Prospective authors are welcome to submit proposals for the series, as outlined on the series website: global.oup.com/academic/content/series/o/oxford-data-protection-and-privacy-law-odppl/

Governing Cross-Border Data Flows

Reconciling EU Data Protection and International Trade Law

SVETLANA YAKOVLEVA

OXFORD
UNIVERSITY PRESS

OXFORD
UNIVERSITY PRESS

Great Clarendon Street, Oxford, OX2 6DP,
United Kingdom

Oxford University Press is a department of the University of Oxford.
It furthers the University's objective of excellence in research, scholarship,
and education by publishing worldwide. Oxford is a registered trade mark of
Oxford University Press in the UK and in certain other countries

Published in the United States of America by Oxford University Press
198 Madison Avenue, New York, NY 10016, United States of America

British Library Cataloguing in Publication Data
Data available

Library of Congress Control Number: 2023948328

ISBN 978–0–19–289924–8

DOI: 10.1093/oso/9780192899248.001.0001

Printed and bound by
CPI Group (UK) Ltd, Croydon, CR0 4YY

Acknowledgements

This book would not have come into existence if it was not for my partner Daniel Gervais, to whom I am deeply indebted for his patience, constant support, and encouragement. My sincere gratitude also goes to my parents for always being there for me, for their unconditional love and support throughout yet another research project of mine. Without their support this book would never have been possible.

I wrote this book on the basis on a PhD thesis produced under the supervision of Professors Joris van Hoboken and Ingo Venzke and defended *cum laude* at the University of Amsterdam on 21 April 2021. I am grateful to my PhD supervisors for their time and effort in guiding me along my PhD journey, for their mentorship and encouragement to publish the thesis as a monograph. I am also thankful to the members of my PhD committee (in alphabetical order, Christina Eckes, Mireille van Eechoud, Kristina Irion, Christopher Kuner, Jürgen Kurtz, and Geraldo Vidigal), whose helpful questions, comments, and suggestions helped me develop my PhD thesis into this book. I am especially grateful to Christopher Kuner, whose work inspired me back in 2015 to start working on cross-border data transfers, for his advice and thorough and insightful comments on my PhD thesis.

This book is a result of work on the topic since 2015. Several working papers, articles, and conference presentations paved the way to what this book has become. In addition to my PhD supervisors Joris van Hoboken and Info Venzke, I am grateful to many brilliant scholars who engaged with me on this topic and provided valuable feedback on my work. In particular, in alphabetical order, Susan Ariel Aaronson, Wolfgang Alschner, Mira Burri, Anupam Chander, Laura Drechsler, Sarah Eskens, Gloria González Fuster, Margot E. Kaminski, William Kovacic, Markus Krajewski, Andrew Lang, Neha Mishra, Milton Mueller, Kenneth Propp, Peter Swire, and Geraldo Vidigal.

I am grateful to the Institute for Information Law (IViR) at the University of Amsterdam for providing time and space for me to work on this project during my appointment as a postdoctoral researcher in 2021–23, and to my IViR colleagues for their support and conversations we had throughout my time at the IViR. I would like to particularly single out, in alphabetical order, Jef Ausloos, Ot van Daalen, Max van Drunen, Mireille van Eechoud, Kristina Irion, Arlette Meiring, Joao Pedro Quintais, Marijn Sax, and Martin Senftleben.

I would also like to acknowledge my colleagues from De Brauw Blackstone Westbroek, where I worked part time while writing this book (and the thesis that led to it). I am now working there full time as this book is going into production. In particular, I am grateful to my colleagues, in alphabetical order, Axel Arnbak,

Mirjam van Dam, Wessel Geursen (who is no longer working for De Brauw), Jonathan de Geus, Andreas Häuselmann, Christien de Kruif, Justyna Niemczyk, Geert Potjewijd, Esther Rosenkrantz, Emma Üstünalp, and Anna Zanathy for listening and giving me space to work on my project. I am also thankful to Helma van der Wal for designing the visuals for this book and to students of the Regulatory Enforcement department for helping to format the footnotes.

I would also like to thank my friends who were always there for me, in particular, Maria Taylor, Maya and Oleg Zupnik, Momchil Tsonev, Radmila Nikitina, and Olga Zrilina.

Last but not least, I am happy to have had my work closely supervised by my cats Charlie and Nefi, who radiated positive vibes while sleeping next to me as I was finalizing the manuscript.

Contents

1.2 COURT OF JUSTICE OF THE EUROPEAN UNION (CJEU): ADVOCATE GENERAL (AG) OPINIONS

1.3 WORLD TRADE ORGANIZATION (WTO)

Table of cases

1.1 COURT OF JUSTICE OF THE EUROPEAN UNION (CJEU): JUDGMENTS

1.4 GENERAL AGREEMENT ON TARIFFS AND TRADE (GATT)

1.5 INTERNATIONAL CENTRE FOR SETTLEMENT OF INVESTMENT DISPUTES

1.6 NATIONAL CASES

1.6.1 Germany

1.6.2 Ireland

1.6.3 Belgium

Table of Legislation

2.1 INTERNATIONAL TREATIES AND CONVENTIONS

2.2 EUROPEAN UNION LEGISLATION

2.2.1 Treaties and Charter

2.2.2 Regulations and Directives

2.2.3 Proposed Legislation

2.2.4 European Commission Implementing Decisions

2.3 NON-EU LEGISLATION

2.3.1 Canada

2.3.2 China

2.3.3 Japan

2.3.4 Russia

2.3.5 United States

2.4 OFFICIAL PAPERS AND POLICY DOCUMENTS

2.4.1 United Nations

2.4.2 Council of Europe

2.4.3 Organisation for Economic Co-operation and Development (OECD)

2.4.4 Asia-Pacific Economic Cooperation (APEC)

2.4.5 World Trade Organization (WTO)

2.4.6 General Agreement on Tariffs and Trade (GATT)

2.4.7 European Union

2.4.8 European Commission

2.4.9 European Parliament

2.4.10 Council of the European Union

2.4.11 Article 29 Working Party

2.4.12 European Data Protection Board (EDPB)

2023-06/edpb_guidelines_042022_calculationofadministrativefines_en.pdf> accessed 10 July 2023. . . . 60–61

Guidelines 05/2021 on the Interplay between the application of Article 3 and the provisions on international transfers as per Chapter V of the GDPR (14 February 2023) <https://edpb.europa.eu/system/files/2023-02/edpb_guidelines_05-2021_interplay_between_the_application_of_art3-chapter_v_of_the_gdpr_v2_en_0.pdf> accessed 10 July 2023 . . . 36, 39, 324–25, 326, 335

Guidelines 2/2018 on derogations of Article 49 under Regulation 2016/679 (25 May 2018) <https://edpb.europa.eu/sites/default/files/files/file1/edpb_guidelines_2_2018_derogations_en.pdf> accessed 10 July 2023. . . . . 39, 53, 71–72, 140–41, 283, 291, 313–14

Guidelines 3/2018 on the territorial scope of the GDPR (article 3) (12 November 2019), <https://edpb.europa.eu/sites/default/files/files/file1/edpb_guidelines_3_2018_territorial_scope_after_public_consultation_en_1.pdf> accessed 10 July 2023. 43–44

Guidelines 9/2022 on personal data breach notification under GDPR (28 March 2023) <https://edpb.europa.eu/system/files/2023-04/edpb_guidelines_202209_personal_data_breach_notification_v2.0_en.pdf> accessed 10 July 2023. 320

Opinion 28/2018 regarding the European Commission Draft Implementing Decision on the adequate protection of personal data in Japan (5 December 2018) <https://edpb.europa.eu/sites/default/files/files/file1/2018-12-05-opinion_2018-28_art.70_japan_adequacy_en.pdf> accessed 10 July 2023. 304–5

Opinion 5/2023 on the European Commission Draft Implementing Decision on the adequate protection of personal data under the EU-US Data Privacy Framework, 28 February 2023 <https://edpb.europa.eu/system/files/2023-02/edpb_opinion52023_eu-us_dpf_en.pdf> accessed 10 July 2023. 15–16

Recommendations 01/2020 on measures that supplement transfer tools to ensure compliance with the EU level of protection of personal data (18 June 2021) <https://edpb.europa.eu/system/files/2021-06/edpb_recommendations_202001vo.2.0_supplementarymeasurestransferstools_en.pdf> accessed 10 July 2023 . . . . 50–51, 97

'Study on the enforcement of GDPR obligations against entities established outside the EEA but falling under Article 3(2) GDPR' (4 November 2021) <https://edpb.europa.eu/system/files/2023-04/call_9_final_report_04112021_en_0.pdf> accessed 10 July 2023 46–47

Thirty-first Plenary session: Establishment of a taskforce on TikTok, Response to MEPs on use of Clearview AI by law enforcement authorities, Response to ENISA Advisory Group, Response to Open Letter NYOB (10 June 2020) <https://edpb.europa.eu/news/news/2020/thirty-first-plenary-session-establishment-taskforce-tiktok-response-meps-use_en> accessed 10 July 2023. . . . . . .72–73, 294–95, 351

2.4.13 European Data Protection Supervisor (EDPS)

Assessing the Necessity of Measures That Limit the Fundamental Right to the Protection of Personal Data: A Toolkit (2017) <https://edps.europa.eu/sites/edp/files/publication/17-04-11_necessity_toolkit_en_0.pdf> accessed 10 July 2023. . . . . . . 97–98, 99, 262–63

Guidelines on assessing the proportionality of measures that limit the fundamental rights to

2.4.14 EU Data Protection Authorities

NETHERLANDS

BELGIUM

ITALY

IRELAND

2.4.15 Non-EU Data Protection Authorities

2.4.16 US Department of Commerce

List of Abbreviations

AI	artificial intelligence
APEC	Asia-Pacific Economic Cooperation
APEC CBPR	Asia-Pacific Economic Cooperation Cross-Border Privacy Rules
APPI	Act on the Protection of Personal Information
BCR	binding corporate rules
CCPA	California Consumer Privacy Act
CETA	Comprehensive Economic and Trade Agreement
CFIUS	Committee on Foreign Investment in the United States
CJEU	Court of Justice of the European Union
CPTPP	Comprehensive and Progressive Agreement for Trans-Pacific Partnership
DEA	Digital Economy Agreement
DEPA	Digital Economy Partnership Agreement
DFFT	Data Free Flows with Trust
DG	Directorate General
DPA	Data Protection Authority
DPC	Data Protection Commission
ECEFP	Executive Committee on Economic Foreign Policy
ECHR	European Convention on Human Rights
ECIPE	European Centre for International Political Economy
ECtHR	European Court of Human Rights
EDPB	European Data Protection Board
EDPS	European Data Protection Supervisor
EEA	European Economic Area
EU	European Union
EU Charter	Charter of the European Union
EU-UK TCA	EU-UK Trade and Cooperation Agreement
FTA	Free Trade Agreement
GATS	General Agreement on Trade in Services
GATT	General Agreement on Tariffs and Trade
GDPR	General Data Protection Regulation
GMO	genetically modified organisms
IAPP	The International Association of Privacy Professionals
ICCPR	International Covenant on Civil and Political Rights
ICO	Information Commissioner's Office
ICT	Information and Communications Technology
IPEF	Indo-Pacific Economic Framework
ITO	International Trade Organization
JEFTA	EU-Japan Economic Partnership Agreement

KORUS FTA	United States-Korea Free Trade Agreement
MFN	most favoured nation
NAFTA	North American Free Trade Agreement
NGO	non-governmental Organization
NTB	non-tariff barriers
OECD	Organisation for Economic Co-operation and Development
OPC	Office of the Privacy Commissioner
PIPEDA	Personal Information Protection and Electronic Documents Act
PNR Agreement	Personal Name Records Agreement
RCEP	Regional and Comprehensive Economic Partnership
SCC	Standard Contractual Clauses
SPS Agreement	WTO Agreement on the Application of Sanitary and Phytosanitary Measures
TBT Agreement	Agreement on Technical Barriers to Trade
TEU	Treaty on European Union
TFEU	Treaty on the Functioning of the European Union
TiSA	Trade in Services Agreement
TPP	Trans-Pacific Partnership
TRIPS	Agreement on Trade-Related Aspects of Intellectual Property Law
TTIP	Transatlantic Trade and Investment Partnership
UDHR	Universal Declaration of Human Rights
UK-Japan CEPA	UK-Japan Comprehensive Economic Partnership Agreement
USIP DEA	US-Indo-Pacific Digital Economy Agreement
USITC	United States International Trade Commission
USJDTA	US-Japan Digital Trade Agreement
USMCA	United States–Mexico–Canada Agreement
VCLT	Vienna Convention on the Law of Treaties
WTO	World Trade Organization

1

Cross-Border Data Flows

Between Trade and Data Privacy

Between 2014 and 2016, a wave of protests swept across Europe. In Brussels, but also Amsterdam, Barcelona, Berlin, Rome, and several other cities, thousands of people filled the streets chanting slogans: 'Stop TTIP, TiSA, & CETA now!' 'No TTIP, TiSA, & CETA!' 'We need TTIP like a fish needs a fishing rod!' The source of the public discontent was the 'new generation' of trade agreements that the European Union (EU) was covertly negotiating with some of its most important trading partners: the Transatlantic Trade and Investment Partnership (TTIP) with the United States, the Comprehensive Economic Trade Agreement (CETA) with Canada, and the Trade in Services Agreement (TiSA) with twenty-two members of the World Trade Organization (WTO), together representing approximately 70 per cent of world trade in services.[1] The protests were sparked not only by the substance of the agreements, namely their perceived threats to EU domestic policy in areas such as the environment, agriculture, culture, and the media, but also by aspects of the negotiation process, namely its secrecy and lack of democratic legitimacy and accountability. Although the possible implications of these agreements—primarily TTIP and TiSA—on the EU policy on privacy and data protection and on the EU *acquis* more broadly had mostly escaped the eye of the broader public at that time, they did not go unnoticed either by digital rights and consumer organizations and activists or by certain EU institutions not involved in those trade negotiations.[2] For the first time, the tension between the liberalization

[1] European Parliament, Legislative Train Schedule: Plurilateral Trade in Services Agreement (TiSA) <https://www.europarl.europa.eu/legislative-train/package-multilateral-and-plurilateral-trade-agreements/file-trade-in-services-agreement-(tisa)> accessed 10 July 2023.

[2] See eg EDRI, 'Data Protection and Privacy Must Be Excluded from TTIP' (8 April 2015) <https://edri.org/our-work/data-protection-privacy-ttip/> accessed 10 July 2023; EDRI, 'TiSA Leaks Set Alarm Bells Ringing' (20 September 2016) <https://edri.org/our-work/tisa-leaks-set-alarm-bells-ringing/> accessed 10 July 2023; Consumers International, 'Why TiSA Should Be in the Global Consumer Spotlight' (1 June 2016) <https://www.consumersinternational.org/news-resources/blog/posts/20160601-why-tisa-should-be-in-the-global-consumer-spotlight/> accessed 10 July 2023; European Parliament resolution of 8 July 2015 containing the European Parliament's recommendations to the European Commission on the negotiations for the Transatlantic Trade and Investment Partnership (TTIP) (2014/2228(INI)); European Parliament resolution of 3 February 2016 containing the European Parliament's recommendations to the Commission on the negotiations for the Trade in Services Agreement (TiSA) (2015/2233(INI)).

Governing Cross-Border Data Flows. Svetlana Yakovleva, Oxford University Press.
DOI: 10.1093/oso/9780192899248.003.0001

of digital trade, on the one hand, and data privacy, on the other, became a broader political issue rather than just the topic of a theoretical debate.

This book explores the difficulties in reconciling these important legal and policy objectives of the European Union. On the one hand, the EU Charter of Fundamental Rights (EU Charter)[3] guarantees the protection of the rights to privacy and the protection of personal data[4] as fundamental rights. On the other hand, in its external trade policy, the EU seeks liberalization of cross-border data flows, maintaining and developing a globally binding rules-based trading system to ensure appropriate access to foreign markets for EU businesses. The fundamental rights protection of data privacy in the EU originated as a prerequisite for the free flow of personal data in the internal market. It was, in other words, intertwined with the economic goals underlying the Union. Until recently, in the EU's external policy the two objectives had little in common and, therefore, did not come into conflict. But then cross-border flows of personal and other data became the 'lifeblood of international trade'.[5] Add to this that digital commerce is taking up a growing share of world trade.[6] Yet, the collection and commercial use of personal data almost always implicates essential non-economic values. Those values explain why personal data is protected by the EU Charter, and why it was instantiated with a high degree of specificity by the General Data Protection Regulation (GDPR).[7] Specifically, the book examines how these two objectives might be pursued simultaneously.

This topic is highly relevant to current policy debate in the EU on the data privacy implications of cross-border data flows, which takes place in parallel to ongoing digital trade negotiations with several trading partners,[8] cooperation on digital issues with the United States as part of the EU-US Trade

[3] Charter of Fundamental Rights of the European Union [2000] OJ C 364/1 (hereafter EU Charter).

[4] Throughout this book, the fundamental rights to privacy and the protection of personal data will also be jointly referred to as fundamental rights to data privacy.

[5] Francesca Casalini and Javier López González, Trade and Cross-Border Data Flows (2019) OECD Trade Policy Papers, No 220, 8, 14 <http://dx.doi.org/10.1787/b2023a47-en> accessed 10 July 2023.

[6] James Manyika and others, 'Digital Globalisation: The New Era of Global Flows' (2016) McKinsey Global Institute, 30–32 <https://www.mckinsey.com/~/media/McKinsey/Business%20Functions/McKinsey%20Digital/Our%20Insights/Digital%20globalization%20The%20new%20era%20of%20global%20flows/MGI-Digital-globalization-Full-report.pdf> accessed 10 July 2023.

[7] Regulation (EU) 2016/679 of the European Parliament and of the Council of 27 April 2016 on the protection of natural persons with regard to the processing of personal data and on the free movement of such data, and repealing Directive 95/46/EC [2016] OJ L 119/1 (hereafter GDPR).

[8] See Communication from the Commission to the European Parliament, the Council, the European Economic and Social Committee, and the Committee of the Regions, 'Trade Policy Review: An Open, Sustainable and Assertive Trade Policy' [2021] COM/2021/66 final (hereafter Communication from the Commission, 'Trade Policy Review').

and Technology Council[9] and digital partnerships with Japan, Korea, and Singapore.[10] Digital trade is a key part of the EU's industrial policy.[11]

This book contributes to the existing academic literature by undertaking a comprehensive and multidimensional analysis of the issue of cross-border data flows from an EU data privacy and international trade perspective, thus bridging the compartmentalization of these two areas of law. As compared to almost all existing literature,[12] which typically takes either an international trade or a data protection perspective,[13] this book undertakes an in-depth engagement with both areas of law with a specific emphasis on the interaction between them. This approach allows the book to propose ways of bridging the gap between international trade and EU rules governing cross-border data flows while preserving the normative values underlying each of these sets of rules. The book goes much further, however. It also proposes concrete paths for short-, medium-, and long-term reforms of both the EU's trade policy approach to cross-border flows of personal data and to specific parts of the GDPR, in particular chapter V, which deals with such flows.

The societal relevance of this work lies in the necessary reconciliation of the fundamental rights, guaranteed under the EU Charter, with the realities of global digital commerce which will contribute to economic growth and job creation. The governance of cross-border flows of personal data must be at once solidly anchored in EU law and values, and capable of being ported to the trade law field. This is important because the outcomes of trade negotiations will affect each and every person in the EU, as almost everybody uses the internet. Guaranteeing sufficient protection of fundamental rights while ensuring that society can benefit from digital commerce is the difficult challenge that this book aims to meet.

[9] European Commission, 'Digital in the EU-US Trade and Technology Council' (5 September 2022) <https://digital-strategy.ec.europa.eu/en/policies/trade-and-technology-council> accessed 10 July 2023.

[10] European Union: Republic of Korea Digital Partnership (30 November 2022) <https://circabc.europa.eu/rest/download/6faad06a-30bc-4207-a46b-3da7e8e496e0> accessed 10 July 2023 (hereafter EU-Korea Digital Partnership); EU-Singapore Digital Partnership (1 February 2023) <https://ec.europa.eu/newsroom/dae/redirection/document/93447> accessed 10 July 2023 (hereafter EU-Singapore Digital Partnership); and Japan-EU Digital Partnership (12 May 2022) <https://www.consilium.europa.eu/media/56091/%E6%9C%80%E7%B5%82%E7%89%88-jp-eu-digital-partnership-clean-final-docx.pdf> accessed 10 July 2023 (hereafter Japan-EU Digital Partnership).

[11] Communication from the Commission to the European Parliament, the European Council, the Council, the European Economic and Social Committee, and the Committee of the Regions, 'A New Industrial Strategy for Europe' [2020] COM/2020/102 final (hereafter Communication from the Commission, 'A New Industrial Strategy').

[12] Another notable publication on the topic, which similarly this book takes a multidimensional approach, is Tobias Naef, *Data Protection without Data Protectionism: The Right to Protection of Personal Data and Data Transfers in EU Law and International Trade Law* (Springer Cham 2023).

[13] See UNCTAD, 'Digital Economy Report. Cross-Border Data Flows and Development: For Whom the Data Flow' (2021) 61 <https://unctad.org/system/files/official-document/der2021_en.pdf> accessed 10 July 2023 (hereafter UNCTAD, 'Digital Economy Report 2021'), stating that '[m]ost of the literature analyses cross-border data flows from a trade perspective. Some of it looks at cross-border privacy issues, but there is a general lack of studies that address cross-border data flows in a multidimensional manner'.

1.1 Setting the Scene: Background and Problem Definition

1.1.1 International trade in data: What's at stake?

The commercial use of personal data enables digital trade[14] and contributes to economic growth. It may also generate individual benefits. However, those benefits often seem both remote and indirect when compared to the risks posed to individuals by the misuse of their data, such as identity theft, access to data by foreign surveillance and law enforcement authorities, profiling, unwanted marketing communications, discrimination, and denial of access to essential services, to name just a few. Unlike data, which can simultaneously be present in multiple locations and fall under the jurisdiction of multiple legal regimes, individuals retain a close connection with a particular State through the institutions of citizenship or residency. It is first and foremost *that* State that must guarantee the individuals' human rights and protect them from the undue actions of other States.

In the realm of digital trade, the level of fundamental rights protection that individuals can expect in the EU member states may not necessarily be upheld once personal data is processed in other countries, such as the United States, China, or Russia. Simply put, while trade in data is *international*, protection of individual rights largely remains the prerogative of *domestic law*,[15] especially when it comes to the protection of the fundamental rights to privacy and the protection of personal data. Although these rights are recognized by important international[16] and regional[17] human rights law instruments, and governed by several regional guidelines,[18] countries across the globe still have important disagreements on the normative rationales underlying the protection of the two rights and the approaches to transfers of personal data.

Cross-border trade in digital goods and services is increasingly dependent on personal data, often dubbed 'the new oil'.[19] Globalization and the decentralization

[14] This book proceeds from the premise that 'digital trade' is qualitatively different 'electronic commerce'. The author agrees with Wolfgang Alschner's argument that while electronic commerce denotes digitally enabled trade in analogue assets, digital trade denotes trade in digital assets. Wolfgang Alschner, 'E-Commerce or Digital Trade? Why the Difference Should Matter to Trade Lawyers' in Michael Geist and David Collins (eds), *Research Handbook on Digital Trade* (Edward Elgar, 2023) <http://dx.doi.org/10.2139/ssrn.4321743> accessed 10 July 2023.

[15] In this book, the EU *acquis* is also referred to as 'domestic' law.

[16] Art 12 Universal Declaration of Human Rights, GA Res 217, UN GAOR, 3d Sess, UN Doc A/810 (1948); art 17 International Covenant on Civil and Political Rights, 16 December 1966, UNTS 999.

[17] Art 8 Council of Europe, European Convention for the Protection of Human Rights and Fundamental Freedoms, as amended by Protocols Nos 11 and 14, 4 November 1950, ETS 5; Modernized Convention for the Protection of Individuals with Regard to the Processing of Personal Data, as amended by the Protocol adopted by the Committee of Ministers at its 128th Session of the Committee of Ministers, 18 May 2018, CETS 223.

[18] Eg, The OECD Guidelines Governing the Protection of Privacy and Transborder Flows of Personal Data (2013) (2013); APEC Privacy Framework (2015), as updated by the Concluding Senior Officials' Meeting on 14–15 November 2016, 2016/CSOM/012app17; and APEC Cross-Border Privacy Rules System (CBPR), as updated in November 2019.

[19] UNCTAD, Digital Economy Report 2021 (n 13), 74–76.

of production and distribution value chains have made the cross-border movement of information—commercial, machine-generated, and personal—crucial for the production and provision of services, both online and offline,[20] as well as the day-to-day management of companies.[21] The large-scale collection and accumulation of data is also essential for developing, fine-tuning, and deploying artificial intelligence (AI) systems. Projecting this economic reality, promising unprecedented efficiency gains, economic development, and growth onto a global legal landscape compartmentalized by multiple domestic legal systems is a sobering exercise. When set against the economic benefits driving globalization, these legal systems must consider how these benefits fit into a broader set of national and regional priorities, such as national security, fundamental rights protection, industrial policy, and cultural values. Differences in the relative weight accorded to each of those priorities vis-à-vis the economic and political gains from cross-border data flows have resulted in a diverse set of diverging domestic rules governing such flows, especially when it relates to identified or identifiable individuals (ie, the definition of personal data in the GDPR).

Companies doing business globally face the challenges of compliance with several data protection regimes and rules for cross-border transfers of personal data in several jurisdictions. Having a lot to gain from dismantling restrictions on the free flow of data, a plethora of industry-funded think-tanks have been trying to shape the global policy agenda by painting a grim picture in which the protection of data privacy is depicted as a barrier to trade and a threat to economic progress.[22] Using an often one-sided narrative of 'digital protectionism', surveillance capitalists portray their practices as 'inevitable expressions of the technology they employ'[23] and digital globalization as the next logical step of economic integration and development.[24] Individuals face a different reality: they must deal with the limitations of domestic legal systems to enforce their rights effectively against the misuse of their personal data on a global scale. Although individuals do also gain from the free flow and ubiquitous monetization of their data by companies, for example, in the form of personalized services, they also have a lot to lose. The potential damage to individuals and society as a whole transcends the direct economic losses from data breaches and identity threats. It includes discrimination and social exclusion; the undermining of human dignity by transforming human experiences into mere

[20] Natali Helberger, Frederik Zuiderveen Borgesius, and Augustin Reyna, 'The Perfect Match? A Closer Look at the Relationship between EU Consumer Law and Data Protection Law' (2017) 54(5) Common Market Law Review 1427, 1430–31.

[21] For discussion, see Ines Willemyns, *Digital Services in International Trade Law* (CUP 2021) 34–39.

[22] See Evgeny Morozov, 'What Happens When Policy Is Made by Corporations? Your Privacy Is Seen as a Barrier to Economic Growth' (*The Guardian*, 12 July 2015) <https://www.theguardian.com/commentisfree/2015/jul/12/ttip-your-data-privacy-is-a-barrier-to-economic-growth?CMP=Share_iOSApp_Other> accessed 10 July 2023 (hereafter Morozov, 'What Happens').

[23] Shoshana Zuboff, *The Age of Surveillance Capitalism: The Fight for a Human Future at the New Frontier of Power* (Public Affairs 2019) 15 (hereafter Zuboff, *The Age of Surveillance Capitalism*).

[24] For a discussion, see Section 3.3.

behavioural data; and the shaping of individuals' behaviour (often using AI) and choices, both on the micro level of what news to read and items to buy, and on the macro level of expressing political preferences.

From a global perspective, massive cross-border appropriation of personal data can be compared to resource extraction.[25] For example, Couldry and Mejias argue that cross-border data flows 'are as expansive as historic colonialism's appropriation of land, resources, and bodies, although the epicenter has somewhat shifted'.[26] In their view, the transformation of human actors and social relations formalized as data, into value, leads to power imbalance (between colonial power and colonized subjects).[27] Against this backdrop, as Morozov puts it, the EU's 'much-cherished commitment to data protection … aimed, above all, at protecting citizens from excessive corporate and state intrusion – is increasingly at odds with the "grab everything" mentality of contemporary capitalism'.[28]

1.1.2 EU data privacy framework

Since 2009 (when the EU Charter went into full effect), the right to the protection of personal data has been a binding fundamental right in the EU (Article 8 of the EU Charter), separate from the fundamental right to privacy (Article 7 of the EU Charter).[29] The EU Charter has the highest legal status in the EU, on a par with the Founding Treaties. Just as personal data has both economic

[25] Nick Couldry and Ulises Mejias, 'Data Colonialism: Rethinking Big Data's Relation to the Contemporary Subject' (2019) 20(4) Television & New Media 336, 337–38 (hereafter Couldry and Mejias, 'Data Colonialism'). See also Danielle Coleman, 'Digital Colonialism: The 21st Century Scramble for Africa through the Extraction and Control of User Data and the Limitations of Data Protection Laws' (2019) 24 Michigan Journal of Race & Law 417; Thomas Streinz, 'International Economic Law's Regulation of Data as a Resource for the Artificial Intelligence Economy' in Shin-yi Peng, Ching-Fu Lin, and Thomas Streinz (eds), *Artificial Intelligence and International Economic Law* (CUP 2021).

[26] Couldry and Mejias, 'Data Colonialism' (n 25). But see Milton Mueller and Karl Grindal, 'Data Flows and the Digital Economy: Information as a Mobile Factor of Production Digital Policy' (2019) 21(1) Regulation and Governance 71, 82 (hereafter Mueller and Grindal, 'Data Flows'), challenging this point of view.

[27] Couldry and Mejias, 'Data Colonialism' (n 25), 337–38.

[28] Morozov, 'What Happens' (n 22).

[29] Despite the separation of the rights to privacy and the protection of personal data in the EU Charter, this book often refers to these two rights jointly. The issue on the relationship between these two rights has generated much academic debate but remains unresolved. For a recount of the state of this debate, see Orla Lynskey, 'General Report Topic 2: The New EU Data Protection Regime' in Jorrit J Rijpma (ed), *The New EU Data Protection Regime: Setting Global Standards for the Right to Personal Data Protection. The XXIX FIDE Congress in The Hague* (Congress Publications 2020, Vol. 2) 29–32. For a deeper analysis of the intricate relationship between the two rights, see Orla Lynskey, *The Foundations of EU Data Protection Law* (OUP 2015) 89–106. For a comprehensive historical account of the issue, see Gloria González Fuster, *The Emergence of Personal Data Protection as a Fundamental Right of the EU* (Springer 2014).

and societal values, the European data protection regime, first introduced by the 1995 Data Protection Directive,[30] has a dual objective: protecting the fundamental rights and freedoms of individuals, in particular their right to the protection of personal data, and ensuring the free flow of personal data within the European Economic Area (EEA).[31] Conflicting at first glance,[32] these objectives are easier to reconcile if seen as cause and effect, or as the 'why' and the 'how'. The harmonization of data protection rules was a prerequisite for the free flow of personal data without undermining individuals' rights to the protection of such data originating from EU member states affording a higher level of protection (the 'why').[33] The fundamental rights approach ('the how') sets the level of protection of personal data which the EU-wide personal data protection framework should attain. However, the constitutionalizing of the EU has put the EU internal market integration needs that necessitated the creation of the EU-wide data protection framework in the first place,[34] to the background, and emphasized the non-economic goals of the current European data protection law.[35] That said, the GDPR, adopted under the EU's competence to legislate on the fundamental right to the protection of personal data, is often cited as one of the pillars of the EU Digital Single Market.[36]

[30] Directive 95/46/EC of the European Parliament and of the Council of 24 October 1995 on the protection of individuals with regard to the processing of personal data and on the free movement of such data [1995] OJ L 281 (hereafter Data Protection Directive).

[31] GDPR (n 7) art 1; art 1 Data Protection Directive (n 30). The European Economic Area consists of the member states of the European Union and countries of the European Free Trade Association (EFTA)—Norway, Iceland, and Lichtenstein. EUROSTAT, Glossary: European Economic Area (EEA), <https://ec.europa.eu/eurostat/statistics-explained/index.php/Glossary:European_Economic_Area_(EEA)#:~:text=The%20European%20Economic%20Area%2C%20abbreviated,force%20on%201%20January%201994> accessed 10 July 2023.

[32] See, eg, Milda Macenaite, 'The "Riskification" of European Data Protection Law through a Two-Fold Shift' (2017) 8(3) European Journal of Risk Regulation 506, 506–07.

[33] Francisco Costa-Cabral and Orla Lynskey, 'Family Ties: The Intersection between Data Protection and Competition in EU Law' (2017) 54 Common Market Law Review 11, 17.

[34] See Directive 95/46/EC of the European Parliament and of the Council of 24 October 1995 on the protection of individuals with regard to the processing of personal data and on the free movement of such data, OJ L 281, 23.11.1995, 31–50, Recitals 3, 5, and 8 (hereafter Data Protection Directive). Safeguarding fundamental rights and freedoms, notably the right to privacy, was another reason for adopting the Data Protection Directive, albeit a secondary one. See Recital 3 of the Data Protection Directive, stating that '[w]hereas the establishment and functioning of an internal market in which, in accordance with Article 7a of the Treaty, the free movement of goods, persons, services and capital is ensured require not only that personal data should be able to flow freely from one Member State to another, *but also* that the fundamental rights of individuals should be safeguarded'. (Emphasis added).

[35] Orla Lynskey, 'From Market-Making Tool to Fundamental Right: The Role of the Court of Justice in Data Protection's Identity Crisis' in Serge Gutwirth and others (eds), *European Data Protection: Coming of Age* (Springer 2013). For further discussion, see Sections 2.2.1 and 2.4.3.

[36] Communication from the Commission to the European Parliament, the European Council, the Council, the European Economic and Social Committee, and the Committee of the Regions, 'Completing a Trusted Digital Single Market for All' [2018] COM (2018) 320 final, 2–3.

1.1.3 EU's digital sovereignty concerns

The emergence of digital trade has brought about a significant reliance on data, which is essential for the growth of data-driven economies and societies. This increased reliance on data has rekindled previous debates on sovereignty and international cooperation.[37]

Under the leadership of Ursula von der Leyen (the president of the European Commission as of June 2023),[38] the robust protection of the fundamental rights to privacy and personal data has become a part of the EU's response to a growing concern about 'technological' or 'digital sovereignty', with regard to the growing economic and social influences of non-EU (primarily American and Chinese) technology companies.[39] This narrative, however, is not entirely new. Already at the dawn of data protection laws in Europe, information sovereignty was one of concerns that regulation of data flows aimed to address.[40]

This discourse resurfaced now with a renewed force as a reaction to the growing concerns about the growing power of non-EU companies, control over data, constraints to the growth of EU technology companies, and the rule-makers' ability to enforce their laws.[41] The EU is increasingly using technological or digital sovereignty labels 'as a means of promoting the notion of European leadership and strategic autonomy in the digital field' in both internal law and policy and international relations.[42] In the international arena, the EU's digital strategy, anchored in European values and fundamental rights, ties into the 'ideal of a social European model'[43] alternative to the American model of 'surveillance capitalism'.[44]

[37] Mira Burri, 'Symposium on Digital Trade and International Law: Digital Trade Law and Human Rights' (2023) 117 AJIL Unbound 110, 110.

[38] European Commission, 'State of the Union Address by President von der Leyen at the European Parliament Plenary' (16 September 2020) <https://ec.europa.eu/commission/presscorner/detail/en/SPEECH_20_1655> accessed 10 July 2023.

[39] Tambiama Madiega, 'Digital Sovereignty for Europe' (2020) EPRS Ideas Paper Towards a More Resilient EU 1 <https://www.europarl.europa.eu/RegData/etudes/BRIE/2020/651992/EPRS_BRI(2020)651992_EN.pdf> accessed 10 July 2023 (hereafter Madiega 'Digital Sovereignty for Europe').

[40] See Section 2.2.1.

[41] Madiega 'Digital Sovereignty for Europe' (n 39) 1. For discussion, see also Svetlana Yakovleva, 'The EU's Trade Policy on Cross-Border Data Flows in the Global Landscape: Navigating the Thin Line between Liberalizing Digital Trade, 'Digital Sovereignty' And Multilateralism' in Elaine Fahey and Isabella Mancini (eds), *Understanding the EU as a Good Global Actor* (Edward Elgar 2022); Svetlana Yakovleva, 'On Digital Sovereignty, New European Data Rules, and the Future of Free Data Flows' (2022) 49(4) Legal Issues of Economic Integration 339.

[42] Madiega 'Digital Sovereignty for Europe' (n 39). See also Communication from the Commission to the European Parliament, the European Council, the Council, the European Economic and Social Committee and the Committee of the Regions, A European Strategy for Data [2020] COM(2020) 66 final; European Commission, 'White Paper on Artificial Intelligence: A European Approach to Excellence and Trust' [2020] COM(2020) 65 final, 3.

[43] Bilyana Petkova, 'Privacy as Europe's First Amendment' (2019) 25(2) European Law Journal 140, 153.

[44] Zuboff, *The Age of Surveillance Capitalism* (n 23); Shoshana Zuboff, 'Big Other: Surveillance Capitalism and the Prospects of an Information Civilization'(2015) 30 Journal of Information Technology, 75; Madiega, 'Digital Sovereignty for Europe' (n 39) 3.

The notion of digital sovereignty reaches into a broad set of policy areas *beyond* privacy and data protection, including digital infrastructure, cybersecurity, competition law, telecommunications, and technology and platform governance.[45] In the area of data governance, 'digital sovereignty' policies create rules for sharing, re-use, and flows of *non-personal data* with a view to unlock the immense potential of industrial data and to create a solid digital economy in the EU based on European values. European legislation (adopted or proposed), which reflects such policies,[46] adds new layers of complexity at the level of substantive rules governing different types of data, relevant institutions, and enforcement mechanisms.

Emerging restrictions on cross-border transfers of *non*-personal data outside the EU raise growing concerns from a trade law perspective.[47] This book, however, focuses solely on transfers of *personal data* outside the EEA and the tensions arising between restrictions on cross-border transfers of such data (motivated by data privacy concerns) and the EU's external trade policy. In international trade negotiations on cross-border data flows, it is data privacy rather than digital sovereignty that is the main point of contention for the EU.

1.1.4 Tension between external trade policy and EU's domestic data privacy framework

The view that domestic restrictions on international data flows in general, and on personal data flows in particular, are a form of undesirable 'protectionism' is now front and centre in academic, public and policy conversations on the topic, as the focus of international trade negotiations shift to digital trade.[48] From this

[45] For an overview, see Huw Roberts and others, 'Safeguarding European Values with Digital Sovereignty: An Analysis of Statements and Policies' (2021) 10(3) Internet Policy Review 1, 9–13. See also Mark Leonard and Jeremy Shapiro, 'Empowering EU Member States with Strategic Sovereignty' European Council on Foreign Relations (June 2019) 6 <https://ecfr.eu/wp-content/uploads/1_Empowering_EU_member_states_with_strategic_sovereignty.pdf> accessed 10 July 2023.

[46] See Regulation (EU) 2022/868 of the European Parliament and of the Council of 30 May 2022 on European data governance and amending Regulation (EU) 2018/1724 (Data Governance Act) PE/85/2021/REV/1 [2022] OJ L 152; Proposal for a Regulation of the European Parliament and of the Council on harmonized rules on fair access to and use of data (Data Act) COM/2022/68 final; Proposal for a Regulation of the European Parliament and of the Council on the European Health Data Space COM/2022/197 final. The EU is also planning to adopt sectoral legislation, which will create European Data Spaces in 10 strategic fields (health, agriculture, manufacturing, energy, mobility, financial, public administration, skills, the European Open Science Cloud and the crosscutting key priority of meeting the Green Deal objectives. See Commission Staff Working Document on Common European Data Spaces [2022] SWD (2022) 45 final; Proposal for a Regulation of the European Parliament and of the Council on the European Health Data Space COM/2022/197 final.

[47] For discussion, see Julie Baloup, 'The Data Governance Act: New Rules for International Transfers of Non-Personal Data Held by the Public Sector (*European Law Blog*, 10 June 2021) <https://europeanlawblog.eu/2021/06/10/the-data-governance-act-new-rules-for-international-transfers-of-non-personal-data-held-by-the-public-sector/> accessed 10 July 2023; Kenneth Propp, 'Cultivating Europe's Data Garden' (*Lawfare Blog*, 4 March 2022) <https://www.lawfareblog.com/cultivating-europes-data-garden> accessed 10 July 2023.

[48] For further discussion, see Section 3.3.

angle, unrestricted cross-border data flows promise global economic growth and are often perceived as a *bonum in se*.[49] However, the tendency of international trade law to liberalize international data flows is at odds with legal regimes that restrict such flows on privacy and data protection grounds, especially that of the European Union.[50] As a result, the data flow issue has become 'the new battlefield'[51] between domestic legal regimes; not only between the European Union and the United States but also between the European Union and its other trading partners,[52] China, the United States, and other Western democracies, between the Global South and the Global North.[53] While the debate often runs along the line of

[49] ibid.

[50] See, eg, Peter Swire and Robert E Litan, *None of Your Business: World Data Flows, Electronic Commerce, and the European Privacy Directive* (Brookings Institution Press 1988) 188–93; Rolf H Weber, Dominic Staiger, *Transatlantic Data Protection in Practice* (Springer 2017) 58–59; Lucas Bergkamp, 'The Privacy Fallacy: Adverse Effects of Europe's Data Protection Policy in an Information-Driven Economy' (2002) 18(1) Computer Law & Security Review 31, 39–40; Joel R Reidenberg, 'E-Commerce and Trans-Atlantic Privacy' (2001) 38 Houston Law Review 717, 735–38; Svetlana Yakovleva and Kristina Irion, 'The Best of Both Worlds? Free Trade in Services and EU Law on Privacy and Data Protection' (2016) 2 European Data Protection Law Review 191, 202–07; But see Gregory Shaffer, 'Globalization and Social Protection: The Impact of EU and International Rules in the Ratcheting Up of U.S. Privacy Standards' (2000) 25 Yale Journal of International Law 1, 46–51 (arguing that a hypothetical US claim regarding WTO inconsistency of the EU's framework for personal data transfers 'would likely not prevail'); Maria Veronica Perez Asinari, 'Is There Any Room for Privacy and Data Protection within the WTO Rules' (2002) 9 Electronic Communication Law Review 249, 277; Yi-Hsuan Chen, 'The EU Data Protection Law Reform: Challenges for Service Trade Liberalization and Possible Approaches for Harmonizing Privacy Standards into the Context of GATS' (2015) 19 The Spanish Yearbook of International Law 211, 218–19 (admitting that although the EU regime for transfers of personal data may violate the EU's WTO commitments, such violation can be justified under the general exception).

[51] Mira Burri, 'The Regulation of Data Flows through Trade Agreements' (2017) 48 Georgetown Journal of International Law 407, 408.

[52] For example, provisions on cross-border flows of information, including personal data, have been and continue to remain a contentious point in the negotiations of the JEFTA. See Marija Bartl and Kristina Irion, 'The Japan EU Economic Partnership Agreement: Flows of Personal Data to the Land of the Rising Sun' (Institute for Information Law, University of Amsterdam 2017) <https://www.ivir.nl/publicaties/download/Transfer-of-personal-data-to-the-land-of-the-rising-sun-FINAL.pdf> accessed 10 July 2023. Not being able to reach an agreement in trade negotiations, instead of such provisions, the parties included a three-year review clause in the final version of the agreement. See Susan Ariel Aaronson and Patrick Leblond, 'Another Digital Divide: The Rise of Data Realms and Its Implications for the WTO' (2018) (21)2 Journal of International Economic Law 245, 261 (hereafter Aaronson and Leblond 'Another Digital Divide'). Cross-border flows of personal data from the EU to Japan were ultimately regulated through an Adequacy Decision. The Adequacy Decision for Japan was adopted on 23 January 2019, shortly before JEFTA took effect. European Commission, 'Press Release: European Commission Adopts Adequacy Decision on Japan, Creating the World's Largest Area of Safe Data Flows' (23 January 2019) <http://europa.eu/rapid/press-release_IP-19-421_en.htm> accessed 10 July 2023. In 2022, the EU is planning to use the above-mentioned review clause to open negotiations for the inclusion of provisions on cross-border data flows in JEFTA, which immediately raised concerns with European Data Protection Supervisor. See European Data Protection Supervisor, Opinion 17/2022 on the Recommendation for a Council Decision authorizing the opening of negotiations for the inclusion of provisions on cross-border data flows in the Agreement between the European Union and Japan for an Economic Partnership (9 August 2022), 6.

[53] See, eg, David McCabe and Adam Satariano, 'The Era of Borderless Data Is Ending' *The New York Times* (23 May 2022) <https://www.nytimes.com/2022/05/23/technology/data-privacy-laws.html> accessed 10 July 2023; Kristina Irion, Margot E Kaminski, and Svetlana Yakovleva, 'Privacy Peg, Trade Hole: Why We (Still) Shouldn't Put Data Privacy in Trade Law' (*The University of Chicago Law Review Online*, 2023) <https://lawreviewblog.uchicago.edu/2023/03/27/irion-kaminski-yakovleva/> accessed

eliminating 'digital protectionism', there is an ideological divide on whether, and to what extent, data privacy protection should fall under or be excluded from the scope of this notion.[54]

Conflicts are thus bound to arise from the fact that while international trade law increasingly aims to liberalize data flows to facilitate digital cross-border trade, EU data protection law restricts cross-border transfers of personal data outside the EEA. Grounded in the fundamental rights to the protection of privacy and personal data under the EU Charter,[55] the rules for transfers of personal data outside the EEA aim to ensure that the level of protection guaranteed in the EU by the GDPR is not undermined as personal data leaves the EEA.[56]

Although the GDPR does not explicitly refer to any fundamental right except for the fundamental right to the protection of personal data, this does not mean that the GDPR furthers this right alone. This is clear from recital 4 of the GDPR, which requires that the 'processing of personal data should be designed to serve mankind'. Furthermore, the right to the protection of personal data itself enables a multitude of other fundamental rights and values.[57] This right is triggered by any processing of personal data (itself defined very broadly[58]), which is now integral to almost any societal activity. It is a proxy to a wide array of public policy interests from the protection of democracy, human dignity, and personality rights to obtaining a fair share of the economic value derived from personal data.[59] According to Rodota,

10 July 2023; Leila Brännström, 'Global Inequality and the EU International Law Position on Cross-Border Data Flows' 92 (2023) Nordic Journal of International Law 119.

[54] For a discussion, see Section 3.3.

[55] *Schrems* [2015] ECLI:EU:C:2015:650, paras 72–73 (hereafter *Schrems I*); *Facebook Ireland and Schrems* [2020] ECLI:EU:C:2020:559 (hereafter *Schrems II*), para 94; Opinion 1/15 (EU-Canada PNR Agreement) [2017] ECLI:EU:C:2017:592 (hereafter *Opinion on EU-Canada PNR Agreement*), para 214.

[56] GDPR (n 7) art 44; *Schrems I* (n 55) paras 72–73; *Schrems II* (n 55) paras 92, 94. See also Gloria González Fuster, 'Un-mapping Personal Data Transfers' (2016) 2(2) European Data Protection Law Review 160, 168.

[57] Manon Oostveen and Kristina Irion, 'The Golden Age of Personal Data: How to Regulate an Enabling Fundamental Right?' in Mor Bakhoum and others (eds), *Personal Data in Competition, Consumer Protection and Intellectual Property Law: Towards a Holistic Approach?* (Springer 2017); Jef Ausloos, *The Right to Erasure: Safeguard for Informational Self-Determination in a Digital Society?* (PhD Dissertation, KU Leuven CiTiP 2018) 62–63; Damian Clifford and Jef Ausloos, 'Data Protection and the Role of Fairness' (2018) 37(1) Yearbook of European Law 130, 147.

[58] For a discussion, see Section 5.3.4.

[59] See eg Orla Lynskey, 'Deconstructing Data Protection: The "Added-Value" of a Right to Data Protection in the EU Legal Order' (2014) 63 International and Comparative Law Quarterly 569, 573–74; Antoinette Rouvroy and Yves Poullet, 'The Right to Informational Self-Determination and the Value of Self-Development: Reassessing the Importance of Privacy for Democracy' in Serge Gutwirth and others (eds), *Reinventing Data Protection?* (Springer 2009) 53–54, 57 (contending that the rights to privacy and data protection have 'an "intermediate" rather than a "final" value, because they are "tools" through which more fundamental values, or more "basic" rights—namely human dignity and individual personality rights—are pursued; that the rights to privacy and personal data protection protect the fundamental value of personal autonomy against the threats of technological evolution, and that they constitute social structural tools for preserving a free and democratic society'). See also Sylvie Delacroix and Neil D Lawrence, 'Bottom-Up Data Trusts: Disturbing the "One Size Fits All" Approach to Data Governance' (2019) 9(4) International Data Privacy Law 236; Wendy Hall and Jérôme Pesenti, 'Growing the Artificial Intelligence Industry in the UK' Report for Government of the United Kingdom

'[d]ata protection can be seen to sum up a bundle of rights that make up citizenship in the new millennium'.[60]

As a result, unlike the internal trade liberalization *within* the EU single market (which led to the emergence of the EU data protection framework in the past), the EU's *external* trade liberalization goal is in tension with the EU data privacy law, due to their opposite normative valences. EU data privacy law can tolerate transfers of personal data outside the EEA only to the extent that these transfers are compliant with the EU Charter and the GDPR. In turn, international trade law can tolerate the EU's restrictions on personal data transfers only to the extent that they comply with the EU's international trade liberalization commitments, including possible exceptions thereto.

1.1.5 Restrictions on personal data flows: A barrier to digital trade?

The WTO is the main body administering international trade rules.[61] Both the EU and its member states are parties to the Marrakesh Agreement establishing the WTO.[62] The WTO notably includes a binding dispute-settlement system. The current framework was established in 1995. It does not regulate specifically cross-border data flows. However, general principles of trade law, such as most-favoured nation and national treatment or market access commitments under the GATS,[63] do apply to EU restrictions on cross-border data flows.

The WTO's role has recently decreased due to political circumstances and the multiplication of regional and bilateral trade agreements. In response to rapid technological change, new international law obligations are emerging through bi- and plurilateral trade venues that by-pass the WTO. So-called 'new generation' free trade agreements, entered into by the EU's most important trading partners, such as Canada, China, Japan, the United Kingdom, and the United States, include binding commitments to allow free cross-border flows of information, including

(2017) <https://www.gov.uk/government/publications/growing-the-artificial-intelligence-industry-in-the-uk> accessed 10 July 2023; Jack Hardinges, 'What Is a Data Trust?' (Open Data Institute, 2018) <https://theodi.org/article/what-is-a-data-trust/> accessed 10 July 2023.

[60] Stefano Rodotà, 'Data Protection as a Fundamental Right' in Serge Gutwirth and others (eds), *Reinventing Data Protection?* (Springer 2009) 77–80.

[61] Marrakesh Agreement Establishing the World Trade Organization [1994] UNTS 154, 33 ILM 1144.

[62] Although the Marrakesh Agreement is a mixed agreement from an EU law perspective, Eckes explains that 'this mixed nature has, in practice, been replaced by EU dominance'. Christina Eckes, *EU Powers under External Pressure: How the EU's External Actions Alter Its Internal Structures* (Oxford Scholarship Online 2019) 186.

[63] General Agreement on Trade in Services, Annex 1B to Marrakesh Agreement Establishing the World Trade Organization [1994] 1869 UNTS 183, 33 ILM 1167 (hereafter GATS).

personal data. These disciplines have, for example, as discussed in Section 3.3.4, been included in the Comprehensive and Progressive Agreement for Trans-Pacific Partnership (CPTPP),[64] the US-Mexico-Canada Agreement (USMCA),[65] the US-Japan Digital Trade Agreement (USJDTA),[66] and the UK-Japan Comprehensive Economic Partnership Agreement (CEPA).[67] In all such agreements, a free data flow obligation is counterbalanced by an exception, strongly resembling that of the GATS Article XIV(c), that allows parties to derogate from it, in order to adopt and maintain regulation in the public interest.[68] This approach, initially heavily influenced by the United States in the court of Trans-Pacific Partnership (TPP) negotiations (which was concluded as CPTPP after the US withdrawal[69]), has spread beyond US trade agreements.[70]

In 2019, under the Japanese presidency, G20 set out Data Free Flows with Trust (DFFT) as a guiding principle for international cooperation on cross-border data flows.[71] Although the concept of DFFT appears appealing in principle (after all, who can oppose trust?), there is a lack of common understanding or consensus on the precise definition of 'trust'.[72] One of the tracks along which multilateral dialogue on cross-border data flows under the flag of DFFT now unfolds is a trade track, which comprises negotiations on digital trade within the WTO Joint Initiative on E-commerce, OECD, G20, and G7.[73]

Cross-border data flows are high on the agenda in the ongoing negotiations at the WTO Joint Initiative on E-commerce between 89 WTO members, and counting,[74] but the feasibility of a multilateral agreement on the issue in the nearest

[64] Art 14.11 Comprehensive and Progressive Agreement for Trans-Pacific Partnership (concluded on 8 March 2018, in force 30 December 2018) (hereafter CPTPP).

[65] Art 19.11 US-Mexico-Canada Agreement (concluded on 30 November 2018, in force 1 July 2020) (hereafter USMCA).

[66] Art 11 US-Japan Digital Trade Agreement (concluded on 7 October 2019, in force 1 January 2020) (hereafter USJDTA).

[67] Art 8.84 UK-Japan Comprehensive Economic Partnership Agreement (concluded 23 October 2020, in force 1 January 2021) (hereafter UK-Japan CEPA).

[68] CPTPP (n 64) art 14.11(3), USMCA (n 65) art 19.11, USJDTA (n 66) art 11(2), and UK-Japan CEPA (n 67) art 8.84(2).

[69] Executive Office of the President, Office of the US Trade Representative [2017] Letter to TPP Depositary.

[70] See Section 3.3.4.

[71] G20 Osaka Leaders' Declaration, 28–29 June 2019, <https://www.consilium.europa.eu/media/40124/final_g20_osaka_leaders_declaration.pdf> accessed 10 July 2023.

[72] The potential risks associated with formulating the normative objective of data privacy protection based on trust are discussed in Section 3.4.

[73] Matthew P Goodman, 'Operationalizing Data Free Flow with Trust (DFFT)' (*Center for Strategic and International Studies*, 13 April 2023) <https://www.csis.org/analysis/operationalizing-data-free-flow-trust-dfft> accessed 10 July 2023. See also Fumiko Kudo, Ryosuke Sakaki, and Jonathan Soble, 'Every Country Has Its Own Digital Laws: How Can We Get Data Flowing Freely between Them?' (*World Economic Forum*, 20 May 2022) <https://www.weforum.org/agenda/2022/05/cross-border-data-regulation-dfft/> accessed 10 July 2023.

[74] E-Commerce Negotiations Maintain Positive Momentum, Focus on Key Issues (*World Trade Organization*, 25 May 2023) <https://www.wto.org/english/news_e/news23_e/jsec_25may23_e.htm> accessed 10 July 2023.

future is limited.[75] The EU has actively embraced the DFFT initiative, which is mentioned in digital trade partnership agreements concluded with Japan, Korea, and Singapore as an anchor point for digital trade cooperation on cross-border data flows.[76] Meanwhile, the United States is propelling the effort to make the non-binding Cross-Border Privacy Rules (CBPR), a certification framework initially established within the Asia Pacific Economic Cooperation (APEC), a global standard for cross-border data flows.[77] Increasingly endorsed in international trade agreements, these frameworks present a competing approach to governing cross-border data flows to that of the fundamental rights protection advanced by the EU.

Taking the view that domestic restrictions on cross-border flows of personal data are a barrier to reaping the benefits of global digital trade,[78] an increasing volume of literature either highlights the risk of inconsistency of personal data protection with the rules of the WTO or asks for new rules to ensure free flows of personal data across borders, or both.[79] The elimination of such restrictions remains one of the contentious issues of most recent trade negotiations in North America, Europe, and Asia. At the same time, as personal data has become an integral part of digital services, the EU's constitutional protection of the rights to privacy and the protection of personal data (of which restrictions on personal data transfers is an important pillar) is actually strengthening.[80] As a result, with the international trade regime increasingly moving towards 'free' digital trade,[81] the risk that the EU's international trade law commitments to liberalize the cross-border movement of services, on the one hand, and the protection of the fundamental rights to data privacy, on the other hand, will clash is very real.

The importance in this context of the 2020 *Schrems II* judgment of the Court of Justice of the European Union (CJEU) must be underscored. It invalidated—for

[75] Mira Burri, 'The Impact of Digitalization on Global Trade Law' (2023) 24 German Law Journal 551, 562.

[76] EU-Korea Digital Partnership (n 10), EU-Singapore Digital Partnership (n 10), and Japan-EU Digital Partnership (n 10).

[77] 'Global Cross-Border Privacy Rules Declaration' (*U.S. Department of Commerce*, 21 April 2022) <https://www.commerce.gov/global-cross-border-privacy-rules-declaration> accessed 10 July 2023. For a discussion, see Jedidiah Bracy, 'US Commerce Dept. Announces 'Historic' Global CBPR Forum for Data Transfers' (*IAPP*, 21 April 2022) <https://iapp.org/news/a/us-commerce-department-announces-historic-global-cbpr-forum-for-data-transfers/> accessed 10 July 2023.

[78] For a discussion on how data protection is being framed as a digital trade barrier in the economic digital trade discourse, see Section 3.3.

[79] See Section 2.3.

[80] See Section 2.2.1.

[81] Some countries, such as India, the African group, and the least developed countries, however, are critical about the e-commerce provisions in trade agreements, including those liberalizing cross-border data flows. See eg Work Programme on Electronic Commerce, 'Report of Panel Discussion on "Digital Industrial Policy and Development": Communication from the African Group' [2017] JOB/GC/133; Work Programme on Electronic Commerce, 'The E-Commerce Moratorium and Implications for Developing Countries, Communication from India and South Africa' [2019] WT/GC/W/774; Catherine Saez, 'E-Commerce: Some Developing Countries Push Back on Idea of New WTO Rules' (Tralac, 2 October 2017) <https://www.tralac.org/news/article/12207-e-commerce-some-developing-countries-push-back-on-idea-of-new-wto-rules.html> accessed 10 July 2023.

the second time—the legal framework negotiated between the United States and the EU for transatlantic flows of personal data, in that case the EU-US Privacy Shield.[82] The judgment asserted the need for a high legal standard for systematic transfers of personal data in general and created additional pressure on the EU's approach to the governance of personal data transfers from an international trade law perspective. In the wake of the judgment, a US commentator suggested that instead of engaging in further negotiations with the EU on its fundamental rights terms, the United States should respond along the lines of international trade law and economic sanctions.[83] For example, the United States should treat the CJEU's judgment as a violation of the WTO rules and retaliate using available US trade law mechanisms or impose sanctions against the EU together with countries like the United Kingdom, Canada, Australia, and India.[84]

Eventually, neither the United States nor other EU's trading partners followed this path. Instead, the EU and the United States resumed dialogue on a new transatlantic framework for transfers of personal data, the EU-US Data Privacy Framework. Following the implementation of additional safeguards for Europeans' personal data by the United States, the EU adopted the adequacy decision for the United States on 10 July 2023.[85] This new agreement ameliorates, for the time being, the risk of clash between the EU's international trade commitments related to the liberalization of cross-border data flows and its restrictions on cross-border transfers of personal data. However, in the long term, this risk prevails. On the day of adoption of the EU-US Data Privacy Framework, privacy activist Max Schrems (whose legal actions led to the invalidation of the two previous EU-US frameworks on personal data flows) reiterated that the new framework is unlikely to resolve issues that led to the invalidation of its predecessors and added that he would challenge the new framework at the CJEU.[86] Both the Civil Liberties Committee of the European Parliament and the European Data Protection Board (EDPB)[87] also

[82] *Schrems II* (n 55).

[83] Stewart Baker, 'How Can the U.S. Respond to Schrems II?'(*Lawfare Blog*, 21 July 2020) <https://www.lawfareblog.com/how-can-us-respond-schrems-ii> accessed 10 July 2023.

[84] ibid.

[85] 'Statement from U.S. Secretary of Commerce Gina Raimondo on the European Union-U.S. Data Privacy Framework' (*U.S. Department of Commerce*, 3 July 2023) <https://www.commerce.gov/news/press-releases/2023/07/statement-us-secretary-commerce-gina-raimondo-european-union-us-data> accessed 10 July 2023; European Commission Implementing Decision of 10 July 2023 pursuant to Regulation (EU) 2016/679 of the European Parliament and of the Council on the adequate level of protection of personal data under the EU-US Data Privacy Framework [2023] C(2023) 4745 final.

[86] 'New Trans-Atlantic Data Privacy Framework Largely a Copy of "Privacy Shield". noyb Will Challenge the Decision' (*noyb*, 10 July 2023) <https://noyb.eu/en/european-commission-gives-eu-us-data-transfers-third-round-cjeu> accessed 10 July 2023. See also '"Privacy Shield 2.0"? First Reaction by Max Schrems' (*noyb*, 25 March 2022) <https://noyb.eu/en/privacy-shield-20-first-reaction-max-schrems> accessed 10 July 2023; 'First reaction: Executive Order on US Surveillance unlikely to satisfy EU law' (*noyb*, 7 October 2022) <https://noyb.eu/en/new-us-executive-order-unlikely-satisfy-eu-law> accessed 10 July 2023.

[87] The EDPB is a consortium of data protection authorities in the EU. See 'EDPB Chairmanship' < https://edpb.europa.eu/about-edpb/who-we-are/edpb-chairmanship_en#:~:text=The%20Europ

raised concerns on whether this framework will allow the United States to meet the EU's essential equivalence standard.[88]

1.1.6 Clash between the EU Charter and the EU's WTO commitments

A clash between the EU's constitutional protection for personal data (as translated into a framework for cross-border transfers of personal data in the GDPR) and the EU's trade liberalization commitments is not in and of itself a reason to cry foul. Both the EU Charter and international trade law contain exceptions that allow each system to tolerate encroachments on their respective rules by the other, within certain limits. As long as the exceptions in both systems are aligned, they can be used to manage the degree of tension between the two systems.

Most prominently among existing exceptions, the majority of international trade agreements governing trade in services provide for a so-called 'general exception' for privacy and data protection. This general exception is either modelled after the general exception contained in Article XIV(c)(ii) of the GATS or incorporates the GATS general exceptoin *mutatis mutandis*.[89] The general exception for privacy and data protection is designed to preserve a degree of regulatory autonomy for parties to an international trade agreement. It enables parties to such an agreement to adopt and maintain measures 'necessary' to protect the privacy of individuals in relation to the processing and dissemination of personal data, even if such measures run counter to the member's international commitments (the 'trade

ean%20Data%20Protection%20Board,Data%20Protection%20Supervisor%20(EDPS)> accessed 10 July 2023.

[88] EDPB, Opinion 5/2023 on the European Commission Draft Implementing Decision on the adequate protection of personal data under the EU-US Data Privacy Framework, 28 February 2023; 'Press Release, MEPs against Greenlighting Personal Data Transfers with the U.S. under Current Rules'(*European Parliament*, 13 April 2023) <https://www.europarl.europa.eu/news/en/press-room/20230411IPR79501/meps-against-greenlighting-data-transfers-with-the-u-s-under-current-rules> accessed 10 July 2023.

[89] See, eg, art 28.3(2)(c)(ii) Comprehensive Economic and Trade Agreement (CETA) between Canada, of the one part, and the European Union and its Member States, of the other part, 14 September 2014 [2017] OJ L11/23; art 8.62(e)(ii) Free trade Agreement between the European Union and the Republic of Singapore, ST/7972/2018/ADD/5, OJ L 294; art 167(1)(e)(ii) Trade Agreement between the European Union and Its Member States, of the One Part, and Colombia and Peru, of the Other Part, 31 May 2012 [2012] OJ L 354/1;aArt 7.50(e)(ii) Free Trade Agreement between the European Union and Its Member States, of the One Part, and the Republic of Korea, of the Other Part, 6 October 2010 [2011] OJ L 127/6; art 203(1)(e)(ii) Agreement Establishing an Association between Central America, on the one hand, and the European Union and its Member States, on the other, 29 June 2012 [2012] OJ L 346/3; art 23.1(2) United States-Korea Free Trade Agreement, 1 April 2007, 46 ILM. 642; art 21.1(2) United States-Singapore Free Trade Agreement, 3 September 2003, 117 Stat. 948; art 21.1(2) Dominican Republic-Central America-United States Free Trade Agreement, 28 May 2004, 43 ILM 514; art 21.1(2) United States-Panama Trade Promotion Agreement, 31 October 2012; art 32.1(2) USMCA (n 65); art 29.1(3) CPTPP (n 64).

necessity test'). This trade necessity test is the core of the first step in the assessment of whether a restriction on cross-border flows of personal data can be justified under the general exception for privacy and data protection.[90]

Because restrictions on cross-border data flows are only an exception in trade agreements, trade rules start from the premise that cross-border flows should be free. Article 52(2) of the EU Charter, conversely, allows the EU to limit fundamental rights if it is 'necessary' to meet objectives of general interest to the EU or to protect the rights and freedoms of others (the EU Charter necessity test). As interpreted by the CJEU, this provision allows EU bodies to conclude an international agreement, which involves transfers of personal data outside the EEA, if the conditions laid out in this clause—and most importantly that of the Charter's necessity test—are fulfilled.[91] The EU Charter protects the fundamental rights implicated by the processing of personal data and contains an exception that might be sufficient, in certain circumstances, to allow the EU to make commitments concerning cross-border flows of personal data in international trade agreements. Among other things, this book explores the tension between these two exceptions and examines various possibilities allowing for the objectives behind them to be met.

Not surprisingly in the light of the above, the possibility of the inclusion of a provision on cross-border data flows accompanied by a GATS Article XIV-type exception for privacy and data protection in TiSA and TTIP[92]—both stalled as of this writing (June 2023)—sparked a strong push-back from European Parliament, academics, and civil society in 2015–2016.[93] Later, in order to avoid any risk of undermining the

[90] The second step in the assessment is the introductory clause of the exception (also referred to as the 'chapeau'). For discussion of the necessity test, see Section 2.4.2, and for the discussion of the test in the chapeau, see Section 4.3.4.

[91] *Opinion on EU-Canada PNR Agreement* (n 55) paras 67, 70.

[92] See Gaël Le Roux, 'TTIP Negotiations, Policy Convergence, and the Transatlantic Digital Economy' (2017) 19(4) Business and Politics 709, 731 ('The USTR includes an essential element that is still not addressed by the European Commission in its initial proposal, which is cross-border data flows. The United States thus remains very offensive on the matter and reproduced what they have already pushed through in the KORUS and the TPP texts.'). A bracketed draft for art 2 of the Annex on Electronic Commerce to TiSA included a prohibition to 'prevent a service supplier of another Party from transferring, accessing processing or storing information, including personal information, within or outside the Party's territory, where such activity is carried out in connection with the conduct of the service supplier's business.' 'Comments of The Coalition for Privacy and Free Trade to the Trade Policy Staff Committee of the United States Trade Representative' (Coalition For Privacy & Free Trade, 2013) <http://www.centerfordigitaldemocracy.org/sites/default/files/Coalition-for-Privacy-and-Free-Trade-Comments-to-USTR-May-9-2013_0.pdf> accessed 10 July 2023 ('The Obama Administration already has recognized the importance of interoperable privacy frameworks to global economic progress and prosperity: ... The United States is committed to engaging with its international partners to increase interoperability in privacy laws by pursuing mutual recognition, the development of codes of conduct through multistakeholder processes, and enforcement cooperation.'). But see James Fontanella-Khan, 'Data Protection Ruled Out of EU-US Trade Talks' *Financial Times* (4 November 2013) <www.ft.com/content/92a14dd2-44b9-11e3-a751-00144feabdc0> accessed 10 July 2023 (noting EU officials' fear that 'finding a middle ground with the U.S. would only lower overall E.U. privacy standards.').

[93] See, eg, Kristina Irion, Svetlana Yakovleva, and Marija Bartl, 'Trade and Privacy: Complicated Bedfellows? How to Achieve Data Protection-Proof Free Trade Agreements' (2016) Independent study commissioned by BEUC and others, 44–45, 59–60 <https://www.ivir.nl/publicaties/download/trade_and_privacy.pdf> accessed 10 July 2023; Fernández Pérez (2016); European Parliament

fundamental rights to privacy and the protection of personal data, the EU ultimately refrained from including such a provision in the Economic Partnership Agreement between the European Union and Japan (JEFTA)[94] and the revision of the EU-Mexico Free Trade Agreement.[95] Instead, the parties agreed to review the necessity to include such a provision in the agreement in three years' time. In the case of Japan, the absence of such a clause was accompanied by the adoption of a mutual adequacy decision under the GDPR shortly before JEFTA took effect.[96]

1.1.7 Cross-border data flows in the EU's digital trade agreements

In 2018, after a thorny interinstitutional dialogue, the EU developed *horizontal provisions* on cross-border data flows and the protection of privacy and personal data for its prospective digital trade agreements.[97] They include a specific exception for privacy and data protection, similar to the national security exception of Article XIV*bis* of the GATS—a text much broader than the above-mentioned general exception. The EU has included those horizontal provisions ever since in its proposals for digital trade chapters in bilateral trade agreements (such as those with Australia, New Zealand, Chile, Indonesia, Tunisia,[98] the United Kingdom

resolution of 8 July 2015 containing the European Parliament's recommendations to the European Commission on the negotiations for the Transatlantic Trade and Investment Partnership (TTIP) (2014/2228(INI)); European Parliament resolution of 3 February 2016 containing the European Parliament's recommendations to the Commission on the negotiations for the Trade in Services Agreement (TiSA) (2015/2233(INI)).

[94] Economic Partnership Agreement between the European Union and Japan, Annex to the Proposal for a Council Decision, COM(2018) 192 final, 18 April 2018 (hereafter JEFTA).

[95] Both agreements include a commitment to reconsider the issue within three years after the agreement enters into force. See art 8.81 of JEFTA (n 94). See also Brett Fortnam, 'EU Punts on Data Flow Language in Japan Deal, Leaving: Position Unresolved' (*Inside US Trade*, 2017) <https://insidetrade.com/inside-us-trade/eu-punts-data-flow-language-japan-deal-leaving-position-unresolved> accessed 10 July 2023 (hereafter Fortnam 'EU Punts on Data Flow Language').

[96] Commission Implementing Decision (EU) 2019/419 of 23 January 2019 pursuant to Regulation (EU) 2016/679 of the European Parliament and of the Council on the adequate protection of personal data by Japan under the Act on the Protection of Personal Information, C/2019/304/ OJ L 76. Although this decision is commonly referred to as 'mutual', from a legal perspective, these are two unilateral decisions adopted at the same time.

[97] European Commission, 'Proposal for Provisions on Cross-Border Data Flows and Protection of Personal Data and Privacy' (31 January 2018) <https://www.politico.eu/wp-content/uploads/2018/02/Data-flow-provisions-POLITICO.pdf> accessed 10 July 2023 (hereafter EU horizontal provisions on cross-border data flows); see also Aaronson and Leblond 'Another Digital Divide' (n 52) 262; Fortnam 'EU Punts on Data Flow Language' (n 95). For background of the horizontal provisions, see Section 4.2.1. For analysis and critique, see Sections 4.2.2–4.2.6.

[98] See EU proposal for a Chapter on Digital Trade of the EU-New Zealand FTA; EU proposal for a Chapter on Digital Trade of the EU-Australia FTA; La proposition de l'Union européenne (UE) relative à Accord de libre-échange UE-Tunisie UE-Tunisie, Titre [] Commerce Numérique, 9 November 2018; Digital Trade Proposals for EU-Chile and EU-Indonesia were drafted before the European Union agreed on the model provisions. Therefore, these proposals only contained a placeholder for a

(following Brexit),[99] and Japan[100]) and in multilateral negotiations on electronic commerce at the WTO.[101] When included in trade agreements, these horizontal provisions are intended not to replace but rather to co-exist with the general exception for privacy and data protection modelled after Article XIV(c)(ii) GATS included in the same agreement.[102]

While the EU managed to maintain the text close to the proposed horizontal provisions in the EU-Chile Interim Trade Agreement[103] (negotiated, but not yet signed, as of June 2023) and the EU-New Zealand FTA (signed but not yet ratified),[104] the exception for privacy and data protection in the 2020 EU-UK TCA seems to be narrower than that in the proposed horizontal provisions.[105] Despite this deviation, the proposed horizontal provisions continue to be the EU's template for cross-border data flow provisions and exceptions from them in international trade negotiations. The discussion in this book, therefore, focuses in significant part on these horizontal provisions.

When compared to the influential US approach to data flows, already implemented in a variety of trade agreements around the world,[106] it is clear that the EU's approach in the 2018 horizontal provisions contains a narrower prohibition

provision on cross-border data flows. EU proposal for a Digital trade title in the Trade Part of a possible modernized EU-Chile Association Agreement, 5 February 2018 (containing a placeholder for provisions on data flows); EU proposal for a Chapter on Digital Trade of the EU-Indonesia FTA, 27 July 2017. The European Union tabled its horizontal provisions on cross-border data flows at a later stage in negotiations with these two countries. See, eg, European Commission, Report of the 5th Round of Negotiations for a Free Trade Agreement between the European Union and Indonesia (July 2018).

99 Draft text of the Agreement on the New Partnership with the United Kingdom, European Commission, 18 March 2020.

100 Relying on the three-year review clause, included in JEFTA instead of a free cross-border data flow provision, in 2022, the EU and Japan launched negotiations on cross-border data flows. See 'EU and Japan Start Negotiations to Include Rules on Cross-Border Data Flows in Their Economic Partnership Agreement' (*European Commission*, 7 October 2022) <https://policy.trade.ec.europa.eu/news/eu-and-japan-start-negotiations-include-rules-cross-border-data-flows-their-economic-partnership-2022-10-07_en> accessed 10 July 2023; Recital 4 of the Recommendation for a Council Decision authorizing the opening of negotiations for the inclusion of provisions on cross-border data flows in the Agreement between the European Union and Japan for an Economic Partnership [2022] COM(2022) 336 final.

101 Joint Statement on Electronic Commerce, EU Proposal for WTO Disciplines and Commitments Relating to Electronic Commerce. Communication from the European Union [2019] INF/ECOM/22, 26 April 2019.

102 See, eg, art 25.1(2)(c)(ii) of the EU-New Zealand Free Trade Agreement (signed on 9 July 2023) (hereafter EU-New Zealand FTA).

103 Arts 19.4 and 19.5 of the EU-Chile Interim Agreement (negotiations concluded on 9 December 2022).

104 EU-New Zealand FTA (n 102) arts 12.4 and 12.5.

105 Art 202 Trade and Cooperation Agreement between the European Union and the European Atomic Energy Community of the one part, and the United Kingdom of Great Britain and Northern Ireland, of the other part [2021] OJ L 149. See Opinion 3/2021 of the European Data Protection Supervisor on the conclusion of the EU and UK trade agreement and the EU and UK exchange of classified information agreement, 22 February 2021. But see Kristina Irion and Mira Burri, '§ 16 Digitaler Handel' in Gesa Kübek, Christian J Tams, and Jörg Philipp Terhechte (Hrsg), *Handels- und Kooperationsvertrag EU/GB Handbuch* (Baden-Baden: Nomos 2022) 343–68, paras 14–16.

106 See Section 3.3.4.

on restrictions of cross-border data flows and a broader exception for domestic privacy and data protection rules.[107] This creates a quandary for countries bound by both. Adherence to the US model by countries that maintain a free flow of personal data from the EU under adequacy decisions, in particular, Canada, Japan, and the United Kingdom, puts pressure on their ability to comply with the EU's restrictions on transfers of personal data.[108] The EU is unlikely and legally unable to agree to the cross-border data flow provisions such as those advanced by the United States just mentioned above, for this would mean an unjustifiable derogation from the EU Charter-based fundamental rights.[109]

1.1.8 Internal critique of EU framework for transfers of personal data

From an EU internal perspective, the EU's own framework for transfers of personal data outside the EEA has been criticized on multiple occasions for its broad reach and insufficient and inconsistent enforcement.[110] An important prerequisite of developing an alternative framework, however, is a deeper understanding of the relationship between Articles 7, 8, and 52(1) of the EU Charter and the GDPR, and the extent to which the EU legislator is free to design the framework for transfers of personal data without overstepping constitutional boundaries. This issue ties into a broader ongoing academic debate on the essence of the EU fundamental rights and the relationship between EU primary and secondary law.

1.2 Research Questions and Methodology

The main research question answered in this book is:

> *How should commitments on cross-border data flows in EU trade agreements be reconciled with the protection of the fundamental rights to privacy and personal data?*

The book answers this question in four steps by addressing the following four sets of sub-questions, relating to (1) compatibility, (2) protectionism, (3) reconciliation, and (4) reform of the EU restrictions.

[107] For discussion, see Sections 3.3.4 and 4.2.1.
[108] See Section 5.3.3.2.
[109] This is because as explained in Section 2.4.4, the trade 'necessity test' that lies at the heart of the exception for privacy and data protection in US-led trade agreements requires a derogation from fundamental rights beyond the limits set by art 52(1) of the EU Charter.
[110] For a discussion, see Section 5.3.

1. *The compatibility question:* Are the obligations of the GATS and EU restrictions on transfers of personal data outside the EEA under the GDPR compatible, and if not, can this incompatibility be justified under the necessity tests the general exception in the GATS and Article 52(1) of the EU Charter?
2. *The protectionism question:* Do EU restrictions on transfers of personal data outside the EEA constitute protectionism? Where should the line be drawn between protection and protectionism? What roles do more general discourses play in determining what amounts to legitimate protection and what to illegitimate protectionism? How does framing the debate on privacy and data protection in terms of 'digital protectionism' affect the normative foundations of domestic regulation on privacy and personal data, and setting appropriate levels of privacy and personal data protection?
3. *The reconciliation question:* Do the proposed horizontal provisions on cross-border data flows, intended to be included in digital trade chapters of the EU digital trade agreements, meet the EU's ambitions of reconciling cross-border data flows under international trade law with the protection of the rights to privacy and personal data as fundamental rights under the EU Charter, while maintaining a global rules-based trading system? If they do not meet the EU's ambitions to reconcile, then what are the issues preventing them from doing so? In which other ways can these policy objectives be reconciled in future trade agreements?
4. *The reform of the EU restrictions question:* Is the EU framework for transfers of personal data outside the EEA still able to perform its constitutional function under the EU Charter? If not, what are the weaknesses of this framework from the EU Charter perspective, and how can they be addressed in a manner both compliant with the EU Charter and conducive to international trade? What are the constitutional boundaries for reforming the EU framework for transfers of personal data outside the EEA? More precisely, does this framework constitute (part of) the essence of the fundamental right to privacy, to the protection of personal data, and to an effective remedy?

Turning to methodological questions, for the most part, the research question calls for a doctrinal analysis of the law from an internal perspective.[111] The main research question is evidently normative, asking how competing values and interests *should* be reconciled. The first normative basis will be the law, even if it will become evident that the law—as an expression of such competition—will not give away the answer.

[111] Jan M Smits, *The Mind and Method of the Legal Academic* (Edward Elgar 2012) 3 (defining the doctrinal method as 'approach, in which rules, principles and case law are considered from the internal perspective and in which law is looked at as being in a relatively autonomous relation to the social, economic and political reality'.).

The book thus engages first in a discussion about what the law is, with a view towards developing it further.[112] This is necessary in order to inform the legal arguments in this book. In doing so, it engages first with the reform of the international trade exception for privacy and data protection in future EU trade agreements. And second, with the reform of the EU framework for transfers of personal data outside the EEA under the GDPR in a manner respectful of EU fundamental rights.[113] The doctrinal analysis systematizes the legislation and jurisprudence of the CJEU and the WTO adjudicating bodies within the scholarly schemes established in secondary literature from the relevant legal domains, in particular, the EU law, European data protection, and international trade law.[114]

In order to further support its normative argument, the book complements the classical doctrinal method by a historical approach to law,[115] elements of economic analysis of law, and critical legal studies.[116] The interplay between these methods plays a central role in the development of the arguments in Chapter 3, addressing the question of where to draw a line between protection and protectionism, and how the framing of the debate on trade and data privacy affects the degree of regulatory autonomy afforded to domestic privacy and data protection rules. Relying on the literature on economics and the political economy of international trade, Chapter 3 takes a historical perspective to trace how the notion of 'protectionism' has evolved over time. The discussion of the role of discourse in shaping the meaning of 'protectionism' is also informed by the literature on language and power, which falls under the umbrella term of 'discourse analysis'. It then applies these insights to the current debate on whether, and to what extent, EU restrictions on transfers of personal data outside the EEA can be viewed as protectionist. The discussion of the dual nature of personal data in Chapter 3 requires a conceptual analysis of personal data, which contraposes its dignitary and economic aspects. An understanding of both the economic nature and life cycle of personal data rests on an external, essentially economic approach. Juxtaposing the legal and economic perspectives on the protection of personal data allows the book to put the tension between the two approaches in sharp contrast. This tension translates into conflicting goals and differing notions as to the right level of regulation, depending on

[112] Armin von Bogdandy, 'The Past and Promise of Doctrinal Constructivism: A Strategy for Responding to the Challenges Facing Constitutional Scholarship in Europe' (2009) 7(3) International Journal of Constitutional Law 364, 377 (hereafter Von Bogdandy 'The Past and Promise').

[113] Robert Cryer and others, *Research Methodologies in EU and International Law* (Hart Publishing 2011) 34ff; Rob Van Gestel, Hans-W Micklitz, and Miguel Poiares Maduro, 'Methodology in the New Legal World'(2012) EUI Working Papers LAW No 2012/13, 2 <https://ssrn.com/abstract=2069872> accessed 10 July 2023; Adrian Vermeule, 'Connecting Positive and Normative Legal Theory' (2007) 10 University of Pennsylvania Journal of Constitutional Law 387, 394–95.

[114] Von Bogdandy 'The Past and Promise' (n 112), 377.

[115] Philip Handler, 'Legal History' in Dawn Watkins and Mandy Burton (eds), *Research Methods in Law* (Routledge 2013).

[116] John Finnis, 'Critical Legal Studies' in John Finnis (ed), *Philosophy of Law: Collected Essays*, vol VI (OUP 2011).

whether personal data is protected as an economic asset or a fundamental right. This part of the discussion draws on the academic literature informed by a law and economics theory of regulation, which addresses regulation from an economic efficiency standpoint.[117] By contrast, a discussion of the dignitary aspect is based on the academic literature embracing a moral and legal approach reflecting the value attached to personal data by international human rights and EU law.

There is a variety of international trade agreements that go a step further than the WTO agreements in regulating issues related to electronic commerce and data (WTO plus agreements).[118] In analysing the governance of cross-border data flows, the book takes an EU perspective, which it juxtaposes, primarily, with that of the United States. For this reason, the scope of WTO plus agreements considered in this book is limited to the recent EU-led trade agreements that have been concluded (the EU-UK TCA), negotiated (EU-Chile Interim Trade Agreement), or signed (EU-New Zealand FTA). These trade agreements are relevant for the analysis in this book because they contain specific provisions on cross-border data flows. Bringing JEFTA and the draft EU-Mexico agreements into the discussion gives a historical perspective to the debate on cross-border data flows in the international trade realm. On the US side, the analysis in this book includes the aforementioned CPTPP, USMCA and the USJDTA, which, as mentioned earlier, set a standard of free cross-border data flow provisions replicated in multiple other trade agreements around the world. Occasionally, the analysis also features the Regional and Comprehensive Economic Partnership (RCEP), which is considered to represent China's model.

The US model for governing cross-border data flows in international trade agreements has been chosen as a point of comparison with the EU model, for the reason that it is the most influential model in international trade agreements. In addition, in the data protection realm, the issue of transfers of personal data from the EEA to the United States has been one of the most contentious within the lifetime of the EU data protection framework. Furthermore, strengthening partnership with the United States is a strategic trade policy priority for the EU.[119] As the European Commission stated in its 2021 Trade Policy Review, '[t]he transatlantic relationship is the biggest and most economically significant partnership in the world'.[120] Cooperation with the United States, in the Commission's words, 'will be critical to ensuring that new regulations are in line with the values of democratic, open and inclusive societies'.[121] In the time of fierce geopolitical competition (not

[117] Anthony Ogus, *Regulation: Legal Form and Economic Theory* (3rd edn, Clarendon Press 1994) 23–54.

[118] For an overview of such provisions, see Mira Burri and Rodrigo Polanco, 'Digital Trade Provisions in Preferential Trade Agreements: Introducing a New Dataset' (2020) 23(1) Journal of International Economic Law 187.

[119] Communication from the Commission, Trade Policy Review (n 8).

[120] ibid.

[121] ibid.

just of economies but also of ideologies) and Russia–Ukraine war, EU–US cooperation is crucial in confronting the rising power of China.[122] The focus on the EU–US relationship, however, does not diminish the fact that the balancing of economic, fundamental rights and other policy objectives in the governance of cross-border data flows is a global issue.

This book does not engage with the debate on the classification of goods and services when it comes to cross-border data flows.[123] The focus of this book is on international agreements covering trade in services and electronic commerce, which is referred to as digital trade in most of the recent trade agreements. The book does not cover trade in goods, even though in some cases, measures restricting cross-border data flows could be targeting 'goods attributes' of a product, such as an internet of things device.

It should also be acknowledged that approaching cross-border data flows from an international trade perspective, as adopted by this book, is only one way of looking at freedom of information flows more generally. In a broader context, restrictions on data flows implicate other policy objectives, such as freedom of speech, as well as (international) media and communications freedom, which in a wider sense support political, social, and economic activities. As Mueller and Grindal rightly observe, the economic value of data flows is a 'by-product of the social, communicative and productive capability caused by untrammelled information flows'.[124]

1.3 Outline of the Book

The chapters of this book tackle in turn the research sub-questions posed in Section 1.2. Chapter 2 explicates the scope and the functioning the EU framework for transfers of personal data outside the EEA under the GDPR against the background of the concerns that led to the emergence of the EU data protection framework in the 1990s. It then demonstrates the possible tension between restrictions imposed on transfers of personal data outside the EEA by this framework and existing EU international trade commitments under the GATS. The chapter further argues that there is a risk that this tension cannot be ameliorated by the application of exceptions provided for in the EU and international trade law, due to the incompatibility of these exceptions when applied simultaneously. Put simply, Chapter 2

[122] Stuart Lauw and Eli Stokols, 'G7 vs. China: US, Europe Unite in Tough Messaging Against Beijing' *Politico* (20 May 2023) <https://www.politico.eu/article/g7-vs-china-us-europe-unite-tough-message-summit-statement/> accessed 10 July 2023.

[123] For a discussion, see eg Nivedita Sen, 'Understanding the Role of the WTO in International Data Flows: Taking the Liberalization or the Regulatory Autonomy Path?' (2018) 21(2) Journal of International Economic Law 323, 330–35; Rajan S Neeraj, 'Trade Rules for the Digital Economy: Charting New Waters at the WTO' (2019), 18(S1) World Trade Review s121.

[124] Mueller and Grindal, 'Data Flows' (n 26) 82.

sets out the main issue addressed by this book: the conflict between commitments to data privacy and trade liberalization.

Chapter 3 takes a step back and investigates whether EU restrictions on transfers of personal data outside the EEA are protectionist. One could argue that the balance between digital trade liberalization and the protection of data privacy should simply be struck by ruling out measures that are protectionist in nature. The problem is, however, that the baseline between legitimate protection and protectionism does not exist. Chapter 3 investigates how views on this baseline are discursively constructed and how this baseline has shifted over time. The chapter demonstrates how discourse affected the conceptualization of the notion of 'protectionism' in international trade negotiations and WTO case law and translates these findings into a number of recommendations for future international trade negotiations on digital trade and cross-border data flows. Chapter 3 also shows how discourse can affect the normative foundations of the public policy objectives incorporated into trade law exceptions, such as privacy and the protection of personal data, and, as a result, the level of protection of such objectives in domestic legal systems.

Chapter 4 turns to the international trade law aspect of the problem identified in Chapter 2, but with a particular focus on future EU digital trade agreements. It questions whether the horizontal provisions on cross-border data flows and the protection of personal data included in its recent digital trade agreements and tabled for all ongoing trade negotiations on these issues would allow the EU to strike the right balance between the fundamental rights protection of privacy and personal data and its trade policy objectives. Having identified the weaknesses of the horizontal provisions, Chapter 4 looks for alternatives.

Chapter 5 examines the EU framework for transfers of personal data outside the EEA through the lens of geopolitical, legal, and economic changes and the constitutional function of those rules in order to establish whether this framework is still fit for purpose or needs to be improved. Having identified the weaknesses of this framework from the EU Charter perspective, this chapter then asks how this framework could be improved to better perform its constitutional function under the EU Charter, while at the same time ameliorating the problem identified in Chapter 2. Engaging with the idea of future reform, Chapter 5 addresses the relatively unexplored issue of the constitutional contours of EU secondary law framework for transfers of personal data outside the EEA. Relatedly, it explores the flexibility that the EU legislator has under the EU Charter to change the rules of the GDPR on transfers of personal data. It also provides three directions of thought on future reform, roughly corresponding to possible short-, medium-, and long-term strategies for the EU.

Chapter 6 offers conclusions structured as responses to the research questions formulated above and envisions paths for further research.

Research in this book is up to date until 1 May 2023. After that, only a small number of substantive additions and changes have been made. This book is based on the author's PhD dissertation, defended *cum laude* on 21 April 2021 at the University of Amsterdam under the supervision of Professors Joris van Hoboken and Ingo Venzke. Some parts of this book are based on the author's published work. In particular, Chapter 2 is based on Svetlana Yakovleva, 'Personal Data Transfers in International Trade and EU Law: A Tale of Two "Necessities"', Journal of World Investment & Trade 21 (2020) 881–919; Chapter 3 is based on Svetlana Yakovleva, 'Privacy Protection(ism): The Latest Wave of Trade Constraints on Regulatory Autonomy', University of Miami Law Review 74 (2) (2020) 416–519. This book also cites individual and co-authored works that preceded and paved the way to this book.

2

Personal Data Transfers in International Trade and EU Law

A Tale of Two 'Necessities'

2.1 Introduction

This chapter identifies and sets out the key issue addressed in this book, namely the increasing tension between the governance of cross-border transfers of personal data by the European Union (EU) and its governance in international trade law. It develops the argument that the EU restrictions on transfers of personal data outside the European Economic Area (EEA) could conflict with the EU's commitments under the General Agreement on Trade in Services (GATS).[1] It contends that such restrictions are unlikely to meet the trade necessity test even in its most lenient interpretation because they arguably go beyond the limits set by the GATS provisions and the general exception. An important contribution of the chapter to the discussion is that the requirement of free cross-border flow of personal data that can be deduced from the EU's existing trade liberalization commitments in the context of digitally provided services is not only inconsistent with the General Data Protection Regulation (GDPR)[2] but is also unlikely to be justified under Article 52(1) of the EU Charter of Fundamental Rights (EU Charter)[3] as a necessary and proportionate derogation from the fundamental right to the protection of personal data. This analysis exposes the EU's constitutional constraints on implementing such a requirement for the cross-border flow of personal data into the GDPR, which may lead to a catch-22 compliance dead lock for the EU. The chapter then argues that adjustments of both international trade and EU data protection rules are necessary to overcome this dead lock.

The chapter proceeds as follows. Section 2.2 presents the historical background and explains the EU restrictions on transfers of personal data outside the EEA.[4] It

[1] General Agreement on Trade in Services, Annex 1B to Marrakesh Agreement Establishing the World Trade Organization [1994] 1869 UNTS 183, 33 ILM 1167 (hereafter GATS).

[2] Regulation (EU) 2016/679 of the European Parliament and of the Council of 27 April 2016 on the protection of natural persons with regard to the processing of personal data and on the free movement of such data, and repealing Directive 95/46/EC [2016] OJ L119/1 (hereafter GDPR).

[3] Charter of Fundamental Rights of the European Union [2000] OJ C364/1 (hereafter EU Charter).

[4] The EEA consists of the member states of the European Union and countries of the European Free Trade Association (EFTA)—Norway, Iceland, and Lichtenstein. 'Glossary: European Economic Area (EEA)' (Eurostat) <https://ec.europa.eu/eurostat/statistics-explained/index.php/Glossary:Euro

Governing Cross-Border Data Flows. Svetlana Yakovleva, Oxford University Press. © Svetlana Yakovleva 2024.
DOI: 10.1093/oso/9780192899248.003.0002

then demonstrates a possible inconsistency between these rules and the EU commitments under the GATS. Section 2.3 juxtaposes the interpretation of the trade necessity test and the EU Charter necessity test and explains why there is a risk of a catch-22 type of compliance dead lock for the EU when the two necessity tests are applied simultaneously. Section 2.4 outlines ways out of the potential dead lock. Section 2.5 concludes.

2.2 The EU Regime for Transfers of Personal Data Outside the EEA

Restrictions on transfers of personal data outside the EEA have been characteristic of the EU data protection framework since its inception. Therefore, this section introduces these restrictions in a historical context, which allows for a deeper understanding of the concerns underlying them. It also explains the prevailing uncertainty surrounding the notion of 'transfer' in the EU data protection framework and its evolution over time.

2.2.1 Historical background

Rules governing cross-border transfers of personal data began to emerge in EU member states, alongside the first data protection laws in the 1970s, in response to the increasingly automated processing of personal data.[5] While the first 1970 data protection laws of the German federal state of Hessen did not contain any restrictions on transfers of personal data, the data protection laws of Austria, Norway, Sweden, Ireland, and Finland, adopted shortly after, did.[6] As classified by Kuner, these restrictions fell into one of the following three categories: (1) requiring an explicit authorization by a Data Protection Authority (DPA); (2) incorporating provisions on data flows from Article 12 of the Council of Europe Convention 108 (Convention 108);[7] and (3) requiring an individual's consent or a similar level of

pean_Economic_Area_(EEA)#:~:text=The%20European%20Economic%20Area%2C%20abbreviated,force%20on%201%20January%201994> accessed 10 July 2023.

[5] Christopher Kuner, *Transborder Data Flows and Data Privacy Law* (OUP 2013) (hereafter Kuner, *Transborder Data Flows and Data Privacy Law*) 26.

[6] ibid 27–28.

[7] Council of Europe, 'Convention for the Protection of Individuals with Regard to the Automatic Processing of Individual Data' (28 January 1981) ETS 108 (hereafter Convention 108). Art 12, 'Transborder flows of personal data and domestic law', of the Convention 108 (prior to reform completed in 2018) states:

1. The following provisions shall apply to the transfer across national borders, by whatever medium, of personal data undergoing automatic processing or collected with a view to their being automatically processed.

protection in the country of destination.[8] Different approaches across EU member states were evidenced not only at the level of the regulations themselves but also at the level of their enforcement.[9] On par with restrictions on the exporting of personal data, some domestic laws also regulated the importation of such data.[10] The strictness of rules governing transfers of personal data at that time was, however, counterbalanced by the relatively small volume of personal data in overall data flows, which mostly comprised non-personal data.[11]

Concerns that motivated the adoption of the rules on *transfers* of personal data, both within EU member states and to other countries, included not only the risk of the circumvention of domestic privacy and data protection rules but also the risk that national,[12] cultural, and economic sovereignty could be undermined by personal data being processed abroad.[13] Examples of risks tied into sovereignty concerns were the inability to administer justice, information dependency on other states, and political risks resulting from information flows being controlled from another country.[14]

The increasing adoption of data protection laws across Europe, as well as on the international level, such as the Convention 108 and the 1980 OECD Guidelines,[15] led to a fragmentation of data protection standards.[16] Despite the recommendation from the European Commission that EU member states should ratify the Convention 108 in an effort to contribute to an organic harmonization of data protection laws across Europe[17], by the end of 1989 only seven EU member states had ratified it.[18] Against the backdrop of increasing cross-border data flows in the

2. A Party shall not, for the sole purpose of the protection of privacy, prohibit or subject to special authorisation transborder flows of personal data going to the territory of another Party.
3. Nevertheless, each Party shall be entitled to derogate from the provisions of paragraph 2:
   a) insofar as its legislation includes specific regulations for certain categories of personal data or of automated personal data files, because of the nature of those data or those files, except where the regulations of the other Party provide an equivalent protection;
   b) when the transfer is made from its territory to the territory of a non-Contracting State through the intermediary of the territory of another Party, in order to avoid such transfers resulting in circumvention of the legislation of the Party referred to at the beginning of this paragraph.

8 Kuner, *Transborder Data Flows and Data Privacy Law* (n 5) 27–28.

9 ibid.

10 For example, Austrian and Luxemburgish data protection acts. Kuner, *Transborder Data Flows and Data Privacy Law* (n 5) 27–28.

11 ibid.

12 Kuner, *Transborder Data Flows and Data Privacy Law* (n 5) 107.

13 ibid 28–29.

14 ibid 29–30.

15 For example, in 1981, the Council of Europe adopted Convention 108 (n 7), and in 1980 the OECD adopted the 1980 Guidelines on the Protection of Privacy and Transborder Flows of Personal Data.

16 Kuner, *Transborder Data Flows and Data Privacy Law* (n 5) 27; Orla Lynskey, *The Foundations of EU Data Protection Law* (OUP 2015) (hereafter Lynskey, *The Foundations of EU Data Protection Law*) 47–48.

17 Commission Recommendation of 29 July 1981 relating to the Council of Europe Convention for the protection of individuals with regard to automatic processing of personal data [1981] OJ L246/31.

18 Lynskey, *The Foundations of EU Data Protection Law* (n 16) 48.

1990s, the lack of a cohesive data protection landscape and the emerging enforcement actions restricting personal data flows *between* the EU member states (such as the so-called *FIAT* case)[19] prompted the need for harmonized European data protection rules.[20] This need was given further impetus by the European Commission's ambition to develop a data processing industry in Europe.[21] These rules, 'clearly intended to improve the functioning of the internal market',[22] were codified in 1995 in the form of the Data Protection Directive.[23] The Data Protection Directive was based on the EU competence to regulate the internal market,[24] although critics have described it as 'a tool of neutralisation of national rights in favour of economic efficiency'.[25]

It should, however, be noted that both furthering the development of the internal market and the protection of fundamental rights were codified as equal objectives of the Directive.[26] As the European Commission noted in its first review of the Data Protection Directive, this Directive 'enshrine[d] two of the oldest ambitions of the European integration project: the achievement of an Internal Market (in this case the free movement of personal information) and the protection of fundamental rights and freedoms of individuals. In the Directive, both objectives are equally important'.[27] Despite the latter statement, in practice, fundamental rights were viewed—at that time and up until 2009 when the EU Charter became legally binding—as merely 'derogat[ions] from internal market freedoms'.[28] From

[19] In the *FIAT* case, which occurred in 1989, the French DPA (Commission nationale de l'informatique et des libertés, CNIL) refused to authorize the transfer of employee personal data from Fiat's French subsidiary to its parent company in Italy due to a lack of data protection legislation in Italy. Fiat could transfer such data only after concluding a data transfer agreement between the two companies.

[20] Lynskey, *The Foundations of EU Data Protection Law* (n 16) 49; Christopher Kuner, 'Regulation of Transborder Data Flows under Data Protection and Privacy Law: Past, Present, and Future' (2010) TILT Law & Technology Working Paper 016/2010 19 <https://papers.ssrn.com/sol3/papers.cfm?abstract_id=1689483> accessed 10 July 2023; Paul M Schwartz, 'Managing Global Data Privacy: Cross-Border Information Flows in a Networked Environment' (2009) Report from the Privacy Projects <https://paulschwartz.net/wp-content/uploads/2019/01/Global_Data_Flows.pdf> accessed 13 July 2023, 11.

[21] Lynskey, *The Foundations of EU Data Protection Law* (n 16) 47.

[22] ibid 49; Gloria González Fuster, *The Emergence of Personal Data Protection as a Fundamental Right of the EU* (Springer 2014) 134 (hereafter González Fuster, *The Emergence of Personal Data Protection as a Fundamental Right of the EU*); Joris van Hoboken, 'The European Approach to Privacy' (TPRC Conference, Schertz, August 2014) <https://ssrn.com/abstract=2418636> accessed 13 July 2023.

[23] Directive 95/46/EC of the European Parliament and of the Council of 24 October 1995 on the protection of individuals with regard to the processing of personal data and on the free movement of such data [1995] OJ L281 (hereafter Data Protection Directive).

[24] Recitals 3, 5, and 8, Data Protection Directive (n 23). For a discussion, see Lynskey, *The Foundations of EU Data Protection Law* (n 16) 47–50.

[25] González Fuster, *The Emergence of Personal Data Protection as a Fundamental Right of the EU* (n 22) 135.

[26] Data Protection Directive (n 23), art 1.

[27] Report from the Commission, First report on the implementation of the Data Protection Directive (95/46/EC) of 15 May 2003 [2003] COM/2003/0265 final 3.

[28] González Fuster, *The Emergence of Personal Data Protection as a Fundamental Right of the EU* (n 22) 135. See also Bilyana Petkova, 'Privacy as Europe's First Amendment' (2019) 25(2) European Law Journal 140, 148 (hereafter Petkova, 'Privacy as Europe's First Amendment').

the rights perspective, the assumption was that those rights would not be violated because the implementation of the Directive would lead to 'equivalent' levels of protection.[29] In its early jurisprudence, the Court of Justice of the European Union (CJEU) tended to prioritize market integration ahead of the fundamental rights limb of the Directive.[30]

Moving forward to the twenty-first century, the Lisbon Treaty,[31] which took effect in 2009 and made the EU Charter legally binding for the EU, transformed the right to the protection of personal data into a *sui generis*, binding fundamental right under Article 8 of the EU Charter, separate from the fundamental right to privacy enshrined in Article 7 of the Charter. It also granted the EU competence to legislate on the protection of personal data as a fundamental right.[32] The EU later relied on this competence to adopt the GDPR.[33] At the same time, just as its predecessor did, the GDPR also pursues the dual objective of safeguarding the fundamental rights, such as that to the protection of personal data, and ensuring the free flow of personal data within the internal market.[34]

The EU data protection reforms that led to the adoption of the GDPR were one of the pillars of the Digital Single Market project, presented by the European Commission as the key for making the European Union thrive in the emerging global data economy.[35] It should also be recalled that back in 2012, the process of drafting the GDPR, which replaced the Data Protection Directive, was initiated with a promise to simplify and streamline the mechanisms for cross-border data transfers and to create more interoperability with the data protection regimes of the EU's strategic partners, including the United States.[36] Despite the 'intense lobbying by and on behalf of US multinationals to limit what are characterized as unnecessarily restrictive rights for individuals',[37] the rules for transfers of personal data became even more stringent and only marginally more flexible.[38]

[29] Data Protection Directive (n 23), Recitals 8 and 9; Lee Andrew Bygrave, *Data Privacy Law: An International Perspective* (Oxford Scholarship Online 2014) 192.

[30] Lynskey, *The Foundations of EU Data Protection Law* (n 16) 51–54.

[31] Treaty of Lisbon amending the Treaty on European Union and the Treaty establishing the European Community [2007] OJ C306/1 (hereafter Lisbon Treaty).

[32] Art 16(1), 'Consolidated Version of the Treaty on the Functioning of the European Union' [2008] OJ C115/47 (hereafter TFEU).

[33] GDPR (n 2), Recitals 1 and 12.

[34] GDPR (n 2), art 1.

[35] Communication from the Commission to the European Parliament, the European Council, the Council, the European Economic and Social Committee and the Committee of the Regions, 'Completing a Trusted Digital Single Market for All' [2018] COM (2018) 320 final 2–3.

[36] Joris van Hoboken, Axel Arnbak, and Nico van Eijk, 'Obscured by Clouds or How to Address Governmental Access to Cloud Data from Abroad' (Privacy Law Scholars Conference, Berkeley, 2013) 28 <https://ssrn.com/abstract=2276103> accessed 13 July 2023; Communication from the Commission to the European Parliament, the European Council, the Council, the European Economic and Social Committee and the Committee of the Regions, 'Safeguarding Privacy in a Connected World: A European Data Protection Framework for the 21st Century' [2012] COM (2012) 09 final, section 5.

[37] Christopher Kuner and others, 'PRISM and Privacy: Will This Change Everything?' (2013) 3(4) International Data Privacy Law 217, 218.

[38] For a discussion of the changes to the EU framework on transfers of personal data outside the EEA introduced by the GDPR (n 2), see Section 5.1.

The constitutionalization of the fundamental rights to privacy and the protection of personal data eventually not only shifted the core normative rationale of protecting these rights within the EU from the predominantly economic goal of ensuring the free flow of personal data in the EU to the protection of individual rights, but also altered the balance between economic and non-economic values in the EU's external economic policy.[39] As Pollicino and Bassini argue, '[w]hile at the very beginning of the European constitutionalism protection of fundamental rights [could] justify restrictions to the economic freedoms provided by the treaties, as exceptions to the same', after the Lisbon Treaty, the level of protection of fundamental rights began 'to determine the degree of openness of the European Union towards other orders'.[40]

Entrusted with the power to interpret the EU Charter, the CJEU has taken up the role of a guarantor of EU fundamental rights. It played an important role in building up jurisprudence on Articles 7 and 8 of the EU Charter as well as in the interpretation of the derogation clause of Article 52(1) of the EU Charter in relation to these rights. Some even argue that in the 2015 Opinion concerning the validity of the draft EU-Canada PNR Agreement (the *Opinion on EU-Canada PNR Agreement*),[41] the CJEU used data protection 'as a vehicle to assert EU fundamental rights in an international context'.[42] The safeguards dealing with privacy and civil liberty of Europeans that the United States introduced in response to the CJEU's *Schrems I*[43] and *Schrems II*[44] judgments and as a condition for a new transatlantic framework for transfers of personal data further illustrate the point.[45]

[39] Under the TEU, as amended by the Treaty of Lisbon, negotiation and conclusion of international trade agreements must be guided by the universality and indivisibility of human rights and fundamental freedoms, respect for human dignity and principles of the United Nations and international law (arts 2(5) and 21 of the Consolidated Version of the Treaty on European Union [2012] OJ C326/13 (hereafter TEU)).

[40] Oreste Pollicino and Marco Bassini, 'Data Truck Can't Get Through … A Critical View of the Schrems Judgement in the Context of the European Constitutionalism' in Giuliana Ziccardi Capaldo (ed), *The Global Community Yearbook of International Law and Jurisprudence* (OUP 2017) 262 (hereafter Pollicino and Bassini, 'Data Truck Can't Get Through … A Critical View of the Schrems Judgement in the Context of the European Constitutionalism').

[41] CJEU Opinion 1/15 *EU-Canada PNR Agreement* [2017] ECLI:EU:C:2017:592 (hereafter CJEU Opinion, *EU-Canada PNR Agreement*).

[42] Christopher Kuner, 'International Agreements, Data Protection, and EU Fundamental Rights on the International Stage: Opinion 1/15 (EU-Canada PNR) of the Court of Justice of the EU' (2018) 55(3) Common Market Law Review 857, 858.

[43] *Maximillian Schrems v Data Protection Commissioner* [2015] ECLI:EU:C:2015:650 (hereafter *Schrems I*).

[44] *Facebook Ireland and Schrems* [2020] ECLI:EU:C:2020:559 (hereafter *Schrems II*).

[45] See U.S. White House, 'FACT SHEET: President Biden Signs Executive Order to Implement the European Union-U.S. Data Privacy Framework' (*The White House*, 7 October 2022) <https://www.whitehouse.gov/briefing-room/statements-releases/2022/10/07/fact-sheet-president-biden-signs-executive-order-to-implement-the-european-union-u-s-data-privacy-framework/>> accessed 10 July 2023. See also Christopher Kuner, 'Protecting EU Data outside EU Borders under the GDPR' (2023) 60(1) Common Market Law Review 77, 99–100 (hereafter Kuner, 'Protecting EU Data outside EU Borders under the GDPR').

The shift of balance between economic and non-economic values is most apparent in a line of post-EU Charter CJEU jurisprudence. In contrast to its prior case law, the Court's jurisprudence now prioritizes the rights to privacy and data protection ahead of other rights, such as the freedom of expression and information (Article 11) and the freedom to conduct a business (Article 16). It conferred on those rights the status of 'leading rights' in Europe.[46] As the CJEU noted in *Google Spain*, '[i]n the light of the potential seriousness of that interference, it is clear that it cannot be justified *by merely the economic interest* which the operator of such an engine has in that processing'.[47] One year before the EU Charter became binding, in the *Satamedia* judgment,[48] the Court took an approach to balancing the right to the protection of personal data against the right to freedom of expression that 'demonstrates that the protection of personal data weighs heavily relative to that part of freedom of expression which falls under "journalistic purposes." In other words, the CJEU place[d] greater weight on the protection of personal data than on freedom of expression in this context'.[49] Similarly, although in the *Schrems I* and *II* cases the CJEU did not explicitly address the underlying issue of balancing trade and privacy, Petkova argues that the Court did implicitly put the protection of fundamental rights to privacy and the protection of personal data above the commercial interests vested in transatlantic data flows.[50]

The higher importance of the fundamental rights to privacy and the protection of personal data, as compared to other fundamental rights, also reveals itself through the higher 'strict necessity' threshold for derogation from these fundamental rights under Article 52(1) of the EU Charter, as is discussed in Section 2.4.3. It is also reflected in the desired level of protection of the right to the protection of personal data—'effective and complete'[51] as pronounced by the CJEU.[52]

[46] Petkova, 'Privacy as Europe's First Amendment' (n 28) 154; Bilyana Petkova, 'Towards an Internal Hierarchy of Values in the EU Legal Order: Balancing the Freedom of Speech and Data Privacy' (2016) 23(3) Maastricht Journal of European and Comparative Law 421, 430–32 (hereafter Petkova, 'Towards an Internal Hierarchy of Values in the EU Legal Order'). See also Kristina Irion, 'A Special Regard: The Court of Justice and the Fundamental Rights to Privacy and Data Protection' (2016) Amsterdam Law School Legal Studies Research Paper No 2016-35, Institute for Information Law Research Paper No 2016-04, 7 <https://ssrn.com/abstract=2836910> accessed 10 July 2023 (noting that 'the relative weight the CJEU accorded to the rights to privacy and data protection steadily expanded corresponding to the increasing significance of personal data processing and flows').

[47] *Google Spain* [2014] ECLI:EU:C:2014:317, para 81, emphasis added (hereafter *Google Spain*).

[48] *Satamedia* [2008] ECLI:EU:C:2008:727, para 56.

[49] Charlotte Bagger Tranberg, 'Proportionality and Data Protection in the Case Law of the European Court of Justice' (2011) 1(4) International Data Privacy Law 239.

[50] Petkova, 'Towards an Internal Hierarchy of Values in the EU Legal Order' (n 46) 431.

[51] *Google Spain* (n 47) para 34; *Wirtschaftsakademie* [2018] ECLI:EU:C:2018:388, para 28 (hereafter *Wirtschaftsakademie*); *Jehovan todistajat* [2018] ECLI:EU:C:2018:551, para 66 (hereafter *Jehovan todistajat*); *Fashion ID* [2019] ECLI:EU:C:2019:629, paras 66, 70 (hereafter *Fashion ID*).

[52] Marie-Pierre Granger and Kristina Irion, 'The Right to Protection of Personal Data: The New Posterchild of European Union Citizenship?' in Sybe de Vries, Henri de Waele, and Marrie-Pierre Granger (eds), *Civil Rights and EU Citizenship* (Edward Elgar Publishing 2018) 4 <https://hdl.handle.net/11245.1/606d4e50-508e-4841-b290-fde00a336621> accessed 10 July 2023 (hereafter Granger and Irion, 'The Right to Protection of Personal Data: The New Posterchild of European Union Citizenship?').

The requirement of 'complete' protection could make the balancing of this right with other competing fundamental rights challenging and leave suboptimal room for respecting those other rights.[53] Hence, although Koen Lenaerts, the president of the CJEU, has contended that 'there is no hierarchy of qualified rights under the Charter',[54] in practice, the CJEU *de facto* tends to rank fundamental rights to privacy and data protection above other rights in the internal hierarchy of values.[55]

In a broader perspective, EU law scholars have linked the European fundamental rights discourse to the growing demand for legitimacy following the expansion of the Union's competences.[56] To Muir, this discourse 'tends to become a legitimating battle horse for the European Union' and an increasingly 'important part of the EU "political messianism"'.[57] The strengthening of the fundamental rights to privacy and the protection of personal data in the CJEU jurisprudence is, arguably, a part of this broader phenomenon and is liable to affect the balance of competences between the Union and its constituencies.[58] For example, the broadening of the scope of EU privacy legislation in relation to foreign countries' surveillance practices involving personal data transferred from the EEA by the CJEU in *Schrems I* and *II* is likely to broaden the scope of EU Charter application to the EU member states' surveillance activities, as Section 2.3.1.2 further elaborates. Furthermore, the EU competence to legislate regarding the fundamental rights to privacy and the protection of personal data increasingly underlies EU ambitions in regulating technology through framing legal challenges, such as those posed by artificial intelligence (AI), as data protection issues.[59] In this sense, despite the shift of the EU competence underlying data protection legislation from internal market to fundamental rights, data protection is still an important pillar of the European integration project. At the same time, asserting the EU values as global is also a part of the EU's political project of expanding the reach of EU law over internet-related

[53] Joris van Hoboken, 'Case Note, CJEU 13 May 2014, C-131/12 (*Google Spain*)' [2014] EHRC <https://ssrn.com/abstract=2495580> accessed 10 July 2023.

[54] Koen Lenaerts, 'Exploring the Limits of the EU Charter of Fundamental Rights' (2012) 8(3) European Constitutional Law Review 375, 392–93.

[55] Pollicino and Bassini, 'Data Truck Can't Get Through ... A Critical View of the Schrems Judgement in the Context of the European Constitutionalism' (n 40) 247–48; Petkova, 'Towards an Internal Hierarchy of Values in the EU Legal Order' (n 46) 430–32; Sandra Seubert and Carlos Becker, 'The Democratic Impact of Strengthening European Fundamental Rights in the Digital Age: The Example of Privacy Protection' (2021) German Law Journal 22(1) 31, 35–37.

[56] Armin von Bogdandy and others, 'Reverse Solange: Protecting the Essence of Fundamental Rights against EU Member States' (2012) Common Market Law Review 49(2) 489, 496; Elise Muir, 'The Fundamental Rights Implications of EU Legislation: Some Constitutional Challenges' (2014) Common Market Law Review 51(1) 219, 223 (hereafter Muir, 'The Fundamental Rights Implications of EU Legislation').

[57] Muir, 'The Fundamental Rights Implications of EU Legislation' (n 56) 223.

[58] Petkova, 'Privacy as Europe's First Amendment' (n 28) 147. See also Granger and Irion, 'The Right to Protection of Personal Data' (n 52) 11–12.

[59] For example, in his opinion in *SCHUFA* case, Advocate General Pikamäe explains the expansive interpretation of art 22(1) of the GDPR by the need to avoid a gap in legal protection that would result from a narrower interpretation of this provision. *OQ v Land Hesse* [2023] ECLI:EU:C:2023:220, Opinion of AG Pikamäe, para 48.

and digital issues globally,[60] as can be seen from the 2020 European Strategy for Data. In this strategy, the European Commission states:

> Building upon the strength of the Single Market's regulatory environment, the EU has a strong interest in leading and supporting international cooperation with regard to data, shaping global standards and creating an environment in which economic and technological development can thrive, in full compliance with EU law.[61]

As Eckes rightly noted eight years before the adoption of this strategy, 'in European law, constitutional law is the new internal market. Indeed, both in importance and in development, European constitutional law is today what the internal market was in the eighties and early nineties'.[62]

In recent years, as mentioned in Section 2.1, robust protection of the fundamental rights to privacy and protection of personal data has also become part of the EU's 'technological' or 'digital sovereignty' narrative.[63] Although these notions are not directly linked by the EU to the regulation of transfers of *personal* data outside the EEA in the present-day EU policy discourse (but rather to transfers of *data* more generally), they do resonate with the concerns that led to the development of such regulation in EU member states back in the 1970s and 1980s. The notion of digital sovereignty reaches into a broad set of policy areas beyond privacy and data protection, including digital infrastructure, cybersecurity, competition law, telecommunications, and technology and platform governance.[64] Part of the

[60] Christopher Kuner, 'The Internet and the Global Reach of EU Law' in Marise Cremona and Joanne Scott (eds), *EU Law beyond EU Borders: The Extraterritorial Reach of EU Law* (OUP 2019) 137–38, criticizing these EU practices.

[61] Communication from the Commission to the European Parliament, the European Council, the Council, the European Economic and Social Committee and the Committee of the Regions, 'A European Strategy for Data' [2020] COM(2020) 66 final (hereafter European Commission, 'A European Strategy for Data').

[62] Christina Eckes, 'Protecting Supremacy from External Influences: A Precondition for a European Constitutional Legal Order?' (2012) 18(2) European Law Journal 230, 230 (hereafter Eckes, 'Protecting Supremacy from External Influences').

[63] Tambiama Madiega, 'Digital Sovereignty for Europe' (2020) EPRS Ideas Paper towards a More Resilient EU 1 <https://www.europarl.europa.eu/RegData/etudes/BRIE/2020/651992/EPRS_BRI(2020)651992_EN.pdf> accessed 10 July 2023 (hereafter Madiega 'Digital Sovereignty for Europe'); Communication from the Commission to the European Parliament, the European Council, the Council, the European Economic and Social Committee and the Committee of the Regions, 'A New Industrial Strategy for Europe' [2020] COM (2020) 102 final 1, 4; European Commission, 'A European Strategy for Data' (n 61); European Commission, 'White Paper on Artificial Intelligence: A European Approach to Excellence and Trust' [2020] COM (2020) 65 final 3; European Commission, 'State of the Union Address by President von der Leyen at the European Parliament Plenary' (16 September 2020) <https://ec.europa.eu/commission/presscorner/detail/en/SPEECH_20_1655> accessed 10 July 2023.

[64] For an overview, see Huw Roberts and others, 'Safeguarding European Values with Digital Sovereignty: An Analysis of Statements and Policies' (2021) 10(3) Internet Policy Review 1, 9–13. See also Mark Leonard and Jeremy Shapiro, 'Empowering EU Member States with Strategic Sovereignty', (June 2019) European Council on Foreign Relations 6 <https://ecfr.eu/wp-content/uploads/1_Empowering_EU_member_states_with_strategic_sovereignty.pdf> accessed 10 July 2023.

idea of 'digital sovereignty', however, is to mobilize non-personal (industrial) data and create a Single European data space—a single market for both personal and non-personal data.[65] Adopted or proposed European legislation, which reflects the digital sovereignty idea, introduces restrictions on transfers of *non-personal* data outside the EEA, which are similar to the restrictions on transfers of *personal* data outside the EEA under the GDPR.[66] These restrictions on transfers of non-personal data, however, are outside the scope of this book.

2.2.2 The concept of transfer

The EU framework governing transfers of personal data outside the EEA is based on a 'prohibition with derogations' principle. Transfers of personal data to a country or territory outside the EEA or to an international organization may only occur if the conditions of Chapter V of the GDPR are met.[67]

Although the concept of 'transfer' is central to triggering the application of the restrictions on transfers of personal data, neither the GDPR nor its predecessor—the Data Protection Directive—defines the concept of 'transfer' of personal data outside the EEA.[68] Though the restrictions on transfers of personal data were in place for more than twenty years, there is still no complete clarity on all the aspects of this concept's meaning.

The CJEU specifically addressed this issue only once, in one of its earliest cases on data protection. In its 2003 *Lindqvist* judgment, the CJEU concluded that uploading materials onto an internet page, which can be consulted, and which is hosted by a person established in a third country, thereby making that data accessible worldwide, does not constitute transfer of data to a third country in the meaning of Article 25 of the Data Protection Directive.[69] The Court also noted that in these circumstances, it is irrelevant whether an individual from a third country has accessed the internet page.[70] The CJEU based its reasoning on what Svantesson calls a 'reasonableness test'.[71] The Court explained that given that, first, the state of

[65] European Commission, 'A European Strategy for Data' (n 61).

[66] For a discussion, seeSvetlana Yakovleva, 'On Digital Sovereignty, New European Data Rules, and the Future of Free Data Flows' (2022) 49(4) Legal Issues of Economic Integration 339 (hereafter Yakovleva, 'On Digital Sovereignty').

[67] GDPR (n 2), art 44.

[68] The European Commission's proposal for the GDPR also failed to define the term 'transfer'. For a discussion and approaches to the notion of 'transfer' in other international frameworks on data flows, see Kuner, *Transborder Data Flows and Data Privacy Law* (n 5) 12. See also EDPB, Guidelines 05/2021 on the Interplay between the application of Article 3 and the provisions on international transfers as per Chapter V of the GDPR (version 2.0, adopted 14 February 2023) 6 (hereafter EDPB, Guidelines 05/2021 on the Interplay between the application of Article 3 and the provisions on international transfers as per Chapter V of the GDPR).

[69] *Lindqvist* [2003] ECLI:EU:C:2003:596, para 4 of the conclusions (hereafter *Lindqvist*).

[70] ibid, para 70.

[71] Dan JB Svantesson, 'Privacy, Internet and Transborder Data Flows: An Australian Perspective' (2010) 4(1) Masaryk University Journal of Law and Technology 1, 15. Kuner agrees that the CJEU's

development of the internet at the time Data Protection Directive was drawn up and, second, the absence (in Chapter IV of the Directive governing transfers of personal data) of criteria applicable to use of the internet:

> one cannot presume that the Community legislature intended the expression transfer [of data] to a third country to cover the loading, by an individual in Mrs Lindqvist's position, of data onto an internet page, even if those data are thereby made accessible to persons in third countries with the technical means to access them.[72]

In other words, there is no 'transfer' in the meaning of the Data Protection Directive whenever there is no 'direct transfer' of personal data between the person posting personal data on the server and the person accessing personal data.[73] The Court further explained that if those rules

> were interpreted to mean that there is 'transfer [of data] to a third country' every time that personal data are loaded onto an internet page, that transfer would necessarily be a transfer to all the third countries where there are the technical means needed to access the internet. The special regime provided for by Chapter IV of the directive would thus necessarily become a regime of general application, as regards operations on the internet.[74]

There are several reasons to treat this rather narrow interpretation of 'transfer' with caution and to adopt instead a broader understanding of this notion today.[75] First, the judgment concerns a case with a rather specific fact pattern that may not justify a universal application to all cases of online data sharing. To illustrate the point, in explaining its position, the CJEU refers to the 'action of a person in Mrs Lindqvist's position' and 'actions such as those of Lindqvist'.[76] Adopting this line of thinking, Kuner argues that making personal data available online can be viewed

decision was 'based partly on pragmatic considerations'. Kuner, *Transborder Data Flows and Data Privacy Law* (n 5) 13.

[72] *Lindqvist* (n 69) para 68.

[73] Kuner, *Transborder Data Flows and Data Privacy Law* (n 5) 13; Samson Yoseph Esayas, 'A Walk in to the Cloud and Cloudy It Remains: The Challenges and Prospects of "Processing" and "Transferring" Personal Data' (2012) 28 Computer Law & Security Review 662, 669; Bygrave, *Data Privacy Law* (n 29) 192.

[74] *Lindqvist* (n 69) para 69.

[75] See Christopher Kuner, 'Article 44 GDPR: General Principles for Transfers' in Christopher Kuner, Lee A Bygrave, and Christopher Dicksey (eds), *The EU General Data Protection Regulation (GDPR): A Commentary* (OUP 2020) 762–63 (hereafter Kuner, 'Article 44 GDPR'); Kuner, 'Protecting EU Data outside EU Borders under the GDPR' (n 45) 96.

[76] See, eg, Dutch Data Protection Authority, 'Guidelines: Publication of Personal Data on the Internet' (*College bescherming persoonsgegevens*, December 2007) 50 <https://cbpweb.nl/sites/default/files/downloads/mijn_privacy/en_20071108_richtsnoeren_internet.pdf> accessed 10 July 2023.

as cross-border data transfer if it involves 'granting access to the data of other parties on a large scale for business purposes'.[77]

Second, unlike the Data Protection Directive, the GDPR was drafted in different economic circumstances, where data was increasingly labelled as 'the new oil',[78] and cross-border data flows as the 'hallmark of 21st-century globalization'.[79] Therefore, one can no longer argue that the legislator could not foresee the application of the rules on transfers of personal data to pervasive transfers on the internet. Third, and most importantly, as already mentioned above, the GDPR was adopted after the right to protection of personal data was elevated to a fundamental right in the EU,[80] and on the basis of the EU competence to legislate on the fundamental right to the protection of personal data, rather than internal market competence, on which the Data Protection Directive was based.[81] In parallel with the CJEU's approach to a broad interpretation of the notions of 'personal data'[82] and 'controller' under the GDPR in a recent line of cases,[83] there is also a broad interpretation of the notion of 'transfer' of personal data, which could be necessary to ensure 'effective and complete'[84] protection of fundamental rights.[85]

[77] Christopher Kuner, *European Data Protection Law: Corporate Compliance and Regulation* (OUP 2007) 83. Factors that could be relevant in assessing the likelihood of data transfer rules being applicable include the presence of an establishment of a data controller in the country of the individual whose data is processed, the targeting of the individual by the company's activity, and the degree of control over the purposes or means used by the individual to process the data. ibid 15. Kuner makes an even stronger point in favour of this position in his 2023 article. See Kuner, 'Protecting EU Data outside EU Borders under the GDPR' (n 45) 96.

[78] See European Commission, 'Keynote Speech of Commissioner Meglena Kuneva in the Roundtable on Online Data Collection: Targeting and Profiling' (*Speech/09/156*, 2009) <https://ec.europa.eu/commission/presscorner/detail/en/SPEECH_09_156> accessed 10 July 2023. See also 'The World's Most Valuable Resource Is no Longer Oil, But Data' (*The Economist*, 6 May 2017) <https://www.economist.com/leaders/2017/05/06/the-worlds-most-valuable-resource-is-no-longer-oil-but-data≥ accessed 10 July 2023. But see Bernard Marr, 'Here's Why Data Is Not the New Oil' (*Forbes*, 5 March 2018) <https://www.forbes.com/sites/bernardmarr/2018/03/05/heres-why-data-is-not-the-new-oil/≥ accessed 10 July 2023.

[79] James Manyika and others, 'Digital Globalisation: The New Era of Global Flows' (2016) McKinsey Global Institute 10 <https://www.mckinsey.com/~/media/McKinsey/Business%20Functions/McKinsey%20Digital/Our%20Insights/Digital%20globalization%20The%20new%20era%20of%20global%20flows/MGI-Digital-globalization-Full-report.pdf> accessed 10 July 2023.

[80] See also Kuner, 'Article 44 GDPR' (n 75) 763.

[81] Lynskey criticizes the qualification of Mrs Lindqvist's activities as falling under the scope of the Data Protection Directive in the first place, calling the judgment 'integrationist'. Lynskey, *The Foundations of EU Data Protection Law* (n 16) 54–55. It could thus be argued that a pragmatic approach of the Court to the scope of the rules on transfers of personal data was aimed at counterbalancing the broader scope of application of the Data Protection Directive.

[82] *Nowak* [2017] ECLI:EU:C:2017:994, para 34 (stating that '[t]he use of the expression "any information" in the definition of the concept of "personal data", within Article 2(a) of Directive 95/46, reflects the aim of the EU legislature to assign a wide scope to that concept, which is not restricted to information that is sensitive or private, but potentially encompasses all kinds of information, not only objective but also subjective, in the form of opinions and assessments, provided that it "relates" to the data subject').

[83] *Google Spain* (n 47) para 34; *Wirtschaftsakademie* (n 51) para 28; *Fashion ID* (n 51) paras 50, 66.

[84] *Google Spain* (n 47) para 34; *Wirtschaftsakademie* (n 51) para 28; CJEU, *Jehovan todistajat* (n 51) para 66; *Fashion ID* (n 51) paras 66, 70.

[85] See also Kuner, 'Protecting EU Data outside EU Borders under the GDPR' (n 45) 96.

The 2018 European Data Protection Board (EDPB)[86] and the CJEU judgment in *Schrems II* clarified that:

(1) 'granting direct access to a database (e.g. via an interface to an IT-application) on a general basis' constitutes a transfer of personal data in the meaning of the GDPR,[87] and
(2) data in transit is equally subject to the rules on transfer of personal data outside the EEA under the GDPR.[88]

The EDPB draft guidelines published in 2021 for public consultation[89] and finalized in 2023[90] are the first and, so far, the only attempt to offer a holistic approach to defining a 'transfer'. These guidelines turned out to be controversial and sparked a lot of critiques.[91] Until this notion is clarified by the CJEU or by a EU legislator, the guidelines are the only and the most elaborate—albeit non-binding—official guidance on the issue, which is likely to be influential in the enforcement of relevant GDPR provisions.[92]

[86] The European Data Protection Board is a consultative body comprising all EU member states' data protection authorities. European Data Protection Board, 'EDPB Chairmanship' <https://edpb.europa.eu/about-edpb/about-edpb_en> accessed 10 July 2023.

[87] EDPB, 'Guidelines 2/2018 on Derogations of Article 49 under Regulation 2016/679' (25 May 2018) 4 <https://edpb.europa.eu/sites/default/files/files/file1/edpb_guidelines_2_2018_derogations_en.pdf> accessed 10 July 2023 (hereafter EDPB, 'Guidelines 2/2018 on Derogations of Article 49 under Regulation 2016/679').

[88] *Schrems II* (n 44) paras 183–85. See also Kuner, *Transborder Data Flows and Data Privacy Law* (n 5) 176, agreeing with such approach, but proposing to consider the fact that data is merely in transit in the analysis of risk of harm to individuals.

[89] Guidelines 05/2021 on the Interplay between the application of Article 3 and the provisions on international transfers as per Chapter V of the GDPR (version for public consultation) (18 November 2021) <https://edpb.europa.eu/system/files/2021-11/edpb_guidelinesinterplaychapterv_article3_adopted_en.pdf> accessed 10 July 2023.

[90] EDPB, Guidelines 05/2021 on the Interplay between the application of Article 3 and the provisions on international transfers as per Chapter V of the GDPR (n 68).

[91] See Svetlana Yakovleva, 'GDPR Transfer Rules vs Rules on Territorial Scope: A Critical Reflection on Recent EDPB Guidelines from both EU and International Trade Law Perspectives' (*European Law Blog*, 9 December 2021) <https://europeanlawblog.eu/2021/12/09/gdpr-transfer-rules-vs-rules-on-territorial-scope-a-critical-reflection-on-recent-edpb-guidelines-from-both-eu-and-international-trade-law-perspectives/> accessed 10 July 2023; Christopher Kuner, 'Exploring the Awkward Secret of Data Transfer Regulation: The EDPB Guidelines on Article 3 and Chapter V GDPR' (*European Law Blog*, 13 December 2021) <https://europeanlawblog.eu/2021/12/13/exploring-the-awkward-secret-of-data-transfer-regulation-the-edpb-guidelines-on-article-3-and-chapter-v-gdpr/> accessed 10 July 2023; Laura Drechsler and Svetlana Yakovleva, 'Contribution to the Public Consultation on the Guidelines 05/2021 on the Interplay between the Application of Article 3 and the Provisions on International Transfers as per Chapter V of the GDPR' (*EDPB*, 27 December 2021) <https://edpb.europa.eu/sites/default/files/webform/public_consultation_reply/20211227.Public_consultation_EDPB_transfers_V8.pdf> accessed 10 July 2023; see also Kuner, 'Protecting EU Data outside EU Borders under the GDPR' (n 45).

[92] Although the EDPB guidance is not legally binding, it is often followed by Data Protection Authorities and courts across the EU.

The guidelines introduced the following three cumulative criteria to determine whether a transmission of personal data qualifies as a 'transfer' under the GDPR:[93]

(1) A controller or a processor ('exporter') is subject to the GDPR for the given processing,
(2) The exporter discloses by transmission or otherwise makes personal data, subject to this processing, available to another controller, joint controller or processor ('importer'), and
(3) The importer is in a third country, irrespective of whether or not this importer is subject to the GDPR for the given processing in accordance with Article 3, or is an international organisation.

Three conclusions important for the discussion in this book follow from this approach to defining a 'transfer'.

First, the EDPB guidelines confirm that providing remote access to personal data constitutes a 'transfer'.[94] Second, according to the EDPB, a *direct transmission* of personal data from individuals in the EEA to a controller or processor outside the EEA—a common situation in the context of online tracking—does *not* qualify as 'transfer' under the GDPR.[95] In other words, in EDPB's view, a 'transfer' in the meaning of the GDPR only exists when personal data flows from a personal data exporter that is subject to the GDPR (and irrespective of its location) to a personal data importer located outside the EEA. This approach assumes that data subjects themselves cannot be data controllers or data exporters.[96] In other words, in situations where there is no data exporter (ie, personal data is collected directly from an individual), there is no 'transfer' of personal data. The wording of the second criterion—'the exporter discloses by transmission'—suggests that the data exporter must perform the actual data processing operation of disclosure, rather than be merely responsible for it (eg, as a joint controller, which does not have access to personal data and is not involved in the actual transmission).

Third, and finally, the EDPB has clarified that the qualification of a personal data transmission as a 'transfer' does *not* depend on whether the recipient of personal data (the data importer) falls under the extraterritorial scope under Article 3 of the GDPR.[97] The EU legal framework for personal data protection includes two sets of rules: *substantive rules* regulating when access to, and processing of, any personal data is lawful; and the *rules governing transfers* of personal data outside the EEA.[98]

[93] EDPB, Guidelines 05/2021 on the Interplay between the application of Article 3 and the provisions on international transfers as per Chapter V of the GDPR (n 68) para 9.
[94] ibid, para 16, example 11, on 12 , 23.
[95] ibid, para 18.
[96] ibid, footnote 15, 8.
[97] ibid, paras 9(3), 23, and 29.
[98] Martina Ferracane and Erik van der Marel, 'The Cost of Data Protectionism' (*ECIPE Blog*, October 2018) <https://ecipe.org/blog/the-cost-of-data-protectionism/> accessed 10 July 2023 stating that: 'We identify two main categories of data policies. The first category covers those policies that impact the

The application of the GDPR's substantive rules is not limited to the geographical territory of the EU. In certain cases, the GDPR also applies when personal data is being processed outside the EEA (ie, by controllers or processors not established in the EEA). This application is often referred to as 'extraterritorial'.

The GDPR applies extraterritorially in the following situations:

- Personal data is being processed by a controller or processor located outside the EEA, and there is an inextricable link between such processing and the activities of this controller's or processor's establishment in the EEA,[99] or
- Personal data is being processed by a controller or processor located outside the EEA, when this processing is related to offering of goods or services to individuals located in the EEA,[100] or
- Personal data is being processed by a controller or processor located outside the EEA, when this processing is related to monitoring of the behaviour of individuals that takes place in the EEA.[101]

Whenever EU personal data is processed outside the EEA borders in any of these situations, it enjoys full GDPR protection. The question is whether application of GDPR rules on transfers of personal data outside the EEA is necessary in these situations, keeping in mind that there is no risk that the GDPR protections of the transferred personal data would be undermined. If no such risk exists, the GDPR transfer rules whose primary aim is to address this risk are simply not necessary.[102]

cross-border transfer of data whilst the second category covers policies that apply to the use of data domestically.'

[99] GDPR (n 2), art 3(1).
[100] GDPR (n 2), art 3(2)(a).
[101] GDPR (n 2), art 3(2)(b).
[102] Arguably, it was precisely this approach that led the European Commission to exclude this type of situations from the scope of application of the 2021 standard contractual clauses (SCCs)—one of the most commonly used mechanisms for transfers of personal data, as explained below. (For a discussion about the inconsistency of the European Commission's approach to the issue, see Kuner, 'Protecting EU Data outside EU Borders under the GDPR' (n 45) 92–93.) Vagueness of the draft version of the SCCs on the limitation of the SCC's scope of application to transmissions of personal data to entities that are *not* subject to the GDPR implied that transmissions of personal data to entities outside the EEA that *are* subject to the extraterritorial application of the GDPR are not 'transfers' in the meaning of the GDPR. (European Commission, Draft Implementing Decision on standard contractual clauses for the transfer of personal data to third countries pursuant to Regulation (EU) 2016/679 of the European Parliament and of the Council, art 1(1) <https://ec.europa.eu/info/law/better-regulation/have-your-say/initiatives/12741-Data-protection-standard-contractual-clauses-for-transferring-personal-data-to-non-EU-countries-implementing-act-_en> accessed 10 July 2023). In their Opinion on the draft SCCs, the EDPB and the European Data Protection Supervisor (EDPS) requested that the Commission does not alter the definition of 'transfers' in the SCCs, which led to a clarification in the final version of the SCCs that definition of the SCC's scope is 'without prejudice to the interpretation of the notion of international transfer in Regulation (EU) 2016/679'. (EDPB, 'EDPS Joint Opinion 2/2021 on the European Commission's Implementing Decision on standard contractual clauses for the transfer of personal data to third countries' (2021) para 28 <https://edpb.europa.eu/sites/default/files/files/file1/edpb_edps_jointopinion_202102_art46sccs_en.pdf> accessed 10 July 2023; European Commission Implementing Decision (EU) 2021/914 of 4 June 2021 on standard contractual clauses for the transfer of personal

The EDPB did not follow this line of reasoning and concluded that even when transferred personal data is already protected through the extraterritorial application of the GDPR, Chapter V rules on transfers of personal data still apply.[103]

On the one hand, the EDPB's interpretation of 'transfer' is logical in the light of the fundamental rights nature of personal data protection in the EU, which, as the CJEU explained in a line of jurisprudence, requires effective and complete protection of personal data, as explained above.[104] On the other hand, this approach creates an overlap of certain GDPR requirements, which exist both under the substantive GDPR regime and the regime applicable to transfers,[105] and adds additional complexity to GDPR compliance by companies that are subject to the extraterritorial application of the GDPR *and* are engaged in transfers of personal data outside the EEA. In an attempt to reduce the overlap and ameliorate this compliance burden, the European Commission and the EDPB have *de facto* created a different legal regime for transfers of personal data in this situation, *de facto* because it is not based on the exact provisions of the GDPR and is aimed to repair the unintended consequences of the definition of 'transfer' adopted by the EDPB. The following section discusses the different legal regimes applicable to transmissions of personal data outside the EEA depending on their configuration.

2.2.3 Legal regimes applicable to personal data transmissions

The upshot of the EDPB's interpretation of the term 'transfer' and of the relationship between the GDPR's extraterritorial application and the rules concerning transfers of personal data outside the EEA in Chapter V is that depending on the technicalities of data flows (the end points of transmissions), there are currently *four different legal regimes* governing transmissions of personal data outside the

data to third countries pursuant to Regulation (EU) 016/679 of the European Parliament and of the Council [2021] OJ L199, recital 7 (hereafter Commission Decision on standard contractual clauses for the transfer of personal data to third countries). Around the same time, the Commission announced its intention to create a separate set of SCCs for this type of transfers, which have not been published at the time of this writing (June 2023). See 'The New Standard Contractual Clauses: Questions and Answers' (*European Commission*, May 2022) question 24 <https://commission.europa.eu/system/files/2022-05/questions_answers_on_sccs_en.pdf> accessed 10 July 2023 (hereafter 'The New Standard Contractual Clauses').

[103] Kuner agrees with this approach, explaining that the rules on territorial scope and on transfers of personal data perform different functions and that, at least in the GDPR's current structure, they are not mutually exclusive. See Kuner, 'Protecting EU Data outside EU Borders under the GDPR' (n 45).

[104] For discussion, see Kuner, 'Protecting EU Data outside EU Borders under the GDPR' (n 45).

[105] For example, principles relating to data processing are contained in both art 5 and in the SCCs for transfers of personal data approved by the European Commission. See Kuner, 'Protecting EU Data outside EU Borders under the GDPR' (n 45) 96. See also 'The New Standard Contractual Clauses' (n 102) question 24.

EEA. Each of these regimes is characterized by a different level of restrictiveness and affords different levels of data protection.

The discussion below distinguishes between two types of data protection rules: (i) GDPR protections by virtue of extraterritorial application of the GDPR and (ii) GDPR protections by virtue of application of Chapter V rules. Depending on the configuration of personal data transmissions, none, some, or all these protections apply. Gaps in legal protection resulting from the application of these different legal regimes, as discussed in Sections 2.3 and 2.4.2, create inconsistency of the legal regime for transfers and increase the tension between the GDPR's framework for transfers of personal data outside the EEA and international trade law. This book returns to these gaps in legal protection in Chapter 5, where it demonstrates that such gaps also undermine the ability of GDPR Chapter V to perform its constitutional function.

Legal Regime 1: Unrestricted transmission, no GDPR protections

This legal regime applies to situations when personal data flows directly from individuals in the EEA to a data importer established outside the EEA, to which the GDPR does not apply (Figure 2.1). An example of this situation is the collection of personal data in the EEA by a Chinese university, which does not fall under the GDPR's extraterritorial application because it does not specifically advertise to students in the EEA and only takes payment in Chinese currency.[106] Another

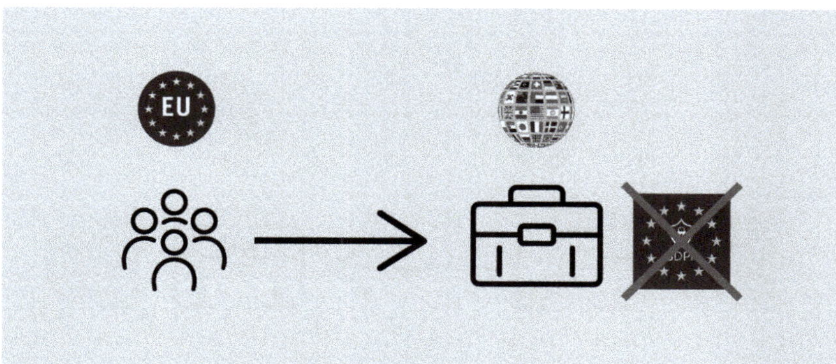

Figure 2.1 Transmission of personal data directly from individuals in the EEA to a data importer established outside the EEA, which is not subject to the GDPR's extraterritorial application (Design: Helma van der Wal)

[106] EDPB, Guidelines 3/2018 on the territorial scope of the GDPR (Article 3) (12 November 2019), example 16 at 19 <https://edpb.europa.eu/sites/default/files/files/file1/edpb_guidelines_3_2018_territorial_scope_after_public_consultation_en_1.pdf> accessed 10 July 2023. The author would like to thank Jeroen Knijff for bringing this example to her attention.

possible example of direct transmissions could be transmissions of personal data from individuals' devices to cookie providers via cookies. In its Guidelines, however, the EDPB clarifies that a situation where personal data is disclosed via cookies is *not* considered as a direct transmission of personal data to the cookie provider. Rather, it is a transmission of personal data from the website provider, which places cookies on a user's device, and the cookie provider.[107] Transmission of personal data to such website providers, when they are located outside the EEA, would, however, *not* be considered as 'transfer'. Such transmissions to website providers not subject to the GDPR would fall under this legal regime.

Because the transmission to the Chinese university does not qualify as a 'transfer' in the interpretation of the EDPB, GDPR restrictions on transfer of this data also do not apply. In sum, personal data falling under Legal Regime 1 is not afforded *any* GDPR protections, thus creating a gap in legal protection of individuals' fundamental rights.

Legal Regime 2: Restricted transfer, GDPR protections of Chapter V

This legal regime applies to situations where personal data flows from a data exporter subject to the GDPR (irrespective of location) to a data importer outside the EEA, to which the GDPR does not apply (Figure 2.2). An example of this situation is a transfer of personal data by an EU-based company to a cloud service provider storing data outside the EEA.

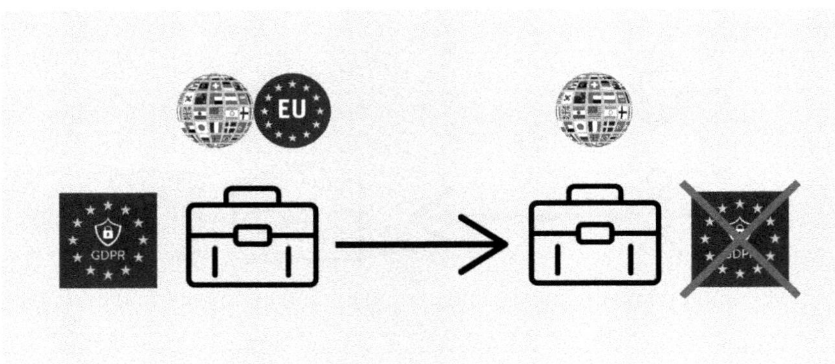

Figure 2.2 Transmission of personal data from a data exporter subject to the GDPR (irrespective of location) to a data importer outside the EEA, which is not subject to the GDPR's extraterritorial application (Design: Helma van der Wal)

[107] EDPB, Guidelines 05/2021 on the Interplay between the application of Article 3 and the provisions on international transfers as per Chapter V of the GDPR (n 68) footnote 15 at 9.

This flow of personal data qualifies as 'transfer' under GDPR's Chapter V; therefore, restrictions on transfers of personal data outside the EEA apply. These restrictions are discussed in Section 2.2.4.

Legal Regime 3: Restricted transfer, extraterritorial GDPR application, and protections of Chapter V 'light'

This legal regime applies to situations where personal data flows from a data exporter subject to the GDPR (irrespective of location) to a data importer outside the EEA, which is subject to the GDPR's extraterritorial application of the GDPR for the same data processing (Figure 2.3). An example of this situation is a transmission of personal data from a website operated by an EEA entity to a cookie provider outside the EEA, which is subject to the extraterritorial application of the GDPR due to its deliberate monitoring of EEA data subjects in the EEA (Article 3(2)(b) GDPR).

This flow of personal data qualifies as a 'transfer' under the GDPR's Chapter V. However, according to the EDPB, in this scenario transfer mechanisms should *not* duplicate the GDPR but rather 'address the elements that are related specifically to the risks associated with the importer being located in a third country, e.g. to address possible conflicting national laws and government access in the third country, as well as the difficulty to enforce and obtain redress against an entity outside the EU'.[108] In other words, Chapter V of the GDPR still applies, but in a 'light' version (this regime is hereinafter referred to as 'Chapter V light').

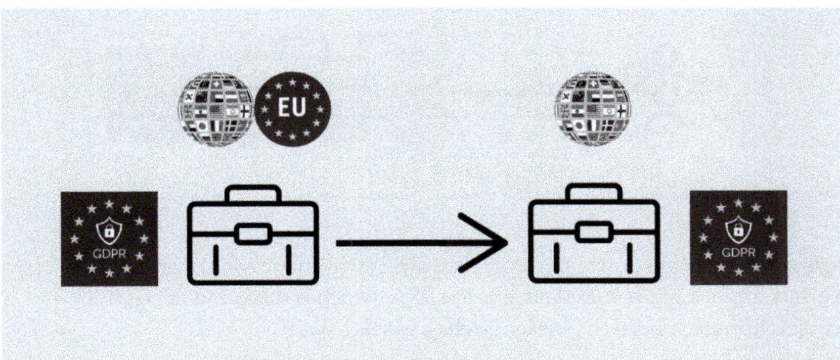

Figure 2.3 Transmission of personal data from a data exporter subject to the GDPR (irrespective of location) to a data importer outside the EEA, which is subject to the GDPR's extraterritorial application (Design: Helma van der Wal)

[108] ibid, para 29.

Legal Regime 4: Somewhat restricted transmission, GDPR protections through extraterritorial application

This legal regime applies to situations where personal data flows directly from individuals in the EEA to a data importer established outside the EEA, to which the GDPR applies extraterritorially under Article 3 of the GDPR (Figure 2.4). An obvious example of this situation, offered by the EDPB, is transmission of personal data from an EU individual shopping in an online shop located outside the EEA, which does not have any establishment in the EU.[109] Situations falling under this legal regime, however, are much more diverse than the EDPB seems to foresee. For example, they also include online monitoring and tracking for the purposes of targeted advertising conducted by entities outside the EEA through websites, which are subject to the extraterritorial application of the GDPR (and, therefore, do not fall under Legal Regime 1) as well as large-scale scraping of EU data subjects' data from the internet for the purpose of designing and training AI algorithms, such as OpenAI's ChatGPT and transmission of personal data to ChatGPT by its users in the EU.[110]

This flow of personal data does not qualify as a 'transfer', and, therefore, the restrictions of GDPR's Chapter V do not apply. However, the flow of personal data to a data importer in this situation is *not completely unrestricted* due

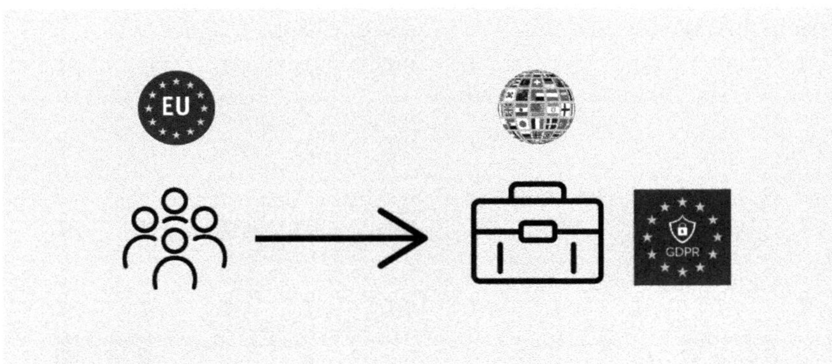

Figure 2.4 Transmission of personal data directly from individuals in the EEA to a data importer established outside the EEA, which is subject to the GDPR's extraterritorial application (Design: Helma van der Wal)

[109] See ibid example 1.

[110] In its 2023 investigation of OpenAI's ChatGPT compliance with the GDPR, Italian DPA (Garante) did not raise the issue of transmissions of personal data to California, USA, where OpenAI is located (OpenAI does not have an EU establishment). See 'Artificial Intelligence: Garante, Stop to ChatGPT by the Italian SA. Personal Data Is Collected Unlawfully, No Age Verification System Is in Place for Children' (*Garante*, 31 March 2023) <https://www.garanteprivacy.it/web/guest/home/docweb/-/docweb-display/docweb/9870847#english> accessed 10 July 2023. Arguably, this issue was not raised because such transmissions do not qualify as 'transfer', following the EDPB guidelines.

to the extraterritorial application of the GDPR, as discussed in Section 2.2.5. Nevertheless, similar to Legal Regime 1, this regime also creates a gap in legal protection as enforcement of the GDPR against controllers or processors not established in the EU can be challenging.[111]

2.2.4 Restrictions on transfers of personal data under Chapter V GDPR

According to the GDPR, a transfer of personal data outside the EEA may only take place if the conditions of the GDPR's Chapter V are met. These conditions, as discussed below, *apply in full* only in Legal Regime 2, that is, when personal data flows from a data exporter subject to the GDPR to a data importer not subject to the GDPR. This section briefly explains these conditions, while Section 2.2.5 focuses on the restrictions that apply to transmissions of personal data in other legal regimes.

Transfers of personal data outside the EEA can occur without restrictions only if the destination country, territory, or international organization ensures an 'adequate' level of personal data protection.[112] First introduced by the 1995 Data Protection Directive, the adequacy mechanism predates the EU Charter. In the 2015 *Schrems I* judgment, however, the CJEU retroactively gave it constitutional meaning.[113]

'Adequate', as interpreted by the CJEU, means 'essentially equivalent' to the level of protection of fundamental rights and freedoms guaranteed by the EU Charter.[114] The European Commission unilaterally evaluates the adequacy of the data protection regime of a country, a territory, or an international organization on a case-by-case basis, taking into account its legal and administrative mechanisms of personal data protection.[115] If the Commission's assessment results in a positive finding, it issues a legally binding 'adequacy decision'.[116]

[111] See EDPB, 'Study on the Enforcement of GDPR Obligations against Entities Established outside the EEA but Falling under Article 3(2) GDPR' (4 November 2021), <https://edpb.europa.eu/system/files/2023-04/call_9_final_report_04112021_en_0.pdf> accessed 10 July 2023. cf Natasha Lomas, 'Italy Orders ChatGPT Blocked Citing Data Protection Concerns' (31 March 2023) <https://techcrunch.com/2023/03/31/chatgpt-blocked-italy/?guccounter=1> accessed 10 July 2023. However, in ChatGPT's case, OpenAI voluntarily acknowledged the jurisdiction of the Italian DPA and agreed to take measures to comply with the DPA's order to stop processing personal data and improve its GDPR compliance.

[112] GDPR (n 2), art 45.

[113] For a discussion, see Section 5.2.

[114] See, eg, *Schrems I* (n 43) para 73; *Schrems II* (n 44) para 94.

[115] For a list of criteria for assessment, see art 45(2) GDPR (n 2).

[116] 'Adequacy decisions' are adopted as Commission implementing acts based on art 288 TFEU (n 32).

Currently, only fifteen countries have a valid adequacy decision,[117] including the new adequacy decision for the United States—the EU-US Data Privacy Framework.[118] This framework is the third adequacy decision that the European Commission has granted to the United States, following the invalidation of the so-called EU-US Privacy Shield framework by the 2020 CJEU judgment in *Schrems II*. In that judgment, the CJEU concluded that the Privacy Shield did not ensure an 'essentially equivalent' level of protection for personal data transferred to the United States, because it could not remedy the absence of (1) necessary limitations and safeguards in US law with regard to the interferences caused by access to personal data by US surveillance authorities in the national security context, and (2) effective judicial protection against such interferences.[119] The *Schrems II* judgment confirmed the CJEU's conclusions in its 2015 *Schrems I* judgment, which invalidated the Privacy Shield's predecessor—the EU-US Safe Harbor. Both *Schrems I* and *II* judgments embodied European discontent with the US foreign surveillance practices[120] exposed by Edward Snowden's revelations.

Increased awareness of the risks of US mass surveillance to Europeans' privacy has put the rules concerning foreign governments' access to EU individuals' data, for national security or law enforcement purposes, in the spotlight of adequacy assessment of any foreign country's data protection framework. Although both *Schrems I* and *Schrems II* concerned transfers of personal data to the United States, the European Commission's subsequent adequacy assessments with respect to third countries' legal frameworks on government access to personal data have become more extensive than prior to *Schrems I* and *Schrems II*.

The Commission has never to date published an assessment finding that a third country does *not* provide an adequate level of protection. In the past, if the Commission was not able to certify the adequacy of personal data protection in the country under assessment, such assessment did not result in any decision at all. This was, for example, the case with Australia.[121]

[117] European Commission, 'Adequacy Decisions. How the EU Determines if a Non-EU Country Has an Adequate Level of Data Protection' <https://commission.europa.eu/law/law-topic/data-protection/international-dimension-data-protection/adequacy-decisions_en> accessed 10 July 2023.

[118] European Commission Implementing Decision of 10 July 2023 pursuant to Regulation (EU) 2016/679 of the European Parliament and of the Council on the adequate level of protection of personal data under the EU-US Data Privacy Framework [2023] C(2023) 4745 final (hereafter EU-US Data Privacy Framework).

[119] *Schrems II* (n 44) paras 168–97. For further discussion, see Section 5.3.1.

[120] See Christopher Kuner, 'Data Nationalism and Its Discontents' (2015) 64 Emory Law Journal 2089, 2092 ('The transfer of national borders to the online space reflects society's ambivalence about the benefits and drawbacks of globalization: on the one hand we have grown accustomed to the global availability of goods and services, but on the other hand we are unsettled by the breakdown of barriers that seems to threaten our national and regional identities. The Snowden revelations and other recent developments have increased the pace and intensity of these anxieties, but the deep-seated nature of these concerns shows the importance of developing an underlying normative framework to address them.').

[121] Abraham L Newman, *Protectors of Privacy: Regulating Personal Data in the Global Economy* (Cornell UP 2018) 109; Bygrave, *Data Privacy Law* (n 29) 194.

In 2017, the European Commission started the review of all adequacy decisions that were in force at that time.[122] The 2019 adequacy decision for Japan was under review since 2020.[123] The European Commission published a report, on 3 April 2023, confirming that Japan continues to ensure adequate level of protection of EU personal data.[124] As of June 2023, the outcome of all other assessments that have been going on for nearly six years has not yet been published. After adopting adequacy decisions for South Korea and the United Kingdom following Brexit, the European Commission is actively exploring the possibility of adequacy assessments of some of the EU's important trading partners in Asia, Africa, and Latin America.[125]

Systematic or regular transfers of personal data to countries, territories, or international organizations that have not been granted an adequacy decision can only lawfully occur subject to 'appropriate safeguards', named in Article 46 of the GDPR, and put in place by the data controller or processor transferring personal data.[126] The most used appropriate safeguards in practice include:

- standard data protection clauses, also known as standard contractual clauses (SCCs), adopted by the European Commission;[127] and
- binding corporate rules (BCRs), approved by competent DPAs, for multinational companies or companies conducting joint economic activity.[128]

In addition to the SCCs, Article 46 of the GDPR includes other contractual tools that can serve as appropriate safeguards: standard data protection clauses adopted by a DPA of an EU member state and approved by the Commission[129] and the so-called bespoke contracts, concluded between a data exporter and a data importer,

[122] Catherine Stupp, 'Commission Conducting Review of All Foreign Data Transfer Deals' (*Euractiv*, 9 November 2017) <https://www.euractiv.com/section/data-protection/news/commission-conducting-review-of-all-foreign-data-transfer-deals/> accessed 10 July 2023.

[123] EDPB, 'Agenda 40th EDPB meeting' (20 October 2020) <https://edpb.europa.eu/sites/default/files/files/file1/20201020plen1.2_agenda_public.pdf> accessed 10 July 2023, mentioning the Review of the Adequacy Decision of Japan.

[124] European Commission, Report from the Commission to the European Parliament and the Council on the first review of the functioning of the adequacy decision for Japan COM(2023) 275 final (3 April 2023) 5 <https://eur-lex.europa.eu/legal-content/EN/TXT/?uri=CELEX%3A52023DC0275> accessed 10 July 2023.

[125] Commission Staff Working Document Accompanying the Document: Communication from the Commission to the European Parliament and the Council, Data Protection as a Pillar of Citizens' Empowerment and the EU's Approach to the Digital Transition: Two Years of Application of the General Data Protection Regulation [2020] COM (2020) 264 final; Communication from the Commission to the European Parliament and the Council, Data Protection as a Pillar of Citizens' Empowerment and the EU's Approach to the Digital Transition - Two Years of Application of the General Data Protection Regulation [2020] COM (2020) 264 final.

[126] GDPR (n 2), arts 46–47.

[127] GDPR (n 2), art 46(2)(c); Commission Decision on standard contractual clauses for the transfer of personal data to third countries (n 102).

[128] GDPR (n 2), art 46(2)(b).

[129] GDPR (n 2), art 46(2)(d).

authorized by a DPA of an EU member state.[130] Neither of these avenues for systematic transfers is currently utilized in practice.[131]

As compared to the Data Protection Directive, the GDPR also introduced two new appropriate safeguards for transfers of personal data. These are approved industry codes of conduct[132] and certification mechanisms,[133] when complemented with binding and enforceable commitments by the controller or processor in the third country to apply the appropriate safeguards, including those in respect of the data subjects' rights. As of this writing, neither of these mechanisms has practical significance, however.

For years, the SCCs were the most widely used mechanism for systematic transfers of personal data to countries without an adequacy decision.[134] Although the CJEU *Schrems II* judgment made reliance on the SCCs more difficult, the SCCs are still the leading transfer mechanism used by companies to transfer personal data outside the EEA.

Part of the questions referred for a preliminary ruling to the CJEU in the *Schrems II* case concerned the validity of the SCCs approved by the European Commission in the light of the EU Charter.[135] Although the CJEU has concluded that the SCCs are valid in the light of the EU Charter, the Court explained that, in practice, the use of the SCCs is only allowed if they yield a standard of protection for the transferred personal data 'essentially equivalent' to that in the EU.[136] If this is not the case, data exporters must put in place supplementary measures to remedy the lack of essential equivalence of personal data protection or, alternatively, suspend or stop transferring personal data.[137] The same

[130] GDPR (n 2), art 46(3)(a).

[131] As of this writing (June 2023), neither of the DPAs has approved standard data protection clauses. The use of bespoke contracts is also very limited, if not non-existent, as DPAs refrain from establishing a process for authorizing such clauses in the absence of an EDPB Guidance. See David Peloquin and others, 'Disruptive and Avoidable: GDPR Challenges to Secondary Research Uses of Data' (2020) 28 European Journal of Human Genetics 697.

[132] GDPR (n 2), arts 40, 46(2)(e).

[133] GDPR (n 2), arts 40(2), 42(2), 46.

[134] See IAPP-EY, Annual Privacy Governance Report (*IAPP*, 2019) 110 <https://f.hubspotuserconten t20.net/hubfs/525875/IAPP_EY_Governance_Report_2019.pdf> accessed 10 July 2023 (showing that in 2019, ie, prior to the CJEU *Schrems II* judgment, 88 per cent of personal data transfers from the EU to the US were based on the SCCs). The use of the SCCs remained the same or even increased after *Schrems II*. See IAPP-FTI Consulting Annual Privacy Governance Report 2020 viii <https://static2. ftitechnology.com/docs/IAPP-FTI+Consulting+-+2020+Privacy+Governance+Report.pdf> accessed 10 July 2023 (showing that 88 per cent of companies surveyed used the SCCs as a transfer mechanism) and Müge Fazlioglu, 'IAPP-EY Annual Privacy Governance Report 2021' (2021) paras 122–49 <https:// ssrn.com/abstract=4227244> accessed 10 July 2023 (hereafter 'IAPP-EY Annual Privacy Governance Report 2021') (showing that 94 per cent of companies surveyed used SCCs as a transfer mechanism).

[135] *Schrems II* (n 44).

[136] *Schrems II* (n 44) paras 96, 99, 100, 133–37, 142; Christopher Kuner, 'The Schrems II Judgment of the Court of Justice and the Future of Data Transfer Regulation' (*European Law Blog*, 17 July 2020) <https://europeanlawblog.eu/2020/07/17/the-schrems-ii-judgment-of-the-court-of-justice-and-the-future-of-data-transfer-regulation/> accessed 10 July 2023.

[137] For a more detailed summary of the CJEU's conclusions regarding the SCCs, see Section 5.3.1.

requirements also apply to other appropriate safeguards under Article 46 of the GDPR.[138]

The SCCs adopted by the European Commission in June 2021 require a data exporter and importer to conduct a so-called Transfer Impact Assessment. This amounts to an obligation to assess whether the laws and practices in the third country of destination applicable to the processing of the personal data by the data importer meet the essential equivalence standard and adopt supplementary measures, where necessary.[139]

EDPB Recommendations on supplementary measures suggest that in some situations transfer of personal data outside the EEA is not allowed at all because supplementary measures that could remedy the lack of essential equivalence of the legal regime of the country of destination are not available.[140] As a result, lawful reliance on the SCCs for transfers of personal data outside the EEA can be problematic, especially when personal data is transferred to non-democratic countries. Following the *Schrems II* judgment, the DPAs are obliged to proactively monitor the use of SCCs for the purposes of transfers of personal data, and must suspend or prohibit personal data transfers when data exporters fail to implement necessary supplementary measures.[141] Since 2020, when the *Schrems II* judgment came out, the DPAs throughout the EU somewhat, but not yet sufficiently, enhanced their enforcement efforts of the GDPR's Chapter V rules.[142]

An example of the *post-Schrems II* enforcement efforts is a line of enforcement cases across the EU (eg, Austria, Denmark, Italy, France), DPAs following 101 complaints by noyb, an NGO led by Max Schrems, investigating the use of Google Analytics and Facebook Connect by certain European websites.[143] All DPAs that conducted investigations have concluded that transfers of personal data by the investigated European websites to the United States by using a Google Analytics or Facebook Connect could not rely on the SCCs, as there were no supplementary

138 EDPB, 'Frequently Asked Questions on the Judgment of the Court of Justice of the European Union in Case C-311/18—Data Protection Commissioner v Facebook Ireland Ltd and Maximillian Schrems' (23 July 2020) question 7 <https://edpb.europa.eu/our-work-tools/our-documents/other/frequently-asked-questions-judgment-court-justice-european-union_en> accessed 10 July 2023; EDPB, Recommendations 01/2020 on measures that supplement transfer tools to ensure compliance with the EU level of protection of personal data (18 June 2021) 13 <https://edpb.europa.eu/system/files/2021-06/edpb_recommendations_202001vo.2.0_supplementarymeasurestransferstools_en.pdf> accessed 10 July 2023 (hereafter EDPB, Recommendations 01/2020 on measures that supplement transfer tools to ensure compliance with the EU level of protection of personal data).

139 Clause 14 of the Annex to the Commission Decision on standard contractual clauses for the transfer of personal data to third countries (n 102).

140 EDPB, Recommendations 01/2020 on measures that supplement transfer tools to ensure compliance with the EU level of protection of personal data (n 138), use cases 6 and 7 at 34–35.

141 *Schrems II* (n 44) paras 108, 121.

142 See Section 5.3.1.

143 See, eg, 'UPDATE: Further EU DPA Orders Stop of Google Analytics' (*noyb*, 5 July 2022) <https://noyb.eu/en/update-further-eu-dpa-orders-stop-google-analytics> accessed 10 July 2023 (hereafter Noyb, 'UPDATE: Further EU DPA Orders Stop of Google Analytics').

measures available to remedy the lack of essential equivalent protection of personal data in the United States.[144] As a result, the DPAs found such transfers unlawful.

The DPAs have also concluded that the risk-based approach does not apply to the interpretation of the GDPR's rules on transfers of personal data.[145] This means that the same standard applies to transfer of personal data irrespective of the risk such transfer carries for the rights of individuals,[146] whether it is (a part of) an online identifier of a website visitor and information about how long this visitor spent on a certain website or complete information about a person's online behaviour. This approach is criticized in Chapter 5 of this book, which makes the case for a risk-based approach to the application of Chapter V of the GDPR. Since the decision on the inapplicability of risk-based approach to transfers has only been taken by national DPAs in specific enforcement cases, there is still a possibility that this position will change. In its report on the work undertaken by the DPAs within the 101 Task Force, formed following Schrems' 101 complaints, the EDPB did not clarify this issue. At the same time, the EDPB referred to the companies' obligation to demonstrate compliance in accordance with Article 24(1) of the GDPR. It is precisely this provision that also codifies the risk-based approach to GDPR compliance under the GDPR. The reference to this provision, as well as the EDPB's unwillingness to make any conclusions on the risk-based approach with GDPR's Chapter V (despite this being a hotly debated topic), suggests that a risk-based approach could still be implemented.[147] Elements of a risk-based approach can also be read into the final EDPB Recommendations on supplementary measures, after the critique of the EDPB's absolutist approach in the draft Recommendations during the public consultation.[148]

The most prominent post-*Schrems II* enforcement action, however, is the decision issued on 12 May 2023 by the Irish DPC to Meta Platforms (following a ten-year inquiry that led to both *Schrems I* and *Schrems II* CJEU judgments) with respect to transfers of personal data to the United States in connection with the

[144] See eg 'Google Analytics' (Danish Data Protection Authority (Datatilsynet) <https://www.datatilsynet.dk/english/google-analytics> accessed 10 July 2023 (hereafter Datatilsynet, 'Google Analytics'); Noyb, 'UPDATE: Further EU DPA Orders Stop of Google Analytics' (n 143).

[145] See, eg, Datatilsynet, 'Google Analytics' (n 144).

[146] See, eg, 'UPDATE on 101 Complaints: Austrian DPA Rejects "Risk Based Approach" for Data Transfers to Third Countries' (*noyb*, 2 May 2022) <https://noyb.eu/en/update-noybs-101-complaints-austrian-dpa-rejects-risk-based-approach-data-transfers-third-countries> accessed 10 July 2023. For analysis and critique, see Lokke Moerel, 'What Happened to the Risk Based Approach to Data Transfers?' (*FPF blog*, 27 September 2022) <https://fpf.org/wp-content/uploads/2022/09/FPF-Guest-Blog-What-Happened-to-the-Risk-Based-Approach-of-Data-Transfers.doc.pdf> accessed 10 July 2023.

[147] For discussion on how risk-based approach is implemented in the GDPR and how the EU framework for transfers of personal data can be reformed with this approach in mind, see Sections 5.3.4 and 5.4.3.

[148] Jetty Tielemans, Daniel Cooper, and Gabe Maldoff, 'EDPB's Data Transfer Recommendations Adopt a Risk-Based Approach with Teeth' (*IAPP*, 22 June 2021) <https://iapp.org/news/a/edpbs-data-transfer-recommendations-adopt-a-risk-based-approach-with-teeth/> accessed 10 July 2023.

delivery of its Facebook service. In this decision (toughened as a result of coordination with other European DPAs within the EDPB, which resulted in a binding EDPB decision[149]), the Irish DPC ordered Meta Platforms to suspend any future transfer of personal data to the United States within the period of five months; and an administrative fine of € 1.2 billion (reflecting the binding EDPB decision); and an order to bring its transfers of personal data in compliance with Chapter V GDPR within six months.[150] The Irish DPC has concluded that Meta Platforms did not implement appropriate supplementary measures to rectify the lack of essentially equivalent protection of Europeans' personal data in US law, and could not rely on specific derogations under Article 49. While this decision is no longer an existential threat for Meta Platforms' Facebook service in the light of the adequacy decision promptly adopted by the European Commission for the United States within two months of the Irish DPC Decision, its practical implications may stretch well beyond this one company. First, because it raises the question of whether SCCs are in practice available for systematic transfers, such as those carried out by Meta Platforms, to a country that does not meet the standard of essential equivalence. And second, because of the narrow interpretation of specific derogations under Article 49, as discussed below.

If it is not reasonably possible for a company to adopt *any* of the appropriate safeguards under Article 46 of the GDPR, a data controller or processor may still be able to rely on one of the specific derogations exhaustively listed in Article 49(1) of the GDPR, such as the explicit consent of a data subject, necessity of transfer for the conclusion or performance of a contract, or necessity for the establishment, exercise, or defence of legal claims. Unlike the adequacy mechanism and appropriate safeguards, however, these derogations—in accordance with the EDPB guidance—are only suitable for 'occasional' or 'non-repetitive' transfers and cannot be relied upon for the purposes of regular and systematic transfers.[151] The layered approach adopted by the EDPB requires that before using these derogations, data exporters should first 'endeavour possibilities to frame the transfer' with one of the adequate safeguards.[152]

[149] EDPB, 'Binding Decision 1/2023 on the Dispute Submitted by the Irish SA on Data Transfers by Meta Platforms Ireland Limited for Its Facebook Service (Art. 85 GDPR)' (13 April 2023) <https://edpb.europa.eu/system/files/2023-05/edpb_bindingdecision_202301_ie_sa_facebooktransfers_en.pdf> accessed 10 July 2023 (hereafter EDPB, 'Binding Decision 1/2023 on the Dispute Submitted by the Irish SA on Data Transfers by Meta Platforms Ireland Limited for Its Facebook Service (Art. 85 GDPR)').

[150] Irish Data Protection Commission, 'Data Protection Commission Announces Conclusion of Inquiry into Meta Ireland' (22 May 2023) <https://www.dataprotection.ie/en/news-media/press-releases/Data-Protection-Commission-announces-conclusion-of-inquiry-into-Meta-Ireland> accessed 10 July 2023.

[151] EDPB, 'Guidelines 2/2018 on Derogations of Article 49 under Regulation 2016/679' (n 87) 4. But see Rob van Eijk and Gabriela Zanfir-Fortuna, 'Schrems II: Article 49 GDPR Derogations May Not Be so Narrow and Restrictive After All?' (*FPF Blog*, 4 February 2021) <https://fpf.org/blog/schrems-ii-article-49-gdpr-derogations-may-not-be-so-narrow-and-restrictive-after-all/> accessed 10 July 2023 (hereafter Van Eijk and Zanfir-Fortuna, 'Schrems II: Article 49 GDPR Derogations May Not Be so Narrow and Restrictive After All?').

[152] EDPB, 'Guidelines 2/2018 on Derogations of Article 49 under Regulation 2016/679' (n 87) 4.

Requirements that derogations under Article 49 are only available for 'occasional' and 'non-repetitive' transfers, however, do not directly follow from the GDPR with respect to all derogations. Article 49 itself requires that transfers must be 'not repetitive' only with respect to transfers, which cannot be based on any of the derogations explicitly listed in Article 49(1) of the GDPR but are necessary for the purposes of compelling legitimate interest.[153] It does not set this requirement with respect to any of the derogations explicitly named in Article 49(1) of the GDPR. Recital 111 of the GDPR states that '[p]rovisions must be made for the possibility for transfers in certain circumstances where the data subject has given his or her explicit consent, where the transfer is occasional and necessary in relation to a contract or a legal claim. . . .' It follows from this recital that requirement that transfers must be occasional only when they are based on a contract or a legal claim, which are only two out of seven specific derogations listed in Article 49(1) of the GDPR.

Therefore, this book contends that based on the GDPR itself specific derogations could be used more broadly than interpreted by the EDPB. In its *Schrems II* judgment, the CJEU seemed to cast doubt on whether the EDPB's layered approach, where only a limited role is afforded for derogations under Article 49, is the correct interpretation of the GDPR. In this judgment, the CJEU stated that invalidation of the EU-US Privacy Shield was not liable to create a legal vacuum, as even in the absence of an adequacy decision or appropriate safeguards, transfers of personal data to third countries could take place on the basis of derogations under Article 49 of the GDPR.[154] Unlike the EDPB, the CJEU does not mention the limitations on the use of these derogations.[155] This leads Drechsler and Kamara to observe that the

[153] GDPR (n 2) para 2 of art 49(1).

[154] *Schrems II* (n 44) para 202.

[155] The judge-rapporteur Von Danwitz in the Schrems cases also stated in an interview that in his opinion, 'the opportunities granted by Article 49 have not been fully explored yet. I believe they are not so narrow that they restrict any kind of transfer, especially when we're talking about transfers within one corporation or group of companies.' See Van Eijk and Zanfir-Fortuna, 'Schrems II: Article 49 GDPR Derogations May Not Be so Narrow and Restrictive After All?' (n 151). cf Christopher Kuner, 'Article 49: Derogations for Specific Situations' in Christopher Kuner and others (eds), The EU General Data Protection Regulation: A Commentary/Update of Selected Articles (4 May 2021) 203 <http://dx.doi.org/10.2139/ssrn.3839645> accessed 10 July 2023, arguing that:

[i]t might be asked whether the restriction that the derogations may not be used for repetitive transfers should be applied only to the derogation based on the compelling legitimate interests of the controller under the second sub-paragraph of Article 49(1), which is the only provision of Article 49 that explicitly states that it does not apply to repetitive transfers, but not to the other derogations. However, the better interpretation is that the condition of transfers being non-repetitive must apply to all the derogations under Article 49, based on the fact that EU law requires that a derogation from a fundamental right not be interpreted in a way that contradicts its exceptional nature. If a derogation is used as the legal basis for transfers which are repetitive, then its use is by definition not exceptional, meaning that the fact that transfers are non-repetitive must be central to the nature of the derogations' (internal footnotes omitted)

CJEU seems to consider derogations to be more widely applicable than previously assumed.[156]

In its decision in the matter of Meta Platforms, the Irish DPC followed the EDPB's interpretation that specific derogations are only available for 'occasional' and 'non-repetitive' transfers.[157] However, the Irish DPC went even further than the EDPB in restricting the availability of specific derogations as mechanisms for transfers of personal data outside the EEA. The DPC held that Meta Platforms could not rely on specific derogations for transfers to the United States because based on Irish DPC's interpretation of CJEU judgments in *Schrems I* and *Schrems II*, US laws that permit data surveillance do not respect the 'essence' of the right to an effective judicial remedy.[158] Assessment of whether an interference with fundamental rights respects the essence of such fundamental rights is the first step in the assessment of lawfulness of such interferences under Article 52(1) of the EU Charter. This assessment is followed by necessity and proportionality assessment, which in application to transfers of personal data outside the EEA is framed as 'essential equivalence' assessment by the CJEU, discussed above.[159] In other words, in Irish DPC's view, before relying on specific derogations, the data exporter must evaluate whether the legal framework of the country of destination respects the essence of fundamental rights under the EU Charter. If such legal framework does not respect the essence of these rights, specific derogations under Article 49 are not available.

This book contends that the Irish DPC's approach is misguided and argues in Section 5.2.2 that in order to rely on specific derogations under Article 49, data exporters are *not* required to conduct either an assessment of whether the country of destination respects the essence of fundamental rights or an essential equivalence assessment of the legal framework of the country of destination. It is also telling that this interpretation by the Irish DPC was not endorsed or in any way commented on by the EDPB in its binding decision in this case.[160]

Following *Schrems II*, specific derogations are the only legal mechanisms companies can rely on for transferring personal data to countries that have not been

See also Christopher Kuner, 'Article 49: Derogations for Specific Situations' in Christopher Kuner and others (eds), *The EU General Data Protection Regulation (GDPR): A Commentary* (OUP 2020) 843–46.

[156] Laura Drechsler and Irene Kamara, 'Essential Equivalence as a Benchmark for International Data Transfers after Schrems II' in Eleni Kosta and Ronald Leenes (eds), *Research Handbook on EU Data Protection* (Edward Elgar Publishing 2022) 349.

[157] Irish Data Protection Commission, 'Decision in the Matter of Meta Platforms Ireland Limited' (previously known as Facebook Ireland Limited) (12 May 2023) paras 8.57–8.61 < https://edpb.europa.eu/system/files/2023-05/final_for_issue_ov_transfers_decision_12-05-23.pdf> accessed 10 July 2023 (hereafter Irish Data Protection Commission, 'Decision in the Matter of Meta Platforms Ireland Limited').

[158] ibid, paras 8.22–8.27, 8.45.

[159] For an elaborate discussion on these points, see Section 5.2.

[160] EDPB, 'Binding Decision 1/2023 on the Dispute Submitted by the Irish SA on Data Transfers by Meta Platforms Ireland Limited for Its Facebook Service (Art. 85 GDPR)' (n 149).

afforded adequacy by the EU and do not meet the essential equivalence standard, when supplementary measures to remedy the lack of essential equivalence are not available. Restrictive interpretation by the derogations by the Irish DPC, which makes them unavailable to countries that do not respect the essence of fundamental rights, adds an additional hurdle in the application of derogations and could potentially deprive these companies of this last opportunity for transferring personal data outside the EEA lawfully. This interpretation increases the tension between the EU framework for transfers of personal data outside the EEA and the EU's international trade obligations, as further discussed in Section 2.3.

2.2.5 Other restrictions on transmissions of personal data under the GDPR

While GDPR's Chapter V, as explained in the previous section, applies in full only in Legal Regime 2, transmissions of personal data outside the EEA in Legal Regimes 3 and 4 are also subject to some form of restrictions, different from those applicable in Legal Regime 2.

In Legal Regime 3, which applies to transfers of personal data from a data exporter to a data importer subject to extraterritorial application of the GDPR, the GDPR's Chapter V applies in its 'light' version. These transfers can proceed without restrictions to countries that have been afforded an adequacy decision by the European Commission. Legal uncertainty persists when it comes to transfers of personal data that fall under Legal Regime 3 on the basis of appropriate safeguards under Article 46 of the GDPR. The EDPB explains that in situations where personal data is transferred to a controller or processor who already falls under the scope of the GDPR, application of appropriate safeguards must be adjusted. The EDPB writes:

> <. . .> for such scenario, when developing relevant transfer instruments under Article 46, namely standard contractual clauses or ad hoc contractual clauses, the Article 3 situation should be taken into account in order not to duplicate the GDPR obligations but rather to address the elements that are related specifically to the risks associated with the importer being located in a third country, e.g. to address possible conflicting national laws and government access in the third country, as well as the difficulty to enforce and obtain redress against an entity outside the EU. Such instruments should, for example, address the measures to be taken in case of conflict of laws between third country legislation and the GDPR and in the event of third country requests for disclosure of data.[161]

[161] EDPB, Guidelines 05/2021 on the Interplay between the application of Article 3 and the provisions on international transfers as per Chapter V of the GDPR (n 68) para 29.

These transfers are explicitly excluded from the scope of existing SCCs adopted in June 2021, meaning no SCCs are currently available for these transfers.[162] With this approach, the EDPB and the European Commission seem to prevent the overlap of legal requirements that follow from the substantive GDPR rules and rules of Chapter V to ensure that non-European companies that fall under the GDPR's extraterritorial application do not have to comply with more extensive requirements compared to (a) their European counterparts and (b) their non-European counterparts that do not fall under the GDPR's extraterritorial application.

As of June 2023, the European Commission was working on a special set of SCCs that would apply to these transfers. In the meantime, companies that fall under the extraterritorial application of the GDPR are disadvantaged because they may not rely on the available SCCs, which, as mentioned above, are the most used transfer mechanism and often the only mechanism available to such companies (in the absence of BCRs and in the light of the low practical significance of certification mechanisms and codes of conduct as mechanisms of transfer). While the SCCs applicable to Legal Regime 3 are in the making, it is unclear how *other* appropriate safeguards under Article 46 of the GDPR, such as the BCRs, and derogations under Article 49 GDPR, should apply to transfers that fall under this Legal Regime.

In Legal Regime 4, which applies to direct transmissions of personal data from individuals to a controller or processor that falls under the extraterritorial application of the GDPR, Chapter V of the GDPR does *not* apply in its entirety. This is because such transmissions, according to the EDPB, do not fall in the definition of 'transfer' under the GDPR. In the Guidelines explaining the concept of 'transfer', the EDPB explains that when the data flow does *not* qualify as a 'transfer', it can still entail risks for individuals, including in relation to disproportionate government access to such data.[163] It is for this reason that the EDPB suggests that these transmissions may not be completely unrestricted.

When the data importer is subject to the extraterritorial application of the GDPR, it is obliged to impose some restrictions on personal data transmissions on the basis of the general GDPR requirements, such as lawfulness and security of personal data processing (Articles 5 and 32 of the GDPR) and the principle of accountability of the controller for processing personal data (Article 24 of the GDPR). The EDPB explains:

> Following from its obligation to be responsible for, and be able to demonstrate compliance with the data protection principles (Article 5) and to implement

[162] Art 1 of Commission Decision on standard contractual clauses for the transfer of personal data to third countries (n 102). See also Answer 24, European Commission, 'The New Standard Contractual Clauses – Questions and Answers' (May 2022) <https://commission.europa.eu/system/files/2022-05/questions_answers_on_sccs_en.pdf> accessed 10 July 2023.

[163] EDPB, Guidelines 05/2021 on the Interplay between the application of Article 3 and the provisions on international transfers as per Chapter V of the GDPR (n 68) paras 31–34.

> technical and organisational measures taking into account, *inter alia*, the **risks with respect to the processing** under Article 32 of the GDPR, a controller may very well conclude that extensive security measures are needed – or even that it would not be lawful – to conduct or proceed with a specific processing operation in a third country although there is no transfer situation.[164] (Bold added)

This interpretation suggests that restrictions on transfers of personal data can stem not only from the specific provisions of Chapter V but also from other GDPR obligations for controllers interpreted in the light of the EU Charter. Interestingly, in the context of a transmission that does *not* qualify as a 'transfer', the EDPB also relies on Article 24 GDPR, which, together with the principle of accountability, endorses the risk-based approach to compliance with the controller's obligations under the GDPR. Considering this approach, it is not logical to disapply the risk-based approach in a situation where a transmission *does* qualify as a transfer, as suggested by several DPAs in Google Analytics and Facebook Connect cases discussed above.

Transmissions that fall under Legal Regime 1 (direct transmissions to a controller or processor that does not fall under the GDPR), unlike Legal Regime 4, are not subject to any restrictions under the GDPR. In other words, personal data transmitted from the EEA to such data importers is deprived of *any* GDPR protection.

2.3 Compatibility of the EU Regime for Data Transfer with International Trade Law

This section positions the EU restrictions on transfers of personal data outside the EEA against the EU commitments under the GATS and other trade agreements that require liberalization of such transfers in the context of international trade in services.

Shortly after the EU data protection framework was introduced in 1995, several commentators flagged the potential inconsistency of the rules for transfers of personal data with the EU's commitments under the GATS, such as most-favoured nation (MFN) treatment, national treatment, and market access and cannot be justified under the Article XIV GATS general exception.[165] The EU is bound by these

[164] ibid, para 32.

[165] See, eg, Peter Swire and Robert E Litan, *None of Your Business: World Data Flows, Electronic Commerce, and the European Privacy Directive* (Brookings Institution Press 1988) 188–96; Joel R Reidenberg, 'E-Commerce and Trans-Atlantic Privacy' (2001) 38 Houston Law Review 717, 736–37; Lucas Bergkamp, 'The Privacy Fallacy: Adverse Effects of Europe's Data Protection Policy in an Information-Driven Economy' (2002) 18(1) Computer Law & Security Review 31, 39–40 <https://www.huntonak.com/images/content/3/2/v3/3292/Privacy-fallacy.pdf> accessed 10 July 2023 (hereafter Bergkamp, 'The Privacy Fallacy'). On the contrary, Shaffer argued that a hypothetical US claim regarding WTO inconsistency of EU's framework for personal data transfers 'would likely not prevail'.

commitments not only under the GATS[166] but also under virtually all the EU's post-GATS bilateral or plurilateral trade agreements.[167] Such warnings have intensified over time[168] under the influence of several factors: the increasing importance

See Gregory Shaffer, 'Globalization and Social Protection: The Impact of EU and International Rules in the Ratcheting Up of U.S. Privacy Standards' (2000) 25 Yale Journal of International Law 1, 46–51 (hereafter Shaffer, 'Globalization and Social Protection'). Asinari admits that the EU regime for transfers of personal data may violate the EU's WTO commitments but concludes that the violation can be justified under the general exception. See Maria Veronica Perez Asinari, 'Is There Any Room for Privacy and Data Protection within the WTO Rules' (2002) 9 Electronic Communication Law Review 249, 277 (hereafter Asinari, 'Is There Any Room for Privacy and Data Protection within the WTO Rules'). It should however be noted that Asinari's article predates the WTO's interpretation of the necessity test in the most recent WTO case law as well as the CJEU's case law on privacy and data protection as fundamental rights. Meddin also argues that the EU restrictions on transfers of personal data are inconsistent with the chapeau, while assuming that the 'necessity test' would be justified without explicating the underlying analysis. See Elisabeth Meddin, 'The Cost of Ensuring Privacy: How the General Data Protection Regulation Acts as a Barrier to Trade in Violation of Articles XVI and XVII of the General Agreement on Trade in Services' (2020) 35 American University International Law Review 997, 1027–28. On the possibility of violation of the chapeau, see also Bygrave, *Data Privacy Law* (n 29) 198; Stewart Baker, 'How Can the U.S. Respond to Schrems II?'(*Lawfare Blog*, 21 July 2020) <https://www.lawfareblog.com/how-can-us-respond-schrems-ii> accessed 10 July 2023; Svetlana Yakovleva and Kristina Irion, 'The Best of Both Worlds? Free Trade in Services and EU Law on Privacy and Data Protection', (2016) 2 European Data Protection Law Review 191(hereafter Yakovleva and Irion, 'The Best of Both Worlds?').

[166] In particular, arts II, XVI, and XVII of the GATS (n 1).

[167] Such obligations are part of most of the EU's international trade agreements, the most recent examples being arts 9.3, 9.5, and 9.6 of the CETA (Comprehensive Economic and Trade Agreement (CETA) between Canada, of the one part, and the European Union and its Member States, of the other part, 14 September 2014 [2017] OJ L11/23 (hereafter CETA)), arts 8.5, 8.6 of the EU-Singapore FTA (Free trade Agreement between the European Union and the Republic of Singapore [2019] OJ L294 (hereafter EU-Singapore FTA)), arts 8.15–8.17 of the JEFTA (Agreement between the European Union and Japan for an Economic Partnership [2018] OJ L330/3 (hereafter JEFTA)); arts 10.14, 10.16, and 10.17 of EU-New Zealand Free Trade Agreement (signed on 9 July 2023) (hereafter EU-New Zealand FTA).

[168] See, eg, Carla L Reyes, 'WTO-Compliant Protection of Fundamental Rights: Lessons from the EU Privacy Directive' (2011) 12 Melbourne Journal of International Law 1, 24–26 <https://law.unimelb.edu.au/__data/assets/pdf_file/0010/1686934/Reyes.pdf> accessed 10 July 2023 (hereafter Reyes, 'WTO-Compliant Protection of Fundamental Rights'); Perry Keller, *European and International Media Law: Liberal Democracy, Trade and New Media* (OUP 2011) (hereafter Keller, *European and International Media Law*); Rolf H Weber, 'Regulatory Autonomy and Privacy Standards under the GATS' (2012) 7(1) Asian Journal of WTO & International Health Law & Policy 25 (hereafter Weber, 'Regulatory Autonomy and Privacy Standards under the GATS'); Rolf H Weber and Dominic Staiger, *Transatlantic Data Protection in Practice* (Springer 2017) 58–59; Diane A MacDonald and Christine M Streatfeild, 'Personal Data Privacy and the WTO' (2014) 36(3) Houston Journal of International Law 625; Yakovleva and Irion, 'The Best of Both Worlds?' (n 165); Nivedita Sen, 'Understanding the Role of the WTO in International Data Flows: Taking the Liberalization or the Regulatory Autonomy Path?' (2018) 21(2) Journal of International Economic Law 323 (hereafter Sen, 'Understanding the Role of the WTO'); Samuel Coldicutt and Nivedita Sen, 'Testing the GDPR's WTO Readiness' (*Linklaters*) <https://www.linklaters.com/en/insights/blogs/digilinks/can-the-wto-save-international-data-transfers> accessed 10 July (hereafter Coldicutt and Sen, 'Testing the GDPR's WTO Readiness'); Aaditya Matto and Joshua P Meltzer, 'International Data Flows and Privacy: The Conflict and Its Resolution' (2018) World Bank Policy Research Working Paper 8431 <http://documents.worldbank.org/curated/en/751621525705087132/pdf/WPS8431.pdf> accessed 10 July 2023; Federica Velli, 'The Issue of Data Protection in EU Trade Commitments: Cross-Border Data Transfers in GATS and Bilateral Free Trade Agreements' (2019) 4(3) European Papers 881; Yi-Hsuan Chen, 'The EU Data Protection Law Reform: Challenges for Service Trade Liberalization and Possible Approaches for Harmonizing Privacy Standards into the Context of GATS' (2015) 19 The Spanish Yearbook of International Law 211, 218 (hereafter Chen,

of cross-border transfers of personal data for digital trade; the above-mentioned Edward Snowden's revelations; the challenge of the validity of the SCCs and the Privacy Shield at the CJEU, which resulted in higher standards for the former and invalidation of the latter;[169] the adoption of the GDPR in 2016 (which introduced a stricter enforcement regime); and the recurring pressure to include cross-border data flow provisions in trade agreements.[170]

Although the GDPR only marginally changed the framework for personal data transfers compared to the 1995 Data Protection Directive, it significantly raised the stakes of violating these rules by introducing harsh penalties, which include a fine of up to 4 per cent of the total worldwide annual turnover of an *undertaking* for the preceding financial year.[171] Under certain circumstances, this fine could be based not just on the turnover of a business unit that has violated the rules but instead on the turnover of a multinational entity as a whole.[172] In addition, following the CJEU *Schrems II* judgment, DPAs across Europe started to more actively (although still insufficiently) enforce the GDPR requirements on transfers of personal data outside the EEA. The most well-known examples of such enforcement actions include the above-mentioned Google Analytics and Facebook Connect enforcement cases and the landmark decision of the Irish DPC in the matter of Meta Platforms.

'The EU Data Protection Law Reform: Challenges for Service Trade Liberalization'); Tobias Naef, *Data Protection without Data Protectionism: The Right to Protection of Personal Data and Data Transfers in EU Law and International Trade Law* (Springer Cham 2023) (hereafter Naef, *Data Protection without Data Protectionism*). Chen and Naef acknowledge that most of the violations of the GATS by EU's restrictions on transfers of personal data outside the EEA could be justified under art XIV(c)(ii) GATS (n 1).

169 *Schrems II* (n 44); Vincent Manancourt, 'The EU Court Ruling That Could Blow Up Digital Trade' (*Politico*, 13 July 2020) <https://www.politico.eu/article/us-china-data-flows-at-risk-in-top-eu-court-ruling/> accessed 10 July 2023.

170 For further discussion, see Kristina Irion, Svetlana Yakovleva, and Marija Bartl, 'Trade and Privacy: Complicated Bedfellows? How to Achieve Data Protection-Proof Free Trade Agreements' (2016) Independent study commissioned by BEUC and others, 41 <https://www.ivir.nl/publicaties/download/trade_and_privacy.pdf> accessed 10 July 2023 (hereafter Irion, Yakovleva, and Bartl, 'Trade and Privacy: Complicated Bedfellows?'); James Fontanella-Khan, 'Data Protection Ruled Out of EU-US Trade Talks' (*Financial Times*, 4 November 2013) <www.ft.com/content/92a14dd2-44b9-11e3-a751-00144feabdc0> accessed 10 July 2023; Yakovleva, 'On Digital Sovereignty' (66); Mira Burri, 'Digital Trade Rulemaking in Free Trade Agreements, Forthcoming' in David Collins and Michael Geist (eds), *Handbook on Digital Trade* (Cheltenham: Edward Elgar 2023) <https://papers.ssrn.com/sol3/papers.cfm?abstract_id=4281650> 15–18.

171 GDPR (n 2) art 83(5).

172 Article 29 Working Party, Guidelines on the application and setting of administrative fines for the purposes of the Regulation 2016/679 WP253 (3 October 2017), 6 <https://ec.europa.eu/newsroom/article29/items/611237> accessed 10 July 2023; EDPB, Guidelines 04/2022 on the calculation of administrative fines under the GDPR (12 May 2022) 22–24, 33–36 <https://edpb.europa.eu/system/files/2023-06/edpb_guidelines_042022_calculationofadministrativefines_en.pdf> accessed 10 July 2023. On the notion of undertaking, see also *Höfner and Elser v Macotron* [1991] ECLI:EU:C:1991:161, para 21; *Confederación Española de Empresarios de Estaciones de Servicio v Compañía Española de Petróleos SA* [2006] ECLI:EU:C:2006:784, para 40; *Akzo Nobel NV and Others v Commission of the European Communities* [2009] ECLI:EU:C:2009:536, para 60; *Elf Aquitaine SA v European Commission* [2011] ECLI:EU:T:2011:217, para 56; *Imperial Chemical Industries Ltd. v Commission of the European Communities* [1972] ECLI:EU:C:1972:70, paras 125–46.

The latter case, however, is also a perfect illustration of the ineffectiveness of the GDPR enforcement, as it took the Irish DPC a decade to adopt a decision.[173] What changes the picture somewhat is that alleged violations of GDPR rules on transfers of personal data outside the EEA are also increasingly becoming the subject of *private* enforcement, in particular, mass claims.[174]

Higher stakes for violating the rules on transfers of personal data outside the EEA increase the risks of a collision between international trade law and the EU's data protection framework. Although the GATS does not specifically regulate cross-border flows of (personal) data, such flows may still be captured by obligations under the GATS (and similar provisions in other more recent FTAs) applicable to trade in services from one WTO member into the territory of another WTO member (cross-border supply of services, or 'mode of supply 1' under the GATS)[175] when data transfers enable cross-border development and provision of such services,[176] for example, cloud computing, search engine, social network, internet of things, and shared economy platform services.[177]

Incompatibility of EU's framework on transfers of personal data outside the EEA stems from both the definition of 'transfer' and from the substance of these rules themselves. The following sections argue that this framework could potentially violate the EU's non-discrimination and market access commitments.[178]

[173] See Irish Data Protection Commission, 'Decision in the Matter of Meta Platforms Ireland Limited' (n 157). This is, however, not the end of the 'saga', as Meta Platforms has already appealed the EDPB's binding decision at the EU's first-tier General Court and at an Irish court. The Irish High Court granted an interim stay on the DPC's decision. Matthew Newman, 'Meta Lodges Appeal against EDPB Data-Transfers Decision at EU Courts' (*MLex Market Insight*, 15 June 2023) <https://content.mlex.com/#/content/1478542/meta-lodges-appeal-against-edpb-data-transfers-decision-at-eu-courts> accessed 10 July 2023 (hereafter Newman, 'Meta Lodges Appeal against EDPB Data-Transfers Decision at EU Courts'); 'Facebook Owner Granted Stay on Order That It Suspend Europe-US Data Transfers' (*The Irish Times*, 9 June 2023) <https://www.irishtimes.com/business/2023/06/09/facebook-owner-granted-stay-on-order-that-it-suspend-europeus-data-transfers/> accessed 10 July 2023 (hereafter The Irish Times, 'Facebook Owner Granted Stay on Order That It Suspend Europe-US Data Transfers').

[174] See, eg, announcement of such a mass claim in the Netherlands: 'Consumentenbond en DPS starten nieuwe zaak na winnen privacyklacht tegen Facebook', (*Telecompaper*, 15 March 2023) <https://www.telecompaper.com/nieuws/consumentenbond-en-dps-starten-nieuwe-zaak-na-winnen-privacyklacht-tegen-facebook--1456816> accessed 10 July 2023.

[175] GATS (n 1) art I(2)(a).

[176] Susannah Hodson, 'Applying WTO and FTA Disciplines to Data Localization Measures' (2019) 18(4) World Trade Review 579, 586.

[177] For an extensive discussion on the application of GATS to data flows enabling these services, see Naef, *Data Protection without Data Protectionism* (n 168), 290–324.

[178] Naef argues that the EU regime for transfers of personal data outside the EEA may also violate domestic regulation obligations under Article VI of the GDPR. See Naef, *Data Protection without Data Protectionism* (n 168), 296–307.

2.3.1 Non-discrimination commitments

Non-discrimination commitments concerning trade in services are the MFN treatment and national treatment principles. The MFN obligation (GATS Article II) requires that WTO members treat services and service suppliers of other WTO members in a manner 'no less favourable' than 'like' services and service suppliers of any other country. National treatment (GATS Article XVII)[179] requires that 'like' foreign services and service suppliers receive a 'treatment no less favourable' than domestic services and service suppliers of the WTO member. The two-prong test for establishing a violation of the MFN and national treatment obligations is essentially the same:[180]

- comparison of service and/or service supplier to determine whether they are 'like', and
- comparison of the treatment of a service and/or service supplier of a complaining WTO member to see if it is 'less favourable' than treatment of a 'like' service and/or service supplier from another country (MFN) or domestic service and/or service supplier of the WTO member accused of violation (national treatment).

An important difference between the MFN and national treatment obligations is that unlike the MFN, which is by default binding on all WTO members, national treatment is a so-called 'specific commitment', which becomes binding only if and to the extent that the member has included it in its Schedules of Specific Commitments (Services Schedules). These schedules constitute an integral part of the GATS (GATS Article XX:3) and of the WTO accession package of a WTO member.

What matters most for the discussion in this book in the interpretation of 'likeness' and 'less favourable' in the context of non-discrimination provisions is whether *regulatory intent* plays a role in the interpretation of whether services or service suppliers are considered as 'like' or different treatments of such services or service suppliers are considered as 'less favourable'.

In the early 1990s, by applying the so-called 'aims and effects' test[181] in the context of trade in goods, adjudicating bodies of the 1947 General Agreement on

[179] National treatment is a specific commitment that only applies in relation to service sectors indicated in a party's schedules of specific commitments (art XVII GATS (n 1)).

[180] WTO, *European Communities – Measures Prohibiting the Importation and Marketing of Seal Products* – Reports of the Appellate Body (22 May 2014) WT/DS400/AB/R/WT/DS401/AB/R para 5.82 (hereafter Appellate Body Reports, *EC – Seal Products*); WTO, *Argentina – Measures Relating to Trade in Goods and Services* – Report of the Appellate Body (14 April 2016) WT/DS453/AB/R and Add.1 para 6.24 (hereafter Appellate Body Report, *Argentina – Financial Services*).

[181] According to Robert E Hudec, 'GATT/WTO Constraints on National Regulation: Requiem for an Aim and Effects Test' (1998) 32(3) The International Lawyer 619, 626–29 (hereafter Hudec, 'GATT/WTO Constraints on National Regulation'). This test was only applied in two cases: *United*

Tariffs and Trade (GATT)[182] (the WTO's predecessor) factored regulatory intent in the assessment of 'likeness', and thus separated it from discriminatory trade effects of the measure.[183] As a result of this subjective approach to 'likeness', goods that were treated differently by domestic regulation based on a legitimate policy objective were not considered 'like'. The 'aims and effects' test was, however, quickly dismissed by the GATT and then WTO adjudicating bodies, partially on formalistic grounds[184] and partially with a view to 'avoiding protectionism'.[185] In late 2000, the 'aims and effects test' was rejected as a relevant test for assessment of 'likeness' of services and service suppliers.[186] Firmly rejecting it, the WTO Appellate Body argued that 'likeness' was a purely economic test that aims to determine the

States – Measures Affecting and Malt Beverages (1992) GATT BISD (39th Supp) DS23/R and 39S/206, paras 5.70–5.77 and GATT panel decision in a 1994 case *United States: Taxes on Automobiles* WT/DS31/R (11 October 1994) (unadopted), paras 5.5–5.16, 5.23–5.36. In the first case in para 7.72, the GATT Panel held: 'In the view of the Panel, therefore, it is imperative that the like product determination in the context of Article III be made *in such a way that it not unnecessarily infringe upon the regulatory authority and domestic policy options of contracting parties*.' (emphasis added).

[182] General Agreement on Tariffs and Trade, 30 October 1947, 61 Stat. A-11, 55 UNTS 194 (1947).

[183] Hudec, 'GATT/WTO Constraints on National Regulation: Requiem for an Aim and Effects Test' (n 181), 628: 'The "aim and effects" approach ... consigned the metaphysics of "likeness" to a lesser role in the analysis, and instead made the question of violation depend primarily on the two most important issues that separate bona fide regulation from trade protection-the trade effects of the measure, and the bona fides of the alleged regulatory purpose behind it.' For discussion, see also Nicolas F Diebold, *Non-Discrimination in International Trade in Services: 'Likeness' in WTO/GATS* (CUP 2010), 75–80 (hereafter Diebold, *Non-Discrimination in International Trade in Services*); Michael H Trebilcock, Robert Howse, and Antonia Eliason, *The Regulation of International Trade* (4th edn, Routledge 2013), 138–45 (hereafter Trebilcock, Howse, and Eliason, *The Regulation of International Trade*).

[184] See WTO, *Japan – Taxes on Alcoholic Beverages – Report of the Appellate Body* (4 October 1996) WT/DS8/AB/R, WT/DS10/AB/R, WT/DS11/AB/R 16 (hereafter Appellate Body Report, *Japan – Alcoholic Beverages II*), citing WTO, *United States – Taxes on Petroleum and Certain Imported Substances – Report of the Panel* (17 June 1987) GATT BISD L/6175 - 34S/136, para 5.1.9; and Appellate Body Report, *Japan – Alcoholic Beverages II*, para 5.5(b). For a more detailed account on the wiping out of the aims and effects approach and the history of this approach, see Hudec, 'GATT/WTO Constraints on National Regulation' (n 181), 629–33; Andrew Lang, *World Trade Law after Neoliberalism* (OUP Online 2011) 257–65 (hereafter Lang, *World Trade Law after Neoliberalism*), Diebold, *Non-Discrimination in International Trade in Services* (n 183) 78–79, Trebilcock, Howse, and Eliason, *The Regulation of International Trade* (n 183) 145–46.

[185] WTO, *Korea: Taxes on Alcoholic Beverages – Report of the Appellate Body* (18 January 1999) WT/DS75/AB/R and WT/DS84/AB/R, para 120; Lang, *World Trade Law after Neoliberalism* (n 284) 255: 'Over the course of the 1990s, the clear trend was incrementally but decisively to eliminate virtually any explicit consideration of intent in the interpretation of GATT non-discrimination norms.' See also Lothar Ehring, 'De Facto Discrimination in WTO Law: National and Most-Favored-Nation Treatment—or Equal Treatment?' (2002) 36(5) Journal of World Trade 921; Gaetan Verhoosel, *National Treatment and WTO Dispute Settlement: Adjudicating the Boundaries of Regulatory Autonomy* (Hart Publishing, Oxford 2002); Hudec, 'GATT/WTO Constraints on National Regulation' (n 181); Henrik Horn and Petros C Mavroidis, 'Economic and Legal Aspects of the Most Favoured Nation Clause' (2001) 17 European Journal of Political Economy 223.

[186] WTO, *European Communities – Regime for the Importation, Sale and Distribution of Bananas – AB-1997-3 – Report of the Appellate Body* (9 September 1997). WT/DS27/AB/R (hereafter Appellate Body Report, *EC – Bananas III*), paras 6.114, 6.115.

existence of a competitive opportunity between the goods and services from a purely economic perspective.[187]

The rejection of the 'aims and effects' test made regulatory intent behind the measure affording different treatment to similar goods and services irrelevant in the interpretation of the 'like' criterion in the context of GATT and GATS. Instead, the focus had shifted towards the economic *impact* on the competitive opportunities of foreign goods[188] and effects on competition between products or services.[189]

In the same vein, the WTO Appellate Body concluded that legal standard of treatment 'no less favourable' does not 'contemplate a separate and additional inquiry into the regulatory objective of, or the regulatory concerns underlying, the contested measure'.[190] The only relevant factor in this assessment is whether a measure at issue modifies the conditions of competition to the detriment of services or service suppliers of any other WTO member.[191] The rationale behind this approach is that public policy objectives that could potentially justify non-compliant measures are more appropriately addressed in the context of relevant exceptions.[192]

[187] Appellate Body Report, *Argentina – Financial Services* (n 180) paras 6.22–6.23, 6.25, 6.34. See also Katherine Connolly, 'Finding Space for Regulatory Autonomy in GATS Article XVII after EC–Seals: Public Services and the "Likeness" of Public and Private Service Providers' (2015) 42 Legal Issues of Economic Integration 57, 61; Mireille Cossy, 'Determining "Likeness" under the GATS: Squaring the Circle?' (2006) World Trade Organization Economic Research and Statistics Division, WTO Staff Working Paper ERSD-2006-08, 331 <https://www.wto.org/english/res_e/reser_e/ersd200608_e.pdf> accessed 10 July 2023; Appellate Body Report, *EC – Bananas III* (n 186) para 241; Appellate Body Reports, *EC – Seal Products* (n 180), 122–29.

[188] As the WTO Panel clarified in WTO, *Argentina – Measures Affecting the Export of Bovine Hides and the Import of Finished Leather – Report of the Panel* (16 February 2001) WT/DS155/R and Corr.1, '[a]rticle III:2, first sentence, is not concerned with taxes or changes as such or the policy purposes Members pursue with them, but with their economic *impact* on the competitive opportunities of imported and like domestic products' (emphasis added).

[189] Robert Howse, 'The World Trade Organization 20 Years On: Global Governance by Judiciary' (2016) 27(1) European Journal of International Law 9, 46 (hereafter Howse, *The World Trade Organization 20 Years On*); Lang, *World Trade Law after Neoliberalism* (n 284) 262.

[190] Appellate Body Report, *Argentina – Financial Services* (n 180) paras 6.106, 6.121. In the 2001 EC-Asbestos report, the Appellate Body brought in the 'aims and effects test' through the interpretation of 'no less favourable' to overturn the Panel's conclusion on the fact of 'likeness' between asbestos and its substitutes. The main argument was that differential treatment is not always 'less favourable' if the difference is grounded by factors unrelated to the foreign origin. See WTO, *European Communities – Measures Affecting Asbestos and Asbestos-Containing Products – Report of the Appellate Body* (5 April 2001) WT/DS135/AB/R (hereafter Appellate Body Report, *EC – Asbestos*), para 100: 'A Member may draw distinctions between products which have been found to be "like", without, for this reason alone, according to the group of "like" imported products "less favourable treatment" than that accorded to the group of "like" domestic products.' (emphasis added). In *Dominican Republic – Import and Sale of Cigarettes* the Appellate Body stated: '... the existence of a detrimental effect on a given imported product resulting from a measure does not necessarily imply that this measure accords less favourable treatment to imports, if the detrimental effect is explained by factors or circumstances unrelated to the foreign origin of the product, such as the market share of the importer in this case.' WTO, *Dominican Republic – Measures Affecting the Importation and Internal Sale of Cigarettes – Report of the Panel* (26 November 2004) WT/DS302/R para 96 (hereafter Panel Report, *Dominican Republic – Import and Sale of Cigarettes*). The approach adopted by the Appellate Body in *EC – Asbestos* was later rejected. See Appellate Body Reports, *EC – Seal Products* (n 180) para 5.92.

[191] Appellate Body Report, *Argentina – Financial Services* (n 180) para 6.106.

[192] ibid, paras 6.114, 6.115.

This economic approach to the interpretation of 'likeness' and 'no less favourable' has key implications for the EU: for the purposes of testing EU rules on transfer of personal data outside the EEA under the non-discrimination commitments, it is irrelevant under WTO law that the different treatments of services and service suppliers from third countries aim to prevent circumvention of the EU data protection framework backed by fundamental rights.

2.3.1.1 Most-Favoured Nation Treatment

Some authors have rightly argued that differences in the treatment by the EU of services and service providers from countries that have, and those from countries that do not have, an adequacy decision may amount to a violation of the MFN principle.[193] Indeed, even the Article 29 Working Party[194] noted in one of its early opinions that 'some third countries might come to see the absence of a finding that they provided adequate protection as politically provocative or at least discriminatory'.[195]

Several scholars as well as the European Commission itself have acknowledged that adequacy assessments are not objective strictly legal assessments but rather a flexible tool to achieve political and economic objectives of the European Union.[196] This implies that adequacy decisions are not equally available to all non-EEA countries. This political dimension also shines through the European Commission's process of reviewing the adequacy decisions after the GDPR was adopted. As mentioned above, the EU Commission started the review of all pre-GDPR adequacy decisions back in 2017, some of which are clearly inadequate from the perspective of the criteria of Article 45 of the GDPR (the 'first generation' adequacy decision

[193] See, eg, Asinari, 'Is There Any Room for Privacy and Data Protection within the WTO Rules' (n 165) 273; Yakovleva and Irion, 'The Best of Both Worlds?' (n 165) 203; Irion, Yakovleva, and Bartl, 'Trade and Privacy: Complicated Bedfellows?' (n 170) 28–30; Bergkamp, 'The Privacy Fallacy' (n 165) 39; Keller, *European and International Media Law: Liberal Democracy, Trade and New Media* (n 168) 353; Reyes, 'WTO-Compliant Protection of Fundamental Rights' (n 168), 14–16; Sen, 'Understanding the Role of the WTO' (n 168) 335–38; see Naef, *Data Protection without Data Protectionism* (n 168) 291–92.

[194] Article 29 Working Party (full name: 'The Working Party on the Protection of Individuals with regard to the Processing of Personal Data') was an advisory body formed under art 29 of the Data Protection Directive (n 23). It consisted of a representative from the data protection authority of each EU member state, the European Data Protection Supervisor, and the European Commission. Article 29 Working Party was replaced by the European Data Protection Board on 25 May 2018, when the GDPR entered into force.

[195] Article 29 Working Party, Working Document Transfers of personal data to third countries: Applying arts 25 and 26 of the EU data protection directive WP 12 (24 July 1998) 26–27 <https://ec.europa.eu/justice/article-29/documentation/opinion-recommendation/files/1998/wp12_en.pdf > accessed 10 July 2023.

[196] See, eg, Paul M Schwartz, 'Global Data Privacy: The EU Way' (2019) 94(4) New York University Law Review 771, 807; Christopher Kuner, 'Developing an Adequate Legal Framework for International Data Transfers' in Serge Gutwirth and others (eds), *Reinventing Data Protection*, 8–9; Kuner, *Transborsder Data Flows and Data Privacy Law* (n 5) 66; Communication from the Commission to the European Parliament and the Council, 'Exchanging and Protecting Personal Data in a Globalised World' [2017] COM (2017) 7 final, 8. For further discussion, see Section 5.3.3.1.

for Canada[197] is the one of the most obvious examples). This almost six-year long review (and counting) is longer than a review period set forth in the EU's most recent adequacy decisions, which must be reviewed at least every four years.[198] The EU is likely waiting for Canada and other countries, whose adequacy decisions are under review since 2017, to strengthen their data protection laws in a way allowing them to maintain their adequacy decisions.[199] The fact that some of these adequacy decisions are still in force (even though they could be suspended or revoked by the European Commission) could be viewed as discriminatory in relation to the United States, whose adequacy decision was invalidated by the CJEU twice, and therefore contrary to the MFN principle.[200]

As mentioned above, and discussed in more detail in Section 2.3.2, in certain situations systematic transfers to countries that do not ensure essentially equivalent protection are not allowed on the basis of appropriate safeguards under Article 46 of the GDPR.[201] Unavailability of such safeguards may conflict with the EU's MFN obligations.[202] This means that services and service providers from these countries are treated less favourably than their counterparts from countries that *do* ensure an essentially equivalent level of personal data protection.[203]

2.3.1.2 National treatment

The 2020 *Schrems II* judgment further intensified the tension between the international trade and EU law frameworks governing transfers of personal data. The central role that access to Europeans' personal data by foreign authorities in the

[197] For example, Adequacy Decision for Canada (Commission Decision 2002/2/EC of 20 December 2001 pursuant to Directive 95/46/EC of the European Parliament and of the Council on the adequate protection of personal data provided by the Canadian Personal Information Protection and Electronic Documents Act [2001] C(2001) 4539 OJ L 2) does not contain any restrictions on onward transfers, as required by art 45(2)(a) GDPR (n 2). For discussion see Section 5.3.3.2.

[198] See art 3(4) and recitals 219–20 of the Adequacy Decision for South Korea (Commission Implementing Decision (EU) 2022/254 of 17 December 2021 pursuant to Regulation (EU) 2016/679 of the European Parliament and of the Council on the adequate protection of personal data by the Republic of Korea under the Personal Information Protection Act [2021] C(2021) 9316) OJ L 44).

[199] For example, both Canada and Israel are in the process of trying to strengthen their data protection legislation. See 'Israel: Ministry launches consultation on draft privacy protection regulations on transfers from the EEA' (Data Guidance, 30 November 2022) <https://www.dataguidance.com/news/israel-ministry-launches-consultation-draft-privacy> accessed 10 July 2023 and Chantal Bernier, '2023 Canada Private-Sector Privacy Law Reform: Keeping Track of Moving Parts' (*IAPP*, 13 January 2023) <https://iapp.org/news/a/2023-canada-private-sector-privacy-law-reform-keeping-track-of-moving-parts/> accessed 10 July 2023. Korff, however, argues that even if the proposed amendments to Israel's data protection law are adopted, Israel would still not meet the EU's essential equivalence standard. See Douwe Korff, 'Update on the Opinion on the Future of Personal Data Transfers from the EU/EEA to Israel & the Occupied Territories' (25 March 2022) <http://dx.doi.org/10.2139/ssrn.4066476> accessed 10 July 2023.

[200] The fact that some of the adequacy decisions that are in force but likely do not meet the essential equivalence standard under the EU Charter (n 3) makes them also problematic from an EU Charter perspective. For discussion, see Section 5.3.3.2.

[201] See Section 2.2.4 and Naef, *Data Protection without Data Protectionism* (n 168) 295.

[202] Naef, *Data Protection without Data Protectionism* (n 168) 295.

[203] ibid.

national security context plays in the CJEU's assessment of 'essential equivalence' of a third country's legal framework has intensified claims of a double standard for personal data flows within and outside the EEA.[204] As the Article 29 Working Party and academics explained, unlike foreign surveillance programmes, such programmes run by the EU member states are generally not subject to EU law, and specifically the EU Charter.[205] The reason for this is that under Article 4(2) of the Treaty on European Union (TEU), national security is excluded from the EU competence and 'remains the sole responsibility of each member state'.[206] As a result, one could argue that by requiring foreign countries to meet the high EU Charter standards for the protection of the fundamental rights to privacy and personal data that the EU's own constituencies are not subject to, the CJEU has adopted a measure[207] violating the GATS *national treatment principle*. For example, it has been argued

[204] See, eg, Anupam Chander, 'Is Data Localization a Solution for Schrems II?' (2020) Journal of International Economic Law <https://ssrn.com/abstract=3662626> accessed 10 July 2023 (hereafter Chander, 'Is Data Localization a Solution for Schrems II?'), 8–11; Peter Swire, 'The Data Protection Commissioner and Facebook Ireland Limited and Maximillian Schrems. Affidavit of Peter Swire' (2016) 18-2 Georgia Tech Scheller College of Business Research Paper <https://ssrn.com/abstract=3097444> accessed 10 July 2023 (hereafter Swire, 'The Data Protection Commissioner'); Paul Roth, 'Adequate Level of Data Protection in Third Countries Post-Schrems and under the General Data Protection Regulation' (2017) 25(1) Journal of Law, Information and Science 49, 65 (hereafter Roth, 'Adequate Level of Data Protection'); Baker, 'How Can the U.S. Respond to Schrems II?' (n 165); Peter Swire, 'Schrems II' Backs the European Legal Regime into a Corner: How Can It Get Out?' (*International Association of Privacy Professionals*, 16 July 2020) <https://iapp.org/news/a/schrems-ii-backs-the-european-legal-regime-into-a-corner-how-can-it-get-out/> accessed 10 July 2023; Kristina Irion, 'Schrems II and Surveillance: Third Countries' National Security Powers in the Purview of EU Law' (*European Law Blog*, 24 July 2020) <https://europeanlawblog.eu/2020/07/24/schrems-ii-and-surveillance-third-countries-national-security-powers-in-the-purview-of-eu-law/> accessed 10 July 2023 (hereafter Irion, 'Schrems II and Surveillance').

[205] Irion, 'Schrems II and Surveillance' (n 204); Article 29 Working Party, 'Opinion 04/2014 on Surveillance of Electronic Communications for Intelligence and National Security Purposes' WP 215 (10 April 2014) 6–7 <https://ec.europa.eu/justice/article-29/documentation/opinion-recommendation/files/2014/wp215_en.pdf> accessed 10 July 2023. See also Anna Buchta and Herke Kranenborg, 'Institutional Report Topic 2: The New EU Data Protection Regime' in Jorrit Rijpma (ed), *The New EU Data Protection Regime. Setting Global Standards for the Right to Personal Data Protection* (The XXIX FIDE Congress in The Hague, 2020 Congress Publications, Vol. 2) 105 <https://cris.maastrichtuniversity.nl/en/publications/institutional-report-topic-2-the-new-eu-data-protection-regime> accessed 10 July 2023 (hereafter Buchta and Kranenborg, 'Institutional Report Topic 2'), arguing that:

> [a]s follows from article 2 TEU the Union is founded on the values of respect for the rule of law and for human rights. As the CJEU has stated in the Opinion on the accession of the EU to the ECHR, the Union is based on the fundamental premise that each Member State shares with all the other Member States a set of common values which implies and justifies the existence of mutual trust between the Member States that those values will be recognised. Against this background it is justified to leave certain matters to the Member State without further assessment, while for third countries a further assessment as regards those values still remains necessary.

[206] TEU (n 39) art 4(2) states that:

> The Union shall respect the equality of Member States before the Treaties as well as their national identities, inherent in their fundamental structures, political and constitutional, inclusive of regional and local self-government. It shall respect their essential State functions, including ensuring the territorial integrity of the State, maintaining law and order and safeguarding national security. *In particular, national security remains the sole responsibility of each Member State.* (emphasis added)

[207] It is established in WTO case law that the notion of 'measure' is not restricted by the requirement to form, and therefore, can also reflect in judicial decisions. See, eg, WTO, *Saudi Arabia – Measures concerning the Protection of Intellectual Property Rights – Report of the Panel* (16 June 2020) WT/DS567/R and WT/DS567/R/Add.1, para 7.49; WTO, *United States – Import Prohibition of Certain Shrimp and*

that in some EU member states (eg, Germany, France, the Netherlands, Sweden, and the United Kingdom), privacy safeguards in the national security context are equally suboptimal or even weaker than those in the United States, which have repeatedly been deemed inadequate by the CJEU.[208] Although all EU member states are also members of the Council of Europe, and are therefore, subject to the requirements of Article 8 of the European Convention on Human Rights (ECHR), it is generally agreed that—in view of the current CJEU and the European Court of Human Rights (ECtHR) case law—the standard of the EU Charter in relation to surveillance laws and measures is higher than that of the ECHR.[209]

In the light of the 2020 CJEU judgments in four cases, including *Privacy International*, the above-mentioned argument on the violation of national treatment cannot be made successfully.[210] From the Advocate General's Opinions in these cases, it follows that the fundamental rights standards developed by the CJEU in a line of cases concerning access to data transmitted by the telecommunications providers[211] equally apply to EU member states legislation governing access to such data in the national security context.[212] These standards, however, do not apply when national security authorities 'exercise that competence directly, using their own resources' without cooperation of private parties.[213] The CJEU

Shrimp Products – Report of the Appellate Body (12 October 1998) WT/DS58/AB/R, para 173 (hereafter Appellate Body Report, *US – Shrimp*); WTO, *United States – Standards for Reformulated and Conventional Gasoline – AB-1996-1 – Report of the Appellate Body* (29 April 1996) WT/DS2/AB/R, 28.

[208] Irion, 'Schrems II and Surveillance' (n 204); Roth, 'Adequate Level of Data Protection' (n 204) 64–65; Didier Bigo and others, 'Mass Surveillance of Personal Data by EU Member States and its Compatibility with EU Law', CEPS Paper in Liberty and Security No 62 (November 2013) <https://www.ceps.eu/wp-content/uploads/2013/11/No%2062%20Surveillance%20of%20Personal%20Data%20by%20EU%20MSs.pdf> accessed 10 July 2023; Swire, 'The Data Protection Commissioner' (n 204) 1–2.

[209] *Facebook Ireland and Schrems* [2020] ECLI:EU:C:2019:1145, Opinion of AG Saugmandsgaard Øe, para 251. Theodore Christakis, 'A Fragmentation of EU/ECHR Law on Mass Surveillance: Initial Thoughts on the Big Brother Watch Judgment' (*European Law Blogs*, 20 September 2018) <https://europeanlawblog.eu/2018/09/20/a-fragmentation-of-eu-echr-law-on-mass-surveillance-initial-thoughts-on-the-big-brother-watch-judgment/> accessed 10 July 2023; Irion, 'Schrems II and Surveillance' (n 204); Monika Zalnieriute, 'Big Brother Watch and Others v. the United Kingdom (case review)' (2022) 116(3) American Journal of International Law 585, arguing that the decision of the Grade Chamber of the European Court of Human Rights (ECtHR) in Strasbourg in *Big Brother Watch and Others v. United Kingdom*—the landmark ECtHR case on bulk government surveillance—'stands for a highly permissive approach to government surveillance'.

[210] *Privacy International* [2020] ECLI:EU:C:2020:790 (hereafter *Privacy International*); *La Quadrature du Net and others* [2020] ECLI:EU:C:2020:791. For a discussion, see, eg, Iain Cameron, 'European Union Law Restraints on Intelligence Activities' (2020) 33(3) International Journal of Intelligence and Counter Intelligence 452.

[211] *Tele2 Sverige* [2016] ECLI:EU:C:2016:970 (hereafter *Tele2 Sverige*); *Digital Rights Ireland and Seitlinger and others* [2014] ECLI:EU:C:2014:238 (hereafter *Digital Rights Ireland*).

[212] See, eg, *Privacy International* (n 210) para 84. See also Court of Justice of the European Union, 'Advocate General Campos Sánchez-Bordona: The Means and Methods of Combating Terrorism Must Be Compatible with the Requirements of the Rule of Law' (15 January 2020) Court of Justice of the European Union Press Release No 4/20 <https://curia.europa.eu/jcms/upload/docs/application/pdf/2020-01/cp200004en.pdf> accessed 10 July 2023.

[213] ibid.

followed the Advocate General's opinion and thus reinstated the equal treatment of EU member states and foreign countries following the two *Schrems* judgments.[214] Furthermore, Buchta and Kranenborg also suggest a way to interpret Article 4(2) of the TEU[215] in a way that 'matters relating to national identities and essential State functions are not as such excluded from the scope of Union law but must be taken into account in the application of Union law'.[216]

The interpretation of the term 'transfer' by the EDPB has somewhat relieved the tension between the restrictions on transfers of personal data outside the EEA and the EU's national treatment obligations under the GATS.[217] From an international trade law perspective, excluding transmission of personal data from individuals from the scope of 'transfer' and thus from the scope of the GDPR's Chapter V (see Legal Regimes 1 and 4, as discussed in Section 2.2.3) is a positive development. Subjecting foreign service providers collecting data directly from individuals, especially those who are already subject to the GDPR's extraterritorial application (like in Legal Regime 4), to all Chapter V rules could lead to a violation of the national treatment. This is because they would face a heavier compliance burden vis-à-vis European service providers. Direct collection of personal data from the EEA would not only require foreign service providers, who are subject to the extraterritorial application of the GDPR, to have a legal basis under Article 6 of the GDPR (just as their European counterparts) but also an additional mechanism for transfers of personal data under Chapter V (requirements their European counterparts are not subject to when collecting personal data in the EU). For example, such foreign providers would not be able to rely on legitimate interest as legal basis for collecting personal data (legitimate interest is not available as a mechanism for transfers under Chapter V); in the case of reliance on consent as a lawful basis, they would need to obtain two separate consents: consent as lawful basis for processing under Article 6(1)(a) and explicit consent under Article 49(1)(a) of the GDPR.

Despite this positive development, tensions between the GDPR rules on transfers of personal data outside the EEA and the EU's national treatment obligation persist in at least two ways. First, in situations where foreign service providers may not rely on appropriate safeguards, as discussed above, these service providers may not provide services in the EEA, for which transfers of personal data are essential.[218] Second, in situations where appropriate safeguards *can* be used, a violation of national treatment can occur with respect to foreign service provider who despite already being subject to the GDPR, nevertheless must comply with GDPR's Chapter V, albeit in its 'light version' (Legal Regime 3, as discussed above).[219] This

214 *Privacy International* (n 210) para 49.

215 TEU (n 39) art 4(2).

216 Buchta and Kranenborg, 'Institutional Report Topic 2' (n 205) 100–03.

217 As explained above, this violation may only occur in specific sectors in which the EU made a specific commitment to grant national treatment in its Schedule of Specific Commitments.

218 Naef, *Data Protection without Data Protectionism* (n 168) 319–20.

219 See also ibid 320.

clearly discriminates these service providers compared to their European counterparts that do not face this heavier compliance burden. What is more, until the European Commission adopts a new set of SCCs for this type of situation, these foreign service providers may not at all rely on existing SCCs as a mechanism for transfers. Given that the SCCs are the transfer mechanism most commonly relied on, the legal tools for systematic transfers of personal data for such foreign service providers are very limited.

2.3.2 Market access

Like national treatment, market access is also a specific commitment under the GATS. A full commitment of market access means a prohibition to maintain, predominantly qualitative,[220] market access barriers included in the exhaustive list of Article XVI:2 of the GATS.[221] In principle, a state that has made a full commitment of market access could nevertheless apply any other limitations.[222] However, in practice, measures, not quantitative on their face, and falling under neither of the prohibited categories of limitations, may still be banned. For example, in *US – Gambling*, the WTO adjudicating bodies qualified total prohibition on the remote supply of gambling and betting services as GATS inconsistent market access limitations. Although per se not a quantitative restriction, the prohibition amounted to a 'zero quota' on the number of service suppliers and total number of service operations (art XVI:2 (a) and (c)).[223]

Because of the way restrictions on transfers of personal data outside the EEA are interpreted by the EDPB following the CJEU *Schrems II* judgment, the EU framework is at risk of violating market access commitments in data processing and database services,[224] as well as other services where transfers of data are essential for the

[220] Mitsuo Matsushita and others, *The World Trade Organization: Law, Practice, and Policy* (OUP 2015) 539–40 (hereafter Matsushita and others, *The World Trade Organization*).

[221] If a party wants to preserve certain market access barriers banned by art XVI:2 GATS in sectors and in relation to modes of supply where it undertook a specific market access commitment, such limitations should be included in the Services Schedule in the column 'Limitations on Market Access'.

[222] Matsushita and others, *The World Trade Organization* (n 220) 539–40.

[223] WTO, *United States – Measures Affecting the Cross-Border Supply of Gambling and Betting Services – AB-2005-1 – Report of the Appellate Body* (7 April 2005) WT/DS285/AB/R paras 238, 251, 252 (hereafter Appellate Body Report, *US – Gambling*).

[224] See, eg, Sen, 'Understanding the Role of the WTO in International Data Flows' (n 168) 335; Reyes, 'WTO-Compliant Protection of Fundamental Rights' (n 168) 22; Weber, 'Regulatory Autonomy and Privacy Standards under the GATS' (n 168) 33–34; Daniel Crosby, 'Analysis of Data Localization Measures under WTO Services Trade Rules and Commitments' (2016) The E15 Initiative, World Economic Forum Policy Brief, 5–7 <http://e15initiative.org/wp-content/uploads/2015/09/E15-Policy-Brief-Crosby-Final.pdf> accessed 10 July 2023; Coldicutt and Sen, 'Testing the GDPR's WTO Readiness' (n 168).

production and delivery of services (the so-called 'integrated services'[225]), even if the EU only liberalized market access for analogue versions of such services.[226]

American scholars labelled the *Schrems II* judgment as 'soft data localization' immediately after it was adopted.[227] Naef rightly argues that data localization is incompatible with cross-border supply of services and may lead to a violation of EU's market access obligations under the GATS.[228]

As discussed above, in its Recommendations on supplementary measures for transfers based on appropriate safeguards under Article 46 GDPR, the EDPB identifies two use case scenarios in which a transfer of personal data outside the EEA is *not allowed* because none of the supplementary measures are available (use cases labelled 6 and 7, which could occur in Legal Regimes 2 and 3).[229] In use case 6, the EDPB describes a situation where a data exporter transfers personal data to a cloud service provider or any other processor in a third country (eg, for the provision of technical support or any type of cloud processing). Personal data in this scenario is not—or cannot be—pseudonymized or encrypted in accordance with the EDPB's recommendations because the processing requires accessing data in the clear.

In use case 7, the EDPB describes another situation where a data exporter transfers personal data to entities in a third country for shared business purposes and this data is not or cannot be pseudonymized or encrypted in accordance with the EDPB's recommendations because the processing requires accessing data in the clear. The EDPB also provides a typical example of a real-life situation where this scenario may occur: cross-border transfers of personal data between controllers and/or processors within a group of companies or a group of companies engaged in a joint economic activity, such as when the data importer in a third country receives the personal data of employees to provide personnel services for the data exporter or communicate with customers of the data exporter who live in the European Union by phone or email. This use case is, however, likely to cover many more situations of transfers of personal data within a group of companies engaged in the same business activity.

Should DPAs across the EU strictly enforce these recommendations (which has not yet been the case), these recommendations would create *de facto* market access restrictions (or a 'zero quota') on cross-border provision of certain types of services

[225] See WTO, *China – Certain Measures Affecting Electronic Payment* Services – Report of the Panel (16 July 2012) WT/DS413/R, para 7.188

[226] See *China – Measures Affecting Trading Rights and Distribution Services for Certain Publications and Audiovisual Entertainment Products – Report of the Appellate Body* (21 December 2009) WT/DS363/AB/R, para 396. For a discussion of whether EU's restrictions on transfers of personal data outside the EEA violate EU's market access obligations under the GATS with respect to cloud computing, search engine, social network, internet of things, and shared economy platform services, see Naef, *Data Protection without Data Protectionism* (n 168) 307–17.

[227] Chander, 'Is Data Localization a Solution for Schrems II?' (n 204) 771–84.

[228] Naef, *Data Protection without Data Protectionism* (n 168) 308–10.

[229] EDPB, Recommendations 01/2020 on measures that supplement transfer tools to ensure compliance with the EU level of protection of personal data (n 138) 34–35.

for which systematic cross-border transfers of personal data outside the EEA are essential by service providers located in countries that do not ensure an essentially equivalent level of protection, for example, PAAS and SAAS cloud services or call centre customer services.[230] In the absence of supplementary measures, none of the appropriate safeguards under Article 46 of the GDPR is available for transfers of personal data to such countries, neither are specific derogations under Article 49 of the GDPR, which, according to the EDPB, are limited to occasional and non-repetitive transfers.[231] For example, in its Questions and Answers on the use of Google Analytics, the Danish DPA states that '[t]he use of consent as the basis for transfers to third countries is ... – in the view of the Danish Data Protection Agency – not compatible with the usual use of Google Analytics, where there is a general transfer of all the data collected by the tool, i.e. where it will be the general rule that data will be transferred to the USA'.[232]

Some courts in the EU member states even tried to—indirectly—restrict market access (so far only in the public procurement sector) to exclude foreign-owned cloud providers from hosting EU personal data within the European Union. In September 2022, the Karlsruhe Higher Regional Court (OLG Karlsruhe) *overturned* on appeal the judgment of the Public Procurement Chamber of the German state of Baden-Württemberg, holding that the very processing of personal data by an EU subsidiary of a US cloud provider constitutes a transfer of personal data, even though the data actually never left the EU. The very risk of access to that data by the US authorities was considered a violation of the GDPR.[233]

So far, most of the tension around transfers of personal data outside the EEA has concentrated around the transfers of personal data to the United States. This tension will subside, at least temporarily,[234] now that the European Commission has adopted the new adequacy decision for commercial transfers to the United States—the EU-US Data Privacy Framework.[235] However, resolving the issue with transfers of personal data to the United States will not resolve the tension between GDPR rules restricting transfers of personal data outside the EEA and

[230] For a discussion, see Naef, *Data Protection without Data Protectionism* (n 168) 311–12.

[231] EDPB, 'Guidelines 2/2018 on derogations of Article 49 under Regulation 2016/679' (n 87).

[232] Datatilsynet, 'Google Analytics' (n 144).

[233] Jane Finlayson-Brown and Gatharina Glugla, 'Germany – Schrems II: German Court Overturns Presumption of International Data Transfer from EU-Subsidiary to Non-EU Parent Company' (*JD Supra*, 13 September 2023) <https://www.jdsupra.com/legalnews/germany-schrems-ii-german-court-2846282/> accessed 10 July 2023.

[234] Max Schrems already announced that he is planning to challenge the new adequacy decision for the US at the CJEU. See 'European Commission Gives EU-US Data Transfers Third Round at CJEU' (*noyb*, 10 July 2023) < https://noyb.eu/en/european-commission-gives-eu-us-data-transfers-third-round-cjeu> accessed 10 July 2023.

[235] EU-US Data Privacy Framework (n 118).

international trade law generally. In particular, transfers of personal data to China are getting increased attention from DPAs,[236] consumer organizations backed by litigation funders in mass claims covering violations of GDPR rules on transfers,[237] and civil society alike.

Under the auspices of a digital sovereignty discourse, restrictions on transfers of data generally (not just personal, but also non-personal) are likely to increase in the future. For example, in their opinion on the proposed Regulation on European Health Data Space, the EDPB and the European Data Protection Supervisor (EDPS) proposed that 'controllers and processors established in the EU processing personal electronic health data within the scope of the Proposal an obligation to store this data in the EU'.[238] This proposal builds, on the one hand, on the proposed restrictions on transfers of non-personal data outside the EEA in the EU proposal for Regulation on European Health Data Space.[239] On the other hand, it is rooted in the CJEU judgments in *Digital Rights Ireland* and *Tele 2*.[240]

[236] Natasha Lomas, 'TikTok Privacy Update in Europe Confirms China Staff Access to Data as GDPR Probe Continues' (*TechCrunch*, 3 November 2022) <https://techcrunch.com/2022/11/03/tiktok-privacy-policy-update-china/> accessed 10 July 2023; Natasha Lomas, 'Ireland Probes TikTok's Handling of Kids' Data and Transfers to China' (*Techcrunch*, 15 September 2021) <https://techcrunch.com/2021/09/15/ireland-probes-tiktoks-handling-of-kids-data-and-transfers-to-china/> accessed 10 July 2023; EDPB, 'Thirty-First Plenary Session: Establishment of a Taskforce on Tiktok, Response to MEPs on Use of Clearview AI by Law Enforcement Authorities, Response to ENISA Advisory Group, Response to Open Letter NYOB' (10 June 2020) <https://edpb.europa.eu/news/news/2020/thirty-first-plenary-session-establishment-taskforce-tiktok-response-meps-use_en> accessed 10 July 2023.

[237] 'Exclusive: Interview with 'Take Back Your Privacy' Foundation on Their Mass Privacy Claim against TikTok in the Netherlands' (*Privacy Perfect*, 28 July 2021) <https://blog.privacyperfect.com/the-privacyperfect-blog/exclusive-interview-with-take-back-your-privacy-foundation-on-their-mass-privacy-claim-against-tiktok-in-the-netherlands> accessed 10 July 2023.

[238] EDPB, EDPB-EDPS Joint Opinion 03/2022 on the Proposal for a Regulation on the European Health Data Space (12 July 2022) 28 <https://edps.europa.eu/system/files/2022-07/22-07-12_edpb_edps_joint-opinion_europeanhealthdataspace_en_.pdf> accessed 10 July 2023; See also European Data Protection Supervisor, 'Opinion 17/2022 on the Recommendation for a Council Decision Authorising the Opening of Negotiations for the Inclusion of Provisions on Cross-Border Data Flows in the Agreement between the European Union and Japan for an Economic Partnership' (2022) 6 <https://edps.europa.eu/system/files/2022-08/22-08-09_edps_opinion_eu_japan_en.pdf> accessed 10 July 2023.

[239] See Yakovleva, 'On Digital Sovereignty' (n 66).

[240] In *Tele2 Sverige*, the CJEU held:

> Given the quantity of retained data, the sensitivity of that data and the risk of unlawful access to it, the providers of electronic communications services must, in order to ensure the full integrity and confidentiality of that data, guarantee a particularly high level of protection and security by means of appropriate technical and organisational measures. In particular, the national legislation must make provision for the data to be retained within the European Union and for the irreversible destruction of the data at the end of the data retention period.

Tele2 Sverige (n 211) para 122.

2.4 Two Necessities: A Catch-22 for the EU

2.4.1 Framing the issue

This section illuminates the clash between the EU law and international trade law regulating trade in services, when it comes to the regulatory framework that both bodies of law require for cross-border transfers of personal data.

In trade agreements, one of the primary mechanisms to accommodate the EU's autonomy to adopt and maintain measures inconsistent with its international trade commitments are the so-called 'general exceptions'. The part of the general exception of GATS Article XIV(c)(ii) that is specifically relevant for privacy and data protection reads as follows:

> Subject to the requirement that such measures are not applied in a manner which would constitute a means of arbitrary or unjustifiable discrimination between countries where like conditions prevail, or a disguised restriction on trade in services, nothing in this Agreement shall be construed to prevent the adoption or enforcement by any Member of measures . . .
>
> (c) *necessary* to secure compliance with laws or regulations which are not inconsistent with the provisions of this Agreement including those relating to . . .
>
> (ii) the protection of the privacy of individuals in relation to the processing and dissemination of personal data and the protection of confidentiality of individual records and accounts . . .

Section 2.4.2 argues that the trade necessity test—the core of the general exception—could be too narrow to accommodate the EU's autonomy to maintain the existing GDPR framework for transfers of personal data. As a result, the EU may be required under the GATS to adjust the rules on cross-border transfers of personal data.

From an EU law perspective, entering into a new international trade agreement or complying with an existing one that limits any of the fundamental rights under EU Charter is a derogation from the rights under the EU Charter and thus is subject to its Article 52(1). According to this provision,

> [a]ny limitation on the exercise of the rights and freedoms recognised by this Charter must be provided for by law and respect the essence of those rights and freedoms. *Subject to the principle of proportionality*, limitations may be made only if they are *necessary* and genuinely meet objectives of *general interest* recognised by the Union or the need to protect the rights and freedoms of others. (emphasis added)

'General interest recognised by the Union', according to the Explanations to the Charter covers, in particular, objectives of the Union in its external relations mentioned in Article 3 of the TEU, which include free and fair trade.[241] As the CJEU has explained, the derogation clause applies equally *to both internal and external legislative acts of the EU*, such as international agreements.[242] Affirming the supremacy of the EU Charter over the EU's international agreements, the CJEU confirmed that the EU may neither conclude nor implement through an EU legislative act, any international agreement (or decision of an international adjudicating body based on this agreement) if the conditions laid out in this derogation clause, namely the proportionality and necessity tests (ie, the 'EU Charter "necessity test"'), are not fulfilled.[243] This conclusion echoes Articles 7 and 207(3)(2) of the Treaty on the Functioning of the European Union (TFEU).[244] Article 7 of the TFEU requires the European Union to 'ensure consistency between its policies and activities'. Article 207(3)(2) TFEU imposes a responsibility on the Council and the European Commission to ensure 'that the agreements negotiated are compatible with internal Union policies and rules'. Then, Article 218(11) of the TFEU provides a mechanism to ensure that an international trade agreement is compatible with the EU's constitutional framework *before* it is concluded by the EU. It allows an EU member state, the European Parliament, the Council, and the European Commission to request an opinion from the CJEU regarding the compatibility of a proposed international agreement with the EU Treaties, including the EU Charter. If the CJEU decides that such an agreement is incompatible with the Treaties, the international agreement cannot take effect until, and unless, it is brought in compliance with the Treaties. This provision was used at the request of the European Parliament concerning the EU-Canada agreement on the transfer and processing of Passenger Name Record data,[245] which, among other things, mandated transfers of Europeans' personal data to Canada. In this landmark ruling, having tested these provisions against the requirements of the derogation clause, including the EU Charter necessity test, the CJEU held that the agreement could not be concluded unless revised.[246]

It is now settled case law at the CJEU that international agreements entered into by the EU must be 'entirely compatible with the Treaties and with the constitutional principles stemming therefrom'.[247] In particular, such agreements must be compatible with the right to privacy and the right to the protection of personal

[241] Explanation on Article 52, Explanations Relating to the Charter of Fundamental Rights, 2007 OJ (C 303), art 3(5) TEU (n 39).

[242] CJEU Opinion, *EU-Canada PNR Agreement* (n 41) para 146.

[243] Arianna Verdaschi, 'Privacy and Data Protection versus National Security in Transnational Flights: The EU-Canada PNR Agreement (2018) 8(2) International Data Privacy Law 124, 138.

[244] TFEU (n 32) arts 7 and 207(3)(2).

[245] CJEU Opinion, *EU-Canada PNR Agreement* (n 41).

[246] ibid, paras 232(2)–232(3).

[247] ibid, paras 67, 70.

data.[248] This is crucial to the analysis in this book because if the EU framework for transfers of personal data outside the EEA was deemed inconsistent with a trade agreement—for example, for failing to meet the requirements of the trade necessity test contained in the general exception—and the EU was required to bring its laws into conformity with the trade agreement, compliance with the decision of a trade adjudicating body establishing such inconsistency would be a derogation from the fundamental rights codified by Articles 7 and 8 of the EU Charter. It follows from the CJEU's jurisprudence, however, that before such a decision of an international trade adjudicating body could be implemented, compliance would have to be tested under the requirements of Article 52(1) of the EU Charter. Yet, trade law's necessity test, when viewed as a derogation from the EU's fundamental right to privacy and the protection of personal data, is unlikely to meet the EU Charter necessity test.[249] Put another way, the trade necessity test obligates the EU to derogate from fundamental rights more than the EU is legally allowed to do under Article 52(1) of the EU Charter.

To sum up, not only could the EU framework for personal data transfers be found to be in violation of the EU's international trade commitments but also international trade commitments requiring (unrestricted) transfers of personal data outside the EEA may be found *inconsistent with the EU Charter*. Simultaneous application of the two necessity tests (trade law and Article 52 of the Charter) thus puts the EU in a catch-22 situation, as discussed in Section 2.4.4 of this chapter.

An important doctrinal point should be clarified before moving on. Although international trade agreements are binding on the EU and constitute an 'integral part' of its legal system,[250] in the hierarchy of the EU legal order, EU primary law (including the EU Charter) prevails over the EU's international trade commitments.[251] Moreover, neither international trade agreements nor the decisions of international trade adjudicating bodies have direct effect in the EU.[252] This

[248] ibid, paras 70, 119.

[249] For further discussion, see Section 2.4.4.

[250] See, eg, *R. & V. Haegeman/Belgian State* [1974] ECLI:C:1974:41, para 5; *Opinion 2/13 (Accession of the European Union to the ECHR)* [2014] ECLI:EU:C:2014:2454, para 180.

[251] *Kadi and Al Barakaat International Foundation v Council and Commission* [2008] ECLI:EU:C:2008:461, paras 282, 307, 308, 316; Recital 11 of the Preamble to Council Decision 94/800/EC of 22 December 1994 concerning the conclusion on behalf of the European Community, as regards matters within its competence, of the agreements reached in the Uruguay Round multilateral negotiations (1986–1994) [1994] OJ L336/1. Although this Decision, unlike the Schedule of Specific Commitments, does not constitute a part of the GATS, the CJEU deferred to it in *Portugal v Council* as an indication of the political will of the EU in concluding the WTO Agreement. *Portugal v Council* [1999] ECLI:EU:C:1999:574, para 48, see also para 42. See also *Air Transport Association of America and others* [2011] ECLI:EU:C:2011:864, para 74; *Germany v Council* [1994] ECLI:EU:C:1994:367, paras 106, 108, 110. See also Christina Eckes, *EU Powers under External Pressure: How the EU's External Actions Alter Its Internal Structures* (Oxford Scholarship Online 2019) 152 (hereafter Eckes, *EU Powers under External Pressure*).

[252] *FIAMM and others/Council and Commission* [2008] ECLI:EU:C:2008:476, paras 120, 125–28. For a discussion, see Aliki Semertzi, 'The Preclusion of Direct Effect in the Recently Concluded EU Free Trade Agreements' (2014) 51(4) Common Market Law Review 1125, 1132–35. See also Szilard Gaspar-Szilagyi, 'The 'Primacy' and 'Direct Effect' of EU International Agreements' (2015) 21(2) European

approach is based on the principle of the autonomy of the EU legal order in relation to international law, which cannot affect the constitutional values and internal division of competences in the EU.[253] From an international law perspective, the absence of direct effects of international court decisions in domestic legal systems is not uncommon.[254] The prerogative of domestic constitutional law to decide how international decisions affect their internal legal frameworks can be viewed as an internal control mechanism that supports the legitimacy of international adjudication.[255] This mechanism, therefore, 'relieves international legal decisions from the burdens of legitimation that they are not always capable of bearing by opening up another mechanism of democratic legitimation'.[256] Furthermore, the principle of autonomy of the EU legal order exemplifies a pluralist approach to the global legal order.[257]

The EU's stance in relation to international law and adjudication, nevertheless, does not make the EU's obligations under international trade law less binding from *an international law* perspective. Under international law, the EU must perform

Public Law 343 (hereafter Gaspar-Szilagyi, 'The "Primacy" and "Direct Effect" of EU International Agreements'); Paul Craig and Graine de Burca, *EU Law: Text, Cases, and Materials* (6th edn, OUP 2015), 362–63; Francesca Martines, 'Direct Effect of International Agreements of the European Union' (2014) 25(1) European Journal of International Law 129. For an elaborate discussion of these issues in the present context, see Yakovleva and Irion, 'The Best of Both Worlds?' (n 165) 200–02. See also Eckes, *EU Powers under External Pressure* (n 251), 187.

253 Starting as early as in 1963 from CJEU case *Van Gend & Loos* [1963] ECLI:EU:C:1963:1. Eckes explains that the CJEU's choice to protect the supremacy of EU law from obligations originating outside the EU 'is a necessary consequence of the Union's complex constitutional set-up'. Eckes, 'Protecting Supremacy from External Influences' (62) 232, 244–49. See also Gaspar-Szilagyi, 'The "Primacy" and "Direct Effect" of EU International Agreements' (n 252) 349.

254 Armin von Bogdandy and Ingo Venzke, *In Whose Name? A Public Law Theory of International Adjudication* (OUP 2014) 196.

255 ibid 196–97.

256 ibid 197. See also Robert Howse, *The WTO System: Law, Politics & Legitimacy* (Cameron May Limited 2007) 128; Robert L Howse and Joanna Langille, 'Permitting Pluralism: The Seal Products Dispute and Why the WTO Should Permit Trade Restrictions Justified by Noninstrumental Moral Values' (2012) 37 Yale Journal of International Law 368, 430 (hereafter Howse and Langille, 'Permitting Pluralism: The Seal Products Dispute').

257 Nico Krisch, *Beyond Constitutionalism: The Pluralist Structure of Postnational Law* (OUP 2012) 103 (hereafter Krisch, *Beyond Constitutionalism*) (describing 'a model that requires each polity, in an exercise of public autonomy through its institutions, to define the terms on which it interacts with others' as an example of example of 'systemic pluralism'). See also De Búrca's reply to Weiler in Dialogical epilogue: Joseph HH Weiler, 'Dialogical Epilogue' in Grainne de Burca and Joseph HH Weiler (eds), *The Worlds of European Constitutionalism* (CUP 2012) 282. In her own contribution to the book, De Búrca criticizes the CJEU's approach and suggests that some version of Solange approach, to which she also refers to as a 'soft constitutionalist' (or 'soft pluralist') approach, would be preferred. Graine de Búrca, 'The ECJ and the International Legal Order: A Re-Evaluation' Grainne de Burca and Joseph HH Weiler, *The Worlds of European Constitutionalism* (CUP 2012). There is, however, some divergence of views in scholarship on the exact meaning of the terms: what De Búrca refers to as 'pluralism', other scholars label 'dualism' for example. See, eg, Samantha Besson, 'European Legal Pluralism after *Kadi*' (2009) 5(2) European Constitutional Law Review 237, 262–63. The CJEU, however, did imply in its decision that the Solange approach could be possible in different circumstances. Juliane Kokott and Christoph Sobotta, 'The *Kadi* Case – Constitutional Core Values and International Law: Finding the Balance?' (2012) 23(4) European Journal of International Law 1015, 1019.

its obligations in good faith.[258] Moreover, the EU may face liability and retaliation under international trade law if it fails to comply with its trade commitments or a decision of a trade-adjudicating body, even if such compliance is not possible due to constraints contained in EU primary law.[259] This is why constitutional restrictions on compliance with such obligations or decisions could present a serious problem.

This problem can manifest itself in at least two different contexts: first, in the context of *existing* international trade norms, specifically those contained in the GATS. Second, in the context of *international negotiations* concerning cross-border data flows and exceptions for privacy and data protection to be included in *future* trade agreements, including the ongoing digital trade talks at the WTO Joint Initiative on E-commerce.

With respect to the *first context*, the possibility of a conflict between the EU law and EU obligations under the (existing) GATS and WTO legal framework cannot be avoided because the rules are already there. Indeed, it could be argued, from a pluralist perspective, that it *should not* necessarily be avoided, given divergent moral convictions and values concerning data privacy.[260] Instead, it can be viewed as an expression of pluralism. In other words, the absence of clear answers at the point of possible conflict could normatively be a preferred option compared to a clear hierarchy between conflicting norms, so that both international trade and EU law legal orders can decide autonomously on their stance on the issue, without having to fully align their perspectives. In such a pluralist structure, the conflict could be addressed in other ways, notably through dialogue and mutual permeation of rules following a potentially unfavourable outcome for the EU of a WTO dispute settlement, should one occur. At the heart of the normative argument in favour of such a pluralist approach is that it provides space for 'intense social contestation about the locus of authority and the right collective for decision-making' on matters surrounded by deep-seated disagreement.[261] Furthermore, '[p]luralism is also closer to foundational ideals of political order – namely public autonomy ... the plural, divided identities, loyalties, and allegiances that characterize postnational society are better reflected in a multiplicity of orders than in an overarching framework that implies ultimate authority'.[262] In addition, a pluralist

[258] Art 31.1 Vienna Convention on the Law of Treaties (entered into force 27 January 1980) 1155 UNTS 331, 8 ILM 679 (hereafter VCLT).

[259] VCLT (n 258) art 27.

[260] For example, Krisch argues that pluralism 'seeks to discern a model of order that relies less on unity and more on the heterarchical interaction of the various layers of law. Legally, the relationship of the parts of the overall order in pluralism remains open—governed by the potentially competing rules of the various sub-orders, each with its own ultimate point of reference and supremacy claim, the relationships between them are left to be determined ultimately through political, not rule-based processes.' Krisch, *Beyond Constitutionalism* (n 257) 23.

[261] ibid 78, 189–90, 206.

[262] ibid 106.

structure offers a potential for adaptation and builds in checks and balances into the global legal order.[263]

The GMO dispute between the EU and the United States, where two fundamentally opposing approaches clashed, is often cited as an example of successful co-operation that can be achieved in a pluralist setting.[264] Despite the clash, found against the EU on narrow, formal grounds, the WTO Panel avoided any pronouncement on the substance of the EU's precautionary approach to GMOs, as opposed the risk-based approach mandated by the WTO Agreement on the Application of Sanitary and Phytosanitary Measures (SPS Agreement).[265] This has been explained by the incentive of the WTO to preserve its own legitimacy and maintain social acceptance of its dispute-settlement system, as well as to avoid the risk that the EU would simply not comply with a 'hard' decision against it (an option, however, that seems available only to more powerful WTO members).[266] On the EU side, WTO dispute-settlement reports have had a profound effect on EU domestic rules on GMOs, and the CJEU has integrated WTO law into its jurisprudence, despite its reluctance to grant it direct effect.[267] The pressure for compliance, arguably, came from the high costs of non-compliance with the WTO reports.[268] In sum, the political dialogue that ensued after the unfavourable WTO dispute-settlement reports led to 'far-reaching convergence on both principles and processes around the SPS approach'.[269]

There are at least three reasons, however, why a pluralist approach is unlikely to play out in the same way in relation to the clash between the rules on data privacy in the current circumstances. First, and most importantly, unlike the GMO debate, the clash between the EU approach to governing cross-border data flows and data privacy protection, and other countries, such as the United States, which could potentially result in a confrontation at the WTO, concerns not only EU secondary but also EU primary law, as this chapter demonstrates. Put differently, the new legal reality, in which the EU Charter is binding and constitutes a part of EU primary law, considerably limits the potential of trade law to shape the EU governance of data privacy protection as compared to the GMO case. As a result, the EU may have to face the costs of trade retaliation—no matter how high—should its framework for transfers of personal data outside the EEA be found to be inconsistent

[263] ibid 78, 103.

[264] ibid 190–222.

[265] ibid, 195–96; Monica Hakimi, 'The Integrative Effects of Global Legal Pluralism' in Paul Schiff Berman (ed), *The Oxford Handbook of Global Legal Pluralism* (OUP 2020) 573 (hereafter: Hakimi, 'The Integrative Effects of Global Legal Pluralism'); Gregory Shaffer, 'A Structural Theory of WTO Dispute Settlement: Why Institutional Choice Lies at the Center of the GMO Case' (2008) 41 JILP 1, 70 (hereafter Shaffer, 'A Structural Theory of WTO Dispute Settlement').

[266] Hakimi, 'The Integrative Effects of Global Legal Pluralism' (n 265) 573; Shaffer, 'A Structural Theory of WTO Dispute Settlement' (n 265), 68–70.

[267] Krisch, *Beyond Constitutionalism* (n 257) 215–16.

[268] ibid 9–10, 20–21.

[269] ibid 216.

with the GATS. If retaliation resulted in a suspension of personal data flows *into* the EU, this would directly cut across the EU digital trade policy, which aims to liberalize such flows.[270] It is, however, possible that WTO adjudicators—in the spirit of a pluralist approach—would not come down too hard on the EU on the data privacy issue. For example, in his 2000 article, Shaffer argues that '[u]nder media scrutiny, WTO dispute settlement panels would prefer to refrain from engaging in a close balancing of competing trade and privacy interests, and rather review the process by which the European Union takes account of foreign privacy protections'.[271] Gervais convincingly argues that after the WTO Appellate Body Report in *Australia – Tobacco Plain Packaging*, the WTO's jurisprudence on TRIPS may have shifted towards a pluralist approach, in which WTO adjudicators rely on non-WTO norms to support domestic policy measures clashing with WTO rules.[272]

Second, although, as mentioned above, the CJEU has used the tool of treaty-consistent interpretation to interpret EU law in the light of international law, including WTO law, it has not done so in areas with high salience, such as issues of the EU's banana market and import of hormone-treated meat.[273] In the latter case, the EU has been incompliant with its WTO commitments and has faced trade retaliation measures from the United States and Canada for more than twenty years.[274] It is equally unlikely that the CJEU will take into account EU trade obligations under the WTO Agreements in its future jurisprudence on the issue of transfers of personal data, as it has already refrained from doing so in both *Schrems I* and *Schrems II* concerning transfers of personal data from the EU to the United States. As explained above, in some of its judgments, the CJEU has implicitly ranked the fundamental rights to privacy and the protection of personal data above other relevant fundamental rights, such as the right to conduct business.

Finally, Howse and Langille argue that pluralism is 'a double-edged sword' as there is 'no guarantee that a largely pluralist legal framework will be deployed'.[275] According to these scholars,

[270] For a discussion, see Section 4.2.5.
[271] Shaffer, 'Globalization and Social Protection' (n 165) 51.
[272] Daniel Gervais, 'TRIPS Pluralism' (2022) 21(2) World Trade Review 185.
[273] Krisch, *Beyond Constitutionalism* (n 257, 205).
[274] Although the EU never adjusted its legislation in compliance with the WTO decisions, the issue has been settled through EU giving Canada and the US concessions on import of hormone free beef. See European Commission, 'Press Release: The European Union and the United States Sign an Agreement on Imports of Hormone-Free Beef' (*European Commission*, 2 August 2019) https://ec.europa.eu/commission/presscorner/detail/en/IP_19_5010 accessed 10 July 2023; Tom Miles, 'EU and Canada Settle Cattle Battle at the WTO' *Reuters* (3 October 2017) <www.reuters.com/article/us-canada-eu-wto-meat-idUSKCN1C81HY> accessed 10 July 2023.
[275] Robert Howse and Joanna Langille, 'Continuity and Change in the World Trade Organization: Pluralism Past, Present, and Future' (2023) 117(1) The American Journal of International Law 1, 25–26.

> [p]recisely because a formally pluralistic legal architecture for cooperation is indeterminate or agnostic as to the ideological or policy projects that it can accommodate, such a framework runs the risk of being coopted or conscripted for a particular project, where its proponents have political, epistemic, or economic power.[276]

Ultimately, the functioning of a pluralist structure is at the mercy of adjudicating bodies in charge of interpreting of trade rules, as they can 'read into' these rules' particular interests and ideologies.[277] As Section 3.2 explains in greater detail, the policy space for domestic regulatory priorities (and the related notion of 'protectionism' that delineates that space) has changed considerably throughout the trade law's history depending on ideologies adopted by WTO adjudicators.

Therefore, in the context of international negotiations of future trade agreements, the risk of a clash between the two necessities, as described above, makes replication of the GATS general exception for privacy and data protection problematic from an EU law perspective. This book addresses that problem in Chapter 4. The main legal reason for this is, as previously mentioned, that the EU institutions must ensure the compatibility of its internal and external policies and ensure that any trade agreements they negotiate accords with internal EU policies and rules.[278]

Preserving uncertainty as to whether the proposed agreement is compatible with the EU *acquis* (which could be viewed as a normatively preferred option from a pluralist perspective) could result in a CJEU judgment under Article 218(11) of the TFEU finding such an agreement incompatible with the EU *acquis*. This would, ultimately, require a re-negotiation of the agreement, which would not only delay the conclusion of the agreement but also result in the additional costs of renegotiation and forfeited benefits from delayed trade concessions under the proposed agreement. It is worth recalling that the conflict about the proper regulatory approach to GMOs in agriculture, which was used to illustrate why a pluralist approach could be normatively more desirable, itself resulted from a situation where European negotiators on the SPS Agreement did not insist on wording that would have shielded the EU approach to sanitary and phytosanitary measures in certain areas (based on the precautionary principle rather than a risk-based approach relying on science as justification for trade-restrictive measures).[279] In view of the above-mentioned TFEU provisions, as well as the fact that the rights to privacy and the protection of personal data are binding fundamental rights in the EU, a similar

[276] ibid.
[277] ibid.
[278] TFEU (n 32) art 207(3)(2).
[279] Krisch, *Beyond Constitutionalism: The Pluralist Structure of Postnational Law* (n 257) 215–16, explaining that 'the EC found itself with few allies and had to give in if negotiations were to continue—it was keen on a successful conclusion because it sought to reduce obstacles to its own market access in other countries and did not want to see this relatively low-priority issue threaten negotiations on other, more central parts of the Uruguay Round'.

outcome is simply not possible as a matter of EU law in the trade negotiations affecting EU data protection framework. Another related reason is that the EU's position, according to which data protection cannot be traded in international trade negotiations, as well as its commitment to safeguard its full autonomy to protect the rights to privacy and the protection of personal data as fundamental rights is an important internal political message to the public.[280] From a political perspective, replication of the GATS general exception for privacy and data protection, in conjunction with a provision on cross-border data flows in the EU's future trade agreements, is also very likely to be opposed by the European Parliament. This may also lead to the European Parliament's refusal to consent to the trade agreement.[281] For example, the European Parliament strongly opposed replication of the GATS general exception in the failed TTIP and TiSA.[282]

2.4.2 Trade law necessity and EU Restrictions on data transfers

To be justified under the general exception contained in GATS Article XIV, a prima facie inconsistent measure must meet one of the material requirements of the general exception set forth in Article XIV(a) to (e) and the introductory clause (or *chapeau*) of this Article. This general exception applies horizontally to measures that violate any obligation under the GATS. The wording of the general exception is remarkably consistent in most post-WTO trade agreements, in that they all closely follow GATS Article XIV.[283] This is why the interpretation of the trade necessity test at the WTO may be relevant also in the context of other trade agreements.

This general exception requires a two-tier assessment: first, it must be established whether the contested measure meets one of the substantive requirements of paragraph (c); second, there is an examination of whether the contested measure

[280] For a discussion, see Section 4.2.1.

[281] For a discussion on the increased role of the European Parliament both at the stage of negotiation and adoption of international trade agreements after the Lisbon Treaty, and how the Parliament has used this role in practice see Eckes, *EU Powers under External Pressure* (n 251) 153–66.

[282] European Parliament Resolution 2014/2228(INI) of 8 July 2015 containing the European Parliament's recommendations to the European Commission on the negotiations for the Transatlantic Trade and Investment Partnership (TTIP) OJ C 265/35. European Parliament Resolution 2015/2233(INI) of 3 February 2016 containing the European Parliament's recommendations to the Commission on the negotiations for the Trade in Services Agreement (TiSA) OJ C 35/21. In its resolution on TiSA (para 1(c)(iii)), the European Parliament recommended European Commission: '. . . to incorporate a comprehensive, unambiguous, horizontal, self-standing and legally binding provision based on GATS Article XIV which fully exempts the existing and future EU legal framework for the protection of personal data from the scope of this agreement, without any conditions that it must be consistent with other parts of the TiSA.' European Parliament Resolution 2015/2233(INI) of 3 February 2016 containing the European Parliament's recommendations to the Commission on the negotiations for the Trade in Services Agreement (TiSA) OJ C 35/21. The above-mentioned Resolution on TTIP contains an identical recommendation in para 2(xii).

[283] The most recent examples of EU trade agreements where the GATS art XIV was closely reproduced include art 8.3 JEFTA (n 167) and art 25.1 of EU-New Zealand FTA (n 167) (not yet in force).

satisfies the requirements of the *chapeau* of the exception.[284] The necessity test is the core of the first stage of the assessment.

Article XIV(c)(ii) has never been applied by a WTO panel. However, privacy and data protection are not the first public policy interests in tension with trade liberalization. The interpretation of the necessity test in WTO cases touching upon other public policy interests listed in GATS Article XIV(c) and Article XX of the General Agreement on Tariffs and Trade (GATT) 1994—applicable to international trade in goods instead of services, which also feeds into the application of 'necessity' in the GATS, and vice versa[285]—can inform the interpretation of paragraph (c)(ii). The method used to interpret 'necessity' applied by WTO adjudicating bodies has been fairly consistent irrespective of the specific public interest invoked to justify the measure, be it the protection of public morals, public health, or securing compliance with a WTO-consistent law.[286] Existing WTO case law has established a high threshold for meeting the necessity test, which in some cases has been almost impossible to meet.[287]

The assessment of the necessity of a GATS-inconsistent measure applied by the WTO adjudicating bodies (first expounded in *Korea – Various Measures on Beef*)[288] requires 'weighing and balancing' of the following factors:[289]

(1) The relative importance of the protected public interest(s) pursued by such contested measure,

[284] Appellate Body Report, *Argentina – Financial Services* (n 180) para 6.161; Appellate Body Report, *US – Gambling* (n 223) para 292.

[285] See eg Appellate Body Report, *US – Gambling* (n 223) para 291.

[286] The WTO adjudicating bodies apply the same interpretation of 'necessity' as pronounced in WTO, *Korea – Measures Affecting Imports of Fresh, Chilled and Frozen Beef – Report of the Appellate Body* (10 January 2001) WT/DS161/AB/R, WT/DS169/AB/R, paras 160–64 (hereafter Appellate Body Report, *Korea – Various Measures on Beef*) irrespective of the specific paragraph of art XIV GATS or art XX GATT 1994. See, eg, in relation to art XX(b) GATT – Appellate Body Report, *EC – Asbestos* (n 190) paras 171–75; in relation to art XIV(a) GATS – WTO, Appellate Body Report, *US – Gambling* (n 223) paras 291, 305–08; in relation to art XIV(c) GATS – Appellate Body Report, *Argentina – Financial Services* (n 180) paras 6.202–205, 6.227ff. See also Panagiotis Delimatsis, 'Protecting Public Morals in a Digital Age: Revisiting the WTO Rulings on US – Gambling and China – Publications and Audiovisual Products' (2011) 14(2) Journal of International Economic Law 257, 262 (hereafter Delimatsis, 'Protecting Public Morals in a Digital Age').

[287] Delimatsis, 'Protecting Public Morals in a Digital Age' (n 286) 266; Ingo Venzke, 'Making General Exceptions: The Spell of Precedents in Developing Art XX GATT into Standards for Domestic Regulatory Policy' (2011) 12(5) German Law Journal 1111, 1118–19 (hereafter Venzke, 'Making General Exceptions').

[288] Appellate Body Report, *Korea – Various Measures on Beef* (n 286) para 164.

[289] WTO, *Argentina – Measures Relating to Trade in Goods and Services – Report of the Panel* (9 May 2016) WT/DS453/R, para 7.661 (hereafter Panel Report, *Argentina – Financial Services*); Appellate Body Report, *US – Gambling* (n 223) paras 304–307; Appellate Body Reports, *EC – Seal Products* (n 180) paras 5.169, 5.214; WTO, *United States – Tariff Measures on Certain Goods from China – Report of the Panel* (15 September 2020) WT/DS543/R (hereafter Panel Report, *US – Tariff Measures*) para 7.158.

(2) The contested measure's contribution to the achievement of objective pursued, manifested in the existence of a 'genuine relationship of ends and means between the objective pursued and the measure at issue',[290] and
(3) The trade restrictiveness of the measure,[291] followed by an assessment of whether, in the light of importance of the interests at issue, a less trade restrictive alternative is 'reasonably available'.

In application to EU restrictions on transfers of personal data, the 'relative importance' factor would be a translation of the requirement that the contested restrictions be designed to secure compliance with the laws and regulations relating to the protection of privacy and personal data. As the WTO Appellate Body stated in *US – Gambling*, the process of assessing 'necessity' 'begins with an assessment of the "relative importance" of the interests or values furthered by the challenged measure'.[292] The more important the interest, the heavier it weighs in the assessment, and the heavier it weighs in the justification of a relatively more restrictive measure. In prior cases, the WTO adjudicating bodies have assigned different values to the various public policy objectives mentioned in the general exceptions of GATS Article XIV and GATT Article XX. For example, the protection of human health and life has been recognized as 'vital and important in the highest degree',[293] the aim of protecting environment as 'important',[294] and the protection of the tax collecting systems against tax evasion as being 'of vital importance'.[295] Some case law suggests that the level of international support of the interest at stake[296] or the actual (as opposed to desired) contribution of the measure to achieve a claimed level of protection of public policy interest[297] could weigh in this assessment.

[290] Panel Report, *US – Tariff Measures* (n 289) para 7.158; Panel Report, *Argentina – Financial Services* (n 289) para 7.688; Appellate Body Report, *US – Gambling* (n 223) para 306; WTO, *Brazil – Measures Affecting Imports of Retreaded Tyres – Report of the Appellate Body* (3 December 2007) WT/DS332/AB/R (hereafter Appellate Body Report, *Brazil – Retreaded Tyres*) para 145; WTO, *Brazil – Certain Measures Concerning Taxation and Charges – Report of the Panel* (11 January 2019) WT/DS472/R, Add.1; WT/DS497/R, Corr.1, para 7.526 (hereafter Panel Report, *Brazil – Taxation*); WTO, *European Union and Its Member States – Certain Measures Relating to the Energy Sector – Report of the Panel* (10 August 2018) WT/DS476/R and Add.1 (under appeal), para 7.1360; WTO, *Colombia – Measures Relating to the Importation of Textiles, Apparel and Footwear – Report of the Panel* (22 June 2016) WT/DS461/R and Add.1; WT/DS461/AB/R, DSR 2016:III para 7.315; WTO, *India – Certain Measures Relating to Solar Cells and Solar Modules – Report of the Panel* (14 October 2016) WT/DS456/R and Add.1 WT/DS456/AB/R, DSR 2016:IV para 7.361; Appellate Body Reports, *EC – Seal Products* (n 180) para 5.210.

[291] Assessment of this factor was left out in Appellate Body Report, *EC – Asbestos* (n 190).

[292] Appellate Body Report, *US – Gambling* (n 223) para 306; Appellate Body Report, *Korea – Various Measures on Beef* (n 286) para 164; Appellate Body Report, *Brazil – Retreaded Tyres* (n 290) para 143; Panel Report, *US – Tariff Measures* (n 289) paras 7.168–7.169.

[293] Appellate Body Report, *EC – Asbestos* (n 190) para 172; Appellate Body Report, *Brazil – Retreaded Tyres* (n 290) para 179.

[294] Appellate Body Report, *Brazil – Retreaded Tyres* (n 290) para 179.

[295] Panel Report, *Argentina – Financial Services* (n 289) para 7.671.

[296] Panel Report, *Argentina – Financial Services* (n 289) paras 7.671, 7.715; Appellate Body Report, *US – Shrimp* (n 207) para 130.

[297] Appellate Body Reports, *EC – Seal Products* (n 180) para 5.502; Ming Du, 'The Necessity Test in World Trade Law: What Now?' (2016) 15 Chinese Journal of International Law 817, 826–27.

Beyond this factor, it is unclear how the WTO adjudicators assess the importance of different non-economic values. No objective has been characterized as 'unimportant'.

Assessment of factors (2) and (3) in the list above comprises a *weighing and balancing* of the contribution of the measure to the protected interest, with the trade restrictiveness of the measure in the light of the relative importance of the protected interest or the underlying values of the objective pursued.[298] On a continuum between 'indispensable' and 'making a contribution to', 'necessity' is understood as being closer to 'indispensable' rather than 'making a contribution to'.[299] Thus, the greater the contribution of the contested measure, and the less restrictive it is, the more likely it is to satisfy the necessity test.[300] It is, however, debatable whether this or the following factor is decisive in the assessment of necessity in practice.

If the defending party has succeeded in making a *prima facie* case of 'necessity', the complaining party may rebut it by showing that a less trade-restrictive measure was 'reasonably available' to the defending party. This assessment includes a 'comparison between the challenged measure and possible alternatives ..., and the results of such comparison should be considered in the light of the importance of the interests at issue'.[301] 'Reasonably available' is interpreted as allowing a WTO member to achieve *the same level of protection* of the public interest or objective pursued without prohibitive cost or substantial technical difficulties.[302] Based on this interpretation, the comparison of alternative measures does not typically involve a full-fledged proportionality assessment, which is arguably the case in the assessment of the trade-restrictiveness of the measure.[303] Rather, this comparison

[298] Appellate Body Report, *Brazil – Retreaded Tyres* (n 290) para 210; Appellate Body Reports, *EC – Seal Products* (n 180) para 5.210; Appellate Body Report, *US – Gambling* (n 223) para 306; Panel Report, *Argentina – Financial Services* (n 289) para 7.684.

[299] Appellate Body Report, *Korea – Various Measures on Beef* (n 286) paras 160–61; Appellate Body Report, *US – Gambling* (n 223) para 310; WTO, Note by Secretariat, 'Necessity tests' in the WTO (2 December 2003) S/WPDR/W/27 8-9.

[300] Panel Report, *Argentina – Financial Services* (n 289) paras 7.685, 7.727, referring to Appellate Body Report, *Korea – Various Measures on Beef* (n 286) para 163.

[301] Appellate Body Report, *US – Gambling* (n 223) para 307.

[302] ibid, para 308; Appellate Body Report, *Korea – Various Measures on Beef* (n 286) paras 176, 178.

[303] Mads Andenas and Stefan Zleptnig, 'Proportionality: WTO Law in Comparative Perspective' (2007) 42 Texas International Law Journal 371, 414 (hereafter Andenas and Zleptnig, 'Proportionality: WTO Law in Comparative Perspective'); Meinhard Hilf and Sebastian Puth, 'The Principle of Proportionality on Its Way into WTO/GATT Law' in Armin Von Bogdandy, Petros C Mavroidis, and Yves Mény (eds), *European Integration and International Co-Ordination* (Wolters Kluwer 2002) 199 (hereafter Hilf and Puth, 'The Principle of Proportionality on Its way into WTO/GATT Law'); Gabrielle Marceau and Joel P Trachtman, 'The Technical Barriers to Trade Agreement, the Sanitary and Phytosanitary Measures Agreement, and the General Agreement on Tariffs and Trade: A Map of the World Trade Organization Law of Domestic Regulation of Goods' (2002) 36(5) Journal of World Trade 811, 826–28, 851–53 (hereafter Marceau and Trachtman, 'The Technical Barriers to Trade Agreement, the Sanitary and Phytosanitary Measures Agreement'); Gabrielle Marceau and Joel P. Trachtman, 'A Map of the World Trade Organization Law of Domestic Regulation of Goods: The Technical Barriers to Trade Agreement, the Sanitary and Phytosanitary Measures Agreement, and the General Agreement on Tariffs and Trade' (2014) 48(2) Journal of World Trade 351, 368–69 (hereafter Marceau and Trachtman, 'A Map of the World Trade Organization Law of Domestic Regulation of Goods'); Weber, 'Regulatory Autonomy and Privacy Standards Under the GATS' (n 168) 43.

involves the balancing of the administrative and enforcement costs of alternative measures granting the same level of protection to a public interest at issue against the trade costs of such measures.[304] It is generally agreed that the factors in the assessment of 'necessity', which, on the one hand, include weighing and balancing, and on the other, the assessment of reasonable availability of a less trade-restrictive measure, contain a logical contradiction and are incompatible: the first assessment leaves WTO members much less regulatory autonomy than the other.[305] This has resulted in a disagreement between two groups of academics, one of which argues that the weighing and balancing in the assessment of necessity requires a full-fledged proportionality or cost–benefits assessment.[306] The other group, however, contends that the analysis of necessity turns on the assessment of reasonable availability of a less trade-restrictive measure.[307]

In most instances, the WTO adjudicating bodies do base their reports on the assessment of reasonable availability of a less trade-restrictive measure,[308] and rightly so. This is a more lenient approach than the proportionality assessment, which arguably allows WTO members to choose the level of protection of the public interest at issue.[309] In *US –Gambling*, the Appellate Body explicitly equated the absence of necessity with the reasonable availability of another WTO consistent measure.[310] However, the risk that those bodies will conduct a full-fledged cost-benefit analysis

[304] Donald H Regan, 'The Meaning of 'Necessary' in GATT Article XX and GATS Article XIV: The Myth of Cost-Benefit Balancing' (2007) 6(3) World Trade Review 347 (hereafter Regan, 'The Meaning of 'Necessary' in GATT Article XX and GATS Article XIV'); Benn McGrady, 'Necessity Exceptions in WTO Law: Retreated Tyres, Regulatory Purpose and Cumulative Regulatory Measures' (2009) 12(1) Journal of International Economic Law 153; Andrew Lang, 'Reflecting on Linkage: Cognitive and Institutional Change in the International Trading System' 2007 70(4) Modern Law Review 523 (hereafter Lang, 'Reflecting on Linkage').

[305] See, eg, Venzke, 'Making General Exceptions' (n 287) 1136; Regan, 'The Meaning of 'Necessary' in GATT Article XX and GATS Article XIV' (n 304) 348; Lang, 'Reflecting on Linkage' (n 304).

[306] Andenas and Zleptnig, 'Proportionality: WTO Law in Comparative Perspective' (n 303) 414; Hilf and Puth, 'The Principle of Proportionality on Its Way into WTO/GATT Law' (n 306) 199; Marceau and Trachtman, 'The Technical Barriers to Trade Agreement, the Sanitary and Phytosanitary Measures Agreement' (n 303) 826–28, 851–53; Marceau and Trachtman, 'A Map of the World Trade Organization Law of Domestic Regulation of Goods' (n 303) 368–69; Weber, 'Regulatory Autonomy and Privacy Standards under the GATS' (n 168) 43; Venzke, 'Making General Exceptions' (n 287) 1136; Naef, *Data Protection without Data Protectionism* (n 168) 333–34.

[307] Jurgen Kurtz, *The WTO and International Investment Law. Converging Systems* (CUP 2016) 199–201; Regan, 'The Meaning of 'Necessary' in GATT Article XX and GATS Article XIV' (n 304) 349; Venzke, 'Making General Exceptions' (n 287) 1136; Csongor István Nagy, 'Clash of Trade and National Public Interest in WTO Law: The Illusion of "Weighing and Balancing" and the Theory of Reservation' (2020) 23(1) Journal of International Economic Law 143, 159.

[308] See also Mira Burri, 'Interfacing Privacy and Trade' (2021) 53 Case Western Reserve Journal of International Law 35 (hereafter Burri, 'Interfacing Privacy and Trade'); Andrew D Mitchell and Caroline Henckels, 'Necessity Testing' in Andrew D Mitchell and Elizabeth Sheargold, *Principles of International Trade and Investment Law* (Edgaronline 2021) 65, 101.

[309] Regan, 'The Meaning of 'Necessary' in GATT Article XX and GATS Article XIV' (n 304) 350; Venzke, 'Making General Exceptions' (n 287) 1138.

[310] Appellate Body Report, *US – Gambling* (n 223) para 307 (stating that: '[i]t is on the basis of this "weighing and balancing" and comparison of measures, taking into account the interests or values at stake, that a panel *determines whether a measure is "necessary" or, alternatively, whether another, WTO-consistent measure is "reasonably available"*'.) (emphasis added).

always remains. For example, in one of the more recent WTO Panel reports, the Panel based its analysis on the weighing and balancing of the three factors mentioned above *without* engaging into a comparison of the contested measure with reasonably available alternative measures.[311]

Furthermore, in practice, the WTO members' autonomy to choose and maintain their own level of protection could be much narrower than it may seem at first glance, notably because it can be narrowed depending on how the adjudicating bodies interpret the term '*same* level' of protection. Does the 'same' level of protection mean a *desired* level of protection (subjectively determined by the State and not (yet) necessarily achieved) or the *actual* level of protection achieved by the disputed measures? The WTO adjudicating bodies have not been consistent in their answer to this question. For example, in *Korea – Various Measures on Beef*, based on the *actual* application of the contested measure, judging by the design of the contested measure the Appellate Body 'assumed' that 'Korea intended to reduce considerably the number of cases of fraud occurring with respect to the origin of beef sold by retailers' rather than to 'totally eliminate fraud'.[312] From this perspective, alternative measures (compared to the contested measure) should not be required to achieve a higher level of protection than that *actually* achieved by the contested measure. The level of protection *desired* by the defending WTO member is thus irrelevant. Remarkably, in that case, the alternative measure that, according to the Appellate Body, was reasonably available to Korea involved significantly higher administrative and enforcement costs.[313] This, however, did not prevent the Appellate Body from concluding that the contested measure did not pass the assessment under the third factor. Conversely, in *US – Gambling*, where the alternative measure proposed by the claiming party was dismissed as 'not an appropriate alternative', the Appellate Body explained that a 'reasonably available' alternative measure should preserve the responding member's 'right to achieve its desired level of protection'.[314] Although the Appellate Body did not elaborate on the degree of deference to the WTO member in the assessment of the '*desired level*',

[311] Panel Report, *US – Tariff Measures* (n 289) paras 7.232–7.238. It could, however, also be argued that in that particular case, the Panel did not consider reasonably available alternatives because the contested measure did not meet step 2 in the assessment. In particular, as a reason for not engaging in such analysis the Panel states that '[t]he Panel's preliminary conclusion, based on a weighing and balancing of the relevant factors, is that the United States has not explained how the chosen measures are apt to contribute to the public morals objective, as invoked by the United States, and how they could therefore be "necessary"'.

[312] Appellate Body Report, *Korea – Various Measures on Beef* (n 286) para 178, internal footnotes omitted.

[313] ibid, para 175.

[314] (Emphasis added.) Appellate Body Report, *US – Gambling* (n 223) paras 308, 317, internal footnotes omitted. The WTO Appellate Body reiterated the same approach in Appellate Body Reports, *EC – Seal Products* (n 180) para 5.261: 'in order to qualify as a genuine alternative, the proposed measure must be not only less trade restrictive than the original measure at issue, but should also preserve for the responding Member its right to achieve its desired level of protection with respect to the objective pursued'. (internal footnotes and quotation marks omitted.)

it could still be argued that the choice of this word requires an assessment of what the WTO member aimed for, rather than an objective assessment of what the contested measure actually achieves. In *EC – Seals*, the WTO Panel found that

> the degree of the EU Seal Regime's *actual contribution* to its identified objective is *diminished* by the scope of the exceptions under the measure and the allowance of certain commercial activities within the European Union. Accordingly, we *do not consider that the level of protection actually achieved by the measure is as high as the European Union claims the measure initially aimed to achieve*. We will bear this in mind in taking into account the risks non-fulfilment would create in our subsequent analysis of the reasonable availability of a less trade-restrictive alternative measure.[315]

Although in that case, both the Panel and the Appellate Body nevertheless concluded that a less restrictive measure was not reasonably available to the EU,[316] clearly the risk that trade adjudicating bodies may not respect the level of protection asserted by a defending party persists.[317]

More generally, even if the adjudicating bodies were to afford sufficient deference to the level of protection desired by the State, the analytical exercise of ensuring that an alternative measure would achieve exactly the same level of protection would be nothing more than educated second guessing. When the public policy goals pursued by contested measures are non-economic values, in practice, it may be especially difficult to accurately define the level of their protection which serves as a benchmark for the comparison of alternative measures. It is equally

[315] WTO, *European Communities – Measures Prohibiting the Importation and Marketing of Seal Products – Report of the Panel* (22 May 2014) WT/DS400/R and Add.1/WT/DS401/R; WT/DS400/AB/R/WT/DS401/AB/R, DSR 2014:II (hereafter Panel Report, *EC – Seal Products*) para 7.466; Appellate Body Report, *EC – Seal Products* (n 180) para 5.203. Emphasis added, internal footnotes omitted.

[316] Appellate Body Reports, *EC – Seal Products* (n 180) para 5.279; Panel Report, *EC – Seal Products* (n 315) para 7.504. Both the Panel and the Appellate Body, however, found that the contested EU ban on seal products did not meet the requirements of the Chapeau of Article XX GATT because the exceptions for some commercial activity with seal products in the EU led to unjustifiable discrimination, and that discrimination could not be reconciled with, or is rationally related to, the policy objective of protecting public morals. Panel Report, *EC – Seal Products* (n 315) para 7.648; Appellate Body Reports, *EC – Seal Products* (n 180) para 5.339.

[317] From a pluralist perspective, there is an argument that by not establishing 'in any meaningful sense ... concrete rules of decision on the public interest exceptions' and not settling 'the lines of authority' the WTO Appellate Body has 'moved toward a more pluralist structure. It has created space for states to use WTO law to keep fighting about the proper balance between the WTO policy on liberalization and their own idiosyncratic regulatory goals. This balance is unstable and consistently at issue in WTO legal disputes'. Hakimi, 'The Integrative Effects of Global Legal Pluralism' (n 265) 569. Thus, from this perspective, leaving the tests for assessing whether trade-inconsistent measures can be justified under public interest exceptions is a desirable outcome conducive to sustaining the WTO as a forum where 'trade governance happens'. See also Shaffer, 'A Structural Theory of WTO Dispute Settlement' (n 265) 71, arguing that by keeping their opinions ambiguous, WTO adjudicating bodies 'can shape their decisions to facilitate [compliance by powerful WTO Members] and amicable settlement, and thereby uphold the WTO legal system'.

difficult to determine *ex ante* whether alternative measures would secure the same level of protection.

Recall that while the assessment of reasonably available alternative measures is conducted in the light of the importance of the public interest at stake, the existing WTO case law does not shed much light on the weight of this factor in the assessment. There is, therefore, a related risk that the importance of the public interest, as determined by the adjudicating bodies, may influence the assessment of whether a less trade restrictive alternative measure is reasonably available. One could argue that the importance of the interest influences the deference to the level of protection chosen by the country. Thus, in *Korea – Various Measures on Beef*, where the Appellate Body did not make any statement as to the importance of the public interest pursued by the contested measure, the level of deference to the chosen level of protection was lower as compared to *US – Gambling*, where the Appellate Body agreed that the contested measure protected 'very important societal interests'.[318]

Relying on the analysis above, one may conclude that the application of trade law's necessity test to the EU framework for transfers of personal data to third countries, as implemented in the GDPR, may not result in the recognition of the 'necessity' of this framework by the WTO adjudicators.[319] Although the chances of this outcome are higher (should trade adjudicating bodies apply the proportionality assessment), the risk remains, even in the case of a more lenient interpretation of 'necessity', which amounts to the assessment of reasonably available

[318] Appellate Body Report, *US – Gambling* (n 223) para 232, referring to WTO, *United States – Measures Affecting the Cross-Border Supply of Gambling and Betting Services – Cigarettes – Report of the Panel* (10 November 2004) WT/DS285/R (hereafter Panel Report, *US – Gambling*) paras 6.492, 6.533.

[319] There are statements in academic literature to the contrary. Most of the publications that contain argumentation on this point are rather outdated and do not take into account the most recent developments in EU data privacy law, most importantly the CJEU's post-2009 jurisprudence on the fundamental rights to privacy and the protection of personal data, in particular the *Schrems I* and *II* decisions. See, eg, Asinari, 'Is There Any Room for Privacy and Data Protection within the WTO Rules' (n 165); Shaffer, 'Globalization and Social Protection' (n 165). Of the most recent literature, Chen does not engage in elaborate discussion and rather presumes that since there is an exception for data protection, there is a chance that EU framework can be justified. He limits the assessment to one sentence: 'Although until now, there hardly has been a case that the responding party won by claiming the general exceptions clause, one could still see the interest of privacy being recognized through the substantial establishment of an exclusive clause for privacy in Article 14 (c) subsection (ii) of the GATS'. Chen, 'The EU Data Protection Law Reform' (n 168) 219. The most elaborate discussion in the most recent literature is by Naef, *Data Protection without Data Protectionism* (n 168) 332–52, who finds that most of the interferences with the GATS obligations can be provisionally justified under art XIV(c)(ii). Naef's arguments are not entirely convincing for at least three reasons. First, in the discussion of less trade-restrictive alternative transfer frameworks reasonably available to the EU, Naef only discussed the principle of accountability and fails to incorporate the framework for transfers of personal data under Convention 108. Second, Naef places a lot of weight on the high level of personal data protection declared and desired by the EU, but fails to acknowledge the inconsistency of the framework, which makes attainment of that level protection nearly impossible in practice. Third, and finally, Naef's work does not consider the controversial interpretation of the concept of 'transfer' by the EDPB, which, as this chapter argues, adds an additional hurdle for the EU framework for transfers of personal data outside the EEA to satisfy the 'necessity test'.

alternatives to a contested measure.[320] There are at least two reasons for this. First, it could be argued that there is an *insufficient nexus* between the contested restrictions on transfers of personal data and the aim of achieving a high level of protection. Second, the EU framework for transfers of personal data may be recognized as *not the least trade restrictive.*

2.4.2.1 Insufficient nexus between restrictions and the aim of high level of protection

On the first point, it could be argued that the link between the existing EU framework for data transfers and the purpose of ensuring a high level of protection of personal data, particularly from foreign governments' ability to access this data, is closer to 'making a contribution to' rather than 'indispensable'. As demonstrated above, mechanisms for systematic personal data transfers under the GDPR must ensure that the level of protection that a particular third country ensures in respect to the transferred data is 'essentially equivalent' to that in the EU,[321] where the 'level of data protection' means not only the quality of the data protection rules but multiple other factors, including the respect for the rule of law and human rights, access of public authorities to personal data, and the existence and effective functioning of independent supervisory authorities.[322] There is, however, a sizeable gap between the level of protection that this framework *should* and *can* deliver in practice.[323] The Transatlantic saga on cross-border data flows is but one illustration of the point.[324]

After the CJEU invalidated the adequacy decision for the United States (the EU-US Safe Harbor framework) in 2015 by the *Schrems I* judgment—which also introduced for the first time the 'essential equivalence' requirement—against a background of a low level of enforcement, personal data continued flowing to the United States despite the absence of 'essentially equivalent' protection of such data.[325] The 2016 EU-US Privacy Shield framework, which replaced the Safe Harbor and underlay transatlantic personal data transfers for almost four years,

[320] Reyes, 'WTO-Compliant Protection of Fundamental Rights' (n 168) 33–34. Generally, several scholars have highlighted the risk of unpredictability in the WTO jurisprudence on the necessity test. See, eg, Bygrave, *Data Privacy Law: An International Perspective* (n 29) 198; Weber, 'Regulatory Autonomy and Privacy Standards under the GATS' (n 168); Reyes, 'WTO-Compliant Protection of Fundamental Rights' (n 168) 12; Venzke, 'Making General Exceptions' (n 287) 191; Neha Mishra, 'Privacy, Cybersecurity, and GATS Article XIV: A New Frontier for Trade and Internet Regulation?' (2020) 19(3) *World Trade Review* 341, 350.

[321] *Schrems I* (n 43) para 73; *Schrems II* (n 44) para 94; Recital 104 GDPR (n 2).

[322] GDPR (n 2) art 45.

[323] Martina F Ferracane, 'Data Protectionism: A Conceptual Framework to Assess Restrictions on Cross-Border Data Flows from a Trade Policy Perspective' (Dissertation, Universität Hamburg 2021) (hereafter Ferracane, 'Data Protectionism') 124–29.

[324] For further discussion, see Section 5.3.

[325] See Sections 5.3.1 and 5.3.3.

did not—as the CJEU confirmed in the *Schrems II* judgment—remedy the absence of 'essentially equivalent' protection of personal data under US law.[326]

Even after *Schrems II*, data has continued to flow across borders. According to the IAPP-EY Annual Privacy Governance Report 2021, only 10 per cent of the firms chose to localize data following that judgment.[327] Compared to the aftermath of *Schrems I*, there was more publicity around enforcement of GDPR rules on transfers of personal data outside the EEA following *Schrems II*, most notably the series of enforcement actions following Max Schrems 101 complaints against Google Analytics and Facebook Connect.[328] In reality, however, as of this writing, these enforcement actions amounted to a few orders to stop using the Google Analytics or Facebook Connect tool issued with respect to individual website owners and only one million Euro fine, while all other millions (or more) of websites across the internet continue using these tools.[329] The above-mentioned Irish DPC's decision in the matter of Meta Platforms, which ordered Meta Platforms to suspend transfers outside the EEA, is the first of its kind in the history of existence of EU restrictions on cross-border data flows, and it should not be underestimated. This order, however, took a long time to come to fruition, and it is currently under appeal.[330]

As Gulczyńska rightly points out, 'a mere prohibition to transfer data to third countries (even subject to appropriate safeguards) is unlikely to stop such processing, and can have the effect of the overall decrease in the level of protection. . . . The Court's lack of flexibility and disregard for other national and international instruments may also act to the detriment of the GDPR's objective of promoting a high standard of the fundamental right to data protection globally.'[331]

Another reason why the nexus between the EU's framework for transfers of personal data outside the EEA and the desired high level of personal data protection may be viewed as insufficient is the exclusion of a large volume of direct transmissions of personal data outside the EEA from the definition of 'transfer' and, therefore, from the scope of the framework for transfers of personal data. This approach creates a gap in legal protection of personal data in situations where personal data is transmitted directly from individuals in the EEA to an entity that has no EEA

[326] *Schrems II* (n 44).

[327] 'IAPP-EY Annual Privacy Governance Report 2021' (n 134) 4.

[328] See, eg '101 Complaints on EU-US transfers filed' (*noyb*, 17 August 2020) <https://noyb.eu/en/101-complaints-eu-us-transfers-filed> accessed 10 July 2023; Noyb, 'UPDATE: Further EU DPA orders stop of Google Analytics' (n 143).

[329] 'noyb Win: First Major Fine (€ 1 million) for Using Google Analytics' (*noyb*, 3 July 2023) <https://noyb.eu/en/noyb-win-first-major-fine-eu-1-million-using-google-analytics> accessed 10 July 2023.

[330] Newman, 'Meta Lodges Appeal Against EDPB Data-Transfers Decision at EU Courts' (n 173); The Irish Times, 'Facebook Owner Granted Stay On Order That It Suspend Europe-US Data Transfers' (n 173).

[331] Zuzanna Gulczyńska, 'A Certain Standard of Protection for International Transfers of Personal Data under the GDPR' (2021) 11(4) International Data Privacy Law 360, 373–74.

Table 2.1 Comparison of Legal Regimes 1 and 2

Legal regime	Type of transmission	Level of protection
Legal Regime 1	Transmission of personal data directly from individuals in the EEA to a data importer established outside the EEA, which is not subject to the GDPR's extraterritorial application	No GDPR protection
Legal Regime 2	Transmission of personal data from a data exporter subject to the GDPR (irrespective of location) to a data importer outside the EEA, which is not subject to the GDPR's extraterritorial application	Protection of GDPR Chapter V

establishment.[332] This can be illustrated, for example, by comparing Legal Regimes 1 and 2 as discussed in Section 2.2.3 (Table 2.1).

This gap in legal protection in Legal Regime 1 compared to Legal Regime 2, solely because of the difference in one of the end points in transmission (and not, eg, due to different levels of risks to individual data privacy rights in each of the legal regimes), weakens the nexus between the EU framework for transfers of personal data outside the EEA and its declared aim of ensuring 'effective and complete' protection of the fundamental right to the protection of personal data under the EU Charter.

2.4.2.2 EU framework for transfers of personal data is not the least trade restrictive

There are at least two ways of arguing that the EU framework for transfers of personal data outside the EEA may be not the least trade restrictive alternative reasonably available to the EU: first, based on the inconsistency of legal protection afforded to personal data transmitted outside the EEA in four legal regimes discussed in Sections 2.2.3 through 2.2.5; second, based on the comparison of the EU's framework for transfers of personal data outside the EEA under the GDPR with other existing international frameworks and EU's emerging international efforts on promoting Data Free Flow with Trust (DFFT) initiative.

[332] See Svetlana Yakovleva, 'Meet the Author Event: Territorial Scope and Data Transfer Rules in the GDPR' (YouTube, 20 January 2022) at 17:30 <https://youtu.be/OlxQLE4lnrM> accessed 10 July 2023; See also Kuner, 'Protecting EU Data outside EU Borders under the GDPR' (n 45).

Table 2.2 Comparison of Legal Regimes 1–4

Legal regime	Type of transmission	Level of protection
Legal Regime 1	Transmission of personal data directly from individuals in the EEA to a data importer established outside the EEA, which is not subject to the GDPR's extraterritorial application	No GDPR protection
Legal Regime 2	Transmission of personal data from a data exporter subject to the GDPR (irrespective of location) to a data importer outside the EEA, which is not subject to the GDPR's extraterritorial application	Protection of GDPR Chapter V
Legal Regime 3	Transmission of personal data from a data exporter subject to the GDPR (irrespective of location) to a data importer outside the EEA, which is subject to the GDPR's extraterritorial application	Protection under the general framework of the GDPR *and* Chapter V 'light'
Legal Regime 4	Transmission of personal data directly from individuals in the EEA to a data importer established outside the EEA, which is subject to the GDPR's extraterritorial application	Protection under the general framework of the GDPR (including some restrictions on transmission deriving from Articles 5, 24, and 32 GDPR) but *not* Chapter V

To illustrate the first point, that is, why the creation of four different Legal Regimes for transmitted personal data may lead to mechanisms for transfers of personal data outside the EEA under Chapter V of the GDPR not being the least trade restrictive alternative available to the EU, let us again reproduce the four legal regimes here for convenience (Table 2.2).

Because these legal regimes are derived from the EDPB's interpretation of the concept of 'transfer' under the GDPR, it should be assumed that, *at least in theory*,[333] the level of protection afforded to transmitted personal data under all four legal regimes is the same and is consistent with the standard of 'effective and

[333] As this book argues in Chapter 5, this assumption is incorrect in practice, as the level of protection afforded to personal data directly transmitted to a controller or processor outside the EEA is lower simply because the standard of 'essential equivalence' determined by the CJEU for 'transfers' of personal data under Chapter V does not apply to direct transmissions that do *not* qualify as 'transfer'.

complete' protection derived by the CJEU from the EU Charter. This would, in turn, mean that protection afforded to transmitted personal data by the rules of Chapter V (Legal Regime 2) is as high as protection afforded to transmitted personal data by virtue of extraterritorial application of the general GDPR framework (minus Chapter V, Legal Regime 4), in particular, the principles of lawfulness, accountability, and security (Articles 5, 24, and 32). At the same time, these latter principles are clearly less trade restrictive than the exhaustive list of transfer mechanisms under Chapter V of the GDPR, in particular to the extent that they require an extensive assessment of essential equivalence of the legal regime in the country of destination. In other words, if protections stemming from GDPR's Articles 5, 32, and 24 are equally able to ensure effective and complete protection of personal data transmitted outside the EEA, the Chapter V's regime is not the least trade restrictive.

On the second point, some authors have noted that the EU's framework for transfers of personal data outside the EEA may not be viewed as least trade restrictive because 'it may be difficult to prove that privacy cannot be otherwise protected'.[334] The fact that compliance with the standard of the recently modified Convention 108—characterized by Greenleaf as 'close to the current global average for data privacy laws'[335]—is in itself insufficient, especially in the light of the CJEU *Schrems II* judgment, to warrant an adequacy decision from the EU,[336] demonstrates that the benchmark set by the EU is higher than that recognized by any other international standard. Under recital 105 of the GDPR, when assessing the adequacy of personal data protection in a third country, the EU Commission should take into account accession of that country to Convention 108.[337] However, Article 14(1) of the Convention 108+ (a modernized version of Convention 108, adopted in 2018)[338] allows a Party to the Convention to restrict transfers from another Party to the Convention if 'bound by harmonised rules of protection shared by States belonging to a regional international organisation'.[339] Given that compliance with the Convention 108+ does not constitute a sufficient ground for adequacy under the

[334] Mira Burri, 'The Governance of Data and Data Flows in Trade Agreements: The Pitfalls of Legal Adaptation' (2017) 51(65) UC Davis Law Review 65, 95–96; Burri, 'Interfacing Privacy and Trade' (n 308) 66. Ferracane, 'Data Protectionism' (n 323) 124–29.

[335] Graham Greenleaf, 'Convention 108+ and the Data Protection Framework of the EU' (2018) UNSW Law & Justice Legal Studies Research Paper No 18-39, 2 <https://papers.ssrn.com/sol3/papers.cfm?abstract_id=3202606> accessed 10 July 2023 (hereafter Greenleaf, 'Convention 108+ and the Data Protection Framework of the EU').

[336] For a discussion, see, eg, Sara L Duque de Carvalho, 'Key GDPR Elements in Adequacy Findings of Countries That Have Ratified Convention 108' (2019) 5(1) European Data Protection Law Review 54; Greenleaf, 'Convention 108+ and the Data Protection Framework of the EU' (n 335) 5.

[337] See also Article 29 Working Party, Working Document on Adequacy Referential, WP 254rev.01 (6 February 2018) <https://ec.europa.eu/newsroom/article29/items/614108> accessed 10 July 2023.

[338] Council of Europe, Modernised Convention for the Protection of Individuals with Regard to the Processing of Personal Data as amended by the Protocol adopted by the Committee of Ministers at its 128th Session of the Committee of Ministers (18 May 2018) CETS 223 (hereafter Convention 108+).

[339] Para 107 of the Explanatory Report to the modernized Convention 108 clarifies that this provision applies in particular to the member States of the EU. Explanatory Report to the modernised Convention

GDPR, it is possible that following the assessment by the European Commission of the legal framework of a Party to this Convention, the adequacy decision will not be granted.

One could assert, as a counter-argument, that the level of protection of the fundamental right to personal data protection chosen by the EU—'effective and complete' protection[340]—makes other, less restrictive alternatives unavailable to the EU.[341] In particular, in contrast to the EU Charter, some international standards on personal data protection, such as the OECD 2013 Guidelines on the Protection of Privacy and Transborder Flows of Personal Data[342] and the 2015 Asia-Pacific Economic Cooperation (APEC) Privacy Framework,[343] take an *instrumental* approach to the protection of personal data and therefore warrant a *lower level* of personal data protection (their primary purpose is to keep restrictions on personal data transfers to a minimum).[344] At the same time, just like the EU Charter and the GDPR, the Convention 108+ recognizes the right to the protection of personal data as a human right.[345] Nevertheless, the restrictions on transfers of personal data to countries that are not Parties to this Convention are still less stringent than those under EU data protection framework.[346]

As explained above, it is entirely possible that given the lack of international harmonization of data privacy rules, trade adjudicators would give little deference to the EU's *desired* high level of protection and would focus instead on the *actual* level of protection achieved.[347] In the absence of reliable statistics on this matter, and the difficulty of producing any concrete evidence of the level of data privacy protection,[348] the adjudicators may buy into empirical arguments, such as those offered by Bamberger and Mulligan, that compared the EU data protection regime

108. Endorsed by Decision of the Committee of Ministers at 128th session (18 May 2018) <https://rm.coe.int/convention-108-convention-for-the-protection-of-individuals-with-regar/16808b36f1> accessed 10 July 2023

[340] *Google Spain* (n 47) para 34; *Wirtschaftsakademie* (n 51) para 28; *Fashion ID* (n 51) paras 50, 66.

[341] See, eg Naef, *Data Protection without Data Protectionism* (n 168) 334–37, who argues precisely along this line of reasoning.

[342] OECD, The OECD Privacy Framework (2013) <https://www.oecd.org/sti/ieconomy/oecd_privacy_framework.pdf> accessed 10 July 2023.

[343] APEC Privacy Framework (2015) <217_ecsg_2015-apec-privacy-framework.pdf> accessed 10 July 2023.

[344] For a comparison of these standards with the European framework, see Svetlana Yakovleva, 'Should Fundamental Rights to Privacy and Data Protection Be a Part of the EU's International Trade "Deals"?' (2018) 17(3) World Trade Review 477, 8–9 (hereafter Yakovleva, 'Should Fundamental Rights to Privacy and Data Protection Be a Part of the EU's International Trade 'Deals'?').

[345] Convention 108+ (n 338) art 1.

[346] While art 14 of Convention 108+ (n 338) conditions transfers of personal data to a State or international organization that is not a party to the Convention on the requirement of securing an 'appropriate' level of protection, the GDPR conditions systematic transfers of personal data to a third country or international organization subject to a requirement that that third country ensures an 'adequate' level of protection, interpreted as 'essentially equivalent' by the CJEU.

[347] Weber, 'Regulatory Autonomy and Privacy Standards under the GATS' (n 168) 40–41, 45.

[348] This issue is discussed in more detail in Section 3.4.2.

to the more liberal US approach, and found that although the latter was not as comprehensive 'on the books,' it operated much more effectively 'on the ground'.[349] Assessment of the 'effectiveness' of data protection on the ground does not take into account the non-instrumental protection of fundamental rights to privacy and the protection of personal data as moral values.[350] Therefore, from an EU law perspective, it could be viewed as incomplete. However, it is precisely the instrumental approach that could be ultimately adopted by trade adjudicating bodies. As Howse and Langille argue:

> where the basis for arguing that a measure is not pretextual is at least partly motivated by noninstrumental moral concerns not universally shared by WTO members, there is a risk that a WTO official or adjudicator who does not share the value in question, or is unfamiliar from its own moral experience with this kind of belief, will begin from a presumption that there is a strong risk of pretextualism. ... [T]he WTO insider community is drawn from a world of diplomats and bureaucrats where a certain kind of instrumental-often economic-rationality dominates conceptions of appropriate public policy. As our analysis of the Seal Products dispute has illustrated, using tests or devices that employ instrumental rationality, such as means/ends reasoning, simply does not work to establish the non-pretextual character of noninstrumental moral regulation.[351]

In addition, some studies suggest that restrictions on transfers of personal data do not sufficiently contribute to ensuring privacy protection against foreign surveillance.[352] The dual facts that the EU framework for transfers of personal data provides the same restrictive approach to any information that qualifies as personal data (which includes a broad range of data under EU law)[353] and does not calibrate restrictiveness in relation to the severity of the risk of interference in individuals'

[349] Deirdre K Bamberger and Kenneth A Mulligan, *Privacy on the Ground: Driving Corporate Behavior in the United States and Europe* (The MIT Press 2015). Koops also underscores 'an enormous disconnect' between European data protection law and reality. Bert-Jaap Koops, 'The Trouble with European Data Protection Law' (2014) 4(4) International Data Privacy Law 250, 256.

[350] For further discussion, see Section 3.4.2.

[351] Howse and Langille, 'Permitting Pluralism' (n 256) 429. See also Robert Howse, Joanna Langille, and Karie Sykes, 'Pluralism in Practice: Moral Legislation and the Law of the WTO after Seal Products' (2015) 48 The George Washington International Law Review 81, 105–06. The authors make an argument in relation to the legislation that can be justified under the general exception for public morals. This reasoning is, however, also applicable to other legislations subject to justification under specific thematic exceptions of the general exceptions, such as the one for privacy and data protection.

[352] Tim Maurer and others, 'Technological Sovereignty: Missing the Point?' in Markus Maybaum, Anna-Maria Osula, and Lauri Lindström (eds), *7th International Conference on Cyber Conflict: Architectures in Cyberspace* (NATO CCD COE Publications 2015) 61 <https://www.ccdcoe.org/uploads/2018/10/Art-04-Technological-Sovereignity-Missing-the-Point.pdf> accessed 10 July 2023; Konstantinos Komaitis, 'The 'Wicked Problem' of Data Localisation' (2017) 2(3) Journal of Cyber Policy 355, 361–62; Chander, 'Is Data Localization a Solution for Schrems II?' (n 204) 778ff.

[353] See Nadezhda Purtova, 'The Law of Everything: Broad Concept of Personal Data and Future of EU Data Protection Law' (2018) 10(1) Law, Innovation and Technology 40.

fundamental rights could also be used as an indication that other (more granular and overall less trade restrictive) frameworks are 'reasonably available' to the EU. Consequently, the importance of the right to the protection of personal data would be given relatively less weight in a trade dispute. While in EU law it is recognized as a fundamental right, and hence one of the highest values in the EU and on a par with other fundamental rights, trade adjudicating bodies may lean towards an economic approach to privacy and data protection that underlies the existing international standards on data protection mentioned above.[354]

What is more, the EU has embraced the Data Free Flow with Trust (DFFT) initiative on removing barriers on cross-border data flows. As part of this initiative, the EU has concluded digital partnership agreements with Japan, Korea, and Singapore.[355] For example, in the digital partnership agreement with Singapore, which does not have an adequacy decision from the EU, the EU has agreed to endeavour to 'support cross-border data flows with trust through model data protection contracts and the use of emerging technologies. Both sides will also explore collaborations on the use of privacy enhancing technologies'.[356] This and other similar endeavours the EU is undertaking as part of the global DFFT initiative could suggest that other means of personal data protection, such as technological measures and privacy enhancing technologies, could be reasonably available to the EU.[357]

2.4.3 Necessity under EU law

From the CJEU case law, it follows that any legislative act of the EU that involves personal data processing, such as the use or transfer of personal data, constitutes 'in itself' a limitation of the fundamental right to the protection of personal data,

[354] Yakovleva, 'Should Fundamental Rights to Privacy and Data Protection Be a Part of the EU's International Trade 'Deals'?' (n 344) 482–85, 489, 496.

[355] European Union-Republic of Korea Digital Partnership (30 November 2022) <https://circabc.europa.eu/rest/download/6faad06a-30bc-4207-a46b-3da7e8e496e0> accessed 10 July 2023; EU-Singapore Digital Partnership (1 February 2023) <https://ec.europa.eu/newsroom/dae/redirection/document/93447> accessed 10 July 2023 (hereafter EU-Singapore Digital Partnership); Japan-EU Digital Partnership (12 May 2022) <https://www.consilium.europa.eu/media/56091/%E6%9C%80%E7%B5%82%E7%89%88-jp-eu-digital-partnership-clean-final-docx.pdf> accessed 10 July 2023

[356] EU-Singapore Digital Partnership (n 355) para 26, see also para 46.

[357] Naef argues, based on the EDPB, Recommendations 01/2020 on measures that supplement transfer tools to ensure compliance with the EU level of protection of personal data (n 138), that technological solutions are unable to deliver compliance with the right to high level of personal data protection under Article 8 of the EU Charter. He then concludes that '[t]here is much to suggest that such technological measures would not be considered reasonably available alternatives'. Naef, *Data Protection without Data Protectionism* (n 168) 337–38. It is worth noting in this regard that EDPB Recommendations, a non-binding guidance document under EU law, would not weigh heavily in the assessment of EU law by international trade adjudicators.

regardless of whether it can be justified.[358] Such a limitation first triggers the assessment under the requirements of Article 8(2) of the EU Charter. Then, any limitation on this right is only lawful if it meets the requirements of Article 52(1) of the EU Charter,[359] which provides a mechanism for balancing different fundamental rights and freedoms with each other, as well as with other competing policy objectives.[360]

It is the prerogative of the CJEU to conduct a fact-based assessment of whether a derogation is 'necessary' in each particular case.[361] As already mentioned above, since 2009, the CJEU has established a higher threshold for derogations from the fundamental rights to privacy and the protection of personal data under Article 52(1) of the EU Charter when balancing these fundamental rights with other competing rights and interests. In a line of cases, most notably *Volker und Markus Schecke*,[362] *Digital Rights Ireland*,[363] *Tele 2*,[364] *Schrems I*,[365] *Schrems II*,[366] and *Opinion on EU-Canada PNR Agreement*,[367] the CJEU elevated the EU Charter necessity test to the level of 'strict necessity' when a derogation from the fundamental rights to privacy and the protection of personal data is at stake. This approach was later taken up by the Article 29 Working Party[368] and the European Data Protection Supervisor (EDPS).[369] It is now settled CJEU case law that the 'strict necessity' standard should apply horizontally in all contexts, to both commercial and national security, if a limitation of the fundamental rights to privacy and data protection is involved.[370]

[358] *Digital Rights Ireland* (n 211) paras 34–36; *Volker und Markus Schecke and Eifert* [2010] ECLI:EU:C:2010:662, para 58 (hereafter *Volker und Markus Schecke and Eifert*). See also European Data Protection Supervisor, 'Assessing the Necessity of Measures That Limit the Fundamental Right to the Protection of Personal Data: A Toolkit' (2017) 7 <https://edps.europa.eu/sites/edp/files/publication/17-04-11_necessity_toolkit_en_0.pdf> accessed 10 July 2023 (hereafter European Data Protection Supervisor, 'Assessing the Necessity of Measures That Limit the Fundamental Right to the Protection of Personal Data: A Toolkit').

[359] Existing CJEU case law suggests that the conditions of lawfulness of personal data processing contained in art 8(2) and art 52(1) of the EU Charter (n 3) should be analysed cumulatively. See, eg, CJEU Opinion, *EU-Canada PNR Agreement* (n 41) paras 137–38, 142ff.

[360] Unlike international trade law, the text of art 52(1) EU Charter (n 3) explicitly mentions that the assessment of 'necessity' should include a fully-fledged proportionality balancing.

[361] European Data Protection Supervisor, 'Assessing the Necessity of Measures That Limit the Fundamental Right to the Protection of Personal Data: A Toolkit' (n 358) 8.

[362] *Volker und Markus Schecke and Eifert* (n 358) paras 77 and 86.

[363] *Digital Rights Ireland* (n 211) paras 51 and 52.

[364] *Tele2 Sverige* (n 211) paras 96 and 103.

[365] *Schrems I* (n 43) para 92.

[366] *Schrems II* (n 44) para 176.

[367] CJEU Opinion, *EU-Canada PNR Agreement* (n 41) para 140.

[368] See eg Article 29 Working Party, Working Document 01/2016 on the justification of interferences with the fundamental rights to privacy and data protection through surveillance measures when transferring personal data (European Essential Guarantees) WP 237 (13 April 2016) 5 <https://ec.europa.eu/newsroom/article29/items/640363/en> accessed 10 July 2023.

[369] European Data Protection Supervisor, 'Assessing the Necessity of Measures That Limit the Fundamental Right to the Protection of Personal Data: A Toolkit' (n 358) 2.

[370] See ibid 7, referring to a line of the CJEU jurisprudence.

Just as with the trade necessity test, 'strict necessity' under Article 52(1) of the EU Charter in relation to privacy and data protection is hard to satisfy. In assessing 'strict necessity', the CJEU determines whether 'it is possible to envisage measures which affect less adversely that fundamental right of natural persons and which still contribute effectively to the objectives . . . in question'.[371] This approach resembles the least-restrictive-means principle in the interpretation of the trade necessity test. While trade law requires that measures aimed at protecting the right to protection of personal data should be least restrictive on trade, conversely, the EU Charter demands that trade rules should be least restrictive of fundamental rights.

According to the CJEU, legislation interfering with fundamental rights to privacy and the protection of personal data can only pass the 'strict necessity' if it:

> lay[s] down clear and precise rules governing the scope and application of the measure in question and imposing minimum safeguards, so that the persons whose data has been transferred have sufficient guarantees to protect effectively their personal data against the risk of abuse. It must, in particular, indicate in what circumstances and under which conditions a measure providing for the processing of such data may be adopted, thereby ensuring that the interference is limited to what is strictly necessary. The need for such safeguards is all the greater where personal data is subject to automated processing.[372]

The CJEU factored in two other general considerations to its analysis: first, the seriousness of the interference that a particular measure limiting the fundamental rights to privacy and the protection of personal data entails[373] and second, the importance of the interest pursued by the measure. Concerning the latter factor, recall that the relative importance of competing interests also takes part in the assessment of trade 'necessity'. According to the CJEU, the objective of *public security can justify even serious interferences* with privacy and data protection, if such measures meet the 'strict necessity test'.[374] However, the economic interests of a private party, as explained above, seem to be at the other end of the importance continuum. Thus, although data protection may not be considered of highest importance in international trade law, cross-border digital trade is unlikely to weigh heavily against data protection in the EU's fundamental rights calculus.

[371] *Volker und Markus Schecke and Eifert* (n 358) para 86.

[372] *Schrems II* (n 44) para 176, internal footnotes omitted. See also *Schrems I* (n 43) paras 93, 95; CJEU Opinion, *EU-Canada PNR Agreement* (n 41) paras 140–41, 154.

[373] European Data Protection Supervisor, 'Assessing the Necessity of Measures That Limit the Fundamental Right to the Protection of Personal Data: A Toolkit' (n 358) 7.

[374] CJEU Opinion, *EU-Canada PNR Agreement* (n 41) paras 149, 154 (emphasis added).

2.4.4 The incompatibility of two 'necessities'

Now that both necessity tests have been explicated, one can see that the risk of tension lies in the fact that neither the EU's trade liberalization commitments to trade in services nor a potential decision of an international trade adjudicating body requiring the EU to reduce the restrictions on cross-border transfers of personal data to comply with such commitments is likely to survive the EU Charter's 'strict necessity' assessment.

To show the polar opposition between the two tests, one could say that because transfers of personal data outside the EEA amount to a limitation of the fundamental rights to privacy and the protection of personal data, the CJEU's assessment of the liberalization of data transfers starts from the question of 'whether transfers *should be allowed* and under what conditions'. In trade law, the question is the opposite, namely 'whether transfers *should be limited*'. Implementing a decision by an international trade adjudicating body requiring the EU to lower the standard of 'essential equivalence,' which all the mechanisms for systematic personal data transfers should meet based on the CJEU jurisprudence,[375] would run afoul of the core of the conditions under which the CJEU considers transfers of personal data outside the EEA compliant with the EU Charter. It follows from the CJEU *Schrems II* judgment that in the context of transfers of personal data outside the EEA, the 'essential equivalence' requirement is an instantiation of the strict necessity test of Article 52(1) of the EU Charter,[376] which makes it a matter of primary rather than secondary EU law.[377]

Two other core conditions for the compliance of a data transfer mechanism with the EU Charter are the existence and effective functioning of an independent supervisory authority, and effective administrative and judicial remedies for individuals. All the mechanisms allowing for systematic transfers of personal data outside the EEA meet, to some extent, this condition.[378] This component of the fundamental right to the protection of personal data alone renders infeasible, under the EU Charter, any approach to data transfers that does meet the following two criteria: first, an approach that does not allow for a preliminary assessment of the legal regime in the country of destination; second, an approach that does not require a commitment from a personal data recipient in a foreign country to grant EU individuals certain safeguards to exercise their rights to judicial remedy. Even

[375] *Schrems I* (n 43) para 73; CJEU Opinion, *EU-Canada PNR Agreement* (n 41) paras 93, 134; CJEU, *Schrems II*, paras 96, 104–05.

[376] *Schrems II* (n 44) paras 184–85.

[377] For further discussion on this issue see Section 5.2.2.

[378] See, eg, art 45(2)(b) GDPR (n 2) on adequacy assessment, arts 47(2)(e), 40(4) and 40(2)(k) GDPR (n 2), Clause 11 and Clause 13 of the Standard Contractual Clauses, Annex to the Commission Decision on standard contractual clauses for the transfer of personal data to third countries (n 102). In *Schrems II*, the CJEU explicitly confirmed that the older version of the SCCs also met the requirement to ensure an effective remedy. *Schrems II* (n 44) paras 144, 145, 148.

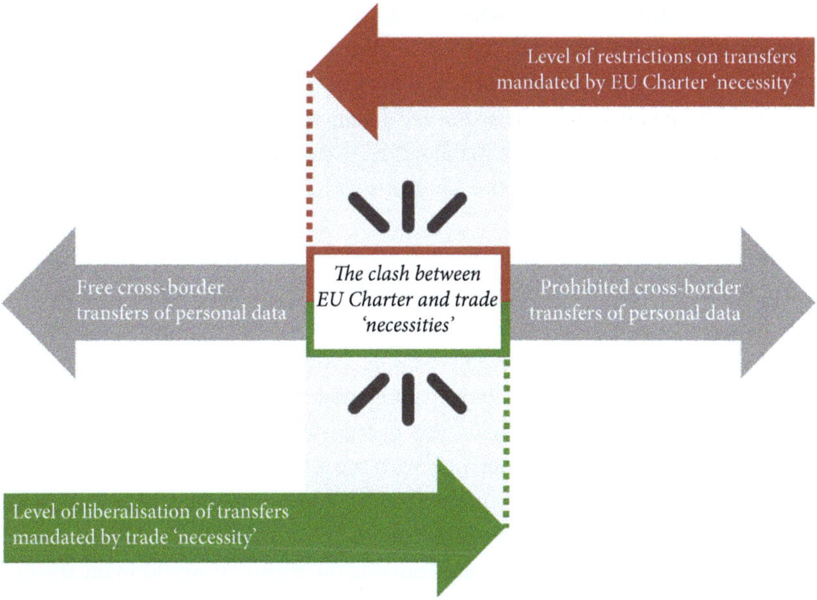

Figure 2.5 Overlap between the EU Charter and Trade 'Necessities' (Design: Helma van der Wal)

if other mechanisms for data transfers are theoretically possible, those mechanisms, if applied horizontally to all types of personal data, would not be less trade restrictive than those already envisaged in the GDPR.

2.5 Ways Forward

The discussion in this chapter has shown that in prior cases concerning the trade-off between the WTO members' autonomy to protect public interests like the environment or public health, on the one hand, and trade liberalization commitments, on the other, the trade necessity test has been interpreted restrictively; too restrictively to accommodate the EU's current approach to transfers of personal data outside the EEA under the EU Charter, as implemented in the GDPR. At the same time, under the strict necessity test contained in the EU Charter (as interpreted by the CJEU), the regulatory autonomy under EU law to derogate from the protection of the fundamental rights to privacy and the protection of personal data may be insufficient to comply with the EU's international trade obligations when it comes to cross-border flows of personal data. The sequential application of the two 'necessities' creates an overlap (see Figure 2.5) where there is a risk that the two 'necessities' may clash, putting the EU in a compliance dead lock between the violation of trade law or unjustifiable derogation from the fundamental right to the protection of personal data, as construed by the CJEU.

In the context of the ongoing digital trade negotiations that the EU is conducting with its trading partners on cross-border data flows, privacy, and data protection, this state of affairs is simply not sustainable. As explained in Section 2.4.1, the EU *should* be able to comply with the Charter *and* its international trade obligations *simultaneously*.

The path forward suggested in this book, and further elaborated on in Chapters 4 and 5, is guided by three principal considerations. First, from a practical perspective, it is risky to wait until EU restrictions are struck down by—or even challenged before—an international trade adjudicating body, which would force the EU's hand. A more proactive approach seems preferable. Second, and relatedly, ongoing uncertainty surrounding the lawfulness of transfers of personal data outside the EEA, on the one hand, and compliance with the restrictions on such transfers with EU's international trade commitments, on the other hand, may have a chilling effect on cross-border trade to the detriment of EU businesses. Third, although the approach to transfers of personal data outside the EEA that would make the most solid contribution to the 'effective and complete' protection of the fundamental rights to privacy and the protection of personal data is a total ban on such transfers, this rather extreme approach would undermine the very existence of digital cross-border trade with the EU and is thus unwarranted.

This book envisions that the clash explicated in this chapter should be addressed from both an international trade and an EU law perspective, not the least because the inconsistency and gaps in legal protection that make the EU framework for transfers of personal data outside the EEA not 'necessary' under trade law is also problematic from the perspective of achieving a high level of personal data protection required by the EU Charter. This book elaborates on the ways this can be done in Chapters 4 and 5, respectively.

From an international trade law perspective, as discussed in Chapter 4, one way out of the quandary is to negotiate a broader exception for the protection of personal data in *future* trade agreements, one that would embrace the EU's restrictions on transfers of personal data without jeopardizing EU trade policy ambitions. Chapter 5 explores, from an EU law perspective, the possibility of reforming the current framework for transfers of personal data outside the EEA in a way that is more compliant with the requirements of the EU's existing and future international trade law obligations and business practices, while keeping within the constitutional boundaries of the EU Charter. However, before the book moves on to those discussions, Chapter 3 uses elements of discourse analysis to explicate the role of narratives in the negotiation and interpretation of trade agreements, and how such narratives could affect the baseline between legitimate protection of data privacy and protectionism in trade negotiations and adjudication. Insights from Chapter 3 then inform proposal for a broader exception for the protection of privacy and personal data in future trade agreements in Chapter 4.

2.6 Conclusion

The pivotal role of personal and other data in the global digital economy intensifies the tension between trade liberalization commitments and the individual rights to privacy and personal data protection. In the EU, where these rights are binding fundamental rights under the EU Charter, this tension could result in a catch-22 situation where the EU would have to choose between adhering to its own constitutional framework and fulfilling its trade obligations. This risk of a compliance dead lock is due to the incompatibility of the exceptions—and, more specifically, the necessity tests lying at their core—that the EU law and international trade agreements have designed to prevent the clash between each other's bodies of rules. This chapter has argued that to prevent this risk from materializing, a reform of the international trade exception for privacy and data protection in future trade agreements and the EU's framework for transfers of personal data is necessary.

3

Privacy Protection(ism)

The Latest Wave of Trade Challenges on Regulatory Autonomy

3.1 Introduction

Labels and frames certainly matter in public policy discussions. So much so, in fact, that they often dictate the outcome. For example, China has spent billions of dollars a year over the past several years to strengthen its *discursive power* to shape specific international policy debates,[1] especially in artificial intelligence (AI), which is an area where countries race for global technological and policy dominance.[2] Similarly, the 'digital protectionism' label has been used in the last decade as a tool to gain control in the domain of digital trade policy debate in relation to personal data protection, and specifically to influence policy outcomes in the European Union (EU), where privacy and personal data are well protected (perhaps even too well protected for those whose business models turn on personal

[1] David Shambaugh, 'China's Soft-Power Push: The Search for Respect' (2015) 94(4) Foreign Affairs 99, 99–100 ('China's diplomatic and development schemes form just one part of a much broader agenda aimed at enhancing its soft power in media, publishing, education, the arts, sports, and other domains. Nobody knows for sure how much China spends on these activities, but analysts estimate that the annual budget for "external propaganda" runs in the neighborhood of $10 billion annually. By contrast, the U.S. Department of State spent $666 million on public diplomacy in fiscal year 2014.'). See Hung Jen Wang, 'Contextualising China's Call for Disclosure Power in International Politics' (2015) 13(3) China: An International Journal 172, 173 and footnote 4 ('Point 5 in Section 7 of "Decision of the Central Committee of the Communist Party of China on Major Issues Pertaining to Deeping Reform of the Cultural System and Promoting the Great Development and Flouring of Social Culture" states that China needs to "strengthen international discourse power, and properly respond to external world concerns".'); see also Jacob Turner, *Robot Rules: Regulating Artificial Intelligence* (Palgrave Macmillan, 2019), 234–35 (citing recommendation III from Chapter 6 of China's 'Artificial Intelligence Standardization White Paper' of 18 January 2018, which advocates 'promotion of international standardization work on artificial intelligence, gathering domestic resources for research and development, participating in the development of international standards, and improving *international discourse power*') (emphasis added); Paul SN Lee, 'The Rise of China and Its Contest for Discursive Power' (2016) 1(1–2) Global Media and China 102, 113 ('Since Xi took over the reins of power in 2013, there have been signs of a shift in China's foreign policy from one that accommodates the existing international rules to a policy that makes new rules and institutions on China's terms.').

[2] See eg Tim Dutton, 'An Overview of National AI Strategies' (*Medium.com*, 28 June 2018) <https://medium.com/politics-ai/an-overview-of-national-ai-strategies-2a70ec6edfd> accessed 10 July 2023 (illustrating the global race for artificial intelligence (AI) dominance by the fact that between 2016 and 2018, Canada, China, Denmark, the EU Commission, Finland, France, India, Italy, Japan, Mexico, the Nordic-Baltic region, Singapore, South Korea, Sweden, Taiwan, the United Arab Emirates, and the United Kingdom published their strategies on AI).

Governing Cross-Border Data Flows. Svetlana Yakovleva, Oxford University Press.
DOI: 10.1093/oso/9780192899248.003.0003

data).[3] As already mentioned in Chapter 1, restrictions on transfers of personal data, such as those adopted by the EU, are routinely criticized as protectionist in trade policy conversations.

'"Protectionism" has become a dirty word'.[4] Yet, discursively, that is far from obvious: in a broader societal context, the term 'protection' is often seen in a positive light, especially when it refers to shelter, safety, or harm prevention. But when it comes to protecting privacy and personal data, trade policy and fundamental rights discourses often seem to work on separate, parallel tracks. Paraphrasing Esty, while the word 'protection' 'warms the hearts' of those seeing data protection and privacy as fundamental rights, it 'sends chills down the spines of free traders'.[5]

This chapter asks where one should draw the line between protection and (digital) protectionism. Set against a discursive backdrop where the label 'protectionism', or 'digital protectionism', is increasingly used in academic, societal, and political debates to refer to regulation that aims to protect privacy and personal data,[6] this chapter considers the implications of this distinction for the autonomy afforded to domestic regulators to protect privacy and personal data by international trade rules and the rules' interpretation. Further, it asks how the framing of the debate on privacy and data protection in terms of (digital) protectionism affects the normative foundations of domestic regulation on privacy and personal data, and the optimal level of privacy and personal data protection.

This chapter tackles these questions by applying elements of 'discourse analysis'[7] methodology, in particular, insights from the work of Michel Foucault on the relationship between discourse and power.[8] According to Foucault, discourse is a 'system that makes possible and governs' the formation of knowledge; it predetermines the objects of knowledge, statements, concepts, and theoretical options as well as the rules of their production.[9] Discourse is not determined once and

[3] See Carole Cadwalladr and Duncan Campbell, 'Revealed: Facebook's Global Lobbying against Data Privacy Laws' (*The Guardian*, 2 March 2019) <https://www.theguardian.com/technology/2019/mar/02/facebook-global-lobbying-campaign-against-data-privacy-laws-investment> accessed 10 July 2023 (revealing Facebook's lobbying around the world, particularly in the United Kingdom, against data privacy legislation).

[4] Dani Rodrik, *The Globalization Paradox: Democracy and the Future of the World Economy* (W. W. Norton & Company 2011) 252 (hereafter Rodrik, *The Globalization Paradox*).

[5] Daniel C Esty, *Greening the GATT: Trade, Environment and the Future* (Peterson Institute for International Economics 1994) 36 (hereafter Esty, *Greening the GATT*) (emphasizing the 'clash of cultures' between environmentalists and free traders and noting that 'the word "protection" warms the hearts of environmentalists but sends chills down the spines of free traders'.).

[6] See Section 3.3.

[7] See James Paul Gee, *An Introduction to Discourse Analysis* (3rd edn, Routledge 2010) 8 ('Discourse analysis is the study of language-in-use. There are many different approaches to discourse analysis. Some of them look only at the "content" of the language being used, the themes or issues being discussed in a conversation or a newspaper article, for example. Other approaches pay more attention to the structure of language ('grammar') and how this structure functions to make meaning in specific contexts. These approaches are rooted in the discipline of linguistics'.).

[8] See, eg, Seumas Miller, 'Foucault on Discourse and Power' (1990) 76 Theoria: A Journal of Social and Political Theory 115, 120–25.

[9] Michel Foucault, *The Archaeology of Knowledge and the Discourse of Language* (Pantheon Books 1972) 72 (hereafter Foucault, *The Archaeology of Knowledge*):

for all—it controls the very *production* of knowledge at a particular moment in history and can evolve over time.[10] Discourse has the power to '*mediate* the dominant view of what constitutes normality or deviance' and to 'produce . . . behaviour that is in conformity with the dominant standard of normality or acceptability'.[11] Language, as Julia Black puts it, 'frames thought, and produces and reproduces knowledge' and is 'intimately related to power'.[12] The use of language places the production of knowledge in a particular discourse, which defines the meaning of terms according to shared practices in line with the ideologies of the social groups controlling the discourse.[13] To Waldman, '[d]iscourse is a tool of power. A given discourse on a topic decides what is up for discussion and what is not, empowering

> We set out with an observation: with the unity of a discourse like that of clinical medicine, or political economy, or Natural History, we are dealing with a dispersion of elements. This dispersion itself with its gaps, its discontinuities, its entanglements, its incompatibilities, its replacements, and its substitutions can be described in its uniqueness if one is able to determine the specific rules in accordance with which its objects, statements, concepts, and theoretical options have been formed: if there really is a unity, it does not lie in the visible, horizontal coherence of the elements formed; it resides, well anterior to their formation, in the system that makes possible and governs that formation.

According to Foucault, '[I]n every society the production of discourse is at once controlled, selected, organised and redistributed according to a certain number of procedures, whose role is to ward off its powers and its dangers, to gain mastery over its chance events, to evade its ponderous, formidable materiality'. Michel Foucault, 'The Order of Discourse' in Robert Young (ed), *Untying the Text: A Post-Structuralist Reader* (Routledge & Kegan Paul Ltd 1981) 52 (hereafter Foucault, 'The Order of Discourse'). See also Julia Black, 'Regulatory Conversations' (2002) 29(1) Journal of Law and Society 163, 168 (hereafter Black, 'Regulatory Conversations'):

Foucault, for example, whose influence is strong, conceptualized discourse as a group of statements that provided the rules for representing the knowledge about a particular topic at a particular historical moment. Discourse is about the production of knowledge, and itself produces the objects of our knowledge. It governs the way that a topic can and cannot be meaningfully talked and reasoned about, and influences how ideas are put into practice and used to regulate the conduct of others Neither contends that nothing exists outside of discourse, that things do not have a real, material existence in the world, but rather that nothing has any meaning outside of discourse.

See also Iara Lessa, 'Discursive Struggles within Social Welfare: Restaging Teen Motherhood' (2006) 36(2) The British Journal of Social Work 283, 285 (defining discourses as 'systems of thoughts composed of ideas, attitudes, courses of actions, beliefs and practices that systematically construct the subjects and the worlds of which they speak'.).

[10] See Foucault, *The Archaeology of Knowledge* (n 9) 73:

As a group of rules for a discursive practice, the system of formation is not a stranger to time. It does not concentrate everything that may appear through an age-old series of statements into an initial point that is, at the same time, beginning, origin, foundation, system of axioms, and on the basis of which the events of real history have merely to unfold in a quite necessary way A discursive formation, then, does not play the role of a figure that arrests time and freezes it for decades or centuries; it determines a regularity proper to temporal processes; it presents the principle of articulation between a series of discursive events and other series of events, transformations, mutations, and processes. It is not an atemporal form, but a schema of correspondence between several temporal series.

[11] Ivan Manokha, 'Foucault's Concept of Power and the Global Discourse of Human Rights' (2009) 23(4) Global Society 429, 430.

[12] Black, 'Regulatory Conversations' (n 9) 165.

[13] ibid 165–69. See also Teun A van Dijk, 'Ideology and Discourse Analysis' (2007) 11(2) Journal of Political Ideologies 115, 138 ('Defined as socially shared representations of groups, ideologies are the foundations of group attitudes and other beliefs, and thus also control the 'biased' personal mental models that underlie the production of ideological discourse'.).

or disempowering those fighting to get themselves and their issues heard'.[14] In other words, control over a discourse ultimately translates into control over the production of 'truth' at a particular point in time and allows the suppression of views outside the prevailing discourse. Not surprisingly, therefore, the power of discourse, or discursive power, is often mentioned in academic, political, and journalistic sources in the context of international relations,[15] domestic trade policy formation,[16] and the functioning of international organizations.[17] States (or governments) use discursive power to advance certain narratives and to shape international discourses and rules on particular topics. In a narrower sense, discourse can also be controlled by 'disciplines', that is, by the social groups practising such disciplines.[18]

Julia Black's work shows that discourse forms the basis of regulation in several respects: it influences regulation by, inter alia, defining the problem and its operational categories; it determines the goals that regulation aims to achieve; and it 'produces shared meanings as to regulatory norms and social practices which then form the basis for action (for example, the formation of regulatory interpretive communities)'.[19] The use of elements of discourse analysis in this chapter aims to show how and why the definition of 'protectionism' came about, and how the interpretation of the legal norms embedding this term in the body of international trade law have evolved over time. This is especially pertinent as international trade rules are often phrased in broad and ambiguous terms,[20] which are operationalized through the interpretation of adjudicating bodies (in case of the law of the World Trade Organization (WTO), by the WTO Panels and the Appellate Body). As Kritsiotis points out, '[a]s such and in the same way as power itself, international law prescribes its own limitations as a language and discipline—in the methods

[14] Ari Ezra Waldman, *Industry Unbound: The Inside Story of Privacy, Data, and Corporate Power* (CUP 2021), 47.

[15] See, eg, Charlotte Epstein, *The Power of Words in International Relations: Birth of an Anti-Whaling Discourse* (The MIT Press 2008), 2–4, 11–14, 16, 19–20, 22–23; Albert J Paolini, 'Foucault, Realism and the Power Discourse in International Relations' (1993) 28(1) Australian Journal of Political Science 98, 98–99; Jennifer Milliken, 'The Study of Discourse in International Relations: A Critique of Research and Methods' (1999) 5(2) European Journal of International Relations 225, 225–26.

[16] See, eg, Gabriel Siles-Brügge 'The Power of Economic Ideas: A Constructivist Political Economy of EU Trade Policy' (2013) 9(4) Journal of Contemporary European Research 597, 605–13.

[17] See, eg, Dongsheng Zang, 'Divided by Common Language: "Capture" Theories in GATT/WTO and the Communicative Impasse' (2009) 32(2) Hastings International and Comparative Law Review 423, 425–28 (hereafter Zang, 'Divided by Common Language').

[18] Foucault, 'The Order of Discourse' (n 9) 59–60. By 'discipline,' Foucault meant 'a domain of objects, a set of methods, a corpus of propositions considered to be true, a play of rules and definitions, of techniques and instruments'. According to Foucault, a discipline controls the production of discourse by recognizing true and false propositions within itself, thus pushing back 'a whole teratology of knowledge beyond its margins'.

[19] Black, 'Regulatory Conversations' (n 9) 165, 178, 188.

[20] See Section 3.2.

and arguments it allows, in its sources, in the interpretations and principles it accepts, and in its own modus operandi'.[21]

The chapter makes two arguments. First, it argues that 'protectionism' is not endowed with an inherent meaning but is socially constructed by the power of the discourse controlling the negotiation, application, and interpretation of anti-protectionist international trade policy and rules. It explicates how shifts in the discourse dominating the negotiation and interpretation of trade law have, in the past, resulted in redefining protectionism as 'new protectionism'. Such redefinition, in turn, triggered the expansion of the scope of domestic policies viewed as protectionist by international trade institutions and elites and the shrinking of domestic autonomy to regulate in the public interest. By extrapolating these historical insights to current policy conversations surrounding digital trade negotiations by the European Union and the United States (referred to in this chapter as 'digital trade' discourse(s)), this chapter shows that despite the fact that the rhetoric of both the EU and the United States on this issue is centred around the same term, 'digital protectionism,' the trading partners advance different discourses based on diverging values, which translate to a different baseline between privacy and data protection, and protectionism. Second, this chapter contends that coining the term 'digital protectionism' to refer to domestic information governance policies that are not yet fully covered by trade law disciplines is *not a logical step* to respond to objectively changing circumstances but a *product of a certain dominant economic 'digital trade' discourse* that has been advanced, in particular, by the United States.[22] This chapter demonstrates how the shift from 'protectionism' to 'digital protectionism' in this particular discourse has resulted in the adoption of international trade rules further restricting domestic autonomy to protect the rights to privacy and the protection of personal data.[23]

This chapter also suggests that the controlling discourse in regulatory conversations on privacy and personal data protection predetermines the baseline between data privacy protection and protectionism and, as a result, affects the level of such protection considered to be necessary and legitimate from a trade perspective. The dominant economic discourse, in particular as advanced by the United States, internalizes an economic approach to personal data and the protection of data privacy.[24] From that perspective, as further discussed in Section 3.4, personal data is viewed as an economic asset and, hence, the extent to which data privacy protection is economically justified is determined against the benchmarks of welfare

[21] Dino Kritsiotis, 'The Power of International Law as a Language' (1998) 34(2) California Western Law Review 397.

[22] This discourse is discussed in more detail in Sections 3.3.1 and 3.3.2.

[23] For a discussion, see Section 3.3.4.

[24] By an economic approach to personal data and the protection of data privacy, this book understands the law and economics approach, which focuses on economic costs and benefits of personal data protection, and does not take full account of protection of personal data as a moral value or value in itself. For a more elaborate discussion, see Section 3.4.

maximization and Pareto efficiency. Within that discourse, any protection beyond what is Pareto efficient is viewed as protectionist.[25] Therefore, conducting policy conversations on domestic regulation protecting privacy and personal data within the boundaries of a purely economic 'digital trade' discourse puts such regulation in an a priori defensive position.[26]

In contrast, within a pluralist discourse, the optimal level of protection will be higher.[27] For the purposes of this book, a pluralist discourse is understood as a discourse which accommodates a broad range of potentially conflicting perspectives, and which, in particular, internalizes economic and non-economic grounds for protecting privacy and personal data as fundamental rights.[28] As a result, some of the policies viewed as protectionist in the economic digital trade discourse will be viewed as protection. Figure 3.1 illustrates this point.

Against this backdrop, this chapter asserts that countries should be conscious of the value frameworks that come with a certain discourse and should ensure that their mutual values determine such discourse, as opposed to the other way around.

On 25 January 2019, seventy-six members of the WTO launched a Joint Initiative on E-commerce, which, among other things, includes rules on cross-border flows of data.[29] As of this writing, eighty-nine countries participated in this multilateral dialogue, representing 90 per cent of global trade.[30] Having emerged

[25] See Susan Strange, 'Protectionism and World Politics' (1985) 39(2) International Organization 233, 235 (hereafter Strange, 'Protectionism and World Politics').

[26] See, eg, Matthias Bauer and others, 'The Economic Importance of Getting Data Protection Right: Protecting Privacy, Transmitting Data, Moving Commerce' (2013) Study by ECIPE for U.S. Chamber of Commerce, 4–9, 20–21 <https://www.uschamber.com/sites/default/files/documents/files/020508_EconomicImportance_Final_Revised_lr.pdf> accessed 10 July 2023 (hereafter Bauer and others, 'The Economic Importance of Getting Data Protection Right'). For a general critique of an economic approach to law, see Arthur Allen Leff, 'Economic Analysis of Law: Some Realism about Nominalism' (1974) 60(3) Virginia Law Review 451, 462 ff.

[27] See, eg, Paul Schwartz and Karl-Nikolaus Peifer, 'Transatlantic Data Privacy Law' (2017) 106 Georgetown Law Journal 115, 121 (hereafter Schwartz and Peifer, 'Transatlantic Data Privacy Law') (comparing the European Union's pluralist, fundamental rights-based approach to data protection with the United States' consumer-based approach).

[28] See William Twining, 'Normative and Legal Pluralism: A Global Perspective' (2010) 20(3) Duke Journal of Comparative and International Law 473, 494.

[29] See European Commission, '76 WTO Partners Launch Talks on E-Commerce' (*European Commission*, 25 January 2019), <https://ec.europa.eu/commission/presscorner/detail/en/IP_19_684> accessed 10 July 2023; Kimberley Botwright, 'Davos Participants Call For Digital Trade Deal' (*World Economic Forum*, 23 January 2019), <https://www.weforum.org/agenda/2019/01/davos-participants-call-for-digital-trade-deal/> accessed 10 July 2023 (hereafter Botwright, 'Davos Participants Call for Digital Trade Deal'); Rana Foroohar, 'Nations Move to Avoid Global Ecommerce "Splinternet"' (*Financial Times*, 24 January 2019), <https://www.ft.com/content/3a8b7458-1fe5-11e9-b2f7-97e4dbd3580d> accessed 10 July 2023; see also Adam Behsudi, 'WTO e-Commerce Talks Could Be a Long Slog' (*Politico*, 11 August 2019), <https://www.politico.com/newsletters/morning-trade/2019/11/08/wto-e-commerce-talks-could-be-a-long-slog-782169> accessed 10 July 2023, indicating that e-commerce talks are likely to take a very long time).

[30] 'Joint Initiative on E-commerce' (*WTO*), <https://www.wto.org/english/tratop_e/ecom_e/joint_statement_e.htm> accessed 10 July 2023. Leaked draft negotiating text as of 14 December 2020 is available here: <https://www.bilaterals.org/IMG/pdf/wto_plurilateral_ecommerce_draft_consolidated_text.pdf> accessed 10 July 2023.

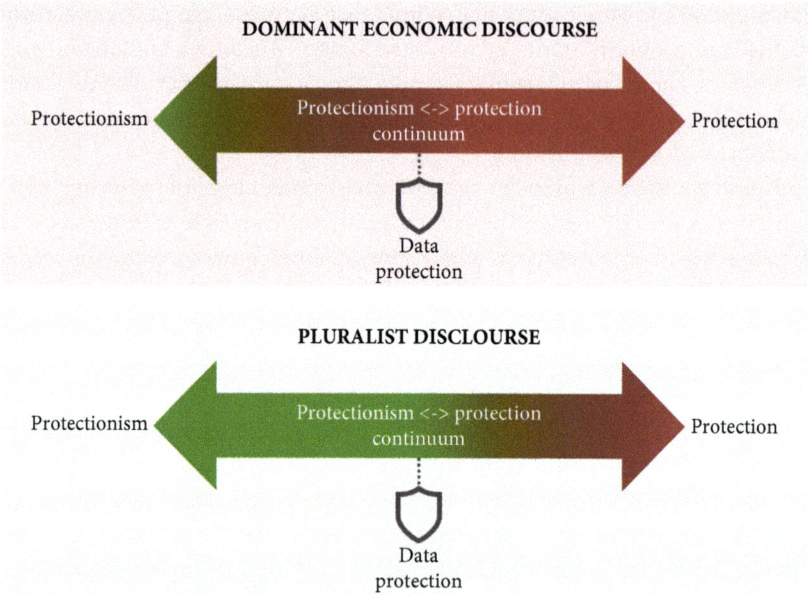

Figure 3.1 Protectionism in economic and pluralist discourses (design: Helma van der Wal)

within the discourse(s) of digital trade, the Joint Initiative on E-commerce aims at 'long-standing, high-standard trade principles to digital trade'.[31] The parties to these negotiations include countries and regions that have different domestic policy priorities and that are situated at different levels of the ladder of economic development—Australia, China, the European Union, Japan, New Zealand, the United States, and Thailand are examples.[32] This chapter suggests that the parties to this multilateral effort should not proceed from the dominant discourse of digital trade as a starting point. Instead, first and foremost, the parties to the effort should agree on the goals of the international trading system in the digital age and the place afforded to essential domestic policy goals within this system. Negotiations conducted within a discourse based on such a mutual understanding would have a much higher chance of producing meaningful results.

This chapter proceeds as follows. Section 3.2 focuses on the most important milestones in the evolution of the notion of 'protectionism', from the mid-eighteenth

[31] Botwright, 'Davos Participants Call for Digital Trade Deal' (n 29).

[32] See WTO, 'Joint Statement on Electronic Commerce' (25 January 2019) WT/L/1056 <https://docs.wto.org/dol2fe/Pages/FE_Search/FE_S_S009-DP.aspx?language=E&CatalogueIdList=251085,251084,251083,251082,251086,251022,251023,251024,251025,251037&CurrentCatalogueIdIndex=4&FullTextHash=371857150&HasEnglishRecord=True&HasFrenchRecord=False&HasSpanishRecord=False> accessed 10 July 2023.

century until the early twenty-first century, using the lens of discourse analysis. Section 3.3 introduces the way in which the discourse of digital trade labels restrictions on transfers of personal data (such as those adopted by the EU), as '(digital) protectionism'. Then, it extrapolates the logic of the reconstruction of the term 'protectionism' in the past on the claims to redefine 'protectionism' as 'digital protectionism'. Section 3.4 explicates how such discourse affects the baseline between data privacy protection and protectionism and influences the right normative rationale behind the regulation of privacy and personal data protection.

3.2 The Expansion of the Notion of 'Protectionism'

Although the notions of 'free trade' and 'protectionism' are among the oldest in economics,[33] there is no uniform understanding of what constitutes 'protectionism'.[34] This section analyses the notion of protectionism and shows that protectionism is not a natural phenomenon—it is a concept socially constructed within a particular discourse.

The core issue in defining protectionism is where to draw the line between regulation that is a precondition for trade (such as a state intervention aimed at correcting market failures, which is economically efficient and socially productive) and protectionist regulation which creates market failures and stifles trade.[35] As Bhagwati, one of the leading twentieth-century trade theorists, noted,

> [S]ince all policies will inevitably affect (directly or indirectly) comparative advantage and (in this sense) there is therefore no purely 'natural' or 'market-determined' comparative advantage, where *should* one draw the line and say that autonomy in this set of policies is fine but not in others?[36]

Eleven years later, Howse argued along similar lines that '[t]here is no natural or self-evident baseline or rule that can solve this basic dilemma'.[37] Defining what

[33] Johannes Overbeek, *Free Trade versus Protectionism* (Edward Elgar Publishing 1999), viii (hereafter Overbeek, *Free Trade versus Protectionism*).

[34] Susan Aaronson, 'What Are We Talking about When We Discuss Digital Protectionism?' (2017) Working Paper for the Economic Research Institute of Asia (Eria)' 1–4, 16, 19 <https://ssrn.com/abstract=3032108> accessed 10 July 2023 (hereafter Aaronson, 'What Are We Talking about When We Discuss Digital Protectionism?').

[35] See, eg, Jagdish N Bhagwati, *Protectionism* (The MIT Press 1989) 126 (hereafter Bhagwati, *Protectionism*).

[36] See Jagdish N Bhagwati, 'Threats to the World Trading Regime: Protectionism, Unfair Trade et al' in Ad Koekkoek and Ludovicus Bernardus Maria Mennes (eds), *International Trade and Global Development: Essays in Honour of Jagdish Bhagwati* (Routledge 1991) 237, 240–41 (hereafter Bhagwati, 'Threats to the World Trading Regime').

[37] See Robert Howse, 'From Politics to Technocracy--And Back Again: The Fate of the Multilateral Trading Regime' (2002) 96 American Journal of International Law 94, 95–96 (hereafter Howse, 'From Politics to Technocracy').

constitutes a precondition for free trade and what is a barrier to trade is, indeed, 'an interpretive act,' to use Lang's terminology.[38] As Tarullo explained, determining what constitutes a trade barrier and what does not depends on the assumption of '"normal" conditions of competitive markets' that is used as a benchmark to identify the deviations.[39] It is the discourse that predetermines what Lang calls 'collective habits of interpretation'[40] or 'the characteristic mindsets and ways of thinking'[41] and ultimately influences the definition of 'normal' market and protectionism. In other words, *defining protectionism is an act of interpretation that occurs within a certain discourse.*

Using a particular theoretical construction of protectionism has two important practical implications. First, such a construction informs the design of international trade rules—an example of this would be the non-discrimination provisions found in current international trade agreements.[42] Second, since these provisions are often phrased in broad and ambiguous terms, which are neither explained nor defined in the agreements,[43] *interpretation* by adjudicating bodies plays a crucial role in recognizing particular domestic policies and rules as 'legitimate' or 'protectionist'.[44] Hence, non-discrimination provisions will be interpreted

[38] See Andrew Lang, *World Trade Law after Neoliberalism* (OUP Online 2011) 169–70 (hereafter: Lang, *World Trade Law after Neoliberalism*):

Since virtually every conceivable form of governmental action has some direct or indirect impact on trade, the selection of a particular set of measures as 'barriers to trade' involves the application of principles of selection and categorization. Similarly, we draw distinctions between government actions which constitute trade 'distortions' on the one hand, and other kinds of government actions which correct pre-existing market distortions on the other.

[39] Daniel K Tarullo, 'Beyond Normalcy in the Regulation of International Trade' (1987) 100(3) Harvard Law Review 546, 549 (discussing trade laws of general application). ('These statutes are based on a regulatory model that assumes that deviations from market principles are "exceptional events"; they correct deviations from market principles by imposing extra duties to raise the low prices of imports to what they would (hypothetically) have been had the foreign producer been operating under "normal" conditions of competitive markets and non-distortion by government.'). See also Lang, *World Trade Law after Neoliberalism* (n 38) 227 (referring to a notion of an 'imagined ideal of a market' that is used as a reference point to characterize a particular governmental policy as a precondition for free trade or 'protectionism').

[40] Lang, *World Trade Law after Neoliberalism* (n 38) 170.

[41] ibid 173.

[42] See, eg, Article II General Agreement on Trade in Services, Annex 1B to Marrakesh Agreement Establishing the World Trade Organization [1994] 1869 UNTS. 183, 33 ILM 1167 (hereafter GATS), discussed in Section 2.3.1.1.

[43] See Daniel K Tarullo, 'Logic, Myth, and the International Economic Order' (1985) 26 Harvard Law Review 533, 535–36 (arguing that 'legal principles are generally indeterminate' and that '[p]olitical or ideological choices are embodied in doctrines that promise a faithful implementation of the principles themselves'.) Using Article I of the General Agreement on Tariffs and Trade, 30 October 1947, 61 Stat A-11, 55 UNTS 194 (hereafter GATT 1947), which codified the principle of non-discrimination in international trade, Tarullo illustrates that the non-discrimination principle 'cannot be administered without political choices about legitimate national policies [and t]he rule cannot be explained or justified simply by reference to the aim of increased trade or the principle of equality'. ibid 536–41.

[44] See, eg, Robert Howse, 'The World Trade Organization 20 Years On: Global Governance by Judiciary' (2016) 27(1) European Journal of International Law 9, 47 (hereafter Howse, 'The World Trade Organization 20 Years On') ('The text of the national treatment provisions of the GATT requires that the adjudicator decide whether less favourable treatment is provided for "like" imported products and/or, in the case of taxation measures only, whether dissimilar treatment is provided for directly competitive and substitutable products'.).

in a broad or narrow sense, largely under the influence of the discourse governing such interpretation.

Against this backdrop, this section shows how shifts in the dominant economic discourse have affected the redefinition of the notion of protectionism. It also demonstrates how such a redefinition has influenced the substance and interpretation of international trade rules, which ultimately *transformed the very goal of the international trade system—from economic stability to liberalization of trade*. This transformation has led to a *shrinking regulatory space left to domestic legal regimes by international trade rules*. It is, however, not the purpose of this section to provide a comprehensive account of all aspects of protectionism in a historical perspective. Instead, this section focuses on the key milestones of the evolution of protectionism to illustrate how the boundaries of discourse and its underlying goals and values affect the predominant conceptualization of protectionism and the functioning of the international trading system. It starts in the mid-eighteenth century with the birth of the classical free trade movement, moves forward to the 1940s and the formation of the first multilateral trading system, and ends with a discussion of the neoliberal discourse which originated in the late 1960s and remained the dominant discourse until recently. Before moving on to a historical account of the evolution of protectionism in Section 3.2.2, however, the following section introduces the key disagreements on the notion of protectionism that weave their way throughout the discussion.

3.2.1 Defining protectionism: The key disagreement

Historically, the main disagreement in understanding what protectionism is lies in the determination of whether protectionism is a subjective or an objective notion. This general disagreement is apparent in the question of whether the *regulatory intent* underlying a domestic regulatory measure that discriminates against foreign competitors matters for the purpose of qualifying such a measure as protectionist.[45]

[45] Compare Alan O Sykes, 'Regulatory Protection and the Law of International Trade' (1999) 66(1) The University of Chicago Law Review 1, 3 (hereafter Sykes, 'Regulatory Protection and the Law of International Trade') (taking an objective approach to protectionism; 'defin[ing] "regulatory protectionism" as any cost disadvantage imposed on foreign firms by a regulatory policy that discriminates against them or that otherwise disadvantages them *in a manner that is unnecessary* to the attainment of some genuine, *nonprotectionist* regulatory objective'; specifically underscoring that in order to qualify as protectionist such regulatory policy 'need not be deliberate and may result simply from regulators' failure to appreciate the trade impact of their policies') (emphasis added), with Douglas A Irwin, *Against the Tide: An Intellectual History of Free Trade* (Princeton UP 1996) 5 (hereafter Irwin, *Against the Tide*) (defining a policy of protection as governmental policies discriminating against imported goods 'in favor of those produced within the country, *usually with the aim* of sheltering domestic producers from foreign competition through tariffs, quantitative restrictions, or other import barriers'.) (emphasis added). While the definition of Sykes puts an emphasis on the *effects* of a regulatory policy, that of Irwin focuses on the *aim* of such policy.

Related questions are *how much* or *how little* protection of domestic industries is sufficient to render regulation protectionist and who bears the burden of proof that a particular regulation is protectionist: the foreign state affected by the measure or the state that has adopted the regulation? As this chapter shows, the answers to these questions have a profound effect on the breadth of the regulatory autonomy left to domestic regulatory regimes by international trade law in order to pursue important societal or public policy objectives, such as protection of human health, the environment, and public morals.[46]

An objective approach to defining protectionism captures a much broader range of regulatory measures, namely any measure that may *de facto* result in discrimination between domestic and foreign firms irrespective of its aim, even if such discrimination is incidental.[47] An objective approach also tends to impose the burden of proving that regulation is not protectionist on the party that has adopted the regulation.[48] The subjective approach, in contrast, only covers regulation intending to shelter domestic markets from foreign competition and places the burden of proof of such intent on the party alleging the protectionist nature of another party's measure.[49]

3.2.2 Protectionism and the classical free trade idea

As a driver of policy, free trade dates back to classical doctrines based on the theories of absolute and comparative advantage developed by Adam Smith and David Ricardo, who argued that just like individuals, countries could gain from international trade by exchanging goods that each country can produce at a lower cost.[50] As summarized by Irwin, 'free trade describes a policy of the nation-state

[46] See Sections 3.3.5 and 3.4.

[47] See Sykes, 'Regulatory Protection and the Law of International Trade' (n 45) 3–4 (providing examples of 'facially neutral regulation[s]' that instituted not *de jure* but *de facto* discrimination, for example, a pharmaceutical regulation 'requir[ing] foreign pharmaceutical manufacturers to engage in more testing and clinical trials than domestic manufacturers with no apparent health justification for this difference in treatment'.).

[48] See, eg, Lang, *World Trade Law after Neoliberalism* (n 38) 268–69 (illustrating WTO panel cases that exemplify how the country that has adopted the challenged regulation has had to show that the regulation is not protectionist, for example, one case regarding Thailand's 'import restrictions and internal taxes on imported cigarettes' and another case regarding France's 'ban on products containing asbestos for public health reasons').

[49] See, eg, ibid 211–14 (illustrating WTO panel cases in which the challenging country had to argue why the other country's measures were intentionally discriminatory and thus illegitimate, for example, one regarding a Pakistani challenge to an Indian measure that Pakistan believed intentionally discriminated against Pakistan, and another regarding a Danish and Norwegian challenge to a Belgian measure that Denmark and Norway believed intentionally discriminated against Denmark and Norway).

[50] Adam Smith, 'Of the Opinion That No Expense at Home Can Be Hurtful' in Edwin Cannan (ed), *Lectures on Justice, Politice, Revenue and Arms* (Clarendon Press 1869) 207, 209 (advocating that eighteenth-century Britain should be 'a free port,' government should not interfere in free trade by measures 'of any kind,' and 'free commerce and liberty of exchange should be allowed with all nations, and for all things'.) See also Adam Smith, 'Of the Balance of Trade' in Edwin Cannan (ed), *Lectures on Justice, Police, Revenue and Arms* (Clarendon Press 1869) 204 ('All commerce that is carried on betwixt

toward international commerce in which trade barriers are absent, implying no restrictions on the import of goods from other countries or restraints on the export of domestic goods to other markets'.[51] While free trade is associated with efficiency gains, barriers to trade are seen as sources of lost gains from trade.[52] The main benchmarks around which classical economic discourse on free international trade revolves are economic efficiency and welfare.[53] With its focus primarily on the enhancement of aggregate national wealth, the logic of comparative advantage does not take into account concerns of distributive justice or morals.[54]

In classical economics, the doctrines of free trade and protectionism are thus fundamentally opposed, as they offer radically different perspectives on the best way to promote a nation's (and the world's) welfare: free trade, by maintaining the utmost freedom of trade between the countries, and protectionism (or mercantilism), by restricting imports, promoting domestic industries, and maintaining self-sufficiency from other countries.[55] Developed in the age of the formation of nation-states in Europe, mercantilist theory aimed to strengthen the power of the state and the accumulation of wealth by stimulating exports and limiting imports.[56] The free trade paradigm developed by Smith and Ricardo was used to oppose and then supplant mercantilism,[57] which dominated trade policy in the

any two countries must necessarily be advantageous to both.'); Howse, 'From Politics to Technocracy' (n 37) 94 ('The Ricardian theory of comparative advantage dictated the removal of import restrictions in almost all circumstances, regardless of any commitment of one's trading partners to liberalize *their* imports.').

[51] Irwin, *Against the Tide* (n 45) 5.

[52] See Howse, 'From Politics to Technocracy' (n 37) 94. ('Smith and Ricardo were concerned in the first instance to disprove the conventional or established mercantilist view that national *wealth* was reduced by (unilateral) free trade, and while they had many important reflections on the relationship of wealth to morals and justice, the basic logic of the theory of comparative advantage does not depend on any of those insights.'). Jan Tumlir, *Protectionism: Trade Policy in Democratic Societies* (American Enterprise Institute for Public Policy Research 1985) 4 (hereafter Tumlir, *Protectionism: Trade Policy in Democratic Societies*) ('Protection imposes costs on the trading economies; when trade restrictions begin to multiply among the main markets, the costs are compounded. When restriction nears the extent indicated, these costs could be large enough to be considered a major cause of the decline in economic growth.')

[53] See Irwin, *Against the Tide* (n 45) 4 ('Debates surrounding the economics of free trade and protection all revolve around the question of efficiency: how does a particular trade policy affect a country's ability to use its limited resources (in terms of primary factors of production, such as land, labor, and capital) to produce the greatest possible real income, which in turn enables it to procure a larger set of all goods.').

[54] See generally ibid 40–41 (providing examples of 'noneconomic arguments for protection that are a perennial feature of trade policy debates'). 'Critics of the economic approach frequently contend that the criterion of wealth is too narrowly materialistic and excludes other more important societal considerations'. ibid.

[55] Overbeek, *Free Trade versus Protectionism* (n 33) viii ('[T]he two doctrines of free trade and protectionism are fundamentally opposed.').

[56] ibid 1–2 ('The two major aims of mercantilist theory and policy were (1) the strengthening of the power of the state (political) and (2) the accumulation of wealth (economic) [M]any of the policy proposals of mercantilist writers consisted of recommendations as to how to stimulate exports and hamper imports.').

[57] See Howse, 'From Politics to Technocracy' (n 37) 94 ('Smith and Ricardo were concerned in the first instance to disprove the conventional or established mercantilist view that national wealth was

early eighteenth century.[58] This shift in the dominant economic ideology was not purely a result of progress in economic thought but a reflection of a '"shared vision" among political economists of Britain's economic future' that represented the views of certain interest groups in Britain at that time.[59] As Venzke notes,

> [i]t is not a coincidence that David Ricardo and others advocated trade liberalization and an international division of labour at a time in which Britain could become the 'Workshop of the World', the centre of valuable production. Members of the British Parliament clearly saw the appeal of free trade so that 'foreign nations would become Colonies to us, without imposing on us the responsibility of governing them'.[60]

3.2.3 Protectionism and 'embedded liberalism' of GATT 1947

During the inter-war period, protectionism was mostly conceptualized in its narrow form, namely as tariffs, import quotas, and exchange controls.[61] In

reduced by (unilateral) free trade'); David Schmidtz, 'Adam Smith on the Dark Side of Capitalism' (2013) 11 Georgetown Journal of Law & Public Policy 371, 378 ('Smith is remembered as a defender of free trade, but his practical goal was to repudiate mercantilism's way of protecting domestic industry'.); see also Nadia Elizabeth Nedzel, 'Rule of Law v. Legal State: Where Have We Come from, Where Are We Going To?' in James R Silkennat, James E Hickey Jr, and Peter D Barenboim (eds), *The Legal Doctrines of the Rule of Law and the Legal State (Rechtsstaat)* (Springer International Publishing 2016) 306 (hereafter Nedzel, 'Rule of Law v. Legal State') ('Adam Smith, in the Wealth of Nations (1776), challenged mercantilism'.).

58 See Nedzel, 'Rule of Law v. Legal State' (n 57) 305 (suggesting the prevalence of mercantilism in the eighteenth century) ('From the sixteenth to the eighteenth century, it was assumed that the amount of gold and silver amassed indicated a nation's wealth and power, and that the world's capital was static'.). 'Since the GATT was designed to be merely a multilateral treaty, it would be similar to the bilateral treaties that preceded it, but designed to operate under the umbrella of the ITO, when the ITO came into being. The general clauses of GATT were the same as those in the chapter of the draft ITO charter which was devoted to trading rules, which in turn had been heavily influenced by clauses in bilateral trade treaties.' ibid. See also Lang, *World Trade Law after Neoliberalism* (n 38) 28 (referring to the Havana Charter, which was the draft of the ITO).

59 Leonard Gomes, *The Economics and Ideology of Free Trade: A Historical Review* (Edward Elgar 2003) 45–46 ('The attitude to foreign trade encapsulated in the principle of comparative costs sprang not only from developments in economic theory but reflected a '*shared vision*' among political economists of Britain's economic future. It so happened that this coincided with the *interests of the new and rising industrial bourgeoisie*'.) (emphasis added); see also Joan Robinson, 'What Are the Questions?' (1977) 15(4) Journal of Economic Literature 1318, 1336 ('When Ricardo set out the case against protection, he was supporting British economic interests.').

60 Ingo Venzke, 'International Law and the Spectre of Inequality' (2019) Inaugural Lecture No 607, University of Amsterdam, 8 < https://dare.uva.nl/search?identifier=a4b88a14-4772-4974-8123-346689262258> accessed 10 July 2023, quoting Bernard Semmel, *The Rise of Free Trade Imperialism: Classical Political Economy, the Empire of Free Trade and Imperialism* (CUP 1970) 8.

61 See, eg, Barry Eichengreen and Douglas A Irwin, 'The Slide to Protectionism in the Great Depression: Who Succumbed and Why?' (2010) 70(4) The Journal of Economic History 871, 871 ('The Great Depression of the 1930s was marked by a severe outbreak of protectionist trade policies. Governments around the world imposed tariffs, import quotas, and exchange controls to restrict spending on foreign goods.').

addition, protectionism was associated with political nationalism, heavy interference by government in economic life, and the quest for increased self-sufficiency that characterized the developed countries' domestic policies at the time.[62]

In 1947, the General Agreement on Tariffs and Trade ('GATT 1947')[63] was signed.[64] It incorporated the trade policy chapter of the charter of the International Trade Organization ('ITO'), the treaty establishing an organization that never saw the light of day.[65] As a legal instrument, GATT 1947 codified efforts to curb protectionist policy. However, GATT 1947 had broader purposes as well. It was executed to avoid future trade wars (similar to those that occurred in the 1930s, and were, in part, seen as a cause of WWII);[66] to preserve international peace; and to prevent the spread of Communism.[67] The newly created trade rules were not about 'comparative advantage as such' but rather about 'the avoidance of protectionist *summum malum*' (or 'beggar-thy-neighbour' policies), that is, when trade barriers introduced by one country led to a chain reaction of trade barriers introduced by other states.[68] In this sense, the post-war trading system only partially remained faithful to the neoclassical free trade idea.[69]

[62] See Overbeek, *Free Trade versus Protectionism* (n 33) 633–34 (stating that up to 1939, 'the belief in political and economic classical liberalism was broken. The prevailing climate of opinion moved increasingly towards a greater role for government, which meant more neo-mercantilism, statism and interventionism'). In the late 1920s and early 1930s, the United States adopted the interventionist New Deal; England ended its free trade policies introduced in the late nineteenth century; Russia, Germany, Italy, and Japan 'adopted totalitarian institutions, subordinating the individual to the state'. ibid.

[63] GATT 1947 (n 43). Throughout this chapter, GATT 1947 refers to the legal text. GATT (without the year) refers to the organization that administered GATT 1947, as well as the agreements and codes that came later, until 1995 when the WTO took over.

[64] WTO, 'Fiftieth Anniversary of the Multilateral Trading System' 27 October 1997 <https://www.wto.org/english/news_e/pres97_e/pr81_e.htm> accessed 10 July 2023.

[65] See John H Jackson, *The World Trade Organization: Constitution and Jurisprudence* (The Royal Institute of International Affairs 1998) 17 (hereafter Jackson, *The World Trade Organization*).

[66] See Douglas A Irwin, Petros C Mavroidis, and Alan O Sykes, *The Genesis of the GATT* (New York: CUP 2008) 5–6 ('To understand the origins of the GATT, one must appreciate the traumatic events of the 1920s and 1930. Although monetary and financial factors were primarily responsible for allowing the recession to turn into the Great Depression of the early 1930s, the spread of trade restrictions aggravated the problem. The commercial policies of the 1930s became characterized as "beggar-thy-neighbor" policies because many countries sought to insulate their own economy from the economic downturn by raising trade barriers.').

See also Lang, *World Trade Law after Neoliberalism* (n 38) 196–97 ('GATT was in part understood as a way of maintaining Western unity during the Cold War, by placing it on a firm and stable economic footing. The fundamental and primary purpose of the post-war regime was international stability, in the specific sense of preventing a repeat of the disastrous trade wars of early 1930s.'); Howse, 'From Politics to Technocracy' (n 37) 94–95 ('A paramount goal is the avoidance of a protectionist *summum malum*—the situation where domestic social or economic pressures lead some states to *increase* or *re-instate* barriers to trade, thus triggering a competitive reaction in kind by other states, and eventually a "race to the bottom" that is disastrous for the global economy'.).

[67] See Lang, *World Trade Law after Neoliberalism* (n 38) 196 footnote 4.

[68] Howse, 'From Politics to Technocracy' (n 37) 103 ('After all … trade law in its original postwar form was not about comparative advantage as such, but about constraining destructive interdependence—of which a race to the bottom is one form'.) See also ibid 94–95; Lang, *World Trade Law after Neoliberalism* (n 38)190–92.

[69] See Howse, 'From Politics to Technocracy' (n 37) 94–95 (discussing how international trade law was not only concerned with 'the classic insights about the gains to wealth and welfare from free trade,' but also the '*interdependency* of different states' trade and other economic policies … .'). 'The postwar

The discursive foundations of the GATT 1947 were not monochromatic; they were laid as a compromise between the two discourses (or 'philosophies,' according to Lang)[70] that influenced its development.[71] On the one hand, according to the discourse advanced by the United States, protectionism was to blame for the Great Depression of the 1930s and the trade wars that 'led in a straight line to the outbreak of the Second World War,' and that discriminatory trade undermined peace.[72] On the other hand, another discourse, advanced by the United Kingdom and influenced by Keynesian thinking, emphasized the boundaries that the international trade regime should not cross in relation to domestic policies affecting trade: in particular, the discourse advocated that an important aspect of an international trade regime is the ability of the state to impose trade restrictions to ensure full employment and domestic economic stability.[73] The delicate compromise between these two views shaped the discourse of 'embedded liberalism'[74]—a term coined by Ruggie,[75] which he described as follows:

> The essence of embedded liberalism ... is to devise a form of multilateralism that is compatible with the requirements of domestic stability. Presumably, then, governments so committed would seek to encourage an international division of labor which, while multilateral in form and reflecting *some* notion of comparative advantage (and therefore gains from trade), *also* promised to minimize socially disruptive domestic adjustment costs as well as any national economic and political vulnerabilities that might accrue from international functional differentiation. However, as neoclassical trade theory defines the term, the overall social profitability of this division of labor will be lower than of the one produced by laissez-faire.[76] (emphasis in the original)

trade and financial order was therefore mainly designed to enable states to manage their domestic economies, in a manner consistent with political and social stability and justice, without the risk of setting off a protectionist race to the bottom'. ibid.

[70] Lang, *World Trade Law after Neoliberalism* (n 38)192 ('There were, broadly speaking, two "philosophies" which emerged at this time, with somewhat different interpretations of the causes and consequences of commercial policy during the 1930s, and different prescriptions for the post-war trading order [B]oth of these philosophies had an important influence on the post-war GATT regime.'). For further discussion, see ibid 24–29 and 192–94.

[71] See ibid 192.

[72] See ibid 192–93.

[73] See ibid 194.

[74] See ibid.

[75] John Gerard Ruggie, 'International Regimes, Transactions, and Change: Embedded Liberalism in the Postwar Economic Order (1982) 36(2) International Organization 379, 392 (hereafter Ruggie, 'International Regimes, Transactions and Change') ('The liberalism that was restored after World War II differed in kind from that which had been known previously. *My term for it is "embedded liberalism"*.') (emphasis added).

[76] ibid 399.

Hence, contrary to the (neo)classical case for free trade discussed above, the discourse of 'embedded liberalism' leaned towards the subjective—and, therefore, narrower—understanding of 'protectionism'.[77] This matters because 'embedded liberalism' was not only reflected in the characteristics and design of the GATT 1947,[78] but it also governed the operation of GATT 1947 for at least two decades after its inception.[79] Put another way, during that period, trade *liberalization* was less important as a goal in itself; it was a component of a broader societal goal of maintaining economic stability.[80]

Although the non-discrimination provisions of the GATT 1947 were formulated broadly,[81] in the first two decades of the existence of GATT 1947 and the dominance of the discourse of 'embedded liberalism', they were interpreted narrowly.[82] Only those discriminatory measures that were 'explicitly or implicitly motivated by a protectionist *intent*' were considered to violate the non-discrimination provisions and thus qualified as protectionism.[83] In other words, the subjective

[77] See Irwin, *Against the Tide* (n 45) 5 (defining the subjective understanding of protectionism) (defining a policy of protection as governmental policies discriminating against imported goods 'in favor of those produced within the country, *usually with the aim* of sheltering domestic producers from foreign competition through tariffs, quantitative restrictions, or other import barriers'.) (emphasis added).

[78] See Lang, *World Trade Law after Neoliberalism* (n 38) 195 ('Key players in the negotiations shared a common view of the legitimacy of state intervention to secure domestic stability, even if they disagreed on the precise form and depth that that intervention should take in particular circumstances'.); see also Howse, 'From Politics to Technocracy' (n 37) 94–95. ('The postwar trade and financial order was therefore mainly designed to enable states to manage their domestic economies, in a manner consistent with political and social stability and justice, without the risk of setting off a protectionist race to the bottom. The legal structure of the General Agreement on Tariffs and Trade (GATT) was designed to facilitate such concessions and make them binding, but it did not require them.').

[79] See Lang, *World Trade Law after Neoliberalism* (n 38) 205 ('These shared ideas were reflected in a set of characteristic institutional forms, social practices, and legal structures which more or less endured over the first two decades of the GATT's existence.'). These 'shared ideas', however, represented the compromise of the Global North and did not factor in the views of countries from the Global South, such as India. Instead of being normalized, Global South countries' preferences were framed as 'special and differential treatment'. ibid. See also Nicolas Lamp, 'How Some Countries Became 'Special': Developing Countries and the Construction of Difference in Multilateral Trade Lawmaking (2015) 18(4) Journal of International Economic Law 743, 745–52, 770.

[80] See Lang, *World Trade Law after Neoliberalism* (n 38) 197 ('[A]lthough the removal of trade barriers was of course an important intermediate purpose of the regime, liberalization was in fact a less important norm during the first two decades of the trade regime's history than is often assumed. Liberalization was pursued not through the application of a rigid principle, but only as far as states were practically able, and only as far as was consistent with the broader norm of economic stability.').

[81] See ibid 208 ('It takes only a moment's reflection to see how broad and intrusive these disciplines had the potential to be'.); see also, eg, Robert E Hudec, *The GATT Legal System and World Trade Diplomacy* (2nd edn, Butterworths 1990) 121 (stating that paragraph 4 of Article III GATT 1947, which contains a national treatment provision, 'covered every internal law and regulation affecting commercial movement of goods, an area that is virtually unlimited in scope').

[82] See Lang, *World Trade Law after Neoliberalism* (n 38) 211 (arguing that orientation towards embedded liberalism 'produced a field of trade law and policy which was narrowly defined (relative to the present day), focused on tariffs and other kinds of trade measures understood at the time as quantitative restrictions, and unwilling to scrutinize "internal" measures except in the clearest circumstances of circumvention of liberalization commitments'.).

[83] See ibid 254 ('From this perspective, the non-discrimination norm contained in Article III of the GATT is essentially an "anti-protectionism" norm and ought to be applied solely to those internal measures which are expressly or implicitly motivated by a protectionist intent'.) (emphasis added); see also Jurgen Kurtz, *The WTO and International Investment Law: Converging Systems* (CUP 2016) 137

view based on regulatory intent had legal significance in the assessment of the protectionist character of a domestic measure challenged under the GATT 1947.[84]

The discourse of 'embedded liberalism'—reflecting the broad consensus on the goals of the multilateral trading system—also governed the practice of challenging other countries' domestic regulations.[85] In the first decades after the formation of GATT 1947, domestic policies that only indirectly intervened with international trade typically were not challenged as inconsistent with international trade rules.[86] In line with this consensus, contracting parties to the GATT 1947 did not resort to trade disciplines in order to 'reshape domestic state-market relations'.[87]

3.2.4 The new protectionism and the neoliberal discourse: Towards an ever-broader conceptualization of 'protectionism'

3.2.4.1 The 'new protectionism'

The notion of protectionism has become much more capacious, a gradual process that began in the early 1970s. In the trade economics literature, the term '*new* protectionism' was coined to refer to a broader range of domestic measures restricting international trade.[88] Unlike traditional protectionism, the new version included not only the more traditional or mercantilist restrictions on trade but also non-tariff barriers ('NTBs,' or 'behind the border' barriers) to trade, such as negotiated

(hereafter Kurtz, *The WTO and International Investment Law*) ('GATT members were free to regulate domestically (behind-the-border) as they saw fit to do so. Trade law would only strike down such interventions if poisoned by protectionist animus'.); Howse, 'From Politics to Technocracy' (n 37) 97 ('The notion of "discrimination" against trading partners seems closely linked to the very idea of protectionism, though in some cases one may discriminate for non-protectionist reasons, which is why at least as a preliminary sorting or sifting mechanism, the nondiscrimination norm has a certain durability and putative legitimacy'.).

[84] See Lang, *World Trade Law after Neoliberalism* (n 38) 211; Howse, 'From Politics to Technocracy' (n 37) 97.

[85] See Ruggie, 'International Regimes, Transactions and Change' (n 75) 399 (describing the 'essence of embedded liberalism'); Lang, *World Trade Law after Neoliberalism* (n 38) 195, 205, 211 (arguing that orientation towards embedded liberalism 'produced a field of trade law and policy which was narrowly defined (relative to the present day), focused on tariffs and other kinds of trade measures understood at the time as quantitative restrictions, and unwilling to scrutinize "internal" measures except in the clearest circumstances of circumvention of liberalization commitments'.).

[86] For a discussion, see Lang, *World Trade Law after Neoliberalism* (n 38) 214–16.

[87] Ibid 215–16 ('[T]oo intrusive an application of GATT disciplines on internal regulation would *undermine* that purpose, as it would run the risk of itself upsetting the delicate balance of concessions embodied in the original agreement, and undermining support for the trading system as a whole'.).

[88] See Dominick Salvatore, 'Protectionism and World Welfare: Introduction' in Dominick Salvatore (ed), *Protectionism and World Welfare* (CUP 1993) 1 (hereafter Salvatore, 'Protectionism and World Welfare: Introduction') ('This phrase, coined in the mid 1970s, refers to the revival of 'mercantilism' whereby nations, particularly the industrial nations, attempt to solve or alleviate their problems of unemployment, lagging growth, and declining industries by imposing restrictions on imports and subsidizing exports'.).

or 'voluntary' export restraining arrangements, and measures allegedly abusing the GATT 1947 non-discrimination provisions, such as anti-dumping measures.[89]

Trade economists also viewed the 'new protectionism' as different in another important respect.[90] While the old protectionism of the 1930s was characterized as 'unsystematic, improvised, and at the end, a result of panic', the 'new protectionism' was seen to be *driven by strong politically organized forces* representing the interests of domestic industries.[91] This approach, as this chapter shows in greater detail later, had a major impact on the acceptability (under trade law) of key domestic policy measures.

Authoritative trade economists have described the rise of non-tariff barriers as a form of circumvention of GATT 1947 disciplines,[92] linked to the tendency of the United States to palliate the decline of its economic dominance (a 'diminished giant syndrome,' in the words of Bhagwati)[93] and to suppress increasing competition from less developed, newly industrializing countries.[94] A number of those countries imposed barriers to US exports in areas where the United States had a comparative advantage, especially knowledge-intensive industries and services.[95]

[89] See Bhagwati, *Protectionism* (n 35) 43–53 (conceptualizing NTBs in the form of domestic regulation on countervailing duties and anti-dumping provisions that was seen as being restrictively used against foreign suppliers); see also Bhagwati, 'Threats to the World Trading Regime' (n 36) 239 (distinguishing between two classes of non-tariff barriers: (1) barriers bypassing the GATT 1947 rules, which include visibly and politically negotiated voluntary export restraints and other export restraining arrangements (eg import quotas, nonautomatic licensing, and variable levies); and (2) protectionist 'captured' provisions that have a legitimate role in a free trade regime (eg countervailing duties and anti-dumping provisions) but are used to 'harass unfairly their successful foreign rivals and thus to deter fair competition and free trade'.); Overbeek, *Free Trade versus Protectionism* (n 33) 555.

[90] See Tumlir, *Protectionism: Trade Policy in Democratic Societies* (n 52) 38–39.

[91] See ibid ('Protectionism in the 1930's was unsystematic, improvised, and at the end, a result of panic. The new protectionism is a very different animal. It has been growing gradually. Industries have used intelligent, long-term planning in creating an expanded system of protection. [T]he new protectionism is politically stronger because it accommodates a broader range of interests'.).

[92] Robert E Baldwin, 'The New Protectionism: A Response to Shifts in National Economic Power' (1986) National Bureau of Economic Research, Working Paper No 1823 <https://www.nber.org/papers/w1823.pdf> accessed 10 July 2023, 1 (hereafter Baldwin, 'The New Protectionism') ('The international trading economy is in the anomalous condition of diminishing tariff protection but the increasing use of nontariff trade-distorting measures'.).

[93] See, eg, Jagdish Bhagwati, 'The Diminished Giant Syndrome' (1993) 72(2) Foreign Affairs 22, 22 (hereafter Bhagwati, 'The Diminished Giant Syndrome') ('America has been struck by a "diminished giant syndrome"—reinforced by the slippage in the growth of its living standards in the 1980s. This affliction has caused a loss of confidence in America's inherited postwar trade policies'.); see also Jagdish N Bhagwati, 'Fair Trade, Reciprocity, and Harmonization: The Novel Challenge to the Theory and Policy of Free Trade' in Dominick Salvatore (ed), *Protectionism and World Welfare* (CUP 1993) 39 (hereafter Bhagwati, 'Fair Trade, Reciprocity, and Harmonization') ('Many of my examples [of demands for fair trade] come from the United States where the diminished giant syndrome has prompted an acute search for unfair trade by others'.).

[94] Baldwin, 'The New Protectionism' (n 92) 1, 20 ('[N]ew nontariff protectionism [is related] to significant structural changes in world industrial production that have brought about a decline in the dominant economic position of the United States, a concomitant rise to international economic prominence of the European Economic Community and Japan, and the emergence of a group of newly industrializing developing countries (NICs)'.)

[95] See Howse, 'The World Trade Organization 20 Years On: Global Governance by Judiciary' (n 44) 17 ('[M]any barriers worldwide hampered America in exploiting its apparent contemporary comparative advantage in knowledge-intensive industries and services. In some, intellectual property was

In addition, new protectionism was viewed as a means of alleviating domestic stability issues, such as growing unemployment and inability, due to economic decline, to deliver on the social obligations of the expanded welfare states.[96] Recall from Section 3.2.3 that it was precisely these measures that were seen as legitimate and not, therefore, protectionist in the 'embedded liberalism' discourse.[97]

In the new protectionism, free trade theorists saw a threat to the legitimacy and to the very existence of the multilateral trading system associated with post-war prosperity and economic growth.[98] Recalling the disastrous consequences of protectionism in the 1930s, Bhagwati, one of the most influential trade theorists of the time, warned that this new protectionism would, just like its predecessor, trigger beggar-thy-neighbour policies and result in new trade wars.[99]

3.2.4.2 'Fair trade'

3.2.4.2.1 The 'new protectionism' in 'fair trade' clothing

Alongside the new protectionism discourse within US business and governmental circles during the 1970s, measures characterized as new protectionism were increasingly re-framed as means to curtail 'unfair trade practices' from (primarily) developing countries.[100] From this perspective, trade-restricting practices, such as import controls and voluntary export restraints, labelled as new protectionism by trade economists, were presented as *responses* to unfair trade.[101] Implicitly using

largely unprotected; in most, competition in network services, such as in telecommunications and finance, was severely restricted or limited, while many others still imposed byzantine and archaic regulatory requirements on products, both imported and domestic. In many cases, a business presence in the other country was necessary for the full exploitation of comparative advantage, and here American firms faced severe foreign investment restrictions.').

[96] See Salvatore, 'Protectionism and World Welfare: Introduction' (n 88) 9; see also Overbeek, *Free Trade versus Protectionism* (n 33) 553–55.

[97] See, eg, Lang, *World Trade Law after Neoliberalism* (n 38) 29, 192–205; Ruggie, 'International Regimes, Transactions and Change' (n 75) 399.

[98] Baldwin, 'The New Protectionism' (n 92) 1 ('[New protectionism] is taking place largely outside the framework of GATT and threatens to undermine the liberal international trading regime established after World War II.') For further discussion, see also Bhagwati, 'Threats to the World Trading Regime' (n 36) 238–44.

[99] See also Bhagwati, 'Threats to the World Trading Regime' (n 36) 238–44. But see Strange, 'Protectionism and World Politics' (n 25) 254–55 ('[T]he next few years will show whether world trade can continue to survive despite the deadlock in the GATT and despite a certain amount of increased protectionism. My contention is that a combination of political and economic interests, reinforced by structural change in the international division of labor brought about by the mobility of capital and technology, is preventing a world depression from seriously arresting or reversing the steady growth in world trade.').

[100] Subsidies, dumping practices, and other discriminatory rules disfavouring US (and other) imports are examples of such 'unfair trade practices'. See Baldwin, 'The New Protectionism' (n 92) 16–19; see also ibid 18 ('*The emphasis on the great need for fair trade* is evident in the 1974 legislation authorizing U.S. participation in the Tokyo Round of multilateral negotiations.') (emphasis added).

[101] See ibid 18–19 ('The most important protectionist action taken by the United States since the late 1960's, namely, the gradual tightening of controls over steel imports, has also been justified mainly on the grounds of unfair trade practices by foreign producers. When a series of voluntary export restraint agreements with leading steel-exporting nations were concluded in late 1984, a spokesperson for the U.S. Trade Representative stated, "We are responding to unfair trade in the U.S.; defending yourself

its domestic market as a primary reference point, the United States used the 'fair trade' discourse to argue that any commercially significant institutional or regulatory difference between its domestic regime and that of other countries distorted the conditions of competition and constituted barriers to US exports.[102] Bhagwati, in contrast, viewed these claims as nothing more than a different rhetoric of protectionist demands in order to make lobbying efforts more successful.[103]

Guided by the new fair trade narrative, the US government saw the changing mission of international trade law as the elimination of unfair trade practices through, in particular, the harmonization (or 'globalization') of a broad range of domestic regulatory frameworks that affect international trade.[104] Demands for 'level playing fields,' 'harmonization,' and 'fair trade' more generally worried trade economists, who saw in such demands a threat to the feasibility of trade liberalization. Not only did these trade economists consider it to be impossible to harmonize every aspect of domestic regulation, but they also argued that it was in these differences between domestic regimes that lay the source of the comparative advantages that make trade beneficial in the first place.[105]

against unfair trade is not, in our opinion, protectionism". The unfair trade argument has been used in support of most other trade-restricting or trade-promoting actions taken by the United States in recent years.').

102 Lang, *World Trade Law after Neoliberalism* (n 38) 227 ('In practice, when one country alleges that another country's measure is an unfair trade practice (or trade distortion), it will implicitly use the institutional form of its own domestic market as the primary reference point against which fairness and distortions are measured.... The result is that the notion of a 'trade distortion' comes to be equated in practice with the existence of a commercially significant institutional or regulatory difference between countries.').

103 See eg also Bhagwati, 'Threats to the World Trading Regime' (n 36) 239 ('[I]f protectionists demand protection, they will today confront politicians who are generally hesitant to supply it because it is not comfortable to be called "protectionist." However, if you cry "foul" and allege that the foreign rival is resorting to "unfair" trade practices and therefore you need protection, your chances of successful lobbying are much greater. Protectionists have increasingly come to appreciate this and to shift their style of complaints accordingly to "unfair trade", opening this notion to ever more areas of concern (eg workers' rights enforcement by foreign countries).'). See also Bhagwati, *Protectionism* (n 35) 123–24 ('The insidious growth of the "fairness" issue poses a yet more disturbing threat to freer trade.').

104 Baldwin, 'The New Protectionism' (n 92) 18 ('In reshaping the proposal of the president [for the Tokyo Round of multilateral negotiations], the Congress stressed that the president should seek "to harmonize, reduce, or eliminate" nontariff trade barriers and tighten GATT rules with respect to fair trading practices. Officials in the executive branch supported these directives not only on their merits but because they deflected attention from more patently protectionist policies.').

105 See Bhagwati, 'Fair Trade, Reciprocity, and Harmonization' (n 93) 18 ('[T]he true and greater crisis that we face with regard to the theory and policy of free trade today comes ... from the growth of demand for "level playing fields", "harmonization", "fair trade", etc., all of which are variously undermining insidiously the legitimacy and feasibility of free trade since it is virtually impossible to harmonize everything so that playing fields are truly level in every way. There will always be something that an opponent of free trade will be able to find that is different in the country of one's successful rival and hence can be argued to make free trade unfair and therefore illegitimate and unacceptable.'). See also Bhagwati, 'Threats to the World Trading Regime' (n 36) 240 ('If differences in national institutions and policies can affect comparative advantage, as they surely can, and if these are now increasingly cited as sources of unfair trade (as they are), then we may be seriously eroding the possibility of free trade and leading towards "managed trade" or towards free trade only when a great deal of policy harmonization has occurred (as in the European Community (EC)).').

In sum, the 'new protectionism' in 'fair trade' clothing 'provided the enabling conditions and leverage for a radical renegotiation of the international rules that had undergirded the profound global economic transformations of the previous era.'[106]

3.2.4.2.2 'Fair trade' and the human rights movement

Another, non-economic, strand of the 'fair trade' debate dealt with background conditions affecting the cost of production in developing countries, such as environmental and labour standards.[107] As the liberalization of capital flows allowed multinational companies from developed countries to move production to developing countries with lower environmental and labour standards, the non-economic fair trade argument raised concerns of a 'race to the bottom' of such standards in developed countries.[108] To prevent this, proponents of the argument called for the creation of an international 'level playing field' and especially with

[106] Andrew Lang, 'Protectionism's Many Faces' (2019) 44 The Yale Journal of International Law Online 1, 3 <https://cpb-us-w2.wpmucdn.com/campuspress.yale.edu/dist/8/1581/files/2018/12/Lang_YJIL-Symposium_Protectionisms-Many-Faces_12.08.18-qedo7n.pdf> accessed 10 July 2023 ('What "new protectionism" signaled above all ... [was] an attempt by many States to rewrite the rules of global trade to establish a new international division of comparative advantage and secure their preferred places in that order .... In retrospect, the "new protectionism" is therefore best understood ... as a successful attempt to transform the system from one type of open global trading order to another.').

[107] See Jagdish Bhagwati, 'The Demands to Reduce Domestic Diversity among Trading Nations' in Jagdish Bhagwati and Robert E Hudec (eds), *Fair Trade & Harmonization. Volume I* (The MIT Press 1996) 10–11 (stating that non-economic fair trade arguments are based on three concerns: a sense of a 'transborder' obligation towards others living in nation-states with lowers standards; concerns of distributive justice that amount to the fear that freer trade with poor countries with abundant unskilled labour will immiserate working people in those countries; and concerns of fair competition that require that costs attributed to environmental and labour standards should not differ across countries in free trade.); see also Jagdish Bhagwati, *In Defense of Globalization* (OUP 2007), 133–34 (hereafter Bhagwati, *In Defense of Globalization*); Robert Howse and Michael J Trebilcock, 'The Fair Trade–Free Trade Debate: Trade, Labor, and the Environment (1996) 16(1) International Review of Law and Economics 61, 74 (hereafter Howse and Trebilcock, 'The Fair Trade–Free Trade Debate') ('Unlike the arguments for trade restrictions on environmental and labor rights grounds ... which have a normative reference point external to the trading system itself, competitiveness-based "fair trade" claims focus largely on the effects on domestic producers and workers of other countries' environmental and labor policies, and not per se on the effects of those policies on the environment and on workers elsewhere.'). See also Robert Wai, 'Countering, Branding, Dealing: Using Economic and Social Rights in and around the International Trade Regime' (2003) 14(1) European Journal of International Law 35, 48–49 ('Free trade based on comparative advantage is agnostic about the production conditions in any particular jurisdiction, including its domestic regulatory standards. Fair trade theory, in contrast, is very much concerned with defining the background of those conditions under which international trade should occur. Production that violate these background conditions would constitute "unfair competition".') For an overview of non-trade rationales for environmental and labour protection, see Howse and Trebilcock, 'The Fair Trade–Free Trade Debate' (n 107) 63–65.

[108] See Howse, 'From Politics to Technocracy' (n 37) 104 ('In the wake of the debt crisis, a range of developing countries ended up removing or modifying restrictions on foreign investment and various other domestic policies that were disincentives to the attraction of foreign capital. This led to fears of "social dumping" in the developed world that would eventually cause a race to the bottom: developed countries would not be able to sustain high environmental and labor standards, or rates of taxation needed to finance the redistributive policies of the welfare state, if they had to compete with these poorer countries for the location of capital investment.').

regard to environmental and labour-rights trade measures.[109] Just like their economic counterpart, these arguments were attacked by opponents as protectionism in disguise.[110] Moreover, even if one views these arguments as not protectionist in nature, addressing non-economic issues through trade measures was perceived as a second-best solution, because the first-best domestic measures are those not interfering with international trade.[111]

Although trade theorists advancing the idea of *free* trade were critical of the *fair* trade narrative, it would be inaccurate to say that this critique applied to *any* domestic interference with free trade.[112] For example, Bhagwati acknowledged that objecting to any state intervention as a departure from fair trade was 'a wrong-headed' approach.[113] He also supported some of the 'fair trade' arguments insofar as they were focused on the importance of creating intra-sectoral level playing fields—especially in the 'context of the few technology-intensive industries in which there are significant scale economies relative to the size of the world market'.[114] Along the same lines, he called for greater tolerance of 'other countries' social objectives'; regulation pursuing such objectives, he argued, should not be labelled as 'unfair'.[115]

[109] ibid 103; see, eg, Howse and Trebilcock, 'The Fair Trade–Free Trade Debate' (n 107) 78–79. For a literature overview on globalization and labour standards, see Eddy Lee, 'Globalization and Labour Standards: A Review of Issues' (1997) 136(2) International Labour Review 173, 176–83 (hereafter Lee, 'Globalization and Labour Standards'). On the 'race to the bottom' argument in relation to environmental standards, see Esty, *Greening the GATT* (n 5) 22–23. The issue of the level-playing field when it comes to social and human rights has resurfaced in the current EU's trade policy discourse. See Josep Borrell, 'Building Global Europe' (*European Union External Action*, 9 September 2020) <https://www.eeas.europa.eu/eeas/building-global-europe_en> accessed 10 July 2023.

[110] See, eg, Bhagwati, *In Defense of Globalization* (n 107) 123–31, 147–50 (arguing that the 'race to the bottom' argument is not supported by empirical evidence; differences in environmental and labour standards are insignificant to affect the location of production; higher labour and environmental standards themselves can be a protectionist move; and finally, attributing such arguments to 'rent seeking'.); see also Overbeek, *Free Trade versus Protectionism* (n 33) 557 ('At present [(1990s)], protectionists in wealthier countries, who are always on the look-out for new reasons for trade barriers, are using labor and environment related arguments to back up demands for additional trade impediments. … [T]his type of argument is extreme protectionism in its crudest possible disguise'.); Lee, 'Globalization and Labour Standards' (n 109) 177. But see Sean D Ehrlich, 'The Fair Trade Challenge to Embedded Liberalism' (2010) 54(4) International Studies Quarterly 1013, 1014, 1026, 1029–30 (providing empirical evidence of genuine nature of concerns with environmental and labour standards); Ronald Davies and Krishna Chaitanya Vadlamannati, 'A Race to the Bottom in Labor Standards? An Empirical Investigation' (2013) 103(C) Journal of Development Economics 1, 11–12 (providing empirical evidence of the race to the bottom in labour standards).

[111] See Howse, 'From Politics to Technocracy' (n 37) 100 ('Thus, the notion that a more effective policy instrument than trade protection is always available to achieve any legitimate public end vastly oversimplifies the problem of politics'.). Bhagwati argued that using trade distorting measures to tackle unemployment is only a second-best measure, while purely domestic measures would be the first best solution. See also Bhagwati, 'Threats to the World Trading Regime' (n 36) 238. On the theory of the second best, see Jagdish Bhagwati, 'The Generalized Theory of Distortions and Welfare' in Jagdish Bhagwati and others (eds), *Trade, Balance of Payments and Growth: Papers in International Economics in Honor of Charles P. Kindleberger* (North-Holland Publishing Co. 1971).

[112] See, eg, Bhagwati, *Protectionism* (n 35) 126–27.

[113] ibid 126.

[114] ibid 127.

[115] ibid.

3.2.4.3 Neoliberal discourse

As this chapter has explicated earlier, redefining 'protectionism' as 'new protectionism' was framed as a necessary and logical step in response to new forms of trade barriers. Ruggie convincingly argues instead that the emergence of the new protectionism was not the cause of but rather the effect of neoliberal discourse, which redefined the *social purposes* of the international trading system.[116] It was, thus, a new vision of the international trading system dictated by neoliberal discourse, and not objective circumstances, which effectuated the transformation of the notion of protectionism.[117]

This evolution of neoliberal discourse happened against the background of a shift in the economic theory of regulation.[118] A neoliberal view that *any* regulation may constitute a potential barrier to trade relies to a large extent on the theory of regulatory capture that became 'common language' in the circles of trade economists and international lawyers associated with the GATT.[119] These economic theories were later embraced in two official GATT reports.[120] In contrast to public interest theory (which advanced analytical arguments that regulation is adopted in the public interest, primarily to correct market failures and pursue non-economic and societal goals),[121] the 'regulatory capture' theory (based on the empirical foundations of the public choice theory) argued that regulation is adopted and implemented primarily in the interest of organized interest groups[122] and that regulatory capture is essentially unavoidable.[123] Captured regulation leads to a reduction of

[116] Ruggie, 'International Regimes, Transactions and Change' (n 75) 410–13. See also Lang, *World Trade Law after Neoliberalism* (n 38) 169–70.

[117] See Ruggie, 'International Regimes, Transactions and Change' (n 75) 410, 412–13.

[118] See generally Zang, 'Divided by Common Language' (n 17) 432–57.

[119] ibid 438 ('During the 1980s, Ordo-liberal and public-choice economics gained influence among trade economists and international lawyers associated with GATT, and 'capture' theory became the common language.').

[120] ibid.

[121] See Robert Baldwin, Martin Cave, and Martin Lodge, *Understanding Regulation: Theory, Strategy and Practice* (2nd edn, OUP 2012) 39–43 (hereafter Baldwin, Cave, and Lodge, *Understanding Regulation*); Anthony Ogus, *Regulation: Legal Form and Economic Theory* (3rd edn, Clarendon Press 1994) 58–71 (hereafter Ogus, *Regulation: Legal Form and Economic Theory*). The private interest theory questioned one of the core assumptions of the public interest theory, the assumption of the 'benevolent regulator,' in other words, that the political process creating regulation is efficient. See, eg, George J Stigler, 'The Theory of Economic Regulation' (1971) 2(1) The Bell Journal of Economics and Management Science 3, 3 ('The second [alternative] view [of regulation] is essentially that the political process defies rational explanation: "politics" is an imponderable, a constantly and unpredictably shifting mixture of forces of the most diverse nature, comprehending acts of great moral virtue (the emancipation of slaves) and of the most vulgar venality (the congressman feathering his own nest)'.).

[122] Ogus, *Regulation: Legal Form and Economic Theory* (n 121) 57–58. For an overview of 'regulatory capture' theory, see Baldwin, Cave, and Lodge, *Understanding Regulation* (n 121) 43–49; Ogus, *Regulation: Legal Form and Economic Theory* (n 121) 55–75; Cass R Sunstein, *After the Rights Revolution: Reconceiving the Regulatory State* (Harvard UP 1993) 69–71 (hereafter Sunstein, *After the Rights Revolution*).

[123] Political economists developed sophisticated models based on empirical data that strongly suggested that not only elected political actors but also non-elected bureaucrats (especially in the case of the European Economic Community) were more prone to adopt protectionist regulation than to adhere to free market principles. See Patrick A Messerlin, 'The Political Economy of Protectionism: The Bureaucratic Case' (1981) 117 Weltwirtschaftliches Archiv 469, 469–71. But see Robert E Baldwin,

social welfare because it merely leads to the transfer of wealth from one industry to another and no longer serves public interest.[124] This explains why, from the perspective of this theory, regulation should be reduced to a minimum.[125]

This theory was also used as a justification of the aggressive pursuit of export interests on the international level for constraining domestic protectionist trade policy making.[126] Binding reciprocal trade rules were thus seen as a tool to contain domestic protectionism through what Baldwin calls a 'juggernaut effect', which is using domestic export-oriented groups who profit from a reduction of trade barriers to fight the domestic protectionist lobby.[127] The new approach to domestic regulation was reinforced by a somewhat simplified version of trade economics that 'professors dole out to journalists'[128] (a 'market fundamentalist ideology' rather than true economic science).[129] Proponents of this ideology argued that trade leads to efficiency gains and enhances domestic welfare while silencing the downsides, such as the lack of consideration of social or distributional effects of free trade policy.[130] Relying on the assumption that any public policy objective can be

'The Political Economy of Trade Policy' (1989) 3(4) Journal of Economic Perspectives 119, 131 ('[T]he individual's various social concerns can play an important role in shaping his or her decisions. To expand their already substantial contributions toward understanding the policymaking process, economists should integrate such social motivations into their microeconomic optimizing framework.').

[124] See, eg, Tumlir, *Protectionism: Trade Policy in Democratic Societies* (n 52) 4 (arguing that '[a]ll protection is a redistribution of income and wealth within the protecting country'); see also Overbeek, *Free Trade versus Protectionism* (n 33) 558 (discussing the policy of managed trade).

[125] See, eg, Sunstein, *After the Rights Revolution* (n 122) 70 (criticizing the capture theory). Sunstein states that '[T]he notion of rent-seeking rejects, as unproductive, nearly all of the basic workings of politics. It treats citizenship itself as an evil. Efforts to enact public aspirations, to counteract discrimination, to protect the environment—all these are seen as the diversion of productive energies into a wasteful place'. ibid 71.

[126] Lang, *World Trade Law after Neoliberalism* (n 38) 234 ('As regards the trade regime itself, public choice theory supported the view that aggressive championing of export interests through trade negotiations was generally beneficial, as it provided a counterweight to the inherent tendency of protectionist special interests to capture domestic trade policy-making processes'.).

[127] Robert Baldwin, *The Great Convergence: Information Technology and the New Globalization* (Belknap Press 2016) 70; see also Howse, 'From Politics to Technocracy' (n 37) 100–101.

[128] See Rodrik, *The Globalization Paradox* (n 4) 77 ('Free market economics was in the ascendancy, producing what has been variously called the Washington Consensus, market fundamentalism, or neoliberalism. This new vision elevated the simplistic case for trade—the one that economics professors dole out to journalists— over the appropriately qualified version. It regarded any obstacle to free trade as an abomination to be removed; caveats to be damned.'). See also Robert Driskill, 'Deconstructing the Argument for Free Trade: A Case Study of the Role of Economists in Policy Debates (2012) 28 Economics and Philosophy 1, 2 (hereafter Driskill, 'Deconstructing the Argument for Free Trade') ('[I]n light of the apparent settled nature of economists' judgement on the issue of trade liberalization, the profession has stopped thinking critically about the question and, as a consequence, makes poor-quality arguments justifying their consensus').

[129] Joseph E Stiglitz, *Globalization and Its Discontents Revisited* (W.W. Norton & Company 2018), xl (hereafter Stiglitz, *Globalization and Its Discontents Revisited*) ('Doubling down on the Washington Consensus was a policy inspired by the special interests that it served, but the belief in the efficacy of these policies was supported by "market fundamentalist" ideologies—the notion that free, unregulated markets were the best way to organize a society'.)

[130] See Howse, 'From Politics to Technocracy' (n 37) 99 ('Put in this crude way, the case for trade liberalization appeared to be totally indifferent to any notion of a just distribution of benefits and burdens from the removal of trade restrictions'.).

more efficiently achieved by domestic regulation not interfering with international trade, this approach judged domestic trade restrictive measures against the benchmark of an imaginary 'toolbox of effective *nontrade* policy instruments'.[131] This perspective was also reinforced by the predisposition that protectionism explains domestic rules that deviate from this benchmark of efficient domestic rules.[132]

Taking an opposite view, Stiglitz argued that '[t]he globalization which emerged at the end of the twentieth century and the beginning of the twenty-first was not based on "free trade," but managed trade—managed for special corporate interests in the United States and other advanced countries'.[133] The 'market fundamentalist' ideologies that created a presumption that 'free, unregulated markets were the best way to organize a society' reinforced the myopic focus of political economy theory on the failures of domestic regulation.[134]

Paradoxically, a policy of deregulation (or not adopting regulation in the first place) and of complete free trade *is* a type of domestic policy, which itself is prone to 'capture' by domestic interest groups that benefit from such policies.[135] This led to questions about why international trade law regulation would be immune to such capture.[136] To illustrate this line of reasoning, an argument can be made that some countries, such as the United States, set their data protection standards *strategically low* in the past in order to increase their competitiveness on a global digital market.[137]

3.2.4.4 The impact of neoliberal discourse on the formation and functioning of the international trading system

The neoliberal discourse had a profound impact on the further rounds of negotiations of the GATT, in particular, the Uruguay Round (1986–1994) that led to

[131] ibid 100 ('One simply *assumed* a certain toolbox of effective nontrade policy instruments, and the stability and viability of the social bargains within states as well, or at least the stability of institutions that construct and reconstruct such social bargains').

[132] ibid ('In its confidence in the prescription of free trade as a timeless truth, the network identified special interest groups as the evil force that explained all, or almost all, deviations from the clearly rational policy prescription to use nontrade instruments for achieving public policy goals.').

[133] Stiglitz, *Globalization and Its Discontents Revisited* (n 129) 20.

[134] ibid xl.

[135] See Howse, 'From Politics to Technocracy' (n 37) 100–01. Dani Rodrik, 'What Do Trade Agreements Really Do?' (2018) 32(2) The Journal of Economic Perspectives 73, 75–76, 88.

[136] ibid.

[137] See, eg, Graham Greenleaf, 'The Influence of European Data Privacy Standards outside Europe: Implications for Globalization of Convention 108' (2012) 2(2) International Data Privacy Law 68, 72, characterizing the US privacy standards as inherently or deliberately weak: '[A]ttempts by US companies and the US government to use their combined economic and political influence to limit the development of data privacy laws in other countries will continue to be important, but may now be on the wrong side of history.'; see also Shamel Azmeh and Christopher Foster, 'The TPP and the Digital Trade Agenda: Digital Industrial Policy and Silicon Valley's Influence on New Trade Agreements' (2016) London School of Economics and Political Science Working Paper No 16–175, 12 <https://www.econstor.eu/bitstream/10419/224801/1/wp175.pdf> accessed 10 July 2023 (hereafter Azmeh and Foster, 'The TPP and the Digital Trade Agenda') ('Over the last few years, the political role of ICT companies has increased substantially with some of these firms becoming key political lobbying forces.').

the creation, design, and functioning of the WTO. The conclusion of the WTO Agreement[138] led to a considerable expansion of the scope of the multilateral trade system.[139] The WTO Agreement not only incorporated the GATT 1947[140] but also introduced new international trade law disciplines on the international trade in services in the GATS,[141] technical standards,[142] sanitary and phytosanitary measures,[143] and intellectual property.[144] Another important outcome of the Uruguay Round was the creation of a binding dispute settlement mechanism.[145]

During the Uruguay Round, 'a specialized policy elite'—employees of the GATT/WTO secretariat and a broad range of 'experts'—took over the gradual development and administration of the multilateral trading system.[146] These elites were 'insulated from, and not particularly interested in, the larger political and

[138] WTO Agreement: Marrakesh Agreement Establishing the World Trade Organization [1994] UNTS 154, 33 ILM 1144.

[139] Howse, 'From Politics to Technocracy' (n 37) 17, 53–54 (showing that the US fair trade agenda became the core of the Uruguay Round, which led to the adoption of trade disciplines implementing the rules dictated by 'the predominant ideology represented by the Washington consensus': extension of disciplines on domestic regulation beyond GATT non-discrimination obligations, greater market access, expansive intellectual property protection, de-monopolization and deregulation of telecommunications and finance, and 'scaling down' governmental health, safety, and environmental protection).

[140] General Agreement on Tariffs and Trade 1994, 15 April 1994, Marrakesh Agreement Establishing the World Trade Organization, Annex 1A, 1867 UNTS 187, 33 ILM 1153 (1994) (hereafter GATT 1994) (incorporating almost all of the provisions of GATT 1947).

[141] GATS (n 42).

[142] Agreement on Technical Barriers to Trade, Annex 1A to Marrakesh Agreement Establishing the World Trade Organization [1994] 1868 UNTS 120 (hereafter TBT Agreement).

[143] Agreement on the Application of Sanitary and Phytosanitary Measures, Annex 1A to Marrakesh Agreement Establishing the World Trade Organization, 1867 UNTS 493 (hereafter SPS Agreement). Kurtz notes in relation to the SPS that it ushered 'in a harder positive integration edge to a member state's commitments in the WTO. The underlying logic is that, by flattening insensible regulatory variances between states, the SPS Agreement can lower compliance costs, enhance efficiency gains and thus lead to an overall improvement in economic welfare'. Kurtz, *The WTO and International Investment Law* (n 83) 138.

[144] Agreement on Trade-Related Aspects of Intellectual Property Rights, Annex 1C to Marrakesh Agreement Establishing the World Trade Organization [1994] 1869 UNTS 299, 33 ILM 1197. See also Daniel J Gervais, *The Trips Agreement* (4th edn, Sweet & Maxwell 2010) 3.

[145] Although there was a dispute settlement mechanism under the GATT 1947 (n 43), the decision of the dispute settlement body ('Panel') had to be adopted by a consensus, which, in practice, meant that a losing party could block the adoption of the decision against it. Jackson, *The World Trade Organization* (n 65) 68. Establishment of the Dispute Settlement System solved this problem. The Dispute Settlement System is embodied in the Understanding on Rules and Procedures Governing the Settlement of Disputes, Marrakesh Agreement Establishing the World Trade Organization, Annex 2, 1869 UNTS; see also Jackson, *The World Trade Organization* (n 65) 72–73; see also Edwin Vermulst and Bart Driessen, 'An Overview of the WTO Dispute Settlement System and Its Relationship with the Uruguay Round Agreements' (1995) 29(2) Journal of World Trade 131, 131 (providing an overview of the WTO dispute settlement system).

[146] Howse, 'From Politics to Technocracy' (n 37) 98 ('This group included some officials employed in the GATT/ WTO Secretariat . . . the larger group of "experts": former or current governmental trade officials; GATT-friendly academics who often sat on GATT/WTO dispute settlement panels and were invited to various conferences and meetings of the GATT/WTO; international civil servants in other organizations (particularly the World Bank, the Organisation for Economic Co-operation and Development, and the International Monetary Fund) preoccupied with trade matters; and a few private attorneys, consultants, and former politicians.').

social conflicts of the age'[147] and shared a common set of neoliberal normative values (ethos or ideology) on the nature and goals of international trade, the relationship between trade law and politics, and the boundaries of domestic regulatory autonomy.[148] The main goal of the international trading system, as advanced by these policy elites, was no longer 'embedded liberalism' but the continued, gradual liberalization of trade.[149] International trade and globalization became an imperative for any trade policy measure, subordinated to the domestic economic, social, and political priorities, and an 'end in itself'.[150] Under the influence of these policy elites, the WTO dispute settlement system, which had exclusive competence to enforce WTO rules, became largely 'self-referential' and gave little weight to other international rules, such as those governing human rights.[151]

This shift in the *dominant discourse* affected the behaviour of WTO members.[152] Compared to the previous system under the GATT 1947, the WTO dispute settlement system was used to challenge a broader range of domestic policy issues.[153]

[147] ibid ('A sense of pride developed that an international regime was being evolved that stood above the "madhouse" of politics (if one can borrow Pascal's image), a regime grounded in the insights of economic "science", and not vulnerable to the open-ended normative controversies and conflicts that plagued most international institutions and regimes, most notably, for instance, the United Nations.').

[148] See Lang, *World Trade Law after Neoliberalism* (n 38) 181 ('[T]rade regime's neoliberal turn was in significant part . . . a transformation of collective ideas about the nature and purpose of the trade regime, collective ideas about the function of law in trade politics, and collective principles and techniques for evaluating the legitimacy of governmental action ... [and] this transformation of the GATT/WTO's "legal imagination" radically reshaped the form, structure, content, and interpretation of international trade law.').

See also Joseph HH Weiler, 'The Rule of Lawyers and the Ethos of Diplomats: Reflections on the Internal and External Legitimacy of WTO Dispute Settlement' (2001) 35(2) Journal of World Trade 191, 193 (hereafter Weiler, 'The Rule of Lawyers and the Ethos of Diplomats') ('The diplomatic ethos which developed in the context of the old GATT dispute settlement tenaciously persists despite the much transformed juridified WTO.').

[149] See Rodrik, *The Globalization Paradox* (n 4) 76 (citing Thomas L Friedman, *The Lexus and the Olive Tree: Understanding Globalization* (Farrar, Straus and Giroux 1999) 61–65). ('[T]he WTO marks the pursuit of a new kind of globalization. Domestic economic management was to become subservient to international trade and finance rather than the other way around. Economic globalization, the international integration of the markets for goods and capital (but not labor), became an end in itself, overshadowing domestic agendas. Globalization became an imperative, apparently requiring all nations to pursue a common strategy of low corporate taxation, tight fiscal policy, deregulation, and reduction of the power of unions.'). See also Howse, 'From Politics to Technocracy' (n 37) 104 ('[Some insiders] moved from free trade as an economic ideology to free trade as embedded in a broader liberal economic ideology. Trade liberalization became part of a general set of prescriptions for growth and prosperity, at odds to a large extent with the progressive welfare state vision of the embedded liberalism bargain.'); WTO, *European Communities – Customs Classification of Frozen Boneless Chicken Cuts – Report of the Appellate Body* (27 September 2005) WT/DS269/AB/R, WT/DS286/AB/R, para 243 (stating that security and predictability of 'the reciprocal and mutually advantageous arrangements directed to the substantial reduction of tariffs and other barriers to trade is an object and purpose of the WTO Agreement, generally, as well as of the GATT 1994').

[150] See Rodrik, *The Globalization Paradox* (n 4) 76.

[151] Weiler, 'The Rule of Lawyers and the Ethos of Diplomats' (n 148) 194 ('A very dominant feature of the GATT was its self-referential and even communitarian ethos explicable in constructivist terms.').

[152] See Lang, *World Trade Law after Neoliberalism* (n 38) 223.

[153] See ibid 223s–24 ('By the end of the 1990s, however, as informal norms limiting the scope of application of the GATT regulatory disciplines were gradually reconstituted, the range of measures subject to challenge under Articles I and III of the GATT had broadened considerably. It was in part the

As a result, in addition to traditional trade-related questions such as tariffs and quotas, WTO dispute settlement bodies increasingly had to evaluate compliance with the new trade rules of domestic health and environment standards, cultural policies, and regulation protecting public morals.[154] In addition to domestic regulation discriminating on the basis of origin ('*de jure* discrimination'),[155] which was a primary matter of concern in the GATT 1947, from the late 1980s onwards, an increasing number of disputes focused on *de facto* discrimination. These were the domestic measures that did not specifically aim to discriminate against foreign goods in favour of domestic ones based on their origin, but rather on a domestic regulatory purpose (eg health or environmental protection).[156]

The WTO caselaw that emerged from these disputes demonstrated a neoliberal shift in the trade adjudicators' interpretative techniques.[157] The WTO adjudicating bodies increasingly refrained from considering regulatory intent (subjective approach injected through the so-called 'aims and effects' test) when assessing whether a particular domestic measure resulting in discrimination between domestic and foreign goods or services violated the relevant trade agreement and was, therefore, protectionist.[158] Instead, the focus shifted towards the *de facto* economic

result of a twofold imaginative change consisting of, first, a redefinition of the common sense concept of "trade barrier," and second, a rethinking of the nature and purpose of the trade regime itself.').

[154] See eg WTO, *United States – Measures Affecting the Cross-Border Supply of Gambling and Betting Services – AB-2005-1 – Report of the Appellate Body* (7 April 2005) WT/DS285/AB/R (hereafter Appellate Body Report, *US – Gambling*); WTO, *European Communities – Measures Affecting Asbestos and Asbestos-Containing Products – Report of the Appellate Body* (5 April 2001) WT/DS135/AB/R; WTO, *United States – Import Prohibition of Certain Shrimp and Shrimp Products – Report of the Panel* (15 May 1998) WT/DS58/R); WTO, *European Communities –Measures Concerning Meat and Meat Products (Hormones) – Report of the Appellate Body* (13 February 1998) WT/DS26/AB/R, WT/DS48/AB/R; WTO, *Canada – Certain Measures Concerning Periodicals – Report of the Appellate Body* (30 July 1997) WT/DS31/AB/R.

[155] Robert E Hudec, 'GATT/WTO Constraints on National Regulation: Requiem for an Aim and Effects Test' (1998) 32(3) The International Lawyer, 619, 620 (hereafter Hudec, 'GATT/WTO Constraints on National Regulation') (defining '*de jure* discrimination' as 'regulatory measures that discriminate explicitly by providing different standards for domestic and foreign goods or services'); see also Nicolas F Diebold, *Non-Discrimination in International Trade in Services: 'Likeness' in WTO/GATS* (CUP 2010) 35–37 (hereafter Diebold, *Non-Discrimination in International Trade in Services*).

[156] See Hudec, 'GATT/WTO Constraints on National Regulation' (n 155) 620 (defining '*de facto* discrimination' as 'regulatory measures that make no explicit distinction between foreign and domestic goods (called "origin-neutral"), but which have a disproportionate impact on foreign goods or services that is for some reason viewed as wrong or illegitimate'.). 'Historically, GATT has been principally occupied with border measures and explicitly discriminatory measures, with *de facto* discrimination only becoming a major concern relatively recently'. ibid 622. Hudec clarifies that '[o]f the first 207 legal complaints filed in GATT between 1948 and 1990, only a small handful involved claims of *de facto* discrimination by internal regulatory measures'. ibid 622 footnote 8; see also Diebold, *Non-Discrimination in International Trade in Services* (n 155) 37–45.

[157] See Lang, *World Trade Law after Neoliberalism* (n 38) 255.

[158] See ibid 255, 257–65 ('Over the course of the 1990s, the clear trend was incrementally but decisively to eliminate virtually any explicit consideration of intent in the interpretation of GATT non-discrimination norms'.); see also Diebold, *Non-Discrimination in International Trade in Services* (n 155) 75–80; Michael H Trebilcock, Robert Howse, and Antonia Eliason, *The Regulation of International Trade* (4th edn, Routledge 2013) 138–45 (examining the Appellate Body's interpretation of the National Treatment Obligation in the GATT and 'rejection of an 'aims and effects' test to determine the validity

impact (narrower, objective approach) on the competitive opportunities of foreign goods and the effects on competition between products or services.[159] These developments led to an equivalence between trade-distorting measures, discrimination, and protectionism.[160]

This equivalence between discrimination/trade distortion and protectionism had two practical implications. First, it altered the baseline between legitimate regulation and protectionism, thus making the term protectionism much more capacious. This, in turn, left a much narrower domestic regulatory space to protect non-economic values, such as the environment, labour rights, animal welfare, and human rights. Second, by refraining from any consideration of regulatory intent in the assessment of violations of international trade commitments, the WTO adjudicating bodies transferred the centre of gravity in the consideration of regulatory purposes towards the all-important general exceptions contained in GATT 1994 Article XX and GATS Article XIV.[161] This shift had an important consequence for the domestic regulatory space: while the burden of proof of an alleged violation of a trade obligation is normally on the complaining party, the burden of proof that all the conditions of a necessity test have been met are on the party whose regulatory measure is contested.[162] This is not just 'a question of technical burden of proof', as Weiler argues,

of an internal tax measure'.); Lothar Ehring, 'De Facto Discrimination in WTO Law: National and Most-Favored-Nation Treatment – or Equal Treatment?' (2002) 36(5) Journal of World Trade 921, 931–46; Hudec, 'GATT/WTO Constraints on National Regulation' (n 155) 629–33. See also discussion in Section 2.3.1.

[159] See, eg, WTO, *Argentina – Measures Affecting the Export of Bovine Hides and the Import of Finished Leather – Report of the Panel* (16 February 2001) WT/DS155/R and Corr1, para 11.182 (clarifying that 'Article III:2, first sentence, is not concerned with taxes or changes as such or the policy purposes. Members pursue with them, but with their economic *impact* on the competitive opportunities of imported and like domestic products'.) (emphasis added); Lang, *World Trade Law after Neoliberalism* (n 38) 262; Howse, 'The World Trade Organization 20 Years On: Global Governance by Judiciary' (n 44) 46: ('Consideration of regulatory intent or of evidence of purposeful discrimination plays no role in this analysis. The adjudicator makes a determination of whether the products are "like" based upon objective criteria, such as physical characteristics and end uses, while consumer preferences can also be dispositive, and then undertakes a formalistic (not empirical) analysis of whether the regulatory intervention in question has detrimental impact on competitive opportunities for imported like products. In this disparate impact or *de facto* discrimination analysis, there is no apparent room for consideration of outside values or legitimate regulatory purposes.').

[160] See Lang, *World Trade Law after Neoliberalism* (n 38) 255 ('[A]n implicit association ... began to be made between the notion of discrimination under Articles I and III and the notion of a "market distortion" from economic analysis'.) '[T]he non-discrimination norm became a much more powerful tool to wield against domestic regulation, even that which was apparently "non-discriminatory" in the sense that that term had been traditionally understood. "Discrimination" began to look very much like "trade-distorting market intervention".' ibid 264.

[161] See WTO, *Argentina – Measures Relating to Trade in Goods and Services – Report of the Appellate Body* (14 April 2016) WT/DS453/AB/R and Add 1, para 6.114; ('[A] Member's commitments under the GATS could in some cases serve to further its national policy objectives. Where measures are found to be inconsistent with a Member's obligations or commitments under the GATS, the GATS provides for various mechanisms, such as Article XIV, which take account of policy objectives underlying such measures'.).

[162] See Donald H Regan, 'The Meaning of "Necessary" in GATT Article XX and GATS Article XIV: The Myth of Cost-Benefit Balancing' (2007) 6(3) World Trade Review 347, 364 (hereafter Regan, 'The Meaning of "Necessary" in GATT Article XX and GATS Article XIV').

but 'a question of cultural identity, the way a society wishes to understand its internal hierarchy of values'.[163] The relegation of values competing with the liberalization of trade to *exceptions* 'establishes the WTO as a system of symbolic normative hierarchy wherein the default norm is the integrity of the market and liberalized trade'.[164] In this way, regulations in the public interest that interfered with international trade commitments were effectively put in a defensive position, facing the requirement of the necessity test and the requirements of the *chapeau* of the general exceptions.[165]

Although the interpretation of the general exceptions and, in particular, the necessity test has been uneven throughout the years,[166] one thing has remained stable: it is a particularly difficult test to meet.[167] The interpretation of the general exceptions, which have become the core mechanism to distinguish between domestic measures that are legitimate and those that are protectionist,[168] has created a 'protectionist bias'; that is, an inclination to protect the interests of trade-oriented stakeholders that 'may be inconsistent with the human rights interests of consumers in maximum equal liberty and open markets'.[169] For example, as discussed in Section 2.3.2, in the interpretation of the 'reasonably available' test—the benchmark for the assessment of whether a particular trade-inconsistent domestic measure meets the 'necessity' requirement of the general exception[170]—WTO

[163] Joseph HH Weiler, 'Law, Culture, and Values in the WTO: Gazing into the Crystal Ball' in Daniel Bethlehem and others (eds), *The Oxford Handbook of International Trade Law* (OUP 2009) 768.

[164] ibid 768.

[165] See Lang, *World Trade Law after Neoliberalism* (n 38) 265 (arguing that '[p]art of the purpose and the effect of the reinterpretation of Article III, in other words, was to shift the centre of gravity of the legal discipline of domestic regulation under the GATT from the non-discrimination test in Article III to the necessity test in Article XX'.).

[166] For a comprehensive overview, see Gabrielle Marceau and Joel P Trachtman, 'A Map of the World Trade Organization Law of Domestic Regulation of Goods: The Technical Barriers to Trade Agreement, the Sanitary and Phytosanitary Measures Agreement, and the General Agreement on Tariffs and Trade' (2014) 48(2) Journal of World Trade 351, 368–77 (hereafter Marceau and Trachtman, 'A Map of the World Trade Organization Law of Domestic Regulation of Goods'); Regan, 'The Meaning of "Necessary" in GATT Article XX and GATS Article XIV' (n 161) 347–66; Ingo Venzke, 'Making General Exceptions: The Spell of Precedents in Developing Art XX GATT into Standards for Domestic Regulatory Policy' (2011) 12(5) German Law Journal 1111, 1116–35 (hereafter Venzke, 'Making General Exceptions') (detailing how various GATT panels and Appellate Bodies have analysed Article XX arguments).

[167] Panagiotis Delimatsis, 'Protecting Public Morals in a Digital Age: Revisiting the WTO Rulings on US – Gambling and China – Publications and Audiovisual Products' (2011) 14(2) Journal of International Economic Law 257, 266; Venzke, 'Making General Exceptions' (n 166) 1118–19. For a discussion, see Section 2.4.2.

[168] See Panagiotis Delimatsis, 'Who's Afraid of Necessity? And Why It Matters?' in Aik Hoe Lim and Bart De Meester (eds), *WTO Domestic Regulation and Services Trade* (CUP 2014) 95

('Since the inception of GATT, necessity tests have formed part of the contract, providing flexibility and "breathing space" to regulators. Necessity has been traditionally considered as the prevailing proxy for the identification and the discipline of protectionist or unduly burdensome regulatory behaviour'.).

[169] Ernst-Ulrich Petersmann, 'Human Rights and International Economic Law in the 21st Century' (2001) 4(1) Journal of International Economic Law 3, 27 (hereafter Petersmann, 'Human Rights and International Economic Law in the 21st Century').

[170] See, eg, WTO, *Korea – Measures Affecting Imports of Fresh, Chilled and Frozen Beef – Report of the Appellate Body* (10 January 2001) WT/DS161/AB/R, WT/DS169/AB/R (hereafter Appellate Body Report, *Korea – Various Measures on Beef*), para 164; WTO, *Argentina – Measures Relating to Trade*

adjudicating bodies assess whether an alternative measure that provides *the same level of protection* of the public interest or objective pursued by a trade-inconsistent measure without *prohibitive cost or substantial technical difficulties* is available.[171] An inconsistent and sometimes very narrow interpretation of what 'the same level of protection' and 'prohibitive' costs entail amounted in some cases to the consideration of an actual level of protection achieved by a contested measure (rather than a desired level of protection subjectively determined by the state and not (yet) necessarily achieved) and a disregard of high administrative and enforcement costs. Such interpretative inconsistencies left WTO members a much narrower regulatory space than the wording of the test might otherwise suggest.[172] The reality is that a less trade-restrictive measure is, in theory, almost always reasonably available in the imaginary 'toolbox of effective nontrade policy instruments' mentioned above.[173] As argued in Section 2.3.2, despite the fairly consistent language in WTO case law that the less restrictive alternative should be real rather than hypothetical, this logic has not always been followed in practice.

In the 2010s, after a decade or so of sharp critiques and public discontent with the WTO's practice of reframing regulatory approaches protecting non-economic values as barriers to trade, the WTO attempted to restore its legitimacy by trying to give more deference to the levels of protection of domestic societal interests.[174] Predictably, those efforts did not produce any tangible effects. As Andrew Lang neatly put it,

in Goods and Services – Report of the Panel (9 May 2016) WT/DS453/R, para 7.729; Appellate Body Report, *US – Gambling* (n 154), paras 304–07; WTO, *European Communities – Measures Prohibiting the Importation and Marketing of Seal Products – Reports of the Appellate Body* (22 May 2014) WT/DS400/AB/R / WT/DS401/AB/R (hereafter Appellate Body Reports, *EC – Seal Products*), paras 5.169, 5.214.

[171] Appellate Body Report, *US – Gambling* (n 154) para 308.

[172] See Appellate Body Report, *Korea – Various Measures on Beef* (n 170) para 178. Based on the actual application of the contested measure, the Appellate Body held the following:

> We think it *unlikely that Korea intended to establish a level of protection that totally eliminates fraud* with respect to the origin of beef (domestic or foreign) sold by retailers. The total elimination of fraud would probably require a total ban of imports. Consequently, *we assume* that in effect Korea *intended to reduce considerably* the number of cases of fraud occurring with respect to the origin of beef sold by retailers. The Panel did find that the dual retail system 'does appear to reduce the opportunities and thus the temptations for butchers to misrepresent foreign beef for domestic beef. (emphasis added)

The alternative measure, which the Appellate Body said was reasonably available to Korea, involved higher administrative and enforcement costs. Korea argued that it lacked the resources necessary for this alternative, but the Appellate Body still concluded that the contested measure did not pass the 'necessity' assessment. ibid paras 175, 180. But see Appellate Body Report, *US – Gambling* (n 154) paras 308, 317 (The Appellate Body dismissed the alternative measure proposed by a claiming party as 'not an appropriate alternative', and stated, '[A] "reasonably available" alternative measure must be a measure that would preserve for the responding Member its right to achieve *its desired level of protection* with respect to the objective pursued under paragraph (a) of Article XIV') (emphasis added).

[173] Howse, 'From Politics to Technocracy' (n 37) 100.

[174] For a detailed account, see Howse, 'The World Trade Organization 20 Years On' (n 44) 13, 45–75.

> [i]n the lingua franca of trade professionals, 'the toothpaste was out of the tube,' and it was simply not possible to return to a trade regime which was narrowly focused on (say) border barriers, and only a small subset of domestic regulations which had direct and immediate impacts on trade flows.[175]

However, this does not mean that restoring such legitimacy is insurmountable in the future. As of this writing (June 2023), the WTO is looking at different ways to use its expertise to re-establish its legitimacy, including through entrenching a more pluralist model of social and economic governance, and reacquire the clout that comes with heightened legitimacy, including through a well-functioning dispute settlement system.[176] The WTO is still hampered by a non-functioning Appellate Body and reeling from the many highly publicized supply chain issues that emerged during the COVID-19 pandemic.[177] Time will tell whether these efforts will succeed.

Indeed, since the Uruguay Round, WTO multilateral negotiations have not made any significant progress in the further liberalization of international trade beyond what could be achieved through a neoliberal interpretation of existing rules.[178] Instead, international trade law-making moved to bilateral and regional fora where multiple bilateral and plurilateral preferential trade and investment agreements have been concluded around the world (some 2219 bilateral investment treaties and 355 regional trade agreements are in force).[179] These agreements

[175] Lang, *World Trade Law after Neoliberalism* (n 38) 315.

[176] See, eg, Ngozi Okonjo-Iweala, 'The Case for Reimagining – Not Abandoning – Globalization' (*Foreign Affairs*, 8 June 2023) <https://www.foreignaffairs.com/world/why-world-still-needs-trade> accessed 10 July 2023; Ngozi Okonjo-Iweala, 'The WTO's Contribution to the Challenges of Global Commons' (2023) 26(1) Journal of International Economic Law 12; Robert Howse and Joanna Langille, 'Continuity and Change in the World Trade Organization: Pluralism Past, Present, and Future' (2023) 117(1) The American Journal of International Law, 1 (hereafter Howse and Langille, 'Continuity and Change in the World Trade Organization').

[177] See, eg, Patricia Cohen, 'Why It Seems Everything We Knew about the Global Economy Is No Longer True' (*The New York Times*, 18 June 2023) <https://www.nytimes.com/2023/06/18/business/economy/global-economy-us-china.html> accessed 10 July 2023.

[178] Mira Burri, 'Should There Be New Multilateral Rules for Digital Trade?' (2013) Think Piece for the E15 Expert Group on Trade and Innovation, 3 <https://ssrn.com/abstract=2344629> accessed 10 July 2023 (2013) ('As the Doha negotiations continue to make little progress, the multilateral venue of rule-making is being seriously undermined, and this triggers forum-shopping—bilaterally, regionally, and through new plurilateral initiatives within clubs of countries, unaffiliated to any international organization, such as the Anti-Counterfeiting Trade Agreement (ACTA)'.).

[179] See WTO, 'Regional Trade Agreements' (*World Trade Organization*) <https://www.wto.org/english/tratop_e/region_e/region_e.htm> accessed 10 July 2023; UNCTAD, 'International Investment Agreements Navigator' (*UNCTAD*) <https://investmentpolicy.unctad.org/international-investment-agreements> accessed 10 July 2023. According to Burri, out of 346 preferential trade agreements (PTAs) concluded between 2000 and 2020, 185 PTAs include digital trade-related provisions, 110 include specific e-commerce provisions, and 80 contain dedicated e-commerce chapters and side agreements. Mira Burri, 'Towards a New Treaty on Digital Trade' (2021) 55(1) Journal of World Trade 77, 80 (hereafter Burri, 'Towards a New Treaty on Digital Trade'). Elsig and Klotz argue that participation in WTO e-commerce or digital trade-related initiatives had some spillover effects on the depth of digital trade provisions in regional trade agreements. See Manfred Elsig and Sebastian Klotz, 'Digital Trade Rules in Preferential Trade Agreements: Is There a WTO Impact?' (2021) 12(4) Global Policy 25.

have shaped a regulatory landscape on digital trade[180] which looks incoherent and highly fragmented.[181] As opposed to WTO negotiations, where consensus of all parties is required, bilateral and regional negotiations make it easier for certain states to advance a new form of the neoliberal discourse—that of global digital trade—to achieve an ever-deeper trade liberalization.[182] Drawing a parallel with the redefinition of protectionism as 'new protectionism' in 1970s, the next section discusses how the redefinition of protectionism as 'digital protectionism' may have contributed to such a transition.

3.3 Digital Protectionism: The Latest Wave of Trade Constraints on Regulatory Autonomy

As noted in Chapter 1, the last decade has witnessed a trend towards regulating electronic commerce and digital trade in bilateral and regional trade agreements.[183] These changes have occurred against a background comprised of the idea that globalization is a net positive, on the one hand, and the development of new information technologies that allow for an almost instant exchange of information, services, and capital, on the other hand. As personal and other data became an essential component of cross-border trade, ensuring its unrestricted cross-border flow became an important yet contentious point in the negotiations of 'new generation' international trade agreements. These negotiations coincided with the discourse of digital trade advanced by the United States, stressing the economic benefits of digital trade and exposing the downsides of restrictions on cross-border flows of personal data—which are also sometimes referred to as data localization requirements[184]—labelling them as 'digital protectionism' or 'data protectionism'.

[180] See Burri, 'Towards a New Treaty on Digital Trade' (n 179) 81.

[181] ibid 78; Mira Burri and Rodrigo Polanco, 'Digital Trade Provisions in Preferential Trade Agreements: Introducing a New Dataset' (2020) 23(1) Journal of International Economic Law 187, 189, 220 (hereafter Burri and Polanco, 'Digital Trade Provisions in Preferential Trade Agreements'); Elaine Fahey, 'The European Union as a Digital Trade Actor: The Challenge of Being a Global Leader in Standard-Setting' (2021) 27(2) International Trade Law and Regulation 1, 9 (hereafter Fahey, 'The European Union as a Digital Trade Actor').

[182] See Joost Pauwelyn, 'The WTO in Crisis: Five Fundamentals Reconsidered' (*WTO*, 2012) <https://www.wto.org/english/forums_e/public_forum12_e/art_pf12_e/art9.htm#:~:text=WTO%20%7C%20The%20WTO%20in%20Crisis%3A%20Five%20Fundamentals%20Reconsidered&text=In%20times%20of%20severe%20crisis,so%20as%20to%20provoke%20discussion> accessed 10 July 2023.

[183] See Robert Wolfe, 'Learning about Digital Trade: Privacy and E-commerce in CETA and TPP' (2019) 18(S1) World Trade Review s63, s63.

[184] It could be argued that 'restrictions on cross-border data flows' and 'data localization' mean different things, as data localization laws do not always restrict cross-border flows of data. See, eg, Francesca Casalini and Javier López González, 'Trade and Cross-Border Data Flows' (2019) OECD Trade Policy Papers No 220, 5<http://dx.doi.org/10.1787/b2023a47-en> accessed 10 July 2023. Some authors view data localization as a form of restrictions on cross-border data flows. See, eg, Susannah Hodson, 'Applying WTO and FTA Disciplines to Data Localization Measures' (2019) 18(4) World Trade Review 579. Given that there is no consensus on the meaning of these terms, and drawing a clear line between them is not the purpose of this book, the author uses them interchangeably.

This label, as the chapter explains later, is often attached to the EU restrictions on cross-border transfers of personal data, explained in Sections 2.2.3 through 2.2.5, by those criticizing the EU approach.[185] It is that set of rules that is more often showcased as being detrimental to international trade and described as protectionist.[186] Accusations of (digital) protectionism resounded with renewed vigour with respect to the EU's new framing of its digital agenda, covering domestic policies beyond data protection, under the label of 'digital sovereignty', as mentioned in Chapter 1.[187]

In spite, or perhaps because, of this, EU politicians also regularly express their disapproval of digital protectionism.[188] Although the EU and US discourses on

[185] Bauer and others, 'The Economic Importance of Getting Data Protection Right' (n 26) 11; Nigel Cory and Luke Dascoli, 'How Barriers to Cross-Border Data Flows Are Spreading Globally, What They Cost, and How to Address Them' (*Information Technology & Innovation Foundation*, 2021) <https://itif.org/publications/2021/07/19/how-barriers-cross-border-data-flows-are-spreading-globally-what-they-cost/> accessed 10 July 2023 (hereafter Cory and Dascoli, 'How Barriers to Cross-Border Data Flows Are Spreading Globally'). For a discussion, see Filippo Maria Lancieri, 'Digital Protectionism? Antitrust, Data Protection, and the EU/US Transatlantic Rift (2019) 7(1) Journal of Antitrust Enforcement 27.

[186] See Avi Goldfarb and Daniel Trefler, 'Artificial Intelligence and International Trade', in Ajay Agrawal, Joshua Gans, and Avi Goldfarb (eds), *The Economics of Artificial Intelligence: An Agenda* (University of Chicago Press 2019) 479–80 <https://www.nber.org/books/agra-1> accessed 10 July 2023 (hereafter Goldfarb and Trefler, 'Artificial Intelligence and International Trade') (viewing restrictions on personal data transfers as a form of data localization that could favour domestic firms and have negative effects on trade); see also Martina Ferracane and Erik van der Marel, 'The Cost of Data Protectionism' (*ECIPE Blog*, October 2018) <https://ecipe.org/blog/the-cost-of-data-protectionism/> accessed 10 July 2023 (hereafter Ferracane and van der Marel, 'The Cost of Data Protectionism') ('We find that restrictions on the cross-border movement of data, as opposed to restrictions on the domestic use of data, significantly reduce imports of services'.); Avi Goldfarb and Catherine E Tucker, 'Privacy Regulation and Online Advertising' (2011) 57(1) Management Science 57, 69–70 (demonstrating that European strict e-privacy rules lead to an average reduction in effectiveness of 65 per cent of banner ads, thus proving to be damaging for the European advertising industry).

[187] See, eg, Cherlene Barshefski, 'EU Digital Protectionism Risks Damaging Ties with the US' (*Financial Times*, 2 August 2020) <https://www.ft.com/content/9edea4f5-5f34-4e17-89cd-f9b9ba698103> accessed 10 July 2023; Trevor Wagener, 'Scholars Identify Costs from EU Digital Agenda' (*Disruptive Competition Project*, 15 December 2022) <https://www.project-disco.org/european-union/121522early-alert-for-eu-digital-protectionism/> accessed 10 July 2023; Nigel Cory, 'How the EU Is Using Technology Standards as a Protectionist Tool in Its Quest for Cybersovereignty' (*Information Technology & Innovation Foundation*, 19 September 2022) <https://itif.org/publications/2022/09/19/how-the-eu-is-using-technology-standards-as-a-protectionist-tool/> accessed 10 July 2023; Cecilia Bonefeld-Dahl, 'European Sovereignty or a Shadow of Protectionism?' (*Euractiv*, 25 August 2022) <https://www.euractiv.com/section/digital/opinion/european-sovereignty-or-a-shadow-of-protectionism/> accessed 10 July 2023.

[188] See, eg, Catherine Stupp 'Lawmakers Rebuke US "Digital Protectionism" Charges' (*Euractiv*, 24 September 2015) <https://www.euractiv.com/section/digital/news/lawmakers-rebuke-us-digital-protectionism-charges/> accessed 10 July 2023; European Parliament resolution of 12 December 2017 on 'Towards a Digital Trade Strategy' (2017/2065(INI)) [2017] OJ C 369, para 12 (hereafter, European Parliament resolution on 'Towards a Digital Trade Strategy') (in which the Parliament 'emphasises that the relevant data protection legislation should be adhered to; regrets attempts to use such requirements as a form of non-tariff barrier to trade and as a form of digital protectionism; considers that such protectionism seriously hampers opportunities for European businesses in third country markets and undermines the efficiency benefits of digital trade'). Communication From the Commission on the Mid-Term Review on the Implementation of the Digital Single Market Strategy A Connected Digital Single Market for All EUR-Lex-52017DC0228-EN-EUR-Lex (europa.eu) (hereafter Communication From the Commission on the Mid-Term Review on the Implementation of the Digital Single Market Strategy); Japan-EU Digital Partnership (12 May 2022) para 36 <https://www.consilium.europa.eu/

digital trade are ostensibly woven with similar terminological threads of digital protectionism, such discourses are inchoate and fundamentally diverge in their views on the underlying values and policy objectives of digital trade.[189] Although in both cases powerful economic interests may have played a role in constructing the discourse, when it comes to the interplay between digital trade and the protection of privacy and personal data, unlike the United States, the European Union is bound by internal *constitutional* constraints, already discussed in Chapter 2, and elaborated upon in more detail in Chapter 5. It is this divergence that could explain why the attempt to redefine protectionism—and narrow domestic regulatory space to protect personal data to a larger extent has been reflected in the US-led trade agreements, while the EU has preferred to safeguard much broader regulatory autonomy on this issue.[190]

The European Union's restrictions on cross-border transfers of personal data undoubtedly impose limitations on international trade. The key question is, however, whether such restrictions can appropriately be labelled as 'protectionist,' and if so, what the consequences of using this label might be in future policy decisions. This chapter addresses this question in Section 3.4.

3.3.1 The digital trade discourse(s)

As shown above, in showcasing the economic benefits of free cross-border data flows, the narrative of digital trade often presents domestic privacy and data protection regimes (as well as their international divergence) as digital trade barriers. A number of economic arguments, advanced primarily by the US government and by European, and US pro-trade think tanks (but also by several academics), are used to explain why restrictions on cross-border flows of personal data or data localization requirements hamper digital trade. For instance, an influential McKinsey & Company report argued that in 2014 alone, cross-border data flows generated $2.8 trillion in value.[191] In an earlier study conducted for the US

media/56091/%E6%9C%80%E7%B5%82%E7%89%88-jp-eu-digital-partnership-clean-final-docx.pdf> accessed 10 July 2023 (hereafter Japan-EU Digital Partnership), in which the EU and Japan 'aim at cooperating and coordinating their approaches regarding digital protectionist measures and trends around the world, which have a detrimental impact on trade and investment flows'.

[189] 'The Rise of Digital Protectionism' (*Greenberg Center for Geoeconomic Studies*, 18 October 2017) <https://www.cfr.org/report/rise-digital-protectionism> accessed 10 July 2023.

[190] See Section 3.3.4.

[191] James Manyika and others, 'Digital Globalisation: The New Era of Global Flows' (2016) McKinsey Global Institute, 10 <https://www.mckinsey.com/~/media/McKinsey/Business%20Functions/McKinsey%20Digital/Our%20Insights/Digital%20globalization%20The%20new%20era%20of%20global%20flows/MGI-Digital-globalization-Full-report.pdf> accessed 10 July 2023 (hereafter Manyika and others, 'Digital Globalisation'). See also 'Business without Borders: The Importance of Cross-Border Data Transfers to Global Prosperity' (2014) US Chamber of Commerce and Hunton & Williams LLP, 1–2 <https://www.huntonak.com/images/content/3/0/v3/3086/Business-without-%20Bord

Chamber of Commerce by the pro-trade think tank, the European Centre for International Political Economy ('ECIPE') warned of the negative welfare effects on the EU economy if cross-border data flows were to be disrupted by the then-draft General Data Protection Regulation (GDPR).[192] A number of other ECIPE studies predicted that the removal of restrictions on cross-border flows of information would increase imports of services, on average by 5 per cent.[193] According to a 2021 study by Frontier Economics prepared for a tech-lobby group Digital Europe, GDPR restrictions on transfers of personal data outside the EEA would cost the EU a reduction in exports of around 4 per cent, and in a 1 per cent loss of GDP per year, amounting to 1.3 trillion euros by 2030.[194] The World Economic Forum claims that as of January 2023, cross-border e-commerce is worth an estimated 2.7 trillion US dollars worldwide, much of which relies on cross-border data flows.[195]

These warnings about the very high stakes associated with cross-border data flows for digital trade being under threat due to domestic restrictions on such flows have fed into the lobbying activities of export-oriented service industries around the world.[196] In a similar vein, in a taxonomy of trade-restricting measures prepared by the United States International Trade Commission ('USITC'), the EU data protection framework (which, unlike US law, requires a higher level of data protection complemented by restrictions on cross-border transfers of personal data), is mentioned as restricting international digital trade in several sectors.[197]

ers.pdf > accessed 10 July 2023 (hereafter US Chamber of Commerce and Hunton & Williams LLP, 'Business without Borders').

[192] Regulation (EU) 2016/679 of the European Parliament and of the Council of 27 April 2016 on the protection of natural persons with regard to the processing of personal data and on the free movement of such data, and repealing Directive 95/46/EC (General Data Protection Regulation) [2016] OJ L119 (hereafter GDPR). See Bauer and others, 'The Economic Importance of Getting Data Protection Right' (n 26) 3.

[193] See Ferracane and van der Marel, 'The Cost of Data Protectionism' (n 186) ('Our analysis predicts that, if countries lifted their restrictions on the cross-border flow of data, the imports of services would rise on average by five percent across all countries, with obvious benefits for local companies and consumers who could access cheaper and better online services from abroad.').

[194] Frontier Economics, 'The Value of Cross-Border Data Flows to Europe: Risks and Opportunities' (2021) Report prepared for DIGITALEUROPE, 6 <https://cdn.digitaleurope.org/uploads/2021/06/Frontier-DIGITALEUROPE_The-value-of-cross-border-data-flows-to-Europe_Risks-and-opportunities.pdf> accessed 10 July 2023.

[195] Fumiko Kudo, 'We Must Enhance Cross-Border Data Flows — Here's Why' (*World Economic Forum*, 16 January 2023) <https://www.weforum.org/agenda/2023/01/data-flows-cross-border-wef23/> accessed 10 July 2023 (hereafter Kudo, 'We Must Enhance Cross-Border Data Flows').

[196] See, eg, 'Global Services Coalition Statement on Digital Trade' (16 October 2017) <http://www.esf.be/new/wp-content/uploads/2017/10/Global-Services-Coalition-Statement-on-Digital-Trade-Final-16-Oct-2017.pdf?> accessed 10 July 2023 (quoting Manyika and others, 'Digital Globalisation' (n 191), and several ECIPE studies and 'calling[ing] for negotiators of ongoing or future negotiations related to data flow including FTAs/EPAs to make their utmost efforts to agree on strong and effective provisions which guarantee free flow of data, and prohibit forced data localization and requirements for provision of software source code, while applying appropriate and effective protection and security for personal data'.) Similarly, Kudo, 'We Must Enhance Cross-Border Data Flows' (n 195) , relies on similar estimates to propel multilateral negotiations on cross-border data flows at the WTO.

[197] 'Global Digital Trade 1: Market Opportunities and Key Foreign Trade Restrictions' (2017) United States International Trade Commission 273 <https://www.usitc.gov/publications/332/pub4716.pdf>

The USITC and ECIPE stress that generally speaking, restrictions on cross-border transfers, in addition to substantive rules restricting the use of personal data and data localization measures, increase the costs of conducting business for multinational companies.[198] More specifically, researchers associated with the ECIPE argue that restrictions on cross-border data flows reduce (or, in other words, restrict) imports of data-intensive services.[199]

As any user of any social media platform can attest, personal data, viewed as an economic asset, also constitutes an important ingredient of AI-based systems and algorithms, an input in the production of many digital services, production processes, and logistics.[200] In other words, it is *a factor of production*.[201] Foreign providers of such services, including targeted advertising companies, are in a less favourable position than domestic providers that do not have to comply with cross-border transfer restrictions to provide the same services domestically.[202]

accessed 10 July 2023 (hereafter United States International Trade Commission, 'Global Digital Trade 1') ('According to input from industry representatives, regulatory and policy measures focused on data protection and privacy affect all kinds of industries. These measures can inhibit global digital trade by U.S. firms due to the increased administrative costs associated with complying with stricter privacy measures that differ from U.S. standards.').

[198] ibid. Ferracane and van der Marel, 'The Cost of Data Protectionism' (n 186); Ines Willemyns, *Digital Services in International Trade Law* (CUP 2021) 58, 61–64.

[199] See Martina Ferracane and Erik van der Marel, 'Do Data Policy Restrictions Inhibit Trade in Services' (2018) ECIPE Working Paper No 2, 15 <https://ecipe.org/wp-content/uploads/2018/10/Do-Data-Policy-Restrictions-Inhibit-Trade-in-Services-final.pdf> accessed 10 July 2023 (showing that 'more restrictive data policies, in particular with respect to the cross-border movement of data, result in lower imports in data-intense services for countries imposing them.').

[200] See Jacques Crémer, Yves-Alexandre de Montjoye, and Heike Schweitzer, 'Competition Policy for the Digital Era', 2019 Final Report to the European Commission Directorate-General For Competition 73 <http://ec.europa.eu/competition/publications/reports/kd0419345enn.pdf> accessed 10 July 2023 ('Data is a core input factor for production processes, logistics, targeted marketing, smart products and services, as well as Artificial Intelligence (AI).').

[201] See Milton Mueller and Karl Grindal, 'Data Flows and the Digital Economy: Information as a Mobile Factor of Production' (2019) 21(1) Digital Policy, Regulation and Governance 71, 80 (concluding that 'information in the form of digital data flows can be considered a mobile factor of production'); see Francisco Costa-Cabral and Orla Lynskey, ' The Internal and External Constraints of Data Protection on Competition Law in the EU' (2015) LSE Law, Society and Economy Working Papers 25/2015, 11 <http://eprints.lse.ac.uk/64887/1/Lynskey_Internal%20and%20External%20Constraints%20of%20Data%20Protection%20_Author_2015.pdf> accessed 10 July 2023 ('Without personal data as an input some goods and services are now ostensibly impossible to produce, leading to the growth of commodity markets for personal data. Thus, personal data is a full-fledged factor of production in a modern economy.'); see Seda Gürses and Joris van Hoboken, 'Privacy after the Agile Turn' in Evan Selinger, Jules Polonetsky, and Omer Tene, *The Cambridge Handbook of Consumer Privacy* (CUP 2018) 595 (showing that users' data has become an integral part of production and testing of digital services and software).

[202] As already explained in Section 2.2.4, foreign companies which fall under the extraterritorial application of the GDPR (n 192) and receive Europeans' personal data from data exporters subject to the GDPR (eg, in a joint controllership situation) not only have to comply with legal grounds for collecting personal data under Articles 5 and 6 of the GDPR (requirements that generally apply to European companies) but *also* with the limitations on transfers of personal data outside the EEA (Chapter V GDPR). EDPB, 'Guidelines 2/2018 on derogations of Article 49 under Regulation 2016/679' (25 May 2018) 3 <https://edpb.europa.eu/our-work-tools/our-documents/guidelines/guidelines-22018-derogations-article-49-under-regulation_en> accessed 10 July 2023. When applying Article 49 of the GDPR, one must bear in mind that according to Article 44 of the GDPR, the data exporter transferring personal data to third countries or international organizations must also meet the conditions of

In addition, restrictions on flows of data are viewed as detrimental not only to ICT services but also for trade in goods and services generally, as they may result in companies choosing a less efficient mode of production (or supply) of services.[203] Global information flows allow multinational companies to operate globally without an international physical presence.[204] Some academics also argue that restrictions on data flows may limit the possibilities of the worldwide aggregation of personal data and are thus threatening technological advances in such areas as cloud computing and AI.[205] In a similar vein, the US Chamber of Commerce and Hunton & Williams warned that such restrictions may turn the 'Internet' into a 'splinternet,' paving the way to economic stagnation.[206]

the other provisions of the GDPR. Each processing activity must comply with the relevant data protection provisions, in particular with Articles 5 and 6 GDPR. Hence, a two-step test must be applied: first, a legal basis must apply to the data processing as such together with all relevant provisions of the GDPR; and as a second step, the provisions of Chapter V GDPR must be complied with. ibid. See also Lucas Bergkamp, 'The Privacy Fallacy: Adverse Effects of Europe's Data Protection Policy in an Information-Driven Economy' (2002) 18(1) Computer Law & Security Review 31, 39 <https://www.huntonak.com/images/content/3/2/v3/3292/Privacy-fallacy.pdf> accessed 10 July 2023.

203 See Ferracane and van der Marel, 'The Cost of Data Protectionism' (n 186) (citing Andrea Andrenelli and others, 'Multinational Production and Trade in Services' (2018) OECD, Trade Policy Paper No 212 <http://dx.doi.org/10.1787/16ec6b55-en> accessed 10 July 2023 ('[A] range of data-intense services from computer services to retail and information services are increasingly being traded over the internet rather than by other means such as foreign establishments. Restricting data would, therefore, also inhibit companies from choosing the most efficient channel of trading many services.').

204 See UNCTAD, 'World Investment Report: Investment and the Digital Economy' (2017) UNCTAD/WIR/2017, 167 < https://unctad.org/system/files/official-document/wir2017_en.pdf> accessed 10 July 2023.

205 See Anupam Chander and Uyên P Lê, 'Data Nationalism' (2015) 64(3) Emory Law Journal 677, 680 (hereafter Chander and Lê, 'Data Nationalism') (Labelling EU restrictions on transfers of personal data as data localization measures and stating that '[b]y creating national barriers to data, data localization measures break up the World Wide Web, which was designed to share information across the globe.... Data localization would dramatically alter this fundamental architecture of the Internet.'). See also ibid 681 (arguing that data localization measures promote 'data nationalism', which 'poses a mortal threat to the new kind of international trade made possible by the Internet—information services such as those supplied by Bangalore or Silicon Valley.'); see also Goldfarb and Trefler, 'Artificial Intelligence and International Trade' (n 186) 29 ('Data localization is an issue for AI because AI requires data. In other words, localization is a way to restrict the possible scale of any country in AI, but at the cost of lower quality overall.'). But see Christopher Kuner, 'Data Nationalism and Its Discontents' (2015) 64 Emory Law Journal 2089, 2090 (hereafter Kuner, 'Data Nationalism') (offering a powerful critique of these arguments).

206 US Chamber of Commerce and Hunton & Williams LLP, 'Business without Borders' (n 191) 2–3 ('Technological advances and an increasingly globalized economy have brought us to a policy crossroads: one path leads to a "splinternet" of economic isolation, characterized by misguided attempts to safeguard data by building protectionist walls this isolationist approach has repeatedly caused economic stagnation.').

3.3.2 Framing data protection as 'digital protectionism' in the digital trade discourse

Discourse matters, and the discourse is changing. Political, academic, and societal debates on cross-border data flows now revolve around terms such as 'digital protectionism', 'data protectionism', 'data nationalism', 'innovation mercantilism', 'data colonialism', and 'digital colonialism'.[207] That said, the view that restrictions on cross-border flows of personal data could favour domestic industries is not new.[208] As early as 1978, John Eger raised a concern that the restrictions on cross-border flows of personal data adopted by some EU countries and envisaged to be introduced on an EU level might, in practice, be used not only to protect privacy and national sovereignty but also 'to protect domestic economic interests' as indirect barriers to trade.[209] It is only recently, however, that the term 'digital protectionism' was coined to refer to such restrictions.[210] For example, in a 2016 non-paper for the discussions on electronic commerce at the WTO, Japan stressed the necessity 'to address emerging "digital protectionism"' as a prerequisite for 'open, secure, and reliable global e-commerce environment that will promote and facilitate cross-border digital trade'.[211] Relying on the definition of barriers to digital trade used by the USITC, Aaronson defined digital protectionism as 'laws and regulations that block the flow of data across borders, impede the provision of services such as

[207] See eg Chander and Lê, 'Data Nationalism' (n 205) 679, 739; Neha Mishra, 'Data Localization Laws in a Digital World: Data Protection or Data Protectionism?' (2016) 4(1) The Public Sphere: Journal of Public Policy 135, 137, 144 (hereafter Mishra, 'Data Localization Laws in a Digital World') ('From a [international political economy] perspective, a dominant view is the emergence of 'innovation mercantilism' in digital trade today.'). Aaronson, 'What Are We Talking about When We Discuss Digital Protectionism?' (n 34) 3; Andrew D Mitchell and Neha Mishra, 'Data at the Docks: Modernizing International Trade Law for the Digital Economy' (2018) 20(4) Vanderbilt Journal of Entertainment & Technology 1073, 1111–12 (hereafter Mitchell and Mishra, 'Data at the Docks'); Nick Couldry and Ulises A Mejias, 'Data Colonialism: Rethinking Big Data's Relation to the Contemporary Subject' (2019) 20(4) Television & New Media 336; Danielle Coleman, 'Digital Colonialism: The 21st Century Scramble for Africa through the Extraction and Control of User Data and the Limitations of Data Protection Laws' (2019) 24 Michigan Journal of Race & Law 417; Susan Ariel Aaronson, 'The Difficult Past and Troubled Future of Digital Protectionism' in Ingo Borchert and L Alan Winters (eds), *Addressing Impediments to Digital Trade* (CEPR Press 2021) 141–68 <https://cepr.org/system/files/publication-files/60026-addressing_impediments_to_digital_trade.pdf> accessed 10 July 2023 (hereafter Aaronson, 'The Difficult Past and Troubled Future of Digital Protectionism'); Cory and Dascoli, 'How Barriers to Cross-Border Data Flows Are Spreading Globally' (n 185); Anupam Chander and Paul Schwartz, 'Privacy and/or Trade' (2023) 90(1) The University of Chicago Law Review 49 (hereafter Chander and Schwartz, 'Privacy and/or Trade').

[208] See John M Eger, 'Emerging Restrictions on Transnational Data Flows: Privacy Protection or Non-Tariff Trade Barriers' (1978) 10 Law and Policy in International Business 1055,1066.

[209] See ibid 1066 ('Many countries in Europe may have no concern other than protecting the privacy of personal data, a concern which neither the American public nor any member of a democratic society can fault. But there is the danger, of course, that these new laws will be used not only to protect just privacy but also to protect domestic economic interests.').

[210] See Aaronson, 'What Are We Talking about When We Discuss Digital Protectionism?' (n 34) 2, 8.

[211] WTO, Work Programme On Electronic Commerce, 'The E-Commerce Moratorium and Implications for Developing Countries, Communication from India and South Africa' [2019] WT/GC/W/774, para 2.2.

cloud computing, or otherwise restrict the ability of firms to take advantage of best-in-class digital services'.[212] Other academics, most notably Chander and Lê, argued that '[w]e must insist on data protection without *data protectionism*. A better, safer Internet for everyone should not require breaking it apart'.[213] Similarly, Burri called upon international legal scholars to 'stress the dangers of data protectionism, often under the disguise of legitimate objectives, such as national security or privacy protection'.[214] At the same time, Burri rightly points out that not only divergent approaches to data privacy and protection (which is arguably the crux of the cross-border data flow problem) but also standards of data protection that are *too low* could be viewed as barriers or obstacles to trade.[215] This is, in part, because consumer confidence and trust, she argues, are a precondition for well-functioning digital trade.[216] This leads to a search for an optimal level (from a trade perspective) of protection rather than a complete absence of protection.[217]

The US administration's rhetoric centred on the notion of data protectionism seems to be based exactly on this logic. US trade experts and the administration have used harsh language to characterize the European Union's privacy and data protection framework.[218] Work by Aaronson demonstrates how the US administration has routinely used the terms 'protectionism' or 'digital protectionism' to refer to EU-style privacy and personal data protection regimes.[219] Yet, in parallel

[212] Aaronson, 'The Difficult Past and Troubled Future of Digital Protectionism' (n 207) 143. Susan Ariel Aaronson, 'Why Trade Agreements Are Not Setting Information Free: The Lost History and Reinvigorated Debate over Cross-Border Data Flows, Human Rights, and National Security' (2015) 14(4) World Trade Review 671, 674; see also Aaronson, 'What Are We Talking about When We Discuss Digital Protectionism?' (n 34) 17–22.

[213] (Emphasis added.) Chander and Lê, 'Data Nationalism' (n 205) 739.

[214] Mira Burri, 'The Regulation of Data Flows through Trade Agreements' (2017) 48 Georgetown Journal of International Law, 407, 448 (hereafter Burri, 'The Regulation of Data Flows through Trade Agreements').

[215] Mira Burri, 'Current and Emerging Trends in Disruptive Technologies: Implications for the Present and Future of EU's Trade Policy' (2017) Study for the European Parliament (EP/EXPO/B/INTA/2017/6) 13–14 <https://www.europarl.europa.eu/RegData/etudes/STUD/2017/603845/EXPO_STU(2017)603845_EN.pdf> accessed 10 July 2023 (hereafter Burri, 'Current and Emerging Trends in Disruptive Technologies'); Mira Burri, 'The Impact of Digitalization on Global Trade Law' (2023) 24 German Law Journal 551, 560 (hereafter Burri, 'The Impact of Digitalization on Global Trade Law').

[216] Burri, 'Current and Emerging Trends in Disruptive Technologies' (n 215) 13–14; see also Neha Mishra, 'Building Bridges: International Trade Law, Internet Governance, and the Regulation of Data Flows' (2019) 52(2) Vanderbilt Journal of Transnational Law 463, 503 (hereafter Mishra, 'Building Bridges') ('Implementing internet privacy is increasingly recognised as one of the fundamental requirements for digital trade.').

[217] Mishra, 'Building Bridges' (n 216) 503.

[218] See, eg, Digital Trade in the US and Global Economies, Part 2 (2014) Inv No 332-540, USITC Pub 4485, 14 <https://www.usitc.gov/publications/332/pub4485.pdf> accessed 10 July 2023 (stating that the EU data privacy and protection requirements are 'obstacles to international digital trade,' among localization requirements, intellectual property rights infringement and customs measures.).

[219] See, eg, Aaronson, 'What Are We Talking about When We Discuss Digital Protectionism?' (n 34) 8–10; see also Susan Ariel Aaronson, 'Digital Protectionism? Or Label the U.S. Government Uses to Criticize Policy It Doesn't Like?' (*Council on Foreign Relations Blog*, 3 March 2016) <https://www.cfr.org/blog/digital-protectionism-or-label-us-government-uses-criticize-policy-it-doesnt> accessed 10 July 2023 (hereafter Aaronson, 'Digital Protectionism? Or Label the U.S. Government Uses to Criticize Policy It Doesn't Like?'). See also Schwartz and Peifer, 'Transatlantic Data Privacy Law' (n 27) ('In the

to attaching the (negative) label 'protectionism' to—what it sees as too much—privacy protection, the US government has also at times criticized situations with *too little* privacy protection on instrumental grounds, arguing that insufficient consumer privacy protection can stifle electronic commerce.[220] It seems to agree that the protection of privacy and personal data is crucial to maintaining consumer trust in digital technologies, which is in turn indispensable for the strong and orderly development of electronic and digital commerce.[221] As this chapter argues in Section 3.4, this is not a mere 'inconsistency' in the US arguments on this issue,[222] but indeed a fundamental question of a baseline—or optimal level of protection—that delineates 'useful' (and possibly indispensable) protection from excessive protection (that one would then label 'protectionist' to try to lower it). In Section 3.4, this chapter returns to the key role of *discourse* in drawing this baseline.

Authors associated with ECIPE and Baker & McKenzie have characterized the EU data protection framework as 'disproportionate and potentially protectionist'.[223] This resonates with Beattie's article in the *Financial Times* comparing the European Union's approach to resistance to genetically modified organisms ('GMOs') on public health grounds—a topic around which the battle between the European Union and United States lasted for at least two decades.[224] Even the then

United States, there has been scepticism about E.U. privacy rights and whether they are merely disguised protectionism'.) Aaronson, 'The Difficult Past and Troubled Future of Digital Protectionism' (n 207).

[220] See Susan Ariel Aaronson, 'Redefining Protectionism: The New Challenge in the Digital Age' (2016) The George Washington University, Institute for International Economic Policy Working Paper Series, Working Paper No 30, 87 <https://ideas.repec.org/p/gwi/wpaper/2016-30.html> accessed 10 July 2023 (hereafter Aaronson, 'Redefining Protectionism'); see also Aaronson, 'What Are We Talking about When We Discuss Digital Protectionism?' (n 34) 21–22.

[221] Aaronson, 'What Are We Talking about When We Discuss Digital Protectionism?' (n 34) 19.

[222] Aaronson, 'Redefining Protectionism' (n 220) 87 ('U.S. arguments against digital protectionism are often inconsistent'.); see also Aaronson, 'What Are We Talking about When We Discuss Digital Protectionism?' (n 34) 21 ('[T]he United States has adopted an inconsistent approach to privacy as a barrier to trade'.).

[223] Bauer and others, 'The Economic Importance of Getting Data Protection Right' (n 26) 4 ('The question of whether the European regulatory model on privacy is disproportionate and potentially protectionist has become one of the most controversial political debates within the EU at this time, and perhaps rightly so'.); see also Lothar Determann, 'Adequacy of Data Protection in the USA: Myths and Facts' (2016) 6(3) International Data Privacy Law 244, 247–48 ('The USA support free global trade and have so far not retaliated against the protectionist data transfer restrictions in "Fortress Europe"'.).

[224] Alan Beattie, 'EU Trade Data Flows Are Becoming the New GMOs' (*Financial Times*, 4 December 2017) <https://www.ft.com/content/9da22968-d8ee-11e7-a039-c64b1c09b482> accessed 10 July 2023 (arguing that the EU privacy and data protection framework is a localization requirement that acts as a form of protectionism in favour of (unnamed) interest groups, just as the EU prohibition on GMOs helped European farmers to protect themselves unfairly from US competition.) Beattie contends that this regulatory framework will benefit European firms and, in the long term, the European Union's 'attitude to cross-border data flows ... will retard European companies' ability to maximise digital technology to full advantage'. ibid. From this book author's perspective, the EU-US controversy on beef treated beef would be a better parallel to the debate surrounding data protection. While mutual permeation of WTO and EU rules governing GMOs within a pluralist governance structure has eventually led—to a large extent—to reconciliation of differences between the EU and US approaches to the GMO issues, the disagreement on governance of beef hormones has never been fully reconciled. For a discussion, see Nico Krisch, *Beyond Constitutionalism: The Pluralist Structure of Postnational Law* (OUP

US President Barack Obama, reacting to the antitrust and data protection enforcement actions against US tech giants Google and Facebook in the European Union, publicly insinuated that the European Union was merely pursuing its own 'commercial interests'.[225]

As alluded to the above, despite being criticized for pursuing potentially protectionist restrictions on transfers of personal data, the EU itself is also actively seeking to remove measures it labels as digital protectionism.[226] If one looks at the EU not as a homogenous institution but as a composition of different subsystems (primarily at the EU and member states levels) with different goals and decision-making processes that determine the European Union's external (trade) and internal policies, then the situation is less clear.[227] The issue becomes even more complicated if one also takes into account that in the European Commission, different departments (directorates general) are responsible for international trade (DG Trade) and fundamental rights (DG Just).

After the 2008 worldwide financial crisis, the European Commission changed its discourse; in its new discourse, trade liberalization was 'consistently presented ... as a desirable and even necessary solution to the *crisis* and protectionism as a mistake from the past that has to be avoided'[228] (emphasis in the original). This rhetoric targeted not only the European Union's trading partners but also the traditionally more protectionist EU member states that were opposed to the European Union's bilateral concessions that could harm their domestic industries.[229] Faithful

2012) 205–16. See also European Commission, 'Press Release: The European Union and the United States Sign an Agreement on Imports of Hormone-free Beef, (*European Commission*, 2 August 2019) https://ec.europa.eu/commission/presscorner/detail/en/IP_19_5010 accessed 10 July 2023.

[225] Ahmed Murad, Duncan Robinson, and Richard Waters, 'Obama Attacks Europe over Technology Protectionism' (*Financial Times*, 16 February 2015) https://www.ft.com/content/41d968d6-b5d2-11e4-b58d-00144feab7de accessed 10 July 2023 ('We have owned the internet. Our companies have created it, expanded it, perfected it in ways that they can't compete. And oftentimes what is portrayed as high-minded positions on issues sometimes is just designed to carve out some of their commercial interests'.).

[226] Julia Fioretti, 'EU Moves to Remove Barriers to Data Flows in Trade Deals' (*Reuters*, 9 February 2018) <https://www.reuters.com/article/us-eu-data-trade-idUSKBN1FT2DC> accessed 10 July 2023. See also European Parliament resolution on 'Towards a Digital Trade Strategy' (n 188) para 12; Communication from the Commission, Mid-Term Review on the Implementation of the Digital Single Market Strategy (n 188); Japan-EU Digital Partnership (n 188) para 36.

[227] See Alasdair R Young and John Peterson, *Parochial Global Europe: 21st Century Trade Politics* (OUP 2014) 23 ('Trade policy might be viewed as one of the most atomistic of all areas of public policy. Each policy decision—whether it is to negotiate a free trade agreement or impose anti-dumping duties on an imported product—involves different calculations, interests, and timeframes'.). Christina Eckes, 'Protecting Supremacy from External Influences: A Precondition for a European Constitutional Legal Order?' (2012) 18(2) European Law Journal 230, 233, explaining that the EU foreign policy is 'first and foremost a task of the executive; and the European executive is more fragmented than the average national executive. Indeed, it consists of "unseen and many layers"'.

[228] (Emphasis added.) Yelter Bollen, Ferdi de Ville, and Jan Orbie, 'EU Trade Policy: Persistent Liberalisation, Contentious Protectionism' (2016) 38(3) Journal of European Integration 279, 288 (hereafter Bollen, de Ville and Orbie, 'EU Trade Policy').

[229] ibid. ('This liberalisation-as-recovery-instrument discourse has been very powerful and difficult to contest by traditionally more protectionist Member States, uncompetitive industries or trade

to its long-standing course towards further liberalization of trade and with an eye towards benefiting from globalization, in its 2015 Communication 'Trade for All,' the European Commission contended that 'the free flow of data across borders has become more *important for European competitiveness* in general'.[230] In November 2016, the EU trade commissioner Cecilia Malström noted that 'in the digital age, restrictions on cross-border data flows inhibit trade of all kinds, and may amount to "digital protectionism." '[231] She committed to using international trade deals as a means for setting the rules for digital trade.

In its more recent 2021 trade policy programme documents developed under the flag of 'digital sovereignty', the European Commission remains faithful to its trade liberalization discourse. It stresses that a critical element of the EU's drive towards open strategic autonomy (an aspect of the EU's 'digital' or 'technological sovereignty' narrative) is the conclusion of the new trade agreements (both not yet ratified), such as those with Chile and New Zealand, both of which contain digital trade chapters and obligations related to cross-border data flows.[232] This, in the European Commission's view will help counter 'protectionist tendencies and distortions affecting EU exports'.[233] The Commission also emphasizes that 'undistorted access to international markets, including new market access and open trade flows' is needed to 'strengthen resilience and support the competitiveness of its various economic sectors'.[234]

As of this writing (June 2023), both the United States and the EU are involved in multistakeholder negotiations under the label of Data Free Flow with Trust (DFFT) coined by Japan's prime minister Abe Shinzo in 2019.[235] One of the tracks[236] along

unions'.); see also Gabriel Siles-Brügge, 'Resisting Protectionism after the Crisis: Strategic Economic Discourse and the EU–Korea Free Trade Agreement' (2011) 16(5) New Political Economy 627, 643 (hereafter Siles-Brügge, 'Resisting Protectionism after the Crisis') ('How did DG Trade manage to convince the Member States to agree to the provisions of the FTA when it was facing the opposition of the powerful car industry . . .? The answer is that, in a sense, it had already won the battle, by recasting liberalisation as *necessary* process, both in terms of the external constraint posed by globalisation but also, more specifically, the competitive pressure emanating from commercial rivals'.).

230 (Emphasis added.) Communication from the Commission to the European Parliament, the European Council, the Council, the European Economic and Social Committee, and the Committee of the Regions, 'Trade for All towards a More Responsible Trade and Investment Policy' [2015] COM (2015) 0497 final, 12.

231 European Commission, 'Commissioner Malmström on the Opportunities of Digital Trade' (*European Commission Press Release*, 17 November 2016.) <http://trade.ec.europa.eu/doclib/press/index.cfm?id=1580.> accessed 10 July 2023.

232 Communication from the Commission to the European Parliament, the Council, the European Economic and Social Committee, and the Committee of the Regions, 'Trade Policy Review: An Open, Sustainable and Assertive Trade Policy' [2021] COM/2021/66 final (hereafter Communication from the Commission, 'Trade Policy Review').

233 ibid.

234 ibid.

235 See 'Data Free Flow with Trust (DFFT): Paths towards Free and Trusted Data Flows' (*World Economic Forum*, May 2020) <https://www3.weforum.org/docs/WEF_Paths_Towards_Free_and_Trusted_Data%20_Flows_2020.pdf> accessed 10 July 2023.

236 Another track is the regulatory one, which includes regulatory cooperation within the OECD, Asia-Pacific Economic Cooperation (APEC), including APEC Cross-Border Privacy Rules (CBPR),

which these negotiations unfold is the trade track (negotiations on digital trade within the WTO Joint Initiative on E-commerce, OECD, G20, and G7), which aims to counteract 'digital protectionism' that has reached 'an all-time high' by setting forth, among other things, multilateral rules facilitating cross-border data flows.[237]

Where, then, one might ask, is the issue if everyone agrees on the benefits of trade liberalization and the ills of digital protectionism? It follows from the fact that when it comes to the rights to privacy and the protection of personal data, the European Union's opposition to digital protectionism is now on a wholly different trajectory. The EU's approach in this respect shifted in 2015 following opposition by the European Parliament,[238] EU member states,[239] academics,[240] and civil society,[241] to the European Union's digital 'free trade' policy, which made it apparent that such a policy 'should not undermine European levels of protection and democratic policy-making'.[242] This shift is apparent, for example, in the 2017 Communication 'Exchanging and Protecting Personal Data in a Globalised World', where the European Commission carefully carved out privacy protection

and the global CBPR system propelled by the United States. See Aidan Arasasingham and Matthew P Goodman, 'Operationalizing Data Free Flow with Trust (DFFT)' (*Center for Strategic and International Studies*, 13 April 2023) <https://www.csis.org/analysis/operationalizing-data-free-flow-trust-dfft> accessed 10 July 2023 (hereafter Arasasingham and Goodman, 'Operationalizing Data Free Flow with Trust (DFFT)').

[237] ibid.

[238] See European Parliament Resolution 2014/2228(INI) of 8 July 2015 containing the European Parliament's recommendations to the European Commission on the negotiations for the Transatlantic Trade and Investment Partnership (TTIP) [2014] OJ C 265/35 ('[T]o ensure that the EU's Acquis on data privacy is not compromised through the liberalisation of data flows ... while recognizing the relevance of data flows as a backbone of transatlantic trade and the digital economy'); European Parliament Resolution 2015/2233(INI) of 3 February 2016 containing the European Parliament's recommendations to the Commission on the negotiations for the Trade in Services Agreement (TiSA) [2015] OJ C 35/21 ('[T]o acknowledge that data protection and the right to privacy are not a trade barrier, but fundamental rights, which are enshrined in Article 39 TEU and Articles 7 and 8 of the Charter of Fundamental Rights of the European Union'.).

[239] See Bollen, de Ville, and Orbie, 'EU Trade Policy: Persistent Liberalisation, Contentious Protectionism' (n 228) 284 ('In the states where TTIP has become most politicised, notably Germany, Austria and the United Kingdom, the openness-protectionism dichotomy is of minor importance. Instead, the debate is dominated by arguments about sovereignty, regulatory paradigms and food safety'.).

[240] See, eg, Kristina Irion, Svetlana Yakovleva, and Marija Bartl, 'Trade and Privacy: Complicated Bedfellows? How to Achieve Data Protection-Proof Free Trade Agreements' (2016) Independent study commissioned by BEUC and others, 54 <https://www.ivir.nl/publicaties/download/trade_and_privacy.pdf> accessed 10 July 2023 (hereafter Irion, Yakovleva, and Bartl, 'Trade and Privacy: Complicated Bedfellows?') ('The risks for privacy and data protection stemming from the sphere of the EU are, broadly speaking, that EU international relations could place more emphasis on international trade in services relative to EU standards on privacy and data protection'.)

[241] See, eg, EDRi, 'BEUC and EDRi Urge the EU Commission Not to Undermine Citizens' Privacy in Trade Agreements' (*EDRi*, 13 June 2016) <https://edri.org/our-work/beuc-edri-urge-eu-commission-not-undermine-citizens-privacy-trade-agreements/> accessed 10 July 2023 ('Discussions on forced data localisation should take place outside trade agreements. Otherwise, our fundamental rights to privacy and data protection can be undermined or challenged as trade barriers'.).

[242] Bollen, de Ville, and Orbie, 'EU Trade Policy: Persistent Liberalisation, Contentious Protectionism' (n 228) 284.

from 'protectionism' by highlighting that 'European companies operating in some third countries are increasingly faced with *protectionist restrictions that cannot be justified with legitimate privacy considerations*'.[243] The EU remains faithful to this approach in its strategy for negotiating trade agreements as of this writing (June 2023). The Digital Trade section of the European Commission's website states regarding the EU's approach to ensuring free flow of data:

> When negotiating trade agreements, the EU proposes the straightforward prohibition of protectionist barriers to cross-border data flows. At the same time, it ensures that trade agreements cannot be used to challenge existing and future EU law on the protection of personal data and privacy, which are fundamental rights in the EU.[244]

In line with this approach, one of the action points for the European Commission trade policy is to

> [s]eek the rapid conclusion of an ambitious and comprehensive WTO agreement on digital trade, including rules on data flows, in full compliance with the EU's data protection framework, and provisions on enhancing consumer trust ensuring a high level of consumer protection.[245]

Interestingly, the United States' opposition against allegedly protectionist data protection rules in Europe has now coexisted for several years with growing restrictions on the outflow of personal data from the United States on national security grounds, broadly defined.[246] These restrictions are motivated primarily by concerns around access to Americans' personal data by non-democratic foreign governments, most notably that of China.[247] There exists a notable distinction

[243] (Emphasis added.) Communication from the Commission to the European Parliament and the Council, 'Exchanging and Protecting Personal Data in a Globalised World' [2017] COM (2017) 7 final, 6 (hereafter Communication from the Commission, 'Exchanging and Protecting Personal Data in a Globalised World').

[244] 'Digital Trade' (*European Commission*) <https://policy.trade.ec.europa.eu/help-exporters-and-importers/accessing-markets/goods-and-services/digital-trade_en> accessed 10 July 2023.

[245] Communication from the Commission, 'Trade Policy Review' (n 232).

[246] For a discussion, see Kristina Irion, Margot E Kaminski, and Svetlana Yakovleva, 'Privacy Peg, Trade Hole: Why We (Still) Shouldn't Put Data Privacy in Trade Law' (2023) The University of Chicago Law Review Online <https://lawreviewblog.uchicago.edu/2023/03/27/irion-kaminski-yakovleva/> accessed 10 July 2023 (hereafter Irion, Kaminski, and Yakovleva, 'Privacy Peg, Trade Hole'). On the broadened concept of national security in the United States, see J Benton Heath, 'The New National Security Challenge to the Economic Order' (2020) 129(4) The Yale Law Journal 1020, 1044; Robert D Williams, 'In the Balance: The Future of America's National Security and Innovation Ecosystem' (*Lawfare Blog*, 30 November 2018) <https://www.lawfareblog.com/balance-future-americas-national-security-and-innovation-ecosystem> accessed 10 July 2023. But see Karl Grindal, 'Trade Regimes as a Tool For Cyber Policy' (2019) 21(1) Digital Policy, Regulation and Governance 19.

[247] For a discussion, see Irion, Kaminski and Yakovleva, 'Privacy Peg, Trade Hole' (n 246). See also Susan Ariel Aaronson, 'What Are We Talking about When We Talk about Digital Protectionism' (2019)

between the United States' apprehension regarding the cross-border transfers of personal data, viewed primarily through the lens of national security, and the European Union's concern over the export of personal data, seen through the lens of fundamental rights. When considering the US perspective, the main focus revolves around the transfers of personal data pertaining to specific groups, such as the military, as well as extensive data collections, as exemplified by the Foreign Investment Risk Review Modernization Act (FIRRMA) enacted in 2020.[248] Rather than concentrating on individual data privacy interests or rights, the US government perceives the collective interest in national security to be at stake.[249] The notion that the United States unequivocally supports unhindered cross-border data transfers is, therefore, no longer an absolute reality.[250]

In sum, while the European Union and the United States frame their digital trade discourses in similar terms, when it comes to the protection of privacy and personal data, they clearly do not agree on the right balance to be struck between the economic benefits of digital trade, on the one hand, and the level of protection of the rights to privacy and personal data, on the other.[251] Both trading partners, however, do seem to agree that the term 'protectionism' has a negative valence. In practice, the European Union and the United States apply their own standards and values to measure what digital protectionism is *abroad* as a result of regulatory divergence on a number of domestic policies that affect digital trade, including privacy and data protection.[252] While the EU decries US national security surveillance in the United States as a threat to European fundamental rights to privacy and data protection, the United States itself blocks data flows to China by invoking its national security. While both the European Union and the United States recognize, in theory, that privacy and data protection are important values, they diverge quite jarringly on what the 'correct' level of such protections should be.[253] In other words, there is a deep disagreement on where to draw the line between protection and protectionism. This ties in a broader tendency of the EU and the United States as powerful players on international arena to advance their version of international

18(4) World Trade Review 541 (hereafter Aaronson, 'What Are We Talking about When We Talk about Digital Protectionism').

248 US Foreign Investment Risk Review Modernization Act (FIRRMA), Pub L No 115-232, §1701-93, 132 Stat. 1636, 2174 (2018) (hereafter FIRRMA).

249 See Irion, Kaminski, and Yakovleva, 'Privacy Peg, Trade Hole' (n 246).

250 For a discussion, see ibid.

251 Susan Ariel Aaronson, 'Why Trade Agreements Are Not Setting Information Free: The Lost History and Reinvigorated Debate over Cross-Border Data Flows, Human Rights, and National Security' (2015) 14(4) World Trade Review 671, 687 (hereafter Aaronson, 'Why Trade Agreements Are Not Setting Information Free') ('Unfortunately, despite their collaboration, the US and the EU do not completely agree on digital rights. In addition, the US and the EU disagree on the role of the state and business in protecting privacy.').

252 See ibid 682 ('Under US law, online privacy is a consumer right, whereas in the EU (as well as in Australia and Canada), privacy is a human and consumer right that must be protected by governments.').

253 ibid 682–83.

digital trade rules, a phenomenon Bradford and Posner call 'universal exceptionalism'.[254] These are the issues to which this chapter returns later. The next section, however, adds one more layer to the analytical edifice and turns to the business interests that underpin the shifts in the discourse.

3.3.3 Business interests behind the 'digital trade' discourse

In Section 3.2.4.3, this chapter explained how a policy favouring trade liberalization, just as a policy favouring domestic regulation limiting free trade (which is often presented by those favouring free trade as 'protectionist'), can be captured. In this section, this chapter demonstrates that not only the economic benefits of cross-border digital trade but also certain business interests profiting from the absence of restrictions on cross-border transfers are shaping the 'digital trade' discourse.[255]

The United States was one of the first WTO members to adopt a so-called 'digital trade' agenda back in 2002.[256] Historically, the United States has a 'strong competitive advantage in the digital economy. . ..'[257] As Aaronson has argued, by making the campaign against digital protectionism an essential element of its international trade policy as demanded by the global US-based internet platforms, the United States is trying to promote a global internet, free of barriers to entry, while preserving its (declining) internet dominance.[258] Some observers suspect that the United States applies the 'digital protectionism' label to any domestic regulation that reduces its market share abroad in this space.[259] This echoes

[254] Anu Bradford and Eric Posner, 'Universal Exceptionalism in International Law' (2011) 52 Harvard International Law Journal 1,12. In particular, the authors argue that 'great powers typically support a view of international law that embodies their own normative commitments but is presented as a universal set of commitments'.

[255] Shamel Azmeh, Christopher Foster, and Jaime Echavarri, 'The International Trade Regime and the Quest for Free Digital Trade' (2020) 22(3) International Studies Review 671, 673 (hereafter Azmeh, Foster, and Echavarri, 'The International Trade Regime and the Quest for Free Digital Trade').

[256] See Mira Burri, 'The Governance of Data and Data Flows in Trade Agreements: The Pitfalls of Legal Adaptation' (2017) 51(65) UC Davis Law Review 65, 99, 129; Sacha Wunsch-Vincent, 'The Digital Trade Agenda of the U.S.: Parallel Tracks of Bilateral, Regional and Multilateral Liberalization' (2003) 58(1) Aussenwirtschaft 7, 7 <https://dx.doi.org/10.2139/ssrn.393961> accessed 10 July 2023.

[257] Azmeh and Foster, 'The TPP and the Digital Trade Agenda' (n 137) 4–5 ('Such policies also represent a long term threat to the US economy which has a strong comparative advantage in the digital economy and related activities which gives it a strong advantage to lead the major technological shifts in the coming decades in different economic sectors'.); see also Aaronson, 'What Are We Talking about When We Discuss Digital Protectionism?' (n 34) 8 (noting the particular importance of digital trade to the US economy).

[258] See Aaronson, 'Digital Protectionism? Or Label the U.S. Government Uses to Criticize Policy It Doesn't Like?' (n 219) ('The United States has conflicting objectives regarding the digital economy. On one hand, it wants to encourage a vibrant global Internet with few barriers to entry. On the other, the United States wants to preserve its Internet dominance, which is clearly declining as China, India, Indonesia and others develop their digital prowess and bring more people online'.). See also Azmeh, Foster, and Echavarri, 'The International Trade Regime and the Quest for Free Digital Trade' (n 255) 683–85.

[259] See Aaronson, 'Digital Protectionism? Or Label the U.S. Government Uses to Criticize Policy It Doesn't Like?' (n 219) ('[T]o some observers, it seems like the United States defines [digital

the above-mentioned 'diminished giant syndrome,' a term coined by Bhagwati to refer to the US trade policy in the 1970s, which used new protectionism to reshape the international trading order to its advantage.[260] American Big Tech companies view initiatives to control domestic data space in several countries, including through restrictions on data flows (eg those adopted in China, Australia, India, Russia, Thailand, Turkey, and the United Arab Emirates), as threats to their business model.[261] As a result, the executives of these companies, often relying on the research of specialized think tanks, activated their lobbying activities with trade policy officials to 'do a better job of limiting digital protectionism.'[262]

Scholars who studied the lobbying of big technological companies demonstrate that tensions around cross-border data flows have intensified, a change marked by an increase in the use of the label 'digital protectionism.'[263] Based on the analysis of data on political spending (lobbying, campaign contributions, and other forms of political activism), those scholars claim convincingly that powerful US tech companies (including large corporations like Google, Facebook, Amazon, Microsoft, and Apple, as well as smaller firms such as LinkedIn, Airbnb, and Expedia) and industry associations (such as the Business Software Alliance, Information Technology Industry Council, and the Software & Information Industry Association)[264] played a crucial role in the formation of the United States'

protectionism] as policies that with or without intent reduce U.S. market share in foreign markets.'). See also Azmeh, Foster, and Echavarri, 'The International Trade Regime and the Quest for Free Digital Trade' (n 255) 684.

260 See Bhagwati, 'The Diminished Giant Syndrome' (n 93) 22 ('The American mood parallels Great Britain's at the end of the nineteenth century.... As was Great Britain at that time, America has been struck by a "diminished giant syndrome"—reinforced by the slippage in the growth of its living standards in the 1980s.').

261 See, eg, Aaronson, 'Why Trade Agreements Are Not Setting Information Free' (n 251) 684 ('[P]olicymakers from [China, Australia, India, Russia, Thailand, Turkey, and the United Arab Emirates] were increasingly determined to control the Internet within their borders and facilitate the rise of domestic Internet firms Many US based Internet companies saw in these actions a threat to their bottom lines.'). For an overview of restrictions on cross-border data flows and their costs to businesses, see also Cory and Dascoli, 'How Barriers to Cross-Border Data Flows Are Spreading Globally' (n 185).

262 Aaronson notes, for example, that Google used the research of a Canadian think-tank to document how more than 40 governments instituted broad scale restrictions of information flows. Aaronson, 'Why Trade Agreements Are Not Setting Information Free' (n 251) 684. See also Evgeny Morozov, 'What Happens When Policy Is Made by Corporations? Your Privacy Is Seen as a Barrier to Economic Growth' (*The Guardian*, 12 July 2015) <https://www.theguardian.com/commentisfree/2015/jul/12/ttip-your-data-privacy-is-a-barrier-to-economic-growth?CMP=Share_iOSApp_Other> accessed 10 July 2023.

263 Azmeh and Foster, 'The TPP and the Digital Trade Agenda' (n 137) 11 ('[T]ensions around cross-border data flows. Such tensions have been brought to the fore by the growing use of so-called "digital protectionism" in a number of countries.').

264 ibid 12–14 ('In the US, political spending by these firms have increased substantially over the last few years making internet and new "tech" companies one of the strongest lobbying sectors in Washington.... This included major spending from large companies such as Google, Facebook, Amazon, Yahoo, Apple, EBay, Microsoft, and Apple, but also younger firms such as Snapchat, Rapidshare, Linkedin, Dropbox, Twitter, Airbnb, Expedia, in addition to industry associations'). See also UNCTAD, 'Digital Economy Report 2019: Value Creation and Capture: Implications for Developing Countries' (2019) UNCTAD/DER/2019, 88–89 <https://unctad.org/en/PublicationsLibr

'digital trade agenda', the prioritization of cross-border data flows in international trade policy, and increase in pressure on domestic regulations restricting such flows.[265] These political efforts, as well as fears concerning the diminishing technological advantage of the United States in the global digital economy, have made the 'digital trade agenda' 'a key part of the US trade policy in future multilateral and bilateral agreements'.[266] At the same time, as China has emerged as the world's second largest home for collectors of data (digital platforms)[267] and the largest e-commerce market in the world,[268] Americans' personal data is being increasingly accumulated by foreign-owned (primarily, Chinese) companies.[269] As a result, the current US digital trade agenda is also motivated by the rationale to counterbalance China's technological and economic ascent,[270] resulting in the policies aimed at facilitating the inflow of data to the United States from all over the world, and restricting the outflow of American data to China.

In the ongoing negotiations on digital trade within the Indo-Pacific Economic Framework (IPEF), the business lobby and the US Congress continue to advocate for free cross-border data flows.[271] Some argue that this time around, these

ary/der2019_en.pdf> accessed 10 July 2023 ('[Global digital platforms]' have an interest in lobbying for international rules and regulations that allow to enable them to leverage their business models. Indeed, in the past few years, technology companies have replaced the financial sector as the biggest lobbyists, and major platforms have spent considerable resources in key locations'.).

265 See Azmeh and Foster, 'The TPP and the Digital Trade Agenda' (n 137) 19 ('Many of the policies demanded by the industry were reflected in the US trade policy and in the 'digital dozen' principles adopted by the USTR. . . . Similarly, the trade promotion authority (TPA) listed digital trade and cross-border data flows as principle negotiating objectives of the United States'.). See also Burcu Kilic, 'Digital Trade Rules: Big Tech's End Run around Domestic Regulations' (*Heinrich-Böll-Stiftung*, 19 May 2021) <https://eu.boell.org/en/2021/05/19/digital-trade-rules-big-techs-end-run-around-domestic-regulations> accessed 10 July 2023. See also Rajan S Neeraj, 'Trade Rules for the Digital Economy: Charting New Waters at the WTO' (2019) 18(S1) World Trade Review s121, s136 ('The overwhelming political and economic influence that the titans of the digital industry exerted over the shaping of the TPP's digital agenda leaves no doubt about the political economy considerations that underpin the TPP').

266 Azmeh and Foster, 'The TPP and the Digital Trade Agenda' (n 137) 30; see also John Selby, 'Data Localization Laws: Trade Barriers or Legitimate Responses to Cybersecurity Risks, or Both?' (2017) 25(3) International Journal of Law and Information Technology 213, 217 ('It is not surprising to see the US government push strongly in the next generation of international trade agreements to restrict efforts to implement data localization in other countries'.).

267 UNCTAD, 'Digital Economy Report. Cross-Border Data Flows and Development: For Whom the Data Flow' (2021), 22 <https://unctad.org/system/files/official-document/der2021_en.pdf> accessed 10 July 2023 (hereafter UNCTAD, '2021 Digital Economy Report').

268 Henry S Gao, 'Data Regulation with Chinese Characteristics' in Mira Burri (ed), *Big Data and Global Trade Law* (CUP 2021) 247.

269 See, eg, Oona A Hathaway, 'Keeping the Wrong Secrets: How Washington Misses the Real Security Threat' (*Foreign Affairs*, 7 December 2021) <https://www.foreignaffairs.com/articles/united-states/2021-12-07/hacking-cybersecurity-keeping-wrong-secrets> accessed 10 July 2023.

270 Leila Brännström, 'Global Inequality and the EU International Law Position on Cross-Border Data Flows' 92 (2023) Nordic Journal of International Law 119, 124.

271 Arasasingham and Goodman, 'Operationalizing Data Free Flow with Trust (DFFT)' (n 236); 'Advancing a Jobs-Centric Digital Trade Policy' (*BSA*, 13 November 2021) <https://www.bsa.org/files/policy-filings/11132021jobscentricdigitrade.pdf> accessed 10 July 2023, arguing that including CPTPP-like provisions on cross-border data flows in IPEF 'would help level the playing field by lowering digital trade barriers that impede exports of goods and services produced by workers at home'. BSA is a lobby group of software companies.

interests may not get the upper hand in trade negotiations due to the current White House's sensitivities to domestic labour groups opposing the current US model on cross-border data flows (discussed in more detail in the following section).[272] However, it remains to be seen how these negotiations play out in practice.[273]

Although there no similar research seems to exist on the lobbying activities on digital trade at the EU level, several NGO and news media reports attest that EU digital trade policy, including that on cross-border data flows, is heavily influenced by powerful US tech companies.[274] Digital platforms from the United States actively engage in lobbying efforts within the European Union, although their expenditure in Brussels has been reported to be comparatively lower than that in Washington, DC.[275] Specifically, Google, Meta Platforms, and Microsoft hold the top three positions on the list of leading lobbying spenders in the European Union as of 15 April 2021, with Apple and Amazon (Amazon Europe Core SARL) ranking within the top 20 and top 30, respectively.[276] Collectively, these US companies allocated over 12 million US dollars towards lobbying activities in the European Union in 2015, and this figure nearly doubled to 24 million US dollars in 2020.[277] As *The New York Times* put it, big tech lobby spending on influencing EU policy-making is thus 'contributing to a Washingtonization of Brussels, giving money and connections an upper hand over the public interest'.[278]

[272] See eg Arasasingham and Goodman, 'Operationalizing Data Free Flow with Trust (DFFT)' (n 236); 'A Worker-Centered Digital Trade Agenda' (*AFL-CIO*, 7 February 2023) <https://aflcio.org/worker-centered-digital-agenda> accessed 10 July 2023 (hereafter AFL-CIO, 'A Worker-Centered Digital Trade Agenda').

[273] See eg the response of the US Chamber of Commerce to the above-cited recommendations by AFL-CIO: Mary Kate Carter and John G Murphy, 'Setting the Record Straight on a "Worker-Centered" Digital Trade Agenda' (*US Chamber of Commerce*, 1 March 2023) <https://www.uschamber.com/international/trade-agreements/setting-the-record-straight-on-a-worker-centered-digital-trade-agenda> accessed 10 July 2023.

[274] Natasha Lomas, 'As Its Data Flows Woes Grow, Google Lobbies For Quickie Fix to EU-US Transfers' (*TechCrunch*, 19 January 2022) <https://techcrunch.com/2022/01/19/google-lobbies-for-new-privacy-shield/?guccounter=1&guce_referrer=aHR0cHM6Ly93d3cuZ29vZ2xlLmNvbS8&guce_referrer_sig=AQAAADTAUg1eK7FULgT-t9SdWOaCU-iAWRomypXA3JgmgXL0foL7DuWJTlSUr85ahiwuK8EbHVw1iG-sYj9WlkbiuRD4Hrj7RN3uAfaIEPB2ismpcHtRWScyKCjsyQ4A1IJRP4Mr0TKbwj7LUUqobS4snXkaCQ84FFnQ3aiG7laPBlHZ> accessed 10 July 2023; UNCTAD, '2021 Digital Economy Report' (n 267) 29; 'The Lobby Network: Big Tech's Web of Influence in the EU' (*Corporate Europe Observatory*, 31 August 2021) <https://corporateeurope.org/en/2021/08/lobby-network-big-techs-web-influence-eu> accessed 10 July 2023 (hereafter Corporate Europe Observatory, 'The Lobby Network: Big Tech's Web of Influence in the EU'). Alexander Fanta, 'Tech Industry Pushes Europe for WTO Data Flows Deal' (*Netzpolitik.org*, 30 June 2021) <https://netzpolitik.org/2021/digital-trade-tech-industry-pushes-europe-for-wto-data-flows-deal/> accessed 10 July 2023 (hereafter Fanta, 'Tech Industry Pushes Europe for WTO Data Flows Deal'); 'Tech Lobby Eyes Opportunities Created by New EU-US Trade and Tech Council' (*Corporate Europe Observatory*, 28 September 2021) <https://corporateeurope.org/en/2021/09/tech-lobby-eyes-opportunities-created-new-eu-us-trade-and-tech-council> accessed 10 July 2023 (hereafter Corporate Europe Observatory, 'Tech Lobby Eyes Opportunities').

[275] UNCTAD, '2021 Digital Economy Report' (n 267) 29. See also Corporate Europe Observatory, 'The Lobby Network' (n 274).

[276] ibid.

[277] ibid.

[278] Adam Satariano and Matina Stevis-Gridneff, 'Big Tech Turns Its Lobbyists Loose on Europe, Alarming Regulators' (*The New York Times*, 14 December 2020) <https://www.nytimes.com/2020/12/14/technology/big-tech-lobbying-europe.html> accessed 10 July 2023.

What is more, big tech companies and large lobby groups have also been reported to engage in 'shadow lobbying', hiding behind the front of small and medium-sized organizations.[279] Corporate Europe Observatory, an NGO that focuses on exposing corporate lobbying in the EU, reports the lobbying efforts exerted by Meta Platforms and big tech industry groups, trying to shape the agenda at the EU-US Trade and Technology Council—a bilateral EU-US forum, created to deepen transatlantic trade and economic relations.[280] The Observatory noted, in particular, the efforts these actors deployed to accelerate the resolution of the issues concerning EU-US data transfers.[281] Relying on the minutes from meetings between Big Tech and EU officials, Netzpolitik demonstrated how prominent tech companies, including Microsoft, Google, Meta Platforms, and industry associations representing the technology sector, are trying to shape an international legal framework on cross-border data flows through influencing the new trade rules being negotiated as part of the Joint Initiative on E-commerce at the WTO, and pushing the EU to adopt a strong commitment against data localization laws in that negotiation.[282]

3.3.4 Measures banning 'digital protectionism' in recent trade agreements

Just as in the neoliberal discourse of the 1970s and 1980s, the modern digital trade discourse is reflected in recent international trade agreements, which increasingly include dedicated chapters on electronic commerce and digital trade ('digital trade chapters').[283] Such chapters tackle a range of domestic policies affecting cross-border digital commerce ('digital trade provisions'),[284] but this book only focuses on those concerning cross-border data flows.

Despite negotiations on cross-border data flows and the above-mentioned Data Free Flow with Trust (DFFT) as part of Joint Initiative on E-commerce ongoing at the WTO since 2019 between, as of this writing, eighty-nine WTO members, a multilateral consensus on the design and scope of cross-border data flow provisions has not yet been achieved.[285] Proposals on electronic commerce submitted

[279] See, eg, Clothilde Goujard, 'Big Tech Accused of Shady Lobbying in EU Parliament' (Politico, 14 October 2022) <https://www.politico.eu/article/big-tech-companies-face-potential-eu-lobbying-ban/> accessed 10 July 2023.

[280] Corporate Europe Observatory, 'Tech Lobby Eyes Opportunities' (n 274).

[281] ibid.

[282] Fanta, 'Tech Industry Pushes Europe for WTO Data Flows Deal' (n 274).

[283] See, eg, Chapter 19 of the Agreement between the United States of America, the United Mexican States, and Canada (30 November 2018) (hereafter USMCA).

[284] For an overview, see eg Burri and Polanco, 'Digital Trade Provisions in Preferential Trade Agreements' (n 181).

[285] See, eg, 'E-Commerce Negotiations Maintain Positive Momentum, Focus on Key Issues' (*World Trade Organization*, 25 May 2023) <https://www.wto.org/english/news_e/news23_e/jsec_25may23_e.htm> accessed 10 July 2023; for discussion, see Mira Burri, 'A WTO Agreement on Electronic

to the WTO negotiations increasingly focus on barriers to digital trade and digital protectionism.[286] Burri argues that despite a clear mandate to negotiate new multilateral rules on e-commerce, 'the feasibility of an agreement that will cover all the pertinent issues that data-driven economy has brought about appears at this point of time somewhat limited'.[287] Issues related to data governance, such as those on cross-border data flows and data privacy are among the most contentious ones.[288] While the DFFT label seems appealing to both the EU and the United States (in general, who can be against trust?), there is *no understanding*, let alone agreement, on what *trust* means (on the potential risks of formulating the normative goal of data privacy protection in terms of trust, see Section 3.4). As a result, digital trade provisions have thus far only appeared in bilateral and regional trade agreements, which have created a web of highly fragmented and sometimes even incoherent rules governing cross-border data flows and data privacy.[289] It remains to be seen how WTO negotiations will play out.[290]

Despite a seemingly firm consensus on the use of the terms 'digital trade' and 'digital protectionism'—the axes around which the discourses governing international negotiations revolve—the value structures underlying these discourses diverge, as the United States and the EU example above illustrates. This section explicates how the international trade provisions on cross-border data flows advanced in recent FTAs mirror this divergence.

In the spirit of its digital trade agenda, the United States has been a pioneer in including provisions on free cross-border data flows in international trade agreements.[291] Although the United States has advocated regulating information flows

Commerce: An Enquiry into Its Legal Substance and Viability' (2021) Trade Law 4.0 Working Paper No 1 <https://ssrn.com/abstract=3976133> accessed 10 July 2023; Burri, 'The Impact of Digitalization on Global Trade Law' (n 215).

[286] See Mitchell and Mishra, 'Data at the Docks' (n 207) 1111 ('The majority of the recent proposals on electronic commerce circulated by WTO Members in recent years tend to focus on regulatory barriers to digital trade. In particular, they emphasize digital protectionism.').

[287] Burri, 'The Impact of Digitalization on Global Trade Law' (n 215) 562.

[288] ibid.

[289] See Burri, 'The Regulation of Data Flows through Trade Agreements' (n 214) 417; Burri, 'The Impact of Digitalization on Global Trade Law' (n 215) 563 ff. Burri and Polanco, 'Digital Trade Provisions in Preferential Trade Agreements' (n 181) 189, 220; Fahey, 'The European Union as a Digital Trade Actor' (n 181) 9.

[290] According to Mitchel and Gyanchandani, the insertion of the new digital trade rules negotiated within the Joint Initiative on E-commerce into the WTO legal framework 'may take a long time in part due to the consensus principle'. In particular, due to persistent objections against the negotiations by a group of developing countries led by India and South Africa. See Andrew D Mitchell and Vandana Gyanchandani, 'Convergence & Divergence in Digital Trade Regulation: A Comparative Analysis of CP-TPP, RCEP, and eJSI' (2023) 19(2) South Carolina Journal of International Law & Business 105 <https://ssrn.com/abstract=4476890> accessed 10 July 2023 (hereafter Mitchell and Gyanchandani, 'Convergence & Divergence in Digital Trade Regulation'). See also Ines Willemyns, 'Agreement Forthcoming? A Comparison of EU, US, and Chinese RTAs in Times of Plurilateral E-Commerce Negotiations' (2020) 23 Journal of International Economic Law 221; Burri, 'Towards a New Treaty on Digital Trade' (n 179).

[291] Susan Ariel Aaronson, 'Redefining Protectionism: The New Challenge in the Digital Age' (2016) The George Washington University, Institute for International Economic Policy Working Paper Series,

via international trade rules roughly since the 1980s,[292] the first time a non-actionable (or non-binding), horizontal provision on free cross-border data flows appeared in its trade agreement was in the electronic commerce chapter of the 2012 US-Korea free trade agreement (KORUS).[293] The United States later proposed a *binding* horizontal provision—a demand of key US lobbies as explained above—in the drafts of the currently stalled TTIP and TiSA.[294] The e-commerce chapter of the CPTPP, heavily influenced by the United States, similarly includes a legally binding horizontal obligation on the free cross-border data flow of information, including personal data, which states that '[e]ach Party shall allow the cross-border transfer of information by electronic means, including personal information, when this activity is for the conduct of the business of a covered person'.[295]

This provision was included in the Comprehensive and Progressive Agreement for Trans-Pacific Partnership (CPTPP)[296] before the US withdrawal from the agreement[297] and remained unchanged in the final version of the agreement concluded

Working Paper No 30, 59 < <https://ideas.repec.org/p/gwi/wpaper/2016-30.html> accessed 10 July 2023 (hereafter Aaronson, 'Redefining Protectionism') ('The United States is the Paul Revere of digital protectionism, using naming and shaming to condemn such policies'.); see also Susan Ariel Aaronson, 'Match Made in Heaven? The Wedding of Trade and Human Rights' in Lisa L Martin (ed), *The Oxford Handbook of the Political Economy of International Trade* (Oxford Handbooks Online 2015) 507; 'Cross-Border Data Flows: Could Foreign Protectionism Hurt U.S. Jobs?' (2014) Hearing Before the Subcommittee on Commerce, Manufacturing, and Trade of the Committee on Energy and Commerce, 3 <https://books.google.nl/books?id=FG2F8oisHWwC&printsec=frontcover&source=gbs_ge_summary_r&cad=0#v=onepage&q&f=false> accessed 10 July 2023; Michael Geist, 'Data Rules in Modern Trade Agreements: Toward Reconciling an Open Internet with Privacy and Security Safeguards' (*CIGI*, 4 April 2018) <https://www.cigionline.org/articles/data-rules-modern-trade-agreements-toward-reconciling-open-internet-privacy-and-security/> accessed 10 July 2023 ('The CPTPP also includes a specific exception for financial services, ironically at the insistence of the US Treasury, which wanted to retain the right to establish restrictions on financial data flows'.).

[292] See Aaronson, 'Why Trade Agreements Are Not Setting Information Free' (n 251) 672 (noting that the issue of free flow of information in trade agreements 'is not new; in the 1980s, with the advent of faster computers, software, and satellites, officials from some states, including the US and Japan, wanted to include language governing the free flow of information in trade agreements'.). For a concise overview of earlier initiatives, see ibid 679–85.

[293] ibid 687 ('[T]his provision does not forbid the use of such barriers, nor does it define necessary or unnecessary barriers. In short, the language is not actionable'.); art 15.8 United States-Korea Free Trade Agreement (1 April 2007) 46 ILM 642 (hereafter KORUS).

[294] See Gaël Le Roux, 'TTIP Negotiations, Policy Convergence, and the Transatlantic Digital Economy' (2017) 19(4) Business and Politics 709, 731. Trade in Services Agreement (TiSA) Annex on Electronic Commerce (Wikileaks, 2016) <https://wikileaks.org/tisa/document/20151001_Annex-on-Electronic-Commerce/> accessed 10 July 2023; 'Comments of the Coalition for Privacy and Free Trade to the Trade Policy Staff Committee of the United States Trade Representative' (*Coalition For Privacy & Free Trade*, 2013), 2–3 <http://www.centerfordigitaldemocracy.org/sites/default/files/Coalition-for-Privacy-and-Free-Trade-Comments-to-USTR-May-9-2013_0.pdf> accessed 10 July 2023. But see James Fontanella-Khan, 'Data Protection Ruled Out of EU-US Trade Talks' (*Financial Times*, 4 November 2013) <www.ft.com/content/92a14dd2-44b9-11e3-a751-00144feabdc0> accessed 10 July 2023 (hereafter Fontanella-Khan, 'Data Protection Ruled Out of EU-US Trade Talks') (noting EU officials' fear that 'finding a middle ground with the U.S. would only lower overall E.U. privacy standards'.).

[295] Art 14.11(2) Comprehensive and Progressive Agreement for Trans-Pacific Partnership (concluded on 8 March 2018, in force 30 December 2018) (hereafter CPTPP).

[296] CPTPP (n 295).

[297] The version of the agreement with the United States as a party was known simply as the Transpacific Partnership ('TPP'). Removing the United States from this agreement was one of President Trump's first

without the United States.[298] The United States-Mexico-Canada Agreement (USMCA)[299]—a revision of the North American Free Trade Agreement ('NAFTA')[300]—includes a similar provision.[301] The US-Japan Digital Trade Agreement (USJTA)[302] and the proposal for the ongoing e-commerce talks at the WTO Joint Initiative on E-commerce replicate the 'golden standard' provisions on digital trade.[303] This move, against the background of trade restricting measures in traditional trade sectors,[304] illustrates the strategic importance of digital trade for the US economy. This model has spread beyond US trade agreements and can be found, for instance, in the UK-Japan Comprehensive Economic Partnership Agreement (CEPA)[305] as well as in other preferential trade agreements, such as Singapore–Australia, Thailand–Australia, New Zealand–Singapore, Japan–Singapore, South Korea–Singapore, and in the Digital Economy Partnership Agreement (DEPA) between Singapore, Chile, and New Zealand.[306]

decisions. See Executive Office of the President, 'Office of the U.S. Trade Representative Letter to TPP Depositary' (2017) <https://ustr.gov/sites/default/files/files/Press/Releases/1-30-17%20USTR%20Letter%20to%20TPP%20Depositary.pdf> accessed 10 July 2023.

[298] See generally CPTPP (n 295).

[299] USMCA (n 283).

[300] North American Free Trade Agreement art 301(2), 8–17 December 1992, 32 ILM 289 [1993] (hereafter NAFTA).

[301] USMCA (n 283) art 19.11(1) ('No Party shall prohibit or restrict the cross-border transfer of information, including personal information, by electronic means if this activity is for the conduct of the business of a covered person.'); see also Susan Ariel Aaronson and Patrick Leblond, 'Another Digital Divide: The Rise of Data Realms and Its Implications for the WTO' (2018) (21)2 Journal of International Economic Law 245, 257 (noting that despite the fact that Trump withdrew from the TPP right after becoming President, 'the Trump administration has built its proposals on those of the Obama administration (namely, the TPP)'.).

[302] Agreement between the United States of America and Japan Concerning Digital Trade (7 October 2019) <https://ustr.gov/sites/default/files/files/agreements/japan/Agreement_between_the_United_States_and_Japan_concerning_Digital_Trade.pdf> accessed 10 July 2023 (hereafter USJDTA).

[303] USJDTA (n 302) art 11(1) ('Neither Party shall prohibit or restrict the cross-border transfer of information, including personal information, by electronic means, if this activity is for the conduct of the business of a covered person.'). WTO, Joint Statement on Electronic Commerce, 'Communication from the United States' INF/ECOM/5 (25 March 2019); WTO, Joint Statement on Electronic Commerce, 'Communication from the United States, INF/ECOM/23' (26 April 2019); Inu Manak, 'U.S. WTO E-Commerce Proposal Reads Like USMCA' (*International Economic Law and Policy Blog*, 8 May 2019) <https://worldtradelaw.typepad.com/ielpblog/2019/05/us-wto-e-commerce-proposal-reads-like-usmca.html> accessed 10 July 2023; Mira Burri, 'Trade Law 4.0: Are We There Yet?' (2023) 26 Journal of International Economic Law 90, 98 (hereafter Burri, 'Trade Law 4.0: Are We There Yet?').

[304] See Daniel CK Chow, Ian M Sheldon, and William McGuire, 'The Revival of Economic Nationalism and the Global Trading System'(2019) 40(5) Cardozo Law Review 2133, 2151 ('[T]he Trump Administration is following a path of economic nationalism and pushing back with threats of not playing by the accepted rules of international governance.'); see also Kyle Handley and Nuno Limão, 'Trade under T.R.U.M.P. Policies' in Chad P Bown (ed), *Economics and Policy in the Age of Trump* (CEPR Press 2017) 141–43 <https://giovanniperi.ucdavis.edu/uploads/5/6/8/2/56826033/ageoftrump_june2017.pdf> accessed 10 July 2023.

[305] Arts 8.80, 8.84 UK-Japan Comprehensive Economic Partnership Agreement (concluded 23 October 2020, in force 1 January 2021).

[306] Mira Burri, 'Approaches to Digital Trade and Data Flow Regulation Across Jurisdictions: Implications for the Future ASEAN-EU Agreement' (2022) 49(2) Legal Issues of Economic Integration 149, 151; Burri, 'The Impact of Digitalization on Global Trade Law' (n

The Biden Administration has been reluctant to negotiate new comprehensive trade agreements.[307] Negotiations of the Indo-Pacific Economic Framework (IPEF) with trading partners in the Asia–Pacific region on strategic issues, including 'digital and emerging technologies-related issues', however, suggests the willingness of the United States to consider new commitments on digital trade.[308] According to some, on digital trade, these negotiations may result in a US-Indo-Pacific Digital Economy Agreement (USIP DEA).[309] According to the Indo-Pacific Strategy of the United States, the United States is planning to 'govern . . . digital economies and cross-border data flows according to open principles, including through a new digital economy framework'.[310] This suggests that the US Government's intention is to use its existing model on regulating cross-border data flows in these negotiations, consistent with several other above-mentioned Digital Economy Agreements concluded around the world already largely replicating the US model.[311] Some argue, however, that the rules on cross-border data flows may deviate from the current US model discussed below (in particular, contain broader public policy exceptions) under pressure from domestic labour groups, arguing for safeguarding a broader right to regulate—in particular, to protect privacy—in digital trade rule-making.[312] These negotiations are conducted in secrecy, and their outcome is unclear.

As compared to prior US-led free trade agreements, the CPTPP, USMCA, and USJTA not only contain an exception from a free data flow provision for regulation

215) 567–68; Mira Burri and Anupam Chander, 'What Are Digital Trade and Digital Trade Law?' (2023) 117 AJIL Unbound 99, 102.

[307] Kenneth Propp, 'More than Adequate: New Directions in International Data Transfer Governance' (2023) Atlantic Council, 14 <https://www.atlanticcouncil.org/wp-content/uploads/2023/06/More-than-Adequate-New-Directions-in-International-Data-Transfer-Governance_-_FINAL.pdf> accessed 10 July 2023 (hereafter Propp, 'More than Adequate').

[308] Mitchell and Gyanchandani, 'Convergence & Divergence in Digital Trade Regulation' (n 290) 101. See also 'Indo-Pacific Strategy of the United States' (*The White House*, February 2022) <https://www.whitehouse.gov/wp-content/uploads/2022/02/U.S.-Indo-Pacific-Strategy.pdf> accessed 10 July 2023 (hereafter The White House, 'Indo-Pacific Strategy of the United States'); Propp, 'More than Adequate' (n 307) 14.

[309] Mitchell and Gyanchandani, 'Convergence & Divergence in Digital Trade Regulation' (n 290) 101. For a discussion of Digital Economy Agreements (DEAs) as innovation of digital trade rule-making, see Burri, 'Trade Law 4.0: Are We There Yet?' (n 203).

[310] The White House, 'Indo-Pacific Strategy of The United States' (n 308) 11.

[311] For example, the 2020 Singapore–Australia Digital Economy Agreement (DEA); the 2020 Digital Economy Partnership Agreement (DEPA) between Chile, New Zealand, and Singapore (Canada, South Korea, and China seeking to join); the 2021 Korea–Singapore Digital Economy Agreement (DEA); and the 2022 UK–Singapore Digital Economy Agreement (DEA). See Burri, 'Trade Law 4.0: Are We There Yet?' (n 203) 96.

[312] See Propp, 'More than Adequate' (n 307) 14. Arasasingham and Goodman, 'Operationalizing Data Free Flow with Trust (DFFT)' (n 236); AFL-CIO, 'A Worker-Centered Digital Trade Agenda' (n 272) (stating that '[c]ommitments to promote reliable, secure cross-border data flows must be offset by corresponding obligations to properly regulate the digital economy, including by addressing a range of issues that threaten workers' rights and privacy in and out of the workplace' and that '[g]overnments should be able to adopt restrictions on cross-border data flows to protect the privacy and security of individuals' personal data.').

pursuing important domestic public policy objectives but also a dedicated article on the protection of personal information.[313] In all three agreements, the structure and text of the exception strongly resemble those of Article XIV(c)(ii) of GATS. For example, Article 19.11(2) of the USMCA states the following:

> This Article does not prevent a Party from adopting or maintaining a measure inconsistent with paragraph 1 that is necessary to achieve a legitimate public policy objective, provided that the measure:
> (a) is not applied in a manner which would constitute a means of arbitrary or unjustifiable discrimination or a disguised restriction on trade; and
> (b) does not impose restrictions on transfers of information greater than are *necessary* to achieve the objective.[314]

Unlike Article XIV(c)(ii) GATS, the exceptions in the CPTPP, USMCA, and USJDTA do not specifically identify privacy and data protection by name, or any other particular policy objective for that matter.[315] It can be reasonably argued that privacy and data protection would fall under such exceptions, as these policy interests are among the public policy goals that are most likely to be affected by the free cross-border data flow provision. Because, unlike in the GATS, legitimate policy objectives are not clearly spelled out, these norms create an even higher degree of uncertainty compared to the exception of Article XIV GATS.[316]

The above-mentioned necessity test—the benchmark to evaluate the consistency of domestic regulation with the conditions of the exception—requires an objective assessment.[317] The USMCA also clarifies that '[a] measure does not meet the conditions of this paragraph if it accords different treatment to data transfers solely on the basis that they are cross-border in a manner that *modifies the conditions of competition* to the detriment of service suppliers of another Party'.[318] This

[313] CPTPP (n 295) art 14.11(2), USMCA (n 283) art 19.11(2), and USJDTA (n 302) art 11(2) contain an exception from the free cross-border data flow provision; art 14.8 CPTPP, art 19.8 USMCA, and art 15 USJDTA contain a provision on the protection of personal information. For a discussion and comparison of these provisions in the CPTPP and USJDTA, see Svetlana Yakovleva, 'Testing Restrictions on Onward Transfers of EU Personal Data against Free Data Flow Obligations in the CPTPP and US-Japan Digital Trade Agreement' (2022) Amsterdam Law School Research Paper No 2023-20, Institute for Information Law Research Paper No 2023-05 <https://ssrn.com/abstract=4423959> accessed 10 July 2023 (hereafter Yakovleva, 'Testing Restrictions on Onward Transfers').

[314] USMCA (n 283) art 19.11(2) (emphasis added).

[315] See ibid; CPTPP (n 295) art 14.11.

[316] Mira Burri, 'Interfacing Privacy and Trade' (2021) 53 Case Western Reserve Journal of International Law 35, 84 (hereafter Burri, 'Interfacing Privacy and Trade').

[317] Instead of the 'necessity' requirement, exception in art 14.11(2) CPTPP (n 295) provides that restrictions should not be 'greater than are *required* to achieve the objective' (emphasis added). This difference seems, however, purely semantic, and according to the WTO Secretariat, 'required' is yet another way to convey the concept of 'necessity'. See WTO, Note by Secretariat, 'Necessity tests' in the WTO (2 December 2003) S/WPDR/W/27, para I.A.5.

[318] (Emphasis added.) Footnote 5 to provision of art 19.11(2)(b) USMCA (n 283).

ties in with the interpretation of the necessity test in the WTO general exceptions discussed in Sections 2.4.2 and 3.2.4.3, and does not recognize regulatory intent as a factor in the necessity test assessment.

The provision for the protection of personal information in the USMCA includes not only aspirational provisions for the protection of personal information but also a number of binding obligations (introduced by 'each party shall'):

(1) '[To] adopt or maintain a legal framework that provides for protection of personal data of users of digital trade,' featuring the APEC Privacy Framework and the 2013 OECD Guidelines governing the Protection of Privacy and Transborder Flows of Personal data as examples of such frameworks;
(2) To implement key data protection principles such as a limitation on the collection of data, data quality, purpose specification and a requirement that 'any restrictions on cross-border flows of personal information are necessary and proportionate to the risks presented';
(3) A transparency requirement that parties publish information on how individuals can pursue a remedy in case of violation of personal information protections and on how companies can comply with the local personal information protection requirements; and
(4) To cooperate with regulations towards developing mechanisms of compatibility between the parties' data protection regimes and an endorsement of APEC Cross-Border Privacy Rules (CBPR) system as a 'valid mechanism' to facilitate cross-border information flows while protecting personal data.[319]

This provision transplants the United States' approach to the protection of personal data as a consumer right. Explicit mention of the 2013 OECD Guidelines and the APEC CBPR reflects the economic approach to the protection of personal data as a precondition for digital trade.[320] This way, privacy and personal data protection become normalized—or redefined—as tools of international trade and are viewed as trade values.[321] Furthermore, endorsement of the OECD Guidelines and APEC CBPR as a benchmark for personal data protection in the trade agreement, both of which set the *minimum* level of protection (the floor, not the ceiling), may make it hard to justify restrictions on cross-border data flows introduced by data protection laws (such as those modelled after the EU's GDPR) on the basis of the

[319] USMCA (n 283) art 19.8. The CPTPP (n 295) and USJDTA (n 302) contain similar but less detailed provisions.

[320] USMCA (n 283) art 19.8; see Svetlana Yakovleva, 'Should Fundamental Rights to Privacy and Data Protection Be a Part of the EU's International Trade "Deals"?' (2018) 17(3) World Trade Review 477, 484–85 (hereafter Yakovleva, 'Should Fundamental Rights Be a Part of Trade "Deals"?').

[321] USMCA (n 283) art 19.8; see Yakovleva, 'Should Fundamental Rights be a Part of Trade "Deals"?' (n 320) 484–85.

exception from the free data flow provisions. It would be hard to argue that such more restrictive laws are the least trade restrictive, when compared to the comparatively more lenient rules on transfers of personal data in the OECD Guidelines and APEC CBPR. These low privacy guarantees clearly prioritize economic rights over protection of data privacy as a non-economic or moral value.[322]

While, as just explained, the United States did not leave itself ample room to derogate from the free data flow provision in its digital trade chapters, it has secured an almost unlimited autonomy to derogate from *any* obligation of the above-mentioned trade agreements, including the free data flow provision, under a broadened national security exception.[323] For example, this national security exception reads as follows in Article 32.2(1)(b) of the USMCA:

> Nothing in this Agreement shall be construed to:
>
> <. . .>
>
> (b) preclude a Party from applying measures that it considers necessary for the fulfilment of its obligations with respect to the maintenance or restoration of international peace or security, or the protection of its own essential security interests

The latter demonstrates a significant departure from the WTO model of the national security exception.[324] As a result, the US-style national security exception can be invoked in *any* circumstances that have at least a remote nexus to good faith 'essential security' interests.[325] This national security exception thus provides a carte blanche for the United States to justify, in particular, its restrictions on cross-border data flows based on its investment screening mechanism and possible future restrictions on such flows that are likely to be based on some form of 'new' national security concerns.[326] At the same time, this national security exception

[322] Burri, 'Interfacing Privacy and Trade' (n 316) 84.

[323] See, eg, art 32.2(1)(b) of the USMCA (n 283); art 4(b) USJDTA (n 302); art 29.2(b) CPTPP (n 295). The United States has included a similarly broad exception in most of its trade agreements since NAFTA (n 300). See also art 22.2 of the United States–Colombia Trade Promotion Agreement (15 May 2012) (hereafter US-Colombia TPA), art 21.2 of the United States–Panama Trade Promotion Agreement (31 October 2012) (hereafter US-Panama TPA), Art 23.2 of the KORUS (n 293).

[324] For discussion, see Section 4.2.3.1.

[325] Dan Ciuriak and Vlada Rodionova, 'Trading Artificial Intelligence' in Shin-yi Peng, Ching-Fu Lin, and Thomas Streinz (eds), *Artificial Intelligence and International Economic Law: Disruption, Regulation, and Reconfiguration* (CUP online 2021).

[326] See, eg, Susan Ariel Aaronson, 'Data Is Disruptive: How Data Sovereignty Is Challenging Data Governance' (2021) Hinrich Foundation Report, 18 <https://www.hinrichfoundation.com/research/article/digital/data-is-disruptive-how-data-sovereignty-is-challenging-data-governance/> accessed 10 July 2023; Jake Harrington and Riley McGabe, 'What the U.S. Innovation and Competition Act Gets Right (and What It Gets Wrong)' (*Center for Strategic and International Studies*, 1 July 2021) <https://www.csis.org/analysis/what-us-innovation-and-competition-act-gets-right-and-what-it-gets-wrong> accessed 10 July 2023; Daniel Lippman, 'Trump Says He Plans to Ban TikTok in the U.S.' (*Politico*, 31 July 2020) <https://www.politico.com/news/2020/07/31/trump-plans-to-ban-tiktok-389956> accessed 10 July 2023; FIRRMA (n 248); U.S. Department of the Treasury Office of Public Affairs, Fact Sheet: Final CFIUS Regulations Implementing FIRRMA (13 January 2020) <https://home.treasury.

is unlikely to be available to countries, such as Japan, that model their restrictions on cross-border data flows on EU's GDPR approach, motivated by the reasons of privacy and data protection, rather than national security.[327]

Unlike the United States, the European Union has taken a more cautious approach to including binding cross-border data flow provisions in trade agreements in trying to defend its regulatory autonomy to protect the fundamental rights to privacy and personal data.[328] In doing so, unlike the United States, the EU prioritizes the protection of privacy and data protection as fundamental rights over economic rights and interests that greater liberalization of cross-border data flows could bring.[329] As already mentioned, in the course of the TTIP and TiSA negotiations, provisions on cross-border flows, especially the exceptions from them for privacy and data protection, became a contentious (and a turning) point in the European Union's approach to regulating cross-border data flows in trade agreements, which has affected its trade negotiations with other trading partners.[330]

In the digital trade chapters of JEFTA and the revision of the EU-Mexico Free Trade Agreements, the European Union explicitly refrained from including a free cross-border data flow provision; these agreements only contain a three-year review clause, which allows parties to reconsider this issue.[331] Cross-border flows of personal data between the European Union and Japan were eventually routed through a mutual adequacy decision granted by both parties to each other (the European Union—in accordance with the GDPR) shortly before JEFTA took effect.[332] Until the 2020 EU-UK Trade and Cooperation Agreement (EU-UK

gov/system/files/206/Final-FIRRMA-Regulations-FACT-SHEET.pdf> accessed 10 July 2023; Salil K Mehra, 'Algorithmic Competition, Trade and Investment: The CFIUS as Privacy Regulator' (2020) 16 University of Pennsylvania Asian Law Review 8, 14–17.

[327] Yakovleva, 'Testing Restrictions on Onward Transfers' (n 313) 4.

[328] See Aaronson, 'Why Trade Agreements Are Not Setting Information Free' (n 251) 685 ('The EU, in contrast, embraced a less combative and more internationalist strategy. The EU pushed for WTO wide data flow principles but did not name and shame other countries for digital protectionism (although it does list some countries' policies as barriers to trade)'.). cf Tobias Naef, *Data Protection without Data Protectionism: The Right to Protection of Personal Data and Data Transfers in EU Law and International Trade Law* (Springer Cham 2023) 368 (hereafter Naef, '*Data Protection without Data Protectionism*'), stating that '[t]he EU has been the pioneer in including data flow clauses in its trade agreements' and referring to a number of aspirational provisions on cross-border data flows since 2002.

[329] Burri, 'Interfacing Privacy and Trade' (n 316) 84.

[330] See Irion, Yakovleva, and Bartl, 'Trade and Privacy: Complicated Bedfellows?' (n 240) 41; see also Fontanella-Khan, 'Data Protection Ruled Out of EU-US Trade Talks' (n 294).

[331] Art 8.81 Agreement between the European Union and Japan for an Economic Partnership [2018] OJ L 330/3 (hereafter JEFTA); art XX EU Proposal for a Chapter on Digital Trade of the modernized EU-Mexico Free Trade Agreement (21 April 2018) <https://circabc.europa.eu/ui/group/09242a36-a438-40fd-a7af-fe32e36cbd0e/library/149d91f8-d2bc-4fca-8a0d-f7b583af2b87/details> accessed 10 July 2023; see also Brett Fortnam, 'EU Punts on Data Flow Language in Japan Deal, Leaving Position Unresolved' (*Inside US Trade*, 2017) <https://insidetrade.com/inside-us-trade/eu-punts-data-flow-language-japan-deal-leaving-position-unresolved> accessed 10 July 2023.

[332] European Commission, 'European Commission Adopts Adequacy Decision on Japan, Creating the World's Largest Area of Safe Data Flows' (*European Commission, Press Release*, 23 January 2019) <http://europa.eu/rapid/press-release_IP-19-421_en.htm> accessed 10 July 2023 (hereafter European Commission, 'European Commission Adopts Adequacy Decision on Japan').

TCA)[333]—which is the first EU trade agreement with binding provisions on cross-border data flows—the EU's digital trade discourse had only produced several 'new generation' international trade agreements that contain, in addition to the usual chapters on trade liberalization, specific chapters on electronic commerce that included predominantly aspirational provisions.[334]

In 2018, the European Union agreed on horizontal provisions on cross-border data flows and protection of personal data and privacy (hereafter EU horizontal provisions on cross-border data flows).[335] The European Union has been including these provisions in its proposals for negotiated trade agreements ever since, in particular, with New Zealand, Australia, Chile, Indonesia, Tunisia, and the United Kingdom and in its proposal for the negotiations at the Joint Initiative on E-commerce at the WTO.[336] The same EU horizontal provisions on cross-border data flows are most likely included in the EU's proposal for negotiation of cross-border data flows with Japan, in accordance with the three-year review clause originally included in the JEFTA, as mentioned above.[337] As of this writing (June

[333] Trade and Cooperation Agreement between the European Union and the European Atomic Energy Community, of the one part, and the United Kingdom of Great Britain and Northern Ireland, of the other part [2021] OJ L 149 (hereafter EU-UK TCA).

[334] See Bollen, de Ville, and Orbie, 'EU Trade Policy: Persistent Liberalisation, Contentious Protectionism' (n 228) 282 ('[S]ince the 2006 Global Europe communication the EU has put bilateral trade deals explicitly at the service of its commercial and wider economic interests'.); ibid 287 (stating that after the 2008 crisis, the European Union significantly intensified 'the (neo)liberal pattern in the bilateral dimension' by opening trade negotiations with the United States, Canada, and Japan); see also Siles-Brügge, 'Resisting Protectionism after the Crisis' (n 229) 629; Jan Orbie and Ferdi de Ville, 'A Boost to Our Economies That Doesn't Cost a Cent: EU Trade Policy Discourse Since the Crisis' in Caterina Carta and Jean-Frederic Morin (eds), *EU Foreign Policy through the Lens of Discourse Analysis: Making Sense of Diversity* (Routledge 2014) 95–110.

[335] European Commission, Proposal for provisions on Cross-border data flows and protection of personal data and privacy (31 January 2018) <https://www.politico.eu/wp-content/uploads/2018/02/Data-flow-provisions-POLITICO.pdf> accessed 10 July 2023 (hereafter EU horizontal provisions on cross-border data flows).

[336] See Joint Statement on Electronic Commerce, EU Proposal for WTO Disciplines and Commitments Relating to Electronic Commerce. Communication from the European Union [2019] INF/ECOM/22, 26 April 2019; EU proposal for a Chapter on Digital Trade of the EU-New Zealand FTA; EU proposal for a Chapter on Digital Trade of the EU-Australia FTA; La proposition de l'Union européenne (UE) relative à Accord de libre-échange UE-Tunisie UE-Tunisie, Titre [] Commerce Numérique, 9 November 2018; Draft text of the Agreement on the New Partnership with the United Kingdom, European Commission (18 March 2020). Digital Trade Proposals for EU-Chile and EU-Indonesia were drafted before the European Union agreed on the horizontal provisions on cross-border data flows (n 335). Therefore, these proposals only contain a placeholder for a provision on cross-border data flows. See EU proposal for a Digital trade title in the Trade Part of a possible modernized EU-Chile Association Agreement, 5 February 2018 (containing a placeholder for provisions on data flows); EU proposal for a Chapter on Digital Trade of the EU-Indonesia FTA, 27 July 2017. The European Union tabled its horizontal provisions on cross-border data flows (n 335) at a later stage in negotiations with these two countries. See, eg, European Commission, Report of the 5th Round of Negotiations for a Free Trade Agreement between the European Union and Indonesia (July 2018) <https://circabc.europa.eu/ui/group/09242a36-a438-40fd-a7af-fe32e36cbd0e/library/ef73321c-1aff-4878-adff-58156280913a/details> accessed 10 July 2023.

[337] See 'EU and Japan Start Negotiations to Include Rules on Cross-Border Data Flows in Their Economic Partnership Agreement' (*European Commission*, 7 October 2022) <https://policy.trade.ec.europa.eu/news/eu-and-japan-start-negotiations-include-rules-cross-border-data-flows-their-economic-partnership-2022-10-07_en> accessed 10 July 2023; Recital 4 of the Recommendation

2023), model provisions have been included in FTAs with Chile and New Zealand, both of which have not yet been ratified.[338]

The exception for privacy and data protection in the EU-UK TCA is an outlier.[339] It is worded differently from and is likely to be narrower than that in the model provisions.[340] So far, it is the only FTA, which deviates from the EU horizontal provisions on cross-border data flows, which, therefore, can still be considered the EU's template in trade negotiations on cross-border data flows.

Unlike an open provision on cross-border data flows in Articles 14.11(2) of the CPTPP, 19.11(1) of the USMCA, and 11(1) USJDTA, the EU model provisions, discussed in greater detail in Chapter 4 of this book, contain an enumerated list of prohibited restrictions on cross-border data flows.[341] These restrictions are formulated in a way that makes the European Union's own restrictions on cross-border transfers of personal data in the GDPR less likely to be subject to the prohibition to restrict cross-border data flows.[342] To Naef, this prohibition of restrictions on cross-border data flows is 'a manifestation of the EU's opposition to digital protectionism'.[343] Furthermore, the provisions also embody the recognition that 'the protection of personal data and privacy is a *fundamental right* and that high standards in this regard contribute to trust in the digital economy and to the development of trade'.[344] In addition, they provide for a broad exception for domestic privacy and data protection rules,[345] which is fundamentally different from, and sufficiently broader than, those included in the CPTPP, USMCA, and USJDTA in at least three ways. First, it integrates into a trade agreement a different normative approach to protecting the rights to privacy and data protection—that of fundamental rights protection as compared to the instrumental approach embedded in the CPTPP, USMCA, and USJDTA explained above. Second, it recognizes rules on cross-border data flows as a valid regulatory tool to protect the rights to privacy and personal data. Third, it incorporates a subjective 'it deems appropriate' test similar to

for a Council Decision authorizing the opening of negotiations for the inclusion of provisions on cross-border data flows in the Agreement between the European Union and Japan for an Economic Partnership [2022] COM(2022) 336 final.

338 Arts 19.4 and 19.5 of EU-Chile Interim Trade Agreement (negotiations concluded on 9 December 2022) (hereafter EU-Chile Interim Trade Agreement); arts 12.4 and 12.5 of the EU-New Zealand Free Trade Agreement (signed on 9 July 2023) (hereafter EU-New Zealand FTA).

339 EU-UK TCA (n 333) art 202.

340 See European Data Protection Supervisor, 'Opinion 3/2021 on the Conclusion of the EU and UK Trade Agreement and the EU and UK Exchange of Classified Information Agreement' (2021) <https://edps.europa.eu/system/files/2021-02/2021_02_22_opinion_eu_uk_tca_en.pdf> accessed 10 July 2023. But see Kristina Irion and Mira Burri, '§ 16 Digitaler Handel' in Gesa Kübek, Christian J Tams, and Jörg Philipp Terhechte (Hrsg), *Handels- und Kooperationsvertrag EU/GB Handbuch* (Nomos 2022), paras 14–16.

341 EU horizontal provisions on cross-border data flows (n 335).

342 See also Naef, '*Data Protection without Data Protectionism*' (n 328) 409.

343 ibid.

344 (Emphasis added.) ibid.

345 (Emphasis added.) ibid.

that employed in national security exceptions in WTO agreements, as opposed to the objective necessity test contained in the CPTPP, USMCA, and USJDTA. To sum up, while the EU model provisions on cross-border data flows and respective exceptions for privacy and data protection aim, on the one hand, to counter protectionist restrictions on cross-border data flows, they, on the other hand, 'offer no solution to address protectionist data protection rules'.[346]

In parallel with the above-mentioned provisions in trade agreements, the EU has continued to channel cross-border data flows with its trading partners through mechanisms for data transfers available in the GDPR, in particular, the so-called 'adequacy decisions'. Most recent adequacy decisions for Japan, the United Kingdom, and South Korea went hand in hand with trade agreements concluded with such partners.[347] The EU's FTA with Chile, which has not yet been ratified, however, deviates from this approach. While it contains binding provisions on cross-border data flows,[348] the EU has not yet afforded or even publicly announced the process to afford an adequacy decision for Chile under the GDPR (admitting that this process is highly untransparent).[349]

Free flow of personal data with a trading partner under an adequacy decision certainly reduces the risk of the EU's restrictions on transfers of personal data under the GDPR being challenged under the trade agreement with such trading partner, but only *as long as the EU maintains the adequacy decision*. As explained in Section 2.2.4, under the GDPR, an adequacy decision can be unilaterally suspended or withdrawn by the European Commission. Provisions prohibiting restrictions on cross-border data flows in trade agreements, however, limit that unilateral right by requiring that such withdrawal—if it violates the prohibition to restrict cross-border data flows—must be justified under the relevant trade law exception.

[346] ibid 413, see also ibid 410–11.

[347] 'Questions & Answers on the Adoption of the Adequacy Decision Ensuring Safe Data Flows between the EU and the Republic of Korea'(*European Commission*, 17 December 2021) <https://ec.europa.eu/commission/presscorner/detail/en/qanda_21_6916> accessed 10 July 2023. European Commission, 'Commission adopts adequacy decisions for the UK' (European Commission, Press Release, 28 June 2021) <https://ec.europa.eu/commission/presscorner/detail/en/ip_21_3183> accessed 10 July 2023; European Commission, 'European Commission Adopts Adequacy Decision on Japan' (n 332). 'Korea Seeks Digital Trade Pact with EU' (*Korea Times*, 13 June 2023) <https://www.koreatimes.co.kr/www/nation/2023/06/113_352846.html?utm_source=substack&utm_medium=email> accessed 10 July 2023.

[348] Arts 19.4 and 19.5 of the EU-Chile Interim Trade Agreement (n 338).

[349] According to the 2019 statement of Bruno Gencarelli, Head of International Data Transfers and Protection Unit at the EU Commission, there is no particular queue of new applicant countries for an adequacy decision. However, future candidates for an adequacy decision could include Brazil and Chile. See 'EU Commission's Review of Existing Adequacy Decisions Well Underway' (*Privacy Laws and Business*, 3 July 2019) <https://www.privacylaws.com/news/eu-commission-s-review-of-existing-adequacy-decisions-well-underway/> accessed 10 July 2023. In its 2017 Communication from the Commission, Exchanging and Protecting Personal Data in a Globalised World (n 243) 8, the European Commission mentioned that the European Commission will 'actively engage' with countries from Latin America, which expressed an interest in obtaining the 'adequacy finding'.

To sum up, in the light of the different digital trade discourses advanced by the United States and the European Union, the contrast in the design of cross-border data flow provisions and exceptions from such provisions for domestic regulation that protects privacy and personal data illustrates the practical implications of a different baseline between protection and protectionism within a particular discourse.

3.3.5 The 'digital protectionism' label as a trigger to redefine 'barriers to trade'

This chapter argues that in the context of the expansion of 'protectionism' into 'new protectionism' in the 1970s and 1980s that led to a fundamental redefinition of 'barriers to trade' and the renegotiation of international trade rules, the coining of the term 'digital protectionism' is a new trigger for another fundamental redefinition of what constitutes a barrier to trade and, thus, deeper trade liberalization. Simply put, by labelling certain domestic policies such as restrictions on cross-border data flows, and data localization measures as digital protectionism, it is much easier to critique them, reject them, and put competing policy interests such as privacy, data protection, or industrial policy in a subordinate position. Moreover, in trade terms, affixing the digital protectionism label to another country's policy decision and insisting on the efficiency gains of free trade automatically puts that measure on the defensive.

At the dawn of the multilateral trading system governed by the discourse of 'embedded liberalism', the term 'protectionism' was meant to target measures *intended* to protect domestic industry (as applied by the GATT for two decades or more).[350] Within the discourse of neoliberalism, the term 'new protectionism' led to a removal of the intent component of the test as a relevant factor in defining a protectionist measure.[351] The increasingly frequent use of the term 'digital protectionism' seems to be heading in the direction of questioning any form of regulation altogether.[352] Despite the notable differences in the scope and types of domestic policies outlawed by digital trade provisions in the EU- and US-led trade agreements discussed in the previous section, they have one trait in common: they are *not* formulated as non-discrimination provisions.[353] While a challenge to restrictions on cross-border data flows or data localization measures would require the contesting party to prove discrimination if such measures were challenged under

[350] See Section 3.2.3.

[351] Aaronson, 'What Are We Talking about When We Discuss Digital Protectionism?' (n 34) 6–7.

[352] ibid 6, 8, 17.

[353] CPTPP (n 295) art 14.11(2); USMCA (n 283); USJDTA (n 302) art 11(1) ; art 1 of EU horizontal provisions on cross-border data flows (n 335); EU-Chile Interim Trade Agreement (n 338) art 19.4; EU-New Zealand FTA (n 338)art 12.4.

the most-favoured nation (MFN) treatment obligation of the GATS, or the services chapters of post-GATS trade agreements,[354] this chapter argues that such a challenge under the digital trade provisions would not impose such a requirement because the measures prohibit restrictions on cross-border data flows or data localization measures irrespective of their discriminatory character.[355] This means that a complainant need not establish discrimination. Put simply, new digital trade provisions make it easier to challenge domestic regulation that interferes with digital trade and make the rate of successful challenges much more probable compared to challenges under non-discrimination provisions.

The non-discrimination requirement appears only in the US model of cross-border data flow provisions, and only in the *exception* from the commitments contained in those provisions. This exception, as discussed in the previous section, allows a party to deviate from the prohibition to restrict cross-border data flows 'that is necessary to achieve a legitimate public policy objective, provided that the measure is not applied in a manner which would constitute a means of arbitrary or unjustifiable discrimination or a disguised restriction on trade'.[356] This exception does not condition the prohibition to restrict cross-border data flows, as Naef argued,[357] but rather delineates a (narrow) policy space for the parties to deviate from that obligation, as discussed in the previous section. Given that exceptions from trade obligations function as affirmative defences, the burden of proof of non-discrimination is the defending party. In contrast, where discrimination is a qualification of a measure prohibited by a trade obligation (such as in, eg, MFN or national treatment obligations), the burden of proof of discrimination is on the claimant.

Aaronson put forward several theoretical arguments about why digital protectionism is unlike other forms of protectionism and called on the United States to lead in redefining 'protectionism' for the digital age.[358] Her arguments are based on the premise that information is different from the objects of trade that the 'old protectionism' is concerned with.[359] The discussion above shows that this redefinition has indeed taken place. While it seems hard to disagree with the proposition

[354] See Marceau and Trachtman, 'A Map of the World Trade Organization Law of Domestic Regulation of Goods' (n 166) 358–60.

[355] See art 14.11(2) CPTPP (n 295); art 19.11(1) USMCA (n 283); art 11(1) USJDTA (n 302); art 1 of EU horizontal provisions on cross-border data flows (n 335); art 19.4 EU-Chile Interim Trade Agreement (n 338); art 12.4 EU-New Zealand FTA (n 338).

[356] USMCA (n 283) art 19.11(2)(a). See also art 14.11(3)(a) CPTPP (n 295); art 11(2)(a) USJDTA (n 302).

[357] Naef, '*Data Protection without Data Protectionism*' (n 328) 380 footnote 47.

[358] Aaronson, 'Redefining Protectionism' (n 291) 58, 87 ('Scholars and policymakers alike need to rethink how we define and measure [digital protectionism] as well as reconsider the appropriate strategies to address it. . . . Given the stakes, the United States should take a leading role in defining protectionism at the World Trade Organization.').

[359] Aaronson, 'What Are We Talking about When We Discuss Digital Protectionism?' (n 34) 6–8; Aaronson, 'What Are We Talking about When We Talk about Digital Protectionism' (n 247) 546–48.

that information is different in nature from goods and services, does that difference imply *ipso facto* that there is a sufficient reason to redefine protectionism? This implication is not obvious, as the characteristics that delineate protectionism from protection—the discriminatory intent or effect of domestic regulation—are not related to the objects of regulation. Therefore, the rhetoric presenting the redefinition of 'protectionism' as 'digital protectionism' as a logical, necessary step to respond to changing circumstances could be self-serving. Put differently, it could be that just as in the case of 'new protectionism,' the emergence of 'digital protectionism' is a product of a new digital trade discourse—and not the consequence of digital transformation of trade—which serves particular business interests and not the broader public interest.

All that said, provisions aiming at curtailing digital protectionism have already been incorporated into several trade agreements, as has been demonstrated in the previous section. Given that a different conceptualization of digital protectionism has already led to diverging and potentially mutually inconsistent digital trade provisions, a consensus on what digital protectionism means is necessary. 'Digital protectionism' is defined and interpreted within a particular discourse. It follows that to be able to reach a consensus on the meaning of 'digital protectionism,' *countries must agree on the discourse in the first place*. As things stand now, though there is an agreement on the use of the terms 'digital trade' and 'digital protectionism,' the value structures underlying the discourse are vastly different. Using the example of privacy and data protection, the following section illustrates how fundamental values on which a discourse is based affect the baseline between protection and protectionism.

3.4 The Baseline between Data Privacy Protection and Protectionism: The Role of Discourse

One variant of the digital trade discourse, advanced in particular by the United States and demonstrated in Sections 3.3.1 and 3.3.2, tends to equate strict privacy and data protection measures, such as restrictions on cross-border data flows, with a non-tariff trade barrier and, potentially, digital protectionism.[360] However, even

[360] It is, however, often recognized that other legitimate concerns could also play a role. See, eg, Mishra, 'Data Localization Laws in a Digital World' (n 207) 150–52 ('The contentious issues with respect to data localization extend well beyond free trade versus protectionism into some delicate, complex and legitimate political concerns, such as technology transfer and IP rights, privacy, human rights, and national security, which is currently missing (and expectedly so) on most trade agendas.'). Mitchell and Hepburn similarly concede that there might be privacy and security concerns behind restrictions on cross-border data flows, but add that 'digital protectionism may also be at play'. Andrew D Mitchell and Jarrod Hepburn, 'Don't Fence Me In: Reforming Trade and Investment Law to Better Facilitate Cross-Border Data Transfer' (2017) 19(1) Yale Journal of Law and Technology 182, 186. Privacy concerns in the context of trade negotiations on cross-border data flows are also increasingly voiced by civil

when some degree of privacy and data protection *are* factored into this discourse of digital trade, the protection of these interests is often presented as an *economic* necessity, a precondition for free trade rather than a fundamental right and societal value beyond its economic utility.[361] It is likely to be presented as such because the use of the digital protectionism label features trade values as natural and obvious, and forces policymakers to defend the measure against a baseline of free trade, as non-protectionist. Regulatory conversations on privacy and data protection within the economic digital trade discourse about the term 'digital protectionism' thus implicitly bring in the normative goal of maximization of wealth rather than a set of goals interacting with, and counterbalancing, each other.[362]

This section unpacks the differences between economic and legal (fundamental rights) approaches to data protection, exposes the limits of the economic approach to privacy and data protection embraced by the economic 'digital trade' discourse, and calls for a pluralist 'digital trade' discourse. It argues that in shaping policy about the protection of privacy and personal data beyond what is economically justified, it is more likely to be labelled as protectionism in an economic discourse than in a pluralist discourse in which the protectionism label loses some of its discursive power.

3.4.1 Normative approaches to privacy and data protection

There are at least two policy approaches to the protection of privacy and personal data: (1) an economic approach in which personal data is viewed as an economic asset and its protection is a precondition of data-intensive trade; and (2) a moral value approach in which personal data is a materialized form of human behaviour and its protection is directed not to data but to an *individual's constitutional rights*.[363] While in the first case, the normative goal of protection is to generate more trade in data, as individuals tend to share more data when they believe it is

society and labour groups in the United States. See, eg, AFL-CIO, 'A Worker-Centered Digital Trade Agenda' (n 272).

[361] Art 19.8 USMCA (n 283); Yakovleva, 'Should Fundamental Rights Be a Part of Trade "Deals"?' (n 320) 484–85.

[362] See Driskill, 'Deconstructing the Argument for Free Trade: A Case Study of the Role of Economists in Policy Debates' (n 128) 2–3 ('[T]he standard argument made by economists in favour of free trade ... implicitly imposes philosophical value judgements about what is good for a nation or society, or it makes leaps of empirical faith about how the world works.').

[363] See Sarah Spiekermann-Hoff and others, 'The Challenges of Personal Data Markets and Privacy' (2015) 25 (2) Electronic Markets 161, 164 ('Interpreting personal data as a tradable good raises ethical concerns about whether people's lives, materialized in their data traces, should be property at all, or whether in fact personal data should be considered inalienable from data subjects.').

protected,[364] in the second case, the aim is the protection of human dignity, autonomy, and privacy as values in themselves.[365]

From an economic perspective, protection of privacy and personal data has several justifications, of which the creation and maintenance of consumers' trust in data-driven goods, services, and their providers is most prominently featured in the economic discourse on digital trade.[366] This justification is explicitly included in the text of several EU- and US-led trade agreements.[367] 'Trust' is also the key

[364] See, eg, Alessandro Acquisti, Laura Brandimarte, and George Loewenstein, 'Privacy and Human Behavior in the Age of Information' (2015) 347(6221) Science 509, 512–13 (hereafter Acquisti, Brandimarte, and Loewenstein, 'Privacy and Human Behavior in the Age of Information') (showing that providing users with explicit control mechanisms over their personal data may lead to sharing more sensitive data by users).

[365] See Cécile De Terwangne, 'Is a Global Data Protection Regulatory Model Possible?' in Serge Gutwirth and others (eds), *Reinventing Data Protection?* (Springer 2009) 180, 185–88 (hereafter De Terwangne, 'Is a Global Data Protection Regulatory Model Possible?'); Julie E Cohen, 'Examined Lives: Informational Privacy and the Subject as Object' (2000) 52 Stanford Law Review 1373, 1423–28 (hereafter Cohen, 'Examined Lives'); Paul M Schwartz, 'Privacy and Democracy in Cyberspace' (1999) 52 Vanderbilt Law Review 1609, 1658–66 (hereafter Schwartz, 'Privacy and Democracy in Cyberspace'); Paul M Schwartz, 'Property, Privacy, and Personal Data' (2004) 117 Harvard Law Review 2056, 2087 (hereafter Schwartz, 'Property, Privacy, and Personal Data'); Shoshana Zuboff, 'Big Other: Surveillance Capitalism and the Prospects of an Information Civilization' (2015) 30(1) Journal of Information Technology 75, 85–86 (hereafter Zuboff, 'Big Other'); François LeSieur, 'Regulating Cross-Border Data Flows and Privacy in the Networked Digital Environment and Global Knowledge Economy' (2012) 2(2) International Data Privacy Law 93, 94–95, 98 (hereafter LeSieur, 'Regulating Cross-Border Data Flows'); Jonathan Cinnamon, 'Social Injustice in Surveillance Capitalism' (2017) 15(5) Surveillance & Society 609, 610–11 (hereafter Cinnamon, 'Social Injustice in Surveillance Capitalism').

[366] See Section 3.3. Looking at the digital economy as a whole, trust meets all the criteria of a public good: it is neither rivalrous nor excludable. Without regulation, the market will not produce an optimal amount of trust necessary for the digital economy to flourish. On trust as a public good, see generally Hans-Bernd Schäfer and Claus Ott, *The Economic Analysis of Civil Law* (1st edn, Edward Elgar Publishing 2004) 359–60 (hereafter Schäfer and Ott, *The Economic Analysis of Civil Law*); George M Cohen, 'The Negligence-Opportunism Tradeoff in Contract Law' (1992) 20(4) Hofstra Law Review 941, 976 ('Economists too have recognized that trust is an extremely valuable and vulnerable resource, which the market alone cannot be counted on to supply.'). For a discussion on the how privacy protection contributes to building trust, see Neil M Richards and Woodrow Hartzog, 'Taking Trust Seriously in Privacy Law' (2016) 19 Stanford Technology Law Review 431, 435; Neil M Richards and Woodrow Hartzog, 'Privacy's Trust Gap: A Review' (2017) 126(4) The Yale Law Journal 1180, 1185–86; Adam N Joinson and others, 'Privacy, Trust, and Self-Disclosure Online' (2010) 25(1) Human–Computer Interaction 1, 4 (hereafter Joinson and others, 'Privacy, Trust, and Self-Disclosure Online'). For an overview of other economic justifications of privacy protection, see, eg, Ian Brown, 'The Economics of Privacy, Data Protection and Surveillance' in Johannes M. Bauer and Michael Latzer (eds), *Handbook on the Economics of the Internet* (Edward Elgar 2016) 248–56 <https://ideas.repec.org/h/elg/eechap/14700_12.html> accessed 10 July 2023.

[367] See, eg, art 19.8(1) USMCA (n 283) ('Personal Information Protection—The Parties recognize the economic and social benefits of protecting the personal information of users of digital trade and the contribution that this makes to enhancing consumer confidence in digital trade.'); see also art 14.8(1) CPTPP (n 295) (a similar provision stating 'The Parties recognise the economic and social benefits of protecting the personal information of users of electronic commerce and the contribution that this makes to enhancing consumer confidence in electronic commerce.'); art 8.57(4) Free Trade Agreement between the European Union and the Republic of Singapore [2019] OJ L 294 (hereafter EU-Singapore FTA); art 16.4 Comprehensive Economic and Trade Agreement (CETA) between Canada, of the one part, and the European Union and its member states, of the other part, 14 September 2014 [2017] OJ L 11/23 (hereafter CETA) (entitled 'Trust and confidence in electronic commerce,' which requires that parties 'should adopt or maintain laws, regulations or administrative measures for the protection of personal information of users engaged in electronic commerce.'). See also art 202(1) EU-UK TCA (n 333); art 19.15 EU-Chile Interim Trade Agreement (n 338); art 12.15(1) EU-New Zealand FTA (n 338).

word in the new paradigm of ongoing trade and other multistakeholder negotiations on cross-border data flows—Data Free Flow with Trust—spearheaded by Japan.[368] This economic approach also serves as a normative rationale for the protection of personal data as a commercial consumer right in the United States.[369] By contrast, the moral value approach views the protection of personal data rights from a broad societal perspective, as contributing to the preservation of a free and democratic society, social equality, individual autonomy, dignity, integrity, and self-determination.[370] In addition, preventing and correcting discriminatory harms caused by inappropriate use of personal data can (and should) be seen as a matter of social justice.[371]

Importantly, these two approaches are not mutually exclusive, as economically motivated protection contributes to the protection of a fundamental right, and fundamental rights protection may have positive effects on digital commerce.[372] The European Union is a good illustration of how these two approaches can coexist, as it simultaneously advances both models in the domestic and international arenas.[373] In the European Union, a strong economic discourse—in which personal data

[368] See eg Kudo, 'We Must Enhance Cross-Border Data Flows' (n 195).

[369] See US The White House, 'Consumer Data Privacy in a Networked World: Framework for Protecting Privacy and Promoting Innovation in the Global Digital Economy' (*The White House*, February 2012), 6 <https://www.hsdl.org/?view&did=700959> accessed 10 July 2023 ('Preserving trust in the Internet economy protects and enhances substantial economic activity. Online retail sales in the United States total $145 billion annually. . . . To preserve these economic benefits, consumers must continue to trust networked technologies. Strengthening consumer data privacy protections will help to achieve this goal.') For a comparison of EU and US data protection regimes, see Paul M Schwartz, 'The EU-U.S. Privacy Collision: A Turn to Institutions and Procedures' (2013) 126 Harvard Law Review 1966, 1966–67 (hereafter Schwartz, 'The EU-U.S. Privacy Collision'); Paul M Schwartz and Daniel J Solove, 'Reconciling Personal Information in the United States and European Union' (2014) 102(4) California Law Review 877, 877 (hereafter Schwartz and Solove, 'Reconciling Personal Information in the United States and European Union').

[370] See De Terwangne, 'Is a Global Data Protection Regulatory Model Possible?' (n 365) 180, 185–88; Priscilla M Regan, *Legislating Privacy: Technology, Social Values, and Public Policy* (The University of North Carolina Press 1995) 213–15; Cohen, 'Examined Lives' (n 365) 1423–28; Schwartz, 'Privacy and Democracy in Cyberspace' (n 365) 1658–66; Schwartz, 'Property, Privacy, and Personal Data' (n 365) 2087; Zuboff, 'Big Other' (n 365) 85–86; LeSieur, 'Regulating Cross-Border Data Flows' (n 365) 94–95, 98; Cinnamon, 'Social Injustice in Surveillance Capitalism' (n 365) 610–11; Sandra Seubert and Carlos Becker, 'The Democratic Impact of Strengthening European Fundamental Rights in the Digital Age: The Example of Privacy Protection' (2021) German Law Journal 22(1) 31, 37ff; Pawan Singh, 'Aadhaar and Data Privacy: Biometric Identification and Anxieties of Recognition in India' (2021) 24(7) Information, Communication & Society 978.

[371] See Khiara M Bridges, *The Poverty of Privacy Rights* (Stanford UP 2017)153 (arguing that 'denying privacy is a mechanism for social control'); Linnet Taylor, 'What Is Data Justice: The Case for Connecting Digital Rights and Freedoms Globally' (2017) 4(2) Big Data and Society 1, 4–8 (showing, based on examples of big data-driven discrimination, that 'a specific articulation of social justice is now required with regard to contemporary data technologies'); Cinnamon, 'Social Injustice in Surveillance Capitalism' (n 365).

[372] cf Bart Custers and Gianclaudio Malgieri, 'Priceless Data: Why the EU Fundamental Right to Data Protection Is at Odds with Trade in Personal Data' (2022) 45 Computer Law & Security Review 1, 10–11 (hereafter Custers and Malgieri, 'Priceless Data'), arguing that the EU needs to choose between its ambitions to build an economy on personal data and the protection of the right to personal data protection as a fundamental right.

[373] EU horizontal provisions on cross-border data flows (n 335) art 1(1). For a discussion on economic and non-economic goals of the EU data protection framework, see Section 2.2.1.

and its protection are presented as enablers of the digital single market and digital agenda—is counterbalanced by a fundamental rights discourse.[374] It is for that reason Polčák and Svantesson label the intertwined nature of economic and fundamental rights considerations in data privacy a 'Gordian knot'.[375] On the one hand, the EU privacy and data protection framework is deeply rooted in a European cultural preference for strong privacy protection and is viewed as an integral part and key instance of the protection of human dignity.[376]

However, as explained in Section 2.2.1, the history of the EU data protection regime shows that the both EU legislative instruments on data protection—the 1995 Data Protection Directive[377] and the GDPR—are underpinned by the goal of establishing a functioning internal market, of which the protection of the fundamental rights of individuals to privacy and data protection is a necessary ingredient.[378] In its communication 'Completing a Trusted Digital Single Market for All', the European Commission noted that it is crucial to 'enable the free flow of personal data within the Union, from which the critical mass of data essential for a strong data economy can be generated'.[379] This rhetoric is clearly linked to the neoliberal internal and external policy discourse of the European Commission discussed earlier. At the same time, the Commission acknowledged the following:

> [r]espect for private life and the protection of personal data are *fundamental rights* in the EU. <. . .>
>
> Strong data protection, confidentiality of communications and data security are crucial to dispel individuals' doubts about misuse of their data and to create

[374] European Data Protection Supervisor, Opinion 4/2015, Towards a new digital ethics data, dignity and technology (11 September 2015), 4, 9–10 (hereafter European Data Protection Supervisor, Opinion 4/2015, Towards a new digital ethics data).

[375] Radim Polčák and Dan Jerker B Svantesson, *Information Sovereignty: Data Privacy, Sovereign Powers and the Rule of Law* (Edward Elgar 2017) 208 (hereafter Polčák and Svantesson, *Information Sovereignty*) ('[D]ata privacy involves multiple fundamental human rights – the right of privacy and the freedom of expression at a minimum – and significant commercial values. Indeed, maybe we are here dealing with a Gordian knot'.).

[376] See Explanations Relating to the Charter of Fundamental Rights [2007] OJ (C 303), Explanation on Article 1; European Data Protection Supervisor, Opinion 4/2015, Towards a new digital ethics data (n 374) 12; Stefano Rodotà, 'Data Protection as a Fundamental Right' in Serge Gutwirth and others (eds), *Reinventing Data Protection?* (Springer 2009) 80; Chris Jay Hoofnagle, Bart van der Sloot, and Frederik Zuiderveen Borgesius, 'The European Union General Data Protection Regulation: What It Is and What It Means' (2019) 28(1) Information & Communications Technology Law 65, 69–72.

[377] Directive 95/46/EC of the European Parliament and of the Council of 24 October 1995 on the protection of individuals with regard to the processing of personal data and on the free movement of such data [1995] OJ L 281 (hereafter Data Protection Directive).

[378] For a discussion, see Gloria González Fuster, *The Emergence of Personal Data Protection as a Fundamental Right of the EU* (Springer 2014) 198; Joris van Hoboken, 'The European Approach to Privacy' (TPRC Conference, Schertz, August 2014), 5 <https://ssrn.com/abstract=2418636> accessed 10 July 2023.

[379] Communication from the Commission to the European Parliament, the European Council, the Council, the European Economic and Social Committee, and the Committee of the Regions, 'Completing a Trusted Digital Single Market for All' [2018] COM (2018) 320 final, 4.

> trust. Without this *trust*, the potential of a thriving data economy will not be met.[380]

In a similar vein, the European Union's horizontal provisions on cross-border data flows in trade agreements, discussed in Section 3.3.4, state that 'the protection of personal data and privacy *is a fundamental right* and that high standards in this regard contribute to *trust in the digital economy* and to the development of trade'.[381] Similarly, the European Commission has endorsed the DFFT narrative in its Digital Partnerships with Japan,[382] South Korea,[383] and Singapore.[384] For example, Digital Trade Principles of the Digital Partnership with South Korea state:

> To harness the opportunities of the digital economy and support the trade of goods and services, data should be able to flow freely across borders with trust, including the trust of individuals and businesses stemming from ensuring a high level of data protection and security.[385]

This illustrates that the Commission does not always separate the economic and moral approaches to privacy and data protection and seems to assign equal importance to each, or even conditioning trust on the presence of a high level of data protection.

In contrast to the European Commission, the Court of Justice of the European Union (CJEU) has grounded the EU restrictions on transfers of personal data outside the EEA in the international context solely on a fundamental rights basis.[386] The CJEU chose this approach despite the fact that Chapter V of the GDPR,

380 ibid 2–3 (emphasis added). Similarly, in the explanatory memorandum to the proposal for the GDPR, the European Commission notes, on the one hand, that building a stronger and more coherent data protection framework in the European Union is essential for building the pan-European digital economy, and, on the other hand, emphasizes the protection of the right to protection of personal data as a fundamental right. Proposal for a Regulation of the European Parliament and of the Council on the protection of individuals with regard to the processing of personal data and on the free movement of such data (General Data Protection Regulation) COM/2012/011 final, 2.

381 See art 2 EU horizontal provisions on cross-border data flows (n 335) (emphasis added). cf EU's 2021 Trade Policy Review where the Commission clearly separates the EU's fundamental rights framework for personal data protection and consumer trust. In the Trade Policy Review, the Commission states that it will 'seek the rapid conclusion of an ambitious and comprehensive WTO agreement on digital trade, including rules on data flows, *in full compliance with the EU's data protection framework*, and provisions on enhancing *consumer trust ensuring a high level of consumer protection*.' (emphasis added). Communication from the Commission, Trade Policy Review (n 232).

382 Japan-EU Digital Partnership (n 188).

383 European Union-Republic of Korea Digital Partnership (30 November 2022) <https://circabc.europa.eu/rest/download/6faad06a-30bc-4207-a46b-3da7e8e496e0> accessed 10 July 2023 (hereafter EU-Korea Digital Partnership).

384 EU-Singapore Digital Partnership, signed on 1 February 2023, https://ec.europa.eu/newsroom/dae/redirection/document/93447

385 EU-Korea Digital Partnership (n 383), Digital Trade Principles, 4.

386 *Maximillian Schrems v Data Protection Commissioner* [2015] ECLI:EU:C:2015:650 paras 38–39, 42 (hereafter *Schrems I*).

which regulates such transfers (as well as the similar rules in the Data Protection Directive) are, at least in theory, guided by both economic *and* non-economic rationales envisaged in Article 1 of the GDPR.[387] As the CJEU explained in the 2015 *Schrems I* judgment, restrictions on transfers of personal data outside the EEA constitute a part of the European Union's 'constitutional' data protection framework and are necessary to avoid circumvention of such a framework.[388]

Although the European Union embraces both the economic and moral value approaches to the protection of privacy and personal data, the latter will always prevail because, as already explained in Chapter 2, the European Union may neither conclude nor implement through an EU legislative act, an international agreement, or decision of an international adjudicating body if it does not comply with the EU Charter of Fundamental Rights (EU Charter).[389] This matters because although the economic and moral value rationales are complementary, the crucial difference between them is, as the next section elaborates, that the economic justification warrants a lower level of protection than the moral value justification.

3.4.2 Limitations of the economic approach to privacy and data protection

There are at least two problems with fitting privacy and data protection's non-economic value (as opposed to the economic value of ensuring consumers' trust in digital trade) into the economic digital trade discourse.

First, non-economic interests in general are difficult to quantify for use in the wealth maximization calculus; it is not always possible to find convincing proof justifying the economic necessity of ensuring a certain level of privacy and data protection.[390] For example, in *Brazil–Retreaded Tyres*, the Appellate Body held that

[387] GDPR (n 192) art 1. See also art 1 Data Protection Directive (n 377). For discussion, see Section 2.2.1.

[388] In the *Schrems I* ruling (n 386), the CJEU stated that '[the adequacy requirement] implements the express obligation laid down in Article 8(1) of the Charter to protect personal data and ... is intended to ensure that the high level of that protection continues where personal data is transferred to a third country'. *Schrems I* (n 386) para 72 (referring to art 25(6) Data Protection Directive (n 377)). However, this does not affect the analysis because art 45 GDPR (n 192) preserved the essential features of the adequacy approach. Lee Andrew Bygrave, *Data Protection Law: Approaching Its Rationale, Logic and Limits* (Wolters Kluwer 2002) 79–80. ('The chief aim of these rules is to hinder data controllers from avoiding the requirements of data protection laws by shifting their data-processing operations to countries with more lenient requirements (so-called "data havens")'.) This approach is now explicitly incorporated in art 44 GDPR (n 192), which requires that the limitations on transfers of personal data outside the EEA 'shall be applied in order to ensure that the level of protection of natural persons guaranteed by [the GDPR] is not undermined'.

[389] Charter of Fundamental Rights of the European Union [2000] OJ C 364/1 (hereafter EU Charter). See Arianna Verdaschi, 'Privacy and Data Protection versus National Security in Transnational Flights: The EU–Canada PNR Agreement (2018) 8(2) International Data Privacy Law 124, 138–39. See also Custers and Malgieri, 'Priceless Data' (n 372).

[390] See Irwin, *Against the Tide: An Intellectual History of Free Trade* (n 45) 221 (showing that empirical evidence 'either played virtually no role' or 'played a small and unproductive role ... in evaluating the

the selection of a methodology to assess a measure's contribution to the claimed objective in the necessity assessment in the context of a general exception 'ultimately also depends on the *nature, quantity, and quality of evidence* existing at the time the analysis is made'.[391] The elaborate discussion on the discrepancy between the levels of protection claimed and actually achieved by the EU Seal Regime in addressing public moral concerns in the EU on seal welfare demonstrates that a defending party in a WTO dispute cannot merely assert a high level of protection.[392] Although in that particular case, arguably because the justification of the EU Seal Regime was based on the public morals exception, rather than on the exceptions aimed at protection of other non-economic objectives, both the WTO Panel and the Appellate Body agreed that it was not necessary to identify 'the exact content of the public morals standard at issue'.[393] In contrast, the Appellate Body noted that while 'such risk-assessment methods do not appear to be of much assistance or relevance in identifying and assessing public morals', 'the focus on the dangers or risks to human, animal, or plant life or health in the context of Article XX(b) may lend itself to scientific or other methods of inquiry'.[394]

One could argue that in respect to the general exception for privacy and data protection in Article XIV(c)(ii) GATS, the analogy with Article XX(b) is closer than that of a public morals exception. The analysis of *EC–Seals* by Howse and Langille, discussed in Section 2.4.2, illustrates that such methods of assessment 'that employ instrumental rationality, such as means/ends reasoning, simply does not work to establish the non-pretextual character of noninstrumental moral regulation'.[395] If we examine more recent WTO cases, trade adjudicators tend to prioritize economic rationality when interpreting vague principles. They are, therefore, more inclined to view data privacy as *an instrument* to enhance trade rather than as a fundamental human right or societal value. Empirical research on the WTO's Dispute Settlement Mechanism provides substantial evidence of the ongoing

substance of an economic argument for protection' and that, rather, the debate about these issues was a 'conceptual debate over economic logic').

391 (Emphasis added.) WTO, *Brazil – Measures Affecting Imports of Retreaded Tyres – Report of the Appellate Body* (3 December 2007) WT/DS332/AB/R, para 145.

392 This discrepancy, in particular, was at the core of the Appeal by Canada and Norway of the WTO Panel Decision in the case. For example, Norway contended that 'the Panel thus erred by holding the alternative measure up to a benchmark level of contribution that was higher than the contribution achieved by the EU Seal Regime. This error, Norway argues, compromised the Panel's analysis of whether the contribution of the alternative was equal to or greater than the level actually achieved by the EU Seal Regime, and of whether the alternative was reasonably available.' Appellate Body Reports, *EC – Seal Products* (n 170), para 2.78.

393 ibid, para 5.199.

394 ibid, para 5.198. Robert L Howse and Joanna Langille, 'Permitting Pluralism: The Seal Products Dispute and Why the WTO Should Permit Trade Restrictions Justified by Noninstrumental Moral Values' (2012) 37 Yale Journal of International Law 368, 429 (hereafter Howse and Langille, 'Permitting Pluralism').

395 Howse and Langille, 'Permitting Pluralism' (n 394) 429.

dominance of developed countries, a bias towards trade liberalization, and a failure to adequately acknowledge non-economic objectives.[396] While there are some recent indications of a growing willingness to consider non-trade norms and values at the WTO, such as public health in the tobacco plain packaging cases, it remains uncertain whether this trend will persist and to what degree it will be embraced.[397]

Although some empirical research exists examining the economic costs of insufficient privacy protection,[398] the aspects of privacy protection contributing to consumers' trust in digital ecosystems,[399] and the value (or price) of privacy for consumers and companies,[400] such research has an inherent limitation: privacy and personal data protection cannot be precisely estimated because consumers' valuation of privacy is highly context dependent and prone to behavioural biases.[401]

[396] Daniel Drache and Marc D Froese, 'An Empirical Analysis of Why the WTO Is Broken and Cannot Be Fixed – Yet' (2007 3(1)) Eurostudia <https://www.erudit.org/en/journals/euro/1900-v1-n1-euro1991/017648ar/> accessed 10 July 2023; Petersmann, 'Human Rights and International Economic Law in the 21st Century' (n 169); Daniel Rangel, 'WTO General Exceptions: Trade Law's Faulty Ivory Tower. Only Two of 48 Attempts to Use the World Trade Organization's GATT Article XX/GATS Article XIV "General Exceptions" Have Ever Succeeded' (2022) Public Citizen's Global Trade Watch <https://www.citizen.org/wp-content/uploads/WTO-General-Exceptions-Paper_-1.pdf> accessed 10 July 2023.

[397] See Daniel Gervais, 'TRIPS Pluralism' (2022) 21(2) Word Trade Review 185.

[398] For empirical research attempting to quantify the chilling effects of governmental surveillance see, eg, PEN America, 'Chilling Effects: NSA Surveillance Drives U.S. Writers to Self-Censor' (2013) Report, 3 <https://pen.org/wp-content/uploads/2022/08/2014-08-01_Full-Report_Chilling-Effects-w-Color-cover-UPDATED.pdf> accessed 10 July 2023; Jonathon W Penney, 'Chilling Effects: Online Surveillance and Wikipedia Use' (2016) 31(1) Berkeley Technology Law Journal 117, 145–61; Alex Marthews and Catherine E Tucker, 'Government Surveillance and Internet Search Behavior' (2017) 2–3 <https://ssrn.com/abstract=2412564> accessed 10 July 2023.

[399] See, eg, World Economic Forum, 'Rethinking Personal Data: A New Lens for Strengthening Trust' (May 2014) Industry Agenda, 21 <http://www3.weforum.org/docs/WEF_RethinkingPersonalData_ANewLens_Report_2014.pdf> accessed 10 July 2023.

[400] See, eg, Nicola Jentzsch, Sören Preibusch, and Andreas Harasser, 'Study on Monetising Privacy: An Economic Model for Pricing Personal Information' (2012) ENISA 1 <https://www.enisa.europa.eu/publications/monetising-privacy> accessed 10 July 2023; Alessandro Acquisti, Leslie K John, and George Loewenstein, 'What Is Privacy Worth?' (2013) 42(2) The Journal of Legal Studies 249, 250 (hereafter Acquisti, John, and Loewenstein, 'What Is Privacy Worth?'); Dan Cvrcek and others, 'A Study on the Value of Location Privacy' (2006) Proceedings of the 5th ACM Workshop on Privacy in Electronic Society, 110 <https://dl.acm.org/citation.cfm?id=1179621> accessed 10 July 2023; Bernardo A Huberman, Eytan Adar, and Leslie R Fine, 'Valuating Privacy: The Value of Privacy' (2005) IEEE Security & Privacy, 22 <http://www.cond.org/deviance.pdf> accessed10 July 2023; Tamara Dinev and Hart Paul, 'An Extended Privacy Calculus Model for E-Commerce Transactions' (2006) 17(1) Information Systems Research 61, 61; Luc Wathieu and Allan Friedman, 'An Empirical Approach to Understanding Privacy Valuation' (2007) Harvard Business School Working Paper No 07-075, 1–2 <https://www.hbs.edu/faculty/Publication%20Files/07-075.pdf> accessed 10 July 2023. Avi Goldfarb and Verina F Que, 'The Economics of Digital Privacy' (2023) Annual Review of Economics, 267 (hereafter Goldfarb and Que, 'The Economics of Digital Privacy').

[401] Alessandro Acquisti, Laura Brandimarte, and George Loewenstein, 'Privacy and Behavioral Economics' in Bart P Knijnenburg and others (eds), *Modern Socio-Technical Perspectives on Privacy* (Springer 2022) 61–77; Acquisti, John, and Loewenstein, 'What Is Privacy Worth?' (n 400) 252 (challenging the premise that privacy valuations can be precisely estimated based on theories from behavioural economics and decision research); ibid 257 ('The dichotomy between [willingness to pay] and [willingness to accept payment] ... suggests that ordinary studies investigating privacy valuations may not tell us much about whether, or how much, consumers will actually pay to protect their data.'); see also Acquisti, Brandimarte, and Loewenstein, 'Privacy and Human Behavior in the Age of Information' (n 364) 505–10; Maria C Wasastjerna, 'The Role of Big Data and Digital Privacy in Merger Review' (2018) 2(3) European Competition Journal 417, 436 (arguing that privacy lacks quantifiable metrics due to

Furthermore, in addition to instrumental (economic) value, consumers may also have intrinsic, non-economic, value of privacy, which is even more subjective.[402]

The second problem is that even if privacy and personal data protection could be priced, an 'optimal' level of protection from an economic perspective, as this chapter argues later, will be lower than the optimal level of such protection determined from the legal (fundamental rights) approach to privacy and data protection, because the economic calculus does not factor in the intrinsic value of privacy and data protection as a fundamental right.[403] Walker argues, for example, that increase of privacy regulation could lead to the *loss* of trust, which is a direct result of communal exchanges and product of society.[404] Therefore, limits on information sharing introduced by legislation 'may exacerbate our declining sense of community, security, accountability, and trust'.[405] From Walker's perspective, '[w]hile legal requirements mandating specific information practices are one way of promoting such trust, they are hardly the only or even the most effective way'.[406] Some empirical studies showing that the GDPR led to reduction in web visits and revenue could be one of illustrations of this argument.[407]

From an economic perspective, the line between privacy and data protection as preconditions of trade, and as trade barriers, should be drawn based on considerations of Pareto efficiency,[408] which is defined as the maximization of social welfare,[409] where social welfare is the aggregated welfare of individual members of society.[410] There is no consensus on how to define welfare; money and utility are the most widely used proxies to evaluate welfare and suggest the most optimal

the subjectivity of consumer preferences about privacy); Jessica Colnago, Lorrie Faith Cranor, and Alessandro Acquisti, 'Is There a Reverse Privacy Paradox? An Exploratory Analysis of Gaps between Privacy Perspectives and Privacy-Seeking Behaviors' (2023) (1) Proceedings on Privacy Enhancing Technologies 455; Goldfarb and Que, 'The Economics of Digital Privacy' (n 400) 270; Danielle Keats Citron and Daniel J Solove, 'Privacy Harms' (2022) 102(973) Boston University Law Review 793, 818.

402 Goldfarb and Que, 'The Economics of Digital Privacy' (n 400) 282, distinguishing between intrinsic (non-economic) and instrumental (economic) value of privacy.

403 Goldfarb and Que, 'The Economics of Digital Privacy' (n 400) 277, arguing that '[i]f enough consumers have an intrinsic value of privacy, the firm cannot infer the instrumental value of an individual's data based on the decision to withhold those data'.

404 Kent Walker, 'The Costs of Privacy' (2001) 25(1) Harvard Journal of Law & Public Policy 87, 102–03.

405 ibid 97.

406 ibid 104.

407 See Guy Aridor, Yeon-Koo Che, and Tobias Salz, 'The Effect of Privacy Regulation on the Data Industry: Empirical Evidence from GDPR' as cited in Goldfarb and Que, 'The Economics of Digital Privacy' (n 400) 280.

408 See Steven Shavell, *Foundations of Economic Analysis of Law* (Belknap Press 2004) 2 (hereafter Shavell, *Foundations of Economic Analysis of Law*); Schäfer and Ott, *The Economic Analysis of Civil Law* (n 366) 46–47; Francesco Parisi, 'Positive, Normative and Functional Schools in Law and Economics, (2004) 18 European Journal of Law and Economics 259, 262.

409 See Schäfer and Ott, *The Economic Analysis of Civil Law* (n 366) 8; see also Richard A Posner, *Economic Analysis of Law* (9th edn, Wolters Kluwer Law 2014) 14–15.

410 See Schäfer and Ott, *The Economic Analysis of Civil Law* (n 366) 8.

regulatory option.[411] In their well-known but controversial *Harvard Law Review* article 'Fairness Versus Welfare', Kaplow and Shavell introduce one of the most comprehensive definitions of 'welfare' that incorporates 'in a positive way everything that an individual might value', including a taste for fairness, and in a negative way anything that the 'individual might find distasteful'.[412] However, even this inclusive understanding of welfare does not (and should not, according to Kaplow and Shavell) include the notion of fairness *as a value in itself*.[413] Kaplow and Shavell emphasize that welfare, defined in this way, should be the sole concern of legal policymakers; they criticize the legal method, which views fairness as an *independent evaluative principle* that should be upheld even at the expense of individuals' well-being, because it can sometimes lead to a decrease of social welfare and make society worse off.[414] Similarly, the economic approach is unable to fully capture the moral value of personal data protection as a fundamental right.[415]

411 See Marco Fabbri and Diogo GC Britto, 'Distributive Justice, Public Policies and the Comparison of Legal Rules: Quantify the "Price of Equity"'(2018) 14(3) Review of Law and Economics 1, 8 (noting that welfare economics theory traditionally maximizes utility, while law and economics tends to 'prefer using wealth as the object of maximization'.); Heico Kerkmeester, 'Methodology: General' in Boudewium Bouckaert and Gerrit De Geest (eds), *Encyclopedia of Law and Economics Volume I: The History and Methodology of Law and Economics* (Edward Elgar Publishing 2020), 386–87; Richard A Posner, 'Wealth Maximization Revisited' (1985) 2 Notre Dame Journal of Law, Ethics and Public Policy 85, 86–87.

412 Louis Kaplow and Steven Shavell, 'Fairness versus Welfare' (2001) 114(4) Harvard Law Review 961, 980–82 (hereafter Kaplow and Shavell, 'Fairness versus Welfare'):

The notion of well-being . . . incorporates in a positive way everything that an individual might value—goods and services that the individual can consume, social and environmental amenities, personally held notions of fulfillment, sympathetic feelings for others, and so forth. Similarly, an individual's well-being reflects in a negative way harms to his or her person and property, costs and inconveniences, and anything else that the individual might find distasteful. Well-being is not restricted to hedonistic and materialistic enjoyment or to any other named class of pleasures and pains. The only limit on what is included in well-being is to be found in the minds of individuals themselves, not in the minds of analysts . . . . We further note a particular source of well-being . . ., namely, the possibility that individuals have a taste for a notion of fairness, just as they may have a taste for art, nature, or fine wine.

This article was criticized by multiple scholars. See, eg, Michael B Dorff, 'Why Welfare Depends on Fairness: A Reply to Kaplow and Shavell' (2002) 75 Southern California Law Review 847; Mark White, 'Preaching to the Choir: A response to Kaplow and Shavell's Fairness versus Welfare' (2004) 16(4) Review of Political Economy 507; Matthew D Adler, 'Book Review: Kaplow, Louis, and Shavell, Steven. Fairness versus Welfare. Cambridge, MA: Harvard University Press, 2002. Pp. 544. $50.00 (cloth)' (2005) Ethics 824.

413 Kaplow and Shavell, 'Fairness versus Welfare' (n 412) 1011–17. Kaplow and Shavell succinctly summarize the argument: 'whenever a notion of fairness leads one to choose a different rule from that favored under welfare economics, everyone is necessarily worse off as a result'. ibid 1012.

414 ibid 967 (stating, as their central claim, that 'the welfare-based normative approach should be exclusively employed in the evaluating legal rules. That is, legal rules should be selected entirely with respect to their effects on the well- being of individuals in society'.).

415 See Wolfgang Kerber, 'Digital Markets, Data, and Privacy: Competition Law, Consumer Law and Data Protection' (2016) 11(11) Journal of Intellectual Property Law & Practice 856, 857 (hereafter Kerber, 'Digital Markets, Data, and Privacy') ('[E]conomic analysis usually focusses on welfare effects alone, which might not always grasp sufficiently the normative dimension of privacy as a fundamental right'.); see also Alessandro Acquisti, 'The Economics of Personal Data and the Economics of Privacy' (2010) Background Paper #3 in Joint WPISP- WPIE Roundtable, The Economics Of Personal Data and Privacy: 30 Years after the OECD Privacy Guidelines, 4 <https://www.oecd.org/sti/ieconomy/46968784.pdf> accessed 10 July 2023 (arguing that not all externalities caused by the use of personal data

A privacy and data protection regulation designed with both economic and non-economic considerations in mind should arguably ensure a higher level of personal data protection than the one designed with only economic efficiency considerations in mind.[416] Put differently, the normative goal of privacy and personal data protection predetermines, in part, both the desired optimal level of protection and the design of the regulatory framework.[417] If the goal is economic and instrumental, then it is justified *only to the extent necessary* to generate and preserve consumers' trust ('bottom-up regulation design').[418] From this perspective, the GDPR fundamental rights-based regulatory design can be viewed as undesirable to the extent that it leads to reduction of trust mentioned above.

Driven by their bottom lines, companies will only invest in privacy and data protection up to the point where the marginal costs of generating more trust will equal marginal benefits.[419] The problem is that trust is a subjective notion. Extensive empirical research has shown that *perceived* trust and control in the service provider can reduce privacy concerns and increases consumer data sharing with companies and participation in digital transactions.[420] Goldfarb and Que argue that '[t]he positive effect of redisclosure on data flows stems from its ability to provide consumers with the perception of control over the use of consented data'.[421] The subjective or perceived level of consumer trust that is sufficient for consumers to enter into digital transactions does not always accurately reflect the actual trustworthiness of digital businesses, as consumers may not have full information or understanding on how well their personal data is actually protected by the company.[422]

can be captured in economic terms); Acquisti, Brandimarte, and Loewenstein, 'Privacy and Human Behavior in the Age of Information' (n 364) 509.

416 Acquisti, Brandimarte, and Loewenstein, 'Privacy and Human Behavior in the Age of Information' (n 364) 509.

417 See Kerber, 'Digital Markets, Data, and Privacy' (n 415) 863–64.

418 Sandra J Milberg, H Jeff Smith, and Sandra J Burke, 'Information Privacy: Corporate Management and National Regulation' (2000) 11(1) Organization Science 35, 49 (hereafter Milberg, Smith, and Burke, 'Information Privacy'); Yakovleva, 'Should Fundamental Rights Be a Part of Trade "Deals"?' (n 320) 483.

419 See Kerber, 'Digital Markets, Data, and Privacy' (n 415) 865.

420 Goldfarb and Que, 'The Economics of Digital Privacy' (n 400) 278–70; see also Catherine E Tucker, 'Social Networks, Personalized Advertising, and Privacy Controls' (2014) 51(5) Journal of Marketing Research 546; Michael Kummer and Patrick Schulte, 'When Private Information Settles the Bill: Money and Privacy in Google's Market for Smartphone Applications' (2019) 65(8) Management Science 3470; Long Chen and others, 'The Data Privacy Paradox and Digital Demand' (2021) NBER Working Paper 28854 <https://www.nber.org/system/files/working_papers/w28854/w28854.pdf> accessed 10 July 2023; Janice Y Tsai and others, 'The Effect of Online Privacy Information on Purchasing Behavior: An Experimental Study' (2011) 22(2) Information Systems Research 254, 266; Joinson and others, 'Privacy, Trust, and Self-Disclosure Online' (n 366) 4–5, 17.

421 Goldfarb and Que, 'The Economics of Digital Privacy' (n 400) 279.

422 See Acquisti, Brandimarte, and Loewenstein, 'Privacy and Human Behavior in the Age of Information' (n 364) 512–13 (showing that the perceived and the actual levels of privacy may not coincide, and that providing users with explicit control mechanisms over their personal data may lead to sharing more sensitive data by users); see also Joinson and others, 'Privacy, Trust, and Self-Disclosure Online' (n 366) 16–17.

This means that by pursuing their strategic self-interest, companies may not necessarily improve the actual trustworthiness of their digital goods or services.[423] For example, companies engage in what is called 'privacy washing' (by analogy with 'green washing') in the context of using privacy enhancing technologies to protect privacy, especially in the context of machine-learning and AI systems.[424] In contrast, if the protection is granted for its own sake as independent normative significance ('top-down regulatory design'), the level of protection will tend to be higher than the level that is necessary to advance social welfare from the welfare economics perspective.[425]

In sum, the protection of personal data as a fundamental right is a type of protection that is not necessarily efficiency-enhancing in an economic sense, but it can create both economic and non-economic effects beneficial for society at large. Setting the economic approach, as just discussed, as the *proper realm* of the discourse (and thus economic efficiency as the proper benchmark) predetermines the outcome.[426] An emphasis on efficiency brands a broader range of domestic policies as protectionist.

When it comes to cross-border transfers of personal data, economic efficiency (or maximization gains from international digital trade) is not the only goal of protection or restrictions.[427] Even if limitations on personal data transfers, such as those imposed by the European Union, do factually restrict trade, a country may well be willing to sacrifice some gains in order to protect its constitutional, cultural, and societal values.[428] As Bhagwati rightly acknowledged, when non-economic objectives, such as the intrinsic value of specific policy objectives, enter the scene,

[423] See Rodrik, *The Globalization Paradox* (n 4) 227 ('Corporations, after all, are motivated by the bottom line. They may be willing to invest in social and environmental projects if doing so buys them customers' goodwill. Yet we shouldn't assume their motives align closely with those of society at large, nor exaggerate their willingness to advance societal agendas. The most fundamental objection to labelling and other market-based approaches is that they overlook the *social* dimension of standard-setting'.).

[424] Sébastien Gambs and others, 'Privacy and AI Ethics – Understanding the Convergences and Tensions for the Responsible Development of Machine Learning (Office of the Privacy Commissioner of Canada, 2021) 39 <https://www.priv.gc.ca/en/opc-actions-and-decisions/research/funding-for-privacy-research-and-knowledge-translation/completed-contributions-program-projects/2020-2021/p_2020-21_09/> accessed 10 July 2023;Stewart Dresner, 'Meaningful Consent and Privacy-Washing' (*Privacy Laws & Business*, 7 December 2022) <https://www.privacylaws.com/reports-gateway/articles/int180/int180blog/> accessed 10 July 2023, referring to a statement of Spanish DPA on privacy washing.

[425] Shavell, *Foundations of Economic Analysis of Law* (n 408) 610. Shavell illustrates the point by the following example: '[I]f promise-keeping is granted independent significance, more promises will be kept than would be best if the goal were to keep promises only to advance individuals' utilities, and whatever utility-based measure of social welfare one endorses will likely be lower than it could be'. ibid; Yakovleva, 'Should Fundamental Rights Be a Part of Trade "Deals"?' (n 320) 483.

[426] See Acquisti, Brandimarte, and Loewenstein, 'Privacy and Human Behavior in the Age of Information' (n 364) 509.

[427] See Kuner, 'Data Nationalism' (n 205) 2097.

[428] Kuner makes a similar point. See ibid 2096 (arguing that the central question that the criticism of the economic effects of data nationalism asks is: '[W]hat if a country has decided that it wants to sacrifice a certain amount of economic efficiency in exchange for promoting other legitimate values that it believes are furthered by data nationalism?').

'free trade will generally cease to be the optimal solution.'[429] Moreover, a country's international trade policy cannot be viewed in clinical isolation from other domestic policies and objectives. In common with all other policies, it is (or at least should be) guided by a shared set of normative values of governmental policy in general, normative goals that are typically safeguarded by domestic constitutions.[430] For the European Union, these principles are those contained in Articles 2, 3(5), and 21 of the Treaty on European Union,[431] and include the universality and indivisibility of human rights and fundamental freedoms, as well as respect for human dignity, for the principles of the United Nations, and for international law. Undoubtedly, societies and governments have goals other than welfare.[432] Susan Strange argued that efficiency falls under only one of the four basic values pursued by a politically organized society—wealth, order, justice, and freedom—and in all politically organized societies, these values will be combined differently and lead to different outcomes.[433]

The EU data protection framework—the result of a difficult political compromise between, at that time, twenty-eight member states with distinct cultures and values—may not be the best regulation, but regulation can never be perfect.[434] In a narrow effects-based definition of 'protectionism' generated by neoliberal discourse, the EU framework indeed may be viewed as protectionist due to its restrictive effects on international trade.[435] However, because of the limitations of economic discourse, this framework is not appropriate when fundamental rights are at stake.[436] The neoliberal conception of protectionism that once drove the

[429] Bhagwati, 'Fair Trade, Reciprocity, and Harmonization' (n 93) 19 (arguing that '[w]hen "non-economic" objectives (such as the *valuation in themselves* of specific outputs such as manufactures or high-tech industry so that a dollar worth of output is valued at four, for instance) are admitted into the analysis, free trade will generally cease to be the optimal solution.') (emphasis added).

[430] See Kuner, 'Data Nationalism' (n 205) 2097.

[431] Treaty on European Union (Consolidated Version), Treaty of Maastricht, 7 February 1992 [2002] OJ EC C 325/5.

[432] Strange, 'Protectionism and World Politics' (n 25) 236 ('The basic premise that state policy should, or even can, be based on the single criterion of maximizing efficiency in the production of goods and services for the market is demonstrably false.').

[433] ibid 237:

Efficiency, in short, is only one of four basic values that any politically organized society seeks to achieve for its members. Wealth, order, justice, and freedom; these are the basic elements of political compounds just as hydrogen, oxygen, and carbon are the essential elements of some chemical compounds. And just as chemical elements can be combined differently to produce oil, wood, or potatoes, so basic values will be combined differently in all politically organized societies to produce, for example, fast-growing authoritarian states or slow-growing democracies, or conversely, fast-growing democracies or slow-growing police states.

See also Polčák and Svantesson, *Information Sovereignty* (n 375) 209 ('While the Internet is often seen as borderless in nature and global in scope, the physical work and the people that inhabit that world are still divided by fundamentally different cultures and values; and even where common values are found, those values are weighted in different ways.').

[434] See Mira Burri and Rahel Schär, 'The Reform of the EU Data Protection Framework: Outlining Key Changes and Assessing Their Fitness for a Data- Driven Economy' (2016) 6 Journal of Information Policy 479, 488–89 (hereafter Burri and Schär, 'The Reform of the EU Data Protection Framework').

[435] United States International Trade Commission, 'Global Digital Trade 1' (n 197) 276.

[436] Burri and Schär, 'The Reform of the EU Data Protection Framework' (n 434) 500.

world trading system towards globalization has reached a turning point where it has become a victim of its own success.[437] A new pluralist discourse is necessary in order to allow each trading party to strike the right balance between globalization (economic gains from digital trade and the right to conduct business), democratic politics, and domestic autonomy to pursue domestic values such as fundamental rights to privacy and data protection.[438]

Yet European integration and the resulting economic power of the European Union not only directs its energies inwards, but is also, to a large extent, an outward-looking strategy: while it improves internal trade within the European Union, it also improves the European Union's negotiating positions in external economic relations and in the negotiations of international treaties.[439] It also contributes to the expansion of European standards and values around the world, a phenomenon labelled by Anu Bradford as the 'Brussels Effect'.[440] The presence of political and economic rationales for the unification of data protection rules in the European Union, however, does not diminish the fact that the level of data protection guaranteed by the unified rules is a projection of a European vision of governance and cultural values.[441]

Schwartz and Peifer attest that '[t]here is no constitutional right to information privacy in the United States analogous to the EU's right to data protection'.[442] The Fourth Amendment[443] only applies to government searches and seizures; it does not apply to government processing of personal data in already existing databases.[444] Neither does it apply to the processing of personal data in the commercial context.[445] In the commercial sphere, protection of information privacy tends to

[437] Rodrik, *The Globalization Paradox* (n 4) xvii–xviii.

[438] ibid 200 (pointing at a 'fundamental political trilemma of the world economy,' meaning that it is impossible to simultaneously pursue democracy, national self-determination, and hyper-globalization). See also Howse and Langille, 'Continuity and Change in the World Trade Organization' (n 176).

[439] See Anu Bradford, 'The Brussels Effect' (2012) 107(1) Northwestern University Law Review 1, 47–48.

[440] ibid.

[441] See Joel R Reidenberg, 'Resolving Conflicting International Data Privacy Rules in Cyberspace' (2000) 52 Stanford Law Review 1315,1319–20 (hereafter Reidenberg, 'Resolving Conflicting International Data Privacy Rules in Cyberspace') ('[S]pecific privacy rules in any particular country have a governance function reflecting the country's choices regarding the roles of the state, market, and individual in the country's democratic structure. Under this governance theory of privacy, national differences derive from distinct visions of governance, and privacy rules strive to protect a state's norm of governance, whether it be a liberal market norm or a socially-protective, citizen's rights norm'.); see also Milberg, Smith, and Burke, 'Information Privacy' (n 418) 47 (based on the empirical study of samples from nineteen different countries, the authors conclude that '[a] country's cultural values are associated strongly with the privacy concerns that are exhibited by its populace (Hypothesis 1) and are associated marginally with its regulatory approach (Hypothesis 2)'.).

[442] Schwartz and Peifer, 'Transatlantic Data Privacy Law' (n 27) 132.

[443] Amendment IV to the US Constitution reads as follows: 'The right of the people to be secure in their persons, houses, papers, and effects, against unreasonable searches and seizures, shall not be violated, and no warrants shall issue, but upon probable cause, supported by oath or affirmation, and particularly describing the place to be searched, and the persons or things to be seized.'

[444] Schwartz and Peifer, 'Transatlantic Data Privacy Law' (n 27) 133.

[445] ibid 132–33.

be anchored in the 'marketplace discourse'.[446] It is aimed at protecting consumer welfare rather than constitutional rights.[447] The legal weight of such protection is thus lower than, for example, that of the constitutional right to freedom of expression.[448] Recall, in addition, that a more liberal approach to data protection in the United States not only echoes US cultural values but also factors in the US strategy of preserving global dominance in the information technology industry.[449]

To sum up, the core of the debate between the European Union and its trading partners is not about *whether* the protection of privacy and personal data is legitimate as such, but rather about *what level* of protection is legitimate. As differences in data protection approaches (including the issue of cross-border transfers of personal data) are fundamentally rooted in a delicate balance between the different values pursued by a politically organized society, a related question arises: whether international trade should be tasked with the mission to reduce or remove this diversity,[450] and if so, how to determine the right level of protection and the right level of deference to domestic interests and values?

3.5 Concluding Remarks: Towards a New Digital Trade Regime

This chapter has demonstrated that it is not possible to strike the right balance between digital trade liberalization and the protection of data privacy by simply ruling out 'protectionism'. It has argued that the choice of the right discourse for

[446] ibid 136.

[447] See Reidenberg, 'Resolving Conflicting International Data Privacy Rules in Cyberspace' (n 441) 1318; Schwartz and Peifer, 'Transatlantic Data Privacy Law' (n 27) 136–37.

[448] Schwartz and Solove, 'Reconciling Personal Information in the United States and European Union' (n 369) 880–81 (stating that the right to privacy in the United States 'may even be secondary to other concerns, such as freedom of speech'.); see also Schwartz, 'The EU-U.S. Privacy Collision' (n 369) 1976–77 ('The First Amendment's protections for freedom of expression … help define the U.S. orientation to privacy regulation'.). Although in some cases the First Amendment can 'bolster privacy,' most of the time it is used to limit privacy: 'statutes that limit information sharing on privacy grounds are subject to constitutional scrutiny of their impact on the speech of the data processor'. ibid. (emphasis omitted). See also Bilyana Petkova, 'Privacy as Europe's First Amendment' (2019) 25(2) European Law Journal 140; James Q Whitman, 'The Two Western Cultures of Privacy: Dignity Versus Liberty' (2004) 113(6) Yale Law Journal 1151.

[449] See Section 3.3.3.

[450] The author of this book is of the position that trade law should not be tasked with this mission. For discussion, see Irion, Kaminski, and Yakovleva, 'Privacy Peg, Trade Hole' (n 246). See also Susan Ariel Aaronson, 'Building Trust in Digital Trade Will Require a Rethink of Trade Policy-Making'(2023) 39 Oxford Review of Economic Policy 98, 99; Patrick Leblond and Susan Ariel Aaronson, 'A Plurilateral "Single Data Area" Is the Solution to Canada's Data Trilemma' (2019) CIGI Papers No 226, 9 <https://www.cigionline.org/static/documents/documents/no.226.pdf> accessed 10 July 2023; Stephen J Schulhofer, 'An International Right to Privacy? Be Careful What You Wish For' (2016) 14(1) International Journal of Constitutional Law 238. cf Chander and Schwartz, 'Privacy and/or Trade' (n 207); Joel R Reidenberg, 'E-Commerce and Trans-Atlantic Privacy' (2001) 38 Houston Law Review 717, 739, 748 (hereafter Reidenberg, 'E-Commerce and Trans-Atlantic Privacy'); Naef, *Data Protection without Data Protectionism* (n 328) 407–08.

policy conversations on domestic privacy and the protection of personal data in the context of negotiating and interpreting international trade law is crucial. The value structures attending it will ultimately predetermine where the line will be drawn between legitimate privacy and personal data protection, and illegitimate protectionism, both in the relevant provisions of international trade agreements and in the interpretation of such provisions by trade adjudicating bodies.

Deliberations on the distinction between protection and protectionism show that it is not clear-cut: drawing a line beyond which protection *should* be viewed as protectionism is ultimately a judgment call.[451] On a spectrum between the two extremes, there is a grey area that includes domestic measures, with an element of uncertainty as to what type of regulatory goal is at stake: protectionism in disguise or genuine protection, which only incidentally benefits domestic industries.[452] Whether measures in this grey area should fall under the label of 'protection' or 'protectionism'—in other words, whether trade adjudicating bodies should err on the side of protection or protectionism—essentially depends on the discourse. Within an economic discourse, where free trade alone is high on the value scale, such regulation should be excluded as protectionist. In contrast, in a pluralist discourse where equal value is assigned to free trade and protection of fundamental rights, letting some disguised protectionist measures slip through in order to safeguard states' domestic autonomy to adopt socially beneficial regulation may be a preferred approach.

This chapter contends that the distinction between privacy and personal data protection, and protectionism is in part a *moral* question, that is, not just a question of economic efficiency. As Romer, a Nobel Prize winning economist, explains '[s]cientific authority never conveys moral authority. No economist has a privileged insight into questions of right and wrong, and none deserves a special say in fundamental decisions about how society should operate'.[453] Therefore, when

[451] Marceau and Trachtman, 'A Map of the World Trade Organization Law of Domestic Regulation of Goods' (n 166) 352 ('The distinction between a protectionist measure—condemned for imposing discriminatory or unjustifiable costs—and a non-protectionist measure restricting trade incidentally (and thus imposing some costs) is sometimes difficult to make'.). See also Sykes, 'Regulatory Protection and the Law of International Trade' (n 45) 33 ('[I]t is exceedingly difficult to devise a workable and palatable legal rule to condemn regulatory measures that are necessary to nonprotectionist regulatory goals but that are nevertheless undesirable because of their trade impact. As a result, this task is left to case-by-case bargaining'.); Robert Howse, 'Regulatory Measures' in Amrita Narlikar, Martin Daunton, and Robert M Stern, *The Oxford Handbook on the World Trade Organisation* (Oxford Handbooks Online 2012) 441–43 ('Regulations serve diverse objectives and reflect compromises between different groups. In such circumstances, it is not simple to draw a line between internal policies that are legitimate exercises of domestic regulatory autonomy (even if they have some trade-restrictive effects) and those that can be considered a form of protectionism or "cheating" on the WTO bargain, in that they undermine the market access reasonably expected from commitments on liberalization of border measures in the multilateral trading system'.); Howse, 'From Politics to Technocracy' (n 37) 96.

[452] Marceau and Trachtman, 'A Map of the World Trade Organization Law of Domestic Regulation of Goods' (n 166) 352.

[453] Paul Romer, 'The Dismal Kingdom: Do Economists Have Too Much Power?' (*Foreign Affairs*, 11 February 2020) <https://www.foreignaffairs.com/reviews/dismal-kingdom> accessed 10 July 2023.

a policy conversation, such as the one on cross-border flows of personal data, involves non-economic spillover effects to individual rights, such conversation should *not* be confined within the straightjacket of trade economics but rather placed in a broader pluralist normative perspective. The economic digital trade discourse, advanced by some states (most notably the United States) and reflected in the CPTPP, USMCA, and USJDTA, subordinates non-economic values, such as the protection of privacy and personal data taken as moral values, to efficiency and to ill-defined welfare enhancement goals.[454] As a result, only an economically justified—and lower—level of privacy and data protection, as compared to that warranted by a pluralist discourse, is able to qualify as not protectionist.[455] This book argues that the political economy arguments against privacy and data protection beyond economic necessity should be taken with a grain of salt, precisely because those who are putting them forward may themselves be suffering from capture by those profiting from unrestricted cross-border data flows.

From a global perspective, the inchoate use of the terms 'protectionism' and 'digital protectionism' in different discourses by the European Union and the United States exposes a deeper challenge to the present-day multilateral trade negotiations.[456] Having chosen digital protectionism as the main stumbling block on the path of digital trade, trading partners focus more on these labels and their definition, while shying away from more fundamental questions about the goals and values of future (digital) trade. This book contends that this path is misguided: there exist as many definitions of (digital) protectionism as there are discourses, which the EU and US examples clearly demonstrate. Using the same terminology, these trading partners advance utterly different discourses built upon different views on where the balance between trade and privacy should be struck. Against this backdrop, this chapter contends that countries should rethink the goals of international trade for the twenty-first century.[457]

On the subject of restrictions on cross-border flows of personal data, this book argues that such restrictions are, and will remain, necessary.[458] Unless approaches to data protection and privacy are harmonized internationally (which, arguably, is not the route to follow due to the lack of a (political) basis for such harmonization, differences between countries, and the danger of settling for the lowest common denominator), countries need more regulatory space to determine the

[454] Additionally, these goals often do not reflect negative externalities of economic growth (eg, environmental degradation) and thus take a narrow view of 'welfare'.

[455] See Section 3.3.4.

[456] See Section 3.3.

[457] Lang, *World Trade Law after Neoliberalism* (n 38) 353. For discussion on what those goal should be, see, eg, Howse and Langille, 'Continuity and Change in the World Trade Organization' (n 176); Harlan G Cohen, 'What Is International Trade Law For?' (2019) 113(2) American Journal of International Law 326; Anthea Roberts, Henrique Choer Moraes, and Victor Ferguson, 'Toward a Geoeconomic Order in International Trade and Investment' (2019) 22(4) Journal of International Economic Law 655.

[458] See also Section 5.2.5 arguing that these restrictions constitute part of the essence of the fundamental rights to privacy and the protection of personal data.

design of domestic data protection regimes.[459] It is precisely because data protection standards in other countries are low (perhaps, strategically low) that countries with higher standards need to impose restrictions on personal data transfers.[460] When it comes to the consequences of removing restrictions on cross-border flows of personal data in domestic privacy and data protection regimes and the ways to avert them, one could draw a parallel with restrictions on financial flows, which are essential to ensure financial stability in a country. Rodrik has eloquently argued the following:

> Financial globalization in effect neutralizes differences in national regulations. This is what is known in the trade as "regulatory arbitrage," a race to the bottom in finance. For this reason, a commitment to regulatory diversity has a very important corollary: the need for restrictions on global finance ... Governments should be able to keep banks and financial flows out—not for financial protectionism but to prevent the erosion of national regulations. Hence a new global financial order must be constructed on the back of a minimal set of international guidelines and with limited international coordination. Most important, the rules would explicitly recognize governments' right to limit cross-border financial transactions, insofar as the intent and effect are to prevent foreign competition from less strict jurisdictions from undermining domestic regulatory standards.[461]

This line of reasoning, this book argues, applies equally to restrictions on cross-border transfers of personal data. Deep harmonization of domestic privacy and data protection standards would also require a more extensive form of global governance, which does not seem realistic.

[459] See Irion, Kaminski, and Yakovleva, 'Privacy Peg, Trade Hole' (n 246), responding to Chander and Schwartz arguing that there should be an international Global Agreement on Privacy. Chander and Schwartz, 'Privacy and/or Trade' (n 207). Chander and Schwartz's work develops an earlier idea of Joel Reidenberg to negotiate a 'General Agreement on Information Privacy' at the WTO. See Reidenberg, 'E-Commerce and Trans-Atlantic Privacy' (n 450) 739, 748.

[460] On the prospects of harmonizing data protection regimes, see, eg, Milberg, Smith, and Burke, 'Information Privacy' (n 418) 53 ('What will or will not meet "societal expectations" is highly contingent on a society itself. Thus, a universal regulatory approach to information privacy seems unlikely and would ignore cultural and societal differences.'); see also Christopher Kuner, 'Regulation of Transborder Data Flows under Data Protection and Privacy Law: Past, Present, and Future' (2011) OECD Digital Economy Papers No 187, 8 <https://www.oecd-ilibrary.org/science-and-technology/regulation-of-transborder-data-flows-under-data-protection-and-privacy-law_5kg0s2fk315f-en> accessed 10 July 2023; Perry Keller, *European and International Media Law: Liberal Democracy, Trade and New Media* (OUP 2011) 348–51. cf Aaditya Matto and Joshua P Meltzer, 'International Data Flows and Privacy: The Conflict and Its Resolution' (2018) 21(4) Journal of International Economic Law 769, 769 (arguing that a common privacy framework could be based on the OECD and APEC data protection frameworks).

[461] See Rodrik, *The Globalization Paradox* (n 4) 263–65.

4

Reconciling Data Privacy and Global Data Flows the EU Way

4.1 Introduction

In Chapter 2, this book demonstrated that if challenged under international trade law, the European Union's (EU) framework for transfers of personal data outside the European Economic Area (EEA)[1] might run afoul of the EU's international trade commitments, such as those under the General Agreement on Trade in Services (GATS),[2] not least because of the rejection by World Trade Organization (WTO) adjudicators of the 'aims and effects' test that factors in the regulatory intent in the assessment of whether a contested measure violates the GATS.[3] This approach to interpretation, as demonstrated in Chapter 3, was one of the manifestations of the neoliberal discourse.[4] If found incompatible with those trade commitments, the EU's framework for transfers of personal data outside the EEA may not be able to be justified under the necessity test of the general exception for the protection of the privacy of individuals in relation to the processing and dissemination of personal data under Article XIV(c)(ii) GATS (for the purposes of this chapter, referred to as the 'general exception for privacy and data protection'). Essentially, the necessity test, as interpreted by the WTO adjudicating bodies within the neoliberal discourse, provides the EU and other WTO members insufficient autonomy—from an EU law perspective—to protect privacy and personal data as fundamental rights. Chapter 2 also shone a spotlight on the EU's constitutional constraints on bringing the EU's legal framework for data transfers into compliance with current international trade rules and, in particular, with the general exception for privacy and data protection.[5] As a result, if the EU restrictions on transfers of personal data were successfully challenged in the WTO, the EU would face a catch-22 situation,

[1] The European Economic Area consists of the member states of the European Union and countries of the European Free Trade Association (EFTA): Norway, Iceland, and Lichtenstein. 'Glossary: European Economic Area (EEA)'(Eurostat) <https://ec.europa.eu/eurostat/statistics-explained/index.php/Glossary:European_Economic_Area_(EEA)#:~:text=The%20European%20Economic%20Area%2C%20abbreviated,force%20on%201%20January%201994> accessed 10 July 2023.

[2] General Agreement on Trade in Services, Annex 1B to Marrakesh Agreement Establishing the World Trade Organization [1994] 1869 UNTS 183, 33 ILM 1167 (hereafter GATS).

[3] See Section 2.3.1.

[4] See Section 3.2.4.3.

[5] See Section 2.4.4.

Governing Cross-Border Data Flows. Svetlana Yakovleva, Oxford University Press. © Svetlana Yakovleva 2024.
DOI: 10.1093/oso/9780192899248.003.0004

having to choose between compliance with its trade commitments, and upholding its constitutional values. A shift in the discourse governing the interpretation of GATS rules from a neoliberal to a pluralist one, as Chapter 3 suggests, would be a way to tackle this problem within the current WTO framework. Giving more weight to the EU's fundamental rights justification (as opposed to a merely economic or instrumental justification) for the protection of the rights to privacy and personal data protection both in the course of assessment of a possible violation of the GATS and in the application of the general exception could certainly tip the balance in favour of the EU.

As explained in Section 3.3.4, free trade agreements (FTAs) concluded outside the WTO framework increasingly address liberalization of cross-border data flows *outside* the traditional non-discrimination and market access commitments in services or goods chapters; instead, they include specific provisions on cross-border data flows and exceptions from those provisions in dedicated e-commerce or digital trade chapters. The EU has already negotiated a few of such FTAs (eg, the FTAs with the United Kingdom, New Zealand, and Chile mentioned in previous chapters) and is in the process of negotiating similar provisions with other trading partners, such as Australia and Japan, as this chapter explicates in the following sections.

A way to avoid the catch-22 problem in *future* trade agreements, as suggested in Chapter 2, is to reform both the exception for privacy and data protection in trade agreements and the EU's framework for transfers of personal data.[6] To be fair, a reform of the EU's framework for transfers of personal data outside the EEA would also reduce tensions with the current GATS framework. This chapter explores the possibilities of developing such an exception for privacy and data protection, while Chapter 5 delves into options for reforming the EU's framework for transfers of personal data outside the EEA.

As already briefly mentioned in Sections 1.1.7 and 3.3.4, in 2018, to address the international trade law aspect of this issue, the EU developed horizontal provisions on cross-border data flows and the protection of privacy and personal data for its prospective digital trade agreements,[7] which need to be distinguished from the standard contractual clauses (SCCs)[8] used as a mechanism for transfers of personal

[6] This book focuses on provisions prohibiting restrictions of cross-border data flows and exceptions from them in the e-commerce and digital trade chapters of future trade agreements concluded by the EU. For a discussion on how the EU could modify the more traditional trade law obligations on trade in services to alleviate the tension between such provisions and EU restrictions on transfers of personal data outside the EEA under the GDPR, see Tobias Naef, *Data Protection without Data Protectionism: The Right to Protection of Personal Data and Data Transfers in EU Law and International Trade Law* (Springer Cham 2023) 316–17, 232 (hereafter Naef, *Data Protection without Data Protectionism*).

[7] European Commission, Proposal for provisions on Cross-border data flows and protection of personal data and privacy (31 January 2018) <https://www.politico.eu/wp-content/uploads/2018/02/Data-flow-provisions-POLITICO.pdf> accessed 10 July 2023.

[8] For discussion on the SCCs, see Section 2.2.4.

data under the General Data Protection Regulation (GDPR)[9] (for the purposes of this chapter referred to as the 'proposed horizontal provisions'). These horizontal provisions contain a broader exception for domestic privacy and data protection rules in trade agreements (for the purposes of this chapter referred to as the 'digital trade exception for privacy and data protection') than the existing general exception for privacy and data protection contained in the GATS. The EU has included these horizontal provisions ever since in its proposals for digital trade chapters in bilateral trade agreements (such as those with Australia, New Zealand, Chile, Indonesia, Tunisia,[10] the United Kingdom (following Brexit),[11] and Japan[12]) and its proposal for the negotiations at the Joint Initiative on E-commerce at the WTO.[13] While the EU managed to maintain the text close to the proposed horizontal provisions in the negotiated (but not yet ratified, as of June 2023) EU-New Zealand FTA and EU-Chile Interim Trade Agreement,[14] the digital trade exception for privacy and data protection in the 2020 EU-UK Trade and Cooperation Agreement (EU-UK TCA) seems to be narrower than the proposed horizontal provisions.[15] Despite

[9] Regulation (EU) 2016/679 of the European Parliament and of the Council of 27 April 2016 on the protection of natural persons with regard to the processing of personal data and on the free movement of such data, and repealing Directive 95/46/EC [2016] OJ L 119/1 (hereafter GDPR).

[10] See EU proposal for a Chapter on Digital Trade of the EU-New Zealand FTA; EU proposal for a Chapter on Digital Trade of the EU-Australia FTA; La proposition de l'Union européenne (UE) relative à Accord de libre-échange UE-Tunisie UE-Tunisie, Titre [] Commerce Numérique, 9 November 2018; Digital Trade Proposals for EU-Chile and EU-Indonesia were drafted before the European Union agreed on the model provisions. Therefore, these proposals only contained a placeholder for a provision on cross-border data flows. EU proposal for a Digital trade title in the Trade Part of a possible modernized EU-Chile Association Agreement, 5 February 2018 (containing a placeholder for provisions on data flows); EU proposal for a Chapter on Digital Trade of the EU-Indonesia FTA, 27 July 2017. The European Union tabled its horizontal provisions at a later stage in negotiations with these two countries. See, eg, European Commission, Report of the 5th Round of Negotiations for a Free Trade Agreement between the European Union and Indonesia (July 2018).

[11] European Commission, Draft text of the Agreement on the New Partnership with the United Kingdom (18 March 2020).

[12] See 'EU and Japan Start Negotiations to Include Rules on Cross-Border Data Flows in Their Economic Partnership Agreement' (*European Commission*, 7 October 2022) <https://policy.trade.ec.europa.eu/news/eu-and-japan-start-negotiations-include-rules-cross-border-data-flows-their-economic-partnership-2022-10-07_en> accessed 10 July 2023; Recital 4 of the Recommendation for a Council Decision authorizing the opening of negotiations for the inclusion of provisions on cross-border data flows in the Agreement between the European Union and Japan for an Economic Partnership [2022] COM(2022) 336 final.

[13] Joint Statement on Electronic Commerce, EU Proposal for WTO Disciplines and Commitments Relating to Electronic Commerce. Communication from the European Union [2019] INF/ECOM/22, 26 April 2019.

[14] Arts 12.4 and 12.5 of EU-New Zealand Free Trade Agreement (signed on 9 July 2023) (hereafter EU-New Zealand FTA); arts 19.4 and 19.5 of the EU-Chile Interim Agreement (negotiations concluded on 9 December 2022) (hereafter EU-Chile Interim Trade Agreement).

[15] Art 202 Trade and Cooperation Agreement between the European Union and the European Atomic Energy Community of the one part, and the United Kingdom of Great Britain and Northern Ireland, of the other part [2021] OJ L 149 (hereafter EU-UK TCA). See European Data Protection Supervisor, 'Opinion 3/2021 EDPS Opinion on the Conclusion of the EU and UK Trade Agreement and the EU and UK Exchange of Classified Information Agreement' (2021) <https://edps.europa.eu/system/files/2021-02/2021_02_22_opinion_eu_uk_tca_en.pdf> accessed 10 July 2023 (hereafter EDPS, 'Opinion 3/2021'). But see Kristina Irion and Mira Burris, '§ 16 Digitaler Handel' in Gesa

this deviation, the proposed horizontal provisions continue to be the EU's template for cross-border data flow provisions and exceptions from them in international trade negotiations. The discussion in this chapter, therefore, focuses mostly on these horizontal provisions.

Because the provisions on cross-border data flows and exceptions from them in the digital trade chapters of EU-New Zealand FTA and EU-Chile Interim Trade Agreement contain slight variations compared to the proposed horizontal provisions, the analysis in this chapter is anchored in the proposed horizontal provisions, but relevant variations in the above-mentioned agreements will be mentioned where this is necessary for the analysis. This chapter will also refer to other relevant provisions of those agreements to provide context or to illustrate how the proposed horizontal provisions are integrated in the broader framework of trade agreements.

In the words of the European Commission, the horizontal provisions 'rule out unjustified restrictions, such as forced data localisation requirements, while preserving the regulatory autonomy of the parties to protect the fundamental right to data protection'.[16] They were designed to serve the goals of 'promoting convergence of data protection standards at international level, as a way to facilitate data flows and thus trade', on the one hand, and 'to tackle digital protectionism', on the other hand.[17] Beyond those specific goals, the proposed horizontal provisions are a part of the EU's broader policy to ground its external relations in EU's values and strengthen its technological sovereignty.[18] For example, in its 2020 Data Strategy, the European Commission communicated its vision to maintain an 'open, but assertive approach to international data flows, based on European values'.[19] Similarly, in its White Paper on Artificial Intelligence (AI), the European Commission stated

Kübek, Christian J Tams, and Jörg Philipp Terhechte (Hrsg), *Handels- und Kooperationsvertrag EU/GB Handbuch* (Nomos 2022) 343–68, paras 14-6 (hereafter Irion and Burri, '§ 16 Digitaler Handel').

[16] Communication from the Commission to the European Parliament and the Council, 'Data Protection as a Pillar of Citizens' Empowerment and the EU's Approach to the Digital Transition – Two Years of Application of the General Data Protection Regulation' [2020] COM (2020) 264 final.

[17] ibid. The Commission has articulated these goals in the earlier policy documents. See, eg, Communication from the Commission to the European Parliament, the European Council, the Council, the European Economic and Social Committee, and the Committee of the Regions, 'A European Strategy for Data' [2020] COM (2020) 66 final (hereafter Communication from the Commission, 'A European Strategy for Data'), 23; European Commission, 'White Paper on Artificial Intelligence. A European Approach to Excellence and Trust' [2020] COM(2020) 65 final (hereafter European Commission, 'White Paper on Artificial Intelligence').

[18] Communication from the Commission to the European Parliament, the European Council, the Council, the European Economic and Social Committee, and the Committee of the Regions, 'Strengthening the Rule of Law within the Union. A Blueprint for Action' [2019] COM (2019) 343 final; European Commission and High Representative of the Union for Foreign Affairs and Security Policy, Joint Communication to the European Parliament and the Council on strengthening the EU's contribution to rules-based multilateralism [2021] JOIN (2021) 3 final (hereafter Joint Communication from the Commission and the High Representative of the Union For Foreign Affairs and Security Policy on strengthening the EU's contribution to rules-based multilateralism).

[19] See Communication from the Commission, 'A European Strategy for Data' (n 17) 23.

that it 'will strive to export its values', such as the protection of privacy and personal data, 'across the world' in its efforts for international cooperation on AI.[20] Simultaneously, the EU trade policy 'champions multilateralism and a rules-based global order'.[21] Some even argue that preserving multilateralism 'represents a key strategy for the EU to prosper and survive'.[22] Creating multilateral rules for digital trade, which include regulation of cross-border data flows, is now part and parcel of the EU's digital trade agenda and a priority for its trade policy:

> The objective is to ensure a leading position for the EU in digital trade and in the area of technology, most importantly by promoting innovation. . . . To achieve this, the WTO needs to set the rules for digital trade and the EU needs to play a central role in creating them.[23]

The EU-proposed horizontal provisions consist of three components: an article on cross-border data flows (Article 1); an article on the protection of personal data and privacy (Article 2); and an article on cooperation on regulatory issues with regard to digital trade (Article X[24]). This proposal is typically included in standalone chapters on digital trade. For the reader's convenience, here is the text of Articles 1 and 2.[25] Article 1 (referred to in this chapter as the 'cross-border data flows provision') reads as follows:

[20] European Commission, 'White Paper on Artificial Intelligence' (n 17).

[21] See European Commission, 'A Stronger Europe in the World: Reinforcing Our Responsible Global Leadership' (*European Commission*) <https://commission.europa.eu/strategy-and-policy/priorities-2019-2024/stronger-europe-world_en> accessed 10 July 2023; Communication from the Commission to the European Parliament, the Council, the European Parliament, the Council, the European Economic and Social Committee, and the Committee of the Regions, 'A Balanced and Progressive Trade Policy to Harness Globalisation' [2017] COM (2017) 492 final, 3 (stating that '[t]he EU is committed to open trade anchored in the rules-based multilateral trading system'); Josep Borrell, 'Building Global Europe' (*European Union External Action*, 9 September 2020) <https://www.eeas.europa.eu/eeas/building-global-europe_en> accessed 10 July 2023 (stating that '[t]he EU has a strong stake in maintaining and developing a rules-based international order within the framework of an effective multilateralism – even if others are clearly trying to weaken it'.) See also Joint Communication from the Commission and the High Representative of the Union for Foreign Affairs and Security Policy on strengthening the EU's contribution to rules-based multilateralism (n 14); Communication from the Commission to the European Parliament, the Council, the European Economic and Social Committee, and the Committee of the Regions, 'Trade Policy Review: An Open, Sustainable and Assertive Trade Policy' [2021] COM (2021) 66 final (hereafter Communication from the Commission, 'Trade Policy Review').

[22] Leonard Schütte and Hylke Dijkstra, 'The Show Must Go On: The EU's Quest to Sustain Multilateral Institutions since 2016' (2023) 61(5) Journal of Common Market Studies 1, showing that since 2016 the EU actively sustained multilateral institutions.

[23] Communication from the Commission, 'Trade Policy Review' (n 21).

[24] The document containing the horizontal provisions does not explain why this article is numbered as 'X' instead of '3'.

[25] Article X is beyond the scope of this book because regulatory cooperation is not relevant to the research question addressed in it. For a discussion and critique of this provision, see Naef, *Data Protection without Data Protectionism* (n 6) 411–13.

1. The Parties are committed to ensuring cross-border data flows to facilitate trade in the digital economy. To that end, cross-border data flows *shall not be restricted* between the Parties by:
   a) requiring the use of computing facilities or network elements in the Party's territory for processing, including by imposing the use of computing facilities or network elements that are certified or approved in the territory of the Party;
   b) requiring the localisation of data in the Party's territory for storage or processing;
   c) prohibiting storage or processing in the territory of the other Party;
   d) making the cross-border transfer of data contingent upon use of computing facilities or network elements in the Party's territory or upon localisation requirements in the Party's territory.
2. The Parties shall keep the implementation of this provision under review and assess its functioning within 3 years of the entry into force of this Agreement. A Party may at any time propose to the other Party to review the list of restrictions listed in the preceding paragraph. Such request shall be accorded sympathetic consideration.

Article 2 deals with the *protection of personal data and privacy* and includes an *exception* from the cross-border data flow provision. It reads as follows:

1. Each Party recognises that the protection of personal data and privacy *is a fundamental right* and that high standards in this regard contribute to trust in the digital economy and to the development of trade.
2. Each Party may adopt and maintain the *safeguards it deems appropriate* to ensure the protection of personal data and privacy, *including through the adoption and application of rules for the cross-border transfer of personal data. Nothing in this agreement shall affect* the protection of personal data and privacy afforded by the Parties' respective safeguards.
3. For the purposes of this agreement, 'personal data' means any information relating to an identified or identifiable natural person.
4. For greater certainty, the Investment Court System does not apply to the provisions in Articles 1 and 2 (emphasis added).

Looking ahead, the digital trade exception[26] for privacy and data protection is likely to be included *in addition to* the *general* exception for privacy and data

[26] There is a degree of uncertainty as to whether the proposed provision of Article 2(2) of the horizontal provisions is actually designed as an exception or rather as a carve-out from the scope of the agreement. This uncertainty originates from the lack of any indication in the provision itself of its actual function. However, comparison of this provision with provisions in existing trade agreements,

protection, replicating almost verbatim the general exception in the GATS, as the already negotiated EU-New Zealand FTA and EU-Chile Interim Trade Agreement demonstrate.[27]

This chapter questions whether the proposed horizontal provisions do indeed allow the EU to overcome the potential catch-22 compliance dead lock in future trade agreements, while at the same time pursuing the goals of facilitating cross-border data flows and promoting a rules-based multilateral trading system. It argues that, superficially, the proposed horizontal provisions do seem to provide the EU with the broad autonomy to protect privacy and personal data as fundamental rights while outlawing a number of measures restricting cross-border data flows. At the same time, the proposed horizontal provisions do have important flaws. Let us begin with what the horizontal provisions might allow.

The prohibition of restrictions on cross-border data flows in Article 1 of the proposed horizontal provisions is formulated more narrowly than in other existing models of similar type provisions deployed in FTAs following the US model (which is for far the most influential)[28] or in the Regional and Comprehensive Economic

which have similar wording (eg the prudential exception in art 2(a) of the GATS Annex on Financial Services and the prudential exceptions in art 195(1) EU-Central America Association Agreement, art 7.38(1) EU-Korea FTA, and art 8.50 EU-Singapore FTA) and are consistently interpreted as exceptions in literature and the WTO case law, suggests that Article 2(2) of the horizontal provisions should be viewed as an exception. See WTO, 'Background Note by the Secretariat Financial Services' (3 February 2010) S/C/W/312, S/FIN/W/73 para 28 (hereafter WTO, 'Background Note by the Secretariat Financial Services'); WTO, *Argentina – Measures Relating to Trade in Goods and Services – Report of the Panel* (9 May 2016) WT/DS453/R (hereafter Panel Report, *Argentina – Financial Services*) para 7.814; WTO, 'Guidelines for the Scheduling of Specific Commitments under the General Agreement on Trade in Services' (GATS) (23 March 2001) S/L/92 (hereafter WTO, 'Guidelines for the Scheduling of Specific Commitments under the GATS'). For further discussion, see Carlo Maria Cantore, '"Shelter from the Storm": Exploring the Scope of Application and Legal Function of the GATS Prudential Carve-Out' (2014) 48(6) Journal of World Trade 1223, 1232, 1242 (hereafter Cantore, 'Exploring the Scope of Application and Legal Function of the GATS Prudential Carve-Out'); Thomas Cottier and Markus Krajewski, 'What Role for Non-Discrimination and Prudential Standards in International Financial Law?' (2010) 13(3) Journal of International Economic Law 817, 826–27 (hereafter Cottier and Krajewski, 'What Role for Non-Discrimination and Prudential Standards in International Financial Law?'); Eric H Leroux, 'Trade in Financial Services under the World Trade Organization' (2002) 36(3) Journal of World Trade 413 (hereafter Leroux, 'Trade in Financial Services under the World Trade Organization'); Juan A Marchetti, 'The GATS Prudential Carve-Out' in Panagiotis Delimatsis and Nils Herger (eds), *Financial Regulation at the Crossroads: Implications for Supervision, Institutional Design and Trade* (Kluwer Law International 2011) (hereafter Marchetti, 'The GATS Prudential Carve-Out'); Armin Von Bogdandy and Joseph Windsor, 'Annex on Financial Services' in Rüdiger Wolfrum, Peter-Tobias Stoll, and Clemens Feinäugle (eds), *WTO – Trade in Services – Max Planck Commentaries on World Trade Law* (Martinus Nijhoff Publishers 2008) (hereafter Von Bogdandy and Windsor, 'Annex on Financial Services'); Mamiko Yokoi-Arai, '"GATS" Prudential Carve Out in Financial Services and Its Relation with Prudential Regulation' (2008) 57(3) International & Comparative Law Quarterly 613 (hereafter Yokoi-Arai, '"GATS" Prudential Carve Out in Financial Services'); Andrew D Mitchell, Jennifer Hawkins, and Neha Mishra, 'Dear Prudence: Allowances under International Trade and Investment Law for Prudential Regulation in the Financial Services Sector' (2016) 19(4) Journal of International Economic Law 787, 807 (hereafter Mitchell, Hawkins, and Mishra, 'Allowances under International Trade').

[27] Art 25.1 of EU-New Zealand FTA (n 14); art 32.1 of EU-Chile Interim Trade Agreement (n 14).

[28] See Section 3.3.4.

Partnership (RCEP),[29] which is considered to represent China's model. While both the US and China models contain a general obligation to allow cross-border data flows, Article 1 of the EU-proposed horizontal provisions contains an *exhaustive* list of restrictions on cross-border data flows that are outlawed by this provision.

Article 2(1) of the proposed horizontal provisions asserts that the normative rationale for the protection of personal data and privacy is the protection of fundamental rights. As demonstrated in Section 3.4.2, this rationale safeguards a higher level of privacy and data protection than that afforded by economic reasons for protecting privacy and personal data, and therefore arguably safeguards a broader autonomy to regulate vis-à-vis international trade commitments. This provision is likely to be interpreted as a part of the digital trade exception for privacy and data protection in Article 2(2) of the proposal. In addition, the breadth of this digital trade exception, modelled after the national security exceptions in the WTO Agreements, secures the EU's ability to maintain restrictions on transfers of personal data outside the EEA under the GDPR. In particular, the 'it deems appropriate' threshold of the proposed exception establishes a significantly lower threshold than the necessity test of the general exception (this issue is discussed in more detail in Section 4.2.3). The digital trade exception in Article 2(2) of the proposed horizontal provisions is formulated more broadly than similar exceptions in both US and China models for any public policy objective other than national security.[30] In addition, the proposed exception explicitly recognizes the rules for cross-border transfers of personal data as an example of the types of measures that would be allowed under the exception. Incorporating the recognition of privacy and personal data protection as fundamental rights in trade agreements, coupled with the possibility of maintaining the above-mentioned GDPR restrictions, serves the goal of exporting EU data protection framework worldwide.[31]

[29] Art 12.15 Regional Comprehensive Economic Partnership (entered into force on 1 January 2022) (hereafter RCEP), which reads as follows:

'Article 12.15: Cross-border Transfer of Information by Electronic Means

1. The Parties recognise that each Party may have its own regulatory requirements concerning the transfer of information by electronic means.

2. A Party shall not prevent cross-border transfer of information by electronic means where such activity is for the conduct of the business of a covered person.'

[30] For comparison with the US model, see Section 3.3.4. Similar to the EU's exception, China's digital trade exception also contains a low threshold 'it considers necessary' modelled after the WTO security exception. However, in addition to this threshold, it also requires that the measure to achieve a legitimate public policy objective 'is not applied in a manner which would constitute a means of arbitrary or unjustifiable discrimination or a disguised restriction on trade'. See art 12.15(3)(a) RCEP (n 29). This wording almost verbatim repeats the chapeau of general exceptions and part of the US model of the digital trade exception. Overall, however, RCEP provides a broader policy space for any legitimate public policy objective than the EU-proposed horizontal provisions because art 12.17 of RCEP excludes all matters arising under Chapter 12 Electronic Commerce (which includes the prohibition to restrict cross-border data flows and exceptions from this prohibition) from the scope of Dispute Settlement mechanism. See Mira Burri, 'Trade Law 4.0: Are We There Yet?' (2023) 26(1) Journal of International Economic Law 90, 97–98.

[31] See Section 5.3.3.

However, the proposed horizontal provisions suffer from at least three essential flaws that could both make them unable to safeguard the fundamental rights to privacy and the protection of personal data and undermine the goals of the EU digital trade policy. First, the unclear relationship of the proposed digital trade exception for privacy and data protection with the general exception creates legal uncertainty as to the material scope of the proposed exception.

Second, the breadth of the proposed digital trade exception for privacy and data protection may nullify the impact of the provision of Article 1, which outlaws what the EU frames as 'digital protectionism'. More generally, this chapter contends that using the extremely low threshold of national security exceptions as a model for a digital trade exception for privacy and data protection could further undermine the stability of the rules-based international trading order. This essentially creates an almost unconditional escape valve from virtually any trade commitment if there is at least a remote nexus to the protection of privacy and personal data. Using this threshold outside the national security context creates a *de facto* hierarchy between privacy and data protection, on the one hand, and other public policy objectives, such as protection of the environment, public health, or EU's emerging rules on data governance in line with its internal digital sovereignty discourse (which are still subject to the stricter necessity test of the general exception),[32] on the other hand. This could lead to the replication of the same threshold in exceptions for those other policy objectives. Such replication could lead to the weakening of the trading system. It could also lead to a more restrictive interpretation of the 'it considers necessary' threshold of the national security exception. This, in turn, would reduce the broad autonomy of states to protect their national security in spite of their international trade commitments—the goal for which this low threshold was introduced into international trade law in the first place.

Third, the proposed horizontal provisions are overly EU-centric in the sense that they require a recognition of the protection of privacy and personal data as fundamental rights—a commitment that not all EU trading partners may be willing to accept.

Based on the analysis of the proposed horizontal provisions, this chapter argues that these provisions could be improved in at least three ways. First, at a minimum, the future trade agreements should include a provision clarifying the relationship between general and digital trade exceptions for privacy and data protection to avoid a situation where EU restrictions on transfers of personal data would still need to meet the general exception for privacy and data protection, which is more onerous compared to the digital trade exception. A more ambitious reform of future trade agreements would contain a single exception for privacy and data

[32] For a discussion on EU's emerging data governance framework and trade policy, see Svetlana Yakovleva, 'On Digital Sovereignty, New European Data Rules, and the Future of Free Data Flows' (2022) 49(4) Legal Issues of Economic Integration 339–48 (hereafter Yakovleva, 'On Digital Sovereignty').

protection, which would apply throughout the agreement. Second, in the course of negotiations, the EU should consider replacing the 'it deems appropriate' threshold of the digital trade exception for privacy and data protection with a specific threshold which is higher than the 'it deems appropriate' standard but lower than the necessity test standard of the general exception. Third, the provision requiring the recognition of the parties that the protection of personal data and privacy is a fundamental right should be rephrased in a way which, on the one hand, safeguards the EU's autonomy to maintain its fundamental rights protection of these rights but, on the other hand, allows other trading partners to adopt a lower or different level of protection, if they so choose, within the bounds of international human rights law.

Considering that the proposed digital trade exception for privacy and data protection is only a starting point in negotiations, Section 4.3 considers alternative thresholds for this exception that the EU could fall back on without compromising on the fundamental rights to privacy and data protection. It looks at other alternatives found in WTO agreements and bilateral and regional trade agreements, which are on a continuum between the 'necessity' in the general exception, which is the current test for privacy and data protection, and the 'it deems appropriate' test proposed for a digital trade exception for privacy and data protection by the EU. Those alternatives are non-circumvention, non-avoidance, reasonableness, and the prohibition of arbitrary or unjustifiable restriction on trade. Relying on the interpretation of these thresholds in WTO case law and academic literature, Section 4.3 demonstrates that the *principles of good faith* and *the prohibition of abuse of rights* are the common denominators of all these thresholds. The flexibility of these principles is both a blessing and a curse. On the one hand, it gives adjudicating bodies wiggle room to adjust the application of these thresholds to the specific circumstances of a given case, but, on the other, it vests adjudicating bodies with broad discretionary powers, which can only be performed responsibly in the presence of appropriate checks and balances.

The chapter then argues that the issue in designing a digital trade exception for privacy and data protection is not only about the wording of the threshold for domestic autonomy to protect these policy interests, but also, and most importantly, about the amount of discretion afforded to the adjudicating bodies. As Chapter 3 has demonstrated, by using their discretion, the adjudicating bodies can—under the influence of a particular discourse—change the breadth of the exception by means of interpretation. Therefore, to ensure more predictability and control for the parties to a trade agreement over the interpretation of the threshold of the digital trade exception, restrictive mechanisms are necessary. In sum, this chapter argues that the standards of non-circumvention, non-avoidance, and reasonableness could be viable alternatives to the 'it deems appropriate' standard, provided that they are accompanied by appropriate restrictive mechanisms constraining the discretion of trade adjudicators and are applied in a nuanced manner. The use of the 'prohibition of arbitrary or unjustifiable restriction on trade' standard, however, is undesirable due to the risks of importation of the existing WTO case law on the chapeau of the general exceptions, which, as this chapter shows, has at times been interpreted in an overly restrictive manner for domestic regulatory autonomy.

The chapter proceeds as follows. Section 4.2 explicates the background of the proposed horizontal provisions, exposes the weaknesses of those provisions against the benchmark of their aims as outlined by the European Commission and in the light of the broader goal of the preservation of the rules-based international trading system, and outlines ways for remedying those weaknesses. Section 4.3 discusses possible alternatives for the threshold of the future digital trade exception for privacy and data protection, instead of the proposed 'it deems appropriate threshold'. Based on their interpretation in WTO case law and academic literature, Section 4.3 also evaluates which of them could be more apt in the light of the above-mentioned goals. Section 4.4 sums up the main conclusions of the chapter.

4.2 EU Horizontal Provisions: A Critical Evaluation

4.2.1 Background

The proposed horizontal provisions represent a political compromise between what can be seen as offensive and defensive strategies coexisting in EU trade policy on cross-border data flows and the protection of privacy and personal data. The offensive strategy is the product of the European 'digital trade' discourse, grounded in the economic benefits of the absence of restrictions on cross-border data flows *abroad* for European businesses. In contrast, the defensive strategy is the product of the fundamental rights discourse, grounded in the moral value of the fundamental rights to privacy and the protection of personal data *at home*, and geared towards protecting EU data protection legislation, most specifically GDPR's restrictions on transfers of personal data outside the EEA from being challenged in a trade forum.

Developed under strong political pressure from the European Parliament, DG Justice, civil society organizations, and academics, the proposed horizontal provisions are not only a set of legal provisions delineating the EU's starting point in international trade negotiations but also largely an inward-looking *political statement*.[33] In terms of regulatory autonomy for domestic privacy and personal data protection rules, the proposed horizontal provisions go a step further than their predecessor—the 2017 EU Council concept paper on data flows in trade agreements, discussed in Section 4.3.1. Unable to reach an internal consensus on the EU Council's proposal, the EU ultimately refrained, as mentioned elsewhere, from

[33] See Section 3.3.2.

including any commitments on cross-border data flows and the protection of privacy and personal data into the E-commerce chapter of the Agreement between the European Union and Japan for an Economic Partnership (JEFTA),[34] which was in the final stages of negotiations at that time. In its 2018 statement outlining the key elements of this agreement, the European Commission clearly laid out the EU's position on this matter: '[d]ata protection is a fundamental right in the European Union and is therefore not up for negotiation. Privacy is not a commodity to be traded'.[35] This statement, however, as Kanetake and de Vries argue, was largely a narrative maintained by the EU for its own constituencies.[36]

Although the final version of JEFTA did not cover cross-border data flows or privacy and data protection, these issues were negotiated within the framework of adequacy assessments under the GDPR which unfolded in parallel with trade negotiations.[37] The EU and Japan agreed to recognize the 'essential equivalence' of each other's data protection frameworks—the key benchmark of adequacy under the GDPR — on the day when both parties signed the trade agreement. Kanetake and de Vries contend that the fact that the EU awarded an adequacy decision to Japan, despite the gaps between the GDPR and the Japanese data protection framework, demonstrates that contrary to the mainstream narrative of the Commission, privacy and data protection were very much 'negotiated and traded'.[38] The weaknesses of the adequacy decision which resulted from these negotiations, in the light of the EU Charter, are addressed in more detail in Chapter 5 of this book. The fact that the EU and Japan are, as of this writing (June 2023), negotiating binding provisions on cross-border data flows and exceptions from them to be included in JEFTA further illustrates the point that, unfortunately, data protection *is very much up to negotiation* even with a trading partner that already enjoys unrestricted cross-border data flows with the EU under the adequacy decision, which was reaffirmed by the European Commission in April 2023 after the first review.[39]

[34] Agreement between the European Union and Japan for an Economic Partnership [2018] OJ L 330/3 (hereafter JEFTA).

[35] European Commission, 'Key Elements of the EU-Japan Economic Partnership Agreement' (*European Commission Press Release*, 18 April 2018) <https://ec.europa.eu/commission/presscorner/detail/en/MEMO_18_3326> accessed 10 July 2023.

[36] Machiko Kanetake and Sybe de Vries, 'EU-Japan Economic Partnership Agreement: Data Protection in the Era of Digital Trade and Economy' (*Renforce Blog*, 18 December 2018), on file with author (hereafter Kanetake and de Vries, 'EU-Japan Economic Partnership Agreement').

[37] As explained in Section 2.2.4, adequacy decisions adopted by the European Commission constitute a primary mechanism for transfers of personal data outside the EEA under the GDPR.

[38] Kanetake and de Vries, 'EU-Japan Economic Partnership Agreement' (n 36).

[39] The GDPR requires that each adequacy decision undergoes a periodic review at least every four years (art 45(3) GDPR (n 9)). European Commission, 'Joint Press Statement on the Conclusion of the First Review of the Japan-EU Mutual Adequacy Arrangement' (*European Commission*, 4 April 2023) <https://commission.europa.eu/news/joint-press-statement-conclusion-first-review-japan-eu-mutual-adequacy-arrangement-2023-04-04_en> accessed 10 July 2023. The EDPS rightly asked the same question in his opinion regarding the start of trade negotiations between the EU and Japan on cross-border data flows ('In view of the Adequacy Decision, the need for having additional rules covering cross-border data flows should be expressed in more detail so that the justification for an amendment of the Agreement is made clearer. In other words, the EDPS recommends to further explain why, despite

It is important to keep in mind that—unlike trade agreements—adequacy decisions, even if said to be adopted 'mutually' by two trading partners, are actually unilateral decisions of each trading partner. This means that they can also be unilaterally repealed without the risk of adverse consequences under the trade agreement. From this perspective, an adequacy decision is not a substitute for a fully binding provision on cross-border data flows in a trade agreement.[40] Conversely, a binding provision on cross-border data flows in a trade agreement limits the EU's ability to unilaterally suspend or repeal an adequacy decision. If such suspension or repeal violates that provision, it can only be done in compliance with the trade agreement if it can be justified under the relevant exceptions. This explains why including binding provisions on cross-border data flows in a trade agreement even with a trading partner that has been granted adequacy may still undermine the EU's autonomy to maintain its data protection under the GDPR.[41] Designing those exceptions in a broad enough manner is thus essential for the effective functioning of the adequacy framework under the GDPR.

4.2.2 Relationship with the general exception

Unlike most other trade law disciplines, the proposed horizontal provisions—intended to form a part of the future digital trade chapters—apply to information flows in electronic commerce in general, irrespective of whether they are related to goods or services or constitute part of financial or telecommunication services.

the Adequacy Decision, further negotiations on cross-border data flows are considered to be necessary.') European Data Protection Supervisor, 'Opinion 17/2022 on the Recommendation for a Council Decision authorising the opening of negotiations for the inclusion of provisions on cross-border data flows in the Agreement between the European Union and Japan for an Economic Partnership' (2022) <https://edps.europa.eu/system/files/2022-08/22-08-09_edps_opinion_eu_japan_en.pdf> accessed 10 July 2023.

40 Jan A Micallef, 'Digital Trade in EU FTAs: Are EU FTAs Allowing Cross Border Digital Trade to Reach Its Full Potential?' (2019) 53(5) Journal of World Trade 855, 867 (hereafter Micallef, 'Digital Trade in EU FTAs').

41 While in the negotiations with the EU Japan is likely to agree to the EU model of provisions on cross-border data flows and exceptions from them, it has already joined multiple FTAs with other trading partners (eg partners to the CPTPP, DEPA, such as Singapore, Malaysia, or Vietnam) that contain the US model of such provisions and exceptions. There is a risk that the latter are incompatible with Japan's obligations to restrict onward transfers of EU personal data to those other trading partners under the EU adequacy decision. For discussion, see Svetlana Yakovleva, 'Testing Restrictions on Onward Transfers of EU Personal Data against Free Data Flow Obligations in the CPTPP and US-Japan Digital Trade Agreement' (2023) Amsterdam Law School Research Paper No. 2023-20, Institute for Information Law Research Paper No. 2023-05 1. The same concerns apply to the United Kingdom. See, eg, EDPS, 'Opinion 3/2021' (n 15). But see Irion and Burri, '§ 16 Digitaler Handel' (n 15) paras 17–19; Elaine Fahey, 'Digital Trade and Data Equivalency: Research Briefing for the Welsh Parliament' (2020) <https://openaccess.city.ac.uk/id/eprint/24721/1/Fahey%20Research%20Briefing%20Digital%20Trade> accessed 10 July 2023; European Parliament resolution of 21 May 2021 on the adequate protection of personal data by the United Kingdom (2021/2594(RSP)) [2022] OJ C 15/218.

They are, in this sense, *horizontal*. For example, the scope of the digital trade chapter in the EU-New Zealand FTA is defined as follows: 'This Chapter applies to measures of a Party affecting trade enabled by electronic means.'[42] Therefore, the provisions of Articles 1 and 2 of the proposed horizontal provisions, when included in the actual FTA, would apply *in addition* to other obligations under the trade agreement on trade in goods and services. For example, information flows can also be relevant in the context of trade in database services, and as such can also be captured by more traditional trade disciplines, such as most-favoured nation treatment (MFN), national treatment, and market access.[43] As Bartl and Irion rightly concluded, removing a data flow provision from the e-commerce chapter 'does not remove personal data from the emergent trade law institutions'.[44]

In a similar vein, the general exception for privacy and data protection—modelled after GATS Article XIV(c)(ii)—is typically included in the Exceptions chapters of the same trade agreements. For example, Article 25.1(2)(c)(ii) of the EU-New Zealand FTA reproduces the GATS Article XIV(c)(ii) for privacy and data protection, which applies to both the FTA's chapter covering trade in services and the digital trade chapter. This creates a situation where *two exceptions must cohabit in the same trade agreement* (one in the digital trade chapter and the other in the general exceptions), with significantly different thresholds for justifying privacy and data protection measures inconsistent with the provisions of the agreement, as the following section illuminates.

Despite the difference in the wording of the privacy and data protection interests in the two exceptions, their scope in the context of present-day international trade is nearly identical. The digital trade exception for privacy and data protection (both in the proposed horizontal provisions[45] and the actual exception included in the EU-New Zealand FTA[46]) exempts domestic measures that 'ensure

[42] EU-New Zealand FTA (n 14) art 12.1(1). See also art 1(1) La proposition de l'Union européenne (UE) relative à Accord de libre-échange UE-Tunisie UE-Tunisie, Titre [] Commerce Numérique). The scope of the digital trade chapter of the EU-Chile Interim Trade Agreement is defined in a similar way: 'This Title shall apply to trade enabled by telecommunications or other information and communication technologies.' EU-Chile Interim Trade Agreement (n 14) art 19.1(1). See also art X.1(1) EU proposal for a Chapter on Digital Trade of the EU-Indonesia FTA. The scope of the digital trade chapters is typically limited. For example, both digital trade chapters in the EU-New Zealand FTA and in the EU-Chile Interim Trade Agreement exempt audio-visual services from their scope. Art 19.1(2) of EU-Chile Interim Trade Agreement (n 14); art 12.1(2)(a) of EU-New Zealand FTA (n 14).

[43] Whether these services are captured by national treatment and market access obligations, which represent specific commitments under trade agreements, depends on whether the EU has liberalized these services in each particular trade agreement. These services are included in the EU's schedules of specific commitments under the GATS. Nivedita Sen, 'Understanding the Role of the WTO in International Data Flows: Taking the Liberalization or the Regulatory Autonomy Path?' (2018) 21(2) Journal of International Economic Law 323, 336.

[44] Marija Bartl and Kristina Irion, 'The Japan EU Economic Partnership Agreement: Flows of Personal Data to the Land of the Rising Sun Study' (2017) Institute for Information Law, University of Amsterdam <https://www.ivir.nl/publicaties/download/Transfer-of-personal-data-to-the-land-of-the-rising-sun-FINAL.pdf> accessed 10 July 2023.

[45] Art 2 of the proposed horizontal provisions.

[46] Art 12.5 of the EU-New Zealand FTA (n 14). See also art 19.5 of the EU-Chile Interim Trade Agreement (n 14).

the protection of personal data and privacy'. The general exception included in the same trade agreement exempts measures protecting 'the privacy of individuals in relation to the processing and dissemination of personal data and the protection of confidentiality of individual records and accounts'.[47] Because of their connection to a particular person, individual records and accounts would constitute personal data under most data protection regimes.[48] Similarly, confidentiality of personal data is a necessary component of most data protection frameworks.[49]

It is worth noting in that respect that during the Uruguay Round (1986–1994), the protection of the privacy of individuals in relation to the processing and dissemination of personal data and the protection of the confidentiality of individual records and accounts could have been different concepts, as at that time many WTO members, including the EU, did not have dedicated data protection laws. Nowadays, the second concept has become a subset of the first, and the difference in wording between the general exception and the proposed digital trade exception for privacy and data protection is better explained by historical reasons than by the intention of the parties to exempt a different scope of privacy and data protection interests.

Digital trade chapters in the EU trade agreements negotiated as of June 2023 (those with New Zealand and Chile) do not contain any explicit provisions regulating the relationship between the digital trade chapter and other provisions of the trade agreements incorporating such a chapter. These agreements do, however, include the digital trade chapter within the scope of the general exceptions, both under the General Agreement on Tariffs and Trade (GATT)[50] and GATS.[51] Furthermore, the article on cross-border data flows in the EU-New Zealand FTA contains an extra clarification regarding the application of the general and other exceptions to the prohibitions to restrict cross-border data flows provided for in that article. According to Article 12.4(3) of EU-New Zealand FTA,

> For greater certainty, the Parties understand that nothing in this Article prevents the Parties from adopting or maintaining measures in accordance with Article 25.1 (General Exceptions) to achieve the public policy objectives referred to therein, which, for the purposes of this Article, shall be interpreted, where

[47] Art 25.1(2)(c)(ii) of the EU-New Zealand FTA (n 14). The same provision is included in art 32.1(2)(c)(ii) of EU-Chile Interim Trade Agreement (n 14).

[48] See DLA Piper, 'Handbook Data Protection Laws of the World' (2023) https://www.dlapiperdataprotection.com/> accessed 10 July 2023.

[49] ibid.

[50] General Agreement on Tariffs and Trade 1994, 15 April 1994, Marrakesh Agreement Establishing the World Trade Organization, Annex 1A, 1867 UNTS 187, 33 ILM 1153 (1994) (hereafter GATT 1994).

[51] Art 25.1 of the EU-New Zealand FTA (n 14); art 32.1 of the EU-Chile Interim Trade Agreement (n 14), mentioning the digital trade chapter within the scope of the general exceptions under the GATS and the GATT. See also art 3 EU proposal for a Chapter on Digital Trade of the EU-Australia FTA; art 3 La proposition de l'Union européenne (UE) relative à Accord de libre-échange UE-Tunisie UE-Tunisie, Titre [] Commerce Numérique; EU proposals for Digital Trade chapters for EU-Indonesia FTA.

relevant, in a manner that takes into account the evolutionary nature of the digital technologies. The preceding sentence does not affect the application of other exceptions in this Agreement to this Article.

Because the digital trade exception from the article on cross-border data flows (based on Article 2 of the proposed horizontal provisions) is solely for privacy and data protection, these clarifications ensure that should the EU restrict cross-border data flows for other public policy objectives (think of the restrictions based on security concerns[52] or emerging restrictions on the outflow of non-personal data[53]), those can still be justified under other exceptions of the FTA.

The absence of a conflict of laws provision in the above-mentioned digital trade chapters stands in sharp contrast to the two other trade agreements priorly concluded by the EU, namely the JEFTA and the Comprehensive Economic and Trade Agreement (CETA).[54] The electronic commerce chapters of both agreements state that in case of any inconsistency between the electronic commerce chapter and other provisions of the trade agreement, those other provisions will prevail to the extent of the inconsistency.[55] If restrictions on transfers of personal data, or any other trade-restrictive privacy or data protection measure, are found to be in violation of the trade in services commitments (alone, or together with a violation of the prohibitions to restrict cross-border data flows based on the Article 1 of the proposed horizontal provisions), which exception will prevail? The inclusion of specific prohibitions on restrictions of cross-border data flows in a digital trade chapter does not prevent an EU trading partner to challenge such restrictions, or restrictions not covered by those prohibitions, in an international trade forum under one of the non-discrimination provisions or a market access provision in the trade in services chapter.[56]

Because the exception contained in Article 2(2) of the proposed horizontal provisions is destined for the digital trade chapter (ie, not for the exceptions chapter), one could argue that this exception would only apply if a measure were challenged under the digital trade chapter, while the general exception would apply to measures challenged under other chapters of the same trade agreement. Following this

[52] Naef, *Data Protection without Data Protectionism* (n 6) 409.

[53] For discussion, see Yakovleva, 'On Digital Sovereignty' (n 32); Kenneth Propp, 'The EU's Proposed Data Act: Regulating International Flows of Non-Personal Data' (*Cross-Border Data Forum*, 11 May 2022) <https://www.crossborderdataforum.org/the-eus-proposed-data-act-regulating-international-flows-of-non-personal-data/> accessed 10 July 2023; Gonzalo Muelas, 'EU: Non-personal Data Transfers under the DGA and the Data Act' (*OneTrust Data Guidance*, July 2022) <https://www.dataguidance.com/opinion/eu-non-personal-data-transfers-under-dga-and-data> accessed 10 July 2023.

[54] Comprehensive Economic and Trade Agreement (CETA) between Canada, of the one part, and the European Union and its member states, of the other part, 14 September 2014 [2017] OJ L 11/23 (hereafter CETA).

[55] Art 8.70(6) of JEFTA (n 34); art 16.7 of CETA (n 54).

[56] For example, arts 10.16 and 10.17 of the EU-New Zealand FTA contain obligations on MFN and National Treatment similar to those in the GATS.

argumentation, the exception of the digital trade chapter would only apply to information flows *in abstracto*, such as flows of employment data between the subsidiaries of a multinational company, and not when such flows (eg, of consumer data) constitute an integral part of a digital service or good. In some cases—for example, when a provision of a service involves the application of an algorithmic system dependent on the processing of personal data—it may be impossible to disentangle the provision of the service from the data flows, however. Yet, the approach where the digital trade exception for privacy and data protection serves as a derogation from the obligation on cross-border data flows in the digital trade chapter (and not other chapters such as the one on trade in services) has been implemented in the US-led trade agreements. For example, the exception for privacy and data protection included in Article 19.11(2) of the digital trade chapter of the United States–Mexico–Canada Agreement (USMCA) states that '[t]his Article does not prevent a Party from adopting or maintaining a measure inconsistent with paragraph 1 ...' where paragraph 1 contains a clause prohibiting restrictions on cross-border data flows. This wording suggests that this exception cannot justify a derogation from any other obligation under the trade agreement except for the one regulating cross-border data flows.

The line of reasoning according to which the scope of the *digital trade exception* for privacy and data protection is limited to the digital trade chapter in the context of the horizontal provisions proposed by the EU could be met, however, by a counter-argument that the proposed digital trade exception should be invoked to justify *any* violation of the trade agreement as long as the challenged measure affects trade enabled by electronic means. There are at least four reasons that lend weight to this counter-argument. First, as follows from the two negotiated trade agreements (EU-New Zealand FTA and EU-Chile Interim Trade Agreement) that include provisions based on the proposed horizontal provisions, the scope of the digital trade chapters covers all measures affecting trade enabled by electronic means.[57] Therefore, both the provision on cross-border data flows and the relevant exception should apply to restrictions on cross-border data flows irrespective of them being embedded in goods, services, or being data flows *in abstracto*. Second, the proposed digital trade exception is not worded as an exception solely to the provision on data flows included in Article 1 of the proposed horizontal provisions but as an independent provision on data protection and privacy, which applies in relation to the whole agreement.[58] Third, since there is no explicit provision on conflict of laws in the EU digital trade chapters or in the general exceptions of the negotiated trade agreements with New Zealand and Chile, the interpretative

[57] Art 19.1(1) of EU-Chile Interim Trade Agreement (n 14); art 12.1(1) of EU-New Zealand FTA (n 14).

[58] cf wording of art XX GATT 1994 (n 50), understood broadly—as exception to any other obligation.

maxim (also recognized as the general principle of law) on the relationship between general and specialized rules *lex specialis derogat legi generali* should apply.[59]

This principle has been applied by WTO adjudicating bodies on several occasions.[60] According to this maxim, the *lex specialis*—that is that the digital trade exception of Article 2 of the proposed horizontal provisions—should prevail over the general exception if a challenged privacy or data protection measure affects trade enabled by electronic means or, in other words, digital trade. If this argumentation is correct, then a conflict between any provision of the trade agreement, which contains the proposed digital trade exception, and the restrictions on cross-border data flows under the GDPR should be resolved under the digital trade exception and *not* the general exception. The reason for this is that the GDPR applies to the processing of personal data wholly or partly *by electronic means*[61] and thus does not apply to the analogue processing of personal data. This means that any privacy and data protection under the GDPR, if trade restrictive, would mainly affect digital trade. Hence, the *digital trade exception should apply*.

Fourth, and finally, in a private conversation with the author European Commission officials opined that the following sentence from Article 2 of the proposed horizontal provisions (included in both digital trade chapters of agreements with New Zealand and Chile) ensures that the digital trade exception for privacy and data protection prevails over the general exception:

> Nothing in this Agreement shall affect the protection of personal data and privacy afforded by the Parties' respective measures.[62]

This interpretative approach reduces the scope of the *general exception* for privacy and data protection to the highly unlikely cases of conflicts between domestic measures concerning *analogue* processing of personal data, and international trade norms. As a result, the general exception for privacy and data

[59] Martti Koskenniemi, 'Fragmentation of International Law: The Function and Scope of the Lex Specialis Rule and the Question of "self-Contained Regimes": An Outline' (2009) 4–5 <https://legal.un.org/ilc/sessions/55/pdfs/fragmentation_outline.pdf.> accessed 10 July 2023.

[60] WTO, 'Analytical Index, GATT 1994 – General (Jurisprudence)' 5–6 <https://www.wto.org/english/res_e/publications_e/ai17_e/gatt1994_general_jur.pdf> accessed 10 July 2023, quoting WTO, *United States – Anti-Dumping Act of 1916 – Complaint by Japan – Report of the Panel* (29 May 2000) WT/DS162/R para 6.269 (hereafter Panel Report, *US – 1916 Act (Japan)*); WTO, *European Communities – Regime for the Importation, Sale and Distribution of Bananas – AB-1997-3 – Report of the Appellate Body* (9 September 1997) WT/DS27/AB/R para 204 (hereafter Appellate Body Report, *EC – Bananas III*); WTO, *United States – Import Prohibition of Certain Shrimp and Shrimp Products – Report of the Panel* (15 May 1998) WT/DS58/R paras 7.159–7.162 (hereafter Panel Report, *US – Shrimp (Thailand)*); WTO, *United States – Customs Bond Directive for Merchandise Subject to Anti-Dumping / Countervailing Duties – Report of the Panel* (29 February 2008) WT/DS345/R paras 7.168–7.171 (hereafter Panel Report, *US – Customs Bond Directive*).

[61] GDPR (n 9) art 2(1).

[62] Second sentence of art 2(2) of the proposed horizontal provisions. See also second sentence of art 12.15(2) of EU-New Zealand FTA (n 14); art 19.5(2) of EU-Chile Interim Trade Agreement (n 14).

protection becomes nearly redundant. In *US – Gasoline*, however, the WTO Appellate Body held that:

> [o]ne of the corollaries of the 'general rule of interpretation' in the Vienna Convention is that interpretation must give meaning and effect to all the terms of a treaty. An interpreter is not free to adopt a reading that would result in reducing whole clauses or paragraphs of a treaty to redundancy or inutility.[63]

If a trade adjudicating body facing the dilemma of the relationship between digital trade and the general exceptions for privacy and data protection adhered to the above approach to interpretation, there is a risk that the *lex specialis* argument would thus not be decisive and the scope of the general exception for privacy and data protection would then be broader than just described. As a result, some of the conflicts between domestic rules on transfers of personal data and international trade disciplines could be still captured by the general exception. Therefore, the question of whether the digital trade exception for privacy and data protection can, in all cases, override the general exception for privacy and data protection remains at least partially open.[64] It is for this reason that the future EU trade agreements—if they were to include both the general exception and the proposed digital trade exception for privacy and data protection—should, as a minimum, clarify the relationship between the two exceptions in a way that makes the general exception inapplicable to domestic measures on the automated processing of personal data.

One may also wonder why the EU does not propose changes to the general exception for privacy and data protection instead of adding another exception overriding it. In theory, this would be the most logical way to solve the issue. It could be that the answer lies in the 'legacy clout' of the general exceptions, which have been replicated in multiple trade agreements for decades.[65] Recall that the general exceptions typically contain exceptions for other public policy interests besides privacy and data protection. Renegotiation of a general exception for privacy and data protection only, with a view of granting parties to a trade agreement a broader autonomy to regulate these interests, would arguably put privacy and data protection above other important policy objectives such as the protection of the environment or public health. Shifting these renegotiations to another forum—the digital trade chapter, despite this leading to the same result of preferring privacy

[63] WTO, *United States – Standards for Reformulated and Conventional Gasoline – AB-1996-1 – Report of the Appellate Body* (29 April 1996) WT/DS2/AB/R, 23 (hereafter Appellate Body Report, *US – Gasoline*).

[64] cf Naef, *Data Protection without Data Protectionism* (n 6) 410, arguing that the digital trade exception for privacy and data protection in Article 2 of the proposed horizontal provisions is 'water-tight'.

[65] For example, Riffle argues that trade agreement negotiators 'are naturally hesitant to tinker with well-established General Agreement on Tariffs and Trade (GATT) language, unless there is a cogent reason'. Christian Riffel, 'The Chapeau: Stringent Threshold or Good Faith Requirement' (2018) 45(2) Legal Issues of Economic Integration 141, 143 (hereafter Riffel, 'The Chapeau').

and data protection to other policy objectives—allows this outcome to be less apparent and avoids the possible discontent of stakeholders defending those other policy objectives on the international trade policy landscape. Therefore, it could be more convenient to negotiate a separate exception for privacy and data protection during digital trade negotiations instead of reopening negotiations on the general exception. Additionally, the transaction costs of renegotiating the general exception may simply be too high.

4.2.3 An undesirable parallel with the national security exception

Let us recall that the digital trade exception for privacy and data protection of Article 2(2) of the proposed horizontal provisions allows each Party to 'adopt and maintain the safeguards *it deems appropriate* to ensure the protection of personal data and privacy' (emphasis added). This wording is replicated verbatim in relevant provisions of EU-New Zealand FTA and EU-Chile Interim Trade Agreement.[66] The threshold that a trade-inconsistent safeguard must meet is the '*it* deems appropriate' test (emphasis added)—as opposed to the necessity test in the general exception—which is similar to that employed in national security exceptions in the WTO agreements.[67] For example, under Article XIVbis(1)(b) of the GATS: [n]othing in this Agreement shall be construed:

<....>

(b) to prevent any Member from taking *any action which it considers necessary* for the protection of its essential security interests:

(i) relating to fissionable materials or the materials from which they are derived;
(ii) relating to the traffic in arms, ammunition and implements of war and to such traffic in other goods and materials as is carried on directly or indirectly for the purpose of supplying a military establishment;
(iii) taken in time of war or other emergency in international relations.[68]

The phrase 'it considers necessary' in the national security exception has been remarkably consistent since the 1947 General Agreement on Tariffs and Trade

[66] Art 12.5(2) of EU-New Zealand FTA (n 14); art 19.5(2) of EU-Chile Interim Trade Agreement (n 14).
[67] See, eg, art XIVbis GATT (n 2); art XXI GATT 1994 (n 50).
[68] Emphasis added.

(GATT 1947),[69] not only in various WTO Agreements[70] but also in post-WTO trade agreements concluded around the world.[71] The wording of the proposed digital trade exception for privacy and data protection allows any safeguards 'it [each Party] deems appropriate'. It is not identical to the 'it considers necessary' phrase contained in the national security exception. Nevertheless, despite this discrepancy in the wording of the two exceptions, the analysis of the national security exception is useful because based on the definition of 'appropriate' and 'necessary' in dictionaries and scholarly interpretations, 'it deems appropriate' seems to afford the same or an even broader margin of appreciation than 'it considers necessary'.[72]

[69] Art XXI of General Agreement on Tariffs and Trade, 30 October 1947, 61 Stat A-11, 55 UNTS 194 (hereafter GATT 1947).

[70] GATT 1994 (n 50) art XXI; art XIVbis GATS (n 2); art 73 Agreement on Trade-Related Aspects of Intellectual Property Rights, Annex 1C to Marrakesh Agreement Establishing the World Trade Organization [1994] 1869 UNTS 299, 33 ILM 1197 (hereafter TRIPS); arts 2.2, 2.10, 5.4, 5.7, and 10.8.3, Agreement on Technical Barriers to Trade, Annex 1A to Marrakesh Agreement Establishing the World Trade Organization [1994] 1868 UNTS 120 (hereafter TBT Agreement); art III:1 Revised Agreement on Government Procurement, Annex 4(b) to Marrakesh Agreement Establishing the World Trade Organization [2012] 1915 UNTS 103 (hereafter Revised Agreement on Government Procurement).

[71] For an overview, see Thomas Cottier and Panos Delimatsis, 'Article XIVbis Security Exceptions' in Rüdiger Wolfrum, Peter-Tobias Stoll, and Clemens Feinäugle (eds), *Max Planck Commentaries on World Trade Law: WTO – Trade in Services Vol. 6* (Martinus Nijhoff Publishers 2008) (hereafter Cottier and Delimatsis, 'Article XIVbis Security Exceptions'). In the most recent FTAs, the same phrase is also used in the EU-New Zealand FTA (art 25.2(b)) and the EU-Chile Interim Trade Agreement (art 32.2(b)), art 32.2(1)(b) of the USMCA and 17.13(b) of RCEP.

[72] From the wording of art 3(1) DSU, it follows that in WTO law 'necessary' and 'appropriate' have different meanings. Under this provision '[a] Member should respond promptly and fully to any request by a panel for such information as the panel considers necessary and appropriate'. See also Rex J Zedalis, emphasizing that 'given the fact that the [GATT's] national security language plainly does not go so far as to authorize an invoking state to take any action *it deems appropriate*, or desirable, or politically popular, that difference in phraseology must be taken as signifying some meaning of real consequence.... [I]n light of the specific phraseology utilized by the drafters in attaching to that exception the requirement of "necessity," it would seem perfectly reasonable to expect that states invoking Article XXI(b) must, at a bare minimum, be able to connect-up, or link the responsive actions taken to the essential security interest deemed threatened.' Rex J Zedalis, 'A Commentary on US 'National Security' Import Restraints: The Situation with Crude Oil' (2019) 53(1) Journal of World Trade 83, 91. In contrast, however, Cottier and Delimatsis use the words 'necessary' and 'appropriate' interchangeably in discussing the national security exception. See Cottier and Delimatsis, 'Article XIVbis Security Exceptions' (n 71) 335 (referring to ICJ and ECJ case law and stating that '[a] Member has indeed the flexibility to choose the measure that it deems appropriate to protect its essential security interests'.). In the *EC – Sardines*, the WTO Panel interpreted 'inappropriate' as referring 'to something which is not "specially suitable", "proper" or "fitting"'. WTO, *European Communities – Trade Description of Sardines – Report of the Appellate Body* (26 September 2002) WT/DS231/AB/R para 285 (hereafter Appellate Body Report, *EC – Sardines*); citing WTO, *European Communities – Trade Description of Sardines – Report of the Panel* (29 May 2002) WT/DS231/R para 7.116 (hereafter Panel Report, *EC – Sardines*). See also WTO, *United States – Measures Concerning the Importation, Marketing and Sale of Tuna and Tuna Products – Report of the Panel* (15 September 2011) WT/DS381/R, as modified by WTO, *United States – Measures Concerning the Importation, Marketing and Sale of Tuna and Tuna Products – Report of the Appellate Body* (16 May 2012) WT/DS381/AB/R para 7.723. Similarly, one of the definitions of 'appropriate' in the *Oxford English Dictionary*, most suitable in the present context, is 'specially fitted or suitable'. 'Appropriate' (*Oxford English Dictionary Online*) <https://www.oed.com/view/Entry/9870?rskey=uGZYsX&result=1#eid> accessed 10 July 2023. The same dictionary defines 'necessary' as 'indispensable, vital, essential; requisite'. 'Necessary' (*Oxford English Dictionary Online*) <https://www.oed.com/view/Entry/125629?redirectedFrom=necessary#eid.> accessed 10 July 2023. According to the same *Dictionary*, 'deem' and 'consider' have synonymous meaning. The *Dictionary* defines the current use of the verb 'to deem' as '[t]o form the opinion, to be of opinion; to judge, conclude, think, consider,

In the following paragraphs, this section first considers the interpretation of the national security exception in general, and its 'it considers necessary' test in particular, by WTO dispute-settlement Panels and then extrapolates the insights to the proposed digital trade exception for privacy and personal data and its 'it deems appropriate' test. Based on this analysis, it explains why modelling a digital trade exception for privacy and data protection after the national security exception is undesirable in the view of the EU's goals to liberalize cross-border data flows and, more generally, the goal of maintaining a multilateral rules-based international trading system.

4.2.3.1 Interpretation of the national security exception at the WTO

The national security exception is the broadest of all the existing exceptions in international trade law. It provides a broad autonomy for states to adopt trade law-inconsistent measures to protect their essential security interests. It is for this reason that this exception has been called 'potentially the biggest loophole',[73] 'an unreviewable trump card',[74] 'the Achilles' heel of international law',[75] and 'all-embracing and seemingly omnipotent'.[76] Until recently, Article XXI GATT had been invoked very infrequently.[77] Although the openness of the security exception has not been abused before, this is changing,[78] as the national security exception is being increasingly invoked in WTO disputes. There have been and continue to be multiple disputes at the WTO involving a national security exception in recent years.[79] To name just a few examples, Russia successfully invoked the exception in

hold'. 'Deem' (*Oxford English Dictionary Online*) <https://www.oed.com/view/Entry/48614?rskey=Ujiiag&result=2&isAdvanced=false#eid> accessed 10 July 2023.

[73] Richard A Westin, *Environmental Tax Initiatives and Multilateral Trade Agreements: Dangerous Collisions* (Kluwer Law International 1997) 181 (hereafter Westin, Environmental Tax Initiatives and Multilateral Trade Agreements).

[74] Roger P Alford, 'The Self-Judging WTO Security Exception' (2011) 3 The Utah Law Review 697, 698 (hereafter Alford, 'The Self-judging WTO Security Exception').

[75] Hannes L Schloemann and Stefan Ohlhoff, ' "Constitutionalization" and Dispute Settlement in the WTO: National Security as an Issue of Competence' (1999) 93(2) American Journal of International Law 424, 426 (hereafter Schloemann and Ohlhoff, ' "Constitutionalization" and Dispute Settlement in the WTO').

[76] Ji Yeong Yoo and Dukgeun Ahn, 'Security Exceptions in the WTO System: Bridge or Bottle-Neck for Trade and Security?' (2016) 19(2) Journal of International Economic Law 417, 426 (hereafter Yoo and Ahn, 'Security Exceptions in the WTO System').

[77] Westin, *Environmental Tax Initiatives and Multilateral Trade Agreements* (n 73) 182; John H Jackson, 'The World Trading System: Law and Policy of International Economic Relations' (1989) MIT 205 (hereafter Jackson, 'The World Trading System'); Alford, 'The Self-Judging WTO Security Exception' (n 74) 699.

[78] Tsai-fang Chen, 'To Judge the Self-Judging Security Exception under the GATT 1994: A Systematic Approach' (2017) 12(2) Asian Journal of WTO and International Health Law and Policy 311, 313–17. For an example of a potential abuse, see WTO, *Saudi Arabia – Measures Concerning the Protection of Intellectual Property Rights – Report of the Panel* (16 June 2020) WT/DS567/R and WT/DS567/R/Add.1 (under appeal) (hereafter Panel Report, *Saudi Arabia – Protection of IPR*).

[79] There were more than twenty of such pending cases as of 2019. See Geraldo Vidigal, 'WTO Adjudication and the Security Exception: Something Old, Something New, Something Borrowed – Something Blue?' (2019) 46(3) Legal Issues of Economic Integration 203, 205 (hereafter Vidigal, 'WTO

a GATT case brought against it by Ukraine; Saudi Arabia—successfully to some extent[80]—invoked the exception contained in Article 73 of the TRIPS Agreement (almost identical to Article XXI GATT) in a case filed by Qatar to defend piracy of Qatari broadcasts as a national security matter;[81] and the United States adopted tariff measures against its trading partners to protect alleged national security interests.[82] Relying on its broadened conception of national security, the United States has invoked (so far unsuccessfully) the national security exception as justification for trade-restrictive measures only vaguely related to national security.[83] Pinchis-Paulsen demonstrates that reimagination of the relationship between essential security interests and trade interests is a broader phenomenon among the WTO members, where 'security and trade pull against one another, each demanding its own "exclusivity" '.[84]

There are two key issues in the interpretation of the 'it considers' threshold in the national security exception: (1) whether it means the exception is entirely *self-judging*, meaning the WTO adjudicating bodies have no jurisdiction to review measures that a WTO member claims to have introduced within the boundaries of the national security exception, and (2) if the exception is *not* entirely self-judging, what is the margin of appreciation afforded to a WTO member to adopt measures to protect national security, and the standard of review that the WTO adjudicating

Adjudication and the Security Exception'). Some of them have led to the issuance of panel reports discussed below.

[80] Saudi Arabia managed to successfully invoke the national security exception in relation to some TRIPS-inconsistent measures but not the others. See WTO, Panel Report, *Saudi Arabia – Protection of IPR* (n 78) paras 7.285–93.

[81] WTO, Panel Report, *Saudi Arabia – Protection of IPR* (n 78).

[82] Mona Pinchis-Paulsen, 'Trade Multilateralism and U.S. National Security: The Making of the GATT Security Exceptions' (2020) 41(1) Michigan Journal of International Law 109, 112–13 (hereafter Pinchis-Paulsen, 'Trade Multilateralism and U.S. National Security').

[83] For a discussion on the transformation in substance and politics of national security, see J Benton Heath, 'The New National Security Challenge to the Economic Order' (2020) 129(4) The Yale Law Journal 1020 (hereafter Heath, 'The New National Security Challenge to the Economic Order'). In a similar vein, Pinchis-Paulsen notes that '[t]he USA, for example, presents an example of national security creep—concerns with international commerce that implicate security risks over time and are dependent on a series of incremental steps rather than a single moment'. Mona Pinchis-Paulsen, 'Let's Agree to Disagree: A Strategy for Trade-Security' (2022) 25 Journal of International Economic Law 527, 532 (hereafter Pinchis-Paulsen, 'A Strategy for Trade-Security'). WTO Panels have concluded in several of those cases that trade-restrictive measures introduced by the United States could not be justified under the national security exception. See, eg, WTO, *United States – Certain Measures on Steel and Aluminium Products – Report of the Panel* (9 December 2022) WT/DS564/R and WT/DS564/R/Suppl. 1 (hereafter Panel Report, *US – Steel and Aluminium Products (Turkey)*) and WTO, *United States – Origin Marking Requirement – Report of the Panel* (21 December 2022) WT/DS597/R and WT/DS597/R/Add. 1 (hereafter Panel Report, *US – Origin Marking (Hong Kong, China)*). The United States appealed both of these decisions at the Appellate Body, which is not able to conduct its work as of June 2023. For an overview of all cases, see Keith Rockwell, 'Recent WTO Ruling against the United States Highlights Challenges in Dispute Resolution' (*Wilson Center*, 15 December 2022) <https://www.wilsoncenter.org/blog-post/recent-wto-ruling-against-united-states-highlights-challenges-dispute-resolution> accessed 10 July 2023.

[84] Pinchis-Paulsen, 'A Strategy for Trade-Security' (n 83) 528ff.

bodies should exercise in assessing whether a contested measure satisfies the conditions of the exception.

The long-standing controversy on whether the national security exception is self-judging emerged in a GATT-1994 dispute between the United States and the European Community, regarding the US Helms–Burton Act imposing sanctions against Cuba with extraterritorial effect bound to affect European companies. In that case, the United States invoked the exception not only as a substantive justification for its GATT-inconsistent measure but also as a jurisdictional defence.[85] In doing so, the United States argued that the WTO, in principle, had no jurisdiction in considering the dispute once this exception has been invoked. The parties ultimately resolved the dispute by agreement and the WTO did not express an opinion on this issue.[86]

In the aftermath of this case, some scholars sided with the United States: based on the wording 'it considers', they argued that it is 'free from any judicial review' and is 'self-judging'.[87] Others argued that the security exception cannot be sensibly interpreted to deny the WTO's jurisdiction on the interpretation and application of the exception (distinguishing between the 'authority to define' and 'authority to interpret').[88] In its *Russia – Traffic in Transit*[89] report, the WTO Panel held that the exception is not 'totally self-judging' and that the WTO adjudicating bodies have the power to review whether the objective requirements of the exception are met.[90] The Panel Report has not been appealed by any of the parties and is final. The WTO Panel in *Saudi Arabia – Measures Concerning the Protection of Intellectual Property Rights* confirmed the general interpretation and the analytical framework

[85] WTO, Dispute Settlement Body, Minutes of Meeting (16 October 1996) WT/DSB/M/24. See WTO, *United States – The Cuban Liberty and Democratic Solidarity Act – Request for the Establishment of a Panel by the European Communities* (8 October 1996) WT/DS38/2.

[86] Vidigal, 'WTO Adjudication and the Security Exception' (n 79) 204.

[87] Alford, 'The Self-judging WTO Security Exception' (n 74) 701–02; See also John H Jackson, *World Trade Organization and the Law of GATT* (Indianapolis, Bobbs-Merrill 1969); Raj Bhala, 'National Security and International Trade Law: What the GATT Says, and What the US Does' (1998) 19(2) University of Pennsylvania Journal of International Economic Law 263; Dapo Akande and Sope Williams, 'International Adjudication on National Security Issues: What Role for the WTO?' (2003) 43(2) Virginia Journal of International Law 365 (hereafter Akande and Williams, 'International Adjudication on National Security Issues').

[88] Schloemann and Ohlhoff, '"Constitutionalization" and Dispute Settlement in the WTO' (n 75) 426–27, 438, and 443ff; Cottier and Delimatsis, 'Article XIVbis Security Exceptions' (n 71) 5 (Referring to ICJ and ECJ case law). See also Richard S Whitt, 'The Politics of Procedure: An Examination of the GATT Dispute Settlement Panel and the Article XX Defense in the Context of the U.S. Embargo of Nicaragua' (1987) 19(3) Law & Policy in International Business 603, 616; Peter Van den Bossche and Werner Zdouc, *The Law and Policy of the World Trade Organization: Text, Cases, and Materials* (3rd edn, CUP 2013) 596 (hereafter Van den Bossche and Zdouc, *The Law and Policy of the World Trade Organization*); Yoo and Ahn, 'Security Exceptions in the WTO System' (n 76) 428.

[89] WTO, *Russia – Measures Concerning Traffic in Transit – Report of the Panel* (5 April 2019) WT/DS512/R and WT/DS512/R/Add. 1 (hereafter Panel Report, *Russia – Traffic in Transit*).

[90] ibid paras 7.102–04. WTO Panels confirmed this conclusion in later cases. See, eg, Panel Report, *US – Steel and Aluminium Products (Turkey)* (n 83) para 7.143; Panel Report, *US – Origin Marking (Hong Kong, China)* (n 83) para 7.160.

established by the Panel in *Russia – Traffic in Transit*.[91] That panel report was not adopted, however, following a settlement between the parties.

The Panels introduced a four-step analytical framework to assess whether a contested measure falls under the national security exception.[92] The discussion below will emphasize the Panels' findings that are most relevant for the analysis of the proposed digital trade exception for privacy and data protection, leaving aside the aspects specific to the wording of the national security exceptions.[93]

Prior to the Panel reports, scholars generally considered that the national security exception afforded WTO members a wide margin of appreciation in choosing an appropriate measure to protect national security in spite of their WTO commitments.[94] In particular, they believed that the state invoking the exception was free to decide *whether* an action was required, no matter how remote the link between the national security and the basis for invoking the exception, and *which* action should be taken: this choice could not be questioned by a trade adjudicating body.[95]

The WTO Panels in *Russia – Traffic in Transit* and in *Saudi Arabia – Measures Concerning the Protection of Intellectual Property Rights* generally confirmed that the phrase 'which it considers' allows a WTO member *itself* to determine 'the "necessity" of the measures for the protection of its essential security interests'.[96] This test is therefore easier to satisfy than the necessity test of the general exception, as the WTO Panel in *Russia – Traffic in Transit* clarified:

> there is no need to determine the extent of the deviation of the challenged measure from the prescribed norm in order to evaluate the necessity of the measure, i.e. that there is no reasonably available alternative measure to achieve the protection

[91] Panel Report, *Saudi Arabia – Protection of IPR* (n 78) para 7.243.

[92] This framework is summarized in Panel Report, *Saudi Arabia – Protection of IPR* (n 78) para 7.241.

[93] For a comprehensive discussion on all the prongs of the assessment developed in *Russia – Traffic in Transit*, see Vidigal, 'WTO Adjudication and the Security Exception' (n 79).

[94] Cottier and Delimatsis, 'Article XIVbis Security Exceptions' (n 71) 4; Westin, *Environmental Tax Initiatives and Multilateral Trade Agreements* (n 73) 181–82; Jackson, 'The World Trading System' (n 77) 205; WTO, 'Analytical Index, GATT Article XXI Security Exceptions', 600–01 (hereafter WTO, 'Analytical Index GATT Article XXI').

[95] Westin, *Environmental Tax Initiatives and Multilateral Trade Agreements* (n 73) 181–82; Jackson, 'The World Trading System' (n 77) 205; Cottier and Delimatsis, 'Article XIVbis Security Exceptions' (n 71); WTO, 'Analytical Index, GATT Article XXI' (n 94) 600–01; GATT Council, Minutes of Meeting Held in the Centre William Rappard on 7 May 1982 (22 June 1982) CIM/157, 10; GATT Council, Minutes of Meeting Held in the Centre William Rappard on 29–30 June 1982 (10 August 1982) CIM/159, 19.

[96] Panel Report, *Russia – Traffic in Transit* (n 89) para 146; Panel Report, *Saudi Arabia – Protection of IPR* (n 78) para 7.249. For a discussion, see Vidigal, 'WTO Adjudication and the Security Exception' (n 79) 216.

Before *Russia – Traffic in Transit*, scholars were sharply divided on whether the national security is self-judging. Compare, eg, Alford, 'The Self-judging WTO Security Exception' (n 74) 701–02 with Schloemann and Ohlhoff, ' "Constitutionalization" and Dispute Settlement in the WTO' (n 75) 426–27, 438, 443ff.

of the legitimate interests covered by the exception which is not violative, or is less violative, of the prescribed norm.[97]

The Panels also explained, however, that the clause 'it considers' does not apply to the assessment of the *three sets of circumstances* under paragraphs (i)–(iii) of Article XXI(b) GATT or Article 73(c) TRIPS, which are subject to an *objective* determination by the WTO adjudicators.[98] On the contrary, these paragraphs operate as 'limitative qualifying clauses' that 'qualify and limit the exercise of the discretion accorded to Members under the chapeau to these circumstances'.[99]

Furthermore, the Panels held that both (a) the WTO member's discretion to designate particular concerns as 'essential security interests' and (b) the subjective assessment of 'necessity' in the national security exception are limited by the obligation to *interpret and apply the exception in good faith,* a general principle of law and a principle of general international law envisaged in Article 31 of the Vienna Convention on the Law of Treaties (VCLT).[100] Whether a WTO member met the obligation of good faith is subject to the objective assessment of the WTO adjudicating bodies.[101] This has two implications.

First, a WTO member cannot use the security exception 'as a means to circumvent their obligations under the GATT 1994'.[102] While each WTO member is free to define what it considers to be its essential security interests, the WTO Panels clarified that such interests 'generally' concern 'those interests relating to the quintessential functions of the state, namely, the protection of its territory and its population from external threats, and the maintenance of law and public order internally'.[103] In *Russia – Traffic in Transit*, the Panel noted that a 'glaring example' of circumvention is when a WTO member tries to 'release itself' from its trade commitments by 're-labelling trade interests that it agreed to protect and promote ... as "essential security interests"'.[104] To satisfy the good faith requirement in relation to the evaluation of 'essential security interests', a WTO member must articulate those

[97] Panel Report, *Russia – Traffic in Transit* (n 89) para 7.108.

[98] ibid para 7.65; Panel Report, *Saudi Arabia – Protection of IPR* (n 78) para 7.244. WTO Panels confirmed this conclusion in later cases. See, eg, Panel Report, *US – Steel and Aluminium Products (Turkey)* (n 83) paras 7.140, 7.143; Panel Report, *US – Origin Marking (Hong Kong, China)* (n 83) paras 7.57, 7.69, 7.89, 7.160. See also Chao Wang, 'Invocation of National Security Exceptions under GATT Article XXI: Jurisdiction to Review and Standard of Review' (2019) 18(3) Chinese Journal of International Law 695, 711.

[99] ibid.

[100] Panel Report, *Russia – Traffic in Transit* (n 89) para 7.132; Panel Report, *Saudi Arabia – Protection of IPR* (n 78) paras 7.249–50, 7.252. See also Pinchis-Paulsen, 'Trade Multilateralism and U.S. National Security' (n 82) 189. Several scholars made the same argument before the Panel Report in *Russia – Traffic in Transit* was adopted. See, eg, Schloemann and Ohlhoff, '"Constitutionalization" and Dispute Settlement in the WTO' (n 75) 446–47.

[101] Panel Report, *US – Steel and Aluminium Products (Turkey)* (n 83) para 7.140; Panel Report, *US – Origin Marking (Hong Kong, China)* (n 83) para 7.89.

[102] Panel Report, *Russia – Traffic in Transit* (n 89) para 7.133.

[103] ibid para 7.130; Panel Report, *Saudi Arabia – Protection of IPR* (n 78) para 7.249.

[104] Panel Report, *Russia – Traffic in Transit* (n 89) para 7.133.

interests in the manner '"minimally satisfactory" in the circumstances', 'sufficiently to enable an assessment of whether the challenged measures are related to those interests'.[105] This requirement, however, 'is not a particularly onerous one, and is appropriately subject to limited review by a panel', in particular because the Panel is not well positioned to make such an assessment.[106] For example, in *Russia – Traffic in Transit*, the Panel concluded that 'there [was] nothing in Russia's expression of [national security] interests to suggest that Russia invoked Article XXI(b)(iii) simply as a means to circumvent its obligations under GATT 1994'.[107]

Second, the connection between the measures at issue and the 'essential security interests' must meet the '*minimum requirement of plausibility* in relation to the proffered essential security interests, i.e. that they are not implausible as measures protective of these interests'.[108] In *Saudi Arabia – Measures Concerning the Protection of Intellectual Property Rights*, the failure by Saudi Arabia to meet this prong of the assessment resulted, for the first time in history, in an *un*successful invocation by a WTO member of the national security exception to justify a trade-inconsistent measure.

This reasoning of the WTO Panels is consistent with the interpretation of the 'it considers necessary' test found in scholarly literature preceding the issuance of the Panel reports. For example, Cottier and Delimatsis had argued that the breadth of the national security exception was not unlimited as this would be incompatible with a rules-based foundation of international trade legal order.[109] Most notably, they argued that the margin of appreciation in determining necessity is limited by the doctrine of abuse of rights or good faith, which amounts to an objective assessment.[110] Similarly, in Sykes's view, 'Article XXI does *not* encompass exigencies such as a member government's financial distress or domestic economic crises that are unrelated to war and international emergencies'.[111]

105 ibid paras 7.134, 7.137; Panel Report, *Saudi Arabia – Protection of IPR* (n 78) paras 7.250, 7.281.

106 Panel Report, *Russia – Traffic in Transit* (n 89) footnote 826; Panel Report, *Saudi Arabia – Protection of IPR* (n 78) para 7.281.

107 Panel Report, *Russia – Traffic in Transit* (n 89) para 7.137.

108 ibid para 7.138; WTO, Panel Report, *Saudi Arabia – Protection of IPR* (n 78) para 7.752 (emphasis added).

109 Cottier and Delimatsis, 'Article XIVbis Security Exceptions' (n 71).

110 ibid 6, 10. See also Lorand Bartels, 'The Separation of Powers in the WTO: How to Avoid Judicial Activism' (2004) 53(4) International & Comparative Law Quarterly 861, 871; Akande and Williams, 'International Adjudication on National Security Issues' (n 79) 389–94; Yoo and Ahn, 'Security Exceptions in the WTO System' (n 68) 429, 442; Schloemann and Stefan Ohlhoff, '"Constitutionalization" and Dispute Settlement in the WTO' (n 67) 446–47; Van den Bossche and Zdouc, *The Law and Policy of the World Trade Organization* (n 80) 442. See also Michael J Hahn, 'Vital Interests and the Law of GATT: An Analysis of GATT's Security Exception' (1991) 12(3) Michigan Journal of International Law 558, 580; Wesley A Cann, 'Creating Standards and Accountability for the Use of the WTO Security Exception: Reducing the Role of Power-Base Relations and Establishing a New Balance between Sovereignty and Multilateralism' (2001) 26(2) Yale Journal of International Law 413; Regis Bonnan, 'The GATT Security Exception in a Dispute Resolution Context: Necessity or Incompatibility?' (2010) 19(1) Currents: International Trade Law Journal 3; Shin-yi Peng, 'Cybersecurity Threats and the WTO National Security Exceptions' (2015) 18(2) Journal of International Economic Law 449.

111 Alan O Sykes, 'Economic 'Necessity' in International Law' (2015) 109(2) American Journal of International Law 296, 303 (emphasis in the original).

The recourse to 'good faith' by the panels is perhaps understandable[112] but fails to provide a clear direction. 'There is no single agreed-upon formulation of a "good-faith test"', although 'proposals generally focus on separating genuine security policies from abuse, pretext, and subversion of the treaty'.[113]

4.2.3.2 Interpretation of the digital trade exception for privacy and data protection

Applying the interpretation of the national security exception explained in the previous section to the proposed digital trade exception for privacy and data protection allows one to make two predictions. First, the proposed digital trade exception is unlikely to be viewed as self-judging and will be subject to the review of trade adjudicating bodies.[114] Second, the 'it deems appropriate' threshold, given its similarity to 'it considers necessary' in the national security exception, is most likely to be interpreted as affording a wide margin of appreciation of what safeguards to protect privacy and personal data are appropriate. In other words, it would allow the defending Party to conduct a subjective assessment of the matter. The fact that the adoption and application of rules on the cross-border transfer of personal data is explicitly mentioned in the proposed exception as an example of 'appropriate safeguards' creates a presumption that such restrictions are covered by the exception.

At the same time, a Party's discretion to adopt and maintain such safeguards is limited by an objective assessment by a trade adjudicating body as to whether the Party's behaviour is in good faith and does not constitute an abuse of right. This objective assessment would include (a) a limited assessment of whether particular concerns are articulated as privacy and data protection interests in a minimally satisfactory manner to allow adjudicators to assess their relationship with the contested measures, and (b) an assessment of whether the nexus between the privacy and data protection interests and the contested measure meets a 'minimum requirement of plausibility'. The objective assessment, however, will be narrower than in the national security exception, as the proposed digital trade exception for privacy and data protection does not contain an analogue of the 'limitative qualifying clauses' present in the national security exception. As a result, the proposed digital trade exception, as well as the actual provisions in the EU-New

112 cf art 31(1) Vienna Convention on the Law of Treaties (entered into force 27 January 1980) 1155 UNTS 331, 8 ILM 679 (hereafter VCLT) (stating that '[a] treaty shall be interpreted in good faith in accordance with the ordinary meaning to be given to the terms of the treaty in their context and in the light of its object and purpose'.).

113 Heath, 'The New National Security Challenge to the Economic Order' (n 83) 1067.

114 Compare with the national security exception from the cross-border data flow provision in the RCEP, which declares itself 'self-judging' by stating that measures invoked by one party as necessary for the protection of essential security interests 'shall not be disputed by other parties'. RCEP (n 29) art 12.15(3)(b). Schill and Vidigal show a broader tendency to include self-judging security exceptions in recent trade and investment agreements. See Stephan Schill and Geraldo Vidigal, 'National Security, Private Actors, and Political Risk: Judicial and Non-Judicial Responses. An Introduction' (2021) 22 Journal of World Investment and Trade 503, 505–06.

Zealand FTA and EU-Chile Interim Trade Agreement reproducing verbatim this exception, affords an even broader regulatory autonomy than the national security exceptions in the WTO agreements.

Applying these predictions to the EU's framework for transfers of personal data under the GDPR, one can conclude that such a framework would pass the 'it deems appropriate' threshold. Although the design of the EU's restrictions on transfers of personal data is unlikely to be the least trade restrictive (as explained in Chapter 2), and arguably no longer fit for its constitutional purpose (as explained in Chapter 5), it does aim to protect the fundamental rights to the protection of personal data and privacy. Therefore, one can argue that restrictions on transfers of personal data are formulated in a minimally satisfactory manner and meet the minimum requirement of plausibility under the 'it deems appropriate' test.[115] Furthermore, the formulation of the EU restrictions cannot be considered a means to circumvent the trade interests it agreed to protect. For one thing, these restrictions were designed in 1995 (the design of the framework has not changed since the 1995 Data Protection Directive[116])—a time when the issue of cross-border data flows was hardly on any country's trade policy agenda.

4.2.4 A different threshold for digital trade exceptions

The previous sections have demonstrated that the 'it deems appropriate' test of the proposed digital trade exception for privacy and data protection is broader than the necessity test of the general exception. Putting these two thresholds on a continuum from most restrictive to least restrictive for domestic autonomy in international trade, these tests would be at the opposite ends of this continuum. That said, although the 'it deems appropriate' test may provide the ultimate protection to the EU's autonomy to protect privacy and personal data as fundamental rights and maintain the design of its framework for transfers of personal data under the GDPR, there are nevertheless at least three key reasons why the digital trade exception for privacy and data protection should not use this threshold, in view of the goals that the EU pursues by introducing the proposed horizontal provisions and the broader goals of EU's trade policy. First, they pose a risk of undermining the international rules-based trading system. Second, the risk of future replication of the 'it deems appropriate' threshold in exceptions for other public policy objectives. Third, and finally, undermining the EU digital trade policy goal of liberalizing

[115] See also Naef, *Data Protection without Data Protectionism* (n 6) 427, arguing that the EU framework for transfers of personal data outside the EEA is not and should not be viewed as protectionist.

[116] Directive 95/46/EC of the European Parliament and of the Council of 24 October 1995 on the protection of individuals with regard to the processing of personal data and on the free movement of such data [1995] OJ L 281.

cross-border data flows, and in particular, facilitating the inflow of personal data to the EU. This chapter reviews each one of them below.

The GATT 1947 parties and WTO members have for many years refrained from using the national security exception and from letting the WTO deliver a report on this exception.[117] There was a good a reason: they were wary of opening Pandora's Box, as abuse of the exception could undermine the rules-based trading system.[118] The reason that the possibility of invoking the national security exception is limited by the 'limitative qualifying clauses'[119] subject to objective assessment, as explained above, was to keep the scope of the national security exception narrow. Adding an exception for personal data and privacy with a threshold very closely resembling that of the national security exception but *without* any 'limitative qualifying clauses' broadens the potential for future departures from international trade rules.

The breadth of the possibilities for escaping trade law disciplines under the proposed exception for privacy and data protection is also explained by the broad conceptualization of the right to the protection of personal data in the EU, as Chapter 1 explains. The broad understanding of data protection also suggests that data protection interests can be placed on a continuum between those integral to the existence of the democratic society and human dignity, and those which are more economic in nature (akin to consumer protection[120]) and which are routinely 'traded' away for online services[121] by individuals on the basis of consent

[117] Until the WTO Panel Report in *Russia – Traffic in Transit*, all prior references to the national security exception did not lead to a binding decision by a WTO adjudicating body.

[118] See Vidigal, 'WTO Adjudication and the Security Exception' (n 79) 204.

[119] Panel Report, *Russia – Traffic in Transit* (n 89) para 7.65.

[120] There is a growing volume of literature highlighting the overlap between data protection and consumer law, which is, at its core, economic regulation. See, eg, Natali Helberger, Frederik Zuiderveen Borgesius, and Agustin Reyna, 'The Perfect Match? A Closer Look at the Relationship between EU Consumer Law and Data Protection Law' (2017) 54(5) Common Market Law Review 1427 (hereafter Helberger, Zuiderveen Borgesius, and Reyna, 'A Closer Look at the Relationship between EU Consumer Law and Data Protection Law'); Nico van Eijk, Chris Jay Hoofnagle, and Emilie Kannekens, 'Unfair Commercial Practices: A Complementary Approach to Privacy Protection' (2017) 3(3) European Data Protection Law Review 325 (hereafter van Eijk, Hoofnagle, and Kannekens, 'Unfair Commercial Practices'). This research also shows that, for example, when it comes to transparency and unfair terms in privacy policies, consumer law is more effective than data protection due to its flexibility and adaptability to changing circumstances. See van Eijk, Hoofnagle, and Kannekens, 'Unfair Commercial Practices' (n 120) 11–12; Helberger, Zuiderveen Borgesius, and Reyna, 'A Closer Look at the Relationship between EU Consumer Law and Data Protection Law' (n 120) 1438–39.

[121] From an economic perspective, personal data in two-sided platforms is increasingly compared to a price or consideration for services. See, eg, Magali Eben, 'Market Definition and Free Online Services: The Prospect of Personal Data as Price' (2018) 14(2) Journal of Law and Policy for the Information Society 227; Ahmed S Bataineha and others, 'Monetizing Personal Data: A Two-Sided Market Approach' (2016) 83 Procedia Computer Science 472. The view that personal data could be viewed as consideration for a service is also represented in some EU legislation. For example, Recital 16 European Electronic Communications Code clarifies that providing personal or other data to a service supplier or allowing such supplier to access personal data without actively supplying it (an example of this would be online tracking) in exchange for a service falls under the concept of remuneration. See also Recital 24 and art 3(1) Directive (EU) 2019/770 of the European Parliament and of the Council of 20 May 2019 on certain aspects concerning contracts for the supply of digital content and digital services [2019] OJ 2019, L 136/1 (hereafter Digital Content Directive). But see European Data Protection

recognized as a legitimate ground for personal data processing under the EU Charter.[122] While for some of the data protection rights a wide autonomy within the international trade regime should be warranted, for others, it may not. This line of reasoning does not imply that measures restricting cross-border data flows can never be a national security issue. However, in that case, they should be defended on the basis of national security—and not under a digital trade exception for privacy and data protection.

Each trade agreement, in which the EU has included a digital trade exception for privacy and data protection based on the proposed horizontal provisions, contains a separate national security exception, which repeats almost verbatim the national security exception of the WTO instruments.[123] Paradoxically, because the digital trade exception for privacy and data protection is broader than the WTO national security exception, defending measures restricting cross-border data flows, in case they are implemented for national security reasons, could be problematic because of the 'limitative qualifying clauses' of that exception. Introducing a broad digital trade exception to ameliorate this deficiency of the national security exception is, however, not an appropriate way forward. Rather, a reform of the national security exception, which was designed in the aftermath of World War II and has remained intact ever since, seems necessary.

For example, since North American Free Trade Agreement (NAFTA)[124], most of the US-led trade agreements demonstrate a significant departure from the GATT 1947 and the WTO model of the national security exception. In the national security exception of the USMCA (and the Comprehensive and Progressive Agreement for Trans-Pacific Partnership (CPTPP) initially led by the United States), the limitative qualifying clauses are no longer present. To illustrate, the respective part of the national security exception in Article 32.2(1)(b) of the USMCA reads as follows:

> 1. Nothing in this Agreement shall be construed to:
>   (b) preclude a Party from applying measures that *it considers necessary* for the fulfilment of its obligations with respect to the maintenance or restoration

Supervisor, Opinion 4/2017 on the Proposal for a Directive on certain aspects concerning contracts for the supply of digital content (2017) 3, sharply criticizing this approach.

[122] Article 8 of the Charter of Fundamental Rights of the European Union [2000] OJ C 364/1 (hereafter EU Charter).

[123] See, eg, art 26.8 CETA (n 54); art 1.5 JEFTA FTA (n 34); art 16.11 Free trade Agreement between the European Union and the Republic of Singapore [2019] OJ L 294 (hereafter EU-Singapore FTA); art 25.2 of EU-New Zealand FTA (n 14); art 32.2 of EU-Chile Interim Trade Agreement (n 14). Namely, they contain an exhaustive list of 'essential security interests' that could justify invocation of the exception.

[124] North American Free Trade Agreement (1993) 32 ILM 289 (hereafter NAFTA).

> of international peace or security, *or the protection of its own essential security interests.*[125]

Unlike the WTO national security exception, this national security exception provides a broader escape valve for any public policy interest that has a nexus to 'essential security'. It could justify restrictions on data flows on privacy and data protection grounds framed as a national security issue. This scenario is plausible, especially given that the Committee on Foreign Investment in the United States (CFIUS) has already interfered with the acquisition of several US companies by Chinese investors by invoking data privacy-related national security concerns.[126] The role of CFIUS in controlling the outflow of personal data from the United States has steadily increased, prompting some to call it 'the privacy regulator'.[127] According to some experts, these concerns are primarily driven by fear of content censorship and surveillance over personal information, which can be exploited in a way threatening to national security.[128]

Whether the US approach to the national security exception is the right way forward is beyond the scope of this book. In broad terms, removing any limitations in relation to the circumstances in which national security can be invoked seems to be a dangerous step that could jeopardize the international trading system, as

[125] See also art 29.2(b) Comprehensive and Progressive Agreement for Trans-Pacific Partnership (concluded on 8 March 2018, in force 30 December 2018) (hereafter CPTPP) (emphasis added).

[126] David McCabe and Cecilia Kang, 'U.S. Pushes for TikTok Sale to Resolve National Security Concerns' (*The New York Times*, 15 March 2023) <https://www.nytimes.com/2023/03/15/technology/tiktok-biden-pushes-sale.html> accessed 10 July 2023; Robert D Williams, 'Reflections on TikTok and Data Privacy as National Security' (*Lawfare Blog*, 15 November 2019) https://www.lawfareblog.com/reflections-tiktok-and-data-privacy-national-security> accessed 10 July 2023 (hereafter Williams, 'Reflections on TikTok and Data Privacy as National Security'); Daniel Lippman, 'Trump Says He Plans to Ban TikTok in the U.S.' (*Politico*, 31 July 2020) https://www.politico.com/news/2020/07/31/trump-plans-to-ban-tiktok-389956> accessed 10 July 2023;Echo Wang, 'China's Kunlun Tech Agrees to U.S. Demand to Sell Grindr Gay Dating App' (*Reuters*, 13 May 2019) <https://www.reuters.com/article/us-grindr-m-a-beijingkunlun-idUSKCN1SJ28N> accessed 10 July 2023; Eduardo Espinosa de los Monteros Pereda and Kimberly Guo, 'TikTok under Investigation for Posing a Threat to National Security: Is Chinese Tech Running Out of Time in the U.S.?' (*Jolt Digest*, 2 December 2019) <https://jolt.law.harvard.edu/digest/tiktok-under-investigation-for-posing-a-threat-to-national-security-is-chinese-tech-running-out-of-time-in-the-u-s> accessed 10 July 2023. For discussion, see Kristina Irion, Margot E Kaminski, and Svetlana Yakovleva, 'Privacy Peg, Trade Hole: Why We (Still) Shouldn't Put Data Privacy in Trade Law' (2023) The University of Chicago Law Review Online <https://lawreviewblog.uchicago.edu/2023/03/27/irion-kaminski-yakovleva/> accessed 10 July 2023.

[127] See Salil K Mehra, 'Algorithmic Competition, Trade and Investment: The CFIUS as Privacy Regulator' (2020) 16 University of Pennsylvania Asian Law Review, 8.

[128] Williams, 'Reflections on TikTok and Data Privacy as National Security' (n 126). In a similar vein, two bipartisan bills aiming to restrict data export to and ban social media platforms from China and other high-risk countries have been proposed in 2022, marking a clear shift in US lawmakers' policy agenda on cross-border data flows. See Justin Sherman, 'New Bill Proposes Banning TikTok in the U.S.' (*Lawfare*, 28 December 2022) <https://www.lawfareblog.com/new-bill-proposes-banning-tiktok-us> accessed 10 July 2023; Alexandra Alper and David Shepardson, 'U.S. Lawmakers Unveil Bill Barring U.S. Data Flows to High-Risk Countries' (*Reuters*, 23 June 2022) <https://www.reuters.com/world/us/us-lawmakers-unveil-bill-barring-us-data-flows-high-risk-countries-2022-06-23/.> accessed 10 July 2023.

constraining the abuse of the national security exception was precisely the reason why the drafters of the Charter of the International Trade Organization (ITO) and the GATT 1947 included the limitative clauses in the exception in the first place.[129] Heath argues that an unintended consequence of the abuse of the exception is that 'potential for *good-faith but novel* national security claims' might not be allowed, as the standards that may result from overuse are likely to increase the threshold to maintain at least a semblance of order in international trade rules.[130] Similarly, the broader use of this threshold for privacy and data protection and other public interests less crucial than national security could lead to the same outcome. The threshold could be narrowed in its interpretation in relation to other public interests, and then this interpretation could be extrapolated back on the national security exception.

By repurposing the broad national security threshold for the purposes of protecting domestic fundamental rights-based framework for privacy and data protection, the EU effectively *normalized* the use of national security threshold outside the national security context and has opened the door for other countries, such as China, to introduce similarly broad exceptions for other public policy interests that fit their own cultural, societal, economic, and political preferences or sensitivities. This could present an even greater existential threat for the rules-based trading system than broadening of the national security exception itself. National security and defence are public interests that, unlike privacy and data protection, are of vital importance to any country's existence and, therefore, unique in their primary importance to any party of an international trade agreement.[131] They stand above trade liberalization goals. National security and defence are also highly political areas for the states, the ones in which any external interference is generally not tolerated. Exception from the free cross-border data flow provision for legitimate public policy objectives other than national security in the RCEP, which represents China's position on the issue, illustrates the point.

Like the EU, China's digital trade exception repurposes the national security threshold outside the national security context with the caveat that China's digital trade exception is *not* limited to privacy and data protection but rather applies to any 'legitimate public policy objective'.[132] According to this exception,

> Nothing in this Article [prohibiting restrictions on cross-border transfer of information] shall prevent a Party from adopting or maintaining:

[129] Pinchis-Paulsen, 'Trade Multilateralism and U.S. National Security' (n 82) 192.
[130] Heath, 'The New National Security Challenge to the Economic Order' (n 83).
[131] Cottier and Delimatsis, 'Article XIVbis Security Exceptions' (n 71) 1.
[132] RCEP (n 29) art 12.15(3)(a). China's digital trade exception is, however, narrower than that of the EU, as it also requires that the measure to achieve such policy objective 'is not applied in a manner which would constitute a means of arbitrary or unjustifiable discrimination or a disguised restriction on trade'. This wording almost verbatim repeats the chapeau of general exceptions and part of the US model digital trade exception.

(a) any measure inconsistent with paragraph 2 [containing the prohibition to restrict cross-border transfer of information] that it considers necessary to achieve a legitimate public policy objective, provided that the measure is not applied in a manner which would constitute a means of arbitrary or unjustifiable discrimination or a disguised restriction on trade.[133]

Introducing a privacy and data protection exception with a repurposed national security threshold makes it hard to argue that other rights—recognized as fundamental by either the EU or its trading partners—do not deserve a similar level of protection. The EU Charter itself protects multiple other fundamental rights and freedoms besides privacy and the protection of personal data, such as the above-mentioned rights to freedom of expression and the freedom to conduct business.[134] Furthermore, some of the EU's partners in international negotiations, especially in the WTO setting, may value other policy interests above privacy and data protection and, therefore, may either demand to raise the threshold for privacy and data protection or lower the threshold for other public policy interests. The participation of China, Russia, and several developing countries in these negotiations is likely to add several other public policy interests (such as economic security, industrial policy, public health, digital divide, and information sovereignty) to the mix of sensitive issues to be balanced against the economic benefits of digital trade liberalization. Each trading partner is likely to strike a different balance between these benefits, on the one hand, and other non-trade policy priorities reflecting their own constitutional traditions, the level of digital and economic development, and the desire to resist 'digital colonialism',[135] on the other hand.

4.2.5 Undermining the goal of liberalization of cross-border data flows

The use of the 'it deems appropriate' threshold in the digital trade exception for privacy and data protection could impair the effectiveness of the prohibitions on restrictions of cross-border data flows under Article 1 of the proposed horizontal

133 RCEP (n 29) art 12.15(3)(a), footnote omitted.
134 EU Charter (n 122) arts 11, 16.
135 See, eg, Danielle Coleman, 'Digital Colonialism: The 21st Century Scramble for Africa through the Extraction and Control of User Data and the Limitations of Data Protection Laws' (2019) 24 Michigan Journal of Race and Law 417;Nick Couldry and Ulises A Mejias, 'Data Colonialism: Rethinking Big Data's Relation to the Contemporary Subject' (2019) 20(4) Television & New Media 336; Dhwani Goel, 'The Global Digital Divide Is Reminiscent of Colonialism' (*LSE Brexit*, 6 May 2021) <https://blogs.lse.ac.uk/brexit/2021/05/06/the-global-digital-divide-is-reminiscent-of-colonialism/> accessed 10 July 2023; Leila Brännström, 'Global Inequality and the EU International Law Position on Cross-Border Data Flows' (2023) 92 Nordic Journal of International Law 119.

provisions, which serve the EU's strategic economic interests.[136] Liberalization of cross-border data flows is also one of the goals pursued by the proposed horizontal provisions. Recall that Article 1 is already formulated in a way which is unlikely to implicate the EU's privacy and data protection framework. Rather, these disciplines serve the EU's economic interests in removing data localization measures in other countries, such as Indonesia,[137] or preventing their introduction in the first place.

In the 2020 European strategy for data, the European Commission noted that 'European companies operating in some third countries are increasingly faced with unjustified barriers and digital restrictions' and promised to address 'these unjustified obstacles to data flows in bilateral discussions and international fora – including the World Trade Organization'.[138] By 'unjustified barriers and digital restrictions', the Commission meant restrictions that cannot be justified by *legitimate* privacy and data protection interests, where 'legitimate' clearly refers to the EU-style data protection framework. A broad digital trade exception for privacy and data protection would grant a broad autonomy to protect privacy and personal data as fundamental rights not only to the EU but also to its trading partners who may have a different view on what measures are necessary to protect these policy objectives. For example, Russia's data localization measures—often criticized as 'protectionist' data localization[139]—are included in Russia's law on the protection of personal data and are, therefore, framed as data protection measures.[140] Ultimately, the economic interests of liberalizing digital trade that the EU factors in in the balancing between trade and fundamental rights to privacy and data protection, should not only include the economic gains from liberalizing personal data flows *from* the EU but also—and perhaps more importantly—the economic gains from personal data flows *to* the EU from its trading partners. To sum up, the risk that the EU's restrictions will be implicated by the proposed obligation not to restrict cross-border data flows under Article 1 of the proposed horizontal provisions is low. As a result, the chances that the EU will have to resort to Article 2 in defence

[136] Micallef, 'Digital Trade in EU FTAs' (n 40) 866, arguing that art 2 'can be used to neutralize the advantages that the first article brings'. See also Naef, *Data Protection without Data Protectionism* (n 6) 411, 413, 416.

[137] See Nigel Cory and Luke Dascoli, 'How Barriers to Cross-Border Data Flows Are Spreading Globally, What They Cost, and How to Address Them' (*Information Technology & Innovation Foundation*, 19 July 2019) <https://itif.org/publications/2021/07/19/how-barriers-cross-border-data-flows-are-spreading-globally-what-they-cost/> accessed 10 July 2023.

[138] Communication from the Commission, 'A European Strategy for Data' (n 17) 23.

[139] See, eg, Matthew Newton, 'Russian Data Localization Laws: Enriching "Security" & the Economy' (*The Henry M. Jackson School of International Studies, University of Washington*, 28 February 2018) <https://jsis.washington.edu/news/russian-data-localization-enriching-security-economy/> accessed 10 July 2023, arguing that Russia is 'using data localization laws to provide capital flow to Russian companies by requiring them to pay to store Russian data on Russian servers' and by doing so is creating barriers to entry for international companies to the Russian market.

[140] Art 18(5) Федеральный закон 'О персональных данных' от 27.07.2006 N 152-ФЗ (Federal Law on Personal Data of 27 July 2006 No 152-FZ).

of its restrictions on transfers of personal data are equally low. Because the prohibitions on data localization in Article 1 primarily target the EU's trading partners, the exception of Article 2 is also most likely to be invoked by EU's trading partners.

As Chapter 3 of this book has explained, exceptions can be seen as a way to distinguish between restrictions on trade that are beneficial for society at large (public interest restrictions) and restrictions on trade captured by domestic industries which create redistribution of welfare and social costs (protectionism). The challenge is to draw a correct line between the two in each particular case, as this balance ultimately affects the balance between the interests of trade liberalization and other public policy objectives. There will always be false positives and false negatives. The necessity test in the general exception uses multiple safeguards to ensure that trade interests are protected. Putting trade liberalization above domestic (non-economic) public interests is likely to produce false positives, that is, to outlaw domestic regulation genuinely pursuing public policy objectives as protectionist. By doing so, the necessity test ends up overprotecting economic trade liberalization interests. On the other hand, the 'it deems appropriate' test—included in the EU proposed horizontal provisions and in digital trade chapters of EU's trade agreements with New Zealand and Chile—is likely to produce false negatives, as it can potentially filter out only cases (if any) where a state invokes the exception in manifestly bad faith.

Figuratively speaking, if the 'it deems appropriate' threshold is used, as compared to the necessity test of the general exception, the pendulum between trade liberalization and competing policy objectives would swing to the other extreme. As discussed in Section 3.2.4.3, in the last several decades of the twentieth century, under the influence of neoliberal discourse, the international trading system has suffered from a 'protectionism bias' that favoured trade liberalization over competing policy objectives. Conversely, an international trading system containing broad exceptions would, in effect, make compliance with trade liberalization commitments voluntary—one might even say no longer fully 'rules-based,' because compliance with actual 'rules' should not be entirely voluntary. The underlying question here is that of the balance between trade liberalization and other public policy interests, which ultimately harkens back to the goals of the international trading system that states want to achieve. This question should be subject to a wide political and societal debate and not buried into the arcane details of negotiations on the wording of one particular exception of a trade instrument.

To sum up, in its future digital trade exceptions for privacy and data protection, the EU should use a threshold different from 'it deems appropriate'. That said, as Chapter 2 has demonstrated, the necessity test (currently used in the general exception for privacy and data protection) is not a suitable option due to its potential incompatibility with the EU's constitutional framework. Given that the horizontal provisions analysed in this section are only a starting point in international trade negotiations, the EU still has sufficient wiggle room to adapt its negotiation strategy going forward.

In Section 4.3, this chapter will take stock of other tests employed in international trade law that strike a balance between trade liberalization and domestic public policy objectives to find an alternative test that would provide enough autonomy for the EU to protect privacy and personal data, while allowing it to pursue the goal of digital trade liberalization and uphold the rules-based international trading system. In other words, Section 4.3 looks for a standard that lies somewhere between an overly broad 'it deems appropriate' or 'it considers necessary' tests and an overly restrictive necessity test. But first, let us consider a last point of critique of Article 2 of the EU's proposed horizontal provisions.

4.2.6 Downsides of the EU-centric approach

As mentioned in Section 4.1, the EU stands out for its commitment to a high level of protection of privacy and personal data as binding fundamental rights guaranteed in Articles 7 and 8 of the EU Charter. International and regional human rights law plays only a limited role in international trade law, however.[141] Therefore, for the EU to safeguard its autonomy to regulate privacy and the protection of personal data as fundamental rights vis-à-vis its international trade obligations, it is essential to include in international trade agreements provisions that reflect the normative foundations of privacy and data protection in the EU and accommodate a regulatory design of domestic frameworks most adequate to this normative goal.[142] This seems to be precisely the rationale behind the provisions in the proposed horizontal provisions stating that, first, '[e]ach Party recognises that the protection of personal data and privacy is a fundamental right' and, second, '[n]othing in this agreement shall affect the protection of personal data and privacy afforded by the Parties' respective safeguards'.[143] This section argues, however, that the first provision is overly EU-centric and can be amended without undermining the EU's autonomy to protect privacy and personal data as fundamental rights in domestic law.

Although privacy is often recognized as a fundamental right,[144] a *sui generis* fundamental right to the protection of personal data is much less common. It is

[141] For a discussion, see Svetlana Yakovleva, 'Should Fundamental Rights to Privacy and Data Protection Be a Part of the EU's International Trade "Deals"?' (2018) 17(3) World Trade Review 477, 487–89, 499–508.

[142] ibid.

[143] Art 2 EU horizontal provisions on cross-border data flows. Naef argues that the EU should have included even more extensive provisions, containing the key elements of the fundamental right to the protection of personal data from art 8 of the EU Charter. Naef, *Data Protection without Data Protectionism* (n 6) 407–08.

[144] The right to privacy is enshrined in art 12 Universal Declaration of Human Rights (1948) GA Res 217, UN GAOR, 3d Sess, UN Doc A/810 (hereafter UDHR); art 17 International Covenant on Civil and

not fully recognized by the UN[145] and reflects to a large degree the European legal tradition. This right is recognized in the Council of Europe Convention 108+—the only binding international legal instrument on data protection—and the EU legal system.[146] Although 67 per cent of independent jurisdictions in the world have a data protection law,[147] few of those countries (outside the European Union and the Council of Europe member states) recognize the protection of personal data as a fundamental right. For example, among the countries that have negotiated or are currently negotiating bilateral trade agreements where the EU has included the proposed horizontal provisions, only Chile[148] and Tunisia[149] recognize data protection as a fundamental or constitutional right, while Australia,[150] Indonesia,[151] and New Zealand[152] do not. This, however, did not prevent New Zealand from agreeing to recognize the protection of personal data and privacy as a fundamental right in the digital trade chapter of the EU-New Zealand FTA. In contrast, even though the United Kingdom recognizes the protection of personal data as a fundamental right,[153] the recognition of the protection of personal data and privacy as a fundamental right was removed from the EU-UK TCA, instead replacing it with

Political Rights (16 December 1966) UNTS 999 (hereafter ICCPR); art 8 Council of Europe, European Convention for the Protection of Human Rights and Fundamental Freedoms, as amended by Protocols Nos 11 and 14 (4 November 1950) ETS 5 (hereafter ECHR).

145 The UN framework was developed long before the rise of personal data protection frameworks. The UN Guidelines for the Regulation of Computerized Personal Data Files adopted by General Assembly resolution 45/95 of 14 December 1990 only refer to the human right to privacy. The UN has recently been also working on harmonizing the data protection standards of the UN members. See, eg, Personal Data Protection and Privacy Principles, Adopted by the UN High-Level Committee on Management (HLCM) at its 36th Meeting on 11 October 2018, which, however, also do not mention specifically the right to the protection of personal data but only the right to privacy.

146 See European Union Agency for Fundamental Rights and Council of Europe, *Handbook on European Data Protection Law* (2018) 21ff <https://www.echr.coe.int/Documents/Handbook_data_protection_ENG.pdf> accessed 10 July 2023.

147 Graham Greenleaf, 'Now 157 Countries: Twelve Data Privacy Laws in 2021/22' (2022) 176 Privacy Laws & Business International Report 3, 9.

148 The right to personal data is protected under the Constitution of Chile. See DLA Piper, 'Data Protection Laws of the World: Chile' (2023) <https://www.dlapiperdataprotection.com/index.html?c=CL&c2=&go-button=GO&t=law> accessed 10 July 2023.

149 Tunisia is a party to the Convention 108 since 2017; it also recognizes the right to protection of personal data in the constitution, albeit to a limited extent. See DLA Piper, 'Data Protection Laws of the World: Tunisia' (2023) <https://www.dlapiperdataprotection.com/index.html?t=law&c=TN&c2=> accessed 10 July 2023. See also Council of Europe, 'Consultative Committee of the Convention for the Protection of Individuals with regard to Automatic Processing of Personal Data (T-PD) Opinion on the Request for Accession by Tunisia' (2015) T-PD(2015)14 <https://rm.coe.int/16806fdcb5> accessed 10 July 2023.

150 DLA Piper, 'Data Protection Laws of the World: Australia' (2022) <https://www.dlapiperdataprotection.com/index.html?t=law&c=AU&c2=> accessed 10 July 2023.

151 DLA Piper, 'Data Protection Laws of the World: Indonesia' (2022) <https://www.dlapiperdataprotection.com/index.html?t=law&c=ID&c2=> accessed 10 July 2023.

152 DLA Piper, 'Data Protection Laws of the World: New Zealand' (2023) <https://www.dlapiperdataprotection.com/index.html?t=law&c=NZ&c2=> accessed 10 July 2023.

153 Irion and Burri, '§ 16 Digitaler Handel' (n 15) para 13. Therefore, as Irion and Burri argue, removal of the reference to the 'fundamental right' has a merely 'symbolic dimension' and no real legal consequence.

'[e]ach Party recognises that individuals have a right to the protection of personal data and privacy'.[154]

Extrapolating this discussion to ongoing negotiations on cross-border data flow provisions, digital trade exceptions, and looking at the Data Free Flow with Trust (DFFT) at the WTO Joint Statement on E-commerce,[155] one can plainly see that not all WTO members that participate in these negotiations adhere to the fundamental rights approach to the protection of personal data. The most obvious examples of countries that do not recognize this right are China,[156] Russia,[157] and the United States.

Although many countries are currently reviewing their data protection framework and strengthening the protection of personal data, it is unclear whether the protection of this right as a fundamental right will become widely recognized. For example, although the United States has recently intensified efforts to adopt a federal privacy law, which would increase the level of protection of personal data in the business context, such protection is still viewed as a consumer—and not a constitutional—right.[158] As Chander, Kaminski, and McGeveran rightly point out, the fundamental difference between the US and the European approaches to their data privacy regimes is not just the different languages used in these two legal systems ('data protection' in Europe versus 'privacy law' in the United States) but also

[154] EU-UK TCA (n 15) art 202(1).

[155] Eighty-nine WTO members as of this writing (June 2023). See WTO, 'Joint Initiative on E-commerce' <https://www.wto.org/english/tratop_e/ecom_e/joint_statement_e.htm> accessed 10 July 2023.

[156] In Chinese law, governance of data and its cross-border flows is, primarily, a matter of cybersecurity, which is directly linked to cyber sovereignty and national security. China's data localization requirements and restrictions on cross-border data flows are scattered throughout the Cybersecurity Law (CSL), the Data Security Law (DSL), and the Personal Information Protection Law (PIPL) as well in sectoral legislation. Although the PIPL framework bears a resemblance to the GDPR, and 'addresses many issues frequently discussed in the context of personal privacy worldwide, it does not directly address "privacy", which is a separate concept in Chinese law'. Rather, it aims to protect individuals, society, and national security from harms, a variety of harms stemming from misuse of personal data. Alexa Lee and others, 'Seven Major Changes in China's Finalized Personal Information Protection Law' (*DIGIChina Stanford*, 15 September 2021) <https://digichina.stanford.edu/work/seven-major-changes-in-chinas-finalized-personal-information-protection-law/> accessed 10 July 2023. See also Henry S Gao, 'Data Regulation with Chinese Characteristics' in Mira Burri (ed) *Big Data and Global Trade Law* (CUP 2021) 251;

Yan Luo, Zhijing Yu, and Vicky Liu, 'The Future of Data Localization and Cross-Border Transfer in China: A Unified Framework or a Patchwork of Requirements?' (*IAPP*, 22 June 2021) <https://iapp.org/news/a/the-future-of-data-localization-and-cross-border-transfer-in-china-a-unified-framework-or-a-patchwork-of-requirements/> accessed 10 July 2023; Xu Ke and others, 'Analyzing China's PIPL and How It Compares to the EU's GDPR' (*IAPP*, 24 August 2021) <https://iapp.org/news/a/analyzing-chinas-pipl-and-how-it-compares-to-the-eus-gdpr/> accessed 10 July 2023.

[157] Russia's constitution protects the right to privacy but does not mention the protection of personal data (Arts 23-24 Конституция Российской Федерации от 12.12.1993 с изменениями от 01.07.2020. (Constitution of the Russian Federation of 12 December 1993 as amended on 1 July 2020)).

[158] Cameron F Kerry, 'Breaking Down Proposals for Privacy Legislation: How Do They Regulate?' (*Brookings Institute*, March 8 2019) <https://www.brookings.edu/research/breaking-down-proposals-for-privacy-legislation-how-do-they-regulate/> accessed 10 July 2023; David Meyer, 'In the Wake of GDPR, Will the U.S. Embrace Data Privacy?' (*Fortune*, 29 November 2018) <https://fortune.com/2018/11/29/federal-data-privacy-law/> accessed 10 July 2023.

that 'data protection' is a fundamental right in Europe, while American law mostly focuses on 'consumer protection'.[159] They argue that the California Consumer Privacy Act (CCPA), despite some facial similarities with the GDPR, was still developed in the American tradition.[160] It is the CCPA, not the GDPR, that is 'catalyzing the development of U.S. data privacy law'.[161] More broadly, as Whitman argues, Americans and continental Europeans perceive privacy differently and have two different cultures of privacy. While '[c]ontinental privacy protection, – he argues – are, at their core, a form of protection of a right to respect and personal dignity', in America it 'is much more oriented toward values of liberty, and especially liberty against the state'.[162] In a similar vein, Schwartz and Peifer conclude that there is a 'conceptual gulf between the data privacy systems of the EU and United States based on the different legal identities that they provide for the individual'.[163] While the 'EU has created a privacy culture around "rights talk" that serves to protect "data subjects" <. . .> [i]n the United States, the focus is on "marketplace discourse" about personal information and the safeguarding of "privacy consumers"'.[164]

From this discussion, it follows that recognition of the protection of personal data as a fundamental right in paragraph 1 of Article 2 of the proposed horizontal provisions can be criticized from outside the EU as EU-centric in that it induces its foreign trading partners to adhere to the EU's values, which are not necessarily in line with their own legal systems. Not every country will see the right to the protection of personal data as a similar public policy target as the EU and its member states do, nor can all countries' approach to personal data be expected to be cut from the same normative cloth. Viewing privacy and data protection as a norm of governance deeply rooted in a country or region's social, political, and democratic structure suggests that to maintain the integrity of their governance structure, countries must retain the autonomy to pursue such priority interests and values.[165] In other words, it is important to acknowledge that not all differences need to be harmonized, as long as there is a mechanism to ensure that the interests of both sides are respected and taken into account.

This section, therefore, suggests that the proposed provision requiring each Party to recognize that the protection of personal data and privacy is a fundamental right could be rephrased in future trade negotiations as requiring each

[159] Anupam Chander, Margot E Kaminski, and William McGeveran, 'Catalyzing Privacy Law' (2019) 105 Minnesota Law Review 1733, 1746–47.
[160] ibid 1756.
[161] ibid 1763.
[162] James Q Whitman, 'The Two Western Cultures of Privacy: Dignity Versus Liberty' (2004) 113(6) Yale Law Journal 1151, 1159–62. See also Bilyana Petkova, 'Privacy as Europe's First Amendment' (2019) 25(2) European Law Journal 140, 153–54.
[163] Paul M Schwartz and Karl-Nikolaus Peifer, 'Transatlantic Data Privacy Law' (2017) 106 Georgetown Law Journal 115, 156.
[164] ibid 119.
[165] Joel R Reidenberg, 'Resolving Conflicting International Data Privacy Rules in Cyberspace' (2000) 52 Stanford Law Review 1315, 1320.

Party to recognize each other's *autonomy to choose the level of protection* of privacy and personal data, *including at the level of fundamental rights*. This approach would also be more conducive to furthering a pluralist discourse in international trade negotiations on cross-border data flows advocated in Chapter 3 of this book.

4.3 Thresholds Alternative to 'Necessity', 'It Considers Necessary', and 'It Deems Appropriate' Tests

This section discusses how far the EU can go in tightening the currently proposed 'it deems appropriate' threshold without compromising on the fundamental rights to privacy and data protection. This identifies the potential fallback options for the EU in relation to a threshold of a digital trade exception for privacy and data protection in international trade negotiations. Moving away from the two 'extremes' of 'necessity' in the general exception and 'it deems appropriate' or 'it considers necessary' tests in the proposed digital trade exception for privacy and data protection, this section explores whether other thresholds could be more suitable in safeguarding the EU's autonomy to protect privacy and personal data as fundamental rights while liberalizing cross-border data flows and preserving the rules-based international trading system.

Considerations applied in the selection of the relevant thresholds for analysis in this section are: (1) presence of the threshold in an existing trade agreement; (2) relevance to privacy and data protection, in particular, whether the threshold is used in an existing provision for privacy and data protection; and (3) availability of case law and academic literature.[166] Thresholds selected with these considerations in mind and analysed in this section are: non-circumvention, non-avoidance, reasonableness, and the prohibition of arbitrary or unjustifiable restriction on trade from the chapeau of the general exception.

This section makes two points. First, any of the following three thresholds are a better alternative to both the 'necessity' and 'it deems appropriate' tests: non-circumvention, non-avoidance, and reasonableness. Second, to ensure more predictability and control for the parties to a trade agreement over the interpretation of the chosen threshold of the digital trade exception, institutional restrictive

[166] The 'Predominant Motive' test proposed by Meyer could also be an appealing alternative. However, it does not meet the third criterion of the selection applied in this book. In addition, given that this test, just as the necessity test, is an objective assessment, the Predominant Motive test seems only marginally different from the necessity test. It only addresses the problem of mixed motives behind a measure, and not the requirement that the contested measure must be least trade restrictive. See Timothy Meyer, 'The Political Economy of WTO Exceptions' (2022) 99 Washington University Law Review 1299 (hereafter Meyer, 'The Political Economy of WTO Exceptions'). In particular, Meyer emphasizes that his proposed approach 'does not call for looking at the subjective intent of government officials. Instead, it looks at the design, architecture, and anticipated application of a measure as objective evidence of what the government intended'.

mechanisms are necessary. Using prohibition of arbitrary or unjustifiable discrimination or of a disguised restriction on trade as a threshold, however, is undesirable primarily because of the 'legacy clout' of its interpretation by the WTO adjudicating bodies in the chapeau of the general exceptions in the GATT and GATS, which has been, at times, dangerously close to 'necessity' in the past.[167]

On the first point, the interpretation of these three standards in academic literature and (scarce) WTO case law is a Venn diagram with a significant intersection in the sense that the interpretation of one often refers to the other. Principles of good faith and the prohibition of abuse of rights, which are a common denominator in the interpretation of all of the three alternative thresholds, as well the indeterminacy of the meaning of these thresholds in case law and literature, would allow a dispute-settlement panel to build the interpretation of any of the thresholds in relation to privacy and data protection almost from scratch. The interpretation of these principles in relation to domestic restrictions on transfers of personal data would amount to a nuanced approach where the strictness of the threshold is situated on the continuum between the necessity test of the general exception and the 'it considers necessary' test of the national security exception, depending on the interference of the trade rules requiring free data flows with the rights to protection of privacy and personal data under domestic law of the Party to the agreement. In the application to EU law, the strictness of the trade law threshold for domestic privacy and data protection measures would be proportionate to the magnitude of the risk of interference with the fundamental rights to privacy and the protection of personal data. In short, a more stringent trade law threshold would cover situations where the risk of interference with the fundamental rights is lower, a more lenient trade law threshold when the risk of interference with the fundamental rights is higher, thus mirroring the granular framework for data transfers in EU law proposed in Section 5.4.3 of this book.

On the second point, this section argues that the precise wording of the threshold used to construct the exception for privacy and data protection (just as any other exception) matters, but only up to a point. The principles of good faith and the abuse of rights that are used to determine their meaning are open norms, the exact meaning of which is essentially determined *in each situation* by adjudicators. This insight harkens back to the conclusions of Chapter 3 of this book—that the discourse governing the interpretation of international trade law norms is just as important, if not more, as their wording. The flexibility of the principles of good

[167] But see Kenneth Propp, suggesting that both the anti-circumvention provisions and the wording of the chapeau of the general exceptions could represent a potential compromise between the EU and the United States in trade negotiations on cross-border data transfers. Kenneth Propp, 'More than Adequate:
New Directions in International Data Transfer Governance' (2023) Atlantic Council 1, 7 <https://www.atlanticcouncil.org/wp-content/uploads/2023/06/More-than-Adequate-New-Directions-in-International-Data-Transfer-Governance_-_FINAL.pdf> accessed 10 July 2023.

faith and the prohibition of the abuse of rights is not only their main advantage but also their main drawback, as it gives broad discretion to adjudicators.

This section proceeds as follows. Sections 4.3.1–4.3.4 provide examples of the use of each of the above-mentioned thresholds in WTO and bilateral and regional trade agreements, discuss the substance and interpretation of each of them, and compare each threshold to the necessity test of the general exception and the 'it considers necessary' test of the national security exception. Section 4.3.5 reflects on the wisdom of using any of them in a digital trade exception for privacy and data protection to replace the currently proposed 'it deems appropriate' test, and the possible restrictive mechanisms limiting the adjudicators' discretion in applying those alternative tests.

4.3.1 Non-circumvention

A non-circumvention clause can be found, for example, in the exceptions from:

(1) the obligation on cross-border information flows in financial services chapters,[168] and
(2) a horizontal provision on cross-border data flows in digital trade agreements of the 2017 EU Council proposal for a data protection exception in digital trade agreements, which preceded the 2018 proposed horizontal provisions discussed in Section 4.2 of this chapter.[169]

[168] Starting from the 1994 Understanding on Commitments in Financial Services and up to recently concluded CETA, rules in EU-led trade agreements on the liberalization of trade in financial services contain a provision that requires the parties 'not to take measures that prevent' or to 'permit' the transfer of information or the processing of financial information, including transfers of data by electronic means, where such transfers of information or processing of financial information are necessary for the conduct of the ordinary business of a financial service supplier (obligation on free flow of financial information). Art B.8 Understanding on Commitments in Financial Services, Results of the Uruguay Round-Legal Texts (15 April 1994) 477 33 ILM 1260-63 (hereafter Understanding on Commitments in Financial Services). Understanding on Commitments in Financial Services is not a part of the GATS, but is an Appendix to the Final Act of the Uruguay Round. Understanding is not legally binding per se; it is 'an optional and alternative approach to making specific commitments on financial services'. See WTO, 'Financial Services' <https://www.wto.org/english/tratop_e/serv_e/finance_e/finance_e.htm> accessed 10 July 2023. See also art 13.15(1) CETA (n 54); art 157(1) Trade Agreement between the European Union and Its Member States, of the One Part, and Colombia and Peru, of the Other Part, 31 May 2012 [2012] OJ L 354/1 (hereafter EU-Colombia-Peru FTA); art 22(1) Economic Partnership, Political Coordination and Cooperation Agreement between the European Community and Its Member States, of the One Part, and the United Mexican States, of the Other Part, 8 December 1997 [2000] OJ L 276/45 (hereafter EU-Mexico Coordination and Cooperation Agreement); art 7.43(a) Free Trade Agreement between the European Union and Its Member States, of the One Part, and the Republic of Korea, of the Other Part, 6 October 2010 [2011] OJ L 127/6 (hereafter EU-Korea FTA); art 198(1) Agreement Establishing an Association between Central America, on the one hand, and the European Union and Its Member States, on the other, 29 June 2012 [2012] OJ L 346/3 (hereafter EU-Central America Association Agreement); art 8.54(1) EU-Singapore FTA (n 123).

[169] Council of the European Union, 'Concept Paper on Data Flows in Trade Agreements' (2017) (on file with author).

According to the WTO's Understanding on Financial Services,

> Nothing in this paragraph restricts *the right of a Member to protect personal data, personal privacy* and the confidentiality of individual records and accounts so long as such right is *not used to circumvent the provisions of the Agreement.*[170]

Similar provisions can be found in several other EU-led trade agreements, including those with Singapore[171] and Japan.[172]

The 'non-circumvention' requirement has never been applied in practice at the WTO. Moreover, it is seldom discussed in literature. According to von Bogdandy and Windsor, although the requirement 'not to circumvent' has not been defined, 'it is reasonably arguable that circumvention is equivalent to avoidance'.[173] Similarly, on the basis of a non-scientific survey of the WTO and GATT dispute-settlement records, Jarreau concluded that '"to circumvent" essentially means "to avoid"'.[174] If 'circumvention' and 'avoidance' are equivalent notions, then the threshold of the data protection exception in the Understanding is functionally the same as the threshold in the prudential exception discussed in the following section.[175]

Another example is useful in shedding additional light on the matter. The provision proposed in the 2017 EU Council's concept paper on data flows reads as follows:

> Nothing in the Agreement restricts the right of a Party to protect personal data and privacy so long as such right is not *used to circumvent* paragraph 1.[176]

170 Art B.8, second sentence of the Understanding on Commitments in Financial Services (n 168) (emphasis added).

171 EU-Singapore FTA (n 123) art 8.54(2).

172 JEFTA (n 34) art 8.63(2).

173 Van Bogdandy and Windsor, 'Annex on Financial Services' (n 26) 658.

174 J Steven Jarreau, 'Interpreting the General Agreement on Trade in Services and the WTO Instruments Relevant to the International Trade of Financial Services: A Lawyer's Perspective' (1999) 25(1) North Carolina Journal of International Law and Commercial Regulation 1, 59–60 (hereafter Jarreau, 'Interpreting the GATS and the WTO Instruments Relevant to the International Trade of Financial Services'). Jarreau refers to WTO, *Indonesia – Certain Measures Affecting the Automobile Industry – Report of the Panel* (2 July 1998) WT/DS54/R, WT/DS55/R, WT/DS59/R, WT/DS64/R paras 4.24, 4.25 (hereafter Panel Report, *Indonesia – Autos*); Dispute Settlement Body, Minutes of Meeting (30 July 1997) WL 908915 Item 4; GATT, *Canada – Import Restrictions on Ice Cream and Yoghurt* (27 September 1989) GATT BISD 361h Supp. 68, 79; GATT, *Japan – Trade in Semi-Conductors* (24 March 1988) GATT BISD 351h Supp. 1988 WL 561373 116, 126.

175 Papaconstantinou calls the non-avoidance clause in the prudential exception the '"anti-circumvention" clause'. George A Papaconstantinou, 'The GATS and Financial Regulation: Time to Clear-House?' (2020) 19 World Trade Review 379, 398 (hereafter Papaconstantinou, 'The GATS and Financial Regulation').

176 (Emphasis added). Council of the European Union, Concept Paper on Data Flows in Trade Agreements (n 169) 2. Para 1 referred to in this provision reads as follows: 'No Party may prevent a person of the other Party from transferring, processing or storing data, within or outside the Party's territory, where such activity is necessary for the conduct of that person's business'.

To ensure greater legal certainty, the concept paper contains a footnote setting out a legally binding interpretation of the standard of 'non-circumvention', which explains that:

> . . . circumvention means *the abuse of the right* to protect personal data and privacy by a Party *with the intention to avoid* the Party's obligations under paragraph 1.[177]

The concept paper explains that the purpose of the 'non-circumvention' clause is to prevent the *intentional* use of the legitimate policy objectives, such as data protection, to *disguise protectionist policies*.[178] The concept paper also explains that the anti-circumvention clause must not allow trade adjudicating bodies to doubt the 'necessity of data protection measures in question'.[179] This suggests that the non-circumvention standard, at least in the EU Council concept paper, is envisaged as a standard *lower* than the 'necessity' test of the general exception. Furthermore, unlike the objective necessity test in the general exception, this interpretation of 'non-circumvention' implies a subjective test, namely intention to evade the law.

Although the available tools to interpret non-circumvention do not allow one to fully explain the meaning of this standard, they do make clear that this standard does not require the party invoking the exception to prove the 'necessity' of the contested measure. Exactly how different the non-circumvention threshold is from 'it considers necessary' or 'it deems appropriate' tests, however, remains difficult to define. As discussed in Section 4.2.3 of this chapter, a prohibition to intentionally circumvent international trade commitments is also a component of the 'it considers necessary' standard, as applied by the WTO Panels in recent cases. The interpretation of non-circumvention as the use of legitimate policy objectives to 'disguise protectionist policies' offered by the footnote in the EU Council concept paper has little value, therefore, in part because there is no uniform understanding of what 'protectionism' is, as demonstrated in Chapter 3 of this book. The discussion of the 'non-avoidance' threshold in the following section—a standard equivalent to 'non-circumvention—brings the investigation of the relationship between non-circumvention standard and 'it considers necessary' test a step further.

[177] ibid (emphasis added).
[178] ibid.
[179] ibid 3.

4.3.2 Non-avoidance

The most well-known 'non-avoidance' clause appears in the prudential exception (also known as prudential carve-out[180]) of Article 2(a) 'Domestic Regulation' of the GATS Annex on Financial Services. It reads as follows:

> Notwithstanding any other provisions of the Agreement, a Member shall not be prevented from taking *measures for prudential reasons* <. . .>. Where such measures do not conform with the provisions of the Agreement, they shall not be *used* as a means of *avoiding* the Member's commitments or obligations under the Agreement.[181]

This clause was later reproduced in the prudential exceptions of other trade agreements, for example, in the KORUS trade agreement[182] and the CPTPP.[183] This demonstrates that the prudential exception provides a widely accepted example of an exception in trade law not based on the necessity test.[184]

In addition to the prudential exception, the non-avoidance clause also appears in the exception for privacy and data protection in a cross-border data flow provision in the financial services chapter of the CPTPP. That exception reads as follows:

[180] As already mentioned above, there is a scholarly debate on whether art 2(a) GATS Annex on Financial Services has a function of an exception or, alternatively, carves out prudential measures from the scope of the agreement. Although the article is entitled 'Domestic Regulation' and—according to Cantore's research into *Travaux Preparatoire*—was intended to work as a 'provision that excludes the application of other provisions', and not an 'exception', this provision is predominantly seen, both by the WTO adjudicative bodies and scholars, as an exception rather than a carve-out. Cantore, 'Exploring the Scope of Application and Legal Function of the GATS Prudential Carve-Out' (n 26) 1242; WTO, 'Background Note by the Secretariat Financial Services' (n 26) para 28; Panel Report, *Argentina – Financial Services* (n 26) para 7.814; WTO, Guidelines for the Scheduling of Specific Commitments under the GATS (n 26). For further discussion, see Cantore, 'Exploring the Scope of Application and Legal Function of the GATS Prudential Carve-Out' (n 26) 1232, 1242; Cottier and Krajewski, 'What Role for Non-Discrimination and Prudential Standards in International Financial Law?' (n 26) 826–27; Leroux, 'Trade in Financial Services under the World Trade Organization' (n 26); Marchetti, 'The GATS Prudential Carve-Out' (n 26); Von Bogdandy and Windsor, 'Annex on Financial Services' (n 26); Yokoi-Arai, '"GATS" Prudential Carve Out in Financial Services and Its Relation with Prudential Regulation' (n 26); Mitchell, Hawkins, and Mishra, 'Allowances under International Trade and Investment Law for Prudential Regulation in the Financial Services Sector' (n 26) 807.

[181] Emphasis added.

[182] Art 13.10(1) United States-Korea Free Trade Agreement (1 April 2007) 46 I LM 642 (hereafter KORUS).

[183] CPTPP (n 125) art 11.11(1).

[184] Yang shows that non-avoidance clause is followed in prudential exceptions of most of the regional trade agreements. Other control mechanisms in the regional trade agreements' prudential exceptions revolve around the reasonableness test or a combination of reasonableness and non-avoidance. Alex Yueh-Ping Yang, 'The Evolving Prudential Exceptions in Regional Trade Agreements' (2018) 13(2) Asian Journal of WTO & International Health Law and Policy 395, 415–20 (hereafter Yang, 'The Evolving Prudential Exceptions in Regional Trade Agreements').

> Nothing in this section restricts the right of a Party to adopt or maintain measures to:
>
> (a) protect personal data, personal privacy and the confidentiality of individual records and accounts; <. . .>
> provided that this right is not used as a means *of avoiding* the Party's commitments or obligations under this section.[185]

The 'non-avoidance' standard has never been interpreted by the WTO adjudicating bodies. In the only WTO case addressing the prudential exception, neither the Panel nor the Appellate Body reached the second sentence of the provision (which contains the non-avoidance clause).[186] However, the meaning of this threshold is discussed in a WTO Background Note[187] and in academic literature. There seems to be a consensus that the 'non-avoidance' standard in the prudential exception provides broad autonomy for WTO Members to adopt financial regulatory measures, that is, unless those measures are 'purely or primarily protectionist in effect'.[188] As explained in the WTO Background Note, the prudential exception is *broader than the general exception*:

> In contrast to health and safety, for example, where only 'necessary' measures are excepted [under the general exception], *all* prudential measures are excepted. As

[185] Section B Annex 11-B to Chapter on Financial services CPTPP. It should be recalled that this exception differs from art 14.11 CPTPP (emphasis added). Financial services are explicitly excluded from the scope of the CPTPP e-commerce chapter; thus, the general obligation on cross-border transfers as well as the exception from it under Article 14.11 do not apply to financial data flows. Art 14.2(4) and (5) CPTPP (n 125). Fefer claims that those were US financial regulators who 'advocated for the explicit ability to restrict cross-border data flows in TPP, in addition to the flexibility provided by the prudential exception'. Rachel F Fefer, 'Trade in Services Agreement (TiSA) Negotiations: Overview and Issues for Congress' (2017) Congressional Research Service 1, 12 <https://fas.org/sgp/crs/misc/R44354.pdf> accessed 10 July 2023. Although the United States later withdrew from the TPP, the provision has remained unchanged in the final version of the CPTPP.

[186] Panel Report, *Argentina – Financial Services* (n 26); WTO, *Argentina – Measures Relating to Trade in Goods and Services – Report of the Appellate Body* (14 April 2016) WT/DS453/AB/R and WT/DS453/AB/R/Add.1 431 (hereafter Appellate Body Report, *Argentina – Financial Services*).

[187] WTO, Background Note by the Secretariat Financial Services (n 26) para 31. Background notes of the WTO Secretariat are of limited interpretative value and can at most be used as supplementary means of interpretation. See WTO, *Mexico – Measures Affecting Telecommunications Services – Report of the Panel* (2 April 2004) WT/DS204/R para 7.43 (hereafter Panel Report, *Mexico – Telecoms*).

[188] Von Bogdandy and Windsor, 'Annex on Financial Services' (n 26) 634–36. See also Jarreau, 'Interpreting the GATS and the WTO Instruments Relevant to the International Trade of Financial Services' (n 173); Mitchell, Hawkins, and Mishra, 'Allowances under International Trade and Investment Law for Prudential Regulation in the Financial Services Sector' (n 26); Panagiotis Delimatsis, 'Financial Innovation and Prudential Regulation: The New Basel III Rules' (2012) 46(6) Journal of World Trade 1309, 1337; Carlo Maria Cantore, *The Prudential Carve-Out for Financial Services* (CUP 2018) 67–68 (hereafter Cantore, *The Prudential Carve-Out for Financial Services*); Papaconstantinou, 'The GATS and Financial Regulation' (n 175) 398–99.

a result, a prudential measure may not be challenged on the grounds of whether it is 'necessary' or 'least trade restrictive'.[189]

The main factors cited as the rationale behind safeguarding such broad regulatory space for domestic financial measures are: first, financial services are crucial for the functioning of today's economies; second, as problems in the financial sector often emerge *ex post*, it is difficult to foresee which measures will be required to address those problems; and third, there is a lack of both coordination and international standards on prudential measures.[190]

Commenting on the meaning of the 'non-avoidance' threshold, the WTO Background Note endorses the approach adopted by Leroux and by von Bogdandy and Windsor. The WTO secretariat agrees with their opinion that the 'non-avoidance' requirement is 'clearly intended to *avoid abuse* in the use of the exception'.[191] For Leroux, the purpose of this requirement is 'to prevent the *abuse of the exception* for prudential measures' and, as a minimum, to impose 'an obligation of *good faith* with respect to the adoption and application of prudential measures'.[192] This interpretation creates a parallel between the 'non-avoidance' standard and the chapeau of the general exception and prompts several scholars to argue that the term 'avoiding' should take into account the rich case law on the *chapeau* of Article XX GATT 1994, as it performs a similar function.[193] Scholars also note that the provision can be read 'as requiring some level of *intent to circumvent* duties under GATS'.[194]

Cantore criticizes the interpretation of 'non-avoidance' through the principle of good faith as circular. In his view, 'good faith is not a self-interpretive concept and depends on the time, context and situations in which it is invoked. As such, this approach leaves considerable discretion for panels to make evaluations

[189] WTO, 'Background Note by the Secretariat Financial Services' (n 26) para 31 (emphasis added). Referring to Sydney J Key, *The Doha Round and Financial Services Negotiations* (American Enterprise Institute Press 2003). See also Papaconstantinou, 'The GATS and Financial Regulation' (n 175) 399.

[190] Mitchell, Hawkins, and Mishra, 'Allowances under International Trade and Investment Law for Prudential Regulation in the Financial Services Sector' (n 26) 791, 814; Cantore, *The Prudential Carve-Out for Financial Services* (n 178) 63, 187.

[191] WTO, 'Background Note by the Secretariat Financial Services' (n 26) para 30 (emphasis added). Referring to Leroux, 'Trade in Financial Services under the World Trade Organization' (n 26).

[192] Leroux, 'Trade in Financial Services under the World Trade Organization' (n 26) 430–31 (emphasis added). See also Von Bogdandy and Windsor, 'Annex on Financial Services' (n 26).

[193] Von Bogdandy and Windsor, 'Annex on Financial Services' (n 26) 635. See also Mitchell, Hawkins, and Mishra, 'Allowances under International Trade and Investment Law for Prudential Regulation in the Financial Services Sector' (n 26) 812; Vu Nhu Thang, 'Applicability of GATS Prudential Exception to Insurance Services: Some Interpretative Issues' (2007) 4(2) Manchester Journal of International Economic Law 88, 116–17; Inu Barbee and Simon Lester, 'Financial Services in the TTIP: Making the Prudential Exception Work' (2014) 45(4) Georgetown Journal of International Law 953, 960; Bart de Meester, 'The Global Financial Crisis and the Government Support for Banks' (2008) 13(1) Journal of International Economic Law 27, 29. This position was also advanced by Argentina in Panel Report, *Argentina – Financial Services* (n 26) paras 7.783, 7.791–7.792. But see Cantore, *The Prudential Carve-Out for Financial Services* (n 188) 180.

[194] Von Bogdandy and Windsor, 'Annex on Financial Services' (n 26) 636 (emphasis added).

on a case-by-case basis'.[195] This book will come back to this interesting argument in Section 4.3.5, where it analyses and compares the alternative thresholds. Furthermore, Cantore rightly warns of the dangers of importing the WTO case law on *chapeau* in the interpretation of the prudential exception due to the absence of similarity in the wording of both provisions, taking into account also the difference in the function they perform, and the practice of the WTO adjudicating bodies of conducting an analysis of domestic policy strategies. As a result, he argues, this would shrink the regulatory autonomy safeguarded under the prudential exception.[196]

As the WTO Appellate Body confirmed in its 2020 *Australia – Tobacco Plain Packaging (Honduras)* report, 'it is well established that different words in a treaty are generally intended to convey a different meaning'.[197] Despite the difference in structure and wording, however, several scholars argue that the non-avoidance standard does not substantially differ from the 'reasonableness' requirement in other prudential exceptions (the reasonableness requirement is discussed in the following section).[198] For example, Mitchell and others contend that the non-avoidance standard implies the reasonableness requirement, which is why the interpretation of 'reasonableness' in WTO case law could be used to interpret 'non-avoidance'.[199]

Although to invoke the prudential exception the defending party need not prove its necessity or trade restrictiveness, the choice of contested prudential measures is not left to the sole discretion of the defending party but is rather subject to an objective assessment.[200] In *Argentina – Financial Services*, the Panel, whose assessment on this point was not reviewed by the Appellate Body, concluded that:

> the use of the word 'for' in the phrase 'measures for prudential reasons' denotes a rational relationship of cause and effect between the measure and the prudential

[195] Cantore, *The Prudential Carve-Out for Financial Services* (n 188) 71–72.

[196] ibid 71–72, 169, 180–83. For a discussion on the importation of standards of review from other provisions by WTO adjudicating bodies, see, more generally, Petros C Mavroidis, '"Driftin" Too Far from Shore – Why the Test for Compliance with the TBT Agreement Developed by the WTO Appellate Body Is Wrong, and What Should the AB Have Done Instead' (2013) 12(3) World Trade Review 509.

[197] WTO, *Australia – Certain Measures Concerning Trademarks, Geographical Indications and Other Plain Packaging Requirements Applicable to Tobacco Products and Packaging – Reports of the Appellate Body* (9 June 2020) WT/DS435/AB/R; WT/DS441/AB/R and WT/DS435/AB/R/Add.1, WT/DS441/AB/R/Add.1 para 6.646 (hereafter Appellate Body Report, *Australia – Tobacco Plain Packaging (Honduras and Dominican Republic)*).

[198] Cantore, *The Prudential Carve-Out for Financial Services* (n 188) 126; Mitchell, Hawkins, and Mishra, 'Allowances under International Trade and Investment Law for Prudential Regulation in the Financial Services Sector' (n 26) 813.

[199] Mitchell, Hawkins, and Mishra, 'Allowances under International Trade and Investment Law for Prudential Regulation in the Financial Services Sector' (n 26) 813.

[200] See also Stephen Simchak, 'Financial Services International Trade Jurisprudence-Revisiting the Prudential Exception and Its Implications for Indonesia' (2022) 25 Currents: Journal of International Economic Law 42, 56, stating that 'the prudential exception is not the carte blanche that some governments had hoped it would be'.

> reason. Thus, the Member taking the measure in question must demonstrate *that in its design, structure or architecture there is a rational relationship of cause and effect* between the measure it seeks to justify under paragraph 2(a) and the prudential reason provided. *A central aspect of this rational relationship of cause and effect is the adequacy of the measure to the prudential reason*, that is, whether the measure, through its *design, structure and architecture*, contributes to achieving the desired effect. Whether a measure has been taken 'for prudential reasons', that is, whether there is a rational relationship of cause and effect between the measure and the reason, can only be determined on a case-by-case basis, taking account of the particular characteristics of each situation and each dispute.[201]

In other words, instead of 'necessity' (as would be the case under the general exception), the party invoking the prudential exception must demonstrate the 'adequacy' of the design, structure, and architecture of the measure. While this threshold, based on the interpretation above, is lower than 'necessity', it is sufficiently higher than that of 'it considers necessary' test, where the nexus between the measure and the national security interests is only subject to a 'minimum requirement of plausibility'.

It is unclear whether the same requirement of adequacy could be extrapolated to other exceptions, in particular, exceptions that, on the one hand (unlike the national security exception), do not denote in their wording that the choice of the measures is at the discretion of the defending party, and on the other hand, do not use the preposition 'for' as in the prudential exception—for example, exceptions mentioned in the previous section of this book. One could, however, argue that the *absence* of a specific wording calling for subjective choice of measures opens the door wider for objective assessment of such choice, as compared to where there *is* such specific wording.

To sum up, the interpretation of the 'non-avoidance' threshold adds a key degree of nuance to the interpretation of 'non-circumvention' for four main reasons. First, the interpretation favoured by the WTO Secretariat clearly sets the non-avoidance, and therefore the non-circumvention standard, apart from the necessity test of the general exception as safeguarding a broader regulatory autonomy. Second, both the WTO and scholarly interpretation further deepen the link between non-circumvention and non-avoidance, on the one hand, and the doctrines of good faith and the abuse of right, on the other. Unfortunately, besides a proposal to import case law from the chapeau of the general exception to interpret the principle of good faith—which is undesirable—there is no guidance on what good faith means in the context of the prudential exception. As a result, the interpretation of non-avoidance does not shed much additional light on the relationship between

[201] Panel Report, *Argentina – Financial Services* (n 26) para 7.891 (emphasis added).

this standard (and the standard of non-circumvention) and the 'it considers necessary' test. Third, unlike the 'it considers necessary' test, which clearly reserves the autonomy of the defending party to determine the appropriateness of the measures, the 'non-avoidance' threshold does not prevent adjudicating bodies from subjecting the appropriateness of defended measures to a fully fledged objective assessment. Therefore, 'non-avoidance' affords less regulatory autonomy than the 'it considers necessary' test. Fourth, some interpretations use the reasonableness standard as a tool to interpret the non-avoidance standard. The following section turns to this third alternative threshold.

4.3.3 Reasonableness

In several trade agreements, the 'non-avoidance' standard in the prudential exception is replaced by the 'reasonableness' one.[202] For example, according to Article 13.16(1) of CETA,

> This Agreement does not prevent a Party from adopting or maintaining *reasonable* measures *for prudential reasons*, including: <. . .>[203]

A similar provision was used in the prudential exception of NAFTA (Article 1410(1)).

To the knowledge of this book's author, the prudential exception under NAFTA was only applied once—in an international investment case—and not actually interpreted by the panel on substance owing to judicial economy. In *Fireman's Fund v Mexico*, the NAFTA investment tribunal only noted that the prudential exception 'permits reasonable measures of a prudential character even if their effect (as contrasted with their motive or intent) is discriminatory. The Tribunal rejected the contention that a measure discriminatory in effect is *eo ipso* unreasonable.'[204]

The tribunal referred to an interpretation of chapter 14 of NAFTA by Wethington, the principal US negotiator:

> Article 1410(1)(a) ... carves out of the national treatment and other obligations of the financial services chapter a right to take reasonable measures even though discriminatory in application, to protect the safety and soundness of the financial system.[205]

[202] See also Yang, 'The Evolving Prudential Exceptions in Regional Trade Agreements' (n 184) 415–20.
[203] CETA (n 54) art 13.16(1) (emphasis added).
[204] *Fireman's Fund v. Mexico*, Award (17 July 2006) ICSID Case No ARB(AF)/02/01, para 162.
[205] ibid paras 163–65. See also Olin L Wethington, *Financial Market Liberalization: The NAFTA Framework* (Sheppard's McGraw Hill 1994) § 5.07.

Analysing this award, Cantore concludes that the 'reasonableness' requirement only targets measures 'that are *manifestly not linked* with a prudential objective and lead to the backhanded *avoidance* of obligations or commitments can be targeted'.[206] Unlike the necessity test in the general exception, it does not require the assessment of costs and benefits or the evaluation of less restrictive means.[207]

In CETA, the standard of reasonableness of the prudential carve-out[208] is explained in the Understanding on the application of the prudential carve-out (hereafter Understanding), which provides guidance on the interpretation of the carve-out in investment disputes.[209] This guidance draws a clear parallel between reasonableness and the *chapeau* of the general exception. One of the non-exhaustive principles, outlined in the Understanding, is that 'a measure is not applied in a manner which would constitute a means of arbitrary or unjustifiable discrimination between investors in like situations, or a disguised restriction on foreign investment'.[210]

Mitchell and Sheargold note that a test of 'reasonableness' is 'inherently flexible and requires case-by-case consideration. This makes the principle of reasonableness difficult, but not impossible, to define'.[211] The term 'reasonable' actually appears more than 200 times in the text of the WTO Agreements in a variety of contexts, but never as a threshold in an exception from trade rules.[212] The context most relevant for this book is the requirement of 'reasonable' administration of measures that appears in Article X:3(a) of the GATT 1994. In *Dominican Republic – Import and Sales of Cigarettes*, the WTO Panel defined this term as meaning '"in accordance with reason", "not irrational or absurd", "proportionate", "having sound judgement", "sensible", "not asking for too much", "within the limits of reason, not greatly less or more than might be thought likely or appropriate", "articulate"'.[213] As Cook explains, WTO adjudicators have also used reasonableness as an unwritten

[206] Cantore, *The Prudential Carve-Out for Financial Services* (n 188) 129 (emphasis added).

[207] ibid.

[208] Although this book has used the term 'prudential exception' rather than 'prudential carve-out', it does refer to 'prudential carve-out' in the context of CETA because this terminology is used in this trade agreement.

[209] Annex 13-B to CETA, Understanding on the Application of Articles 13.16.1 and 13.21.

[210] ibid para 8(e).

[211] Andrew D Mitchell and Elizabeth Sheargold, 'Reasonableness' in Andrew D Mitchell and Elizabeth Sheargold (eds), *Principles of International Trade and Investment Law* (Edgaronline 2021) 55 (hereafter Mitchell and Sheargold, 'Reasonableness').

[212] Graham Cook, 'Reasonableness in WTO Law' (2013) 1(2) Latin American Journal of International Trade Law 1–26, 3 (hereafter Cook, 'Reasonableness in WTO Law').

[213] WTO, *Dominican Republic – Measures Affecting the Importation and Internal Sale of Cigarettes – Report of the Panel* (26 November 2004) WT/DS302/R para 7.385 (hereafter Panel Report, *Dominican Republic – Import and Sale of Cigarettes*) quoting from *The New Shorter Oxford English Dictionary*. Reasonableness also appears in Article VI(1) of the GATS, which requires that '[i]n sectors where specific commitments are undertaken, each Member shall ensure that all measures of general application affecting trade in services are administered in a reasonable, objective and impartial manner'. There is little guidance on how to interpret this provision. Naef argues that this provision should be interpreted in the same was as similar provision in art X:3(a) of the GATT in the WTO Panel Report mentioned above in this footnote. Naef, *Data Protection without Data Protectionism* (n 6) 249.

norm, even in the absence of a direct reference to it in a particular provision.[214] The most relevant of such cases is the interpretation of the chapeau of the general exception, which is discussed in the following section.[215]

According to Mitchell and Sheargold, in application to a measure, reasonableness requires justification and the test applied to determine reasonableness is 'essentially one of rationality'.[216] They further explain that

> [i]n contrast to necessity testing ... where the principle of reasonableness is employed in international economic law, it does not require that a measure be the least trade or investment restrictive alternative, or the best option for achieving a particular purpose. In international economic law, reasonableness typically only requires a basic level of rationality or suitability.[217]

Despite the fact that, based on the scarce available literature, the reasonableness standard is very similar to both non-circumvention and non-avoidance, it is important to highlight one notable difference. While both the non-circumvention and non-avoidance requirements in the provisions discussed in previous sections relate to how a contested measure *is used or applied*, the reasonableness requirement in the provisions referred to in this section is addressed *to the measure itself*.[218] It could be argued that for this reason, the reasonableness requirement provides less regulatory autonomy than the other two standards. From this perspective, on the continuum between 'necessity' and 'it considers necessary' tests, the standard of reasonableness is somewhat closer to 'necessity'. In addition, while both non-circumvention and non-avoidance requirements give deference to the party's intent not to circumvent or abuse its trade law obligations, the reasonableness requirement leans more towards the objective consideration of rationality and justification. However, as is explained in the following section, in investigating how the measure is applied, the WTO adjudicating bodies have also consistently inquired into the architecture and design of the measure.

214 Cook, 'Reasonableness in WTO Law' (n 212) 12. See also Mitchell and Sheargold, 'Reasonableness' (n 211) 52.

215 Mitchell and Sheargold also discuss other instances of when WTO adjudicating bodies used reasonableness as an unwritten norm, eg reasonable expectations in non-violation complaints and 'reasonableness' in rational relationship tests. Mitchell and Sheargold, 'Reasonableness' (n 211) 73–74.

216 ibid 53, 55–56.

217 ibid 56–57, see also 75.

218 In other provisions of international economic law, 'reasonableness' may also refer to the administration of measures, terms and conditions, 'reasonable periods of time', or 'reasonable intervals'. See ibid 52.

4.3.4 Prohibition of 'arbitrary or unjustifiable discrimination' or a 'disguised restriction on international trade'

The most well-known provision where the formula stated in the heading of this section is used is the chapeau of the general exceptions contained in Articles XX GATT and XIV GATS (both of which are reproduced almost verbatim or incorporated *mutatis mutandis* in most post-WTO trade agreements around the world).[219] Recall from Chapter 2 that the WTO adjudicating bodies follow a two-step assessment of whether a contested measure can be justified under one of the general exceptions.[220] The chapeau requirement is the second step in that assessment.[221] The chapeau requires that measures justified under one of the exceptions should not be 'applied in a manner which would constitute a means of arbitrary or unjustifiable discrimination between countries where the same conditions prevail, or a disguised restriction on international trade'.[222]

The same wording appears in Article 5(d) of the GATS Annex on Telecommunications—together with the necessity test. This provision allows a WTO member to derogate from an obligation to provide access to public telecommunications infrastructure if this is '*necessary* to ensure the security and confidentiality of messages, subject to the requirement that such measures are not applied in a manner which would constitute a means of arbitrary or unjustifiable discrimination or a disguised restriction on trade in services'. While the GATS Annex on Telecommunications does not specifically mention privacy, CETA and some of the US-led trade agreements refer to privacy in addition to the security and confidentiality of the communications.[223] Some Telecommunication chapters in EU-led

[219] See, eg, art 28.3(2)(c)(ii) CETA (n 54); art 8.62(e)(ii) EU-Singapore FTA (n 123); art 167(1)(e)(ii) EU-Colombia-Peru FTA (n 168); art 7.50(e)(ii) EU-Korea FTA (n 168); art 203(1)(e)(ii) EU-Central America Association Agreement (n 168); art 23.1(2) KORUS (n 182); art 21.1(2) United States-Singapore Free Trade Agreement (3 September 2003) 117 Stat. 948 (hereafter US-Singapore FTA); art 21.1(2) Dominican Republic-Central America-United States Free Trade Agreement (28 May 2004) 43 ILM 514 (hereafter Dominican Republic-Central America-US FTA); art 21.1(2) United States-Panama Trade Promotion Agreement (31 October 2012) (hereafter US-Panama TPA); art 32.1(2) Agreement between the United States of America, the United Mexican States, and Canada (30 November 2018) (hereafter USMCA); art 29.1(3) CPTPP (n 125).

[220] Section 2.4.2.

[221] See, eg, Appellate Body Report, *US – Gasoline* (n 63) 22; WTO, *Brazil – Measures Affecting Imports of Retreaded Tyres – Report of the Appellate Body* (3 December 2007) WT/DS332/AB/R para 139 (hereafter Appellate Body Report, *Brazil – Retreaded Tyres*); WTO, *United States – Import Prohibition of Certain Shrimp and Shrimp Products – Report of the Appellate Body* (12 October 1998) WT/DS58/AB/R paras 119–20 (hereafter Appellate Body Report, *US – Shrimp*); WTO, *United States – Measures Affecting the Cross-Border Supply of Gambling and Betting Services – AB-2005-1 – Report of the Appellate Body* (7 April 2005) WT/DS285/AB/R para 7.586 (hereafter Appellate Body Report, *US – Gambling*); WTO, Panel Report, *Argentina – Financial Services* (n 26) para 7.586.

[222] GATS (n 2) art XIV; art XX GATT 1994 (n 67).

[223] CETA (n 54) art 15.3(4); US-Singapore FTA (n 219) art 9.2(4); Dominican Republic-Central America-US FTA (n 219) art 13.2(4); US-Panama TPA (n 219); art 13.2(4) United States-Chile Free Trade Agreement, US-Chile (6 June 2003) KAV 6375 (hereafter US-Chile FTA); art 13.2(4) United States-Morocco Free Trade Agreement (15 June 2004) 44 I.L.M. 544 (hereafter US-Morocco FTA), art 14.2(4) United States-Peru-Trade Promotion Agreement (12 April 2006) (hereafter US-Peru TPA); art

bilateral trade agreements include this wording, but without an accompanying necessity test.[224] Then, in a 2019 article, Micallef proposed complementing Article 2 of the EU-proposed horizontal provisions discussed in Section 4.2 of this chapter with a proviso that the right to protection of personal data and privacy 'is not to be unjustifiably used to circumvent rules for cross-border data transfers for reasons other than the protection of personal data'.[225] Because the provision in the Annex on Telecommunications has not yet been interpreted in practice, however, the rest of this section focuses solely on the chapeau.

The language of the chapeau has been criticized as unclear,[226] 'rife with ambiguity',[227] and 'the vaguest, and therefore the most problematic' requirement of all those found in exception clauses.[228] Just like the interpretation of the necessity test, the interpretation of the chapeau in general exceptions has been uneven throughout the years. Back in 1947, during negotiations of the general exceptions in the ITO Charter, the US Executive Committee on Economic Foreign Policy (ECEFP) warned that the language of the chapeau (which was later included verbatim in the GATT 1947 and subsequently in the GATT 1994 and the GATS) was 'vague and diffuse, making it difficult, if not impossible, to assign specific content to it'.[229] Furthermore, the ECEFP noted that the broad language of the chapeau could 'preclude the possible application of the exceptions to meet the legitimate circumstances for which the exceptions were designed'.[230]

Fast forward to present day, this characterization turned out to be not far from the truth. Reflecting on the interpretation of the chapeau in WTO case law, Riffel neatly describes the interpretative conflict of the chapeau as revolving around the two extremes:

> On one end of the spectrum, the chapeau is read as a stringent threshold requirement, thus reducing the policy space of states to regulate public welfare matters.

14.2(4) United States-Colombia Trade Promotion Agreement (15 May 2012) (hereafter US-Colombia TPA); USMCA (n 219) art 18.3(4); art 13.4(4) CPTPP (n 125).

224 CETA (n 54) art 15.3(4); EU-Central America Association Agreement (n 168) art 192.

225 Micallef, 'Digital Trade in EU FTAs' (n 40) 868.

226 ibid 96 (stating that although the disputes in *US – Gasoline, US – Shrimp, US – Gambling, Brazil – Retreaded Tyres*, and *EC – Seal Products* 'have given the chapeau a high profile, and yet it is still not clear what it requires'). See also Lorand Bartels, 'The Chapeau of the General Exceptions in the WTO GATT and GATS Agreements: A Reconstruction' (2015) 109(55) American Journal of International Law 95.

227 Riffel, 'The Chapeau' (n 65) 143.

228 ibid 176.

229 The chapeau in the New York Draft Charter, which was the subject of the critique, was formulated as follows:

> Subject to the requirement that such measures are not applied in a manner which would constitute a means of arbitrary or unjustifiable discrimination between countries where the same conditions prevail, or a disguised restriction on international trade.

Quoted from Pinchis-Paulsen, 'Trade Multilateralism and U.S. National Security' (n 82) 147, footnote 274 at 151.

230 ibid.

On the other end, the chapeau reaffirms the tenet of good faith, which guides the performance of every treaty in any event.[231]

Just as the necessity test of the general exception, the standard of the chapeau is rather hard to meet and has a very low success rate so far.[232]

4.3.4.1 Blurring the borderline between the chapeau and the necessity test of the general exception

The wording of the test of the chapeau seems to refer to the manner in which a measure is *applied*, rather than the measure itself or its content. This is how this provision was interpreted in one of the early cases applying Article XX GATT 1994.[233] In later cases, however, the Appellate Body departed from this narrow interpretation of the chapeau requirement. It determined that the application of a measure can also 'most often be discerned from the *design, the architecture, and the revealing structure* of a measure'.[234] A WTO Panel took the same approach in the interpretation of the chapeau under Article XIV GATS.[235]

In *US – Shrimp*, the Appellate Body underlined that the 'standards established in the chapeau are ... necessarily broad in scope and reach'. To Cantore, the Appellate Body's 'pervasive analyses regarding the design and structure of the measures under scrutiny' set a high threshold for domestic measures to meet in order to satisfy the test.[236] Put differently, it brings the standard of the chapeau dangerously close to the necessity test of the general exception, which, by definition should be different given that the two standards are a part of the same general exception.[237] Similarly, Riffel argues that because of the Appellate Body's scrutiny of substantive

[231] Riffel, 'The Chapeau' (n 65) 143.

[232] See, eg, ibid; Daniel Rangel, 'WTO General Exceptions: Trade Law's Faulty Ivory Tower Only Two of 48 Attempts to Use the World Trade Organization's GATT Article XX/GATS Article XIV "General Exceptions" Have Ever Succeeded, Public Citizen's Global Trade Watch' Public Citizen (February 2022) <https://www.citizen.org/wp-content/uploads/WTO-General-Exceptions-Paper_-1.pdf> accessed 10 July 2023 (hereafter Rangel 'WTO General Exceptions').

[233] Appellate Body Report, *US – Gasoline* (n 63) 22. See also Appellate Body Report, *US – Shrimp* (n 221) 115; Appellate Body Report, *Brazil – Retreaded Tyres* (n 221) 215. The WTO Panel reiterated the same interpretation of chapeau of art XIV GATS in WTO, *United States – Measures Affecting the Cross-Border Supply of Gambling and Betting Services – Cigarettes – Report of the Panel* (10 November 2004) WT/DS285/R para 6.581 (hereafter Panel Report, *US – Gambling*).

[234] WTO, *European Communities – Measures Prohibiting the Importation and Marketing of Seal Products – Reports of the Appellate Body* (22 May 2014) WT/DS400/AB/R / WT/DS401/AB/R WTO, para 5.302 (hereafter Appellate Body Reports, *EC – Seal Products*), internal footnotes omitted, emphasis added. See also WTO, *Japan – Taxes on Alcoholic Beverages – Report of the Appellate Body* (4 October 1996) WT/DS8/AB/R, WT/DS10/AB/R, WT/DS11/AB/R 29 (hereafter Appellate Body Report, *Japan – Alcoholic Beverages II*); WTO, Appellate Body Report, *US – Shrimp* (n 221) 160.

[235] Panel Report, *Argentina – Financial Services* (n 26) 7.748 (referring to Appellate Body Report, *EC – Seal Products* (n 234) 5.302) and para 7.761.

[236] Cantore, *The Prudential Carve-Out for Financial Services* (n 188) 179. See also Petros C Mavroidis, 'Sealed with a Doubt. EU, Seals, and the WTO' (2015) 3 European Journal of Risk Regulation, Symposium on the EU-Seal Product Case 388, 390.

[237] See also Christian Delev, 'A Moral Stretch? US–Tariff Measures and the Public Morals Exception in WTO Law' (2022) 21 World Trade Review, 249, 255.

exceptions under the chapeau, 'the distinction between substance and administration of the measure became blurred'.[238] He warns that 'false interpretation' of the ambiguities of the chapeau 'could lead adjudicatory bodies to seriously encroach on the Members' regulatory autonomy'.[239]

4.3.4.2 Chapeau as an expression of the principles of good faith and prohibition of abuse of right

The matter was not clarified much when, in relation to the legal standard set by the requirements of 'arbitrary discrimination', 'unjustifiable discrimination' and 'disguised restriction' on international trade of the chapeau, the Appellate Body in *US – Gasoline* held that taking into consideration the object and purpose of the provision and the drafting history, their meaning overlaps.[240] It focused on the 'fundamental theme' behind them rather than the exact meaning of each phrase.[241] The Appellate Body concluded that the 'purpose and object' of the chapeau 'is generally the *prevention of abuse* of the exceptions' of Article XX GATT and to ensure that the exceptions are not invoked 'as to frustrate or defeat the legal obligations of the holder of the right under the substantive rules of the General Agreement'.[242]

In *US – Shrimp*, the Appellate Body had explained that the chapeau is 'a fundamental part of *the balance of rights and obligations* struck by the original framers of the GATT 1947'.[243] This balancing of the rights and obligations according to the Appellate Body is linked to the principle of good faith:[244]

> The chapeau of Article XX is, in fact, but one *expression of the principle of good faith*. This principle, at once a general principle of law and a general principle of international law, controls the exercise of rights by states. *One application of this*

[238] Riffel, 'The Chapeau' (n 65) 176. See also Emily Reid, *Balancing Human Rights, Environmental Protection and International Trade: Lessons from the EU Experience* (Hart Publishing 2015) 247.

[239] Riffel, 'The Chapeau' (n 65) 173.

[240] Appellate Body Report, *US – Gasoline* (n 63) 25. This interpretation has been repeated in relation to art XIV GATS chapeau in WTO, Panel Report, *US – Gambling* (n 233) 6-579–6.580. See also Cantore, *The Prudential Carve-Out for Financial Services* (n 188) 173.

[241] Appellate Body Report, *US – Gasoline* (n 63) 25.

[242] Appellate Body Report, *US – Gasoline* (n 63) 22, 25 (emphasis added). See also WTO, Panel Report, *US – Gambling* (n 233) 6.579–6.580.

[243] Appellate Body Report, *US – Shrimp* (n 221) 157–59.

[244] Whether good faith here is applied as a general principle of international law, or is implied in the text of the chapeau, or by way of interpretation of the chapeau in good faith under art 31(1) VCLT, is debatable. For further discussion, see Thomas Cottier and Krista N Schefer, 'Good Faith and the Protection of Legitimate Expectations in the WTO' in Marco Bronckers and Reinhard Quick (eds), *New Directions in International Economic Law, Essays in Honour of John H. Jackson* (Kluwer Law International 2000) 64–65; Marion Panizzon, *Good Faith in the Jurisprudence of the WTO. The Protection of Legitimate Expectations, Good Faith Interpretation and Fair Dispute Settlement* (Hart Publishing 2006) 109–10 (hereafter Panizzon, *Good Faith in the Jurisprudence of the WTO*); Yoo and Ahn, 'Security Exceptions in the WTO System' (n 76) 442. See also Van den Bossche and Zdouc, *The Law and Policy of the World Trade Organization* (n 80) 573; Alexandre Kiss, 'Abuse of Rights' in Max Planck Encyclopedia of Public International Law (Oxford Public International Law 2006) 14 (hereafter Kiss, 'Abuse of Rights').

> *general principle*, the application widely known as the doctrine of *abus de droit*, prohibits the abusive exercise of a state's rights and enjoins that whenever the assertion of a right impinges on the field covered by [a] treaty obligation, it must be exercised *bona fide, that is to say, reasonably*.[245]

In the same report, the Appellate Body also explained that the location of the 'line of equilibrium' between the rights and obligations of the Members, which the chapeau aims to achieve, 'is not fixed and unchanging; *the line moves* as the kind and the shape of the measures at stake vary and as the facts making up specific cases differ'.[246] The 'actual contours and contents' of 'arbitrary or unjustifiable discrimination' and 'disguised restriction on trade' themselves vary depending on the type of measure under examination and the public policy interest which that measure aims to protect.[247]

Generalizing the application of the good faith and abuse of right standards to the chapeau by the WTO adjudicators, Panizzon concludes that these standards' primary function is to control or push back 'expansive or creationist readings of the exceptions to the liberalization obligation of GATT Article XX', in other words, 'to separate the "wheat" of real trade disputes from the "chaff" of non-trade disputes'.[248] This approach at least suggests that what the standard of the chapeau means is impossible to define *in general*, that is, without its application to the facts of a particular dispute.

4.3.4.3 Factors in assessment of 'arbitrary or unjustifiable discrimination'

Turning to the assessment of whether discrimination is 'arbitrary' or 'unjustifiable', the Appellate Body has primarily considered the *cause or the rationale* of the discrimination in the light of the objectives listed in paragraphs of Article XX.[249] In *US – Tuna II*, the Appellate Body also considered whether 'discrimination can be *reconciled with, or is rationally related to*, the policy objective with respect to which the measure has been provisionally justified under one of the subparagraphs of Article XX.'[250] These are, however, not the only factors that

[245] Appellate Body Report, *US – Shrimp* (n 221) 158–59, internal footnotes omitted, emphasis added. See also Appellate Body Report, *US – Gasoline* (n 63) 22. The same 'reasonableness' requirement the Appellate Body read in art XIV GATS the chapeau in WTO, Appellate Body Report, *US – Gambling* (n 221) 339.

[246] Appellate Body Report, *US – Shrimp* (n 221) 158–59, emphasis added.

[247] Appellate Body Report, *US – Shrimp* (n 221) 120. For a discussion, see Donald McRae, 'GATT Article XX and the WTO Appellate Body' in Marco Bronckers and Reinhard Quick (eds), *New Directions in International Economic Law, Essays in Honour of John H. Jackson* (Kluwer Law International 2000) 225.

[248] Panizzon, *Good Faith in the Jurisprudence of the WTO* (n 244) 115.

[249] Appellate Body Report, *Brazil – Retreaded Tyres* (n 221) 225, 229–30; WTO, *United States – Measures Concerning the Importation, Marketing and Sale of Tuna and Tuna Products – Recourse to Article 21.5 of the DSU by Mexico – Report of the Appellate Body* (20 November 2015) WT/DS381/AB/RW (hereafter Appellate Body Report, *US – Tuna II (Mexico) Article 21.5 – Mexico)* para 7.316.

[250] Appellate Body Report, *US – Tuna II (Mexico) Article 21.5 – Mexico* (n 249) 7.316 (quoting Appellate Body Report, *EC – Seal Products* (n 234) 5.321). See also WTO, *Indonesia – Importation*

could be relevant in the assessment of 'unjustifiable discrimination', depending on the nature of the measure and the circumstances at hand, the effects of the discrimination[251] as well as other factors could also be relevant for the assessment.

Looking at the *cause or rationale* behind a contested measure, the Appellate Body considered, in particular, the following factors:[252] (a) whether the contested measure was a 'rigid and unbending requirement' in that it required other countries to adopt a regulatory programme that is '*essentially the same*' as opposed to '*comparable in effectiveness*';[253] (b) whether the contested measure took into account different circumstances that may occur in territories of other WTO members;[254] and (c) whether the defending party negotiated seriously with all WTO members, as opposed to doing so with some but not with others.[255] In prior cases, the Appellate Body considered a requirement to adopt an 'essentially the same' regulatory framework as failure to take into account different circumstances in other WTO members and negotiating with some but not with others as inconsistent with the chapeau requirement.[256]

Finally, in *US – Gambling*, in applying the chapeau of Article XIV GATS, the key factor that the WTO panel considered in the assessment of 'arbitrary and unjustifiable discrimination between countries where like conditions prevail' and/or a 'disguised restriction on trade' was the *consistency* of the contested measure in which it was applied and enforced domestically.[257] In that particular case, the Panel concluded that the contested measure did not meet the chapeau requirement because of inconsistency between the US federal measure prohibiting the remote supply of gambling and betting services and the interstate measure that permitted interstate pari-mutuel wagering over the telephone or other modes of electronic communication.[258]

of Horticultural Products, Animals and Animal Products – Report of the Appellate Body (9 November 2017) WT/DS477/AB/R, WT/DS478/AB/R, para 5.99.

[251] Appellate Body Report, *Brazil – Retreaded Tyres* (n 221) 229–30.

[252] Appellate Body Report, *Brazil – Retreaded Tyres* (n 221) 225 (referring to Appellate Body Report, *US – Shrimp* (n 221) 163–66, 172, and 177). These factors were also reiterated in Appellate Body Report, *US – Shrimp* (n 221) 5.305.

[253] Appellate Body Report, *US – Shrimp* (n 221) 177(emphasis added); see also Appellate Body Report, *Brazil – Retreaded Tyres* (n 221) 163.

[254] Appellate Body Report, *US – Shrimp* (n 221) 163–65.

[255] ibid 166 and 172.

[256] Appellate Body Report, *US – Shrimp* (n 221) 166, 172.

[257] Panel Report, *US – Gambling* (n 233) 6.584, 6.607.

[258] ibid 6.599.

4.3.5 Towards the goldilocks exception for privacy and data protection in future EU trade agreements

Building on the discussion in Sections 4.3.1–4.3.4, this section first explains why any of the standards of non-circumvention, non-avoidance, and reasonableness are better equipped as a prototype for a new threshold in the future digital trade exception than the standard of the chapeau of the general exception. Second, it argues that the wording of the exception matters only up to a point and that a limiting mechanism ensuring more predictability and parties' control over the interpretation of the exception is needed.

4.3.5.1 Undesirability of replicating the standard of chapeau in digital trade exception for privacy and data protection

As explained in previous sections, the interpretation of the prohibition of 'arbitrary or unjustifiable discrimination' or of a 'disguised restriction on international trade' contained in the chapeau of the general exceptions is much more elaborate and nuanced than the current understanding of the other three standards considered in Sections 4.3.1–4.3.3. However, it is precisely the availability of extensive WTO case law on the chapeau that presents the biggest risks in replicating the same standard in the future digital trade exception for privacy and data protection.

First, on the face of it, the standard of the chapeau appears to be less stringent than that of the necessity test of the general exception, because it aims at the assessment of the administration of a contested measure rather than its content and does not require that the measure should be the least trade restrictive. However, in practice, its interpretation has moved it dangerously close to the necessity test. The latter, as explained in Chapter 2 of this book, does not leave the EU enough regulatory autonomy to protect privacy and the protection of personal data in line with its constitutional framework.

Second, one of the factors in the assessment of 'arbitrary or unjustifiable discrimination', namely, whether the contested measure requires other countries to adopt a regulatory framework that is '*essentially the same*' as opposed to '*comparable in effectiveness*', is likely to be at odds with the requirement of 'essential equivalence' that the EU constitutional framework (as interpreted by the highest court of the EU, the Court of Justice of the European Union) imposes on other countries' legal frameworks as a condition for unrestricted transfers of personal data from the EEA to their territory.[259]

In relation to these risks, one could raise two objections. First, 'unjustifiability', which appears in the standard of the chapeau, imposes a lower threshold for contested measures than 'necessity'. As the Appellate Body explained in

[259] See Section 2.2.4. For a discussion about the 'essential equivalence' requirement in EU data protection law, see Section 5.2.2.

Australia – Tobacco Plain Packaging (Honduras) Report in relation to Article 20 of the TRIPS Agreement (which prohibits unjustifiable encumbrance on the use of trademarks) and the 'necessity' requirement in other provisions of the TRIPS Agreement:

> reference to the notion of justifiability rather than necessity in Article 20 suggests that the degree of connection between the encumbrance on the use of a trademark imposed and the objective pursued reflected through the term 'unjustifiably' is lower than it would have been had a term conveying the notion of 'necessity' been used in this provision. Accordingly, a consideration of whether the use of a trademark has not been 'unjustifiably' encumbered should not be equated with the necessity test within the meaning of Article XX of the GATT 1994 or Article 2.2 of the TBT Agreement.[260]

This insight could be used to argue that the standard of the chapeau—due to the absence of similarity with 'necessity'—imposes a lower threshold than 'necessity'.

The second objection is that despite similarity of wording, even if the chapeau standard is replicated in the future digital trade exception for privacy and data protection, it does not necessarily have the same meaning. For example, in *Australia – Tobacco Plain Packaging (Honduras)*, the Appellate Body also held that 'arbitrary or unjustifiable discrimination' in the chapeau of Article XX of the GATT 1994 'does not imply that the meaning imparted to this term in other contexts can be easily transplanted to the interpretation of Article 20 of the TRIPS Agreement'.[261] Similarly, the WTO Secretariat, in its Note on 'Necessity Tests' in the WTO, explained that 'even if there are similar thematic issues arising in the "necessity tests" in the different provisions in the WTO agreements, an interpretation developed in the context of a specific case or specific provision is *not necessarily transposable* to other provisions'.[262] As a result, '"necessity tests" contained in different WTO Agreements or in different provisions of the same Agreement cannot necessarily be used interchangeably'.[263]

In response to these objections, this book contends that although the meaning of the same terms is not 'easily' or 'necessarily' transplantable or transposable, such transplantation or transposition is certainly not impossible, especially when the same words are used in another exception. WTO practice contains several circumstances in which this has happened. For example, there has been extensive cross-pollination between the interpretation of the notion of 'likeness' in the MFN, and

[260] Appellate Body Report, *Australia – Tobacco Plain Packaging (Honduras and Dominican Republic)* (n 197), para 6.647.

[261] ibid 6.646. See also ibid 6.627.

[262] WTO, Note by Secretariat, 'Necessity tests' in the WTO (2 December 2003) S/WPDR/W/27 para 12 (emphasis added).

[263] ibid 83.

national treatment provisions in the GATT 1994 and the GATS (despite the differences between them[264]), as well as between the general exceptions in Article XX GATT 1994 and Article XIV GATS—irrespective of the public policy objective involved—in WTO case law.[265] Even outside the WTO system, the WTO case law is likely to be very influential on adjudicators appointed in the framework of bilateral and regional trade agreements. For example, Article 26.22(2) the EU-New Zealand FTA explicitly states:

> The panel shall also take into account relevant interpretations in reports of WTO panels and the Appellate Body adopted by the Dispute Settlement Body of the WTO.[266]

Prevailing uncertainty on whether, and to what extent, trade adjudicators may import WTO jurisprudence on the chapeau of the general exception when interpreting the digital trade exception on privacy and data protection weighs strongly against the use of the chapeau's threshold in such exception.

4.3.5.2 The need for a restrictive mechanism in the digital trade exception for privacy and data protection

As opposed to the standard of the chapeau, the non-circumvention, non-avoidance, and reasonableness standards would be more suitable than the 'it deems appropriate' test to achieve the EU's goals in liberalizing cross-border data flows while preserving its autonomy to protect privacy and the protection of personal data as fundamental rights, as well as the broader goal of preserving the rules-based international trading system. This book argues that *any* of these three standards are suitable, because, as illustrated above, each of them is interpreted in reference to the others. Substantively, each of those standards affords broader regulatory space than the necessity test of the general exception, on the one hand, but narrower regulatory space than the 'it considers necessary' test of the national security exception (and, therefore, the 'it deems appropriate test' proposed in the EU horizontal provisions), on the other hand. The fact that the principles of good faith and the prohibition of abuse of right constitute the common denominator for

264 See, eg, Mireille Cossy, 'Determining "Likeness" under the GATS: Squaring the Circle?' (2006) World Trade Organization Economic Research and Statistics Division, WTO Staff Working Paper ERSD-2006-08, 4 <https://www.wto.org/english/res_e/reser_e/ersd200608_e.pdf> accessed 10 July 2023.

265 On cross-pollination between the interpretation of the general exceptions in the GATT and the GATS, see Section 2.4.2. On cross-pollination between the interpretation of 'likeness' in the GATT and the GATS, see, eg, WTO, *Argentina – Measures Relating to Trade in Goods and Services – Report of the Appellate Body* (14 April 2016) WT/DS453/AB/R and Add.1, para 6.119, referring to WTO, Appellate Body Report, *EC – Seal Products* (n 234) 5.90, 5.87–5.88, and 5.101 (noting that '[its] interpretation of Articles II:1 and XVII of the GATS chimes with the Appellate Body's interpretation of the most-favoured-nation and national treatment obligations in the context of the GATT 1994'.).

266 See also art 28.12(3) CPTPP (n 125).

the interpretation of those thresholds ensures their flexibility and the possibility of tailoring their interpretation to different situations.

This flexibility, however, also has drawbacks. For example, the WTO case law on the chapeau and the national security exceptions—the bodies of WTO jurisprudence interpreting the principles of good faith and the abuse of right in relation to exceptions from trade obligations—suggest that the content of these principles is a moving target. Academic research on these principles confirms this conceptualization.

Good faith is a 'broad and value oriented concept'.[267] When interpreting good faith, the WTO adjudicators usually uncover the underlying conflict of interests, which they then balance according to the case-by-case context.[268] The legal value that the principle of good faith has in a particular (WTO) trade dispute depends on the functions of adjudicators, and ranges between regulative (*infra legem*, in particular as applied in the *US – Shrimp* by the Appellate Body), corrective or jurisdictional (*contra legem*, in particular as embodied by the principle of prohibition of the abuse of right), and gap-filling or constitutive (*praeter legem*) functions.[269] Panizzon rightly notes in relation to the abuse of right that its '"elasticity" risks giv[ing] too much power into the hands of international tribunals'.[270]

Kotzur emphasizes that given the abstractness of the principle of good faith, 'it may inevitably contain the risk of an all too ambitious judicial activism'.[271] These risks are exacerbated by the absence of 'checks and balances to guarantee that international tribunals will dispose of this power responsibly'.[272] It is for these reasons that even the proponents of the good faith doctrine, such as Lauterpacht, call for its application with caution and restraint.[273] Ziegler and Baumgartner likewise warn that 'in the absence of limitations on the adjudicatory mandate, tribunals should be careful not to engage in an overly broad use of the principle of good faith, which could negatively impact the quality of the legal reasoning and thus the legitimacy

[267] Andreas R Ziegler and Jorun Baumgartner, 'Good Faith as a General Principle of (International) Law' in Andrew D Mitchell, M Sornarajah, and Tania Voon (eds), *Good Faith and International Economic Law* (OUP (2015), 31–32 (hereafter Ziegler and Baumgartner, 'Good Faith as a General Principle'); Markus Kotzur, 'Good Faith (Bona Fide)' in *Max Planck Encyclopedias of International Law* (Oxford Public International Law 2009) (hereafter Kotzur, 'Good Faith (Bona Fide)') para 26.

[268] Panizzon, *Good Faith in the Jurisprudence of the WTO* (n 244) 109–10. See Ziegler and Baumgartner, 'Good Faith as a General Principle' (n 267) 31–34; Kiss, 'Abuse of Rights' (n 244) 4.

[269] Panizzon, *Good Faith in the Jurisprudence of the WTO* (n 244) 110, relying on the work of Schwarzenberger.

[270] ibid 34.

[271] Kotzur, 'Good Faith (Bona Fide)' (n 267) para 26; Ziegler and Baumgartner, 'Good Faith as a General Principle' (n 267) 10 (noting that 'good faith has a firm place as both a facilitating and a restraining agent'. Yet, as 'an inherently abstract notion,' it leaves 'a broad margin of discretion to the person deciding whether the principle of good faith has been respected'.).

[272] Panizzon, *Good Faith in the Jurisprudence of the WTO* (n 244) 34.

[273] Hersch Lauterpacht, *The Development of International Law by the International Court* (Stevens & Sons 1958) 164 (stating that '[t]he doctrine of abuse of rights is therefore an instrument which, apart from other reasons calling for caution in the administration of international justice, must be wielded with studied restraint'.).

of the arbitral process'.[274] What 'careful' and 'responsibly' means in international trade context is a judgment call. For Panizzon, this means 'in accordance with the requirements of international peace and justice and in the light of the "growing integration of the international community," as opposed to giving in to unilateral pressure by militaries or economically superior world powers'.[275] In practice, the normative values guiding trade adjudicators in the application of these general concepts, as Chapter 3 has demonstrated, are often determined by the dominant discourse adopted by those adjudicators.

To sum up, the circular interpretation of 'non-circumvention', 'non-avoidance', and 'reasonableness' and their ultimate anchoring in the general principles of good faith and the prohibition of abuse of right, as interpretative tools, allow adjudicators to determine the meaning of these standards on a case-by-case basis. This also means that after a trade agreement has been negotiated, the parties to such an agreement have little influence on the interpretation of the agreement. This book contends that it is to a large extent the *lack of trust* in international trade adjudication, as well as internal policy agenda, that has led the EU to use the broadest of trade law exceptions—the national security exception—as a prototype for the digital trade exception for privacy and data protection to minimize the risk that trade adjudicators will shift the meaning of the exception towards a higher threshold for domestic privacy and data protection rules than intended by the drafters. This argument ties into the broader debate on the WTO legitimacy crisis and the rule-making power of adjudicating bodies.[276]

To ameliorate such lack of trust, the use of 'non-circumvention', 'non-avoidance', and 'reasonableness' thresholds in the future digital trade exception (rather than the 'it deems appropriate' threshold) should be accompanied by a restrictive mechanism controlling the adjudicators' power of interpretation. To be sufficiently robust, this restrictive mechanism should include an *institutional* component and not merely amount to a change of wording of exceptions.[277] A mere change of

[274] Ziegler and Baumgartner, 'Good Faith as a General Principle' (n 267) 36.

[275] Panizzon, *Good Faith in the Jurisprudence of the WTO* (n 244) 34.

[276] For a discussion, see, eg, Ingo Venzke, *How Interpretation Makes International Law: On Semantic Change and Normative Twists* (OUP 2012) 190–95. See also Daniel C Esty, 'The World Trade Organization's Legitimacy Crisis' (2002) 1(1) World Trade Review 7; Joseph HH Weiler, 'The Rule of Lawyers and the Ethos of Diplomats: Reflections on the Internal and External Legitimacy of WTO Dispute Settlement' (2001) 35(2) *Journal of World Trade* 191; Robert Howse, 'From Politics to Technocracy--And Back Again: The Fate of the Multilateral Trading Regime' (2002) 96 American Journal of International Law 94; Andrew Lang, *World Trade Law after Neoliberalism* (OUP Online 2011) 313ff; Manfred Elsig, 'The World Trade Organization's Legitimacy Crisis: What Does the Beast Look Like?' (2007) 41(1) Journal of World Trade 75; Robert Howse and Kalypso Nicolaidis, 'Enhancing WTO Legitimacy: Constitutionalization or Global Subsidiarity?' (2003) 16(1) Governance: An International Journal of Policy, Administration, and Institutions 73; Robert Howse, 'The World Trade Organization 20 Years On: Global Governance by Judiciary' (2016) 27(1) European Journal of International Law 9, 11, 75.

[277] cf Rangel, 'WTO General Exceptions' (n 232) 7. See also Meyer, 'The Political Economy of WTO Exceptions' (n 166), proposing to introduce a 'predominant motive test' when interpreting and drafting exception clauses.

wording of the exceptions is not enough to limit the discretion of adjudicating bodies. As Chapter 3 has demonstrated, the interpretation of exceptions changes with the shift in the discourse governing such interpretation, for it provides the normative lens with which the interpretation is examined.

One example of such an institutional mechanism is the mechanism created under the Understanding on the interpretation of the prudential carve-out in CETA, already mentioned above.[278] On the one hand, the Understanding contains high-level principles intended to guide the interpretation of the prudential carve-out by investment tribunals. For example, Principle 8.a states that 'a Party may establish and enforce measures that provide a higher level of prudential protection than those set out in common international prudential commitments', while Principle 8.b requires investment tribunals to 'defer to the highest degree possible to regulations and practices in the Parties' respective jurisdictions and to the decisions and factual determinations, including risk assessments, made by financial regulatory authorities'. On the other hand, the Understanding regulates the role of the Financial Services Committee (which includes representatives of authorities in charge of financial services policy with expertise in the field)[279] in investment disputes concerning the prudential carve-out. In particular, the Understanding determines that the Committee 'shall decide whether and, if so, to what extent the prudential carve-out is a valid defence to a claim'. This decision, as well as the decision of the CETA Joint Committee (which is competent to make this decision if the Financial Services Committee does not provide its position within a specified term), is binding on the investment tribunal in the dispute in question.[280] Thus, if the Financial Services Committee or the CETA Joint Committee conclude that the prudential carve-out is the valid defence to all parts of the claim in their entirety, the 'investor is deemed to have withdrawn its claim and the proceedings are discontinued'.[281]

Looking ahead, if the EU should decide to create a committee for privacy and data protection in a future trade agreement, further research is required to determine what the structure, composition, and exact role of such a committee should be. This research is, however, beyond the scope of this book. What can be said at this juncture is that it is important to ensure that the conferral of certain powers on such a committee does not overstep the EU's competence and constitutional

[278] Annex 13-B CETA (n 54), Understanding on the Application of Articles 13.16.1 and 13.21.

[279] CETA (n 54) art 13.18. For Canada, the Committee representative is an official from the Department of Finance Canada or its successor, and for the European Union, the Committee representative is an official of the Directorate-General for Financial Stability, Financial Services and Capital Markets Union (DG FISMA). See Patrick Leblond, 'CETA and Financial Services: What to Expect?' (2016) CIGI Papers No 91, p. 3 <https://www.cigionline.org/sites/default/files/cigi_paper_no.91_web.pdf> accessed 10 July 2023.

[280] Annex 13-B CETA (n 54), Understanding on the Application of Articles 13.16.1 and 13.21; art 13.21(4) CETA.

[281] CETA (n 54) art 13.21(4).

boundaries and that such committee does not undermine supervision of data protection rules in the EU by an independent authority required by Article 8(3) of the EU Charter.[282]

4.4 Conclusion

This chapter has addressed the international trade aspect of the catch-22 problem identified in Chapter 2 of this book, represented by a possible clash between the EU's constitutional framework on privacy and data protection, on the one hand, and existing international trade commitments relating to cross-border data flows, on the other. It has demonstrated that the horizontal provisions on cross-border data flows and the protection of privacy and personal data, proposed by the European Commission in 2018, are not an optimal way to achieve the goals of the EU's digital trade policy on data. They are unlikely to contribute to the liberalization of cross-border data flows from other countries into Europe and may contribute to further undermining of the rules-based international trading system. This chapter has proposed several ways to improve the horizontal provisions with a specific focus on the threshold of the future digital trade exception for privacy and data protection. It has argued that a 'non-circumvention', 'non-avoidance,' or 'reasonableness' threshold, anchored on the principles of good faith and prohibition of abuse of rights, and complemented by a restrictive mechanism controlling for trade adjudicators' rule-making power, would be better suited to achieve the EU's digital trade policy goals, as compared to the 'it deems appropriate' threshold proposed in the EU's horizontal provisions.

282 For a discussion on this issue, see, eg, Wolfgang Weiß, 'Delegation to treaty Bodies in EU Agreements: Constitutional Constraints and Proposals for Strengthening the European Parliament' (2018) 14 European Constitutional Law Review 532.

5

EU Framework for Transfers of Personal Data

Critique and Directions for Reform

5.1 Introduction

This chapter discusses potential solutions to the problem of the 'two necessities' identified in Chapter 2 of the book from an EU Charter of Fundamental Rights (EU Charter)[1] and the European data protection law perspectives. Chapter 2 explained that several elements of the current EU framework for transfers of personal data outside the European Economic Area (EEA)[2] could be found in violation of the European Union's (EU) international trade obligations under the General Agreement on Trade in Services (GATS)[3] and that these violations may not be justified under the trade law necessity test of the GATS general exception for privacy and data protection. At the same time, Chapter 2 also argued that the trade law necessity test requires the EU to derogate from the fundamental rights to the protection of privacy and personal data further than the EU Charter necessity test of Article 52(1) of the EU Charter permits, *assuming* that the current General Data Protection Regulation (GDPR)[4] framework for transfers of personal data outside the EEA (which is the source of tension between the EU data protection law and the EU's trade law commitments) is fit for its constitutional function under the EU Charter. This chapter goes a step further and challenges this assumption, arguing that the current GDPR framework is not or no longer able to perform its constitutional functions.

Chapter 2 proposed that the solution to the 'two necessities' problem should be twofold: on the one hand, the EU should negotiate a more lenient exception for

[1] Charter of Fundamental Rights of the European Union [2000] OJ C 364/1 (hereafter EU Charter).

[2] The European Economic Area consists of the member states of the European Union and countries of the European Free Trade Association (EFTA): Norway, Iceland, and Lichtenstein. 'Glossary: European Economic Area (EEA)'(*Eurostat*) <https://ec.europa.eu/eurostat/statistics-explained/index.php/Glossary:European_Economic_Area_(EEA)#:~:text=The%20European%20Economic%20Area%2C%20abbreviated,force%20on%201%20January%201994> accessed 10 July 2023.

[3] General Agreement on Trade in Services, Annex 1B to Marrakesh Agreement Establishing the World Trade Organization [1994] 1869 UNTS 183, 33 ILM 1167 (hereafter GATS).

[4] Regulation (EU) 2016/679 of the European Parliament and of the Council of 27 April 2016 on the protection of natural persons with regard to the processing of personal data and on the free movement of such data, and repealing Directive 95/46/EC [2016] OJ L 119/1.

Governing Cross-Border Data Flows. Svetlana Yakovleva, Oxford University Press. © Svetlana Yakovleva 2024.
DOI: 10.1093/oso/9780192899248.003.0005

privacy and data protection in its future trade agreements (the issue discussed in Chapter 4) and, on the other hand, the EU framework itself should be reformed in a way more compliant with EU's existing and future international trade law obligations and business practices, while respecting the EU's constitutional boundaries. This chapter argues that this reform is also necessary to restore the constitutional function of the EU framework for transfers of personal data outside the EEA and proposes directions of such reform within the boundaries of the EU Charter.

The arguments in this chapter are structured along the following three broad issues: (1) the constitutional boundaries that the EU Charter imposes on EU secondary law governing transfers of personal data outside the EEA; (2) the inability of the current EU framework for transfers of personal data outside the EEA to perform its constitutional function; and (3) the reform proposal for such framework in response to changing (geo)political and economic circumstances.

The *first* issue (the constitutional boundaries set by the EU Charter on EU secondary law) is a relatively unexplored and highly dynamic topic in current case law of the Court of Justice of the European Union (CJEU) and academic debates. Against the backdrop of rising geopolitical tensions, the interpretation of the EU framework for transfers of personal data, including its constitutional content and boundaries, has also become a (geo)political issue. The key CJEU judgments on transfers—the *Schrems I*[5] and *Schrems II*[6], coloured by the (geo)political tensions between the EU and the United States—have created uncertainty as to exactly what the constitutional content and boundaries of this framework are.[7] This uncertainty not only makes it challenging to apply the relevant GDPR rules in practice, it also contributes to the tensions of the EU framework for transfers of personal data outside the EEA with international trade law (as Chapter 2 explains) and complicates efforts to reform the GDPR framework in a way that would not overstep such constitutional boundaries.

This chapter approaches this issue through the prism of Article 52(1) of the Charter, which contains two layers of requirements with respect to derogations from fundamental rights:[8] such derogations must respect the 'essence' of those

[5] *Maximillian Schrems v Data Protection Commissioner* [2015] ECLI:EU:C:2015:650 (hereafter *Schrems I*).

[6] *Facebook Ireland and Schrems* [2020] ECLI:EU:C:2020:559, paras 150–202 (hereafter *Schrems II*).

[7] See eg Lorenzo Dalla Corte, 'On Proportionality in the Data Protection Jurisprudence of the CJEU' (2022) 12(4) International Data Privacy Law 259 (hereafter Dalla Corte, 'On Proportionality in the Data Protection Jurisprudence of the CJEU'), stating at 272 that '[t]he Luxemburg court's adjudication of data protection controversies involved a broad variety of issues that have clear and weighty political relevance, from trans-Atlantic data sharing to mass surveillance, bulk collection, and data retention.' and at 275 '. . . the emergence of the concept of essence in the Luxemburg court's jurisprudence, by introducing a means of adjudication alternative to proportionality testing, increases the potential arbitrariness of its limitations analysis, while providing a very marginal addition to the protective capacity of the right to personal data protection'.

[8] This so-called bifurcated model (where a constitutional right is divided into an irreducible core and periphery) discussed in more detail in Section 5.2.3, as opposed to a relativist model, has become more prominent in recent literature and CJEU case law. For discussion, see Jacob Weinrib, 'The Essence of Rights and the Limits of Proportionality' (2023) The Promise of Legality: Critical Reflections upon

fundamental rights and be 'strictly necessary'[9] and proportionate. In other words, the essence (or the core) of fundamental rights cannot be interfered with by secondary EU law. Derogations from fundamental rights that respect the essence of the fundamental rights are possible, provided they meet the necessity and proportionality tests. Against this backdrop, this chapter argues that there is a dynamic relationship between the GDPR (as a secondary EU law instrument) and the EU Charter (as a primary law instrument), in that EU secondary law has, to some extent, influenced the essence of the fundamental rights to the protection of personal data. At the same time, only a few aspects of the current framework for transfers of personal data constitute the *essence* of the fundamental rights to privacy, to the protection of personal data, and to effective judicial remedy (in the context of the first two rights), which cannot be changed by secondary EU legislation. The standard of 'essential equivalence', which, following the CJEU *Schrems II* judgment, can be seen as the constitutional benchmark for the secondary law framework on transfers of personal data, does not constitute a part of the essence of the above-mentioned fundamental rights.[10] Instead, this concept is an instantiation of the strict necessity and proportionality requirements under Article 52(1) of the EU Charter in the context of transfers of personal data. It governs the balancing of the above-mentioned fundamental rights against competing policy objectives, primarily economic benefits inherent in unrestricted cross-border flows of personal data, and the national security interests of foreign countries. Building on this normative legal framework under EU law, this chapter contends that the EU legislator has sufficient flexibility to change the design of the rules currently codified in Chapter V of the GDPR.

The *second* issue is the inability of the current EU framework for transfers of personal data under Chapter V of the GDPR to perform its constitutional function against the background of circumstances that have changed since this framework was first designed. As already discussed in detail in previous chapters, this framework's main function is to prevent circumvention of the high level of personal data protection in the EU and, ultimately, to ensure 'effective and complete' protection of fundamental rights.[11] The problem is, however, that there is a widening

the Work of TRS Allan <https://ssrn.com/abstract=4321570> accessed 10 July 2023 (forthcoming) (hereafter Weinrib, 'The Essence of Rights and the Limits of Proportionality'); Orlando Scarcello, 'Preserving the 'Essence' of Fundamental Rights under Article 52(1) of the Charter: A Sisyphean Task?' (2020) 16(4) European Constitutional Law Review 647 (hereafter Scarcello, 'Preserving the 'Essence' of Fundamental Rights under Article 52(1) of the Charter').

[9] As explained in Section 2.3.3, in the context of the derogations from the fundamental rights to privacy and data protection under the EU Charter, the CJEU has elevated the 'necessity' threshold under Art. 52(1) EU Charter to 'strict necessity'.

[10] See also Tobias Naef, *Data Protection without Data Protectionism: The Right to Protection of Personal Data and Data Transfers in EU Law and International Trade Law* (Springer Cham 2023) 206 (hereafter Naef, *Data Protection without Data Protectionism*).

[11] *Google Spain* [2014] ECLI:EU:C:2014:317, para 34 (hereafter *Google Spain*); *Wirtschaftsakademie* [2018] ECLI:EU:C:2018:388, para 28 (hereafter *Wirtschaftsakademie*); *Jehovan todistajat* [2018]

gap between 'reality and illusion' in the EU framework for transfers of personal data,[12] to be more specific: an *illusion* that the current EU legal framework can effectively provide continuous and high level of fundamental rights protection with respect to European data irrespective of its location, and the *reality* which is that the EU framework for transfers of personal data is rife with uncertainties and existing mechanisms do not meet that standard in practice, because of faults in their design, challenges of enforcement, or both.

In legal terms, this gap between reality and illusion translates into a gap in legal protection of the fundamental rights to privacy and the protection of personal data. Article 7 of the Treaty on the Functioning of the European Union (TFEU)[13] requires that the EU 'shall ensure consistency between its policies and activities, taking all of its objectives into account and in accordance with the principle of conferral of powers'. Consistency and uniformity in the interpretation of EU law are also essential to preserve the autonomy of the EU legal order.[14] Gaps in the protection of fundamental rights, which result from failure to ensure such consistency by the EU, however, risk undermining the effective and complete protection of fundamental rights required by the EU Charter.[15] Avoiding gaps in the protection of fundamental rights, therefore, is an important consideration in the course of GDPR interpretation by the CJEU.[16]

This chapter breaks down this gap in legal protection into four major weaknesses of the EU framework for transfers of personal data outside the EEA. The overall lack of enforcement of the EU rules on transfers of personal data outside the EEA in general and the requirements introduced by the CJEU *Schrems I* and *Schrems II* judgments in particular, as already alluded to earlier in this book, have widened the gap between the high, idealistic level of protection of personal data

ECLI:EU:C:2018:551, para 66 (hereafter *Jehovan todistajat*); *Fashion ID* [2019] ECLI:EU:C:2019:629, paras 66–70 (hereafter *Fashion ID*).

[12] Christopher Kuner raised this problem already back in 2017, following the CJEU *Schrems I* judgment. The gap between reality and illusion of EU data transfers' regime discussed by Kuner has not only closed but even widened since then, as Section 5.3 explains. See Christopher Kuner, 'Reality and Illusion in EU Data Transfer Regulation Post Schrems' (2017) 18(4) German Law Journal 881 (hereafter Kuner, 'Reality and Illusion in EU Data Transfer Regulation Post Schrems').

[13] Consolidated Version of the Treaty on the Functioning of the European Union [2008] OJ (C 115) 47 (hereafter TFEU).

[14] See Peter Van Elsuwege, 'Judicial Review and the Common Foreign and Security Policy: Limits to the Gap-Filling Role of the Court of Justice' (2021) 58(6) Common Market Law Review 1731, 1755.

[15] See Christopher Kuner, 'Protecting EU Data outside EU Borders under the GDPR' (2023) 60(1) Common Market Law Review 77, 94 (hereafter Kuner, 'Protecting EU Data outside EU Borders under the GDPR').

[16] See, eg, Andreas Häuselmann, 'The ECJ's First Landmark Case on Automated Decision-Making: A Report from the Oral Hearing before the First Chamber' (*European Law Blog*, 20 February 2023) <https://europeanlawblog.eu/2023/02/20/the-ecjs-first-landmark-case-on-automated-decision-making-a-report-from-the-oral-hearing-before-the-first-chamber/> accessed 10 July 2023, showing a particular focus of the CJEU on not leaving a lacuna in the protection of data subjects' rights when interpreting the GDPR. See also *OQ v Land Hesse* [2023] ECLI:EU:C:2023:220, Opinion of AG Pikamäe, para 43.

aspired by the GDPR, and the actual level of protection on the ground. It underlies the entire discussion as a *fil rouge* of all the weaknesses discussed in this chapter.

The first weakness is the foreign surveillance issue. As already mentioned in Section 2.4.2.2, restrictions on transfers of personal data in general are unlikely to be able to protect Europeans against foreign countries' surveillance practices. But even assuming that such restrictions could *in theory* address the foreign surveillance issue, Section 5.3.1 argues that this is not the case with respect to the current GDPR mechanisms for systematic transfers of personal data outside the EEA. Despite the recent *Schrems II* judgment, there is a persistent qualitative gap between adequacy decisions, on the one hand, and appropriate safeguards under Article 46 of the GDPR, on the other (both of which serve as mechanisms for systematic transfers). In other words, the level of protection ensured by adequacy decisions, even after considering their flaws, is higher than the level of protection that can be achieved through private law mechanisms under Article 46 of the GDPR.

In *Schrems II*, the CJEU shifted the requirements of assessing the adequacy of foreign legal frameworks towards data controllers (in most cases companies) that transfer data, many if not most of which lack the necessary expertise, resources, and incentives to conduct those assessments, or even to the Data Protection Authorities (DPAs),[17] which lack human and financial resources. This is unlikely to solve the problem. The fact is that three years after the *Schrems II* judgment, most public and private enforcement cases with respect to the mechanisms under Article 46 concern transfers of personal data to the United States, whose legal regime for the protection of personal data was pronounced not being 'essentially equivalent' by the CJEU itself, or to China, whose legal framework lacks democratic controls over government surveillance and, therefore, is unlikely to meet the 'essentially equivalent' standard. This chapter argues that the EU should address the foreign surveillance problem—which is the main reason why issues relating to transfers of personal data land at the CJEU—on the international level rather than through its own secondary law.

The second weakness lies, as this chapter argues, in the inconsistent interpretation of the scope of application of GDPR Chapter V rules and their interaction with Article 3 of the GDPR in such a way that protection does not (fully) apply to certain transmissions of personal data outside the EEA.[18]

The third weakness concerns the deficiencies of adequacy decisions. These decisions are prone to political pressures in the context of EU trade policy. In addition, adequacy decisions create a gap in legal protection of fundamental rights due to lack of regular reviews of the assessment on which the adequacy decisions are based (the 'snapshot' problem), the difficulties of enforcing individual rights in

[17] DPAs are independent supervisory authorities under Article 8(3) of the EU Charter and Chapter VI of the GDPR.

[18] See also Kuner, 'Protecting EU data outside EU borders under the GDPR' (n 15) 90.

foreign jurisdictions (the 'heavy burden' problem), and the inadequacy of onward transfer mechanism embedded in the adequacy decisions (the 'onward transfer' problem).

The fourth and last weakness is, on a more abstract level, the limited scalability of the current regime for personal data transfers in Chapter V of the GDPR in view of the technological developments that have occurred since the 1990s, when the core of the framework was first designed. While the GDPR and the EU Charter set a high standard for the protection of personal data transferred outside the EEA, this standard is unattainable in practice when applied to tens or hundreds of gigabytes of data flowing across borders each second.

The *third* and final issue addressed in this chapter is a proposal for a new EU framework for transfers of personal data outside the EEA. Relying on the analysis in this book and existing reform proposals in the literature, this chapter suggests three directions or lines of thought on how to improve the framework of Chapter V of the GDPR, reflecting possible short-, medium-, and long-term strategies for the EU in this area.

The chapter proceeds as follows. Section 5.2 examines the constitutional contours of the EU's framework for transfers of personal data, including the *marge de manoeuvre* available to the EU legislator in designing such a framework. Section 5.3 addresses the weaknesses of the current framework in Chapter V of the GDPR. Section 5.4 elaborates on three directions of thought on how to ameliorate these weaknesses through a reform of the GDPR's Chapter V. Section 5.5 concludes.

5.2 Constitutional Contours of the EU's Framework for Transfers of Personal Data

The EU maintains a 'multi-level protection of fundamental rights' comprised of primary and secondary law, which applies equally to the rights to privacy and the protection of personal data.[19] As already explained, Articles 7 and 8 of the EU Charter protect the rights to privacy and the protection of personal data as fundamental rights. The EU legislator's competence underlying the adoption of the GDPR is provided by Article 16 TFEU, namely, the competence to 'lay down the rules relating to the protection of individuals with regard to the processing of personal data'.[20]

This section tackles two questions regarding the relationship between the EU's primary and secondary data protection rules in the context of cross-border

[19] Maja Brkan, 'The Essence of the Fundamental Rights to Privacy and Data Protection: Finding the Way through the Maze of the CJEU's Constitutional Reasoning' (2019) 20 German Law Journal, 864, 865 (hereafter Brkan 'The Essence of the Fundamental Rights to Privacy and Data Protection').

[20] Consolidated Version of the Treaty on the Functioning of the European Union [2008] OJ (C 115) 47.

transfers of personal data. First, whether, and to what extent, the *design of the current framework* for transfers of personal data in Chapter V of the GDPR is grounded in the EU Charter. Another way to approach this question is to ask which parts of the framework cannot be changed without running afoul of the EU Charter requirements for data transfers. The second, and more general, question is how much leeway, in the view of the EU Charter, the EU legislator has in designing the mechanisms for transfers of personal data in the GDPR.

5.2.1 The relationship between the EU Charter and EU secondary data protection law

In the hierarchy of the EU law, secondary law is, as the name suggests, below primary law, which, in turn, has the highest legal force in the EU.[21] Therefore, from a formalistic perspective, secondary law should be consistent with primary law. However, in practice—as demonstrated by CJEU jurisprudence—this relationship is not as clear-cut as it may seem[22] and is somewhat underexplored in academic literature, especially when it comes to the relationship between the EU Charter and the EU framework for data transfers.

Based on CJEU case law, Syrpis argues that EU secondary law may relate to EU primary law in at least three different ways. First, as just mentioned, in some cases, the CJEU views primary law as hierarchically superior to secondary law, meaning that secondary law is rendered inapplicable when in conflict with primary law. Second, in other cases, the CJEU interprets primary and secondary law 'neutrally', meaning that interpretation of primary law affects the interpretation of secondary law and vice versa. Third, in yet other cases, secondary law has a significant impact on the CJEU's interpretation of primary law and, to some extent, determines its content.[23] In sum, Syrpis claims that the CJEU's approach on this issue has been inconsistent, which gives the EU legislator the power to affect the CJEU's interpretation of EU Treaties.[24]

Thus, the modes of relationship between primary and secondary law that can be deduced from CJEU case law broadly represent two diverging approaches to the 'proper' relationship between EU primary and secondary law. The first, which this chapter calls a *static* approach, puts the emphasis on the formal powers of the CJEU to interpret secondary law in the light of primary law and invalidate the former when contrary to the latter,[25] and can be seen as a hierarchical relationship

[21] Paul Craig and Gráinne de Búrca, *EU Law: Text, Cases, and Materials* (6th edn, OUP 2015) 105, 110.

[22] Phil Syrpis, 'The Relationship between Primary and Secondary Law in the EU' (2009) 52 Common Market Law Review 461, 465.

[23] ibid 465–67.

[24] ibid 466.

[25] ibid 482–83.

between EU primary and secondary law. The second, which this chapter calls a *dynamic* approach, adopts a less hierarchical view of primary and secondary law, in which secondary law, although limited by the primacy of primary law (and should be annulled if the legislature has 'manifestly' or 'manifestly and gravely' exceeded the limits of its powers[26]), reflects the '(democratic) will expressed by the political [EU] institutions' and, therefore, should be able to affect the interpretation of EU primary law by the Court.[27] This dynamic approach corresponds to the second and third ways of interaction between primary and secondary law, as identified by Syrpis.

Following the dynamic approach to the relationship between EU primary and secondary law, Muir explains that EU secondary legislation can implicate fundamental rights in three ways.[28] First, based on the EU competence to legislate on fundamental rights, some EU secondary legislation is *designed* to 'give specific expression' to a fundamental right.[29] Second, legislative instruments designed to implement an 'ordinary' EU competence—a competence other than fundamental rights protection—can incidentally set fundamental rights standards.[30] Finally, EU secondary legislation can merely define the scope of the EU courts' fundamental rights jurisdiction.[31]

Based on the ways of thinking about the relationship between EU primary and secondary law proposed by Syrpis and Muir, this section contends, first, that Chapter V of the GDPR (as well as Section V of the GDPR's predecessor—the Data Protection Directive[32]) should be viewed as secondary legislative instruments 'giving specific expression' to the fundamental rights, and establishing a system of checks and balances on the limitations of those fundamental rights. Second, the chapter argues that there is a dynamic relationship between the EU framework on transfers of personal data and the EU Charter. This relationship manifests itself in the standard of 'essential equivalence', first introduced through the interpretation of the concept of 'adequacy' in Article 25 of the Data Protection Directive in the light of the EU Charter and later injected into Chapter V of the GDPR as the central constitutional requirement for compliance of *any transfer* of personal data outside the EEA, rather than just adequacy. The discussion below elaborates on each of these points.

[26] ibid 484.
[27] ibid 483–85.
[28] Elise Muir, 'The Fundamental Rights Implications of EU Legislation: Some Constitutional Challenges' (2014) 51(1) Common Market Law Review 219, 223 (hereafter Muir, 'The Fundamental Rights Implications of EU Legislation').
[29] ibid 223–26.
[30] ibid 226–27.
[31] ibid 227–29.
[32] Directive 95/46/EC of the European Parliament and of the Council of 24 October 1995 on the protection of individuals with regard to the processing of personal data and on the free movement of such data [1995] OJ L 281 (hereafter Data Protection Directive).

The relationship between EU primary and secondary law in the area of data protection is not clear-cut. On the one hand, the limited CJEU case law concerning the fundamental right to the protection of personal data enshrined in Article 8 of the Charter leans towards a more hierarchical approach between the two. For example, in *Digital Rights Ireland*, the CJEU invalidated the EU Data Retention Directive because by adopting it 'the legislature exceeded the limits imposed by compliance with the principle of proportionality in the light of Articles 7, 8, and 52(1) of the Charter (of Fundamental Rights)'.[33] In *Schrems I*, the CJEU invalidated the Commission's implementing act approving the EU-US Safe Harbor,[34] and in *Schrems II*, the Commission's implementing act approving the Safe Harbor's successor—the EU-US Privacy Shield.[35] In the *Opinion on EU-Canada PNR Agreement*, the CJEU found the draft EU-Canada PNR Agreement inconsistent with the EU Charter, treating the agreement as an 'equivalent externally, of that which is a legislative act internally'.[36] On the other hand, the origins of this fundamental right, as well as the evolution of the standard of 'essential equivalence' in the design of the EU framework for transfers of personal data outside the EEA, show that EU secondary law also influenced the conceptualization of this right. This influence demonstrates a dynamic approach between the two.

The Data Protection Directive was adopted before the Lisbon Treaty[37] and, as mentioned earlier, was based on the EU internal market competence.[38] It had a profound effect on the formation and the content of the fundamental right to the protection of personal data in the EU Charter.[39] According to the Explanations relating to the EU Charter, one of the foundations of Article 8 of the EU Charter is that the Data Protection Directive contains 'conditions and limitations for the exercise of the right to the protection of personal data'.[40] Indeed, paragraph 2 of Article 8 can be seen as codifying the secondary law principles of fair and lawful

[33] *Digital Rights Ireland and Seitlinger and others* [2014] ECLI:EU:C:2014:238, para 69 (hereafter *Digital Rights Ireland*).

[34] *Schrems I* (n 5).

[35] *Schrems II* (n 6) paras 150–202.

[36] CJEU Opinion 1/15 *EU-Canada PNR Agreement* [2017] ECLI:EU:C:2017:592, para 146 (hereafter CJEU Opinion, *EU-Canada PNR Agreement*).

[37] Treaty of Lisbon amending the Treaty on European Union and the Treaty establishing the European Community [2007] OJ C 306/1

[38] See Section 2.2.1.1.

[39] Lorenzo Dalla Corte, 'A Right to a Rule: On the Substance and Essence of the Fundamental Right to Personal Data Protection' in Dara Hallinan and others (eds), *Data Protection and Privacy: Data Protection and Democracy* (Hart Publishing 2020) 44–45 (hereafter Dalla Corte, 'A Right to a Rule') (arguing that '[t]he right to data protection has been strongly shaped by the evolution of the secondary legislation'). See also Muir, 'The Fundamental Rights Implications of EU Legislation: Some Constitutional Challenges' (n 28) 226 (stating that '[a]lthough adopted in the mid-1990s as an internal market instrument on the basis of the equivalent of today's Article 114 TFEU, in substance the Directive is specifically designed to give shape to a fundamental right'). cf Maria Tzanou, *The Fundamental Right to Data Protection, Normative Value in the Context of Counter-Terrorism Surveillance* (Bloomsbury Publishing 2017) 38–39, arguing that the meaning of Article 8 should be independent from EU secondary law.

[40] Explanation to art 8, Explanations Relating to the Charter of Fundamental Rights, 2007 OJ (C 303).

data processing, the right of individuals to access their personal data, the right to rectification, as well as the establishment of an independent supervisory authority to ensure compliance with the fundamental right—all of which were already present in the Data Protection Directive.[41] In its 2015 *Schrems I* judgment, the CJEU pointed to a reverse relationship between the Data Protection Directive and the EU Charter (which was already legally binding at that time). The CJEU held that the Directive's Article 25(6) governing the adequacy mechanism for transfers of personal data outside the EEA '*implements the express obligation laid down in Article 8(1) of the Charter* to protect personal data and . . . is intended to ensure that the high level of that protection continues where personal data is transferred to a third country'.[42] This demonstrates that the relationship between the fundamental right to the protection of personal data and the EU Data Protection Directive was a two-way street.

Unlike the Data Protection Directive, the GDPR was '*specifically* adopted in order to give expression' to the fundamental right to the protection of personal data.[43] It constitutes secondary legislation adopted on the basis of Article 16 of the TFEU and the Charter. As rightly pointed out by Ausloos, the GDPR 'has a primarily enabling or instrumental role' of putting in 'place an infrastructure of checks and balances to ensure fairness [of personal data processing]' and setting 'the parameters for legitimate processing of personal data in the light of the Charter as a whole'.[44] This includes not only articles codifying the substantive fundamental rights but also Article 52(1) of the EU Charter setting the boundaries for derogation from those fundamental rights. In general terms, while 'Article 8 [of the] Charter is substantive, the GDPR is procedural'.[45] This, however, does not mean that the right to the protection of personal data is the only fundamental right operationalized by the GDPR.[46] In addition, just like the Data Protection Directive, the GDPR *limits* the fundamental rights enshrined in the EU Charter,[47] as any processing of personal data constitutes a derogation from the fundamental right under

[41] See arts 6, 7, 12, and 28 of the Data Protection Directive, respectively. Art 8 EU Charter is also based on art 8 ECHR and Convention 108, which has been ratified by all the member states.

[42] *Schrems I* (n 5) para 72. This goal is now explicitly incorporated in art 44 GDPR (emphasis added).

[43] Muir, 'The Fundamental Rights Implications of EU Legislation' (n 28) 224.

[44] Jef Ausloos, *The Right to Erasure: Safeguard for Informational Self-Determination in a Digital Society?* (PhD Dissertation, KU Leuven CiTiP 2018) 62–63 (hereafter Ausloos, 'The Right to Erasure'). See also Damian Clifford and Jef Ausloos, 'Data Protection and the Role of Fairness' (2018) 37(1) Yearbook of European Law 130–87, 147 (hereafter: Clifford and Ausloos, 'Data Protection and the Role of Fairness') (arguing that 'the GDPR is a clear manifestation of a secondary framework built on checks and balances in order to respect "control" as the essence of the right to data protection'). See also Dalla Corte, 'A Right to a Rule' (n 39) 45.

[45] Ausloos, 'The Right to Erasure' (n 44) 63.

[46] Oostveen, Irion (2017); Ausloos, 'The Right to Erasure' (n 44) 62–63; Clifford and Ausloos, 'Data Protection and the Role of Fairness' (n 43) 147. See also Section 1.1.3.

[47] For a discussion, see Clifford and Ausloos, 'Data Protection and the Role of Fairness' (n 44) 148, 152–54.

Articles 7 and 8 of the Charter.[48] The GDPR sets the rules for lawful processing of personal data, which must remain within the boundaries of Article 52(1) of the Charter governing derogations from the fundamental rights. This also means that the requirements of this article serve as a constitutional compass in the interpretation and application of the GDPR.

5.2.2 'Essential equivalence': From EU secondary law to EU Charter and then back again

In the spirit of the dynamic relationship between EU primary and secondary law on data protection, in its *Schrems I* judgment, the CJEU interpreted the term 'adequate level of protection' from Article 25(6) of the Data Protection Directive in the light of the EU Charter 'as requiring the third country in fact to ensure, by reason of its domestic law or its international commitments, a level of protection of fundamental rights and freedoms that is "*essentially equivalent*" to that guaranteed within the European Union by virtue of [the Data Protection Directive] read in the light of the Charter'.[49] This Article's aim is to ensure continuity of the high level of personal data protection after personal data is transferred outside the EEA and to prevent circumvention of the EU data protection framework.[50] Several scholars have argued that by interpreting 'adequacy' as 'essential equivalence', the CJEU has elevated the standard of data protection that a third country must meet to be afforded an adequacy decision.[51]

In the *Opinion on EU-Canada PNR Agreement*, the CJEU applied the 'essentially equivalent' standard outside the context of the Data Protection Directive, in relation to the draft EU-Canada PNR Agreement. Just as in *Schrems I*, the Court invoked the standard of 'essential equivalence' as an *interpretation of the notion of 'adequacy'* incorporated into the text of the draft Article 5 of the EU-Canada PNR Agreement.[52] In that Opinion, the CJEU referred to the *Schrems I*

[48] *Digital Rights Ireland* (n 33) paras 34–36; *Volker und Markus Schecke and Eifert* [2010] ECLI:EU:C:2010:662, para 58. See also European Data Protection Supervisor, 'Assessing the Necessity of Measures That Limit the Fundamental Right to the Protection of Personal Data: A Toolkit' (2017) <https://edps.europa.eu/sites/edp/files/publication/17-04-11_necessity_toolkit_en_0.pdf> accessed 10 July 2023, p. 7 (hereafter European Data Protection Supervisor, 'Assessing the Necessity of Measures').

[49] *Schrems I* (n 5) para 73 (emphasis added).

[50] ibid; CJEU Opinion, *EU-Canada PNR Agreement* (n 36) para 214; *Schrems II* (n 6) para 93.

[51] See, eg, Paul Roth, 'Adequate Level of Data Protection in Third Countries Post-Schrems and under the General Data Protection Regulation' (2017) 25(1) Journal of Law, Information and Science 49, 63 (hereafter Roth, 'Adequate Level of Data Protection'); Bilyana Petkova, 'Privacy as Europe's First Amendment' (2019) 25(2) European Law Journal 140, 153.

[52] This Article states that '[s]ubject to compliance with this Agreement, the Canadian Competent Authority is deemed to provide an *adequate level of protection, within the meaning of relevant European Union data protection law*, for the processing and use of PNR data'. CJEU Opinion, *EU-Canada PNR Agreement* (n 36) para 86 (emphasis added).

judgment—without referring to the adequacy provision of the Data Protection Directive—and stated that:

> the transfer of personal data, such as PNR data, from the European Union to a non-member country is lawful only if there are rules in that country which ensure a level of protection of fundamental rights and freedoms that is *essentially equivalent* to that guaranteed within the European Union.[53]

This led Kuner to conclude that the CJEU's reference to the standard of essential equivalence 'leaves no doubt that this standard also applies to data transfers under international agreements'.[54]

Although the CJEU did not explain the relationship between the standard of 'essential equivalence' and the assessment under Article 52(1) of the EU Charter, this chapter contends that the Court used the standard of 'essential equivalence' as an instantiation of proportionality balancing under Article 52(1) of the EU Charter in application to the EU secondary law's concept of 'adequacy'. In other words, by ensuring that an adequacy decision guarantees that the level of personal data protection abroad is 'essentially equivalent' to that in the EU, the European Commission can strike the right balance under the strict necessity test of Article 52(1) of the EU Charter. This indirectly follows from the fact that in *Schrems I*, the CJEU first conducted an assessment under Article 52(1) of the EU Charter (paragraphs 92–95) but then in paragraph 96 returned to the standard of 'essential equivalence' and finally in paragraph 98 concluded that the Commission's decision was incompliant with Article 25(6) of the Directive read in the light of the EU Charter.

The relationship between restrictions on transfers of personal data as a component of the fundamental right under Article 8 of the EU Charter and its implementation in secondary law can also be illustrated by this quote from the CJEU *Opinion on EU-Canada PNR Agreement*:

> That right to the protection of personal data requires, inter alia, that the high level of protection of fundamental rights and freedoms conferred by EU law *continues* where personal data is transferred from the European Union to a non-member country. Even though the means intended to ensure such a level of protection may differ from those employed within the European Union *in order to ensure that the requirements stemming from EU law are complied with*, those means must nevertheless prove, *in practice*, effective in order to ensure *protection essentially equivalent to that guaranteed within the European Union*.[55]

[53] CJEU Opinion, *EU-Canada PNR Agreement* (n 36) paras 93, 134, and 214.

[54] Christopher Kuner, 'International Agreements, Data Protection, and EU Fundamental Rights on the International Stage: Opinion 1/15 (EU-Canada PNR) of the Court of Justice of the EU' (2018) 55(3) Common Market Law Review 857–82, 872 (hereafter: Kuner, 'International Agreements, Data Protection, and EU Fundamental Rights on the International Stage').

[55] CJEU, *Opinion on EU-Canada PNR Agreement* (n 36) para 134 (emphasis added).

This quote suggests that the standard of 'essential equivalence' is also a *practical implementation of the constitutional requirement* of continuity of protection in EU secondary law. Extrapolating the relationship between the fundamental right in Article 8 of the EU Charter and secondary data protection law, to the relationship between Article 52(1) of the EU Charter and the standard of 'essential equivalence', one can thus conclude that the first is substantive and the second is procedural; it is but one of the tools in the toolbox of secondary law ensuring that the fundamental right is not derogated from further than is allowed under Article 52(1) of the EU Charter.

The interpretation of 'adequacy' as 'essential equivalence' later found its way to the text of the GDPR. Recital 104 of the GDPR states, in relation to the adequacy framework in Article 45 of the GDPR, that [t]he

> third country should offer guarantees ensuring an adequate level of protection *essentially equivalent* to that ensured within the Union, in particular where personal data are processed in one or several specific sectors. In particular, the third country should ensure effective independent data protection supervision and should provide for cooperation mechanisms with the Member States' data protection authorities, and the data subjects should be provided with effective and enforceable rights and effective administrative and judicial redress. (emphasis added)

The criteria to assess whether a foreign legal framework affords 'essentially equivalent' protection are listed in Article 45 of the GDPR. For systematic transfers of personal data to third countries not afforded an adequacy decision by the EU, however (such as those governed by Article 46 GDPR), the GDPR sets forth a requirement of 'appropriate safeguards'.[56] It should, therefore, be emphasized that until *Schrems II*, the 'essential equivalence' requirement featured both in the CJEU case law discussed earlier and in the GDPR, as the instantiation of the proportionality and strict necessity balancing under Article 52(1) of the EU Charter was interpreted *solely in relation to the adequacy mechanism* for transfers of personal data, rather than in relation to the EU secondary law framework for transfers of personal data *as a whole*. This created a qualitative gap—criticized in academic and policy discourse and discussed in more detail in Section 5.3.1—between the level of protection that must be guaranteed to transferred personal data by an adequacy decision, on the one hand, and by appropriate safeguards under Article 46, such as the standard contractual clauses (SCCs) and the binding corporate rules (BCRs), on the other hand. In *Schrems II*, the CJEU confirmed its prior analysis of what the 'essential equivalence' standard requires in relation to an adequacy decision,[57]

[56] See also recital 107 GDPR.
[57] *Schrems II* (n 6) para 176.

but it also took an important step towards reinstating a consistent and holistic approach to the EU framework for transfers of personal data.[58] In particular, the Court held that:

> data subjects whose personal data are transferred to a third country pursuant to standard data protection clauses are afforded, as in the context of a transfer based on an adequacy decision, a level of protection *essentially equivalent* to that which is guaranteed within the European Union.[59]

The CJEU further explained that the level of protection of fundamental rights required by Article 46(1) of the GDPR 'must be determined on the basis of the provisions of that regulation, read in the light of the fundamental rights enshrined in the Charter'.[60] The factors that should be taken into account for such assessment in the context of Article 46 'correspond to those set out, in a non-exhaustive manner, in Article 45(2) of [the GDPR]'.[61] One could, therefore, argue that not only adequacy decisions but indeed all mechanisms for transfers of personal data outside the EEA should provide an 'essentially equivalent' level of protection.

Hence, despite the fact that factors outlined in Article 45(2) of the GDPR—based on the textual interpretation—only apply to adequacy decisions, they should, when interpreted in the light of the EU Charter, be considered in the assessment related to any other mechanism for transfer of personal data. By doing so, as explained earlier, the CJEU asserted the 'essential equivalence' standard as an instantiation of the strict necessity and proportionality balancing under Article 52(1) of the EU Charter in the context of the whole framework for systematic transfers of personal data in EU secondary data protection law. It is no longer a constitutional *interpretation* of 'adequacy'; instead, 'essential equivalence' has acquired a meaning independent of 'adequacy'. As a result, the factors for an adequacy assessment became a part of such 'essential equivalence' standard. This outcome fits with the understanding of the GDPR as a legal framework creating a system of checks and balances that enable the protection of the fundamental rights. Based on this, all provisions of the GDPR, and therefore, all mechanisms for transfers of personal data, should meet the strict necessity test provided in Article 52(1) of the Charter.[62]

[58] For a discussion, see Theodore Christakis, 'After Schrems II: Uncertainties on the Legal Basis for Data Transfers and Constitutional Implications for Europe' (*European Law Blog*, 21 July 2020) <https://europeanlawblog.eu/2020/07/21/after-schrems-ii-uncertainties-on-the-legal-basis-for-data-transfers-and-constitutional-implications-for-europe/> accessed 10 July 2023 (hereafter Christakis, 'After Schrems II'); Christopher Kuner, 'Schrems II Re-Examined' (*Verfassungsblog*, 25 August 2020) <https://verfassungsblog.de/schrems-ii-re-examined/> accessed 10 July 2023 (hereafter Kuner, 'Schrems II Re-Examined').

[59] *Schrems II* (n 6) paras 96, 105.

[60] *Schrems II* (n 6) para 101.

[61] ibid para 104.

[62] Clifford and Ausloos, 'Data Protection and the Role of Fairness' (n 44), 148, 152.

Stating that all mechanisms for transfers of personal data should meet the strict necessity test does *not* mean that the *application* of each of such mechanisms by personal data controllers and processors involves such an assessment. Under the GDPR, such assessment is mandated by the EU legislator only for *systematic* transfers of personal data outside the EEA by requiring that such mechanisms must ensure adequate or appropriate safeguards for personal data. In the case of adequacy decisions, such assessment must be conducted by the European Commission and in the case of appropriate safeguards, by controllers or processors transferring personal data outside the EEA.

This book also contends that such an assessment is *not* necessary when personal data is transferred on the basis of the derogations of Article 49 of the GDPR, which provide derogations from the 'essentially equivalent' level of protection required under the adequacy decisions and appropriate safeguards.[63] In the case of derogations, a strict necessity assessment has already been done by the legislator and is built in the design and content of those derogations.[64] It is, therefore, logical that in *Schrems II*, the CJEU stated, as already explained in Section 2.2.4, that invalidation of the EU-US Privacy Shield was not liable to create a legal vacuum, as even in the absence of an adequacy decision or appropriate safeguards, transfers of personal data to third countries could take place on the basis of derogations under Article 49 of the GDPR.[65] This also follows from the European Data Protection Board (EDPB)[66] Recommendations[67] and the text of Article 49 of the GDPR itself,

[63] The question of whether the standard of 'essential equivalence' also applied to derogations under art 49 is, however, not viewed as clear-cut in literature. See, eg, Laura Drechsler and Irene Kamara, 'Essential Equivalence as a Benchmark for International Data Transfers after Schrems II' in Eleni Kosta and Ronald Leenes (eds), *Research Handbook on EU Data Protection* (Edward Elgar Publishing 2022) 349 (hereafter Drechsler and Kamara, 'Essential Equivalence as a Benchmark for International Data Transfers after Schrems II'), arguing that, on the one hand, derogations have to be measured against the same high level of protection as adequacy and appropriate safeguards, but on the other hand, 'derogations are meant to be exceptions to be applicable when the other mechanisms do not apply. The point of such exceptions could be said to be lost if they also have to fulfil the same high standard than adequacy and appropriate safeguards'. See also Naef, *Data Protection without Data Protectionism* (n 10) 205–06.

[64] See also Vera Jungkind and Susanne Koch, 'The Risk-Based Approach in the GDPR: Restating the Obvious and Reinstating a Guiding Principle' (2022) ZD 656, 658 (hereafter Jungkind and Koch, 'The Risk-Based Approach in the GDPR'), stating that 'justifications for data transfers under Art. 49 GDPR reflect a prior risk assessment of the legislator that allows for a derogation from Artt. 45, 56 GDPR. . . . In these specific situations, the legislator weighs the interest of data controllers in a data transfer higher than the interest of data subjects in the protection of their personal data, even if there are no safeguards in the sense of Artt. 45, 46 GDPR in place.'

[65] *Schrems II* (n 6) para 202.

[66] Article 29 Working Party (full name: 'The Working Party on the Protection of Individuals with regard to the Processing of Personal Data') was an advisory body formed under Article 29 of the Data Protection Directive (n 32). It consisted of a representative from the data protection authority of each EU member state, the European Data Protection Supervisor and the European Commission. Article 29 Working Party was replaced by the European Data Protection Board on 25 May 2018, when the GDPR entered into force.

[67] See EDPB, Recommendations 01/2020 on measures that supplement transfer tools to ensure compliance with the EU level of protection of personal data (18 June 2021) <https://edpb.europa.eu/system/files/2021-06/edpb_recommendations_202001vo.2.0_supplementarymeasurestransferstools_en.pdf> accessed 10 July 2023, para 25, stating that 'Article 49 GDPR has an exceptional nature. The derogations it contains must be interpreted in a way which does not contradict the very nature of the derogations as

according to which a transfer or a set of transfers shall take place on the basis of one of the conditions listed in this article '[i]n the absence of an adequacy decision pursuant to Article 45(3), or appropriate safeguards pursuant to Article 46'.

As Kuner rightly explains in this respect in a leading commentary on the GDPR,

> the derogations in effect function as a 'safety valve' to allow transfers when there is an overriding societal interest that they take place, whether because the risks to the transfers are small, or because such risks are overridden by other important rights and interests. As the CJEU has held, data protection is not an absolute right, which implies that there must be situations when respect for other important rights and freedoms requires that international data transfers be allowed.[68]

This conceptualization of derogations as a 'safety valve' narrowly crafted by the EU legislator illustrates that transfers of personal data outside the EEA under Article 49 of the GDPR is only a limited interference with the fundamental rights of individuals. Article 49 of the GDPR *in itself* already represents the right balance between different societal interests, risks and benefits of transfers in an exhaustive list of specific situations listed in that article. Therefore, there is *no* need to conduct an assessment under Article 52(1) of the EU Charter of each transfer or set of transfers under the derogations of Article 49 of the GDPR: neither an essential equivalence assessment nor an assessment of whether transfers under the derogations to a specific country respect the essence of fundamental rights.[69] This conforms with the argument made above that the GDPR gives specific expression to fundamental rights and establishes a system of checks and balances for legitimate processing of personal data in the light of the EU Charter. Unlike Articles 45 and

being exceptions from the rule that personal data may not be transferred to a third country unless the country provides for an adequate level of data protection or, alternatively, appropriate safeguards are put in place' (hereafter EDPB, Recommendations 01/2020 on measures that supplement transfer tools).

[68] Christopher Kuner, 'Article 49 Derogations for Specific Situations' in Christopher Kuner and others (eds), *The EU General Data Protection Regulation (GDPR): A Commentary* (OUP 2020) 843. See also Naef, *Data Protection without Data Protectionism* (n 10) 206–14. Internal footnotes omitted.

[69] Irish Data Protection Commission, 'Decision in the Matter of Meta Platforms Ireland Limited' (previously known as Facebook Ireland Limited) (12 May 2023) paras 8.21–8.45 < https://edpb.europa.eu/system/files/2023-05/final_for_issue_ov_transfers_decision_12-05-23.pdf> accessed 10 July 2023 (hereafter Irish Data Protection Commission, 'Decision in the Matter of Meta Platforms Ireland Limited'), where the DPC wrongly argues that transfers to the United States may not rely on derogations because US law does not respect the essence of the fundamental right to effective remedy under Article 47 of the EU Charter. cf Koen Lenaerts, 'Limits on Limitations: The Essence of Fundamental Rights in the EU' (2019) 20 German Law Journal 779, 792 (hereafter Lenaerts, 'Limits on Limitations'), stating that '[i]t follows from the case law of the CJEU that the essence of a fundamental right is not compromised where the measure in question limits the exercise of certain aspects of such a right, leaving others untouched, or applies in a specific set of circumstances with regard to the individual conduct of the person concerned. Conversely, in order for an EU or national measure to compromise the essence of a fundamental right, such a measure must constitute a particularly intense and broad limitation on the exercise of such a right.'

46 from the GDPR, which set not specific enough standards as a condition of transfers (adequacy and appropriateness) serving as a gateway for the assessment under Article 52(1) of the EU Charter, Article 49 of the GDPR is already very specific, and like most other specific GDPR rules, already embeds the Article 52(1) of the EU Charter assessment in its specific provisions.

To sum up, 'essential equivalence' is the EU Charter requirement in relation to the level of personal data protection that any EU secondary law mechanism for any transfers of personal data should ensure. Recall, in addition, that the standard of 'essentially equivalent' protection is not only the CJEU's creation in the line of cases on cross-border transfers of personal data.[70] It closely resembles the 'essentially comparable' standard used by the German Constitutional court in the 1986 *Solange II* case when assessing the level of fundamental rights protection in the EU as compared to the German legal order, and codified in Article 23 of the German Basic Law.[71] The fact that the *Solange I* was one of the reasons that prompted the EU transition from an economic to a constitutional union[72] supports the conclusion that the standard of 'essential equivalence' is very likely to 'stick' even without adequacy being mentioned in the EU secondary law. In any event, what matters is that the CJEU determined that this standard constitutes a yardstick to gauge the permissible derogations from the fundamental rights set forth in Article 52(1) of the EU Charter in the context of transfers of personal data outside the EEA.

5.2.3 The concept of the 'essence' of fundamental rights

The previous section has argued that the GDPR sets up a system of checks and balances for the legitimate processing of personal data in the light of the EU Charter. It has concluded that the EU primary law, and more specifically the EU Charter, set the boundaries for the legislature to regulate transfers of personal data outside the EEA in the form of the 'essential equivalence' standard. This section considers the question of those boundaries more specifically and circumscribes the degree of discretion that the EU legislature has in designing the framework of cross-border transfers of personal data outside the EEA.

[70] Loïc Azoulai and Marijn van der Sluis, 'Institutionalizing Personal Data Protection in Times of Global Institutional Distrust: Schrems' 53(5) Common Market Law Review 1343, 1363.

[71] ibid 1363; Franz C Mayer, 'The Force Awakens: The Schrems Case from a German Perspective' (*Verfassunsblog*, 16 October 2015) <https://verfassungsblog.de/the-force-awakens-the-schrems-case-from-a-german-perspective-2/> accessed 10 July 2023; BVerfGE, Wünsche Handelsgesellschaft (*Solange II*), 2 BvR 197/83, 22 October 1986, 73, 339 (1987) 3 Common Market Law Review 225. Unofficial translation <https://law.utexas.edu/transnational/foreign-law-translations/german/case.php?id=572> accessed 10 July 2023.

[72] For a discussion, see, eg, Vlad F Perju, 'On Uses and Misuses of Human Rights in European Constitutionalism' in Silja Vöneky and Gerald L Neumann (eds), *Human Rights, Democracy, and Legitimacy in a World in Disorder* (CUP 2017).

The EU law concept that seems to be most helpful in drawing a red line between the elements of a fundamental right that can and cannot be restricted is the concept of the 'essence' of fundamental rights, which appears in Article 52(1) of the EU Charter.[73] This provision requires that any limitation on the exercise of the fundamental rights must (a) be provided for by law (first sentence), (b) respect the essence of those rights (first sentence), and (c) meet the principles of proportionality and necessity (second sentence).

The concept of the 'essence' of fundamental rights in general, and of the fundamental rights to privacy and the protection of personal data in particular, remains 'elusive' in the CJEU case law and relatively unexplored in academic literature.[74] It is 'a construct with blurry boundaries'.[75] It was only in 2015 in *Schrems I* judgment that the CJEU invalidated an EU measure due to its lack of respect for the essence of the fundamental rights to privacy and effective remedy.[76] It is, therefore, unsurprising that in their 2013 article Gellert and Gutwirth even dismiss the 'assumption that there is, eventually and behind all descriptions, such thing as an essence of privacy and data protection'.[77]

This section looks into the meaning of the 'essence' of fundamental rights, in general and in application to the fundamental rights to privacy and the protection of personal data, with the aim to determine what—if anything—constitutes the essence of those fundamental rights in relation to transfers of personal data outside the EEA. In doing so, this section relies on the relatively scarce literature and CJEU case law available on this topic.

Scholars generally agree that the notion of 'essence' is an 'absolute limit to balancing, i.e. to underline that a certain interference actually "destroys" a certain right or strips it of any content'.[78] Relying on the CJEU case law on the fundamental

[73] Mark Dawson, Orla Lynskey, and Elise Muir, 'What Is the Added Value of the Concept of the 'Essence of EU Fundamental Rights?' (2019) 20(6) German Law Journal 763, 767 (hereafter Dawson, Lynskey, and Muir, 'What Is the Added Value of the Concept of the "Essence" of EU Fundamental Rights?').

[74] Orla Lynskey, *The Foundations of EU Data Protection Law* (OUP 2015) 270–72 (hereafter Lynskey, *The Foundations of EU Data Protection Law*). See also Dalla Corte, 'A Right to a Rule' (n 39) 48; Maria G Porcedda, 'On Boundaries: Finding the Essence of the Right to the Protection of Personal Data' in Ronald Leenes and others (eds), *Privacy and Data Protection: The Internet of Bodies* (Hart Publishing 2018) 2 (hereafter Porcedda 'On Boundaries'); Kathleen Gutman, 'The Essence of the Fundamental Right to an Effective Remedy and to a Fair Trial in the Case-Law of the Court of Justice of the European Union: The Best Is Yet to Come?' (2019) 20(6) German Law Journal 884, 884, calling the standard of 'essence of fundamental rights' a 'late bloomer'.

[75] Dalla Corte, 'On Proportionality in the Data Protection Jurisprudence of the CJEU' (n 7) 274.

[76] ibid 273.

[77] Raphael Gellert and Serge Gutwirth, 'The Legal Construction of Privacy and Data Protection' (2013) 29 Computer Law & Security Review 522, 522.

[78] Armin von Bogdandy and others, 'Reverse Solange: Protecting the Essence of Fundamental Rights against EU Member States' (2012) 49(2) Common Market Law Review 489, 511 (hereafter Von Bogdandy and others, 'Reverse Solange'). See also Clifford and Ausloos, 'Data Protection and the Role of Fairness' (n 44) 146–47; Porcedda 'On Boundaries' (n 74) 3; Dalla Corte, 'A Right to a Rule' (n 39) 50; Dalla Corte, 'On Proportionality in the Data Protection Jurisprudence of the CJEU' (n 7) 274; Tuomas Ojanen, 'Making the Essence of Fundamental Rights Real: The Court of Justice of the European Union Clarifies the Structure of Fundamental Rights under the Charter: ECJ 6 October 2015, Case C-362/

rights to privacy and the protection of personal data, Brkan convincingly argues that the concept of the 'essence' of fundamental rights contained in Article 52(1) of the EU Charter is 'an independent constitutional concept that is not a part of the principle of proportionality'.[79] This means that an interference with the essence of a fundamental right cannot be justified based on a necessity and proportionality assessment.[80] Along similar lines, CJEU's president Koen Lenaerts noted that where an 'EU measure fails to take due account of the essence of a fundamental right, that measure is incompatible with the Charter and must be annulled or declared invalid'.[81] As Advocate General Henrik Saugmandsgaard Øe argued in the *Schrems II* case,

> when an interference compromises [the essence of] those rights and freedoms, no legitimate objective can justify it. The interference is then deemed to be contrary to the Charter without it being necessary to examine whether it is appropriate and necessary for the purpose of achieving the objective pursued.[82]

In other words, a measure interfering with the essence of a fundamental right is 'automatically disproportionate',[83] which makes, in Lenaerts' view, the 'essence test' and the 'proportionality test' (including where there is a particularly serious interference with a fundamental right at stake) two separate lines of inquiry under Article 52(1) of the EU Charter.[84] Building on the CJEU's judgment in *Schrems I*, Lenaerts further explains that the 'essence' of a fundamental right refers to its 'hard nucleus' (also referred to as the 'core' by other scholars[85]), which is *absolute* and 'must always remain free from interference'.[86] This concept thus suggests that the EU legislator may only 'determine non-essential elements' of those rights, and that secondary law may not affect the absolute 'nucleus' of those rights under the Charter.[87] More generally and relatedly, the EU legislator's discretion in using

14, Maximillian Schrems v Data Protection Commissioner' (2016) 12(2) European Constitutional Law Review 318.

[79] Brkan 'The Essence of the Fundamental Rights to Privacy and Data Protection' (n 19) 868.
[80] ibid 883.
[81] Lenaerts, 'Limits on Limitations' (n 69) 779, 782.
[82] *Facebook Ireland and Schrems* [2020] ECLI:EU:C:2019:1145, Opinion of AG Saugmandsgaard Øe, para 272 (hereafter Opinion of AG Saugmandsgaard Øe in *Schrems II*). See also European Data Protection Supervisor, 'Guidelines on Assessing the Proportionality of Measures that Limit the Fundamental Rights to Privacy and to the Protection of Personal Data' (2019), 8 <https://edps.europa.eu/sites/default/files/publication/19-02-25_proportionality_guidelines_en.pdf> accessed 10 July 2023.
[83] Lenaerts, 'Limits on Limitations' (n 69) 781.
[84] ibid 781.
[85] See, eg, Scarcello, 'Preserving the "Essence" of Fundamental Rights under Article 52(1) of the Charter' (n 8) 651–53; Weinrib, 'The Essence of Rights and the Limits of Proportionality' (n 8).
[86] ibid 782.
[87] Dawson, Lynskey, and Muir, 'What Is the Added Value of the Concept of the 'Essence' of EU Fundamental Rights?' (n 74) 767.

secondary law to operationalize fundamental rights is proportionate to the level of interference with fundamental rights that the legislation in question entails.[88]

Applying this line of reasoning to the GDPR, one can conclude that the GDPR, which operationalizes the fundamental rights to privacy and data protection by setting the limits within which these fundamental rights can be interfered with,[89] may only permit derogations from these fundamental rights to the extent it does not interfere with their 'nucleus'. Put differently, any GDPR rule must respect the 'essence' of the fundamental rights affected by data processing, and primarily the rights to privacy (Article 7 of EU Charter), the protection of personal data (Article 8 of EU Charter), and judicial remedy (Article 47 of EU Charter), which most often feature in the CJEU case law touching upon the 'essence' of fundamental rights in the context of personal data processing.

To sum up, unlike the shades of grey in balancing in the assessment of necessity and proportionality under Article 52(1) of the EU Charter, the assessment of whether the 'essence' of fundamental rights was respected is binary: either the interference with the fundamental right respects the essence of that right or it does not.

5.2.4 The 'essence' of the fundamental rights to privacy, protection of personal data, and judicial remedy

In order to operationalize the concept of the 'essence' of fundamental rights in the context of this book, it is important to understand what—if anything—constitutes the essence of the fundamental rights to privacy and the protection of personal data, as well as the right to effective remedy in the context of interferences with the first two fundamental rights, as applied in a line of CJEU jurisprudence. Unfortunately, neither the role of the 'essence' nor the definition of the 'essence' in relation to the above-mentioned fundamental rights is yet fully developed in CJEU jurisprudence and academic literature.[90]

The CJEU's approach to the conceptualization of essence and its conclusions have been criticized as 'contentious',[91] lacking 'coherence' and 'conceptual clarity',[92]

[88] Lenaerts, 'Limits on Limitations' (n 69) 793.

[89] As noted above, in the view of the CJEU and the EU Data Protection Authorities, any processing of personal data constitutes a derogation from the fundamental right to privacy and the protection of personal data. *Digital Rights Ireland* (n 33) paras 34–36; *Volker und Markus Schecke and Eifert* (n 48) para 58. See also European Data Protection Supervisor, 'Assessing the Necessity of Measures' (n 48) 7.

[90] Dawson, Lynskey, and Muir, 'What Is the Added Value of the Concept of the 'Essence' of EU Fundamental Rights?' (n 74) 769; Kuner, 'International Agreements, Data Protection, and EU Fundamental Rights on the International Stage' (n 54) 87; Lynskey, *The Foundations of EU Data Protection Law* (n 74) 268; Clifford and Ausloos, 'Data Protection and the Role of Fairness' (n 44) 130–87.

[91] See, eg, Brkan 'The Essence of the Fundamental Rights to Privacy and Data Protection' (n 19) 865.

[92] Dawson, Lynskey, and Muir, 'What Is the Added Value of the Concept of the 'Essence' of EU Fundamental Rights?' (n 74) 769. See also Maria Tzanou and Plixavra Vogiatzoglou, 'In Search of Legal

and methodology.[93] It is beyond the scope of this book to engage fully with such critiques. Using available CJEU jurisprudence on the topic and its interpretation in literature, this book only addresses three issues that are germane to it. First, it considers the aspects that constitute the essence of the fundamental rights to privacy, the protection of personal data, and the right to effective remedy in the context of the first two rights based on the existing CJEU case law. Second, it analyses whether restrictions on transfers of personal data outside the EEA, and the standard of 'essential equivalence', constitute a part of the essence of the right to the protection of personal data. Third, it examines whether there is a 'rule of thumb' on how to identify the essence of the relevant fundamental rights in situations not yet addressed by the CJEU, in particular, in relation to transfers of personal data outside the EEA.

The CJEU has interpreted the notion of the 'essence' of the fundamental rights to privacy, the protection of personal data, and judicial remedy (in the context of the other two rights) in six judgments thus far: *Digital Rights Ireland*, *Tele2 Sverige*, *Schrems I and II*, *Ligue des droits humains*, and *Opinion on EU-Canada PNR Agreement*.[94] In *Schrems I*, the CJEU held that 'legislation permitting the public authorities to have access on a generalised basis *to the content of electronic communications* must be regarded as compromising the essence of the fundamental right to respect for private life, as guaranteed by Article 7 of the Charter'.[95] In contrast, legislation, which 'authorises, on a generalised basis, *storage of all the personal data of all the persons* whose data has been transferred ... without any differentiation, limitation or exception being made' does not interfere with the 'essence' of the right to privacy, but rather violates the principles of strict necessity under the second sentence of Article 52(1) of the Charter.[96] The Court reached the same conclusion in *Digital Rights Ireland*[97] and *Tele2 Sverige*.[98]

In his Opinion in *Schrems II*, the Advocate General continued the CJEU's approach in prior cases that as long as there is no 'generalised access by the public

Certainty Regarding 'Effective Redress' in International Data Transfers: Unpacking the Conceptual Complexities and Clarifying the Substantive Requirements' (2023) 16(1) Review of European Administrative Law Review 11, 17–23 (hereafter Tzanou and Vogiatzoglou, 'In Search of Legal Certainty Regarding 'Effective Redress' in International Data Transfers').

[93] See, eg, Weinrib, 'The Essence of Rights and the Limits of Proportionality' (n 8) 5.

[94] There are other cases in which the CJEU ruled on whether a contested EU measure respects the essence of the relevant fundamental rights. However, in those cases, the CJEU merely held that a certain measure respects the essence without explaining what that essence constitutes. See, eg, *Orde van Vlaamse Balies and Others* [2022] ECLI:EU:C:2022:963, paras 39–40; *Luxembourg Business Registers* [2022] ECLI:EU:C:2022:912, paras 52–54.

[95] *Schrems I* (n 5) para 94 (emphasis added). Brkan extensively criticizes this distinction between the data that constitutes the content of electronic communications and the metadata, as large volumes of metadata can reveal almost as much personal data about the individuals as, or even more than, the content of communications. Brkan, 'The Essence of the Fundamental Rights to Privacy and Data Protection' (n 19) 872–73, 879.

[96] *Schrems I* (n 5) para 93.

[97] *Digital Rights Ireland* (n 33) paras 37, 39, 69, 73.

[98] *Tele2 Sverige* [2016] ECLI:EU:C:2016:970, para 101 (hereafter *Tele2 Sverige*).

authorities to the content of the electronic communications', there is no 'breach of the very essence' of the right to privacy.[99] In its *Schrems II* judgment, the CJEU, however, followed neither its own line of reasoning in *Schrems I* nor that of the Advocate General; it remained silent on whether the EU-US Privacy Shield interfered with the essence of the right to privacy or the right to protection of personal data.[100] Instead, it held that EU-US Privacy Shield did not ensure 'essential equivalent' protection because 'limitations on the protection of personal data arising from the domestic law of the United States ... are not circumscribed in a way that satisfies requirements that are essentially equivalent to those required, under EU law, by the second sentence of Article 52(1) of the Charter'.[101] The CJEU also failed to mention the issue of generalized access by public authorities to the content of electronic communications. In the *Opinion on EU-Canada PNR Agreement*, where access to content or other electronic communications data was not at issue, the CJEU concluded that the EU-Canada PNR Agreement did not interfere with the right to privacy because although 'PNR data may, in some circumstances, reveal very specific information concerning the private life of a person, the nature of that information *is limited to certain aspects of that private life*, in particular, relating to air travel between Canada and the European Union'.[102] The CJEU confirmed this line of reasoning in *Ligue des droits humains* with respect to the challenged EU PNR Directive, concluding that the PNR Directive does not adversely affect the essence of fundamental rights enshrined in Articles 7 and 8 of the EU Charter:

> it is true that PNR data may, in some circumstances, reveal very specific information on the private life of a person. However, in so far as, on the one hand, the nature of that information is limited to certain aspects of a person's private life, concerning that person's air travel in particular, and, on the other hand, the PNR Directive expressly prohibits in Article 13(4) thereof the processing of sensitive data within the meaning of Article 9(1) of the GDPR, the data covered by that directive do not by themselves allow for a full overview of the private life of a person.[103]

In relation to the right to effective remedy under Article 47 of the EU Charter, in the context of the rights to privacy and the protection of personal data, the CJEU interpreted the essence of this right in two cases. In *Schrems I* and *Schrems II*, the CJEU held that 'legislation *not providing for any possibility* for an individual to

[99] Opinion of AG Saugmandsgaard Øe in *Schrems II* (n 82) para 278.

[100] *Schrems II* (n 6) para 185. This deviation from *Schrems I* could be attributed to the critique of the *Schrems I* (n 5) approach to finding the interference with essence of the fundamental right. See eg Brkan, 'The Essence of the Fundamental Rights to Privacy and Data Protection' (n 19) 877–78.

[101] ibid.

[102] CJEU Opinion, *EU-Canada PNR Agreement* (n 36) para 150.

[103] *Ligue des Droits Humains* [2022] ECLI:EU:C:2022:491 (hereafter *Ligue des Droits Humains*).

pursue legal remedies in order to have access to personal data relating to him, or to obtain the rectification or erasure of such data, does not respect the essence of the fundamental right to effective judicial protection, as enshrined in Article 47 of the Charter'.[104] However, as Drechsler and Kamara rightly observed, the CJEU 'ultimately never fully pronounced whether or not the remedy system established violated the essence of the right to effective judicial protection'.[105]

Unlike the fundamental right to privacy, the CJEU has not yet found a violation of essence of the fundamental right to the protection of personal data. As a general observation, the CJEU tends to assess interference with the essence of the right to the protection of personal data jointly with that of the right to privacy. In *Digital Rights Ireland*, the Court concluded that there was no such interference because the contested Data Retention Directive required respect of 'certain principles of data protection and data security' in order to 'ensure that appropriate technical and organisational measures are adopted against accidental or unlawful destruction, accidental loss or alteration of the data'.[106] In *Tele2 Sverige*, where the CJEU discussed the right to privacy and to the protection of personal data jointly, the CJEU held that as long as the contested legislation 'does not permit retention of the content of a communication', it does not affect adversely the essence of the right to the protection of personal data.[107] In the *Opinion on EU-Canada PNR Agreement*, the CJEU found that the EU-Canada PNR Agreement did not interfere with the essence of the fundamental right to data protection for two reasons: first, because it limited 'the purposes for which PNR data may be processed', and second, because it contained the rules to ensure 'the security, confidentiality and integrity of that data, and to protect it against unlawful access and processing'.[108] The CJEU reiterated the same conclusion in its later *Ligue des droits humains* judgment without drawing a distinction between the essence of the fundamental right to the protection of personal data and the fundamental right to privacy.[109] The Advocate General in his

104 (Emphasis added) *Schrems I* (n 5) para 95; *Schrems II* (n 6) para 187.

105 Drechsler and Kamara, 'Essential Equivalence as a Benchmark for International Data Transfers after Schrems II' (n 63) 336. See also Scarcello, 'Preserving the "Essence" of Fundamental Rights under Article 52(1) of the Charter' (n 8) 664. Irish Data Protection Commission, 'Data Protection Commission Announces Conclusion of Inquiry into Meta Ireland' (22 May 2023) <https://www.dataprotection.ie/en/news-media/press-releases/Data-Protection-Commission-announces-conclusion-of-inquiry-into-Meta-Ireland> accessed 10 July 2023 (hereafter Irish Data Protection Commission, 'Data Protection Commission Announces Conclusion of Inquiry into Meta Ireland'), arguing that in *Schrems I* the CJEU concluded that Safe Harbour was invalid without engaging in proportionality analysis (para 8.31), and that the CJEU made the same conclusion *Schrems II*, albeit indirectly (paras 8.36–8.41). See also Tzanou and Vogiatzoglou, 'In Search of Legal Certainty Regarding "Effective Redress" in International Data Transfers' (n 92) 21, arguing that the CJEU took a different approach in *Schrems II* compared to *Schrems I*. While in *Schrems I* the CJEU evaluated US law on the basis of the 'essence' of the right to effective remedy under Article 47, in *Schrems II* the CJEU, arguably, adopted 'the flexible approach' and constructed a four-pronged test.

106 *Digital Rights Ireland* (n 33) para 40.

107 *Tele2 Sverige* (n 98) para 101. The Court discusses the right to privacy and the right to the protection of personal data at the same time by referring to 'these rights'.

108 CJEU Opinion, *EU-Canada PNR Agreement* (n 36) para 150.

109 *Ligue des Droits Humains* (n 103) para 120.

Opinion in *Schrems II* followed the CJEU's line of reasoning in *Opinion on EU-Canada PNR Agreement*, namely that the

> essence of the right to protection of personal data, guaranteed in Article 8 of the Charter, is preserved when the purposes of the processing are limited and the processing is accompanied by rules designed to ensure, inter alia, the security, confidentiality and integrity of the data, and also to protect them against unlawful access and processing.[110]

The Advocate General further noted that although there was a doubt whether the US surveillance programmes, allowed under the EU-US Privacy Shield, defined the purposes of processing of personal data 'with sufficient clarity and precision to ensure a level of protection essentially equivalent to that prevailing in the legal order of the Union', 'those possible weaknesses would not suffice ... to substantiate a finding that such programmes would ... violate the essence of the right to protection of personal data'.[111] In its *Schrems II* judgment, the CJEU did not separate the issue of interference with the essence of the fundamental right to protection of personal data from the interference with the fundamental right to privacy.[112]

Brkan criticizes the CJEU's approach to the essence of fundamental rights, noting that in relation to privacy it is quantitative instead of qualitative,[113] and in relation to the protection of personal data 'extremely restrictive and technical'.[114] In the latter case, she argues that the Court reduced the essence of the right to certain aspects of it, turning the core of the right to a minimum rather than a maximum standard.[115] In contrast, Lenaerts argues that the essence of the fundamental rights to privacy and the right to effective judicial remedy is only compromised when 'the limitation in question empties those rights of their content or calls their very existence into question'.[116] The same logic arguably applies to the protection of personal data. From his perspective, the 'essence' should be interpreted restrictively so that it can only be compromised in 'extreme cases', because a broad understanding of this concept would make fundamental rights absolute, which is undesirable in a democratic society.[117]

This overview of the CJEU case law shows that the nucleus of the fundamental right to privacy and, even more so, the fundamental right to the protection of

[110] Opinion of AG Saugmandsgaard Øe in *Schrems II* (n 82) para 279.
[111] ibid para 280.
[112] See, eg, *Schrems II* (n 6) paras 169–72, 178, 199.
[113] Brkan 'The Essence of the Fundamental Rights to Privacy and Data Protection' (n 19) 872, 877.
[114] ibid 878–79.
[115] ibid.
[116] Lenaerts, 'Limits on Limitations' (n 69) 784.
[117] ibid 793.

personal data is rather small. To sum up, the CJEU case law suggests that secondary EU law must:

- Not permit generalised access to the content of electronic communications *in order to respect the essence of the fundamental right to privacy*
- (a) Limit the purposes of processing (i.e. respect the purpose limitation principle); (b) require that the processing of personal data is accompanied by rules designed to ensure, inter alia, the security, confidentiality and integrity of the data, and also to protect them against unlawful access and processing, and (c) not permit retention of the content of communications *in order to respect the essence of the fundamental right to the protection of personal data; and*
- Provide scope for an individual to pursue legal remedies in order to have access to personal data relating to him, or to obtain the rectification or erasure of such data, in order to respect the *essence of the fundamental right to judicial remedy in the context of privacy and data protection*.

From this summary, it is clear that rather than defining the 'essence' of the fundamental rights to privacy, protection of personal data, and effective remedy, the CJEU has chosen to distil, on a case-by-case basis, a number of requirements that EU secondary law should meet in order for the essence of the respective rights to be respected. The existing CJEU case law does not provide for any methodology on how to determine the essence of a particular fundamental right thus leaving ample room for 'arbitrariness, inconsistencies, and political compromise'.[118]

The next question is whether restrictions on transfers of personal data and in particular the standard of 'essential equivalence' constitute the essence of the fundamental rights to privacy and the protection of personal data. At the outset, it should be mentioned that restrictions on transfers of personal data are not mentioned among the elements of this fundamental right codified in Article 8(2) of the EU Charter. This, however, is not a decisive factor, because as Brkan convincingly argues, although these elements are 'constitutive of this fundamental right' they do not automatically constitute its essence.[119] Conversely, the fact that a certain element of the right is not mentioned in this provision does not mean that it does not constitute the essence of the right.

Based on the fact that both in *Schrems I* and *II* as well as in *Opinion on EU-Canada PNR Agreement* the CJEU assessed whether EU law instruments ensured

[118] Dalla Corte, 'On Proportionality in the Data Protection Jurisprudence of the CJEU' (n 7) 274.

[119] Brkan, 'The Essence of the Fundamental Rights to Privacy and Data Protection' (n 19) 881–82. See also Dalla Corte, 'A Right to a Rule' (n 39) 46 (expressing the same point of view.) cf Christopher Kuner, 'Extraterritoriality and Regulation of International Data Transfers in EU Data Protection Law' (2015) 5(4) International Data Privacy Law 235, 243–44 (hereafter Kuner, 'Extraterritoriality and Regulation of International Data Transfers') (suggesting as a preliminary thought that rights listed in Article 8 of the EU Charter could be viewed as the 'essence' of the fundamental right to the protection of personal data.).

an 'essentially equivalent' level of protection by conducting a balancing exercise on the basis of the second sentence of Article 52(1) of the EU Charter, one can conclude that the 'essential equivalence' standard does not constitute (part of) the essence of any of the fundamental rights discussed in this section.[120] The assessment of whether the standard of 'essential equivalence' is met is the second step in the assessment under Article 52(1) of the EU Charter. This conclusion confirms the finding above that 'essential equivalence' is the substantiation of the strict necessity and proportionality requirement of Article 52(1) of the EU Charter in regard to its application to transfers of personal data outside the EEA.

As noted earlier, until now the CJEU has dealt with the question of the essence of the fundamental rights to privacy, the protection of personal data, and the presence of a judicial remedy (in the context of the first two rights) on a case-by-case basis. One could ask whether there is, or could be, a rule of thumb which would allow a line to be drawn between the absence of respect of the essence of a fundamental right and a particularly serious interference with the right, which should be balanced with an overriding public interest on the basis of principles of necessity and proportionality.

Although the requirements listed above apply to all secondary data protection rules, including those governing transfers of personal data outside the EEA, the CJEU case law does not offer a rule of thumb to determine, more generally, what constitutes the essence of the fundamental rights to privacy, data protection, and judicial remedy (in the context of the first two rights), and whether a specific *design* of rules on transfers of personal data outside the EEA is necessary in order to respect this essence. While some scholars argue that there is no 'fixed or universally valid essence of rights that can be conceptually deduced' and that the '"European essence" of fundamental rights' can only be determined 'inductively by analysing the jurisprudence of the courts with regard to certain infringements upon certain rights that cannot be justified',[121] others offer ways of thinking about the essence of the fundamental rights, which could be useful in answering the question posed above. Generalizing the Court's approach, Lenaerts for instance concludes that the limitation of a fundamental right respects its essence if it 'does not call [it] into question as such'.[122] Therefore, if a limitation concerns only 'certain aspects of a

[120] Brkan's analysis of whether an essentially equivalent level of protection and the concept of essence of fundamental rights should be equated supports this conclusion. Brkan, 'The Essence of the Fundamental Rights to Privacy and Data Protection' (n 19) 865.

[121] Von Bogdandy and others, 'Reverse Solange' (n 78) 511. See also Scarcello, 'Preserving the "Essence" of Fundamental Rights under Article 52(1) of the Charter' (n 8) 667, arguing that '[t]he idea that we can establish the essence of a right in vacuo is deeply problematic. The interest theory of right entails that the core-periphery distinction, although meaningful, is not sharp, but scalar. It can only amount to a relatively fuzzy and relative distinction: drawing a firm line, as the absolute theory requires, is impossible.'

[122] Lenaerts, 'Limits on Limitations' (n 69) 785, 792. Brkan proposes a second prong to this test, namely that to establish whether there is an interference with the essence of a fundamental right it is also necessary to evaluate whether there is an overriding public interest that can justify such interference. As long as there exists such an interest, the CJEU should engage in proportionality assessment and

fundamental right, leaving others untouched, or that only applies in a specific set of circumstances regarding the individual conduct of the person concerned', the essence of the fundamental right is respected.[123] The key factors the Court uses in this assessment are the *intensity* and the *extent* of the limitation of the fundamental right at issue.[124] The next section discusses how this analysis can be applicable to rules on transfers of personal data outside the EEA.

5.2.5 The 'essence' and restrictions on transfers of personal data outside the EEA

Although transfers of personal data outside the EEA affect not only the fundamental right to the protection of personal data but also the right to privacy, this section focuses on the essence of the fundamental right to the protection of personal data. The reason for this is that the 'home' of the EU secondary law framework on transfers of personal data outside the EEA is in the GDPR, which, in the first place, manifests and effectuates the fundamental right to the protection of personal data. This right is thus most relevant for the purposes of this section, which considers approaches to the essence of fundamental rights proposed in the context of the governance of data processing in the GDPR.

The most useful ways of thinking about the essence of the fundamental right to the protection of personal data for our purposes are those proposed by Clifford and Ausloos and by Dalla Corte.[125] Clifford and Ausloos claim that 'control constitutes the essence of the right to data protection. "Control" here - they argue - should be interpreted broadly and not simply as an individual's "control" over their personal data but as a *robust architecture of control* that actively pursues individual autonomy'.[126] In arriving at such a conclusion, they emphasize the flexibility of the notion of 'respect' in Article 52(1) of the EU Charter in the protection of the

rule out the breach of essence of the fundamental right at issue. Brkan, 'The Essence of the Fundamental Rights to Privacy and Data Protection' (n 19) 869.

123 Lenaerts, 'Limits on Limitations' (n 69) 785, 792.

124 ibid. See also Brkan, 'The Essence of the Fundamental Rights to Privacy and Data Protection' (n 19) 877–78 (arguing that in the EU-Canada PNR Opinion, the CJEU 'adopts a position that the interference with the essence of the right to privacy is a question of a degree of interference with the fundamental right, given that it takes as a benchmark the limited nature of the acquired and processed data'.).

125 Porcedda also extensively discusses the essence of the fundamental right to data protection in her work. See, eg, Porcedda 'On Boundaries' (n 74). Her proposal to defining the essence of the fundamental right to the protection of personal data by using the concept of 'attributes' of the right is less helpful for the purposes of analysis in this section as she does not touch upon the rules on transfers of personal data outside the EEA.

126 (Emphasis added). Clifford and Ausloos, 'Data Protection and the Role of Fairness' (n 44) 144–45. These authors also argue—as opposed to what has been discussed above—that the essence of the right to data protection can be limited, provided that 'effective balancing mechanisms are in place as specified in Articles 8(2) and 8(3) of the Charter'.

essence of a right.[127] In other words, it seems that in these authors' views, the requirement of 'respect' allows a filtering out of the most serious interferences with the right. Once the threshold of 'respect' is passed, interferences with the 'essence' of the rights are subject to a balancing test under the second sentence of Article 52(1) of the EU Charter. The checks and balances effectuating control as the essence of all fundamental rights and freedoms under the EU Charter (and not only the right to the protection of personal data), they argue, play a role at the level of the secondary framework, such as the GDPR.[128]

Dalla Corte contends that the value of the fundamental right to data protection (as opposed to the right to privacy and other rights implicated by data processing) is 'in the very existence of a system of rules and norms applying to the processing of personal data, regardless of its connection with concepts like privacy, or the secrecy and confidentiality of the information processed.'[129] In other words, from his perspective, the fundamental right to the protection of personal data is 'our fundamental "right to a rule" regulating personal data processing', 'a system of rules and norms applying to the processing of personal data.'[130] These are, in the understanding of this book, rules governing the processing of personal data, rather than, for example, rules concerning applicable law.[131] Thus, '[a] violation of the essence of the right to data protection would ... exist in cases where the interference with the right challenges, explicitly or implicitly, the very societal choice of having an omnibus regime regulating the processing of personal data'.[132] It 'endangers ... the very functioning and legitimacy of the collective posture towards personal data processing in its entirety, and hence ultimately its deepest roots: the rule of law and the democratic legitimacy of EU regulation'.[133] In this context, it is worth recalling that in a line of cases, the CJEU established that the objective pursued by the EU secondary data protection law (and, in particular, the Data Protection Directive) is to ensure 'effective and complete' protection of the rights of individuals.[134]

Applying—in a way similar—approaches to the essence of the right to the protection of personal data proposed by these authors, one could conclude that in relation to the governance of transfers of personal data outside the EEA, *the very presence of the restrictions* (in general) on transfers of personal data outside the

[127] ibid 145.
[128] ibid 152.
[129] Dalla Corte, 'A Right to a Rule' (n 39) 48.
[130] ibid 53.
[131] For example, Kuner has argued that rules on transfers of personal data outside the EEA are a form of private international law rule. See Kuner, 'Extraterritoriality and Regulation of International Data Transfers' (n 119) 235–45. These rules that merely affect the choice of applicable law would not be sufficient to constitute the essence of the fundamental right to the protection of personal data understood as 'the right to a rule'.
[132] ibid 51–52.
[133] ibid 53.
[134] *Google Spain* (n 11) para 34; *Wirtschaftsakademie* (n 11) para 28; *Jehovan todistajat* (n 11) para 66; *Fashion ID* (n 11) paras 66–70.

EEA constitutes a part of the essence of the right to the protection of personal data, as their complete absence would strip this fundamental right, and the system of checks and balances instantiating it in secondary law, of their meaning and content. This is because, in the absence of any restrictions on transfers of personal data, the entire EU legal framework governing the processing of personal data could be easily circumvented. It is the prevention of this circumvention, as has been shown earlier, that constitutes the very constitutional function of such restrictions. In a similar vein, restrictions on onward transfers of personal data from the first country of destination outside the EEA to other countries outside the EEA are equally essential in performing this function and, therefore, should also be considered a part of the essence of the fundamental right to protection of personal data. At the same time, the *particular design* of restrictions on transfers and onward transfers of personal data, apart from the rules identified in Section 5.2.4, is a matter of strict necessity and proportionality balancing.

To sum up, this section has argued that there is a dynamic relationship between EU primary and secondary data protection law. 'Essential equivalence' is the constitutional benchmark for strict necessity and proportionality balancing in the design and application of rules on transfers of personal data outside the EEA. The essence of the fundamental rights to privacy, protection of personal data, and judicial remedy (in the context of the first two rights) will be respected—based on state of the art of CJEU case law and academic literature—when secondary data protection law meets all of the following conditions:

- provides for some limitations on transfers of personal data outside the EEA and on onward transfers,
- contains safeguards preventing generalised access of foreign authorities to the content of electronic communications,
- ensures that purposes for processing personal data are limited,
- requires that the processing of personal data is accompanied by rules designed to ensure, inter alia, the security, confidentiality and integrity of the data, and also to protect them against unlawful access and processing,
- does not permit retention of the content of communications, and
- provides for some possibility for an individual to pursue legal remedies in order to have access to personal data relating to him or her, or to obtain the rectification or erasure of such data.

5.3 Weaknesses of the EU's Framework for Transfers of Personal Data from the EU Charter Perspective

The previous section has argued that the EU secondary law framework for transfers of personal data outside the EEA under Chapter V of the GDPR *can* and *should* be evaluated for compliance with the EU primary law envisaged in the EU Charter. This section conducts such an evaluation in the light of the constitutional function of this framework to prevent circumvention of the EU data protection framework and, ultimately, to ensure that the aim of the EU secondary data protection legislation—'effective and complete' protection of fundamental rights in the course of processing personal data—is not undermined. This evaluation is conducted against the backdrop of ever-changing political, geopolitical, and economic circumstances, which contrasts with the comparatively static nature of the EU secondary law framework for transfers of personal data outside the EEA. The discussion in this section presumes, and does not question, the fact that current GDPR rules respect the essence of the fundamental rights to privacy, the protection of personal data, and judicial remedy and meet the strict necessity and proportionality tests under Article 52(1) of the EU Charter. The starting point for the analysis is different, namely that the rules on transfers of personal data in Chapter V of the GDPR may not be the most fit for the constitutional purpose of the framework.

As already explained in this book, the EU framework for transfers of personal data outside the EEA was designed in early 1990s and first introduced by the 1995 Data Protection Directive. The GDPR changed the particularities of the framework by adding some flexibilities, but it did not alter its core structure. For the reader's convenience, this section briefly reiterates the structure of the EU's framework for transfers of personal data outside the EEA. For a detailed discussion of the issues, however, the reader is referred to Section 2.2.

Just like the Data Protection Directive, the GDPR, as interpreted by the EDPB, adopts a layered approach to transfers of personal data, where each of the subsequent layers is subsidiary to the one above it.[135] The first (top) layer is an adequacy decision by the European Commission establishing that a third country's legal framework—both in general and in relation to the protection of personal data—is 'essentially equivalent' to that of the EU.[136] Personal data can flow freely to a third country that has been afforded an adequacy decision, as if it is being processed within the EEA. The second layer of mechanisms for transfers of personal data, which apply in the absence of an adequacy decision, is the 'appropriate safeguards' put in place by the data controller or possessor (such as SCCs, BCRs, certification mechanisms, or codes of conduct).[137] Data exporters and data importers must include the model SCCs, approved by the European Commission, *verbatim* into their agreements involving transfers of personal data.[138] BCRs are codes of conduct regulating the processing of personal data by a group of undertakings or group of enterprises engaged in a joint economic activity.[139] As clarified by the CJEU in

135 Kuner questions, however, whether this is still the case following the CJEU *Schrems II* judgment. Kuner, 'Schrems II Re-Examined' (n 58).

136 Art 45 GDPR; *Schrems I* (n 5) para 73.

137 Arts 46–47 GDPR.

138 Recital 81, art 46(2)(c) GDPR.

139 Art 47 GDPR.

Schrems II, when using appropriate safeguards for transfers of personal data to third countries that have not been afforded an adequacy decision, data exporters and importers must conduct a comprehensive case-by-case assessment of whether the use of such safeguards will ensure *in practice* a level of personal data protection 'essentially equivalent' to that in the EU.[140]

In exceptional circumstances, exporters of personal data may resort to the third layer of data transfer mechanisms, that is, limited derogations under Article 49 of the GDPR (such as unambiguous consent of the data subject or the performance or conclusion of a contract with or in the interest of the data subject).[141] According to the EDPB, the derogations may only be used for non-repetitive and occasional transfers, however.[142] The layered approach requires that before using any of the derogations, data exporters should first 'endeavour possibilities to frame the transfer' with one of the appropriate safeguards.[143]

As discussed in Section 2.2.4, these restrictions apply in varying degrees only to transmissions of personal data that fall under the definition of a 'transfer'. As explained in Section 2.2.2, the way this concept is defined by the EDPB creates different legal regimes with different legal mechanisms applicable to transfers of personal data within each legal regime and, as a result, different levels of protection of transmitted personal data. This approach contributes to the inconsistency of the EU framework for transfers of personal data with the EU international trade law obligations (as discussed in Sections 2.3 and 2.4.2) and creates a gap in legal protection in the protection of personal data from an EU law perspective with respect to certain types of transmissions of personal data outside the EEA not recognized as 'transfers' by the EDPB.

Between 1995, when the Data Protection Directive was adopted, and 2016, the year of adoption of the GDPR, at least three key changes occurred, and they are crucial for the discussion in this section. First, as mentioned in Section 2.2.1, the rights to the protection of privacy and personal data became binding fundamental rights in the EU. Second, following the Edward Snowden revelations,[144] access to personal data transferred outside the EEA in a commercial context by the public authorities of a third country, and the availability of judicial redress against such authorities, became the most contentious issue in assessing the essential equivalence of third countries' legal systems by the EU, not only for the purposes of

[140] For a discussion, see Section 5.3.1.

[141] Art 49 GDPR.

[142] EDPB, Guidelines 2/2018 on derogations of Article 49 under Regulation 2016/679 (25 May 2018) 4ff < https://edpb.europa.eu/our-work-tools/our-documents/guidelines/guidelines-22018-derogations-article-49-under-regulation_en> accessed 10 July 2023 (hereafter EDPB, 'Guidelines 2/2018 on derogations of Article 49 under Regulation 2016/679').

[143] ibid 4.

[144] See, eg, Wen Macaskill and Gabriel Dance, 'NSA Files: Decoded' (*The Guardian*, 1 November 2013) <https://www.theguardian.com/world/interactive/2013/nov/01/snowden-nsa-files-surveillance-revelations-decoded#section/1> accessed 10 July 2023.

affording adequacy decisions under the GDPR but, in general, for the EU framework for transfers of personal data outside the EEA.[145] Recall that in the aftermath of those revelations, in its 2015 *Schrems I* judgment, the CJEU invalidated the EU-US Safe Harbor framework for transfers of personal data from the EU to the United States.[146] *Schrems I* marked a watershed moment in the history of transfers of personal data. By injecting the foreign surveillance issue in the mix of the EU data protection law's framework for transfers of personal data outside the EEA—the issue that is typically one of national security nature—the CJEU disrupted the framework that was designed to account for what data exporters and importers can and cannot do with personal data originating in the EU. Five years later, in its *Schrems II* judgment, the CJEU invalidated the Safe Harbor's successor—the EU-US Privacy Shield—on similar grounds.[147] Furthermore, as explained earlier, the Court expanded the application of the 'essential equivalence' standard to all mechanisms for systematic personal data transfers under the GDPR.[148]

The third and final change is that the last twenty-five years have seen an exponential growth of cross-border commerce powered by personal and other data.[149] The importance of data flows for pan-European and global trade forms an integral part of the EU's economic digital trade discourse advanced in parallel and, at times, contrary to the fundamental rights discourse.[150] The ubiquitous character of data flows in digital commerce and online activities has further intensified global economic interdependence. It puts extraordinary pressure on the legal framework setting boundaries for the flows of personal data.

The changes introduced into the EU's framework for transfers of personal data in the GDPR, as compared to the Data Protection Directive, tried addressing some of the political, legal, and economic changes identified earlier. Indeed, several recitals of the GDPR acknowledge the challenges for the data protection regime brought by technological developments and globalization.[151] In its 2017 Communication 'Exchanging and Protecting Personal Data in a Globalised World', the European Commission praised the GDPR for providing 'a diverse set of mechanisms that are flexible enough to adapt to a variety of different transfer situations', citing notably the SCCs, the codes of conduct, and certification mechanisms.[152] It is true that as

[145] EDPB, 'Recommendations 02/2020 on the European Essential Guarantees for Surveillance Measures' (10 November 2020) <https://edpb.europa.eu/sites/default/files/files/file1/edpb_recommendations_202002_europeanessentialguaranteessurveillance_en.pdf > accessed 10 July 2023 (hereafter EDPB, 'Recommendations 02/2020 on the European Essential Guarantees for Surveillance Measures').

[146] *Schrems I* (n 5).

[147] *Schrems II* (n 6) paras 184–87.

[148] For a discussion, see Section 5.2.2.

[149] See Chapter 1 to this book.

[150] See Section 3.3.2.

[151] Recitals 5–7 GDPR.

[152] Communication from the Commission to the European Parliament and the Council, 'Exchanging and Protecting Personal Data in a Globalised World' [2017] COM (2017) 7 final, 10 (hereafter

compared to the Data Protection Directive, the GDPR's transfer mechanisms are somewhat more flexible. For example, the GDPR allows for the adoption of an adequacy decision not only to a third country overall but also to an international organization, a territory or one or more specified sectors within that third country.[153] In addition, the GDPR has explicitly recognized BCRs—which were applied in practice, but were merely implied in the text of the Directive—as one of the appropriate safeguards for transfers of personal data. The GDPR also added two new appropriate safeguards, namely certification mechanisms and codes of conduct,[154] which, at the time of writing, have not yet been operationalized. Finally, the specific derogations allowed under Article 49 of the GDPR were complemented by an open-ended, but extremely hard to comply with, safeguard allowing the transfer of personal data for the purposes of compelling legitimate interests of the data controller.[155]

On a more critical note, more than four years after the GDPR took effect, few of these flexibilities have ever been used or operationalized. To wit: no adequacy decisions have been adopted for international organizations,[156] territories, or sectors of economy; only three adequacy decisions for a third country have been adopted under the GDPR (Japan, the United Kingdom, and South Korea); certification mechanisms and codes of conduct are not yet used as mechanisms for data transfers; and BCRs take several years to be approved by the DPAs.[157]

In practice, most of the systematic transfers of personal data outside the EEA still rely on SCCs, which are currently only available for transfers of personal data to data importers *not* subject to the extraterritorial application of the GDPR, as explained in Section 2.2.4.[158] SCCs for transfers of personal data to foreign controllers

Communication from the Commission, 'Exchanging and Protecting Personal Data in a Globalised World').

[153] Compare art 25(1) Data Protection Directive and art 45(1) GDPR. Note, however, that three adequacy decisions under the Data Protection Directive (namely, adequacy decision for Canada, the EU-US Safe Harbor, and the EU-US Privacy Shield), despite the absence of a direct mentioning of the possibility to adopt and adequacy decision for a specific sector the text of the Data Protection Directive, were adopted solely for commercial sector transfers.

[154] Art 46(2)(e) and (f) GDPR.

[155] Second paragraph of art 49(1) GDPR.

[156] See Christopher Kuner, 'The GDPR and International Organizations' (2020) 114 AJIL Unbound 15.

[157] As of 2023, waiting time for BCR approval by the Dutch DPA constitutes seven more years. See Autoriteit Persoonsgegevens, Jaarplan 2023. Toezichthouden in een digitaliserende samenleving (April 2023), 2 <https://www.autoriteitpersoonsgegevens.nl/uploads/2023-05/AP_jaarplan_-_2023.pdf> accessed 10 July 2023.

[158] IAPP-EY Annual Privacy Governance Report (*IAPP*, 2019) < https://f.hubspotusercontent20.net/hubfs/525875/IAPP_EY_Governance_Report_2019.pdf> accessed 10 July 2023, 110 (hereafter IAPP-EY Annual Privacy Governance Report) (showing that in 2019 (ie prior to the CJEU *Schrems II* judgment), 88 per cent of personal data transfers from the EU to the United States are based on the SCCs.) The use of the SCCs remained the same or even increased after *Schrems II*. See IAPP-FTI Consulting Annual Privacy Governance Report 2020 < https://static2.ftitechnology.com/docs/IAPP-FTI+Consulting+-+2020+Privacy+Governance+Report.pdf> accessed 10 July 2023 (showing that 88 per cent of companies surveyed used the SCCs as a transfer mechanism) and Müge Fazlioglu, 'IAPP-EY Annual

and processors who *are* subject to the extraterritorial application of the GDPR were announced back in 2021 by the European Commission, but have not been released as of this writing (June 2023).[159] As a result, no transfer mechanism is available for systematic transfers of personal data to such data importers located in countries not afforded an adequacy decision. This raises the question of whether the above-mentioned flexibilities are merely paying lip service to the EU's economic discourse on digital trade, as discussed in Chapter 3 of this book, rather than reflecting a genuine effort to reform the framework for transfers of personal data.

This section argues that although the framework did—on paper—become more flexible, the changes did not rectify key structural issues inherent within it. Against the backdrop of the three developments mentioned at the beginning of this section, the discussion below is centred around the *four principal weaknesses* of the EU's framework under Chapter V of the GDPR that undermine effective and complete protection of the fundamental rights to privacy and the protection of personal data in practice.[160] These weaknesses also harken back to the discussion of the Chapter V framework from an international trade law perspective in Sections 2.3 and 2.4.2.

First, although the CJEU's *Schrems II* judgment contributed to bridging the qualitative gap between adequacy decisions and private law mechanisms for systematic transfers of personal data, it did not eliminate the problem completely. This section contemplates that *Schrems II* may instead lead to other problems, such as the fragmentation of standards for transfers of personal data across the EU due to: (a) the deficiencies of coordination between European DPAs; (b) limitations of enforcement resources of European DPAs and a resulting shift towards private enforcement, which will, in turn result in (c) a fragmentation of case law across the EU member states in the short and medium terms. It also argues that, overall, in the future the secondary EU framework for transfers of personal data may not be the right tool to address the foreign surveillance issue in transfers of personal data outside the EEA.

Second, there is a gap in legal protection of personal data transmitted outside the EEA in a situation when such transmission falls outside the scope of the definition

Privacy Governance Report 2021' (2021) <https://ssrn.com/abstract=4227244> accessed 10 July 2023 (showing that 94 per cent of companies surveyed used SCCs as a transfer mechanism).

[159] See 'The New Standard Contractual Clauses: Questions and Answers' (*European Commission*, May 2022) < https://commission.europa.eu/system/files/2022-05/questions_answers_on_sccs_en.pdf> accessed 10 July 2023.

[160] The CJEU has highlighted both in *Schrems I* and *Schrems II* judgments that essentially equivalent level of protection must be guaranteed in practice. *Schrems I* (n 5) paras 73–74; *Schrems II* (n 6) para 248 ('248. As the Court made clear in the judgment in Schrems, [the essentially equivalent] standard does not mean that the level of protection must be "identical" to that required in the Union. Although the means which a third country employs in order to protect the data subjects' rights may differ from those prescribed by the GDPR read in the light of the Charter, "those means must ... prove, *in practice*, effective in order to ensure protection essentially equivalent to that guaranteed within the European Union".') (emphasis added, internal footnotes omitted). See also Kuner, 'Protecting EU Data outside EU Borders under the GDPR' (n 15) 97–99.

a 'transfer' and the scope of the EU framework for transfers of personal data outside the EEA. As a result, such personal data is not afforded the same level of protection as personal data transmitted outside the EEA as a result of a 'transfer'.[161]

The third weakness is the gap in legal protection of personal data due to the inadequacies of the adequacy decisions. These are: (a) the lack of regular reviews of the assessment on which the adequacy decisions are based (the 'snapshot' problem), (b) the difficulties of enforcing individual rights in foreign jurisdictions (the 'heavy burden' problem), and (c) the inadequacy of onward transfer mechanism embedded in the adequacy decisions (the 'onward transfer' problem).

The fourth and final weakness is a mismatch between the transformation of the role of personal data in cross-border commerce since 1995, when the core of the EU framework for transfers of personal data was designed, on the one hand, and the rigidity of this framework in the sense that it does not take into account the different degrees of risks to fundamental rights inherent in transfers of personal data in different circumstances, on the other hand. The section therefore contends that the rules of Chapter V of the GDPR lack scalability and are thus not fully adequate for the digital age. The discussion below elaborates on each of these arguments.

5.3.1 The foreign surveillance issue after *Schrems II*

The interpretation of 'adequacy' of personal data protection as 'essential equivalence' by the CJEU in *Schrems I* created a qualitative gap between the level of protection that, in theory, is given to personal data transferred on the basis of adequacy decisions, on the one hand, and the level of protection afforded to personal data transferred on the basis of so-called 'appropriate safeguards', on the other hand. The CJEU's conclusions and the ensuing guidance by the European DPAs[162]—as well as the above-mentioned qualitative gap—were later codified in the GDPR. As compared to Article 25(2) of the Data Protection Directive, the list of factors set forth in Article 45(2) of the GDPR (that the European Commission must consider when assessing the adequacy of the level of protection of personal data in a third country) has been sufficiently expanded. In particular, it requires the Commission to evaluate the access of public authorities to personal data, as well as the implementation of the foreign legislation to see whether it contains effective and enforceable data subject rights and effective administrative and judicial redress for the data subjects whose personal data are being transferred.[163] By strengthening the adequacy assessment, however, the GDPR inadvertently created a situation where

[161] See also Kuner, 'Protecting EU data outside EU Borders under the GDPR' (n 15) 90–94.

[162] EDPB, Recommendations 02/2020 on the European Essential Guarantees for surveillance measures (n 145).

[163] Art 45(2)(a) GDPR.

the level of personal data protection achieved by all other mechanisms for systematic data transfers (most importantly, appropriate safeguards under Article of the 46 GDPR, which on a par with adequacy, can underlie systematic transfers of personal data) became lower than that afforded (in theory) by an adequacy decision.

Adequacy decisions are adopted by implementing acts of the Commission after a thorough assessment of the third country's legal system and data protection framework. For example, the adequacy decision for Japan—which is one of the new generation of adequacy decisions adopted after the GDPR entered into force—contains commitments by Japan in relation to personal data transferred from the EEA. These commitments are included in the 'Supplementary Rules under the Act on the Protection of Personal Information for the Handling of Personal Data Transferred from the EU based on an Adequacy Decision' (hereafter referred to as the 'Supplementary Rules'), which are legally binding for Japanese businesses.[164] In contrast, the appropriate safeguards and specific derogations are merely private law mechanisms.

An adequacy decision certifies (in theory) that a particular third country ensures a level of personal data protection 'essentially equivalent' to that in the EU.[165] The 'level of personal data protection' means here not only the quality of the data protection rules but multiple other factors, including the respect for the rule of law and human rights, access of public authorities to personal data, existence and effective functioning of independent supervisory authorities, and existence of effective judicial review designed to ensure compliance with provisions of EU law.[166] None of the other mechanisms for systematic data transfers required—until the *Schrems II* judgment—such a thorough assessment. Most specifically, these mechanisms as described in the GDPR, did *not* seem to provide individuals with any safeguards against the access to their data by third country's public authorities. After the CJEU's invalidation of the Safe Harbor framework in *Schrems I* in 2015, Kuner rightly noted that:

> [t]he conclusions of the CJEU in *Schrems* have thus undermined the logical consistency of using adequate safeguards to transfer personal data. The European Commission and the DPAs have allowed standard contractual clauses and BCRs to be used for years although it has been clear that they cannot provide effective protection against intelligence surveillance, suggesting that until now they have implicitly factored the possibility of such surveillance into the definition of

[164] Annex 1 to Commission Implementing Decision (EU) 2019/419 of 23 January 2019 pursuant to Regulation (EU) 2016/679 of the European Parliament and of the Council on the adequate protection of personal data by Japan under the Act on the Protection of Personal Information [2019] C/2019/304/ OJ L 76 (hereafter 'Adequacy Decision for Japan').

[165] *Schrems I* (n 5) para 73.

[166] Art 45 GDPR; *Schrems I* (n 5) paras 91–96; Article 29 Working Party, Working document on Adequacy Referential, WP 254rev.01, 6 February 2018, Chapter 4.

"adequate safeguards." The strict standard for data protection rights applied by the CJEU in *Schrems* judgments raises the question of whether this is compatible with EU fundamental rights law.[167]

It is precisely this deficiency of private law mechanisms for transfers of personal data that led to a challenge of the validity of the European Commission's Decision approving the SCCs, along with the EU-US Privacy Shield, in the light of the EU Charter, which resulted in the CJEU's 2020 *Schrems II* judgment.[168] In particular, in the judgment of the Irish High Court referring the case to the CJEU, Justice Costello argued that neither the 'Privacy Shield' nor the SCCs are sufficient to protect the fundamental rights that apply to personal data in the EU Charter. In particular, they limit the right to an effective remedy before an independent tribunal guaranteed by Article 47 of the EU Charter beyond the limits set by Article 52(1) of the EU Charter.[169] Justice Costello also noted that '[i]f there are inadequacies in the laws [of the foreign country] within the meaning of Union law, the SCCs cannot and do not remedy or compensate for these inadequacies'.[170]

As has already been mentioned earlier, in *Schrems II*, the CJEU reinstated the logical consistency of the EU framework for transfers of personal data outside the EEA.[171] Despite running the risk of being repetitive, for the purposes of discussion below, it is important to summarize *all* the CJEU's conclusions in relation to the validity of the SCCs and, indirectly, all other appropriate safeguards under Article 46 of the GDPR:

(1) The standard of 'essential equivalence' equally applies to all appropriate safeguards under Article 46 GDPR, also in the context of access to personal data by foreign authorities in a national surveillance context;[172]

[167] Kuner, 'Reality and Illusion in EU Data Transfer Regulation Post Schrems' (n 12) 907–08.

[168] CJEU, *Schrems II*, referred to the CJEU by Irish High Court (Commercial), *The Data Protection Commissioner v. Facebook Ireland Limited and Maximillian Schrems* 2016 No 4809 P, 3 October 2017.

[169] Irish High Court (Commercial), *The Data Protection Commissioner v. Facebook Ireland Limited and Maximillian Schrems* 2016 No 4809 P, 3 October 2017, para 334, stating that

> the limitations on the exercise of the right to an effective remedy before an independent tribunal, as required by Article 47 [of the EU Charter], for EU citizens whose data privacy rights are infringed by the intelligence agencies are not proportionate or necessary or needed to protect the rights and freedoms of others. Neither the introduction of the Privacy Shield Ombudsperson mechanism nor the provisions of Article 4 of the SCC decisions eliminate the well-founded concerns raised by the [Irish Data Protection Commissioner] in relation to the adequacy of the protection afforded to EU data subjects whose personal data is wrongfully interfered with by the intelligence services of the United States once their personal data has been transferred for processing to the United States.

[170] *Schrems II* (n 6) para 154.

[171] Christopher Kuner, 'The Schrems II Judgment of the Court of Justice and the Future of Data Transfer Regulation' *European Law Blog* (17 July 2020) <https://europeanlawblog.eu/2020/07/17/the-schrems-ii-judgment-of-the-court-of-justice-and-the-future-of-data-transfer-regulation/> accessed 10 July 2023 (hereafter Kuner, 'The Schrems II Judgment of the Court of Justice and the Future of Data Transfer Regulation').

[172] *Schrems II* (n 6) paras 96, 105; see also Opinion of AG Saugmandsgaard Øe in *Schrems II* (n 82) para 117. See also EDPB, Frequently Asked Questions on the Judgment of the Court of Justice of the European Union in Case C-311/18 – *Data Protection Commissioner v Facebook Ireland Ltd and*

(2) 'Essential equivalence' of the level of protection in third countries that have been afforded an adequacy decision is presumed;[173]

(3) The SCCs 'are solely intended to provide contractual guarantees … independently of the level of protection guaranteed in each third country',[174] and are valid;[175]

(4) Prior to using the SCCs and other appropriate safeguards for third countries that have not been granted an adequacy decision, the data exporter must conduct a comprehensive assessment, in particular, on the basis of factors 'set out, in a non-exhaustive manner, in Article 45(2) [GDPR]' of whether those safeguards can, *in practice*, ensure essentially equivalent protection of personal data[176] (so-called 'mini-adequacy' assessments[177]);

(5) If, based on the assessment above, the data exporter concludes that an 'essentially equivalent' level of data protection cannot be ensured by appropriate safeguards, the data exporter must implement what the CJEU calls 'additional safeguards' or 'supplementary measures', which should be determined on a case-by-case basis;[178]

(6) If the data exporter established in the EU is not able to take 'supplementary measures' to guarantee 'essentially equivalent' protection of personal data, the data exporter must suspend or end the transfer; this is, in particular, the case where the law of the third country imposes obligations on the recipient of personal data, which are contrary to the SCCs;[179]

(7) The DPAs must proactively monitor transfers of personal data under appropriate safeguards and suspend or prohibit data transfers that do not meet the standard of 'essential equivalence';[180] and

(8) To prevent the fragmentation of rules, which could result from different EU member states' DPAs arriving at different conclusions regarding lawfulness of transfers, DPAs must work together through coordination mechanisms under the GDPR.[181]

Maximillian Schrems (23 July 2020), questions 6 and 7 <https://edpb.europa.eu/our-work-tools/our-documents/other/frequently-asked-questions-judgment-court-justice-european-union_en> accessed 10 July 2023.

[173] *Schrems II* (n 6) para 118.
[174] ibid para 133.
[175] ibid paras 136, 147. See also Opinion of AG Saugmandsgaard Øe in *Schrems II* (n 82) para 126.
[176] ibid para 105.
[177] Kuner, 'The Schrems II Judgment of the Court of Justice and the Future of Data Transfer Regulation' (n 171).
[178] *Schrems II* (n 6) paras 131–34, 137, 142.
[179] ibid para 135.
[180] ibid paras 108, 121.
[181] ibid para 147.

Facially, the CJEU closed the qualitative gap between adequacy decisions and appropriate safeguards under Article 46 GDPR, while preserving the lawfulness of the most commonly used mechanism for data transfers in the absence of an adequacy decision.[182] The way the CJEU answered the questions referred to it in *Schrems II* is, indeed, perhaps, the only logical way the Court could restore the consistency of the EU secondary law framework for transfers of personal data[183] and assert the importance of fundamental rights vis-à-vis the economic interests embedded in data transfers, on the one hand, and without upsetting the delicate institutional balance in the EU, on the other hand. If the CJEU had invalidated the SCCs as a mechanism for transfers of personal data, it would have undermined the validity of all other private law mechanisms in the GDPR—not only the BCRs but also the certification mechanisms and codes of conduct added into the GDPR, which the European Commission frequently emphasizes as bringing extra flexibility to the modernized 'toolbox' for data transfers.[184] Such a state of affairs would also undermine the system of cross-border transfers in the GDPR as a whole.[185] Thus, this approach would have created—*de jure—data* localization in respect of all countries not afforded adequacy decisions,[186] which would be contrary to the EU's external digital trade policy and digital trade discourse (discussed in Chapters 3 and 4). Recall that specific derogations under Article 49 of the GDPR, which were not considered in *Schrems II*, can only be used for occasional and non-repetitive transfers, at least in their interpretation by the EDPB.[187] Neither could the CJEU invalidate the model SCCs approved by the European Commission: as the CJEU demonstrated itself, they do provide the safeguards required under Article 45(2) of the GDPR, provided that a third country's legal framework does not interfere with their application.[188]

The CJEU also did not use the window of opportunity—opened by the Advocate General's opinion—to modify its position in *Schrems I* and apply a lower threshold

[182] IAPP-EY Annual Privacy Governance Report (n 158) 110 (showing that in 2019 (ie prior to the CJEU *Schrems II* judgement) 88 per cent of personal data transfers from the EU to the US are based on the SCCs.).

[183] See , 'The Schrems II Judgment of the Court of Justice and the Future of Data Transfer Regulation' (n 171); Christakis, 'After Schrems II' (n 58).

[184] See Communication from the Commission, 'Exchanging and Protecting Personal Data in a Globalised World' (n 152); Communication from the Commission to the European Parliament and the Council, Data Protection as a Pillar of Citizens' Empowerment and the EU's Approach to the Digital Transition – Two Years of Application of the General Data Protection Regulation [2020] COM (2020) 264 final (hereafter Communication from the Commission, Two Years of Application of the General Data Protection Regulation).

[185] For a discussion of this scenario, see Peter Swire, 'The Data Protection Commissioner and Facebook Ireland Limited and Maximillian Schrems. Affidavit of Peter Swire' (2016) 18-2 Georgia Tech Scheller College of Business Research Paper <https://ssrn.com/abstract=3097444> accessed 10 July 2023.

[186] There were twelve adequacy decisions as of the judgment in *Schrems II*, fourteen as of June 2023.

[187] EDPB, Guidelines 2/2018 on derogations of Article 49 under Regulation 2016/679 (n 142). For discussion of a different viewpoint, see Section 2.2.4.

[188] *Schrems II* (n 6) paras 126–48.

for situations where foreign authorities' access transferred personal data for national security purposes, thus amplifying the tension between the CJEU's approach to national security measures interfering with fundamental rights abroad and in the EU member states.[189] In particular, the Advocate General had noted that:

> 'essential equivalence' test should therefore ... be applied in such a way as to preserve a certain flexibility in order to take the various legal and cultural traditions into account. That test implies, however, if it is not to be deprived of its substance, that certain minimum safeguards and general requirements for the protection of fundamental rights that follow from the Charter and the ECHR have an equivalent in the legal order of the third country of destination.[190]

Thus, the Advocate General had argued that both the standards of the Charter and the ECHR are the relevant comparators for the assessment of the foreign legal framework. He had also observed that 'the standards resulting from Articles 7, 8 and 47 of the Charter, as interpreted by [the CJEU], are in certain respects stricter than those arising under Article 8 of the ECHR according to the interpretation of those provisions by the European Court of Human Rights ("the ECtHR")'.[191]

In practice, the CJEU pushed the foreign surveillance problem in the context of personal data transfers further down the line. As argued in Chapter 2, the *Schrems II* judgment has restricted the possibility of using the SCCs in practice.[192] Furthermore, and most importantly, it is questionable whether in practice the *Schrems II* judgment has allowed to bridge the qualitative gap between the adequacy assessments and appropriate safeguards under Article 46 for several reasons. It is unclear whether companies are in the right position to conduct assessments of the third country's legal regime similar to adequacy assessments, which the European Commission typically conducts for several years and which, even then, do not always result in bullet-proof adequacy decisions as this section illuminates below. Many companies, especially small and medium enterprises, will have neither the resources nor the expertise to conduct comprehensive research into third countries' legal frameworks. It is also questionable whether the lack of 'essential equivalence' can be remedied by additional guarantees that companies must implement in order to continue data transfers.[193] With respect to transfers

[189] See Section 2.2.2.

[190] Opinion of AG Saugmandsgaard Øe in *Schrems II* (n 82) para 249.

[191] ibid para 251. See also Monika Zalnieriute, 'Big Brother Watch and Others v. the United Kingdom (case review)' (2022) 116(3) American Journal of International Law 585–86, stating that the decision of the Grand Chamber of the European Court of Human Rights (ECtHR) in Strasbourg in *Big Brother Watch and Others v. United Kingdom*—the landmark ECtHR case on bulk government surveillance—'stands for a highly permissive approach to government surveillance'.

[192] See Section 2.2.2.

[193] See EDPB, Recommendations 01/2020 on measures that supplement transfer tools (n 67) paras 34–35, use cases 6 and 7.

to the United States, which was recognized by the CJEU itself as lacking essentially equivalent protection, even companies that have both the resources and expertise to do such an assessment are simply not able to rectify the deficiencies of the US legal framework identified by the CJEU, short of stopping transfers to the United States entirely.[194]

Even more importantly, the CJEU's approach gives companies—the very actors which 'encroach upon the private sphere'—a crucial role in setting the boundaries for data transfers and resulting interference with fundamental rights.[195] While companies are driven by their bottom lines, it is the role of governments and European institutions to ensure that fundamental rights are protected. Thus, on the one hand, it is clear that many countries in the world do not meet the 'essential equivalence' standard as formulated by the CJEU. On the other hand, it is similarly clear that additional private law guarantees cannot remedy those deficiencies. In the present-day interconnected world, data flows will not simply stop and, in practice (in the view of low risk of enforcement by DPAs), many companies are likely to continue with 'business as usual', unless ordered by a DPA to stop doing so.

Within almost three years after *Schrems II*, such orders were issued only a few times, and only with respect to transfers to the United States.[196] Most of these orders concern the use of Google Analytics and Facebook Connect tools by public bodies or private companies, addressed to the latter rather than to Google or Meta Platforms (that provides the Facebook service). Given that millions of websites use these tools, orders to stop using them for even a few tens or hundreds of companies is merely a drop in the ocean. Only one of orders to suspend transfers of personal data issued since 2015 (when the CJEU *Schrems I* judgment was rendered) is likely to have tangible practical consequences for transfers of personal data outside the EEA. This is the decision issued on 12 May 2023 by the Irish DPC to Meta Platforms (following a ten-year inquiry that led to both *Schrems I* and *Schrems II* CJEU judgments) with respect to transfers of personal data to the United States in connection

[194] As discussed in Section 2.3.2, in certain circumstances identified by the EDPB, systematic transfers of personal data are not allowed to countries that do not ensure an essentially equivalent level of personal data protection. For discussion, see Anupam Chander and Joe Jones, 'What if It Were Illegal to Transfer Personal Data from the European Union to the United States?' (*Lawfare*, 22 June 2023) <https://www.lawfaremedia.org/article/what-if-it-were-illegal-to-transfer-personal-data-from-the-european-union-to-the-united-states> accessed 10 July 2023.

[195] For a discussion on why giving companies too much power in setting the boundaries for data processing could be a problem, see Claudia Quelle, 'Privacy, Proceduralism and Self-Regulation in Data Protection Law' (2017) Teoria Critica della Regolazione Sociale <https://ssrn.com/abstract=3139901> accessed 10 July 2023, 86.

[196] See EDPB, 'Report of the Work Undertaken by the Supervisory Authorities within the 101 Task Force' (28 March 2023) <https://edpb.europa.eu/system/files/2023-04/edpb_20230328_report_101task_force_en.pdf> accessed 10 July 2023 (hereafter EDPB, 'Report of the Work Undertaken by the Supervisory Authorities within the 101 Task Force'). See also Christopher Kuner, 'Op-Ed: "International Data Transfers after Five Years of the GDPR: Postmodern Anxieties' (2023) EU Law Live <https://eulawlive.com/op-ed-international-data-transfers-after-five-years-of-the-gdpr-postmodern-anxieties-by-christopher-kuner/> accessed 10 July 2023 (hereafter Kuner, 'Op-Ed: "International Data Transfers after Five Years of the GDPR: Postmodern Anxieties').

with the delivery of its Facebook Service. In this decision (toughened as a result of coordination with other European DPAs within the EDPB, which resulted in a binding EDPB decision[197]), the Irish DPC ordered Meta Platforms to suspend any future transfer of personal data to the United States within the period of five months; an administrative fine of EUR 1.2 billion (reflecting the EDPB binding decision); and an order to bring its transfers of personal data in compliance with Chapter V of the GDPR within six months.[198] The impact of this decision is not going to affect transfers to the United States, at least for the time being, in the light of the newly adopted adequacy decision (EU-US Data Privacy Framework).[199] It may, however, have real consequences for transfers to other countries that have not been afforded adequacy by the EU. Another notable order to stop transfers to the United States was issued by the Belgian DPA, which prohibited transfer of tax data of Belgian 'Accidental Americans' to the United States due to violations of Chapter V of the GDPR.[200] This order, however, was promptly overturned by the Belgian court.[201]

Furthermore, in the light of the low enforcement rate following *Schrems I* and *Schrems II*, it is questionable whether the DPAs themselves are well situated to assess the adequacy of legal frameworks in third countries and monitor compliance with the new rules, given the pervasiveness of data flows and the lack of financial and human resources.[202] Most enforcement actions concerning transfers of personal data outside the EEA following *Schrems II* focus either on transfers to the

[197] EDPB, 'Binding Decision 1/2023 on the dispute submitted by the Irish SA on data transfers by Meta Platforms Ireland Limited for its Facebook service (Art. 65 GDPR)' (13 April 2023) < https://edpb.europa.eu/system/files/2023-05/edpb_bindingdecision_202301_ie_sa_facebooktransfers_en.pdf> accessed 10 July 2023.

[198] Irish Data Protection Commission, 'Data Protection Commission Announces Conclusion of Inquiry into Meta Ireland' (n 105).

[199] European Commission Implementing Decision of 10 July 2023 pursuant to Regulation (EU) 2016/679 of the European Parliament and of the Council on the adequate level of protection of personal data under the EU-US Data Privacy Framework [2023] C(2023) 4745 final (hereafter European Commission Implementing Decision on EU-US Data Privacy Framework).

[200] Autorité de protection des données (Gegevensbeschermingsautoriteit), 'Press Release: Belgian DPA prohibits the transfer of tax data of Belgian "Accidental Americans" to the USA' (24 May 2023) <https://www.dataprotectionauthority.be/citizen/belgian-dpa-prohibits-the-transfer-of-tax-data-of-belgian-accidental-americans-to-the-usa> (accessed 10 July 2023).

[201] GDPRhub, 'Court of Appeal of Brussels - 2023/AR/801' (2023) <https://gdprhub.eu/index.php?title=Court_of_Appeal_of_Brussels_-_2023/AR/801&mtc=today> accessed 10 July 2023.

[202] According to the EDPB's 2021 study, over 80 per cent of national DPAs have insufficient budget to carry out their statutory activities, and for 86 per cent of DPAs staffing levels are below what is necessary to perform their tasks. EDPB, 'Overview on Resources Made Available by Member States to the Data Protection Authorities and on Enforcement Actions by the Data Protection Authorities' (05 August 2021) < https://edpb.europa.eu/system/files/2021-08/edpb_report_2021_overviewsaressourcesandenforcement_v3_en_0.pdf> accessed 10 July 2023. The EDPB and the European Data Protection Supervisor (EDPS), monitoring compliance with data protection laws by European institutions and bodies, are equally underfunded. See EDPB, 'Open Letter on EDPB Budget Proposal for 2023' (12 September 2022) < https://edpb.europa.eu/system/files/2022-09/letteronbudget_out2022-0068.pdf> accessed 10 July 2023.

United States, where such assessment has already been done by the CJEU,[203] or China, which is unlikely to meet the essential equivalence standard in the view of its 'government's vast and unlimited access to personal data'.[204] The fact that there is only one tangible enforcement action since 2015 concerning transfers of personal data outside the EEA, and the reluctance of the Irish DPA to take a firm action against Facebook's transfers to the United States for ten years,[205] is telling. Yet, the situation is even worse than this. Following *Schrems I* and despite the CJEU having found that the *essence* of the fundamental rights was violated by transfers to the United States on the basis of the EU-US Safe Harbor, there were virtually zero enforcement cases brought by the DPAs for transfers under the Safe Harbor. Thus, although in *Schrems II* the CJEU restored, in theory, the coherence of the framework for systematic transfers of personal data, it did not close the gap between the 'reality and illusion' of personal data protection in the context of transfers of personal data outside the EEA.[206]

While it has put the DPAs at centre stage for ensuring the lawfulness of transfers, the CJEU has explicitly dismissed the risk of divergent decisions by the EU DPAs to suspend or prohibit transfers by referring to coordination mechanisms within the EDPB under the GDPR.[207] This coordination mechanism, however, has not been effective until now, in part due to differences in administrative procedures in EU

[203] The most notable examples include: a series of enforcement cases regarding the use of Google Analytics and Facebook Connect following 101 complaints by noyb (an NGO affiliated with digital rights activist Max Schrems) (see EDPB, 'Report of the Work Undertaken by the Supervisory Authorities within the 101 Task Force' (n 196)); decision by Irish DPC in the matter of Meta Platform ordering to bring transfers of personal data to the United States in compliance with the GDPR (see Irish Data Protection Commission, Decision in the matter of Meta Platforms Ireland Limited (n 69)); and a collective action concerning transfers of personal data to the United States launched against Meta in the Netherlands (see Data Privacy Stichting, 'Why Did We Launch Two Actions against Meta?' <https://dataprivacystichting.com/our-actions/> accessed 10 July 2023.

[204] Centre for IT and IP Law of KU Leuven, 'Government Access to Data in Third Countries', Final Report, EDPS/2019/02-13 (November 2021) <https://edpb.europa.eu/system/files/2022-01/legalstudy_on_government_access_0.pdf>, 24, accessed 10 July 2023. Transfers of personal data from the EEA to China have attracted some attention of European DPAs recently, and are a relatively easy target amidst broader public debates on the risks of Chinese government's access to data among Western governments. See, eg, EDPB, 'Thirty-First Plenary Session: Establishment of a Taskforce on TikTok, Response to MEPs on Use of Clearview AI by Law Enforcement Authorities, Response to ENISA Advisory Group, Response to Open Letter NYOB' (10 June 2020) <https://edpb.europa.eu/news/news/2020/thirty-first-plenary-session-establishment-taskforce-tiktok-response-meps-use_en> accessed 10 July 2023; John Culatto, 'Dutch Parents Sue TikTok for €1.4 Billion' (*DW*, 6 February 2021) <https://www.dw.com/en/dutch-parents-sue-tiktok-for-14-billion/a-57762350> accessed 10 July 2023; Shiona McCallum, 'TikTok under Investigation by Canadian Privacy Authorities' (*BBC News*, 24 February 2023) <https://www.bbc.com/news/technology-64759365> accessed 10 July 2023; Glenn Thrush and Sapna Maheshwari, 'Justice Dept. Investigating TikTok's Owner over Possible Spying on Journalists' (*The New York Times*, 17 March 2023) <https://www.nytimes.com/2023/03/17/us/politics/tik-tok-spying-justice-dept.html> accessed 10 July 2023.

[205] See, eg, 'Is the DPC Actually Stopping Facebook's EU-US Data Transfers?! Maybe Half-Way!' (*noyb*, 9 September 2020) <https://noyb.eu/en/dpc-actually-stopping-facebooks-eu-us-data-transfers-maybe-half-way> accessed 10 July 2023.

[206] Kuner, 'Reality and Illusion in EU Data Transfer Regulation Post Schrems' (n 12), discussing the 'reality and illusion' in EU personal data transfer regulation post *Schrems I*.

[207] *Schrems II* (n 6) para 147.

member states.[208] This issue is very well recognized by the European legislator.[209] To address the issue, the European Commission has proposed rules harmonizing procedural rules regarding cross-border enforcement of the GDPR.[210]

Importantly, the relatively new possibilities for mass damages claims under Articles 80 and 82 of the GDPR and EU member states' laws are becoming increasingly attractive for NGOs and professional litigation funders.[211] The GDPR provisions allow a not-for-profit body, organization or association that has been mandated by an individual and meets certain requirements, to exercise individual rights to judicial remedy, including an ability to claim compensation.[212] In 2023, a Dutch data privacy foundation and a Dutch consumer association started a mass claim against Meta Platforms in connection to transfers of personal data to the United States by its Facebook service.[213] Sooner or later, domestic courts will need to evaluate whether transfers to certain jurisdictions with the use of the SCCs meet the *Schrems II* requirements and which supplementary measures are appropriate in specific circumstances. This may result in a fragmentation of the case law throughout the EU in short and medium terms, and in more references to the CJEU in the long term.

Despite this critique, it is undeniable that the *Schrems* cases set an important agenda for law and policy on cross-border transfers of personal data outside the EEA. The *Schrems II* judgment marks an important milestone in asserting the fundamental rights to privacy and the protection of personal data in the context of digital trade. The fact that the CJEU put the burden on private companies and the

[208] See EDPB, 'Contribution of the EDPB to the Evaluation of the GDPR under Article 97' (18 February 2020), 3 <https://edpb.europa.eu/sites/default/files/files/file1/edpb_contributiongdprevaluation_20200218.pdf> accessed 10 July 2023 (hereafter EDPB, 'Contribution of the EDPB to the Evaluation of the GDPR'); Communication from the Commission, 'Two Years of Application of the General Data Protection Regulation' (n 184) 5 (noting that 'developing a truly common European data protection culture between data protection authorities is still an on-going process. Data protection authorities have not yet made full use of the tools the GDPR provides, such as joint operations that could lead to joint investigations.').

[209] See Communication from the Commission, 'Two Years of Application of the General Data Protection Regulation' (n 184).

[210] Proposal for a Regulation of the European Parliament and of the Council laying down additional procedural rules relating to the enforcement of Regulation (EU) 2016/679 [2023] COM/2023/348 final.

[211] For discussion, see Geert Potjewijd and others, 'Mass Damage Claims for GDPR Infringements: A Multi-Jurisdictional Perspective' (2021) 1 Mass Claims 5 (hereafter Potjewijd and others, 'Mass Damage Claims for GDPR Infringements').

[212] For an overview of collective damage compensation systems for data protection violations in different EU member states, see Alexia Pato, 'The Collective Private Enforcement of Data Protection Rights in the EU' (2019) MPI-IAPL Summer School 3rd edn <https://ssrn.com/abstract=3303228> accessed 10 July 2023; Alexia Pato, 'The National Adaptation of Article 80 GDPR, Towards the Effective Private Enforcement of Collective Data Protection Rights' in Karen McCullagh, Olivia Tambou, and Sam Bourton (eds), *National Adaptations of the GDPR* (Collection Open Access Book 2019) 98ff <https://wp.me/p6OBGR-3dP> accessed 10 July 2023. See also Potjewijd and others, 'Mass Damage Claims for GDPR Infringements' (n 211).

[213] Wouter Hoeffnagel, 'Consumentenbond en DPS Starten Opnieuw Rechtszaak Tegen Facebook' (*Dutch IT Channel*, 16 March 2023) <https://www.dutchitchannel.nl/news/221853/consumentenbond-en-dps-starten-opnieuw-rechtszaak-tegen-facebook> accessed 10 July 2023.

DPAs should be taken as an intermediary solution: the lesser of two evils, the other being the prohibition of systematic data transfers on the basis of appropriate safeguards. It is a wake-up call to the EU and its trading partners to start a dialogue on the interplay between digital trade, fundamental rights, and national security. Such a dialogue has finally become a part of international conversations on cross-border data flows and is ongoing in multiple fora, in particular, at the OECD, WTO, G7, and G20, and is now part of the Data Free Flow with Trust agenda, discussed in Chapter 3.[214] The OECD Declaration on trusted government access to data, which sets non-binding principles governing such access, is an important step in this dialogue.[215]

The core issue raised in *Schrems I* and *II* cannot be fully addressed by businesses, DPAs, or even the EU secondary rules, such as the GDPR or the adequacy decisions.[216] As rightly noted by several commentators in relation to the invalidation of the EU-US Privacy Shield and the standards the EU Charter requires from foreign legal frameworks, 'any hope of a stable and viable accommodation for data transfers between the EU and the US can only be based on changes to US law'.[217] This is also true for other third countries: as discussed in the following section, few of the existing adequacy decisions can meet the high threshold of essential equivalence standard set by the CJEU in *Schrems I* and confirmed in *Schrems II* judgments.

In a global or, at a minimum, multilateral setting, reconciling the policy objectives of digital trade, national security, and fundamental rights is an intricate political challenge. As Farrell and Newman demonstrate, global economic interdependence and seamless data flows have been 'weaponized' by surveillance authorities that leveraged global networks for surveillance purposes (authors call this phenomenon 'weaponized interdependence').[218] *Schrems II*, they argue, is an opportunity to address this changed relationship between national security and civil liberties by democratic states, and primarily by the United States and the

[214] See Aidan Arasasingham and Matthew P Goodman, 'Operationalizing Data Free Flow with Trust (DFFT)' (*Center for Strategic and International Studies*, 13 April 2023) <https://www.csis.org/analysis/operationalizing-data-free-flow-trust-dfft> accessed 10 July 2023.

[215] Declaration on Government Access to Personal Data Held by Private Sector Entities (*OECD*, 14 December 2022) <https://legalinstruments.oecd.org/en/instruments/OECD-LEGAL-0487> accessed 10 July 2023.

[216] For example, Reidenberg noted that Safe Harbor 'offered a mechanism to delay facing tough decisions about international privacy'. Joel R Reidenberg, 'E-Commerce and Trans-Atlantic Privacy' (2001) 38 Houston Law Review 717, 739 (hereafter Reidenberg, 'E-Commerce and Trans-Atlantic Privacy').

[217] Kuner, 'Schrems II Re-Examined' (n 58); Kuner, 'The Schrems II Judgment of the Court of Justice and the Future of Data Transfer Regulation' (n 171); Kenneth Propp and Peter Swire, 'After Schrems II: A Proposal to Meet the Individual Redress Challenge' (*Lawfare Blog*, 13 August 2020) <https://www.lawfareblog.com/after-schrems-ii-proposal-meet-individual-redress-challenge> accessed 10 July 2023; Genna Churches and Monika Zalnieriute, '"Contracting Out" Human Rights in International Law: Schrems II and the Fundamental Flaws of U.S. Surveillance Law' (2020) Harvard International Law Journal Online, UNSW Law Research Paper No 20–44, 7–8 <https://ssrn.com/abstract=3679671> accessed 10 July 2023.

[218] Henry Farrell and Abraham L Newman, 'Weaponized Interdependence: How Global Economic Networks Shape State Coercion' (2020) 44(1) International Security 42.

EU.[219] Arguably, putting the burden on companies to assess essential equivalence of third countries' legal frameworks and hoping for companies operating in legal regimes with insufficient privacy protection to push their governments to change this regime—a bottom-up change—has not worked in the past. Improvements to bring US law governing government access to Europeans' data and create a redress mechanism for European data subjects may signal that the bottom-up change is in fact working.[220] Whether these improvements will be sufficient to meet the essential equivalence standard is likely to be a matter for the CJEU's consideration in the near future.[221]

To break the vicious circle of invalidations of transatlantic frameworks for transfers of personal data, setting the binding standards for foreign government access to personal data and agreeing on the redress mechanisms at the international, or at least bilateral, level[222] are much more in line with the EU's ambition to 'promote convergence of data protection standards at international level, as a way to facilitate data flows and thus trade'.[223] As former UK Information Commissioner Elizabeth Denham said at the IAPP Global Privacy Summit 2023, '[d]emocracies, especially the G7, should be able to get together and come to an agreement around standards for government access to private sector data'.[224]

What the optimal forum for addressing this issue should be is a broader question, one which is outside the scope of this book. At this stage, one could, however,

[219] Henry Farrell and Abraham L Newman, 'Schrems II Offers an Opportunity—If the U.S. Wants to Take It' (*Lawfare Blog*, 28 July 2020) <https://www.lawfareblog.com/schrems-ii-offers-opportunity-if-us-wants-take-it> (accessed 10 July 2023) (hereafter Farell and Newman, 'Schrems II Offers an Opportunity').

[220] See European Commission Implementing Decision on EU-US Data Privacy Framework (n 199). For an overview of those changes, see Theodore Christakis, Kenneth Propp, and Peter Swire, 'The Redress Mechanism in the Privacy Shield Successor: On the Independence and Effective Powers of the DPRC' (*IAPP*, 11 October 2022) <https://iapp.org/news/a/the-redress-mechanism-in-the-privacy-shield-successor-on-the-independence-and-effective-powers-of-the-dprc/> accessed 10 July 2023; EDPB, EDPB Welcomes Improvements under the EU-U.S. Data Privacy Framework, but Concerns Remain (28 February 2023) <https://edpb.europa.eu/news/news/2023/edpb-welcomes-improvements-under-eu-us-data-privacy-framework-concerns-remain_en> accessed 10 July 2023.

[221] See 'New Trans-Atlantic Data Privacy Framework Largely a Copy of "Privacy Shield". noyb Will Challenge the Decision' (*noyb*, 10 July 2023) <https://noyb.eu/en/european-commission-gives-eu-us-data-transfers-third-round-cjeu> accessed 10 July 2023; '"Privacy Shield 2.0"? First Reaction by Max Schrems' (*noyb*, 25 March 2022) <https://noyb.eu/en/privacy-shield-20-first-reaction-max-schrems> accessed 10 July 2023; 'First Reaction: Executive Order on US Surveillance Unlikely to Satisfy EU Law' (*noyb*, 7 October 2022) <https://noyb.eu/en/new-us-executive-order-unlikely-satisfy-eu-law> accessed 10 July 2023.

[222] Unfortunately, these topics are not part of the issues and points of cooperation addressed within the EU-US Trade and Technology Council. See European Commission, EU-US Trade and Technology Council <https://commission.europa.eu/strategy-and-policy/priorities-2019-2024/stronger-europe-world/eu-us-trade-and-technology-council_en>.

[223] Communication from the Commission, 'Two Years of Application of the General Data Protection Regulation' (n 184) 12.

[224] Alex LaCasse, 'In Wake of Global Data Transfer Complexity, Need for Multilateral Treaty Grows' (*IAPP*, 25 April 2023) <https://iapp.org/news/a/schrems-3-transborder-data-flows-become-hot-button-topic-at-iapp-gps-2023/> accessed 10 July 2023.

argue that this dialogue should *not* be part of international trade negotiations.[225] As noted several times throughout this book, privacy and data protection as well as national security interests are built into the international trading system as exceptions. The economic ethos of the international trading system, as argued in Chapter 3, could lead to a lower level of fundamental rights protection. Furthermore, this would be against the current EU approach to digital trade negotiations discussed in Chapter 4.

5.3.2 Inconsistent interpretation of the concept of 'transfer'

As discussed in Section 2.2.2, when Europeans' personal data flows outside the EEA, it may benefit from the GDPR protections by virtue of two sets of rules: first, rules extending the application of the GDPR outside the territory of the EEA under Article 3 of the GDPR and, second, rules on transfers of personal data outside the EEA under Chapter V of the GDPR. The EDPB's interpretation of the notion of 'transfer', which determines the scope of application of Chapter V of the GDPR, and of the interplay between Chapter V and Article 3 of the GDPR, led to the inconsistency of and gaps in the legal protection of Europeans' personal data transmitted outside the EEA.

As explained in Section 2.2.2, the EDPB's guidelines created four different legal regimes applicable to personal data transmitted outside the EEA. The divergence of legal protection of personal data in each of these legal regimes can be illustrated by Table 2.2 from Section 2.4.2.2, which is reproduced here for readers' convenience.

Legal Regime 1, in which no GDPR protections whatsoever are afforded to transmitted personal data, clearly creates a gap in legal protection of fundamental rights of individuals. This gap stems from the opinion of the EDPB, discussed in Section 2.2.2, that Chapter V rules only apply to transmissions of personal data between a data exporter and a data importer. Given that an individual themselves do not qualify as data exporters, Chapter V rules are inapplicable to transmissions of personal data outside the EEA *directly from individuals*. This conclusion, however, is inconsistent with the constitutional function of the EU framework for transfers of personal data to ensure 'effective and complete'

[225] See Hielke Hijmans, 'The Transatlantic Trade and Investment Partnership and the Developments in the Area of Privacy and Data Protection' (2016) 43(4) Legal Issues of Economic Integration 385, 394–98; Kristina Irion, 'Panta Rhei: A European Perspective on Ensuring a High-Level of Protection of Digital Human Rights in a World in Which Everything Flows' in Mira Burri (ed), *Big Data and Global Trade Law* (CUP 2021). cf Reidenberg, 'E-Commerce and Trans-Atlantic Privacy' (n 216) 739, 748, proposing to negotiate a 'General Agreement on Information Privacy' at the WTO; see also Anupam Chander and Paul Schwartz, 'Privacy and/or Trade' (2023) 90(1) The University of Chicago Law Review 49, developing Reidenberg's proposal further. cf Kristina Irion, Margot E Kaminski, and Svetlana Yakovleva, 'Privacy Peg, Trade Hole: Why We (Still) Shouldn't Put Data Privacy in Trade Law' (*The University of Chicago Law Review Online*, 2023) <https://lawreviewblog.uchicago.edu/2023/03/27/irion-kaminski-yakovleva/> accessed 10 July 2023.

Table 5.1. Comparison of Legal Regimes 1–4

Legal regime	Type of transmission	Level of protection
Legal Regime 1	Transmission of personal data directly from individuals in the EEA to a data importer established outside the EEA, which is not subject to the GDPR's extraterritorial application	No GDPR protection
Legal Regime 2	Transmission of personal data from a data exporter subject to the GDPR (irrespective of location) to a data importer outside the EEA, which is not subject to the GDPR's extraterritorial application	Protection of GDPR Chapter V
Legal Regime 3	Transmission of personal data from a data exporter subject to the GDPR (irrespective of location) to a data importer outside the EEA, which is subject to the GDPR's extraterritorial application	Protection under the general framework of the GDPR *and* Chapter V 'light'
Legal Regime 4	Transmission of personal data directly from individuals in the EEA to a data importer established outside the EEA, which is subject to the GDPR's extraterritorial application	Protection under the general framework of the GDPR (including some restrictions on transmission deriving from Articles 5, 24 and 32 GDPR) but *not* Chapter V

protection of personal data and prevent circumvention of the high level of personal data protection in the EU. It also does not follow from the GDPR, which does not contain such a restriction. Moreover, derogation under Article 49(1)(b) of the GDPR allows a transfer of personal data to take place when it is necessary for the performance of a contract between the data subject and the controller. In such a situation, in most cases, there is a direct contact between the data importer and the individual, and personal data flows directly from the individuals.

Although the EDPB does not substantiate its approach, it could be reasoned by the fact that if the EDPB recognized direct transmissions of personal data from individuals as transfers, in the absence of an adequacy decision, there would be no mechanisms for systematic transfers available for such transfers, as appropriate safeguards under Article 46 of the GDPR all seem to cover transmissions of personal data between a data importer and a data exporter. Thus, derogations under Article 49 of the GDPR, which are not available for systematic transfers, would be the only available transfer mechanisms for such transfers. This situation, as explained in Section 2.3, would be contrary to the EU's international trade obligations.

Whether there is a gap of legal protection in Legal Regimes 2 and 4, in which either rules of Chapter V or GDPR rules and principles (but not Chapter V) apply, compared to Legal Regime 3, in which both sets of rules apply, is unclear, and its detailed consideration is beyond the scope of this book. For the purposes of this book, it suffices to say that in the light of the principle of consistency under Article 7 of the TFEU, ideally, the level of protection afforded to Europeans' personal data abroad by virtue of either the extraterritorial application of the GDPR under Article 3 or the rules of Chapter V of the GDPR, as well as the corresponding obligations on data controllers and processors, must be the same. The aim of Chapter V to prevent circumvention of GDPR rules should lead it to step in where the GDPR no longer applies. A crucial condition for this to work, however, is that the rest of the GDPR should lead to the same level of protection for transferred data as Chapter V mechanisms for transfers of personal data outside the EEA. This does not seem to be the case, at least in the EDPB's opinion, which extends the application of Chapter V also to situations where the GDPR applies extraterritorially, which suggests that something is missing in the protection of personal data solely by virtue of extraterritorial application of the GDPR.

It could be that following the CJEU interpretation of various Chapter V provisions especially in the light of foreign surveillance risks, Chapter V ends up providing a higher level of protection to personal data transmitted outside the EEA. Following the *Schrems I* and *Schrems II* judgments, systematic transfers of personal data outside the EEA on the basis of Chapter V are conditioned not only by the implementation of certain GDPR rules and principles by data importers but also by certain level of guarantees implemented in domestic law of the data importer. In contrast, Article 3 of the GDPR, which extends the application of GDPR rules extraterritorially, is agnostic to the legal regime in which a data controller or processor operates.

5.3.3 Deficiencies of adequacy decisions

This section argues that although—based on the criteria for assessment in Article 45(2) of the GDPR—adequacy decisions, in theory, must ensure an essentially equivalent level of protection, in practice this mechanism for data transfers suffers not only from political pressures, which result in assessment less rigorous than required by Article 52(1) of the EU Charter, but also from the problems inherent in any domestic legal instrument with extraterritorial reach, namely, the 'snapshot', the 'heavy burden', and the 'onward transfer' problems. As a result, as Kuner argues, 'while adequacy purports to provide a strong level of protection for personal data, such protection is actually difficult to enforce outside the borders of the EU'.[226] The flaws of adequacy decisions discussed in this section strongly suggest that the adequacy framework does not fully prevent, in practice, the circumvention of the EU data protection framework when personal data leaves the EEA borders and does not fulfil the function of securing 'effective and complete' protection of the fundamental rights to the protection of privacy and personal data in the EU.

5.3.3.1 Adequacy decisions: Between protection of fundamental rights and trade politics

Despite being the primary mechanism for transfers of personal data outside the EEA in the layered structure of the EU legal framework, the adequacy assessments mechanism lacks a clear procedure and moreover it is extremely slow. From 1995 when the adequacy mechanism was first introduced, the EU has granted adequacy only seventeen times. The EU Commission's adequacy decisions were challenged twice at the CJEU, both times for the United States, and both challenges resulted in the invalidation of the decisions.[227] It takes on average several years to obtain adequacy.[228]

The adequacy mechanism is a powerful negotiation tool between the EU and its trading partners.[229] For example, in its 2017 Communication, the European Commission stated that it will 'actively engage with key trading partners in East and South-East Asia', starting with Japan and Korea in 2017 and, depending on progress towards the modernization of its data protection laws, with India, but also with countries in Latin America (in particular Mercosur members), and countries in the 'the European neighbourhood' that have expressed an interest in obtaining an 'adequacy finding'.[230]

Several leading scholars have argued that adequacy decisions are not strict legal assessments.[231] For example, Schwartz contends that in evaluating adequacy 'the EU has demonstrated a wide range of flexible approaches with regard to this

[226] Christopher Kuner, 'Developing an Adequate Legal Framework for International Data Transfers' in Serge Gutwirth and others (eds), *Reinventing Data Protection?* (Springer 2009) 8–9 <https://ssrn.com/abstract=1464323> accessed 10 July 2023 (hereafter Kuner, 'Developing an Adequate Legal Framework').

[227] In *Schrems I* (n 5), the CJEU invalidated the EU-US Safe Harbor, and in *Schrems II* (n 6), the CJEU invalidated the EU-US Privacy Shield.

[228] One of the recent examples is the Adequacy Decision for Japan (n 164).

[229] Paul M Schwartz, 'Global Data Privacy: The EU Way' 2019 94(4) New York University Law Review 771 807(hereafter Schwartz, 'Global Data Privacy: The EU Way').

[230] Communication from the Commission, Exchanging and Protecting Personal Data in a Globalised World (n 152) 8.

[231] For a discussion, see Svetlana Yakovleva and Kristina Irion, 'The Best of Both Worlds? Free Trade in Services and EU Law on Privacy and Data Protection' (2016) 2 European Data Protection Law Review 191, 205.

standard'.[232] Although under the GDPR, adequacy is a unilateral assessment, the EU negotiators have not 'exercised unilateral power', but rather 'flexibly assessed the adequacy of different legal systems as it suits the EU's goals at the time'.[233] Similarly, Kuner argues that 'adequacy decisions are far from always being objective and logical, and do not provide a watertight standard of data protection',[234] and that '[i]n practice, it can be difficult for a State or regional organization to pass judgment on a foreign regulatory system without political considerations playing some role'.[235] He illustrates his point by referring to the adequacy decision for Argentina, where serious human rights abuses were flagged by Amnesty International right after that decision was granted.[236] The assessment of Argentina's adequacy by Article 29 Working Party was conducted 'on the basis of ... assumptions and explanations and in the absence of any substantial experience with the practical application of the legislation, both at federal or provincial level'.[237] In a similar vein, one of the factors that played a role in the assessment and finding of adequacy of New Zealand was the volume of EU's trade with this country.[238] Concerns regarding the absence of onward transfer restrictions in New Zealand law were addressed by simply pointing out the remote geographical location of the country and low likelihood of such transfers.[239] The adequacy decision for Israel, despite documented Israeli intelligence agency practices, is yet another example of a political compromise in the assessment of adequacy.[240]

The invalidated EU-US Privacy Shield (which superseded the EU-US Safe Harbor, invalidated by the CJEU in 2015) was hastily negotiated and concluded in record time: eight months as opposed to the 'lengthy and troubled negotiations

[232] Schwartz, 'Global Data Privacy: The EU Way' (n 229) 806.

[233] ibid 806–07.

[234] Kuner, 'Developing an Adequate Legal Framework' (n 226) 8–9.

[235] Christopher Kuner, *Transborder Data Flows and Data Privacy Law* (OUP 2013) 66 (hereafter Kuner, *Transborder Data Flows and Data Privacy Law*).

[236] Kuner, 'Developing an Adequate Legal Framework' (n 226) 8–9. See also Roth, 'Adequate Level of Data Protection' (n 51) 61–62; Christopher Wolf, 'Delusions of Adequacy? Examining the Case for Finding the United States Adequate for Cross-Border EU-U.S. Data Transfers' (2014) 43 Washington University Journal of Law & Policy 227, 242–43.

[237] Article 29 Working Party, Opinion 4/2002 on the level of protection of personal data in Argentina, WP 63 (3 October 2002) 17 <https://ec.europa.eu/justice/article-29/documentation/opinion-recommendation/files/2002/wp63_en.pdf> accessed 10 July 2023.

[238] Lee Andrew Bygrave, *Data Privacy Law: An International Perspective* (Oxford Scholarship Online 2014) 194 referring to Article 29 Working Party, Opinion 11/2011 on the level of protection of personal data in New Zealand, WP 182 (4 April 2011) https://ec.europa.eu/justice/article-29/documentation/opinion-recommendation/files/2011/wp182_en.pdf accessed 10 July 2023.

[239] Roth, 'Adequate Level of Data Protection' (n 51) 60–61.

[240] Kuner, *Transborder Data Flows and Data Privacy Law* (n 235) 66. Based on the analysis of the modernization of Israel's data protection framework currently being adopted in Israel, Korf argues that even if these amendments are adopted, Israel's framework will still not meet the EU's essential equivalence standard. See Douwe Korff, 'Update on the Opinion on the Future of Personal Data Transfers from the EU/EEA to Israel & the Occupied Territories' (25 March 2022) <http://dx.doi.org/10.2139/ssrn.4066476> accessed 10 July 2023 (hereafter Korff, 'Update on the Opinion on the Future of Personal Data Transfers from the EU/EEA to Israel & the Occupied Territories').

of the Safe Harbor'[241] and other adequacy decisions.[242] Political pressure from the US government and powerful transatlantic business stakeholders not only explains the faster pace of the negotiations but also the fact that this adequacy decision for the United States was adopted despite reservations from the Article 29 Working Party (the EDPB's predecessor), the European Parliament, and the European Data Protection Supervisor (EDPS).[243] It therefore comes as no great surprise that, just like its predecessor, the Privacy Shield did not survive CJEU scrutiny.[244]

The adequacy decision for Japan is a more recent example of the same phenomenon. As mentioned in Chapter 4, trade negotiations with Japan played a significant role in granting Japan an adequacy decision, which indeed coincided with the conclusion of the bilateral trade agreement. Japan's adequacy decision contains (besides the Commission's assessment of Japan's regulatory framework) additional rules that Japan agreed to implement specifically in relation to personal data transferred from the EEA, thus creating a double standard for personal data protection within the country.[245] As rightly mentioned by France in its submission for the 2020 review of the GDPR, the purpose of the adequacy decision is the assessment of an existing framework, not the creation of an additional layer of rules specifically for the EEA data to rectify gaps in a foreign country's legal system.[246] Thus, by adding Supplementary Rules to the adequacy decision, the European Commission has, in effect, re-designed the adequacy framework under the GDPR. Furthermore, the adequacy decision for Japan was adopted despite the concerns of the EDPB and the European Parliament regarding, in particular, the compliance of the surveillance measures employed by the Japanese government with the adequacy standard established by the CJEU in *Schrems I*, and relatively mild enforcement mechanisms

[241] House of Representatives, Hearing before the Subcommittee on Commerce, Trade and Consumer Protection of the Committee on Energy and Commerce (The EU Data Protection Directive: Publications for the U.S. Privacy Debate 2001) 72 <https://books.google.nl/books?printsec=frontcover&vid=ISBN0160658942&redir_esc=y#v=onepage&q&f=false> accessed 10 July 2023.

[242] The EU-US Safe Harbor was invalidated in October 2015, and the EU-US Privacy Shield was adopted on 12 July 2016.

[243] European Parliament resolution of 26 May 2016 on transatlantic data flows (2016/2727(RSP)) [2016] OJ C 76; European Data Protection Supervisor, Opinion 4/2016 on the EU-US Privacy Shield draft adequacy decision (30 May 2016); Article 29 Working Party, Opinion 01/2016 on the EU-US Privacy Shield draft adequacy decision, WP 238 (13 April 2016).

[244] Farell and Newman, 'Schrems II Offers an Opportunity' (n 219) (arguing that 'no one—including the European Union officials who negotiated it—ever thought that the Privacy Shield agreement that succeeded Safe Harbor had much chance of surviving CJEU scrutiny.'). See also Christakis, 'After Schrems II' (n 58); Kuner, 'The Schrems II Judgment of the Court of Justice and the Future of Data Transfer Regulation' (n 171).

[245] Annex 1 to Adequacy Decision for Japan (n 164).

[246] In its comments to the EU Council on the evaluation of the GDPR, France calls this approach an 'ingenious solution,' which, nonetheless, 'should not be considered as a precedent for future adequacy decisions'. Council of the European Union, Preparation of the Council position on the evaluation and review of the General Data Protection Regulation (GDPR): Comments from Member States, 12756/1/19 REV 1 (9 October 2019) 24 <https://data.consilium.europa.eu/doc/document/ST-12756-2019-REV-1/en/pdf> accessed 10 July 2023 (hereafter Council of the European Union, Comments from Member States).

(compared to those under GDPR) under Japanese law.[247] Although the 2020 reform of Japan's Act on the Protection of Personal Information brought it closer to the GDPR, it did not alter the provisions on administrative fines.[248] Not surprisingly, Greenleaf criticized the adequacy decision for Japan, which, in his words, 'discounts' the EU law's adequacy standard on several grounds, most importantly in that (a) the Japanese enforcement regime is not 'essentially equivalent' to that of the EU; (b) consent cannot be a sufficient ground for onward transfers (this issue is further discussed in Section 5.3.2.2); and (c) there was a lack of expert involvement in the assessment of the Japanese legal system.[249]

The adequacy decision mechanism has been, and continues to be, a powerful tool for the EU to export its data protection standards and seek further convergence of other countries' data protection rules on the basis of EU standards (*de jure* 'Brussels Effect'[250]). The political component, however, has an impact on the robustness of the adequacy decisions and their ability to safeguard an 'essentially equivalent' level of protection of personal data transferred outside the EEA. Although none of the adequacy decisions (except those for the United States) have yet been challenged at the CJEU, it is questionable whether most of them—given that eleven out of fifteen adequacy decisions in force were granted before the 2015 *Schrems I* judgment—would meet the 'essential equivalence' standard articulated by the CJEU in *Schrems I* and *Schrems II* in respect to the access of foreign surveillance authorities to transferred data, and right to effective judicial remedy.[251] This problem of staticity of adequacy assessments and other limitations of the adequacy framework is discussed in the following section.

[247] EDPB, Opinion 28/2018 regarding the European Commission Draft Implementing Decision on the adequate protection of personal data in Japan (5 December 2018), paras 122, 128, 137ff; European Parliament resolution of 13 December 2018 on the adequacy of the protection of personal data afforded by Japan (2018/2979(RSP)) [2018] OJ C 388, paras 21–25. See also Yuliya Miadzvetskaya, 'What Are the Pros and Cons of the Adequacy Decision on Japan?' (*KU Leuven CiTiP Blog*, 4 April 2019) <https://www.law.kuleuven.be/citip/blog/what-are-the-pros-and-cons-of-the-adequacy-decision-on-japan/> accessed 10 July 2023.

[248] For an overview of amendments, see Takeshige Sugimoto, Akihiro Kawashima, and Tobyn Aaron, 'A New Era for Japanese Data Protection: 2020 Amendments to the APPI' (*Future of Privacy Forum*, 13 April 2021) <https://fpf.org/blog/a-new-era-for-japanese-data-protection-2020-amendments-to-the-appi/> accessed 10 July 2023.

[249] Graham Greenleaf, 'Japan: EU Adequacy Discounted' (2018) 155 Privacy Laws & Business International Report, 8 <https://ssrn.com/abstract=3276016> accessed 10 July 2023 (hereafter Greenleaf, 'Japan: EU Adequacy Discounted'); see also Graham Greenleaf, 'Japan's Proposed EU Adequacy Assessment: Substantive Issues and Procedural Hurdles' (2018) UNSW Law Research Paper No 18-53 4-8 <https://ssrn.com/abstract=3219728> accessed 10 July 2023; Graham Greenleaf, 'Questioning "Adequacy" (Pt I) – Japan' (2017) 150 Privacy Laws & Business International Report 6-11 <https://ssrn.com/abstract=3096370> accessed 10 July 2023.

[250] René Mahieu and others, 'Has the European General Data Protection Regulation Influenced the Data Protection Rights of Canadian Citizens?' (2021) 11 Journal of Information Policy 301, 307.

[251] See Christakis, 'After Schrems II' (n 58).

5.3.3.2 Limitations of adequacy decisions inherent in legal instruments with extraterritorial reach

This section argues that, as domestic legal instruments with extraterritorial reach,[252] adequacy decisions suffer from at least three weaknesses. First, they embody an assessment of a third country's legal framework at a particular point in time and do not provide effective dynamic mechanisms for ensuring that the third country will maintain the same level of personal data protection throughout the life of the adequacy decision (the 'snapshot' problem). Second, if a foreign data controller or processor violates the third country's data protection rules when processing a European's personal data, enforcement of such rules abroad is burdensome (the 'heavy burden' problem). Third, adequacy decisions, at best, guarantee that personal data transferred from the EEA is equally protected in the *first country of destination—the* one granted an adequacy decision—but often fail to provide the same level of protection in relation to *onward transfers* of such data to other countries (the 'onward transfer' problem).

On the first point (*the 'snapshot' problem*), as mentioned earlier, an adequacy decision for a third country (international organization, territory, or a sector of industry[253]) is the result of an assessment of that country's system based on a snapshot of rules at a particular point in time. The GDPR requires that the adequacy decision should provide for a periodic review, at least every four years.[254] In a fast-paced globalized present-day environment, review of the legal framework once in four years is simply not frequent enough. In addition, the GDPR requires the Commission to monitor developments in third countries and international organizations that could affect the functioning of the adequacy decisions and may, to the extent necessary, repeal, amend, or suspend such adequacy decisions.[255] Although the Data Protection Directive did not contain specific rules on the monitoring and review of adequacy decisions, similar requirements were initially included in the text of adequacy decisions themselves.[256] These requirements were later expanded to include the monitoring of the developments on foreign authorities' access to

[252] Kuner, 'Extraterritoriality and Regulation of International Data Transfers' (n 119) 236, 239 (arguing that although the EU rules for transfers of personal data are not 'extraterritorial in scope within a literal meaning of the term, they do have extraterritorial effect'.).

[253] For simplicity, this section refers to country only but implies organization, territory, and sector of industry.

[254] Art 45(3) GDPR.

[255] Arts 45(4) and (5) GDPR.

[256] See, eg, art 4 of Adequacy decision for Canada (Commission Decision 2002/2/EC of 20 December 2001 pursuant to Directive 95/46/EC of the European Parliament and of the Council on the adequate protection of personal data provided by the Canadian Personal Information Protection and Electronic Documents Act [2001] C(2001) 4539 OJ L 2); art 4 Adequacy decision for Uruguay (Commission Implementing Decision 2012/484/EU of 21 August 2012 pursuant to Directive 95/46/EC of the European Parliament and of the Council on the adequate protection of personal data by the Eastern Republic of Uruguay with regard to automated processing of personal data [2012] C(2012) 5704) OJ L 227).

personal data in the aftermath of the CJEU *Schrems I* judgment.[257] There is, however, no information on whether and how, if at all, the Commission actually conducts the monitoring of legal regimes in third countries that have been afforded adequacy. Furthermore, none of the pre-GDPR adequacy decisions—except for the invalidated EU-US Privacy Shield, which was reviewed on an annual basis[258]—have ever been reviewed.

Of the eleven adequacy decisions adopted prior to the GDPR, which are currently in force, some have been in force more than twenty years (eg, adequacy for Switzerland adopted in 2000, for Canada, in 2001). Neither the 2013 Snowden revelations, followed by European Parliament reports and calls on the Commission to review adequacy decisions for New Zealand and Canada because of these countries' participation in the 'Five Eyes' programme, nor the 2015 *Schrems I* judgment triggered a review of such adequacy decisions by the Commission.[259] Similarly, the Commission did not take action to remedy the deficiencies of the Safe Harbor, despite having identified its weaknesses in its 2013 Communications, preceding the Safe Harbor's invalidation by the CJEU in *Schrems I*.[260] What is more, already back in 2001, just one year after the Safe Harbor framework came into being, a leading US academic proclaimed Safe Harbor 'only a weak, seriously flawed solution for e-commerce'.[261]

[257] Implementing Decision (EU) 2016/2295 of 16 December 2016 amending Decisions 2000/518/EC, 2002/2/EC, 2003/490/EC, 2003/821/EC, 2004/411/EC, 2008/393/EC, 2010/146/EU, 2010/625/EU, 2011/61/EU and Implementing Decisions 2012/484/EU, 2013/65/EU on the adequate protection of personal data by certain countries, pursuant to art 25(6) of Directive 95/46/EC of the European Parliament and of the Council [2016] C(2016) 8353) C/2016/8353 OJ L 344 (hereafter European Commission, Implementing Decisions amending Adequacy Decisions after Schrems I).

[258] The third annual review was completed in October 2019. See Report from the Commission to the European Parliament and the Council on the Third Annual Review of the Functioning of the EU-US Privacy Shield COM (2019) 495 final (18 October 2017) <https://eur-lex.europa.eu/legal-content/EN/TXT/?uri=CELEX%3A52019DC0495> accessed 10 July 2023.

[259] See Committee on Civil Liberties, Justice and Home Affairs, Report on the US NSA surveillance programme, surveillance bodies in various Member States and their impact on EU citizens' fundamental rights and on transatlantic cooperation in Justice and Home Affairs. No 2013/2188(INI) (European Parliament, 21 February 2014) https://www.europarl.europa.eu/doceo/document/A-7-2014-0139_EN.html accessed 10 July 2023; European Parliament Resolution of 12 March 2014 on the US NSA surveillance programme, surveillance bodies in various Member States and their impact on EU citizens' fundamental rights and on transatlantic cooperation in Justice and Home Affairs 2013/2188(INI) [2014] OJ C 378. For a discussion, see Roth, 'Adequate Level of Data Protection' (n 51) 64. In the aftermath of *Schrems I*, the European Commission did, however, amend the adequacy decisions in force at that time to include provisions regarding the monitoring of developments in third countries regarding government agencies' access to personal data, the communication between the European Commission and EU member states, and between the European Commission and third countries on the issue. See European Commission, Implementing Decisions Amending Adequacy Decisions after *Schrems I* (n 257).

[260] See Communication from the European Commission to the European Parliament and the Council, 'Rebuilding Trust in EU-US Data Flows' COM(2013) 846 final [2013], paras 2 and 3.2; Communication from the European Commission to the European Parliament and the Council on the Functioning of the Safe Harbour from the Perspective of EU Citizens and Companies Established in the EU COM(2013) 847 final [2013], paras 3–5, 7–8.

[261] Reidenberg, 'E-Commerce and Trans-Atlantic Privacy' (n 216) 719.

The European Commission announced the first review of all pre-GDPR adequacy decisions in 2017.[262] Almost six years later, this review is still ongoing. The time it takes the Commission to review these adequacy decisions is, therefore, at least 150 per cent longer than the four-year review period mandated by the GDPR. First, the publication of the report on the review of adequacy decisions was postponed until after *Schrems II*. Prior to *Schrems II* judgment, the Commission indicated that it is discussing 'additional safeguards' with some of the countries and territories 'to address relevant differences in protection'.[263] It is plausible that the EU is hoping for Canada and other countries to strengthen their data protection laws in a way allowing them to maintain their adequacy decisions.[264] It remains to be seen whether this review will result in qualitative improvements of the adequacy decisions. A 2023 study found that the effect of adequacy decisions on digital trade is driven largely by adequacy decisions granted to the United States; 'no significant trade effects were found for other countries that received adequacy.'[265] This finding, in this book's opinion, is not only a manifestation of the volume of transatlantic digital trade but can also be explained by the fact that adequacy decisions for the United States are the only ones that have actually been enforced by the EU.

One way or the other, at this juncture, it seems clear that adequacy decisions do not fully factor in developments in the third countries' legal systems, and practice of application after adequacy has been granted. Besides, the EU has little or no control over the way personal data transferred from the EEA is processed abroad. One of the reasons why the review of adequacy decisions has not been an effective mechanism is that as discussed earlier, granting and maintaining an adequacy decision is not purely a legal matter but largely a political act, especially when the EU's trade interests are at stake. Another reason is the design of the adequacy decision as a unilateral assessment by the EU. To constantly monitor developments in all countries that have been granted adequacy, especially in relation to the practice of application of the legal framework governing the processing of personal data,

[262] See Paul Jordan, 'Notes from the IAPP Europe Managing Director, 17 November 2017' (IAPP, 16 November 2017) https://iapp.org/news/a/notes-from-the-iapp-europe-managing-director-17-november-2017/ accessed 10 July 2023.

[263] Communication from the Commission, 'Two Years of Application of the General Data Protection Regulation' (n 184).

[264] As mentioned in Chapter 2, both Canada and Israel are in the process of trying to strengthen their data protection legislation. See 'Israel: Ministry Launches Consultation on Draft Privacy Protection Regulations on Transfers from the EEA' (*Data Guidance*, 30 November 2022) <https://www.dataguidance.com/news/israel-ministry-launches-consultation-draft-privacy> accessed 10 July 2023; and Chantal Bernier, '2023 Canada Private-Sector Privacy Law Reform: Keeping Track of Moving Parts' (*IAPP*, 13 January 2023) <https://iapp.org/news/a/2023-canada-private-sector-privacy-law-reform-keeping-track-of-moving-parts/> accessed 10 July 2023. As noted above, however, Korff argues that even if the proposed amendments to Israel's data protection law are adopted, Israel would still not meet the EU's essential equivalence standard. See Korff, 'Update on the Opinion on the Future of Personal Data Transfers from the EU/EEA to Israel & the Occupied Territories' (n 240).

[265] Martina F Ferracane and others, 'Digital Trade, Data Protection and EU Adequacy Decisions' (2023) EUI Working Paper RSC 2023/37, 24 https://cadmus.eui.eu/handle/1814/75629 accessed 10 July 2023.

would require a substantial investment and granular expertise from the European Commission. In turn, third countries do not have any notification obligations regarding the changes of rules or practices related to personal data protection and national security programmes, which makes the discovery of such changes burdensome for the EU. Even at the stage of negotiations, as the practice of negotiating the adequacy decision with Japan has shown, the Commission may not commission independent expert opinions from the third country and instead relies solely on the statements of the foreign government.[266]

On the second point (*the 'heavy burden' problem*), seeking judicial or administrative redress abroad under the rules of a foreign legal system may incur prohibitive costs for individuals.[267] This is even assuming that the level of personal data protection guaranteed in a third country, including the level of administrative fines, does comply with the standard of 'essential equivalence'. In the case of Japan, which, as discussed earlier, has created a higher level of protection of personal data from the EEA as compared to Japanese citizens' data, enforcement of those higher protections may also be more difficult as there will be scarce domestic practice on which Supplementary rules (applicable only to personal data transferred from the EEA) can be grounded. Similarly, even when the GDPR applies to the processing of personal data abroad (eg under Article 3(2) of the GDPR) and grants EU member state courts jurisdiction over the issue—for example, in relation to damage compensation under article 79(2) GDPR—the costs of enforcing such a decision against a foreign controller in a third country are likely to be much higher than the amount of damages the individual may obtain. In addition, the harm caused to individuals as a result of violation of their fundamental rights cannot be fully undone. Then, a lack of enforceability significantly reduces the effectiveness of data protection rules, as Section 5.3.3 discusses in more detail.

On the third point (*the 'onward transfer' problem*), assessment of the rules for onward transfers of personal data from country A (which is undergoing the adequacy assessment) to country B (which does not have adequacy) is one of the factors in the adequacy assessment under Article 45(2)(a) of the GDPR. This means that in order to preserve continuity of personal data protection and prevent circumvention of the EU data protection framework, the mechanism for transfers of personal data under country A's legal framework should be 'essentially equivalent' to that of the EU. Although most countries' legislation provides for some form of restrictions on international transfers of personal data, those restrictions are typically milder than those under the GDPR.[268]

[266] Greenleaf, 'Japan: EU Adequacy Discounted' (n 249) 9.

[267] Kuner, 'Developing an Adequate Legal Framework' (n 226) 8–9.

[268] Graham Greenleaf, 'European' Data Privacy Standards Implemented in Laws outside Europe' (2017) 149 Privacy Laws & Business International Report 21 <https://ssrn.com/abstract=3096314> accessed 10 July 2023. For an overview of restrictions, see Martina Ferracane, 'Restrictions on Cross-Border Data Flows: A Taxonomy' (2017) ECIPE Working Paper No 1/2017, 10-27 <https://ecipe.org/

Onward transfer mechanisms in existing adequacy decisions adopted by the Commission, which aim to compensate for the absence of restrictions on transfers of personal data from countries granted adequacy, provide for a lower level of protection to personal data transferred from country A (that has been granted adequacy) to countries B, C, and D (that have not been granted adequacy) than the level of protection that would have been granted to this data if it was transferred to countries B, C, and D directly from the EEA. In other words, onward transfer mechanisms under the adequacy decisions could allow circumvention of the EU's high level of personal data protection and restrictions on transfers of personal data to third countries that have not been granted adequacy.

Another challenge in this context is that the rules for onward transfers of personal data included in the adequacy decisions only apply to data obtained from the EEA and not to any other data processed in country A. Different legal regimes applicable to different datasets within the same country make monitoring of compliance difficult and therefore diminish the effectiveness of restrictions on onward transfers. This makes rules on onward transfers under adequacy decisions the Achilles' heel of the adequacy mechanism. Furthermore, and relatedly, just as there is no effective mechanism to monitor the rules in countries afforded adequacy, the EU framework does not have any monitoring mechanisms for the application of onward transfer rules.[269]

To illustrate the point, the discussion below looks at specific provisions on onward transfer mechanisms under the adequacy decisions for Canada and Japan. There are two reasons for selecting these specific adequacy decisions. First, these countries are important trading partners of the EU, with which the EU has recently concluded a trade agreement.[270] Second, Japan's decision is one of the newest adequacy decisions adopted by the EU under the GDPR. In contrast, the adequacy decision for Canada is one of the oldest, adopted in 2001. Bringing both of them into analysis demonstrates the evolution of adequacy decisions over the last twenty years.

wp-content/uploads/2017/11/Restrictions-on-cross-border-data-flows-a-taxonomy-final1.pdf> accessed 10 July 2023.

269 The same argument was made by France in its submission to the Council of the European Union. See Council of the European Union, 'Comments from Member States' (n 246) 24 ('the existence of a precise and effective mechanism for monitoring these rules, in particular in regard to subsequent transfers of the European data transmitted, must be a sine qua non for the adoption of an adequacy decision, and must be regularly assessed by the European authorities.'). The importance of such monitoring is also highlighted by the EDPB. See EDPB, 'Contribution of the EDPB to the Evaluation of the GDPR' (n 208) 6.

270 CETA with Canada (Comprehensive Economic and Trade Agreement (CETA) between Canada, of the one part, and the European Union and its member states, of the other part, 14 September 2014 [2017] OJ L 11/23) and JEFTA with Japan (Agreement between the European Union and Japan for an Economic Partnership [2018] OJ L 330/3).

As mentioned earlier, onward transfers of EU personal data from Japan to third countries are regulated in the Adequacy Decision for Japan and 'Supplementary Rules' included in Annex 1 to the Decision. These rules oblige Japanese businesses 'to ensure (e.g. by technical ("tagging") or organizational means (storing in a dedicated database)) that they can identify personal data transferred from the EEA throughout their "life cycle." '[271] Recital 75 of the Adequacy Decision requires that further recipients of EU personal data outside Japan are subject to rules ensuring a 'similar' level of protection to that of the Japanese legal order.[272]

Just like under the EU GDPR, onward transfers of EU personal data from Japan are only possible under certain conditions. The adequacy decision for Japan, including the Supplementary Rules, provides for three principal options for onward transfers of EU personal data from Japan. The first option allows onward transfers based on an individual's consent.[273] Under Japan's data protection law—Act on the Protection of Personal Information (APPI)[274]—consent to transfer personal data to a third party in a foreign country is different from the consent to transfer personal data to a third party *within Japan*.[275] Supplementary Rule 4 specifies that 'consent' means that the individual has been 'provided information on the circumstances surrounding the transfer necessary for the principal[276] to make a decision on his/her consent'. According to Recital 76 of the adequacy decision, this provision ensures that 'such consent will be particularly well informed and will allow [individuals] to assess the risk for the privacy involved in the transfer'.[277] The legal standard of consent for onward transfer of EU personal data is thus higher than the general standard for consent in Japanese law. The second and third options allow an onward transfer of EU personal data from Japan without consent if:

(1) the country of destination of the onward transfer has been recognized by the Japanese data protection authority as providing a level of protection of personal data *equivalent* to that of Japan; or

[271] Recital 15 of Adequacy Decision for Japan (n 164).

[272] The 'similar' as opposed to 'essentially equivalent' standard suggests that the adequacy decision sets a lower threshold for the legal framework in a country of onward transfer to meet than that threshold applicable to initial transfers of EU personal data to Japan.

[273] Recital 76 of Adequacy Decision for Japan (n 164), Supplementary rule 4.

[274] Act on the Protection of Personal Information (APPI), Act No 57 of May 30, 2003, Consolidated text as of 1 April 2023. Informal English translation <https://www.japaneselawtranslation.go.jp/en/laws/view/4241/en> accessed 10 July 2023 (hereafter APPI).

[275] Consent for transfer of personal data to a third party within Japan is regulated in art 23 APPI (n 274), and consent for transfer of personal data to a third party in a foreign country is regulated in art 24 APPI. The lawfulness and information requirements as well as exceptions from the consent requirement in both cases are different. This suggests that a consent obtained under art 23 APPI (n 274) could be insufficient for transfer of personal data to a third party in a foreign country.

[276] In terms of the GDPR, 'principal' means 'data subject'.

[277] Greenleaf argues that Japanese consent requirements are lower than those under the GDPR. Greenleaf, 'Japan: EU Adequacy Discounted' (n 249) 8.

(2) if the data exporter from Japan and importer in a third country have together implemented binding arrangements that guarantee an *equivalent* level of data protection to that in Japan by means of a contract, other forms of binding agreements or binding arrangements within a corporate group.[278]

The adequacy decision for Canada simply does not address at all the issue of onward transfers of personal data.[279] Under Canadian federal law (the Personal Information Protection and Electronic Documents Act (PIPEDA)), transfers of personal data outside Canada are regulated by the principle of accountability. The 2009 Guidance by the Office of the Privacy Commissioner (OPC) of Canada explains that a transfer of personal data to a third party for the purposes of processing (including when such party is outside Canada) does not constitute disclosure of such personal data; therefore, additional consent is not required for such a transfer.[280] It stipulates that such transfers are subject to the accountability of the Canadian organization transferring personal data outside Canada, which means that such an organization remains responsible for protecting personal data under its control. The primary means of compliance with this principle is through contractual arrangements to ensure that the third party will provide a *comparable* (not 'essentially equivalent' as required by the CJEU) level of personal data protection.[281] The Canadian OPC also requires organizations to assess the risks and benefits of transferring personal data outside Canada, and recommends applying higher standards of protection to sensitive data, such as financial data, and to refrain from such transfers when the risks are too high (eg due to the 'uncertain nature of the foreign regime').[282] In its opinion on the adequacy of PIPEDA, the Article 29 Working Party noted that such contractual or other binding provisions

[278] Recital 79 of the Adequacy Decision for Japan (n 164) explicitly states that APEC Cross-Border Privacy Rules cannot be used as a mechanism for onward transfers of EEA personal data from Japan.

[279] Kuner, 'Developing an Adequate Legal Framework' (n 226) 5 ('It is also striking that in its own adequacy decisions, the European Commission does not always require that third countries found adequate themselves prohibit the transfer of personal data to non-adequate countries. For example, the Canadian Personal Information Protection and Electronic Documents Act (PIPED Act (PIPEDA)) has been found adequate, even though the Act itself contains no such prohibition.').

[280] Office of the Privacy Commissioner of Canada, 'Guidelines for Processing Personal Data across Borders' (January 2009) <https://www.priv.gc.ca/en/privacy-topics/airports-and-borders/gl_dab_090127/> accessed 10 July 2023 (hereafter Office of the Privacy Commissioner of Canada, 'Guidelines for Processing Personal Data across Borders').

[281] Principle 1 of the CSA Model Code for the Protection of Personal Information, Schedule 1 to Personal Information Protection and Electronic Documents Act (PIPEDA) 13 April 2000 S.C. 2000 states:

An organization is responsible for personal information in its possession or custody, including information that has been transferred to a third party for processing. The organization shall use contractual or other means to provide a comparable level of protection while the information is being processed by a third party.

[282] Office of the Privacy Commissioner of Canada, 'Guidelines for Processing Personal Data across Borders' (n 280).

are able to provide a comparable level of data protection.[283] After a public consultation concluded in September 2019, the OPC decided that the 2009 Guidelines should remain 'unchanged under the current law'.[284] At the same time, the Privacy Commissioner acknowledged that the 'PIPEDA's accountability principle is not always effective in protecting Canadians in the context of international transfers' and requires reform.[285] Similar to the situation with Japan's adequacy decision, this shows that the standard required for onward transfers is lower than that required by the GDPR for transfers of personal data outside the EEA.

To sum up, the adequacy decision for Japan devotes significantly more attention to the question of onward transfers of personal data than the earlier adequacy decision for Canada. Analysis of the onward transfer mechanisms in the adequacy decision for Japan shows, however, that the range of onward transfer mechanisms is narrower than the range of mechanisms for transfers of personal data available under Chapter V of the GDPR and is limited solely to contractual arrangements or binding arrangements within a group and an individual consent. Despite the fact that the choice of onward transfer mechanisms is restricted, in substance their application is unlikely to meet the standard of 'essential equivalence' to the EU framework, and, therefore, the strict necessity and proportionality tests for derogation from these fundamental rights under Article 52(1) of the Charter.

In relation to consent, for example, Greenleaf convincingly argues that it cannot serve as a sufficient basis for onward transfers of personal data for at least three reasons.[286] First, the Supplementary Rules annexed to the adequacy decision for Japan do not require, when obtaining consent, individuals to be informed that their data will be subject to an onward transfer to a country with a lower level of data protection.[287] Second, as mentioned earlier, the standard for actually obtaining consent under Japanese law is lower than that under the GDPR.[288] The third, and more systemic, issue is that under the GDPR, consent is a specific derogation that

[283] Article 29 Working Party, 'Opinion 2/2001 on the Adequacy of the Canadian Personal Information and Electronic Documents Act', WP 39 (26 January 2001) 6 <https://ec.europa.eu/justice/article-29/documentation/opinion-recommendation/files/2001/wp39_en.pdf> accessed 10 July 2023.

[284] 'Commissioner Concludes Consultation on Transfers for Processing' (*Office of the Privacy Commissioner of Canada*, 23 September 2019) <https://www.priv.gc.ca/en/opc-news/news-and-announcements/2019/an_190923/> accessed 10 July 2023

[285] '2018–2019 Annual Report to Parliament on the Privacy Act and the Personal Information Protection and Electronic Documents Act. Data Protection Law Reforms Have Been Announced in December 2019 by Canada's Prime Minister Trudeau' (*Office of the Privacy Commissioner of Canada*, 2019) < https://www.priv.gc.ca/en/opc-actions-and-decisions/ar_index/201819/ar_201819/> accessed 10 July 2023. See also Mia Hunt, 'Trudeau Outlines Canadian Data Privacy Reforms' (*Global Government Forum*, 26 December 2019) <https://www.globalgovernmentforum.com/trudeau-outlines-canadian-data-privacy-reforms/> accessed 10 July 2023.

[286] Greenleaf, 'Japan: EU Adequacy Discounted' (n 249) 8.

[287] ibid ('Supplementary Rule (4) requires that the individuals concerned shall be "provided information on the circumstances surrounding the transfer necessary for the principal to make a decision on his/her consent". However, there is no obligation to tell the person that their data will be transferred to a country with very weak privacy laws such as the US'. Internal footnotes omitted.).

[288] ibid.

is inappropriate for systematic transfers of personal data. The fact that it can be used as a legal ground for systematic onward transfers of personal data from Japan is inconsistent with the logic of the GDPR, where under Article 49 of the GDPR, as interpreted by the EDPB, consent can be used only for non-repetitive and occasional transfers.[289] This book contends that it is precisely because of the fact that specific derogations, such as consent, are not intended for systematic transfers, that the CJEU in *Schrems II* did not impose the 'essential equivalence' standard on transfers using such derogations.[290] As the Article 29 Working Party noted in the 2014 Opinion on data protection in Québec, 'consent should not be promoted as the general legal basis for onward transfers as the recipient then does not commit to take any action to ensure an adequate level of protection; this situation should thus remain an exception.'[291] In essence, by allowing regular transfers on the basis of consent, the adequacy decision for Japan allows the circumvention of the GDPR rules restricting transfers of personal data on the basis of consent. This places Japanese companies in a more favourable position than those from third countries that have not been afforded adequacy, as unlike Japanese companies, those companies cannot rely on consent for systematic transfers of personal data from the EEA.

In respect of using contractual arrangements and binding agreements within the group as mechanisms for onward transfers, there are at least two potential problems. The first is that unlike the SCCs and the BCRs in the GDPR framework, there are no specific requirements that such contractual and intra-group arrangements must incorporate. Recall that the model SCCs in the EU are approved by the Commission and must be incorporated verbatim in the contract. As confirmed by the CJEU in *Schrems II*, these provide for 'effective mechanisms' for protection of personal data, but only to the extent that transfers are suspended or prohibited when the recipient of data is unable to comply with those clauses.[292] In addition, the GDPR provides for extensive requirements as to the content of the BCRs, further elaborated in the EDPB guidance.[293] Furthermore, the compliance of BCRs with the GDPR is ultimately certified by the EDPB, which approves BCRs before they take effect.[294] The absence of similar requirements in relation to contractual

[289] EDPB, 'Guidelines 2/2018 on Derogations of Article 49 under Regulation 2016/679' (n 142).
[290] For discussion, see Section 5.2.2.
[291] Article 29 Working Party, 'Opinion 7/2014 on the Protection of Personal Data in Quebec, WP 219 (4 June 2014) 10 <https://ec.europa.eu/justice/article-29/documentation/opinion-recommendation/files/2014/wp219_en.pdf> accessed 10 July 2023.
[292] *Schrems II* (n 6) para 148.
[293] Art 47(2) GDPR; Article 29 Working Party, Working Document setting up a table with the elements and principles to be found in Binding Corporate Rules, WP 256 rev.01 (6 February 2018) <https://ec.europa.eu/newsroom/article29/items/614109/en> accessed 10 July 2023; Article 29 Working Party, Working Document setting up a table with the elements and principles to be found in Processor Binding Corporate Rules, WP 257 rev.01 (6 February 2018) <https://ec.europa.eu/newsroom/article29/items/614110/en> accessed 10 July 2023.
[294] Art 47(1) GDPR.

and intra-group arrangements used for onward transfers of personal data from Japan and Canada is likely to lead to a lower level of data protection as compared to that under SCCs and BCRs.

The second problem, as discussed in Section 5.3.1, is that appropriate safeguards like SCCs and BCRs can be used as mechanisms for systematic transfers of personal data to third countries that have not been afforded adequacy only subject to prior comprehensive case-by-case assessment by data exporters of such third country's legal framework. Relying on the logic of the EU framework for transfers of personal data as interpreted by the CJEU in *Schrems II*, and in the light of the aims pursued by the EU framework for transfers of personal data, the same assessment must be conducted whenever contractual or intragroup arrangements are used for onward transfers of personal data. This requirement could indeed be one of the outcomes of the above-mentioned ongoing review of adequacy decisions by the European Commission.

In its Report on the first review of the functioning of the adequacy decision for Japan, the European Commission did suggest that the Japan's Personal Information Commission could clarify the 'content (in terms of safeguards) of "equivalent measures" used for international transfers, be it in the form of guidelines or model data protection clauses'.[295] This suggestion, however, is formulated in vague terms[296] and does not mention that the use of private law mechanisms, such as standard contracts, must be conditioned by an 'essential equivalence' assessment of the country of destination, as mandated by the CJEU *Schrems II* judgment for similar transfer mechanisms under the GDPR. Until this deficiency is rectified through amendment by the Commission, or interpretation in the light of *Schrems II* by the EDPB or domestic courts, this adequacy decision is unlikely to yield an essentially equivalent protection of personal data in the context of onward transfers.

A further complicating factor is that both Japan and Canada, as well as other countries that have been afforded an EU adequacy decision (such as the United Kingdom), are subject to binding cross-border data flow provisions in digital trade agreements.[297] For example, Canada, Japan, and the United Kingdom are all parties to the Comprehensive and Progressive Agreement for Trans-Pacific Partnership (CPTPP), and Canada is party to the United States-Mexico-Canada Agreement (USMCA). Both trade agreements include, as parties, countries that have not been

[295] European Commission, Report from the Commission to the European Parliament and the Council on the first review of the functioning of the adequacy decision for Japan COM(2023) 275 final (3 April 2023) 5 <https://eur-lex.europa.eu/legal-content/EN/TXT/?uri=CELEX%3A52023DC0275> accessed 10 July 2023.

[296] ibid. The European Commission states that '[t]hese further clarifications ... could notably be based on the exchange of information and best practices between the PPC and the Commission'.

[297] Art 14.11(2) CPTPP (Comprehensive and Progressive Agreement for Trans-Pacific Partnership (concluded on 8 March 2018, in force 30 December 2018); art 19.11 USMCA (Agreement between the United States of America, the United Mexican States, and Canada (30 November 2018)). For discussion, see Section 3.3.4.

afforded an adequacy decision by the EU, such as Australia, Mexico, Singapore, and Viet Nam. These trade agreements prohibit the parties to restrict cross-border data flows, unless such restrictions can be justified by an exception. This exception, however, may be insufficiently broad to justify restrictions on onward transfers of personal data mandated by an adequacy decision granted by the EU to one of such countries.[298] In this situation, countries such as Canada, Japan, and the United Kingdom may well serve as a 'backdoor' for data flows from the EU to countries that have not been afforded adequacy decisions, thus undermining the high level of protection that must be afforded to personal data from the EEA.

5.3.4 Limited scalability of EU framework for transfers of personal data

Against the backdrop of the broad understanding of the notion of 'personal data' in the EU, this section argues that the EU regime for transfers of personal data outside the EEA in Chapter V of the GDPR lacks granularity in the sense that the same rules apply irrespective of the context, volume, and type of data transferred and other parameters of data transfers.

In a world where massive volumes of personal data are transferred every second, it is unrealistic to expect that the stringent EU framework under Chapter V of the GDPR will be observed in all those transfers. It is even more unrealistic to believe that the EU DPAs endowed with the powers to enforce this compliance can have the capacity to monitor such compliance and enforce against non-compliance in order to produce an effective level of deterrence to violate such rules. As a result, there is a mismatch between the legal framework, which requires a high level of personal data protection, and the reality of data transfers in the digitalized world, in which such high level cannot be achieved in practice. This section explains that such a mismatch is a direct consequence of (a) lack of granularity of EU rules on transfers of personal data in the sense that the same rules apply to any personal data, which is broadly defined in the EU and, relatedly, (b) lack of the risk-based approach to regulating transfers of personal data.

EU law maintains a distinction between personal data and non-personal data, which are governed by two different legal frameworks.[299] In the digital

[298] For a discussion, see Svetlana Yakovleva, 'Testing Restrictions on Onward Transfers of EU Personal Data against Free Data Flow Obligations in the CPTPP and US-Japan Digital Trade Agreement' (2022) Amsterdam Law School Research Paper No 2023-20, Institute for Information Law Research Paper No 2023-05 <https://ssrn.com/abstract=4423959> accessed 10 July 2023. See also EDPB, Opinion 14/2021 regarding the European Commission Draft Implementing Decision pursuant to Regulation (EU) 2016/679 on the adequate protection of personal data in the United Kingdom (13 April 2021) para 94 <https://edpb.europa.eu/system/files/2021-04/edpb_opinion142021_ukadequacy_gdpr.pdf_en.pdf> accessed 10 July 2023.

[299] Bert-Jaap Koops, 'The Trouble with European Data Protection Law' (2014) 4(4) International Data Privacy Law 250, 257 (hereafter Koops, 'The Trouble with European Data Protection Law') ('EU

environment, where almost any data can be linked to an identifier, the distinction between what constitutes personal data and what remains non-personal data—and therefore not subject to the scrutiny of stringent data protection rules—is often difficult to make.[300] While cross-border transfers of personal data are subject to a 'border control'[301] regime (in contrast to the United States' 'open skies' policy[302]), transfers of non-personal data outside the EEA are not subject to the same restrictions on transfers under the GDPR.[303] In sum, while in reality it is hard to draw a distinction between personal and non-personal data, the European law maintains two different legal regimes for personal and non-personal data, and nothing in between.[304]

Schwartz and Solove succinctly summarize four main problems with this distinction. First, almost any data online can be qualified as personal data. The

data protection law applies an all-or-nothing approach: data is either personal data (triggering the whole regime), or it is not (triggering nothing), but it cannot be something in between or something else.'). While processing of personal data is regulated by the GDPR, non-personal data is governed by Regulation on Non-Personal Data.

[300] Recital 9 of the Regulation (EU) 2018/1807 of the European Parliament and of the Council of 14 November 2018 on a framework for the free flow of non-personal data in the European Union PE/ 53/2018/REV/1 [2018] OJ L 303 (hereafter Regulation on Non-Personal Data). For a discussion, see Omer Tene and Jules Polonetsky, 'Big Data for All: Privacy and User Control in the Age of Analytics' (2013) 11(5) Northwestern Journal of Technology and Intellectual Property 239; Dániel Kondor and others, 'Towards Matching User Mobility Traces in Large-Scale Datasets' (2018) IEEE Transactions on Big Data <https://arxi.org/pdf/1709.05772.pdf> accessed 10 July 2023; Paul M Schwartz and Daniel J Solove, 'The PII Problem: Privacy and a New Concept of Personally Identifiable Information' (2011) 86 New York University Law Review 1814 (hereafter Schwartz and Solove, 'The PII Problem'); Nadezhda Purtova, 'The Law of Everything: Broad Concept of Personal Data and Future of EU Data Protection Law' (2018)10(1) Law, Innovation and Technology 40, 78 (hereafter Purtova, 'The Law of Everything'); Michèle Finck and Frank Pallas, 'They Who Must Not Be Identified—Distinguishing Personal from Non-Personal Data under the GDPR' (2020) 10(1) International Data Privacy Law 11 (hereafter Finck and Pallas, 'They Who Must Not Be Identified'); Paul Ohm, 'Broken Promises of Privacy: Responding to the Surprising Failure of Anonymization' (2010) 57 UCLA Law Review 1701, 1706 (hereafter Ohm, 'Broken Promises of Privacy') (warning about the problems of re-identification of personal data and stressing that even truly anonymized personal data at some point in time may be re-identified.).

[301] Dan Jerker B Svantesson, 'The Regulation of Cross-Border Data Flows' (2011) 1(3) International Data Privacy Law 180,184 (hereafter Svantesson, 'The Regulation of Cross-Border Data Flows'); François LeSieur, 'Regulating Cross-Border Data Flows and Privacy in the Networked Digital Environment and Global Knowledge Economy' (2012) 2(2) International Data Privacy Law 93, 101, 103–04 (hereafter LeSieur, 'Regulating Cross-Border Data Flows and Privacy').

[302] See Svantesson, 'The Regulation of Cross-Border Data Flows' (n 301) 184; LeSieur, 'Regulating Cross-Border Data Flows and Privacy' (n 301) 101, 103–04; Paul M Schwartz and Karl-Nikolaus Peifer, 'Transatlantic Data Privacy Law' (2017) 106 Georgetown Law Journal 115, 135 (stating that '[u]nlike EU law, U.S. law starts with a principle of free information flow and permits the processing of any personal data unless a law limits this action').

[303] Regulation on Non-Personal Data (n 300) does not provide for any restrictions on cross-border transfers of non-personal data outside the EEA. For a discussion on the emerging restrictions on transfers of non-personal data outside the EEA, see Section 2.2.1.

[304] This distinction between personal and non-personal data is also built in the EU Regulation on Non-Personal Data (n 300) and Regulation (EU) 2022/868 of the European Parliament and of the Council of 30 May 2022 on European data governance and amending Regulation (EU) 2018/1724 (Data Governance Act) PE/85/2021/REV/1 [2022] OJ L 152. See Nine Riis, 'Shaping the Field of EU Data Law' (2023) 14(1) JIPITEC 54, 64.

'built-in identifiability' in cyberspace makes anonymity online a 'myth', as all online data can be linked to some identifier.[305] Second, non-personal information can be transformed into personal data over time. Third, the distinction between personal and non-personal data has a dynamic nature, as the line between the two depends on technological developments. Fourth and finally, the borderline between personal and non-personal data is not firm, but rather contextual, as many kinds of data are not non-identifiable or identifiable in the abstract.[306]

Maintaining this distinction between personal and non-personal data in a situation where almost any data element can be qualified as personal at a specific point in time can also be very costly.[307] The transition of data from non-personal to personal leads to higher compliance costs and the risks of multimillion Euro fines.[308] As a result, the problems of distinguishing personal and non-personal data exemplify a tendency of any data potentially becoming personal in the future and being treated as personal.[309] Purtova predicts that the application of the GDPR's 'highly intensive and non-scalable regime' to virtually any data processing will strip this data protection framework of meaning,[310] by leading to paper compliance and selective enforcement.[311] This is precisely what is happening in the area of transfers of personal data outside the EEA.

[305] See also Ohm, 'Broken Promises of Privacy' (n 300) 1706.

[306] Schwartz and Solove, 'The PII Problem' (n 300) 1836–48. Stating that:

[f]irst, many people believe in an 'anonymity myth',-that is, a belief that individuals remain anonymous if they have not formally used their name. This belief is especially prevalent for cyberspace activity. Yet, the growth of static IP addresses and other developments creates some built-in identifiability when one enters cyberspace. Second, information that is initially non- PII can be transformed into PII. Third, technology itself is constantly evolving, which means that the line between PII and non-PII is not fixed but rather depends upon changing technological developments. Fourth, the ability to distinguish PII from non-PII is frequently contextual. Many kinds of information are not inherently non- identifiable, or identifiable as an abstract matter.

[307] A 2019 OECD study shows that businesses across sectors overwhelmingly report that separating personal from non-personal data is likely to be costly or very costly. Francesca Casalini and Javier López González, 'Trade and Cross-Border Data Flows' (2019) OECD Trade Policy Papers No 220 <http://dx.doi.org/10.1787/b2023a47-en> accessed 10 July 2023, 33 and Figure 6 ('The extent to which firms can identify and split personal from non-personal data was also identified as an issue for firms. Respondents to the business questionnaire overwhelmingly reported that separating data was likely to be costly or very costly, a response consistent across most sectors').

[308] Art 83(4)–(5) GDPR.

[309] Ohm, 'Broken Promises of Privacy' (n 300) 1742. ('No matter how effectively regulators follow the latest re-identification research, folding newly identified data fields into new laws and regulations, researchers will always find more data field types they have not yet covered. The list of potential PII categories will never stop growing until it includes everything.' Internal footnotes omitted); Purtova, 'The Law of Everything' (n 300) 41, arguing that 'literally any data can be plausibly argued to be personal'.

[310] Purtova, 'The Law of Everything' (n 300) 75 ('a highly intensive and non-scalable regime of rights and obligations created by the GDPR will not simply be difficult but impossible to maintain in a meaningful way'.).

[311] ibid 77–78 ('Facing the threat of effective and deterring sanctions, the controllers, instead of engaging in a meaningful assessment of fairness and necessity, will be pushed to create the formal appearance of compliance by using "compliance surrogates", such as compliance roadmaps, "accountability tools," trust marks and certification schemes'.); ibid 78 ('Alternatively, or in addition, enforcement of the data protection rights and obligations will likely become selective, determined by priority lists and short-cuts that the data protection authorities would develop to cope with the workload, including

The point about the broad definition of personal data is not made here with a view to criticize the breadth of this definition in the GDPR, as there are good normative reasons to support a broad definition of this notion.[312] Given that the rights to privacy and the protection of personal data are protected as fundamental rights, maintaining a broad concept of 'personal data' is essential to ensure a high level of protection of these fundamental rights.[313] Furthermore, to be clear, this book also does not propose to eliminate a legal distinction between personal and non-personal data and, as Purtova has suggested, to treat *all* data as personal,[314] as this would water down the legal data governance framework even further. Rather, this chapter is best seen as a call for a reform of the rules on transfers of personal data outside the EEA to make them more scalable, in particular by taking account of the *risks* associated with different sets of transfers and, therefore, more effective in practice.

To some extent, the GDPR has already made steps towards greater scalability by implementing a risk-based approach to data protection.[315] In particular, the very determination of whether data constitutes 'personal data' embraces a risk-based approach.[316] The GDPR also singles out a separate category of personal data (special categories of personal data listed in Article 9 of the GDPR, such as personal data relating to health, race, or sexual orientation), the processing of which is associated with higher risks for individuals, and provides for stricter rules for the processing of such data. Personal data about criminal convictions, the content of electronic communications, and financial and location data have also been recognized as sensitive by the Article 29 Working Party and its successor, the EDPB, due to the higher risks of processing these types of data for individual rights. They are, therefore, subject to a higher level of protection than personal data falling into

the "compliance surrogates". Selective enforcement and the pretence of compliance will reinforce each other, ridiculing data protection law, and depriving its protection of meaning.').

312 See, eg, Katerina Demetzou, 'Risk to the "Rights and Freedoms": A Legal Interpretation of the Scope of Risk under the GDPR' in Dara Hallinan and others (eds), *Data Protection and Privacy Data Protection and Democracy* (Hart Publishing 2020) 131 (hereafter Demetzou, 'Risk to the "Rights and Freedoms"').

313 Purtova, 'The Law of Everything' (n 300) 78; Article 29 Working Party, Opinion 4/2007 on the Concept of Personal Data' WP 136 (20 June 2007) <https://ec.europa.eu/justice/article-29/documentation/opinion-recommendation/files/2007/wp136_en.pdf> accessed 10 July 2023 (hereafter Article 29 Working Party, Opinion 4/2007 on the Concept of Personal Data).

314 Purtova, 'The Law of Everything' (n 300) 79–80.

315 cf Raphaël Gellert, *The Risk-Based Approach to Data Protection* (Oxford Data Protection & Privacy Law 2020) 154 (hereafter Gellert, *The Risk-Based Approach to Data Protection*), arguing that the only risk-based provisions can be found in Chapter IV of the GDPR. For discussion, see also Jungkind and Koch, 'The Risk-Based Approach in the GDPR (n 64). See also Finck and Pallas, 'They Who Must Not Be Identified' (n 300) 24; Giovanni De Gregorio and Pietro Dunn, 'The European Risk-Based Approaches: Connecting Constitutional Dots in the Digital Age' (2022) 59 Common Market Law Review 473, 480 (hereafter De Gregorio and Dunn, 'The European Risk-Based Approaches').

316 Finck and Pallas, 'They Who Must Not Be Identified' (n 300) 14–15.

what one might call the general category.[317] In addition, in several contexts (eg, in the balancing between the legitimate interest of the data controller as the legal ground for processing personal data with the risk to the fundamental rights of data subjects, data breach notification, accountability of data controller), the GDPR allows data controllers to calibrate their obligations in accordance with the risk that certain processing of personal data may pose to the fundamental rights of individuals.[318]

Furthermore, the GDPR has codified a notion of *pseudonymized data*.[319] Recital 28 of the preamble to the GDPR explicitly states that the 'application of pseudonymisation to personal data can reduce the risks to the data subjects concerned'. As noted by various experts in the field and EDPB, the GDPR already provides for more lenient rules for pseudonymized data when it comes to the rights of individuals, data breach notification requirement, and the possibilities of using the data for purposes other than that for which it was originally collected.[320]

None of these flexibilities, however, are taken into account in the GDPR's framework for transfers of personal data *outside the EEA* in Chapter V. What is more, as explained in Section 2.2.4, in a series of investigations of transfers of personal data with the use of Google Analytics and Facebook Connect, several DPAs have concluded that the risk-based approach does *not* apply to the interpretation of the GDPR's rules on transfers of personal data.[321] In other words, according to the DPAs, the same standard should apply to transfer of personal data irrespective of the risk such transfer carries for the rights of individuals.[322]

[317] Article 29 Working Party, 'Guidelines on Data Protection Impact Assessment (DPIA)' WP 248rev.01 (4 October 2017) <https://ec.europa.eu/newsroom/article29/items/611236/en> accessed 10 July 2023.

[318] Article 29 Working Party, 'Opinion 06/2014 on the Notion of Legitimate Interests of the Data Controller under Article 7 of Directive 95/46/EC' WP 217 (9 April 2014) <https://ec.europa.eu/justice/article-29/documentation/opinion-recommendation/files/2014/wp217_en.pdf> accessed 10 July 2023 (hereafter Article 29 Working Party, 'Opinion 06/2014 on the Notion of Legitimate Interests'). As of this writing, the EDPB is working on the new guidelines on the topic.

[319] Art 4(5) GDPR.

[320] Recitals 29, 50, and 156, arts 6(4), 11(1), 12(2), 14(5)(b) GDPR; Article 29 Working Party, 'Guidelines on Transparency under Regulation 2016/679' WP260 rev. 1 (11 April 2018) 31 <https://ec.europa.eu/newsroom/article29/items/622227/en> accessed 10 July 2023 (hereafter Article 29 Working Party, 'Guidelines on Transparency'); EDPB, 'Guidelines 9/2022 on Personal Data Breach Notification under GDPR' (28 March 2023) 25 <https://edpb.europa.eu/system/files/2023-04/edpb_guidelines_202209_personal_data_breach_notification_v2.0_en.pdf> accessed 10 July 2023 (hereafter EDPB, 'Guidelines 9/2022 on Personal Data Breach Notification under GDPR'); Niall McCreanor, 'Pseudonymisation Is the GDPR's "Escape Hatch"' (*IT Governance Blog*, 14 May 2018) <https://www.itgovernance.eu/blog/en/pseudonymisation-is-the-gdprs-escape-hatch> accessed 10 July 2023 (hereafter McCreanor, 'Pseudonymisation Is the GDPR's "Escape Hatch"'); Gabe Maldoff, 'Top 10 Operational Impacts of the GDPR: Part 8 – Pseudonymization' (*IAPP*, 12 February 2016) <https://iapp.org/news/a/top-10-operational-impacts-of-the-gdpr-part-8-pseudonymization/> accessed 10 July 2023 (hereafter Maldoff, 'Top 10 Operational Impacts of the GDPR: Part 8 – Pseudonymization').

[321] See, eg, 'Google Analytics' (*Danish Data Protection Authority (Datatilsynet)* <https://www.datatilsynet.dk/english/google-analytics> accessed 10 July 2023

[322] See eg, 'UPDATE on 101 Complaints: Austrian DPA Rejects "Risk Based Approach" for Data Transfers to Third Countries' (*noyb*, 2 May 2022) <https://noyb.eu/en/update-noybs-101-complaints-austrian-dpa-rejects-risk-based-approach-data-transfers-third-countries> accessed 10 July 2023.

Therefore, the criticism of non-scalability, lack of nuance, and a catch-all method fully applies to this set of rules. Moreover, as compared to the substantive data protection framework, which, to some extent has embraced a risk-based approach, the provisions on data transfers do not differentiate between different degrees of risks to fundamental rights that transfers of personal data may entail for individuals. Given the expansive scope of information that may constitute personal data, this 'one size-fits-all' approach to cross-border transfers is not sustainable in the long run as it applies to growing datasets including 'Big Data' corpora systematically crossing EEA borders.

While by prohibiting the risk-based approach to transfers of personal data the DPAs clearly intended to enhance the protection of personal data transferred outside the EEA, this book contends that by failing to adopt a risk-based approach, the DPAs have in effect weakened such protection. Fortunately, the decision to disapply the risk-based approach to the rules on transfers of personal data outside the EEA by the DPAs have not yet been endorsed by the EDPB. In its report on the work undertaken by the DPAs within the 101 Task Force, formed following Schrems' 101 complaints against Google Analytics and Facebook Connect, the EDPB did not mention the (in)applicability of the risk-based approach to Chapter V of the GDPR.[323] At the same time, the EDPB referred to the companies' obligation to demonstrate compliance in accordance with Article 24(1) of the GDPR, which endorses the risk-based approach. This suggests that the risk-based approach to the interpretation of Chapter V of the GDPR may not be completely off the table. Furthermore, the EDPB may not be totally against the risk-based approach in the context of transfers of personal data outside the EEA. For example, elements of a risk-based approach have been read into the final EDPB Recommendations on supplementary measures following *Schrems II* judgment, after the critique of the EDPB's absolutist approach in the draft Recommendations during the public consultation.[324]

It is hardly realistic to expect that the same level of 'effective and complete' protection of *all* personal data transferred internationally can be achieved in practice. Requiring the same level of compliance with a strict regime for transfers of personal data for such a broad scope of data is simply inoperable. Kuner thus seems to be correct when he argues that '[t]he definition of transborder data flows is so

For analysis and critique, see Lokke Moerel, 'What Happened to the Risk Based Approach to Data Transfers? How the EDPB Is Rewriting the GDPR' (*FPF Blog*, 27 September 2022) <https://fpf.org/wp-content/uploads/2022/09/FPF-Guest-Blog-What-Happened-to-the-Risk-Based-Approach-of-Data-Transfers.doc.pdf> accessed 10 July 2023.

323 EDPB, 'Report of the Work Undertaken by the Supervisory Authorities within the 101 Task Force' (n 196).

324 Jetty Tielemans, Daniel Cooper, and Gabe Maldoff, 'EDPB's Data Transfer Recommendations Adopt a Risk-Based Approach with Teeth' (*IAPP*, 22 June 2021) <https://iapp.org/news/a/edpbs-data-transfer-recommendations-adopt-a-risk-based-approach-with-teeth/> accessed 10 July 2023.

broad that it can cover most acts of data processing on the Internet, and no national regulation could ever be consistently enforced with regard to such a vast amount of data processing on a global scale'.[325] It is therefore entirely unsurprising that enforcement of the rules on cross-border data flows has so far been ineffective, as already alluded to in this chapter.[326]

Throughout the lifetime of the EU data protection framework, the only significant enforcement actions came from the CJEU, which, as discussed earlier, invalidated adequacy decisions issued by the European Commission for the United States.[327] As Kuner rightly points out, these enforcement actions were driven not by the DPAs but by an Austrian activist Max Schrems.[328] Just as there was 'very little enforcement related to the *Schrems [I]* judgement',[329] *Schrems II* has not led to a surge of enforcement actions in the context of data transfers. Apart from a few enforcement actions related to transfers of personal data outside the EEA through Google Analytics and Facebook Connect, and the landmark decision by the Irish DPC in the matter of Meta Platforms ordering to suspend transfers of personal data by its Facebook service (which took ten years to materialize), *Schrems II* has not been subject to vigorous enforcement.[330] The Irish DPC's order to suspend transfers outside the EEA is the first of its kind in the history of existence of EU restrictions on cross-border data flows, and it should not be underestimated. This order, however, took a long time to come to fruition, and it is not yet final.[331]

The risk of enforcement is one of the major drivers behind companies' compliance with data protection rules. Thus, a lack of enforcement reduces the risks of non-compliance with the cross-border transfer rules, making them even less effective in performing their function of preventing the circumvention of the EU's high level of personal data and privacy protection.

[325] Kuner, *Transborder Data Flows and Data Privacy Law* (n 235) 154–55. See also Koops, 'The Trouble with European Data Protection Law' (n 299) 259:

The regulatory disconnection of data protection law, with risks being enlarged rather than diminished through stretching the scope of data protection law to embrace new regulatory issues, together with a narrow focus on command-and-control law, demonstrate a fallacy of regulators to believe that every problem related to Internet data flows can be regulated by data protection law in the books. It does not work, as any realist looking at 21st century data processing practices will acknowledge.

[326] Kuner, *Transborder Data Flows and Data Privacy Law* (n 235) 144; Kuner, 'Op-Ed: "International Data Transfers after Five Years of the GDPR: Postmodern Anxieties' (n 196).

[327] *Schrems I* (n 5) and *Schrems II* (n 6).

[328] Kuner, 'Op-Ed: "International Data Transfers after Five Years of the GDPR: Postmodern Anxieties' (n 196).

[329] Kuner, 'Reality and Illusion in EU Data Transfer Regulation Post Schrems' (n 12) 885.

[330] See also Sections 2.2.4, 2.4.2.1, and 5.3.1.

[331] Matthew Newman, 'Meta Lodges Appeal against EDPB Data-Transfers Decision at EU Courts' (*MLex Market Insight*, 15 June 2023) <https://content.mlex.com/#/content/1478542/meta-lodges-appeal-against-edpb-data-transfers-decision-at-eu-courts> accessed 10 July 2023; 'Facebook Owner Granted Stay on Order That It Suspend Europe-US Data Transfers' (*The Irish Times*, 9 June 2023) <https://www.irishtimes.com/business/2023/06/09/facebook-owner-granted-stay-on-order-that-it-suspend-europeus-data-transfers/> accessed 10 July 2023.

5.4 Directions of Thought on How to Improve the EU Framework for Transfers of Personal Data outside the EEA

A reform of the GDPR's framework for transfers of personal data outside the EEA is necessary to address the weaknesses identified in the previous section and restore its ability to perform its constitutional function. This reform will also make this framework more consistent with the EU's international trade obligations. Many of the weaknesses, identified in the previous section from the perspective of the EU Charter, are also problematic from the international trade law perspective, as discussed in Sections 2.3 and 2.4.2 of this book.

This section suggests and elaborates upon three possible lines of thought on how to improve the framework in a way more suitable to perform its constitutional function and more consistent with the EU's international trade obligations. A full-fledged reform proposal cannot be developed within the boundaries of this book for a few reasons, among them the fact that the aim of this book is to situate the need for reform in the context of international trade law and the EU's approach to existing and future trade commitments. A comprehensive reform of the GDPR would require an interdisciplinary effort based on a host of both domestic and international factors, an endeavour which goes well beyond the scope of this book. Hence, this section's objective is to inform and suggest reform paths, but not to offer an *exhaustive* overview of opportunities for reform of the GDPR's Chapter V.

The three proposed paths or lines of thought that this section considers are as follows. The first, and the most moderate, is to improve *specific elements* of the framework for transfers of personal data already present in Chapter V of the GDPR but without changing the design and composition of the framework. The second, intermediate, path incorporates the first but goes a step further by suggesting adding several new elements to the extant framework based on key recent developments in EU data protection law and technology. The third, and the most radical, path is a complete redesign of GDPR Chapter V's framework, for example by re-anchoring it on a risk-based approach, with elements proposed as a part of the second line of thought. The three paths roughly correspond to short-, medium-, and long-term strategies for the reform of Chapter V of the GDPR.

Before moving on to the discussion of each path, two remarks are in order. First, recall that while some form of restrictions on transfers of personal data form part of the essence of the fundamental rights to privacy and the protection of personal data, their specific design—with some specific exceptions[332]—is subject to

[332] Based on the current CJEU case law, the elements of the design of the framework for transfers of personal data, which constitute a part of the essence of the fundamental rights to privacy and the protection of personal data, include: (a) restrictions on generalized access to the content of electronic communications; (b) compliance with the purpose limitation principle, the rules designed to ensure, inter alia, the security, confidentiality, and integrity of the data, and to protect them against unlawful access and processing; (c) limitations on the retention of the content of communications; (d) rules that provide for some possibility for an individual to pursue legal remedies in order to have access to personal

balancing with the aim of ensuring 'essentially equivalent' protection of personal data. This balancing must be conducted on the basis of the principles of strict necessity and proportionality (Article 52(1) of the EU Charter), which, as Section 5.2.2 explained, underlie the 'essential equivalence' standard. Second, the standard of 'essential equivalence' itself does not constitute the essence of the fundamental rights to privacy and the protection of personal data under the EU Charter. It does, however, constitute a part of the constitutional meaning of the above-mentioned fundamental rights and is not merely an interpretation of the secondary EU data protection law concept of 'adequacy'.

5.4.1 Improving the operation of the current framework

This line of thought considers a number of improvements to the existing framework for transfers of personal data outside the EEA. These are (a) amending the interpretation of the concept of 'transfer' by the EDPB, (b) improving administration and enforcement of adequacy decisions, the SCCs and bespoke contracts, and (c) making broader use of derogations for specific situations under Article 49.

Although this line of thought does not resolve all the conceptual drawbacks of the framework of Chapter V of the GDPR, its modesty makes it easier to implement, at least in the short term. Furthermore, proposed improvements could yield an incremental improvement through fairly minor changes to the GDPR and CJEU jurisprudence without having to redesign the framework for transfers of personal data at its core, which seems a much longer-term exercise.

To restore consistency of application of the rules on transfers of personal data outside the EEA and their interaction with the GDPR's extraterritorial application by virtue of Article 3 of the GDPR, the EDPB should amend its definition of 'transfer' in two ways. First, the EDPB should recognize that direct transmissions of personal data outside the EEA also qualify as a 'transfer' under the GDPR. Second, the EDPB should exclude the application of Chapter V rules in situations where personal data is transferred to a data importer that is already subject to the extraterritorial application of the GDPR. Amendment of the definition of 'transfer' in such a way will ensure that Europeans' personal data always benefits from the GDPR protection irrespective of the end points of transmissions. Such an approach is also the most consistent with the EU's international trade obligations, as simultaneous application of Article 3 and Chapter V of the GDPR to foreign service providers would discriminate them vis-à-vis their European counterparts.

This solution is not ideal from an EU law perspective because due to the centrality of the notion of 'transfer' and the interplay between Article 3 and Chapter

data relating to him, or to obtain the rectification or erasure of such data. For a detailed discussion see Section 5.2.4.

V of the GDPR, these issues are best left to be defined by the EU legislator.[333] However, in the short term, addressing these issues through a revised EDPB guidance is the most feasible solution.

In addition, there are two possible objections to this proposal, one from an international trade law, and the other from the EU fundamental rights perspective. The first objection is that recognition of direct transmissions of personal data outside the EEA as 'transfers' would mean that the most commonly used mechanisms for systematic transfers of personal data (the SCCs and the BCRs) in the absence of an adequacy decision would not be available for such transfers. These mechanisms are only available for transfers between a data exporter and a data importer and, as explained in Section 2.2.2, individuals are not considered as exporters of their own personal data.

In the absence of an adequacy decision, such transmissions may only rely on the derogations of Article 49 of the GDPR, which: (a) are, in the interpretation by the EDPB, only available for occasional and non-repetitive transfers and (b) create stricter rules for the collection of personal data from outside the EEA. For example, legitimate interest is not available as a mechanism for transfers of personal data and, therefore, cannot be relied on by a foreign service provider as a ground for a collection of personal data from an individual in the EEA. Therefore, the inclusion of direct transfers into the scope of Chapter V of the GDPR is likely to violate the EU's national treatment obligations under the GATS, as demonstrated in Section 2.3.1.2. While the characteristic of derogations under (b) above cannot be changed without amending the GDPR itself, the characteristic under (a) can be changed as the limitation of specific derogations to occasional and non-repetitive transfers, as explained in Section 2.2.4, stems from the EDPB guidelines. These EDPB guidelines can be reviewed more easily than the GDPR.

Compared to the current state of affairs, the proposed solution is preferable from an international trade law perspective. While both the current and the proposed approaches may be in conflict with the EU's international trade obligations under the GATS, the proposed approach can be easily justified under the trade necessity test, because it eliminates inconsistencies and gaps in legal protection of fundamental rights created by four legal regimes applicable to personal data transmitted outside the EEA[334] stemming from the current definition of

[333] Kuner, 'Protecting EU Data outside EU Borders under the GDPR' (n 15) 105; EDPB, Guidelines 05/2021 on the Interplay between the application of Article 3 and the provisions on international transfers as per Chapter V of the GDPR (14 February 2023), para 8 <https://edpb.europa.eu/system/files/2023-02/edpb_guidelines_05-2021_interplay_between_the_application_of_art3-chapter_v_of_the_gdpr_v2_en_0.pdf> accessed 10 July 2023 (hereafter EDPB, Guidelines 05/2021 on the Interplay between the application of Article 3 and the provisions on international transfers as per Chapter V of the GDPR).

[334] See Section 2.2.3.

'transfer' and the relationship between Article 3 and Chapter V of the GDPR by the EDPB.[335]

From an EU fundamental rights perspective, Kuner argues that 'since the data transfer rules provide for a greater possibility of enforcement than extraterritorial application of the GDPR under Article 3 does, it would be best to provide that the GDPR does not apply to data processing that has been transferred subject to one of the data transfer mechanisms set out in Chapter V, rather than vice versa'.[336] However, the extra enforcement possibilities only exist, as Kuner himself explains, when personal data is transferred from a data exporter in the EU to a data importer, in particular, under the SCCs. Thus, they only cover some, but not all personal data transmitted outside the EEA, if direct transmissions of personal data from individuals were also to be recognized as transfers. This approach, yet again, would create a gap between the enforcement possibilities depending on the end points of the transfer, and, potentially, a gap in legal protection of fundamental rights. Furthermore, similar enforcement possibilities against a data exporter in the EU (in a data exporter to data importer transfer situation) would exist even when Chapter V of the GDPR does not apply. A transfer of personal data outside the EEA by a controller or processor constitutes processing of personal data[337] and, therefore, the data exporter must comply with all GDPR requirements for such processing and remains accountable for its processing activities.[338] Before transferring personal data to a data importer, even if Chapter V of the GDPR does not apply, the data exporter must evaluate the risks due to processing of personal data in a foreign country, and refrain from transfer if it would not be lawful to process personal data in that country.[339] Individuals may exercise all remedies available under the GDPR against such data exporter, if it transfers personal data unlawfully.

To address the proneness of adequacy decisions to political influence, the EU could adopt a transparent procedure governing such assessments. According to Kuner, the European Commission already has internal guidelines for evaluating adequacy, though they have never been published.[340] A renewed procedure could, in particular, regulate the process of the selection of countries (or application by countries themselves) in relation to which the adequacy assessment is to be conducted and the detailed procedure for an adequacy assessment, including the due involvement of all stakeholders (such as the EDPB and European Parliament), the time frame for the whole process as well as for each step of the assessment.

[335] For discussion on why the current interpretation of 'transfer' and the relationship between Article 3 and Chapter V of the GDPR thwarts justification of the EU restrictions on transfers of personal data outside the EEA under the trade necessity test, see Section 2.4.2.

[336] Kuner, 'Protecting EU Data outside EU Borders under the GDPR' (n 15) 105.

[337] Art 4(2) GDPR.

[338] Guidelines 05/2021 on the Interplay between the application of Article 3 and the provisions on international transfers as per Chapter V of the GDPR (n 333) 31.

[339] ibid paras 31–32.

[340] Kuner, 'Reality and Illusion in EU Data Transfer Regulation Post Schrems' (n 12) 901.

All this would ensure, among other things, that stakeholders have sufficient time and opportunity to review the assessment.[341] The Commission could be required to respond and substantiate its deviation from the recommendations or opinion of stakeholders, and to involve experts in the assessment, so as to exclude situations where the review of the foreign legal system is conducted by the European Commission's employees on the basis essentially consisting of submissions by the foreign government. Such a procedure could be adopted by a Commission's Implementing Regulation, which, however, would require including a relevant enabling provision in the GDPR.

To enhance ongoing monitoring of the foreign legal framework, and in order to mitigate the fact that an adequacy assessment (and its review once in four years) constitutes a snapshot of the foreign legal framework at a particular point in time, adequacy decisions could transition from a unilateral instrument to a reciprocal agreement, under which the foreign country would undertake certain obligations. For example, such an agreement could include a mechanism of notifications by the foreign government of any changes to legislation taken into account during the adequacy assessment, and provide for negative consequences for non-notification, if discovered during the periodic review. This change would not require any amendments to the GDPR.[342]

The European Commission should conduct rigorous and timely review of adequacy decisions. This is essential if the EU wants to maintain the credibility of adequacy mechanisms as capable of safeguarding a high level of fundamental rights protection of privacy and personal data, and to prevent adequacy decisions being trumped by US-style binding cross-border data flow provisions in digital trade agreements, to which countries afforded adequacy decisions increasingly adhere (eg, Canada, Japan, and the United Kingdom, as mentioned earlier). In particular, the EU must complete the reviews of pre-GDPR adequacy decisions launched in 2017 and suspend or revoke those that do not meet the 'essential equivalence' standard mandated by the CJEU in *Schrems I* and *Schrems II*.

The onward transfer mechanisms should, as much as possible, mirror the appropriate safeguards provided for in the GDPR as interpreted by the CJEU in *Schrems II*. This is necessary in order to avoid discrimination between transfers of personal data on the basis of appropriate safeguards to countries not afforded adequacy from the EEA (under Article 46 of the GDPR) and *onward transfers* of personal

[341] EDPB, 'Contribution of the EDPB to the Evaluation of the GDPR' (n 208) 4–6 (noting that the EDPB should have sufficient time to review adequacy decisions.).

[342] For example, as discussed above, Adequacy Decision for Japan (n 164) contains Supplementary Rules, which Japan undertook in order to compensate for the deficiency of its legal framework for protection of personal data as compared to that of the EU. Similarly, the two adequacy decisions for the United States—the invalidated EU-US Safe Harbor and the EU-US Privacy Shield—contained representations by the US government in relation to the protection of personal data. The same is true with respect to the new EU-US Data Privacy Framework. See European Commission Implementing Decision on EU-US Data Privacy Framework (n 199).

data from a country that has been afforded adequacy to another country that has not been afforded adequacy. In particular, consent should not be generally allowed as a legal ground for systematic onward transfers (as discussed earlier, consent serves as one of the grounds for onward transfers in the EU adequacy decision for Japan). In addition, contractual mechanisms used for onward transfers should incorporate the SCCs approved by the European Commission; their wording should not be left to the discretion of the parties.

To enhance the effectiveness of the SCCs, the European DPAs should also enhance their enforcement efforts on this issue, for example, through conducting industry scans and requests for information, while prioritizing the transfers that carry the greatest risks for individuals.[343] To address the legal vacuum for transfers of personal data to data importers that are subject to the extraterritorial application of the GDPR (Legal Regime 3 as discussed in Sections 2.2.3 and 2.2.5), the European Commission should adopt the SCCs for such type of transfers. The EDPB should also adopt guidance on the requirements for bespoke contracts as mechanisms for transfer of personal data under Article 46 GDPR.

To prevent the risk of *de facto* data localization with respect to transfers of personal data to countries that do not meet the 'essential equivalence' standard, the EDPB could also amend its guidelines to allow a broader use of specific derogations under Article 49. While transfers of personal data under these derogations should remain limited to specific situations, as prescribed in Article 49, the EDPB could relax the requirement that such transfers should be limited to 'occasional' and 'non-repetitive' transfers to the extent that such requirements do not follow from the text of the GDPR itself.[344]

5.4.2 Greater scalability

A second, intermediate line of thought suggests adjustments to the GDPR's framework for transfers of personal data *complementing* those encompassed by the first line of thought discussed in the previous section. It would require a more substantial revision of the GDPR and, therefore, could realistically be addressed only in the medium term. For example, it could be introduced as a result of the next review of the GDPR's Chapter V under Article 97 of the GDPR, which is scheduled for 2024.

The two principal adjustments that could be introduced into Chapter V of the GDPR are (a) the introduction of the more lenient rules for transfers of

[343] See Christopher Kuner, 'Regulation of Transborder Data Flows under Data Protection and Privacy Law: Past, Present, and Future' (2011) OECD Digital Economy Papers No 187, 27 <https://www.oecd-ilibrary.org/science-and-technology/regulation-of-transborder-data-flows-under-data-protection-and-privacy-law_5kg0s2fk315f-en> accessed 10 July 2023.

[344] For discussion, see Section 2.2.4.

pseudonymized data as long as such data does not include sensitive data;[345] and (b) a codification of the legal significance of technological means for protection of personal data, including as a means of ensuring that pseudonymized data will not be re-identified after the transfer. In his 2014 article, Koops suggested that pseudonymized data could become a 'useful in-between category' between personal and non-personal data.[346] He proposed, accordingly, the creation of a special legal regime for pseudonymized data that would be 'milder' than the regime for personal data but stricter than that for non-personal data.[347] Kuner proposed relaxing restrictions on cross-border transfers of pseudonymized and encrypted data under appropriate circumstances,[348] and data in transit.[349] Similarly, but in more general form, Schwartz and Solove have suggested calibrating the intensity of the data protection regime depending on the risk of identification of individuals, based on three categories of personal information (or data): (a) identified, (b) identifiable, and (c) non-identifiable.[350]

As one of the advantages of their proposed approach, Schwartz and Solove name the incentives to companies to invest resources in maintaining data in the less identifiable form. In contrast, in the current EU regime that treats identifiable and identified data as equal, such incentive is absent.[351] Most recently, some data protection authorities and scholars proposed to use encryption, pseudonymization,

345 Just like pseudonymized personal data remains personal, pseudonymized sensitive data remains sensitive data. This means that processing pseudonymized sensitive data still involves a higher risk than processing pseudonymized 'ordinary' personal data.

346 Koops, 'The Trouble with European Data Protection Law' (n 299) 257, footnote 40. At the same time, Koops criticizes the definition of 'pseudonymised data' in the (then draft) GDPR. That wording, however, has not changed in the final version of the GDPR.

347 ibid 257 ('. . . not all identifiers function in the same way, and it makes sense to differentiate in the legal regimes for different types of identifiers'.).

348 Kuner, *Transborder Data Flows and Data Privacy Law* (n 235) 97, 99:

> Pseudonymization is used on a wide scale in some important areas (eg, in clinical trials of pharmaceutical products), and can be regarded as a form of encryption, since it allows identification of an individual only under limited conditions and by certain parties; it should be encouraged by relaxing restrictions on transborder data flows under appropriate circumstances. ... [G]reater use should be made of technology in the context of transborder data flow regulation, such as by the creation of "safe harbours" to ease regulatory approval of transborder flows of encrypted data.

See also W Kuan Hon and Christopher Millard, 'Data Export in Cloud Computing: How Can Personal Data Be Transferred outside the EEA? The Cloud of Unknowing, Part 4' (2012) 9(1) SCRIPTed 25, 27 <http://script-ed.org/wp-content/uploads/2012/04/hon.pdf> accessed 10 July 2023.

349 Kuner, *Transborder Data Flows and Data Privacy Law* (n 235) 175.

350 Schwartz and Solove, 'The PII Problem' (n 300) 1877. See also Paul M Schwartz and Daniel J Solove, 'Reconciling Personal Information in the United States and European Union' (2014) 102(4) California Law Review 877, 905.

351 Schwartz and Solove, 'The PII Problem' (n 300) 1883. In particular, Schwartz and Solove quote Article 29 Working Party Guidance for ISPs and search engine operators, where the Working Party introduced an 'absolutely certainty test' requiring companies to treat data as personal unless they can demonstrate 'with absolute certainty that the data correspond to users that cannot be identified'. See Article 29 Working Party, Opinion 4/2007 on the concept of personal data (n 313) 17; Article 29 Working Party, Opinion 1/2008 on data protection issues related to search engines, WP 148 (4 April 2008) 8 <https://ec.europa.eu/justice/article-29/documentation/opinion-recommendation/files/2008/wp148_en.pdf> accessed 10 July 2023.

and other privacy enhancing technologies as one of the additional safeguards that data exporters can implement while transferring personal data to countries that do not ensure an essentially equivalent level of personal data protection based on the SCCs.[352] The EDPB recognizes both strong encryption and pseudonymization as effective measures that are able to guarantee an essentially equivalent level of protection to that in the EEA, even when the legal framework in the country of destination does not ensure an essentially equivalent level of protection.[353] Courts in France and Belgium reached the same conclusion with respect to encryption.[354]

Since the adoption of the GDPR, pseudonymized data, defined in Article 4(5) of the GDPR, gained more prominence in the EU data protection framework. Recital 28 of the preamble to the GDPR explicitly states that the 'application of pseudonymisation to personal data can reduce the risks to the data subjects concerned'. As noted by various experts in the field and the EDPB, the GDPR already provides for more lenient rules for pseudonymized data, when it comes to the rights of individuals, data breach notification requirements, and the possibilities of using the data for purposes other than that for which it was originally collected.[355] Relaxation of these data protection principles, two of which are explicitly mentioned in Article 8 of the EU Charter, in relation to pseudonymized data, suggests that a lighter touch regulatory approach to transfers of such data outside the EEA could be compliant with the EU Charter and the GDPR.

In particular, in circumstances such as scientific or academic research, where societal benefits of data processing are high and risks of interference with fundamental rights could be minimized through various technological means, such as differential privacy and ethical safeguards of the profession, the transfer of pseudonymized data could be allowed without restrictions. Such a possibility would be welcome, for example, in the area of public health research,[356] especially in global health crises such as the one triggered by the COVID-19 pandemic in

[352] See eg Bjørn Aslak Juliussen and others, 'The Third Country Problem under the GDPR: Enhancing Protection of Data Transfers with Technology' (2023) International Data Privacy Law 1 <https://doi.org/10.1093/idpl/ipad013> accessed 1 August 2023; Christakis, 'After Schrems II' (n 58).

[353] EDPB, Recommendations 01/2020 on measures that supplement transfer tools (n 67) 28ff, in particular, use cases 2–4.

[354] 'French Highest Court Rejects Suspension of Partnership with EU Service Provider Using AWS; Extends Application of the Schrems II Requirements' (*Privacy & Information Security Law Blog*, 15 March 2021), <https://www.huntonprivacyblog.com/2021/03/15/french-highest-court-rejects-suspension-of-partnership-with-eu-service-provider-using-aws-extends-application-of-the-schrems-ii-requirements/> accessed 10 July 2023; 'Belgian Council of State Considers Encryption a Sufficient Measure for U.S. Data Transfers' (*Privacy & Information Security Law Blog*, 9 September 2021) <https://www.huntonprivacyblog.com/2021/09/09/belgian-council-of-state-considers-encryption-a-sufficient-measure-for-u-s-data-transfers/> accessed 10 July 2023.

[355] Recitals 29, 50, and 156, arts 6(4), 11(1), 12(2), 14(5)(b) GDPR; Article 29 Working Party, Guidelines on transparency (n 320) 31; EDPB, Guidelines 9/2022 on personal data breach notification under GDPR (n 320) 15–16, 21; McCreanor, 'Pseudonymisation is the GDPR's "Escape Hatch"' (n 320); Maldoff, 'Top 10 Operational Impacts of the GDPR: Part 8 – Pseudonymization' (n 320).

[356] See, eg, Heidi Beate Bentzen and others, 'Remove Obstacles to Sharing Health Data with Researchers outside of the European Union' (2021) 27 Nature Medicine 1329.

2020.[357] It should, however, be acknowledged that pseudonymization is effectively a security measure that reduces the risks associated with personal data processing. The way in which this measure should be taken into account in designing more flexible rules for transfers of personal data outside the EEA requires further research.

In relation to the role of technology in governing information flows, Reidenberg in his seminal 1998 article 'Lex Informatica' showed that 'for network environments and the Information Society ... law and government regulation are not the only source of rule- making ... . The creation and implementation of information policy are embedded in network designs and standards as well as in system configurations.'[358] He argued that Lex Informatica—'the set of rules for information flows imposed by technology and communication networks'—had an equally important role to play, along with the law, in governing information flows online.[359] Similarly, Kuner argued more recently that 'technology could play a greater role in transborder data flow regulation'; in particular, through the principle of 'privacy by design' (which is now codified in the GDPR), it could explicitly include a possibility to regulate cross-border data flows in part by technological solutions.[360] He also noted that companies already routinely configure their international IT systems to regulate cross-border flows of data and access rights in their IT networks.[361]

Gürses and van Hoboken suggest that the question of information flows should be tackled at the level of the design and production of functionality, where some of the individual harms due to reidentification of data can be mitigated though privacy technologies, such as differential or pan-privacy.[362] In addition, those

[357] For a discussion, see ALLEA, EASAC, FEAM, 'International Sharing of Personal Health Data for Research' (April 2021) 38 <https://easac.eu/fileadmin/PDF_s/reports_statements/Health_Data/2021_ALLEA_EASAC_FEAM_Policy-Report_International_Sharing_Health_Data_en.pdf> accessed 10 July 2023, arguing that the GDPR presents 'significant hurdles for sharing data with researchers outside the EU/EEA' and that '[t]he measures introduced by the GDPR to transfer data outside the EU/EEA do not provide workable mechanisms for sharing personal data with public sector research institutions outside the EU/EEA.' cf Christopher Kuner, 'Data Crossing Borders: Data Sharing and Protection in Times of Coronavirus' (*Information and Policy Center Blog*, 27 April 2020) <https://infolawcentre.blogs.sas.ac.uk/2020/04/27/data-crossing-borders-data-sharing-and-protection-in-times-of-coronavirus-christopher-kuner/> accessed 10 July 2023, who concludes that the current GDPR framework is flexible enough for the times of pandemic, while emphasizing its limitations.

[358] Joel R Reidenberg, 'Lex Informatica: The Formulation of Information Policy Rules through Technology' (1998) 76 Texas Law Review 553, 554–55.

[359] ibid 555, 562–65, 568–76. Similar arguments were also made by Lessig. See Larry Lessig, *Code and Other Laws of Cyberspace* (Basic Books 1999) (hereafter Lessig, *Code and Other Laws of Cyberspace*).

[360] Kuner, *Transborder Data Flows and Data Privacy Law* (n 235) 96. ('But technology could play a greater role in transborder data flow regulation than is now the case. ... Data controllers routinely configure information technology systems so as to regulate the transborder flow of data, and it is not uncommon for an international company to structure its IT system so that certain types of data may not be accessed by its employees outside a specific country or region.').

[361] ibid.

[362] Seda Gürses and Joris van Hoboken, 'Privacy after the Agile Turn' in Evan Selinger, Jules Polonetsky, and Omer Tene, *The Cambridge Handbook of Consumer Privacy* (CUP 2018) 597:

If every form of digital functionality has the potential to be transformed into a data intensive machine learning product, the application of principles such as data minimization, purpose specification and policies that enforce some sort of control over data on the side of end-users is going to be challenging.

authors note that certain privacy intrusive practices adopted by service providers can be leveraged by 'automated privacy support that allows users to evaluate which information flows they want to engage in and how they can control these when they use services'.[363] There are other promising technological solutions, such as user-held data model, federated learning, distributed analytics, and multi-party computation, that substantially reduce the need for cross-border transfers of personal data or the risk to fundamental rights of individuals associated with such transfers.[364]

Giving legal significance to privacy-enhancing technologies in the context of transfers of personal data outside the EEA is also in line with the endeavours the EU has promised to Japan and Singapore in digital partnership agreements.[365]

It should, of course, be acknowledged that technology is not a panacea to correct inefficiencies of the legal framework in governing transfers of personal data, but it could provide an effective complementary regime to mitigate those inefficiencies.[366] Already in 2009, in his OECD study, Schwartz demonstrated based on several case studies that cross-border transfers of data are 'not a finite event' and 'occur in a multi-directional fashion throughout the globe, and involve more companies and entities in the processing activities'.[367] In other words, they 'occur as part of a networked series of processes made to deliver a business result'.[368] The implication of this transformation is that regulating cross-border transfers of personal data based on the outdated views of information flows as point-to-point transfers is increasingly challenging, and is perhaps missing the forest for the trees. Technological tools in combination with data privacy industry standards could be more effective

At the same time, much of service capture creates prime opportunities to apply privacy technologies such as differential or pan privacy. The application of these techniques could protect users from individual harms due to reidentification of data.

[363] ibid.

[364] For an overview, see OECD, 'Emerging Privacy Enhancing Technologies. Current Regulatory and Policy Approaches' (2023) OECD Digital Economy Papers No 351<https://www.oecd.org/publications/emerging-privacy-enhancing-technologies-bf121be4-en.htm> accessed 10 July 2023. See also Paulius Jurcys, Marcelo Corrales Compagnucci, and Mark Fenwick, 'The Future of International Data Transfers: Managing Legal Risk with a 'User-Held' Data Model'(2022) 46 Computer Law & Security Review 2.

[365] EU-Singapore Digital Partnership, signed on 1 February 2023, para 26 <https://ec.europa.eu/newsroom/dae/redirection/document/93447> accessed 10 July 2023 ('26. Both sides endeavour to support cross-border data flows with trust through model data protection contracts and the use of emerging technologies. Both sides will also explore collaborations on the use of privacy enhancing technologies.') Japan-EU Digital Partnership, signed on 12 May 2022, paras 3, 34, 82 <https://www.consilium.europa.eu/media/56091/%E6%9C%80%E7%B5%82%E7%89%88-jp-eu-digital-partnership-clean-final-docx.pdf> accessed 10 July 2023 ('34. On data, both sides envisage working towards strengthening Data Free Flow with Trust (DFFT), including by promoting technologies enhancing trust . . . .')

[366] Kuner, *Transborder Data Flows and Data Privacy Law* (n 235) 99. See also Lessig, *Code and Other Laws of Cyberspace* (n 359) 138.

[367] Paul M Schwartz, 'Managing Global Data Privacy: Cross-Border Information Flows in a Networked Environment' (2009) Report from the Privacy Projects 12, 36 <https://paulschwartz.net/wp-content/uploads/2019/01/Global_Data_Flows.pdf> accessed 13 July 2023.

[368] ibid 16.

in tracing cross-border data flows and ensure that the legal regime for protection of personal data is not circumvented. The EU has already to some extent resorted to technological means in governing cross-border data flows in its adequacy decision for Japan, because the adequacy decision creates—through Supplementary Rules—a higher level of data protection for data from the EEA in contrast to Japanese data. The Supplementary Rules require that Japanese business operators 'ensure (e.g. by technical ("tagging") or organisational means (storing in a dedicated database)) that they can identify such personal data throughout its "life cycle"'.[369]

Implementing these ideas in Chapter V of the GDPR would add more scalability to the regime for transfers of personal data, and facilitate and enhance enforcement of compliance with the framework.

5.4.3 Redesign

In the longer term, addressing all the weaknesses of the GDPR's Chapter V framework for transfers of personal data outside the EEA identified in Section 5.3 may require a much more thorough redesign. This redesign could grow organically out of improvements to the GDPR proposed as a part of the first and second lines of thought. One way of doing so would be to create a single set of rules 'dealing with protection against external threats to EU data'[370] based on a *risk-based approach*.[371] This approach would eliminate the problem of the interplay between Article 3 and Chapter V, discussed in Section 5.3.2, which presents problems from both EU fundamental rights and international trade law perspectives.[372]

Basing this new set of rules protecting personal data against external threats on a risk-based approach would fit better into the logic of the GDPR. As De Gregorio and Dunn argue,

> transition from a market-driven to a constitutional-oriented perspective was translated into law through the adoption of a risk-based approach that ... ultimately represents an attempt to strike an 'optimal' balance among conflicting constitutional interests. The principle of accountability, pursuant to which data controllers must be able to prove they comply with the general principles set by the GDPR, is itself strictly intertwined with the rationale of this approach.[373]

369 Para 15 Adequacy Decision for Japan (n 164).

370 Kuner, 'Protecting EU Data outside EU Borders under the GDPR' (n 15) 105.

371 For an in-depth discussion on the role of the concept of risk in the GDPR, see, eg, Gellert, *The Risk-Based Approach to Data Protection* (n 315); Demetzou, 'Risk to the "Rights and Freedoms"' (n 312).

372 For discussion of the issues this approach creates for EU's compliance with its international trade obligations, see Sections 2.3 and 2.4.1.

373 De Gregorio and Dunn, 'The European Risk-Based Approaches' (n 315) 479. Internal footnotes omitted.

Furthermore, Article 24 of the GDPR requires controllers to be accountable and to be able to demonstrate that processing of personal data is performed in accordance *with the whole GDPR*, not only Chapter IV of this regulation, where this article is located. Disclosure by transmission, dissemination, or otherwise making available of personal data whether within or outside the EEA constitutes a form of such processing.[374]

Part of the GDPR already reflects a risk-based approach.[375] In particular, this is the case in relation to some data protection elements explicitly or implicitly envisaged in Article 8 of the Charter, such as the legitimate interest that can be used as a legal ground for processing of personal data,[376] the stricter rules for processing special categories of personal data,[377] the principle of accountability,[378] the provisions on records of processing activities,[379] the data breach notification requirement,[380] provisions on security of processing,[381] the obligation of prior consultation with a data protection authority,[382] and finally in the data protection impact assessment process.[383] This strongly suggests that a risk-based approach to data transfers would also feasible, and indeed arguably preferable.[384] The EDPB has also embraced the risk-based approach to GDPR compliance with respect to transmissions of personal data outside the EEA, when such transmissions do not fall under the EDPB's definition of 'transfer'. The EDPB stated:

[374] Art 4(2) GDPR.

[375] It is, however, worth keeping in mind that the implementation of the risk-based approach in the GDPR is incomplete and is, arguably, in tension with the rights of the data subject envisaged in Chapter III GDPR. See, eg, Claudia Quelle, 'The "Risk Revolution" in EU Data Protection Law: We Can't Have Our Cake and Eat It, Too' (2017) Tilburg Law School Legal Studies Research Paper Series No 17/2017, 20–21 <http://ssrn.com/abstract=3000382> accessed 10 July 2023 (hereafter Quelle, 'The "Risk Revolution"'). See also Gellert, *The Risk-Based Approach to Data Protection* (n 315) Chapter 7.

[376] In its pre-GDPR but post EU Charter Opinion, Article 29 Working Party explicitly suggests to use the terminology and methodology of traditional risk assessment as a helpful tool to assess the impact of data processing on the individual. Article 29 Working Party, Opinion 06/2014 on the notion of legitimate interests (n 318) 37–38. Similarly, in its guidance on UK GDPR on the application of legitimate interest (which, as of this writing is almost identical to the GDPR), the UK Information Commissioner's Office (ICO) equates the legitimate interest assessment with a light-touch risk assessment based on the specific context and circumstances. 'Legitimate interests' (*ICO*, 19 May 2023) <https://ico.org.uk/for-organisations/uk-gdpr-guidance-and-resources/lawful-basis/a-guide-to-lawful-basis/lawful-basis-for-processing/legitimate-interests/> accessed 10 July 2023.

[377] Recital 51, art 9 GDPR.

[378] Recitals 74–77, arts 24 GDPR.

[379] Recital 82, art 30(5) GDPR.

[380] Recitals 85–88, arts 33–34 GDPR.

[381] Recital 83, art 32 GDPR.

[382] Recitals 94–96, art 36 GDPR.

[383] Recitals 84, 89, 90–93, 95, art 35 GDPR.

[384] There is, however, some critique of this approach. See, in particular, Claudia Quelle, 'Enhancing Compliance under the General Data Protection Regulation: The Risky Upshot of the Accountability and Risk-Based Approach' (2018) 9(3) European Journal of Risk Regulation, 502; Claudia Quelle, 'Does the Risk-Based Approach to Data Protection Conflict with the Protection of Fundamental Rights on a Conceptual Level?' (2015) <https://ssrn.com/abstract=2726073> accessed 10 July 2023; Quelle, 'The "Risk Revolution"' (n 375).

> although a certain data transmission may not qualify as a transfer to a third country in accordance with Chapter V of the GDPR . . ., such processing can still be associated with increased risks because it takes place outside the EU . . . . These risks must be considered when taking measures to ensure compliance with the GDPR, including under Article 5 ('Principles relating to processing of personal data'), Article 24 ('Responsibility of the controller'), 32 ('Security of processing'), 33 ('Notification of a personal data breach'), 35 ('Data Protection Impact Assessment'), 48 ('Transfers or disclosures not authorised by Union law') etc. Following from its obligation to be responsible for, and be able to demonstrate compliance with the data protection principles (Article 5) and to implement technical and organisational measures taking into account, *inter alia*, the risks with respect to the processing under Article 32 of the GDPR, a controller may very well conclude that extensive security measures are needed – or even that it would not be lawful – to conduct or proceed with a specific processing operation in a third country although there is no transfer situation.[385]

This line of thinking can also be implemented in the context of the new set of rules against external threats to Europeans' personal data.

Against the backdrop the *function* of the current framework for restrictions on transfers of personal data based on the EU Charter, as discussed in the previous sections of this chapter, the main risk that the new should address is the circumvention of the EU data protection regime when personal data is processed abroad.[386] In fundamental rights terms, this can be reformulated as the risk that processing of personal data outside the EEA can interfere with the fundamental rights to privacy and the protection of personal data more than is strictly necessary and proportionate to pursue a legitimate public policy objective.

Safeguards required for processing of personal data outside the EEA could be differentiated in the GDPR depending on the remoteness of link between personal data and individuals to which it relates or, in other words, the risk of reidentification (which can serve as a proxy for the risk to a particular individual, including where data is accessed by foreign surveillance authorities) and threat of harm.[387] One could, for instance, use Ohm's non-exhaustive list of five factors for assessing the

[385] Guidelines 05/2021 on the Interplay between the application of Article 3 and the provisions on international transfers as per Chapter V of the GDPR (n 333), paras. 31-32..

[386] Kuner, 'International Agreements, Data Protection, and EU Fundamental Rights on the International Stage: Opinion 1/15 (EU-Canada PNR) of the Court of Justice of the EU' (n 54) 872. See also Kuner, *Transborder Data Flows and Data Privacy Law* (n 235) 107–13.

[387] For a discussion on this approach to regulating privacy in general, see Ohm, 'Broken Promises of Privacy' (n 300) 1761, 1764. Schwartz and Solove are critical of this approach as it requires ex ante cost–benefit assessment of information flows, which, in their view, is not only speculative in nature but may also amount to rejecting potentially beneficial collections and use of large datasets. Schwartz and Solove, 'The PII Problem' (n 300) 1868–69.

risk of privacy harms in general, and apply it to harms associated with processing of personal data outside the EEA:[388]

(1) data-handling techniques (risk of re-identification can be labelled as high, medium or low based on a rough relative ordering of different techniques that could potentially be developed by computer scientists[389]);
(2) private versus public release (the level of protection of publicly released data should be higher than that of data shared between trusted parties due to higher privacy risks inherent in public release of data for privacy[390]);
(3) quantity (larger volumes of data sets are more susceptible to reidentification through matching different data sets[391]);
(4) motive (the legal constraints on sharing data, the motives of owners of data sets to share them as well as the economic incentives for reidentification also have an impact on the risk of reidentification.[392]); and
(5) trust (society's trust in people and institutions in privacy regulatory framework[393]).

In line with the first of those five factors, and incorporating the proposals made as a part of the second line of thought above, more lenient rules for processing of personal data outside the EEA could be designed for data that only has a remote link with individuals, such as pseudonymized data, when such data is transmitted outside the EEA without additional information necessary to link the data to particular individuals. By definition, pseudonymized data cannot be attributed to a specific individual without the use of additional information, *provided* such information is kept separately and adequately protected.[394] Beyond this, differentiation between the intensity of restrictions on processing of personal data outside the EEA should not be solely or mostly based on the distinctions between different categories of data (such as sensitive data), because such distinctions are often highly contextual,[395] which makes differentiation between such categories difficult in practice.[396]

Another factor that could be useful in designing the new set of rules against external threats to Europeans' data based on risk-based approach is the *sector* in

[388] Ohm, 'Broken Promises of Privacy' (n 300) 1765–68.
[389] ibid 1765.
[390] ibid 1766.
[391] ibid 1766–67.
[392] ibid 1767.
[393] ibid.
[394] Art 4(5) GDPR.
[395] Koops, 'The Trouble with European Data Protection Law' (n 299) 260; Lokke Moerel, 'EU Data Protection Laws Are Flawed: They Undermine the Very Autonomy of the Individuals They Set Out to Protect' (*IAPP*, May 2020) <https://iapp.org/resources/article/gdpr-at-two-expert-perspectives/> accessed 10 July 2023.
[396] Purtova, 'The Law of Everything' (n 300) 79, 80.

which the transfer of personal data occurs. For example, as one of the measures to increase availability of data for businesses, the European Commission is developing sectoral data spaces within the EU in strategic areas such as manufacturing, agriculture, health, and mobility.[397] This approach could also be usefully explored for transfers of personal data outside the EEA.

5.5 Conclusion

This chapter has demonstrated that the framework for transfers of personal data outside the EEA in Chapter V of the GDPR represents only *one* possible design of such a framework in the light of the EU Charter requirements. Only the presence of *some* restrictions and a few aspects of such restrictions constitute the essence of the fundamental rights to privacy, the protection of personal data and the right to judicial remedy (in the context of the first two rights) and, therefore, cannot be altered by EU secondary law. Other elements of such a framework can be determined by the EU secondary legislator on the basis of strict necessity and proportionality assessment, with the aim of ensuring its constitutional function, which is to prevent circumvention of the high level of personal data protection in the EU. Section 5.3 of this chapter has shed light on several weaknesses of the current framework's elements and overall design, and argued that due to economic, political, geopolitical, and legal changes, this framework is no longer actually fit for its constitutional purpose. To ameliorate these weaknesses within the boundaries set by the EU Charter, this chapter has proposed three paths to how to reform this framework, corresponding to a short-, medium-, and long-term strategy for the EU.

[397] Communication from the Commission to the European Parliament, the European Council, the Council, the European Economic and Social Committee and the Committee of the Regions, 'A European Strategy for Data' [2020] COM(2020) 66 final, 6; Proposal for a Regulation of the European Parliament and of the Council on the European Health Data Space COM/2022/197 final.

6

Reconciling EU Data Protection and International Trade Law

Four Propositions and Avenues for Further Research

This book has tackled the timely issue of reconciling the governance of cross-border data flows from the perspectives of European Union (EU) data protection and international trade law. It has demonstrated a real clash between international trade and European data privacy law when it comes to the governance of cross-border flows of personal data. This clash is the result of the coming together of a multitude of factors. Among them, the following three are of particular importance: (a) the pivotal importance of personal data in digital commerce; (b) the increased level of protection of the rights to privacy and the protection of personal data since 2009 as binding fundamental rights under the EU Charter of Fundamental Rights (EU Charter)[1]; and (c) the recent trend of governing cross-border data flows by regional, plurilateral, and multilateral trade agreements.

This book has provided the necessary background and analysis of EU rules governing cross-border transfers of personal data outside the European Economic Area (EEA)[2] in the light of the EU Charter and the ways in which this issue is addressed in the current and proposed trade agreements led by the EU and the United States. It also put the developments in both areas against the background of EU constitutionalization and trade policy. In order to resolve the tensions caused by the above-mentioned clash, this book has analysed and proposed ways to ameliorate the situation from both ends (trade and personal data protection), specifically through reforms of both international trade rules in future trade agreements and EU General Data Protection Regulation (GDPR).[3] To explain how such reforms could be effectuated, the book has also aimed to fill in a significant lacuna in existing literature by looking at the role of discourse in the evolution of trade law,

[1] Charter of Fundamental Rights of the European Union [2000] OJ C 364/1 (hereafter EU Charter).

[2] The European Economic Area consists of the member states of the European Union and countries of the European Free Trade Association (EFTA): Norway, Iceland, and Lichtenstein. EUROSTAT, Glossary: European Economic Area (EEA), <https://ec.europa.eu/eurostat/statistics-explained/index.php/Glossary:European_Economic_Area_(EEA)#:~:text=The%20European%20Economic%20Area%2C%20abbreviated,force%20on%201%20January%201994> accessed 10 July 2023.

[3] Regulation (EU) 2016/679 of the European Parliament and of the Council of 27 April 2016 on the protection of natural persons with regard to the processing of personal data and on the free movement of such data, and repealing Directive 95/46/EC [2016] OJ L 119/1 (hereafter GDPR).

Governing Cross-Border Data Flows. Svetlana Yakovleva, Oxford University Press.
DOI: 10.1093/oso/9780192899248.003.0006

in particular in its relation to cross-border data flows. In doing so, the book considered the digital trade discourses currently advanced by the EU and the United States in the course of negotiations of digital trade agreements, revolving around the issue of whether, and to what extent, restrictions on cross-border data flows amount to 'digital protectionism'. The book has shown the importance of discourse in any attempt to reform trade rules.

This book answered the following research question:

> How should commitments on cross-border data flows in EU trade agreements be reconciled with the protection of the fundamental rights to privacy and personal data?

In answering this research question, this book has concluded that in order to reconcile cross-border data flows with data protection and privacy without undermining fundamental rights, a reform of both trade law rules in the EU's future trade agreements and the GDPR rules on transfers of personal data outside the EEA is necessary. Tackling each of the research sub-questions specifically, the book has made the following propositions.

> ***Proposition 1.*** *Simultaneous application of international trade and EU Charter rules to the restrictions on transfers of personal data outside the EEA may create a catch-22 compliance dead lock for the EU. On the one hand, there is a risk of inconsistency between the obligation on cross-border flows of personal data, which can be deduced from the EU's commitments under the General Agreement on Trade in Services (GATS)*[4] *in the context of digitally provided services and the restrictions on transfers of personal data under the GDPR. This inconsistency may not be justifiable under the general exception for privacy and data protection in trade agreements. On the other hand, from an EU Charter perspective, the level of liberalization of cross-border data flows required by the GATS constitutes an interference with the fundamental rights to privacy and the protection of personal data under the EU Charter. This interference may not be justifiable under Article 52(1) of the Charter.*

Although the GATS does not specifically regulate cross-border data flows, in Section 2.3, the book concludes that the different treatments of transfers of personal data outside the EEA to countries that have been granted an adequacy decision, and other countries, could be in violation of the most-favoured nation treatment clause contained in the GATS. Similarly, limited number of legal tools available for transfers of personal data to service providers located in countries that have not been afforded an adequacy decision and do not ensure an essentially

[4] General Agreement on Trade in Services, Annex 1B to Marrakesh Agreement Establishing the World Trade Organization [1994] 1869 UNTS 183, 33 ILM 1167 (hereafter GATS).

equivalent level of protection could be viewed as discrimination of such service providers vis-à-vis their counterparts in the EEA in violation of the national treatment. Prohibition to transfer personal data to service providers located in countries that do not ensure an essential equivalent level of personal data protection also creates a risk of *de facto* data localization and a violation of the EU's market access obligations under the GATS. Incoherence added to the GDPR's framework for transfers of personal data following the inconsistent interpretation of the concept of 'transfer' and the relationship between Article 3 and Chapter V of the GDPR by the European Data Protection Board (EDPB)[5] puts more pressure on that framework from an international trade perspective.

Next, Section 2.4 concludes that the scope of the general exception contained in GATS Article XIV(c)(ii)—perhaps the most important legal mechanism to accommodate the EU's autonomy to adopt and maintain rules that would otherwise be inconsistent with its GATS commitments—may not be broad enough to justify the EU's restrictions on transfers of personal data outside the EEA. The main reason for that insufficiency is that these restrictions are unlikely to pass the necessity test (referred to as the 'trade necessity test' in this book), which lies at the core of this exception. The trade necessity test requires, in particular, that a GATS-inconsistent trade-restrictive measure be the least trade restrictive of all reasonably available measures to achieve the level of protection of the public interest at stake. Relying on existing case law of the World Trade Organization (WTO), the book concludes that there are at least two reasons for the tension.

First, within the 'range of degrees of necessity' in WTO caselaw, the nexus between the existing EU framework for transfers of personal data outside the EEA and the underlying purpose of ensuring a high level of protection of personal data is closer to 'making a contribution' rather than 'indispensable'. The sizeable gap between what the EU framework for transfers of personal data outside the EEA *should* and *can* deliver makes it far from clear that it would pass the necessity test of the general exception in trade agreements.

Second, the EU's restrictions on transfers of personal data are among the most restrictive in the world. Against the backdrop of the weaknesses that the EU framework for transfers of personal data contains (elaborated upon in greater detail in Section 5.3), one could argue that other approaches to personal data transfers could be 'reasonably available' to the EU to achieve the same level of protection. Such other approaches could, for example, include the Organisation for Economic Development and Cooperation (OECD) 2013 Guidelines on the Protection of Privacy and Transborder Flows of Personal Data[6] and the 2015 Asia-Pacific

[5] The EDPB is a consortium of data protection authorities in the EU. See 'EDPB Chairmanship' < https://edpb.europa.eu/about-edpb/who-we-are/edpb-chairmanship_en#:~:text=The%20European%20Data%20Protection%20Board,Data%20Protection%20Supervisor%20(EDPS)> accessed 10 July 2023.

[6] The OECD Privacy Framework (2013).

Economic Cooperation (APEC) Privacy Framework,[7] or the framework codified in the Council of Europe Convention 108+[8]. This argument is, however, only valid if the '*same*' level of protection is viewed as that *actually achieved* by the current framework as opposed to the *desired* level of protection in the light of the EU Charter.

The book then flips the analysis by looking at it from the perspective of the EU Charter, which requires that rules, including international agreements, interfering with the fundamental rights to privacy and the protection of personal data, should be least restrictive of such rights. While international trade law starts from the premise that cross-border data flows should be allowed, the EU Charter instead posits that those data flows outside the EEA should be conditionally restricted. As a result, should a WTO adjudicating body find EU restrictions inconsistent with the GATS and unable to be justified under the general exception, compliance with such a decision could be inconsistent with the necessity test under Article 52(1) of the EU Charter. This provision sets constitutional limits on the extent to which the EU institutions can derogate from the fundamental rights, including the rights to privacy and the protection of personal data. Although the EU Charter does not establish any hierarchy between fundamental rights, in a line of cases (that include most notably *Volker und Markus Schecke*,[9] *Digital Rights Ireland*,[10] *Tele 2*,[11] *Schrems I*,[12] *Opinion on EU-Canada PNR Agreement*,[13] and *Schrems II*[14]), the Court of Justice of the European Union (CJEU) has elevated the EU Charter necessity test to the level of 'strict necessity' in relation to derogations from the fundamental rights to privacy and the protection of personal data. Relaxing restrictions on transfers of personal data to the extent consistent with the requirement of being the least trade restrictive is unlikely to pass the strict necessity test under the EU Charter. In other words, international trade obligations governing cross-border data flows may require the EU to derogate from these fundamental rights further than it is allowed within its own constitutional boundaries. Facing the choice of violating its trade obligations or the EU Charter, the EU may find itself in a catch-22 compliance dead lock.

[7] APEC Privacy Framework (2015), as updated by the Concluding Senior Officials' Meeting on 14–15 November 2016, 2016/CSOM/012app17; APEC Cross-Border Privacy Rules System (CBPR), as updated in November 2019.

[8] Modernized Convention for the Protection of Individuals with Regard to the Processing of Personal Data, as amended by the Protocol adopted by the Committee of Ministers at its 128th Session of the Committee of Ministers, 18 May 2018, CETS 223.

[9] *Volker und Markus Schecke and Eifert* [2010] ECLI:EU:C:2010:662.

[10] *Digital Rights Ireland and Seitlinger and others* [2014] ECLI:EU:C:2014:238.

[11] *Tele2 Sverige* [2016] ECLI:EU:C:2016:970.

[12] *Schrems* [2015] ECLI:EU:C:2015:650, paras 72–73 (hereafter *Schrems I*).

[13] Opinion 1/15 (EU-Canada PNR Agreement) [2017] ECLI:EU:C:2017:592 (hereafter *Opinion on EU-Canada PNR Agreement*).

[14] *Facebook Ireland and Schrems* [2020] ECLI:EU:C:2020:559 (hereafter *Schrems II*).

Although in the hierarchy of EU law, the EU Charter, as primary EU law, is situated above international trade agreements, this does not make international trade law less binding on the EU. From an international law perspective, the EU must perform its international trade obligations in good faith and may face liability and retaliation for failing to do so. This is why constitutional restrictions on compliance with trade obligations or decisions of trade adjudicating bodies could present a serious problem, especially in the context of international trade negotiations of future trade agreements, for at least two reasons. First, the Treaty on the Functioning of the European Union (TFEU)[15] requires that in the course of international trade negotiations, the EU institutions must ensure compatibility of any trade agreements with the internal EU policies and rules. Failure to do so may result in a CJEU judgment under Article 218(11) of the TFEU, finding that a prospective trade agreement is inconsistent with the EU *acquis* and ultimately requiring EU institutions to renegotiate a (part) of the agreement. Second, the EU's rhetoric in trade policy discourse, which is that personal data and privacy cannot be traded, is an important internal political message. An attempt to negotiate an exception for privacy and data protection that could potentially undermine the EU's domestic framework safeguarding such protection is likely to be opposed by the European Parliament, both during the negotiations and the actual legislative process. Therefore, to alleviate the possible tension between the trade and EU Charter necessity tests, this book has concluded that, from a trade law perspective, the EU's future trade agreements containing more elaborate provisions governing cross-border data flows *should not* replicate the general exception for privacy and data protection from GATS Article XIV.

> ***Proposition 2.*** *It is not possible to strike the right balance between domestic data privacy protection and liberalization of digital trade by just ruling out 'protectionism'. Where the line should be drawn between legitimate protection and protectionism is strongly influenced by the discourse governing policy conversations on domestic privacy and the protection of personal data in the context of international trade. Therefore, it is crucial for the EU to frame future digital trade negotiations in terms of pluralist—as opposed to purely economic—discourse. Under the narrow effects-based definition of 'protectionism' generated by neoliberal discourse on international trade, EU restrictions on transfers of personal data outside the EEA can be viewed as protectionist. A broader pluralist discourse is necessary to allow the EU to strike the right balance between globalization, democratic politics, and the domestic autonomy to pursue domestic values such as the fundamental rights to privacy and data protection.*

[15] Consolidated Version of the Treaty on the Functioning of the European Union [2008] OJ (C 115) 47.

Before diving into the discussion of the ways in which to reform the exception for privacy and data protection in future trade agreements in Chapter 4, in Chapter 3, the book takes a step back and offers a bird's eye perspective on the dynamics of international trade reforms through trade negotiations and the interpretation of trade rules by adjudicating bodies. Informed by established methods of discourse analysis, Section 3.2 demonstrates the role of discourse in the redefinition of 'protectionism' in trade negotiations and in the interpretation of trade rules throughout the history of the development of the international trading system. It explicates that the term 'protectionism' is not endowed with a specific meaning and shows that its definition is, to a large extent, a product of discourse. Against this backdrop, Section 3.3 juxtaposes the digital trade discourses of the EU and the United States and shows how the meaning of what these trading partners label as 'digital protectionism' differs depending on the values underlying each discourse. Using the economics-based 'digital trade' discourse advanced by the United States, this section demonstrates how 'digital protectionism' and similar terms that are often used to label restrictive data protection regimes trigger a fundamental redefinition of what constitutes a barrier to trade and, thus, pushes towards deeper trade liberalization and favours the deregulation of personal data transfers. Furthermore, Section 3.4 of the book concludes that the value structures attending the discourse ultimately predetermine where the line will be drawn between legitimate privacy and personal data protection, and illegitimate protectionism—both in the relevant provisions of international trade agreements and in the interpretation of such provisions by trade adjudicating bodies. Exposing the limitations of the dominant economic discourse when it comes to protection of privacy and personal data as fundamental rights, the book highlights the importance for the EU of maintaining a pluralist discourse.

Ultimately, the *definitional* distinction between privacy and personal data protection and protectionism is in part a *moral* question, that is, it should not be viewed just as a question of economic efficiency. Therefore, when a policy conversation, such as the one on cross-border flows of personal data, involves non-economic spillover effects to individual rights, such conversation should not be confined within the straightjacket of trade economics but rather placed in a broader normative perspective.

From a global perspective, the book concludes that a consensus on discourse and its underlying values is likely to be essential for the success of ongoing multilateral trade negotiations. This discourse should be defined on the basis of the goals of international trade for the twenty-first century and how far domestic regimes are willing to let trade rules interfere in their autonomy to protect their societal, cultural, and political values. What actually constitutes 'protectionism' should be defined based on the outcome of this discussion.

> ***Proposition 3.*** *The trade law horizontal provisions on cross-border data flows and the protection of personal data and privacy proposed by the EU*[16] *do not allow the EU to strike the right balance between the fundamental rights protection and the EU digital trade policy objectives. These provisions, however, afford the EU a broad autonomy to protect the rights to privacy and the protection of personal data as fundamental rights. They also send a clear message to the public about the EU's commitment to do so. Nevertheless, these horizontal provisions are unlikely to fulfil the EU's ambition to liberalize the flows of data into the EU and maintain a multilateral rules-based trading system. One of the important ways to improve the horizontal provisions is to replace the threshold 'it deems appropriate', contained in the proposed exception for privacy and data protection, with a standard of non-circumvention, non-avoidance, or reasonableness. When implemented in trade agreements, these standards should be complemented by an institutional restrictive mechanism imposing checks and balances on trade adjudicators' powers of interpretation.*

As this book concludes in Chapter 2, the exception for privacy and data protection in the EU's future trade agreements requires a lower threshold than the necessity test in the GATS general exception. In an attempt to design such a new exception, in 2018, the EU proposed horizontal provisions for its prospective digital trade agreements, which included a provision on cross-border data flows and an exception for the protection of privacy and personal data (the 'digital trade exception'). These horizontal provisions are a part of the current EU's digital trade policy aiming, in particular, at removing 'protectionist' restrictions on cross-border data flows from other countries into the EU. As a part of its general trade policy, the EU promotes multilateralism and a rules-based global trading system.

The provision on cross-border data flows prohibits an enumerated list of restrictions on such flows. None of these prohibitions is likely to affect the EU's own restrictions on transfers of personal data outside the EEA under the GDPR. The digital trade exception includes a subjective 'it deems appropriate' test—modelled after the 'it considers necessary' test of the national security exceptions in the WTO Agreements (eg, Article XXI GATT and Article XIV*bis* GATS). That is the broadest of all current exceptions in international trade law. If one were to put the trade necessity test and the 'it deems appropriate' test on a continuum, from most restrictive to least restrictive thresholds for domestic autonomy in international trade, they would be at the opposite ends of such a continuum.

Chapter 4 of this book concludes that the proposed horizontal provisions suffer from at least three weaknesses and should be improved. As a result, they do not

[16] European Commission, 'Proposal for Provisions on Cross-Border Data Flows and Protection of Personal Data and Privacy (31 January 2018) <https://www.politico.eu/wp-content/uploads/2018/02/Data-flow-provisions-POLITICO.pdf> accessed 10 July 2023.

allow the EU to reconcile fundamental rights protection with its digital trade policy, while promoting a rules-based trading system. First, the material scope of the proposed digital trade exception is uncertain due to unclear relationship between this exception and the general exception for privacy and data protection, which is simultaneously included in the EU (proposals for) digital trade agreements. The best way to address this concern would be to replace the two separate exceptions with a consolidated one that would apply throughout the trade agreement. However, this may be hard to achieve in practice due to the high costs of renegotiating the general exception, and its 'legacy clout'. Therefore, as a minimum, the relationship between the two exceptions should be clarified.

Second, modelling the threshold for the proposed digital trade exception on the national security exception is undesirable. Because the prohibitions on cross-border data flows are targeted at the EU's trading partners, it is these partners—and not the EU itself—who are most likely to invoke the digital trade exception. The breadth of the 'it deems appropriate' threshold, on which this exception is based, can justify almost any derogation from a prohibition of restrictions on data flows. As a result, it may undermine the EU's trade policy objective of removing restrictions on cross-border data flows *abroad*. In addition, including such a low threshold (until now reserved only for national security interests that are vital for any state) in an exception for privacy and data protection, on the one hand, puts the latter policy objectives on par with national security and above other policy objectives that still fall under the general exception (eg, public health). This creates an incentive to frame a broader set of policy objectives as privacy and data protection to escape international trade law disciplines. On the other hand, this also opens the door for using the same low threshold in other exceptions in the future. This is exactly what happened in China-led Regional Comprehensive Economic Partnership (RCEP)[17], where an exception from a cross-border data flow provision allowing to restrict data flows to achieve a legitimate public policy objective contains the same threshold as the WTO national security exception but is accompanied by a clause similar to a chapeau of the general exception. Ultimately, including such a low threshold in the digital trade exception may contribute to further undermining of the international rules-based trading system. Therefore, the proposed digital trade exception should be based on a different threshold—somewhere in between an overly broad 'it deems appropriate' test and an overly restrictive 'necessity' test.

Based on an in-depth analysis of academic literature and the WTO case law concerning other thresholds used in WTO agreements to balance trade liberalization against other public policy objectives, Chapter 4 of this book concludes that a 'non-circumvention', 'non-avoidance', or 'reasonableness' threshold would be

[17] Regional Comprehensive Economic Partnership (entered into force on 1 January 2022).

a better option than the 'it deems appropriate' threshold proposed in the digital trade exception. All of these thresholds are interpreted by recourse to the *principle of good faith and the prohibition of abuse of right*, which preserves the flexibility of the 'it deems appropriate' test but acts as a counterweight to the almost unrestricted nature of the latter. To control for the drawbacks that come with the flexibility of those principles, the use of any of these thresholds should be complemented by restrictive mechanisms, such as institutional controls already implemented in the Understanding on the interpretation of the prudential carve-out in Comprehensive Economic and Trade Agreement (CETA)[18]. In particular, this mechanism requires involving competent domestic authorities in the adjudicating process and deferring to their opinion on the interpretation of relevant concepts.

Third, and finally, the proposed digital trade exception requires the EU's trading partners to recognize the protection of privacy and personal data as fundamental rights. Given that not all EU trading partners assign the same importance to these policy objectives, this provision is EU-centric. This book has proposed to rephrase this provision in a way that would allow the EU to maintain its high level of privacy and personal data protection as fundamental rights while allowing other parties to adopt a lower level of protection if they so choose. This approach would also be more conducive to furthering a pluralist discourse in international trade negotiations on cross-border data flows advocated in Chapter 3 of this book.

> ***Proposition 4.*** *Some form of restrictions on transfers of personal data outside the EEA constitutes a part of the essence of the fundamental rights to privacy and the protection of personal data under the EU Charter. However, the actual design of the framework for such transfers is not a part of such essence. Although Article 52(1) of the EU Charter places some constraints on the EU legislator, the latter has sufficient flexibility to reform the GDPR rules governing transfers of personal data outside the EEA. This is necessary in order to make those rules more scalable and apt for performing their constitutional function of preventing the circumvention of 'effective and complete' protection of the fundamental rights to privacy and the protection of personal data in the EU. The book proposes three lines of thought for accomplishing this reform corresponding to a short-, medium-, and long-term strategy.*

Section 5.2 concludes that the EU Charter, as EU primary law, and the GDPR, as EU secondary law, are in a dynamic relationship with each other. While the GDPR has been adopted to effectuate the fundamental right to the protection of personal data (and other rights enabled by it), interpretation of its rules and the rules of the

[18] Comprehensive Economic and Trade Agreement (CETA) between Canada, of the one part, and the European Union and its member states, of the other part, 14 September 2014 [2017] OJ L 11/23.

1995 Data Protection Directive[19] has informed the constitutional content of that fundamental right. To illustrate the point, from a mere constitutional interpretation of the secondary law concept of 'adequacy', the standard of 'essential equivalence' has become the constitutional benchmark and an instantiation of the strict necessity and proportionality requirements under Article 52(1) of the EU Charter in respect of the *whole* secondary law framework on transfers of personal data outside the EEA.

Next, Section 5.2 concludes that restrictions on transfers of personal data per se constitute a part of the essence of the fundamental rights to privacy and the protection of personal data, as their complete absence allows these rights to be easily circumvented and deprives them of their content. However, the *particular design* of those restrictions, as well as the standard of 'essential equivalence' setting constitutional boundaries on such a design, does not constitute a part of the essence of the above-mentioned fundamental rights. Based on the current CJEU case law, Section 5.2 argues that in order to respect the essence of the fundamental rights to privacy and the protection of personal data, the EU secondary law framework for transfers of personal data outside the EEA must incorporate at least the following elements:

- provide for some limitations on transfers of personal data outside the EEA and on onward transfers,
- contain safeguards preventing generalized access of foreign authorities to the content of electronic communications,
- ensure that purposes for processing personal data are limited,
- require that the processing of personal data is accompanied by rules designed to ensure, inter alia, the security, confidentiality, and integrity of the data, and also to protect them against unlawful access and processing,
- not permit retention of the content of communications, and
- provide for some possibility for an individual to pursue legal remedies in order to have access to personal data relating to him or her, or to obtain the rectification or erasure of such data.

Using the constitutional function of the EU rules for transfers of personal data outside the EEA to prevent the circumvention of the 'effective and complete' protection of privacy and personal data in the EU, Section 5.3 identifies four weaknesses of those rules. These weaknesses are put in the context of broader political, societal, and technological changes between 1995 (when those rules were first adopted) and this writing (June 2023).

[19] Directive 95/46/EC of the European Parliament and of the Council of 24 October 1995 on the protection of individuals with regard to the processing of personal data and on the free movement of such data [1995] OJ L 281 (hereafter Data Protection Directive).

First, this book argues that the CJEU *Schrems II* judgment has reinstated—on the books—the logical consistency of the tools for systematic transfers of personal data: the adequacy mechanisms, and appropriate safeguards under Article 46 of the GDPR, such as the SCCs and the BCRs. However, it is questionable whether in practice the *Schrems II* judgment has allowed to bridge the qualitative gap between the adequacy assessments and appropriate safeguards for several reasons. This judgment has both led to an increased risk of data localization and a fairly low level of compliance—on the ground. The problem is that as a matter of fact, personal data continues flowing across borders. At the same time, (most) companies have insufficient expertise and resources to ensure that all personal data transferred on the basis of appropriate safeguards is protected to the level of protection abroad that is essentially equivalent to the protection in the EU. Furthermore, the DPAs have neither financial nor human resources to monitor such compliance. Section 5.3, therefore, argues that the problem of foreign surveillance, which lies at the core of this issue, should rather be addressed by the EU and its trading partners in an international forum, which should not coincide with international trade negotiations.

Second, the inconsistent interpretation of the concept of 'transfer' and the relationship between Article 3 and Chapter V of the GDPR by the EDPB in such a way that protection does not (fully) apply to certain transmissions of personal data outside the EEA has created a gap in legal protection of fundamental rights to privacy and the protection of personal data.

Third, the book argues that the adequacy framework itself suffers from political pressures as well as from what the book has called the 'snapshot', the 'heavy burden', and the 'onward transfer' problems. Fourth, and more generally, the book contends that the EU framework for transfers of personal data outside the EEA lacks granularity in the sense that the same rules apply irrespective of the context, volume, and type of data transferred, and other parameters of data transfers. In a world where massive volumes of various kinds of personal data are transferred every second, it is unrealistic to expect that the stringent EU framework under Chapter V of the GDPR will be fully observed, and most importantly, monitored and enforced by authorities in all those transfers.

Section 5.4 suggests and elaborates upon three possible lines of thought on how to improve the current GDPR framework for transfers of personal data outside the EEA. The first, and the most moderate, line of thought proposes to improve *specific* elements of mechanisms for transfers of personal data, without changing the design and composition of the framework. In particular, it proposes to:

(1) amend the definition of 'transfer' in two ways: (1) to recognize that direct transmissions of personal data outside the EEA also qualify as a 'transfer' under the GDPR and (2) exclude the application of Chapter V rules in

situations where personal data is transferred to a data importer that is already subject to the extraterritorial application of the GDPR;

(2) adopt a transparent procedure governing adequacy assessment to address proneness of adequacy mechanism to political influence;
(3) transition adequacy assessments from a unilateral instrument to a reciprocal agreement, under which the foreign country would undertake certain obligations, such as to notify about any changes in legislation considered during the adequacy assessments, and to accept negative consequences of the failure to notify;
(4) conduct rigorous and timely review of adequacy decisions. In particular, to complete the reviews of pre-GDPR adequacy decisions launched in 2017 and suspend or revoke those that do not meet the 'essential equivalence' standard mandated by the CJEU in *Schrems I* and *Schrems II* judgments;
(5) ensure that onward transfer mechanisms in adequacy decisions, as much as possible, mirror the appropriate safeguards provided for in the GDPR and as interpreted by the CJEU in *Schrems II*. Consent should not be allowed as a legal ground for systematic onward transfers;
(6) more actively enforce the SCCs, for example, through conducting industry scans and requests for information, while prioritizing the transfers that carry the greatest risks for individuals;
(7) adopt the SCCs for transfers of personal data to data importers subject to the extraterritorial application of the GDPR (Legal Regime 3 as discussed in Sections 2.2.3 and 2.2.5);
(8) adopt guidance on the requirements for bespoke contracts as mechanisms for transfer of personal data under Article 46 of the GDPR;
(9) allow a broader use of specific derogations under Article 49 of the GDPR.

The second, intermediate, line of thought proposes to add greater scalability to the framework while improving its particularities. It requires a more substantial revision of the GDPR and, therefore, could realistically be addressed only in the medium term—for example, in the next review of the GDPR's Chapter V under Article 97 of the GDPR in 2024. In addition to the reform proposals outlined in the first line of thought, the second line of thought proposes two principal adjustments to Chapter V of the GDPR:

(1) introducing more lenient rules for transfers of personal data in relation to pseudonymized data, with the exception of pseudonymized sensitive data, and data in transit; and
(2) giving legal significance in Chapter V of the GDPR to technological means for protection of personal data, including as a means of ensuring that pseudonymized data will not be reidentified after the transfer.

The third, long-term, line of thought proposes a more fundamental redesign of the EU framework for transfers of personal data. One way of doing so would be to create a single set of rules 'dealing with protection against external threats to EU data'[20] based on a *risk-based approach*. This approach would eliminate the problem of the interplay between Article 3 and Chapter V of the GDPR, which presents problems from both EU fundamental rights and international trade law perspectives. This new set of rules should be based on a risk-based approach, which would better into the logic of the GDPR compared to the current one-size-fits-all approach. In the light of the constitutional function of the EU framework for transfers of personal data, as mentioned above, the main risk that the redesigned framework should address is the circumvention of the 'effective and complete' protection of privacy and personal data protection that the EU affords, when personal data is transferred outside the EEA. Reformulating this in fundamental rights terms, it is a risk that transfers of personal data outside the EEA can interfere with the fundamental rights to privacy and the protection of personal data more than is strictly necessary and proportionate to pursue a legitimate public policy objective. Safeguards required for transfers of personal data could be differentiated depending on the remoteness of link between personal data and the individuals to which it relates or, in other words, on the risk of the reidentification of individuals and threat of harm to their fundamental rights.

Avenues for Further Research

This book has proposed, among other things, that a reform of the EU framework for transfers of personal data outside the EEA in Chapter V of the GDPR is needed. In the case of the GDPR, an effort based on a host of both domestic and international factors that goes well beyond this work is needed to design a full-fledged reform proposal.

Beyond strictly legal questions, cross-border transfers of personal and other data also raise questions of social justice, especially in the context of using personal data to develop, fine-tune, and regulate the use of AI systems. So far, privacy and data protection are the only policy objectives that are juxtaposed with those of digital trade liberalization in EU digital trade discourse. However, in designing rules on cross-border data flows, questions of how these rules will affect the digital divide and global inequality, who benefits and who loses from data flows, should also be considered, especially in a multilateral setting. Put simply, more research is necessary to explore how distributional issues should be incorporated in the design of digital trade provisions on cross-border data flows.

[20] Christopher Kuner, 'Protecting EU Data outside EU Borders under the GDPR' (2023) 60 Common Market Law Review 77, 105.

Finally, national security interests are increasingly taking centre stage in governments' policy on data flows and trade policy. This topic has four dimensions. First, national security interests lead some governments, like the United States, to restrict transfers of personal data to non-democratic countries like China, viewing such transfers as a national security threat. Second, the United States' national security programmes, which allow the US authorities to access Europeans' data for national security purposes, led the CJEU to invalidate, two times around, transatlantic mechanisms for transfers of personal data (The EU-US Safe Harbor[21] and the EU—US Privacy Shield[22]). Similarly (albeit for different reasons), DPAs across Europe are investigating TikTok's data processing practices in Europe, and specifically transfers of personal data to China.[23] Third, as confirmed by the CJEU in the *Schrems II* and *Privacy International* cases,[24] the EU Charter guarantees under Articles 7 and 8 apply to rules governing surveillance authorities' access to personal data for national security purposes, when such data is obtained by authorities from private parties (such as telecommunication services providers or platforms), both under EU member states law and the law of foreign states receiving personal data from the EEA. Fourth, the national security exception plays a special role in international trade agreements due to its breadth, and it has been invoked recently by countries trying to derogate from their trade commitments for reasons only marginally related to national security. Furthermore, as discussed in Chapter 4, the United States has broadened the national security exception in its digital trade agreements by removing the factual circumstances in which it can be invoked, present in the WTO exception, thus removing an important objective constraint on the invocation of the exception.

At the same time, cross-border data flows are increasingly regulated by international trade agreements, which means that in a trade setting, countries could potentially invoke a national security exception to restrict data flows as well. As a result, there is a tension between the tendency, on the one hand, to keep the national security exception as broad as possible due to the quintessential importance of national security for the very existence of the states and, on the other hand, to use the national security exception as a means to derogate from the increasingly

[21] Commission Decision of 2000/520/EC 26 July 2000 pursuant to Directive 95/46/EC of the European Parliament and of the Council on the adequacy of the protection provided by the safe harbour privacy principles and related frequently asked questions issued by the US Department of Commerce [2000] 2441 OJ L 215.

[22] Commission Implementing Decision (EU) 2016/1250 of 12 July 2016 pursuant to Directive 95/46/EC of the European Parliament and of the Council on the adequacy of the protection provided by the EU-U.S. Privacy Shield [2016] OJ L 207.

[23] EDPB, Thirty-first Plenary session: Establishment of a taskforce on TikTok, Response to MEPs on use of Clearview AI by law enforcement authorities, Response to ENISA Advisory Group, Response to Open Letter NYOB (10 June 2020) <https://edpb.europa.eu/news/news/2020/thirty-first-plenary-session-establishment-taskforce-tiktok-response-meps-use_en> accessed 10 July 2023.

[24] *Privacy International* [2020] ECLI:EU:C:2020:790; *Facebook Ireland and Schrems* [2020] ECLI:EU:C:2020:559. See also *La Quadrature du Net and others* [2020] ECLI:EU:C:2020:791.

broader scope of trade commitments on the grounds unrelated to traditional security interests. This tension will either lead to the narrowing of the regulatory autonomy of states to invoke national security or erode the foundations of the rule-based multilateral trading system. Using the issue of cross-border data flows as a case study to demonstrate how national security concerns can drive countries towards imposing data localization, further research is needed to consider whether a reform of the national security exception in trade agreements is necessary. This research could also include finding an international law solution to the problem of foreign surveillance authorities' access to personal data from companies that received such data in the course of conducting business.

Bibliography

'101 Complaints on EU-US Transfers Filed' (*noyb*, 17 August 2020) <https://noyb.eu/en/101-complaints-eu-us-transfers-filed> accessed 10 July 2023

'A Worker-Centered Digital Trade Agenda' (*AFL-CIO*, 7 February 2023) <https://aflcio.org/worker-centered-digital-agenda> accessed 10 July 2023

'Advancing a Jobs-Centric Digital Trade Policy' (*BSA*, 13 November 2021) <https://www.bsa.org/files/policy-filings/11132021jobscentricdigitrade.pdf> accessed 10 July 2023

'Belgian Council of State Considers Encryption a Sufficient Measure for U.S. Data Transfers' (*Privacy & Information Security Law Blog*, 9 September 2021) <https://www.huntonprivacyblog.com/2021/09/09/belgian-council-of-state-considers-encryption-a-sufficient-measure-for-u-s-data-transfers/> accessed 10 July 2023

'Business without Borders: The Importance of Cross-Border Data Transfers to Global Prosperity.' (2014) US Chamber of Commerce and Hunton & Williams LLP <https://www.huntonak.com/images/content/3/0/v3/3086/Business-without-%20Borders.pdf> accessed 10 July 2023

'Comments of the Coalition for Privacy and Free Trade to the Trade Policy Staff Committee of the United States Trade Representative' (*Coalition For Privacy & Free Trade*, 2013) <http://www.centerfordigitaldemocracy.org/sites/default/files/Coalition-for-Privacy-and-Free-Trade-Comments-to-USTR-May-9-2013_0.pdf> accessed 10 July 2023

'Consumentenbond en DPS starten nieuwe zaak na winnen privacyklacht tegen Facebook', (*Telecompaper*, 15 March 2023) <https://www.telecompaper.com/nieuws/consumentenbond-en-dps-starten-nieuwe-zaak-na-winnen-privacyklacht-tegen-facebook--1456816> accessed 10 July 2023

'Cross-Border Data Flows: Could Foreign Protectionism Hurt U.S. Jobs?' (2014) Hearing before the Subcommittee on Commerce, Manufacturing, and Trade of the Committee on Energy and Commerce <https://books.google.nl/books?id=FG2F8oisHWwC&printsec=frontcover&source=gbs_ge_summary_r&cad=0#v=onepage&q&f=false> accessed 10 July 2023

'Data Free Flow with Trust (DFFT): Paths towards Free and Trusted Data Flows' (*World Economic Forum*, May 2020) <https://www3.weforum.org/docs/WEF_Paths_Towards_Free_and_Trusted_Data%20_Flows_2020.pdf> accessed 10 July 2023

Digital Trade in the U.S. and Global Economies, Part 2 (2014) Inv No 332-540, USITC Pub 4485 <https://www.usitc.gov/publications/332/pub4485.pdf> accessed 10 July 2023

'EU Commission's Review of Existing Adequacy Decisions Well Underway' (*Privacy Laws and Business*, 3 July 2019) <https://www.privacylaws.com/news/eu-commission-s-review-of-existing-adequacy-decisions-well-underway/> accessed 10 July 2023

'European Commission Gives EU-US Data Transfers Third Round at CJEU' (*noyb*, 10 July 2023) <https://noyb.eu/en/european-commission-gives-eu-us-data-transfers-third-round-cjeu> accessed 10 July 2023

'Exclusive: Interview with "Take Back Your Privacy" Foundation on Their Mass Privacy Claim against TikTok in the Netherlands' (*Privacy Perfect*, 28 July 2021) < https://blog.privacyperfect.com/the-privacyperfect-blog/exclusive-interview-with-take-back-your-priv acy-foundation-on-their-mass-privacy-claim-against-tiktok-in-the-netherlands> accessed 10 July 2023

'Facebook Owner Granted Stay on Order That It Suspend Europe-US Data Transfers' (*The Irish Times*, 9 June 2023) <https://www.irishtimes.com/business/2023/06/09/facebook-owner-granted-stay-on-order-that-it-suspend-europeus-data-transfers/> accessed 10 July 2023

'First reaction: Executive Order on US Surveillance Unlikely to Satisfy EU law' (*noyb*, 7 October 2022) <https://noyb.eu/en/new-us-executive-order-unlikely-satisfy-eu-law> accessed 10 July 2023

'French Highest Court Rejects Suspension of Partnership with EU Service Provider Using AWS; Extends Application of the Schrems II Requirements' (*Privacy & Information Security Law Blog*, 15 March 2021), <https://www.huntonprivacyblog.com/2021/03/15/french-highest-court-rejects-suspension-of-partnership-with-eu-service-provider-using-aws-extends-application-of-the-schrems-ii-requirements/> accessed 10 July 2023

'Global Services Coalition Statement on Digital Trade' (16 October 2017) <http://www.esf.be/new/wp-content/uploads/2017/10/Global-Services-Coalition-Statement-on-Digital-Trade-Final-16-Oct-2017.pdf?> accessed 10 July 2023

'Global Digital Trade 1: Market Opportunities and Key Foreign Trade Restrictions' (2017) United States International Trade Commission https://www.usitc.gov/publications/332/pub4716.pdf accessed 10 July 2023

'Google Analytics' (*Danish Data Protection Authority (Datatilsynet)*) <https://www.datatilsynet.dk/english/google-analytics> accessed 10 July 2023

'Is the DPC Actually Stopping Facebook's EU-US Data Transfers?! ..Maybe Half-Way!' (*noyb*, 9 September 2020) <https://noyb.eu/en/dpc-actually-stopping-facebooks-eu-us-data-transfers-maybe-half-way> accessed 10 July 2023

'Israel: Ministry Launches Consultation on Draft Privacy Protection Regulations on Transfers from the EEA' (*Data Guidance*, 30 November 2022) <https://www.dataguidance.com/news/israel-ministry-launches-consultation-draft-privacy> accessed 10 July 2023

'Korea Seeks Digital Trade Pact with EU' (*Korea Times*, 13 June 2023) <https://www.koreatimes.co.kr/www/nation/2023/06/113_352846.html?utm_source=substack&utm_medium=email> accessed 10 July 2023

'New Trans-Atlantic Data Privacy Framework Largely a Copy of "Privacy Shield". noyb Will Challenge the Decision' (*noyb*, 10 July 2023) <https://noyb.eu/en/european-commission-gives-eu-us-data-transfers-third-round-cjeu> accessed 10 July 2023

'"Privacy Shield 2.0"? First Reaction by Max Schrems' (*noyb*, 25 March 2022) <https://noyb.eu/en/privacy-shield-20-first-reaction-max-schrems> accessed 10 July 2023

'Tech Lobby Eyes Opportunities Created by New EU-US Trade and Tech Council' (*Corporate Europe Observatory*, 28 September 2021) <https://corporateeurope.org/en/2021/09/tech-lobby-eyes-opportunities-created-new-eu-us-trade-and-tech-council> accessed 10 July 2023

'The Lobby Network: Big Tech's Web of Influence in the EU' (*Corporate Europe Observatory*, 31 August 2021) <https://corporateeurope.org/en/2021/08/lobby-network-big-techs-web-influence-eu> accessed 10 July 2023

'The World's Most Valuable Resource Is No Longer Oil, but Data' (*The Economist*, 6 May 2017) <https://www.economist.com/leaders/2017/05/06/the-worlds-most-valuable-resource-is-no-longer-oil-but-data> accessed on accessed 10 July 2023

'UPDATE on 101 Complaints: Austrian DPA Rejects "Risk Based Approach" for Data Transfers to Third Countries' (*noyb*, 2 May 2022) <https://noyb.eu/en/upd

ate-noybs-101-complaints-austrian-dpa-rejects-risk-based-approach-data-transfers-third-countries> accessed 10 July 2023

'UPDATE: Further EU DPA Orders Stop of Google Analytics' (*noyb*, 5 July 2022) < https://noyb.eu/en/update-further-eu-dpa-orders-stop-google-analytics> accessed 10 July 2023

Aaronson SA, 'Why Trade Agreements Are Not Setting Information Free: The Lost History and Reinvigorated Debate over Cross-Border Data Flows, Human Rights, and National Security' (2015) 14(4) World Trade Review 671

—— 'Match Made in Heaven? The Wedding of Trade and Human Rights' in Martin LL (ed), *The Oxford Handbook of the Political Economy of International Trade* (Oxford Handbooks Online 2015)

—— 'Redefining Protectionism: The New Challenge in the Digital Age' (2016) The George Washington University, Institute for International Economic Policy Working Paper Series, Working Paper No 30 <https://ideas.repec.org/p/gwi/wpaper/2016-30.html> accessed 10 July 2023

—— 'Digital Protectionism? Or Label the U.S. Government Uses to Criticize Policy It Doesn't Like?' (*Council on Foreign Relations Blog*, 3 March 2016) <https://www.cfr.org/blog/digital-protectionism-or-label-us-government-uses-criticize-policy-it-doesnt> accessed 10 July 2023

—— 'What Are We Talking about When We Discuss Digital Protectionism?' (2017) Working Paper for the Economic Research Institute of Asia (Eria) <https://ssrn.com/abstract=3032108> accessed 10 July 2023

—— 'What Are We Talking about When We Talk about Digital Protectionism' (2019) 18(4) World Trade Review 541

—— 'Data Is Disruptive: How Data Sovereignty Is Challenging Data Governance' (2021) Hinrich Foundation Report <https://www.hinrichfoundation.com/research/article/digital/data-is-disruptive-how-data-sovereignty-is-challenging-data-governance/> accessed 10 July 2023

—— 'The Difficult Past and Troubled Future of Digital Protectionism' in Borchert I and Winters LA (eds), *Addressing Impediments to Digital Trade* (CEPR Press 2021)

—— 'Building Trust in Digital Trade Will Require a Rethink of Trade Policy-Making'(2023) 39 Oxford Review of Economic Policy 98

—— and Leblond P, 'Another Digital Divide: The Rise of Data Realms and Its Implications for the WTO' (2018) 21(2) Journal of International Economic Law 245

Acquisti A, 'The Economics of Personal Data and the Economics of Privacy' (2010) Background Paper #3 in Joint WPISP-WPIE Roundtable, The Economics of Personal Data and Privacy: 30 Years after the OECD Privacy Guidelines <https://www.oecd.org/sti/ieconomy/46968784.pdf> accessed 10 July 2023

—— Brandimarte L, and Loewenstein G, 'Privacy and Human Behavior in the Age of Information' (2015) 347(6221) Science 509

—— Brandimarte L, and Loewenstein G, 'Privacy and Behavioral Economics' in Knijnenburg BP and others (eds), *Modern Socio-Technical Perspectives on Privacy* (Springer 2022)

—— John LK, and Loewenstein G, 'What Is Privacy Worth?' (2013) 42(2) The Journal of Legal Studies 249

Adler MD, 'Book Review: Kaplow, Louis, and Shavell, Steven. Fairness versus Welfare. Cambridge, MA: Harvard University Press, 2002. Pp. 544. $50.00 (cloth)' (2005) Ethics 824

Akande D and Williams S, 'International Adjudication on National Security Issues: What Role for the WTO?' (2003) 43(2) Virginia Journal of International Law 365

Alford RP, 'The Self-judging WTO Security Exception' (2011) 3 The Utah Law Review 697

ALLEA, EASAC, and FEAM, 'International Sharing of Personal Health Data for Research' (April 2021) 38 <https://easac.eu/fileadmin/PDF_s/reports_statements/Health_Data/2021_ALLEA_EASAC_FEAM_Policy-Report_International_Sharing_Health_Data_en.pdf> accessed 10 July 2023

Alper A and Shepardson D, 'U.S. Lawmakers Unveil Bill Barring U.S. Data Flows to High-Risk Countries' (*Reuters*, 23 June 2022) <https://www.reuters.com/world/us/us-lawmakers-unveil-bill-barring-us-data-flows-high-risk-countries-2022-06-23/> accessed 10 July 2023

Alschner W, 'E-Commerce or Digital Trade? Why the Difference Should Matter to Trade Lawyers' in Geist M and Collins D (eds), *Research Handbook on Digital Trade* (Edward Elgar, 2023) <http://dx.doi.org/10.2139/ssrn.4321743> accessed 10 July 2023

Andenas M and Zleptnig S, 'Proportionality: WTO Law in Comparative Perspective' (2007) 42 Texas International Law Journal 371

Andrenelli A and others, 'Multinational Production and Trade in Services' (2018) OECD, Trade Policy Paper No 212 <http://dx.doi.org/10.1787/16ec6b55-en> accessed 10 July 2023

Arasasingham A and Goodman MP, 'Operationalizing Data Free Flow with Trust (DFFT)' (*Center for Strategic and International Studies*, 13 April 2023) <https://www.csis.org/analysis/operationalizing-data-free-flow-trust-dfft> accessed 10 July 2023

Asinari MVP, 'Is There Any Room for Privacy and Data Protection within the WTO Rules' (2002) 9 Electronic Communication Law Review 249

Ausloos J, *The Right to Erasure – Safeguard for Informational Self-Determination in a Digital Society?* (PhD Dissertation, KU Leuven CiTiP 2018)

Azmeh S and Foster C, 'The TPP and the Digital Trade Agenda: Digital Industrial Policy and Silicon Valley's Influence on New Trade Agreements' (2016) London School of Economics and Political Science Working Paper No 16-175 <https://www.econstor.eu/bitstream/10419/224801/1/wp175.pdf> accessed 10 July 2023

Azmeh S, Foster C, and Echavarri J, 'The International Trade Regime and the Quest for Free Digital Trade' (2020) 22(3) International Studies Review 671

Azoulai L and van der Sluis M, 'Institutionalizing Personal Data Protection in Times of Global Institutional Distrust: Schrems' 53(5) Common Market Law Review 1343

Baker S, 'How Can the U.S. Respond to Schrems II?'(*Lawfare Blog*, 21 July 2020) <https://www.lawfareblog.com/how-can-us-respond-schrems-ii> accessed 10 July 2023

Baldwin R, *The Great Convergence: Information Technology and the New Globalization* (Belknap Press 2016)

Baldwin R, Cave M, and Lodge M, *Understanding Regulation: Theory, Strategy and Practice* (2nd edn, OUP 2012)

Baldwin RE, 'The New Protectionism: A Response to Shifts in National Economic Power' (1986) National Bureau of Economic Research, Working Paper No 1823 <https://www.nber.org/papers/w1823.pdf> accessed 10 July 2023

—— 'The Political Economy of Trade Policy ' (1989) 3(4) Journal of Economic Perspectives 119

Baloup J, 'The Data Governance Act: New Rules for International Transfers of Non-Personal Data Held by the Public Sector (*European Law Blog*, 10 June 2021) <https://europeanlawblog.eu/2021/06/10/the-data-governance-act-new-rules-for-international-transfers-of-non-personal-data-held-by-the-public-sector/> accessed 10 July 2023

Bamberger DK and Mulligan KA, Privacy on the Ground: Driving Corporate Behavior in the United States and Europe (The MIT Press 2015)

Barbee I and Lester S, 'Financial Services in the TTIP: Making the Prudential Exception Work' (2014) 45(4) Georgetown Journal of International Law 953

Barshefski C, 'EU Digital Protectionism Risks Damaging Ties with the US' (*Financial Times*, 2 August 2020) <https://www.ft.com/content/9edea4f5-5f34-4e17-89cd-f9b9ba698103> accessed 10 July 2023

Bartels L, 'The Separation of Powers in the WTO: How to Avoid Judicial Activism' (2004) 53(4) International & Comparative Law Quarterly 861

—— 'The Chapeau of the General Exceptions in the WTO GATT and GATS Agreements: A Reconstruction' (2015) 109(55) American Journal of International Law 95

Bartl M and Irion K, 'The Japan EU Economic Partnership Agreement: Flows of Personal Data to the Land of the Rising Sun Study' (2017) Institute for Information Law, University of Amsterdam <https://www.ivir.nl/publicaties/download/Transfer-of-personal-data-to-the-land-of-the-rising-sun-FINAL.pdf> accessed 10 July 2023

Bataineha AS and others, 'Monetizing Personal Data: A Two-Sided Market Approach' (2016) 83 Procedia Computer Science 472

Bauer M and others, 'The Economic Importance of Getting Data Protection Right: Protecting Privacy, Transmitting Data, Moving Commerce' (2013) Study by *ECIPE* for US Chamber of Commerce <https://www.uschamber.com/sites/default/files/documents/files/020508_EconomicImportance_Final_Revised_lr.pdf> accessed 10 July 2023

Beattie A, 'EU Trade Data Flows Are Becoming the New GMOs' (*Financial Times*, 4 December 2017) <https://www.ft.com/content/9da22968-d8ee-11e7-a039-c64b1c09b482> accessed 10 July 2023

Behsudi A, 'WTO E-commerce Talks Could Be a Long Slog' (*Politico*, 11 August 2019) <https://www.politico.com/newsletters/morning-trade/2019/11/08/wto-e-commerce-talks-could-be-a-long-slog-782169> accessed 10 July 2023

Bentzen HB and others, 'Remove Obstacles to Sharing Health Data with Researchers outside of the European Union' (2021) 27 Nature Medicine 1329

Bergkamp L, 'The Privacy Fallacy: Adverse Effects of Europe's Data Protection Policy in an Information-Driven Economy' (2002) 18(1) Computer Law & Security Review 31 <https://www.huntonak.com/images/content/3/2/v3/3292/Privacy-fallacy.pdf> accessed 10 July 2023

Bernier C, '2023 Canada Private-Sector Privacy Law Reform: Keeping Track of Moving Parts' (*IAPP*, 13 January 2023) <https://iapp.org/news/a/2023-canada-private-sector-privacy-law-reform-keeping-track-of-moving-parts/> accessed 10 July 2023

Besson S, 'European Legal Pluralism after Kadi' (2009) 5(2) European Constitutional Law Review 237

Bhagwati J, 'The Generalized Theory of Distortions and Welfare' in Jagdish Bhagwati and others (eds), *Trade, Balance of Payments and Growth: Papers in International Economics in Honor of Charles P. Kindleberger* (North-Holland Publishing Co 1971)

—— *Protectionism* (The MIT Press 1989)

—— 'Threats to the World Trading Regime: Protectionism, Unfair Trade et al', in Koekkoek A and Mennes LBM (eds), *International Trade and Global Development: Essays in Honour of Jagdish Bhagwati* (Routledge 1991)

—— 'The Diminished Giant Syndrome' (1993) 72(2) Foreign Affairs 22

—— 'Fair Trade, Reciprocity, and Harmonization: The Novel Challenge to the Theory and Policy of Free Trade' in Salvatore D (ed), *Protectionism and World Welfare* (CUP 1993)

—— 'The Demands to Reduce Domestic Diversity among Trading Nations' in Bhagwati J and Hudec RE (eds) *Fair Trade & Harmonization. Volume I* (The MIT Press 1996)

—— *In Defense of Globalization* (OUP 2007)

Bhala R, 'National Security and International Trade Law: What the GATT Says, and What the US Does' (1998) 19(2) University of Pennsylvania Journal of International Economic Law 263

Bigo D and others, 'Mass Surveillance of Personal Data by EU Member States and Its Compatibility with EU Law', CEPS Paper in Liberty and Security No 62 (November 2013) <https://www.ceps.eu/wp-content/uploads/2013/11/No%2062%20Surveillance%20of%20Personal%20Data%20by%20EU%20MSs.pdf> accessed 10 July 2023

Black J, 'Regulatory Conversations' (2002) 29(1) Journal of Law and Society 163

Bollen Y, De Ville F, and Orbie J, 'EU Trade Policy: Persistent Liberalisation, Contentious Protectionism' (2016) 38(3) Journal of European Integration 279

Bonefeld-Dahl C, 'European Sovereignty or a Shadow of Protectionism?' (*Euractiv*, 25 August 2022) <https://www.euractiv.com/section/digital/opinion/european-sovereignty-or-a-shadow-of-protectionism/> accessed 10 July 2023

Bonnan R, 'The GATT Security Exception in a Dispute Resolution Context: Necessity or Incompatibility?' (2010) 19(1) Currents: International Trade Law Journal 3

Borrell J, 'Building Global Europe' (*European Union External Action*, 9 September 2020) <https://www.eeas.europa.eu/eeas/building-global-europe_en> accessed 10 July 2023

Botwright K, 'Davos Participants Call for Digital Trade Deal' (*World Economic Forum*, 23 January 2019) <https://www.weforum.org/agenda/2019/01/davos-participants-call-for-digital-trade-deal/> accessed 10 July 2023

Bracy J, 'US Commerce Dept. Announces 'Historic' Global CBPR Forum for Data Transfers' (*IAPP*, 21 April 2022) <https://iapp.org/news/a/us-commerce-department-announces-historic-global-cbpr-forum-for-data-transfers/> accessed 10 July 2023

Bradford A, 'The Brussels Effect' (2012) 107(1) Northwestern University Law Review 1

—— and Posner E, 'Universal Exceptionalism in International Law' (2011) 52 Harvard International Law Journal 1

Brännström L, 'Global Inequality and the EU International Law Position on Cross-Border Data Flows' 92 (2023) Nordic Journal of International Law 119

Bridges KM, *The Poverty of Privacy Rights* (Stanford UP 2017)

Brkan M, 'The Essence of the Fundamental Rights to Privacy and Data Protection: Finding the Way through the Maze of the CJEU's Constitutional Reasoning' (2019) 20(6) German Law Journal 864

Brown I, 'The Economics of Privacy, Data Protection and Surveillance' in Bauer JM and Latzer M (eds), *Handbook on the Economics of the Internet* (Edward Elgar 2016) <https://ideas.repec.org/h/elg/eechap/14700_12.html> accessed 10 July 2023

Buchta A and Kranenborg H, 'Institutional Report Topic 2: The New EU Data Protection Regime' in Rijpma J (ed), *The New EU Data Protection Regime: Setting Global Standards for the Right to Personal Data Protection* (The XXIX FIDE Congress in The Hague, 2020 Congress Publications, Vol 2) <https://cris.maastrichtuniversity.nl/en/publications/institutional-report-topic-2-the-new-eu-data-protection-regime> accessed 10 July 2023

Burri M, 'Should There Be New Multilateral Rules for Digital Trade?' (2013) Think Piece for the E15 Expert Group on Trade and Innovation <https://ssrn.com/abstract=2344629> accessed 10 July 2023

—— 'Current and Emerging Trends in Disruptive Technologies: Implications for the Present and Future of EU's Trade Policy' (2017) Study for the European Parliament (EP/EXPO/B/INTA/2017/6) <https://www.europarl.europa.eu/RegData/etudes/STUD/2017/603845/EXPO_STU(2017)603845_EN.pdf> accessed 10 July 2023

—— 'The Governance of Data and Data Flows in Trade Agreements: The Pitfalls of Legal Adaptation' (2017) 51(65) UC Davis Law Review 65

—— 'The Regulation of Data Flows through Trade Agreements' (2017) 48 Georgetown Journal of International Law 407

—— 'A WTO Agreement on Electronic Commerce: An Enquiry into Its Legal Substance and Viability' (2021) Trade Law 4.0 Working Paper No 1 <https://ssrn.com/abstract=3976133> accessed 10 July 2023

—— 'Interfacing Privacy and Trade' (2021) 53 Case Western Reserve Journal of International Law 35

—— 'Towards a New Treaty on Digital Trade' (2021) 55(1) Journal of World Trade 77

—— 'Approaches to Digital Trade and Data Flow Regulation across Jurisdictions: Implications for the Future ASEAN-EU Agreement' (2022) 49(2) Legal Issues of Economic Integration 149

—— 'Symposium on Digital Trade and International Law: Digital Trade Law and Human Rights' (2023) 117 AJIL Unbound 110

—— 'The Impact of Digitalization on Global Trade Law' (2023) 24 German Law Journal 551

—— 'Trade Law 4.0: Are We There Yet? ' (2023) 26(1) Journal of International Economic Law 90

—— and Chander A, 'What Are Digital Trade and Digital Trade Law?' (2023) 117 AJIL Unbound 99

—— and Polanco R, 'Digital Trade Provisions in Preferential Trade Agreements: Introducing a New Dataset' (2020) 23(1) Journal of International Economic Law 187

—— and Schär R, 'The Reform of the EU Data Protection Framework: Outlining Key Changes and Assessing Their Fitness for a Data-Driven Economy' (2016) 6 Journal of Information Policy 479

Bygrave LA, *Data Protection Law: Approaching Its Rationale, Logic and Limits* (Wolters Kluwer 2002)

—— *Data Privacy Law: An International Perspective* (Oxford Scholarship Online 2014)

Cadwalladr C and Campbell D, 'Revealed: Facebook's Global Lobbying against Data Privacy Laws' (*The Guardian*, 2 March 2019) <https://www.theguardian.com/technology/2019/mar/02/facebook-global-lobbying-campaign-against-data-privacy-laws-investment> accessed 10 July 2023

Cameron I, 'European Union Law Restraints on Intelligence Activities' (2020) 33(3) International Journal of Intelligence and Counter Intelligence 452

Cann Jr WA, 'Creating Standards and Accountability for the Use of the WTO Security Exception: Reducing the Role of Power-Base Relations and Establishing a New Balance between Sovereignty and Multilateralism' (2001) 26(2) Yale Journal of International Law 413

Cantore CM, '"Shelter from the Storm": Exploring the Scope of Application and Legal Function of the GATS Prudential Carve-Out' (2014) 48(6) Journal of World Trade 1223

—— *The Prudential Carve-Out for Financial Services* (CUP 2018)

Carter MC and Murphy JG, 'Setting the Record Straight on a "Worker-Centered" Digital Trade Agenda' (*US Chamber of Commerce*, 1 March 2023) <https://www.uschamber.com/international/trade-agreements/setting-the-record-straight-on-a-worker-centered-digital-trade-agenda> accessed 10 July 2023

Casalini F and López González J, 'Trade and Cross-Border Data Flows' (2019) OECD Trade Policy Papers No 220 <http://dx.doi.org/10.1787/b2023a47-en> accessed 10 July 2023

Centre for IT and IP Law of KU Leuven, 'Government Access to Data in Third Countries' Final Report, EDPS/2019/02-13 (November 2021) <https://edpb.europa.eu/system/files/2022-01/legalstudy_on_government_access_0.pdf> accessed 10 July 2023

Chander A, 'Is Data Localization a Solution for Schrems II?' Journal of International Economic Law <https://ssrn.com/abstract=3662626> accessed 10 July 2023

—— and Jones J, 'What if It Were Illegal to Transfer Personal Data from the European Union to the United States?' (*Lawfare*, 22 June 2023) <https://www.lawfaremedia.org/article/what-if-it-were-illegal-to-transfer-personal-data-from-the-european-union-to-the-united-states> accessed 10 July 2023

—— Kaminski ME, and McGeveran W, 'Catalyzing Privacy Law' (2019) 105 Minnesota Law Review 1733

—— and Lê UP, 'Data Nationalism' (2015) 64 Emory Law Journal 677

—— and Schwartz P, 'Privacy and/or Trade' (2023) 90(1) The University of Chicago Law Review 49

Chen L and others, 'The Data Privacy Paradox and Digital Demand' (2021) NBER Working Paper 28854 <https://www.nber.org/system/files/working_papers/w28854/w28854.pdf> accessed 10 July 2023

Chen TF, 'To Judge the Self-Judging Security Exception under the GATT 1994: A Systematic Approach' (2017) 12(2) Asian Journal of WTO and International Health Law and Policy 311

Chen Y-H, 'The EU Data Protection Law Reform: Challenges for Service Trade Liberalization and Possible Approaches for Harmonizing Privacy Standards into the Context of GATS' (2015) 19 The Spanish Yearbook of International Law 211

Chow DCK, Sheldon IM, and McGuire W, 'The Revival of Economic Nationalism and the Global Trading System' (2019) 40(5) Cardozo Law Review 2133

Christakis T, 'A Fragmentation of EU/ECHR Law on Mass Surveillance: Initial Thoughts on the Big Brother Watch Judgment' (*European Law Blog*, 20 September 2018) <https://europeanlawblog.eu/2018/09/20/a-fragmentation-of-eu-echr-law-on-mass-surveillance-initial-thoughts-on-the-big-brother-watch-judgment/> accessed 10 July 2023

—— 'After Schrems II: Uncertainties on the Legal Basis for Data Transfers and Constitutional Implications for Europe' (*European Law Blog*, 21 July 2020) <https://europeanlawblog.eu/2020/07/21/after-schrems-ii-uncertainties-on-the-legal-basis-for-data-transfers-and-constitutional-implications-for-europe/> accessed 10 July 2023

—— Propp K, and Swire P, 'The Redress Mechanism in the Privacy Shield Successor: On the Independence and Effective Powers of the DPRC' (*IAPP*, 11 October 2022) <https://iapp.org/news/a/the-redress-mechanism-in-the-privacy-shield-successor-on-the-independence-and-effective-powers-of-the-dprc/> accessed 10 July 2023

Churches G and Zalnieriute M, '"Contracting Out" Human Rights in International Law: Schrems II and the Fundamental Flaws of U.S. Surveillance Law' (2020) Harvard International Law Journal Online, UNSW Law Research Paper No 20-44 <https://ssrn.com/abstract=3679671> accessed 10 July 2023

Cinnamon J, 'Social Injustice in Surveillance Capitalism' (2017) 15(5) Surveillance & Society 609

Citron DK and Solove DJ, 'Privacy Harms' (2022) 102(973) Boston University Law Review 793

Ciuriak D and Rodionova V, 'Trading Artificial Intelligence' in Peng S, Lin C, and Streinz T (eds), *Artificial Intelligence and International Economic Law: Disruption, Regulation, and Reconfiguration* (CUP online 2021)

Clifford D and Ausloos J, 'Data Protection and the Role of Fairness' (2018) 37(1) Yearbook of European Law 130

Cohen GM, 'The Negligence-Opportunism Tradeoff in Contract Law' (1992) 20(4) Hofstra Law Review 941

Cohen HG, 'What Is International Trade Law For?' (2019) 113(2) American Journal of International Law 326

Cohen JE, 'Examined Lives: Informational Privacy and the Subject as Object' (2000) 52 Stanford Law Review 1373

Cohen P, 'Why It Seems Everything We Knew about the Global Economy Is no Longer True' (*The New York Times*, 18 June 2023) <https://www.nytimes.com/2023/06/18/business/economy/global-economy-us-china.html> accessed 10 July 2023

Coldicutt S and Sen N, 'Testing the GDPR's WTO Readiness' (*Linklaters*) <https://www.linklaters.com/en/insights/blogs/digilinks/can-the-wto-save-international-data-transfers> accessed 10 July 2023

Coleman D, 'Digital Colonialism: The 21st Century Scramble for Africa through the Extraction and Control of User Data and the Limitations of Data Protection Laws' (2019) 24 Michigan Journal of Race and Law 417

Colnago J, Cranor LF, and Acquisti A, 'Is There a Reverse Privacy Paradox? An Exploratory Analysis of Gaps between Privacy Perspectives and Privacy-Seeking Behaviors' (2023)(1) Proceedings on Privacy Enhancing Technologies 455

Connolly K, 'Finding Space for Regulatory Autonomy in GATS Article XVII after EC–Seals: Public Services and the "Likeness" of Public and Private Service Providers' (2015) 42 Legal Issues of Economic Integration 57

Consumers International, 'Why TiSA Should Be in the Global Consumer Spotlight' (1 June 2016) <https://www.consumersinternational.org/news-resources/blog/posts/20160601-why-tisa-should-be-in-the-global-consumer-spotlight/> accessed 10 July 2023

Cook G, 'Reasonableness in WTO Law' (2013) 1(2) Latin American Journal of International Trade Law 1

Cory N, 'How the EU Is Using Technology Standards as a Protectionist Tool in Its Quest for Cybersovereignty' (*Information Technology & Innovation Foundation*, 19 September 2022) <https://itif.org/publications/2022/09/19/how-the-eu-is-using-technology-standards-as-a-protectionist-tool/> accessed 10 July 2023

—— and Dascoly L, 'How Barriers to Cross-Border Data Flows Are Spreading Globally, What They Cost, and How to Address Them' (*Information Technology & Innovation Foundation*, 2021) <https://itif.org/publications/2021/07/19/how-barriers-cross-border-data-flows-are-spreading-globally-what-they-cost/> accessed 10 July 2023

Cossy M, 'Determining "Likeness" under the GATS: Squaring the Circle?' (2006) World Trade Organization Economic Research and Statistics Division, WTO Staff Working Paper ERSD-2006-08 <https://www.wto.org/english/res_e/reser_e/ersd200608_e.pdf> accessed 10 July 2023

Costa-Cabral F and Lynskey O, The Internal and External Constraints of Data Protection on Competition Law in the EU' (2015) LSE Law, Society and Economy Working Papers 25/2015 <http://eprints.lse.ac.uk/64887/1/Lynskey_Internal%20and%20External%20Constraints%20of%20Data%20Protection%20_Author_2015.pdf> accessed 10 July 2023

—— 'Family Ties: The Intersection Between Data Protection and Competition in EU Law' (2017) 54 Common Market Law Review 11

Cottier T and Delimatsis P, 'Article XIVbis Security Exceptions' in Wolfrum R, Stoll P-T, and Feinäugle C (eds), *Max Planck Commentaries on World Trade Law: WTO - Trade In Services Vol. 6* (Martinus Nijhoff Publishers 2008)

Cottier T and Krajewski M, 'What Role for Non-Discrimination and Prudential Standards in International Financial Law?' (2010) 13(3) Journal of International Economic Law 817

Cottier T and Schefer KN, 'Good Faith and the Protection of Legitimate Expectations in the WTO' in Bronckers M and Quick R (eds), *New Directions in International Economic Law, Essays in Honour of John H. Jackson* (Kluwer Law International 2000)

Couldry N and Mejias UA, 'Data Colonialism: Rethinking Big Data's Relation to the Contemporary Subject' (2019) 20(4) Television & New Media 336

Craig P and de Burca G, *EU Law: Text, Cases, and Materials* (6th edn, OUP 2015)

Crémer J, De Montioye YA, and Schweitzer H, 'Competition Policy for the Digital Era' 2019 Final Report to the European Commission Directorate-General for Competition <http://ec.europa.eu/competition/publications/reports/kd0419345enn.pdf> accessed 10 July 2023

Crosby D, 'Analysis of Data Localization Measures under WTO Services Trade Rules and Commitments' (2016) The E15 Initiative, World Economic Forum Policy Brief <http://e15initiative.org/wp-content/uploads/2015/09/E15-Policy-Brief-Crosby-Final.pdf> accessed 10 July 2023

Cryer R and others, *Research Methodologies in EU and International Law* (Hart Publishing 2011)

Culatto J, 'Dutch Parents Sue TikTok for €1.4 Billion' (*DW*, 6 February 2021) <https://www.dw.com/en/dutch-parents-sue-tiktok-for-14-billion/a-57762350> accessed 10 July 2023

Cvrcek D and others, 'A Study on the Value of Location Privacy' (2006) Proceedings of the 5th ACM Workshop on Privacy in Electronic Society <https://dl.acm.org/citation.cfm?id=1179621> accessed 10 July 2023

Dalla Corte L, 'A Right to a Rule: On the Substance and Essence of the Fundamental Right to Personal Data Protection' in Hallinan D and others (eds), *Data Protection and Privacy: Data Protection and Democracy* (Hart Publishing 2020)

—— 'On Proportionality in the Data Protection Jurisprudence of the CJEU ' (2022) 12(4) International Data Privacy Law 259

Data Privacy Stichting, 'Why Did We Launch Two Actions against Meta?' <https://dataprivacystichting.com/our-actions/> accessed 10 July 2023

Davies RB and Chaitanya Vadlamannati K, 'A Race to the Bottom in Labor Standards? An Empirical Investigation' (2013) 103(C) Journal of Development Economics 1

Dawson M, Lynskey O, and Muir E, 'What Is the Added Value of the Concept of the Essence of EU Fundamental Rights?' (2019) 20(6) German Law Journal 763

De Búrca G, 'The ECJ and the International Legal Order: A Re-Evaluation' in de Burca G and Weiler JHH (eds), *The Worlds of European* Constitutionalism (CUP 2012)

De Gregorio G and Dunn P, 'The European Risk-Based Approaches: Connecting Constitutional Dots in the Digital Age' (2022) 59 Common Market Law Review 473

De Meester B, 'The Global Financial Crisis and the Government Support for Banks' (2008) 13(1) Journal of International Economic Law 27

De Terwangne C, 'Is a Global Data Protection Regulatory Model Possible?' in Gutwirth S and others (eds), *Reinventing Data Protection?* (Springer 2009)

Delacroix S and Lawrence ND, 'Bottom-Up Data Trusts: Disturbing the "One Size Fits All" Approach to Data Governance' (2019) 9(4) International Data Privacy Law 236

Delev C, 'A Moral Stretch? US–Tariff Measures and the Public Morals Exception in WTO Law' (2022) 21 World Trade Review 249

Delimatsis P, 'Protecting Public Morals in a Digital Age: Revisiting the WTO Rulings on US – Gambling and China – Publications and Audiovisual Products' (2011) 14(2) Journal of International Economic Law 257

—— 'Financial Innovation and Prudential Regulation: The New Basel III Rules' (2012) 46(6) Journal of World Trade 1309

—— 'Who's Afraid of Necessity? And Why It Matters?' in Hoe Lim A and De Meester B (eds), *WTO Domestic Regulation and Services Trade* (CUP 2014)

Demetzou K, 'Risk to the "Rights and Freedoms": A Legal Interpretation of the Scope of Risk under the GDPR' in Hallinan D and others (eds), *Data Protection and Privacy Data Protection and Democracy* (Hart Publishing 2020)

Determann L, 'Adequacy of Data Protection in the USA: Myths and Facts' (2016) 6(3) International Data Privacy Law 244

Diebold NF, 'Non-Discrimination in International Trade in Services: "Likeness"' in *WTO/GATS* (CUP 2010)

Dinev T and Hart P, 'An Extended Privacy Calculus Model for E-Commerce Transactions' (2006) 17(1) Information Systems Research 61

DLA Piper, 'Handbook Data Protection Laws of the World' (2023) <https://www.dlapiperdataprotection.com/> accessed 10 July 2023

Dorff MB, 'Why Welfare Depends on Fairness: A Reply to Kaplow and Shavell' (2002) 75 Southern California Law Review 847

Drache D and Froese MD, 'An Empirical Analysis of Why the WTO Is Broken and Cannot Be Fixed – Yet' (2007 3(1)) Eurostudia <https://www.erudit.org/en/journals/euro/1900-v1-n1-euro1991/017648ar/> accessed 10 July 2023

Drechsler L and Kamara I, 'Essential Equivalence as a Benchmark for International Data Transfers after Schrems II' in Kosta E and Leenes R (eds), *Research Handbook on EU Data Protection* (Edward Elgar Publishing 2022)

Drechsler L and Yakovleva S, 'Contribution to the Public Consultation on the Guidelines 05/2021 on the Interplay between the Application of Article 3 and the Provisions on International Transfers as per Chapter V of the GDPR' (*EDPB*, 27 December 2021) <https://edpb.europa.eu/sites/default/files/webform/public_consultation_reply/20211227.Public_consultation_EDPB_transfers_V8.pdf> accessed 10 July 2023

Dresner S, 'Meaningful Consent and Privacy-Washing' (*Privacy Laws & Business*, 7 December 2022) <https://www.privacylaws.com/reports-gateway/articles/int180/int180blog/> accessed 10 July 2023

Driskill R, 'Deconstructing the Argument for Free Trade: A Case Study of the Role of Economists in Policy Debates' (2012) 28 Economics and Philosophy 1

Du M, 'The Necessity Test in World Trade Law: What Now?' (2016) 15 Chinese Journal of International Law 817

Duque de Carvalho SL, 'Key GDPR Elements in Adequacy Findings of Countries That Have Ratified Convention 108' (2019) 5(1) European Data Protection Law Review 54

Dutton T, 'An Overview of National AI Strategies' (*Medium.com*, 28 June 2018) <https://medium.com/politics-ai/an-overview-of-national-ai-strategies-2a70ec6edfd> accessed 10 July 2023

Eben M, 'Market Definition and Free Online Services: The Prospect of Personal Data as Price' (2018) 14(2) Journal of Law and Policy for the Information Society 227

Eckes C, 'Protecting Supremacy from External Influences: A Precondition for a European Constitutional Legal Order?' (2012) 18(2) European Law Journal 230

—— *EU Powers under External Pressure: How the EU's External Actions Alter Its Internal Structures* (OUP 2019)

EDRI, 'Data Protection and Privacy Must Be Excluded from TTIP' (8 April 2015) <https://edri.org/our-work/data-protection-privacy-ttip/> accessed 10 July 2023

—— 'TiSA Leaks Set Alarm Bells Ringing' (20 September 2016) <https://edri.org/our-work/tisa-leaks-set-alarm-bells-ringing/> accessed 10 July 2023

Eger JM, 'Emerging Restrictions on Transnational Data Flows: Privacy Protection or Non-Tariff Trade Barriers' (1978) 10 Law and Policy in International Business 1055

Ehring L, 'De Facto Discrimination in WTO Law: National and Most-Favored-Nation Treatment—or Equal Treatment?' (2002) 36(5) Journal of World Trade 921

Ehrlich SD, 'The Fair Trade Challenge to Embedded Liberalism' (2010) 54(4) International Studies Quarterly 1013

Eichengreen B and Irwin DA, 'The Slide to Protectionism in the Great Depression: Who Succumbed and Why?' (2010) 70(4) The Journal of Economic History 871

Elsig M, 'The World Trade Organization's Legitimacy Crisis: What Does the Beast Look Like?' (2007) Journal of World Trade 41(1) 75

—— and Klots S, 'Digital Trade Rules in Preferential Trade Agreements: Is There a WTO Impact?' (2021) 12(4) Global Policy 25

Epstein C, *The Power of Words in International Relations: Birth of an Anti-Whaling Discourse* (The MIT Press 2008)

Esayas SY, 'A Walk in to the Cloud and Cloudy It Remains: The Challenges and Prospects of "Processing" and "Transferring" Personal Data' (2012) 28 Computer Law & Security Review 662

Espinosa de los Monteros Pereda E and Guo K, 'TikTok under Investigation for Posing a Threat to National Security: Is Chinese Tech Running Out of Time in the U.S.?' (*Jolt Digest*, 2 December 2019) <https://jolt.law.harvard.edu/digest/tiktok-under-investigation-for-posing-a-threat-to-national-security-is-chinese-tech-running-out-of-time-in-the-u-s> accessed 10 July 2023

Esty DC, *Greening the GATT: Trade, Environment and the Future* (Peterson Institute for International Economics 1994)

—— 'The World Trade Organization's Legitimacy Crisis' (2002) 1(1) World Trade Review 7

European Union Agency for Fundamental Rights and Council of Europe, *Handbook on European Data Protection Law* (European Union Agency for Fundamental Rights and Council of Europe 2018) <https://www.echr.coe.int/Documents/Handbook_data_protection_ENG.pdf> accessed 10 July 2023

Executive Office of the President, 'Office of the U.S. Trade Representative Letter to TPP Depositary' (2017) <https://ustr.gov/sites/default/files/files/Press/Releases/1-30-17%20USTR%20Letter%20to%20TPP%20Depositary.pdf> accessed 10 July 2023

Fabbri M and Britto DGC, 'Distributive Justice, Public Policies and the Comparison of Legal Rules: Quantify the "Price of Equity"' (2018) 14(3) Review of Law and Economics 1

Fahey E, 'Digital Trade and Data Equivalency: Research Briefing for the Welsh Parliament' (2020) <https://openaccess.city.ac.uk/id/eprint/24721/1/Fahey%20Research%20Briefing%20Digital%20Trade> accessed 10 July 2023

—— 'The European Union as a Digital Trade Actor: The Challenge of Being a Global Leader in Standard-Setting' (2021) 27(2) International Trade Law and Regulation 1 <https://openaccess.city.ac.uk/id/eprint/26428/8/THE%20EU%20AS%20A%20DIGITAL%20TRADE%20ACTOR%20%20THE%20CHALLENGE%20OF%20BEING%20A%20GLOBAL%20LEADER%20IN%20STANDARD-SETTING.pdf> accessed 10 July 2023

Fanta A, 'Tech Industry Pushes Europe for WTO Data Flows Deal' (*Netzpolitik.org*, 30 June 2021) <https://netzpolitik.org/2021/digital-trade-tech-industry-pushes-europe-for-wto-data-flows-deal/> accessed 10 July 2023

Farrell H and Newman AL, 'Weaponized Interdependence: How Global Economic Networks Shape State Coercion' (2020) 44(1) International Security 42

—— 'Schrems II Offers an Opportunity: If the U.S. Wants to Take It' (*Lawfare Blog*, 28 July 2020) <https://www.lawfareblog.com/schrems-ii-offers-opportunity-if-us-wants-take-it> (accessed 10 July 2023)

Fazlioglu M, 'IAPP-EY Annual Privacy Governance Report 2021' (2021) <https://ssrn.com/abstract=4227244> accessed 10 July 2023

Fefer RF, 'Trade in Services Agreement (TiSA) Negotiations: Overview and Issues for Congress' (2017) Congressional Research Service 1, 12 <https://fas.org/sgp/crs/misc/R44354.pdf> accessed 10 July 2023

Ferracane MF, 'Restrictions on Cross-Border Data Flows: A Taxonomy' (2017) ECIPE Working Paper No 1/2017 <https://ecipe.org/wp-content/uploads/2017/11/Restrictions-on-cross-border-data-flows-a-taxonomy-final1.pdf> accessed 10 July 2023

—— *A Conceptual Framework to Assess Restrictions on Cross-Border Data Flows from a Trade Policy Perspective* (Dissertation, Universität Hamburg 2021)

—— and van der Marel E, 'Do Data Policy Restrictions Inhibit Trade in Services' (2018) ECIPE Working Paper No 2 <https://ecipe.org/wp-content/uploads/2018/10/Do-Data-Policy-Restrictions-Inhibit-Trade-in-Services-final.pdf> accessed 10 July 2023

—— and van der Marel E, 'The Cost of Data Protectionism' (*ECIPE Blog*, October 2018) <https://ecipe.org/blog/the-cost-of-data-protectionism/> accessed 10 July 2023

—— and others, 'Digital Trade, Data Protection and EU Adequacy Decisions' (2023) EUI Working Paper RSC 2023/37 <https://cadmus.eui.eu/handle/1814/75629> accessed 10 July 2023

Finck M and Pallas F, 'They Who Must Not Be Identified: Distinguishing Personal from Non-Personal Data under the GDPR' (2020) 10(1) International Data Privacy Law 11

Finlayson-Brown J and Glugla G, 'Germany – Schrems II: German Court Overturns Presumption of International Data Transfer from EU-Subsidiary to Non-EU Parent Company' *JD Supra* (13 September 2023) <https://www.jdsupra.com/legalnews/germany-schrems-ii-german-court-2846282/> accessed 10 July 2023

Finnis J, 'Critical Legal Studies' in Finnis J (ed), *Philosophy of Law: Collected Essays, vol VI* (OUP 2011)

Fioretti J, 'EU Moves to Remove Barriers to Data Flows in Trade Deals' (*Reuters*, 9 February 2018) <https://www.reuters.com/article/us-eu-data-trade-idUSKBN1FT2DC> accessed 10 July 2023

Fontanella-Khan J, 'Data Protection Ruled Out of EU-US Trade Talks' (*Financial Times*, 4 November 2013) <www.ft.com/content/92a14dd2-44b9-11e3-a751-00144feabdc0> accessed 10 July 2023

Foroohar R, 'Nations Move to Avoid Global Ecommerce "Splinternet"' (*Financial Times*, 24 January 2019) <https://www.ft.com/content/3a8b7458-1fe5-11e9-b2f7-97e4dbd3580d> accessed 10 July 2023

Fortnam B, 'EU Punts on Data Flow Language in Japan Deal, Leaving Position Unresolved' (*Inside US Trade*, 2017) <https://insidetrade.com/inside-us-trade/eu-punts-data-flow-language-japan-deal-leaving-position-unresolved> accessed 10 July 2023

Foucault M, *The Archaeology of Knowledge and the Discourse of Language* (Pantheon Books 1972)

—— 'The Order of Discourse' in Robert Young (ed), *Untying the Text: A Post-Structuralist Reader* (Routledge & Kegan Paul Ltd 1981)

Friedman TL, *The Lexus and the Olive Tree: Understanding Globalization* (Farrar, Straus and Giroux 1999)

Frontier Economics, 'The Value of Cross-Border Data Flows to Europe: Risks and Opportunities' (2021) Report Prepared for DIGITALEUROPE <https://cdn.digitaleur

ope.org/uploads/2021/06/Frontier-DIGITALEUROPE_The-value-of-cross-border-data-flows-to-Europe_Risks-and-opportunities.pdf> accessed 10 July 2023

Gambs S and others, 'Privacy and AI Ethics: Understanding the Convergences and Tensions for the Responsible Development of Machine Learning (*Office of the Privacy Commissioner of Canada*, 2021) <https://www.priv.gc.ca/en/opc-actions-and-decisions/research/funding-for-privacy-research-and-knowledge-translation/completed-contributions-program-projects/2020-2021/p_2020-21_09/> accessed 10 July 2023

Gao HS, 'Data Regulation with Chinese Characteristics' in Burri M (ed), *Big Data and Global Trade Law* (CUP 2021)

Gáspár-Szilágyi S, 'The "Primacy" and "Direct Effect" of EU International Agreements' (2015) 21(2) European Public Law 343

Gee JP, *An Introduction to Discourse Analysis* (3rd edn, Routledge 2010)

Geist M, 'Data Rules in Modern Trade Agreements: Toward Reconciling an Open Internet with Privacy and Security Safeguards' (*CIGI*, 4 April 2018) <https://www.cigionline.org/articles/data-rules-modern-trade-agreements-toward-reconciling-open-internet-privacy-and-security/> accessed 10 July 2023

Gellert R, *The Risk-Based Approach to Data Protection* (Oxford Data Protection & Privacy Law 2020)

—— and Gutwirth S, 'The Legal Construction of Privacy and Data Protection' (2013) 29 Computer Law & Security Review 522

Gervais DJ, *The Trips Agreement* (4th edn, Sweet & Maxwell 2010)

—— 'TRIPS Pluralism' (2022) 21(2) Word Trade Review 185

Goel D, 'The Global Digital Divide Is Reminiscent of Colonialism' (*LSE Brexit*, 6 May 2021) <https://blogs.lse.ac.uk/brexit/2021/05/06/the-global-digital-divide-is-reminiscent-of-colonialism/> accessed 10 July 2023

Goldfarb A and Trefler D, 'Artificial Intelligence and International Trade' in Agrawal A, Gans J, and Goldfarb A (eds), *The Economics of Artificial Intelligence: An Agenda* (University of Chicago Press 2019) <https://www.nber.org/books/agra-1> accessed 10 July 2023

Goldfarb A and Tucker CE, 'Privacy Regulation and Online Advertising' (2011) 57(1) Management Science 57

Gomes L, *The Economics and Ideology of Free Trade: A Historical Review* (Edward Elgar 2003)

González Fuster G, *The Emergence of Personal Data Protection as a Fundamental Right of the EU* (Springer 2014)

—— 'Un-mapping Personal Data Transfers' (2016) 2(2) European Data Protection Law Review 160

Goujard C, 'Big Tech Accused of Shady Lobbying in EU Parliament' (*Politico*, 14 October 2022) <https://www.politico.eu/article/big-tech-companies-face-potential-eu-lobbying-ban/> accessed 10 July 2023

Granger M-P and Irion K, 'The Right to Protection of Personal Data: The New Posterchild of European Union Citizenship?' in de Vries S, de Waele H, and Granger M-P (eds), *Civil Rights and EU Citizenship* (Edward Elgar Publishing 2018) <https://hdl.handle.net/11245.1/606d4e50-508e-4841-b290-fde00a336621>accessed 10 July 2023

Greenberg Center for Geoeconomic Studies, 'The Rise of Digital Protectionism' (*Greenberg Center for Geoeconomic Studies*, 18 October 2017) <https://www.cfr.org/report/rise-digital-protectionism> accessed 10 July 2023

Greenleaf G, 'The Influence of European Data Privacy Standards outside Europe: Implications for Globalization of Convention 108' (2012) 2(2) International Data Privacy Law 68

—— 'European' Data Privacy Standards Implemented in Laws outside Europe' (2017) 149 Privacy Laws & Business International Report 21 <https://ssrn.com/abstract=3096314> accessed 10 July 2023

—— 'Questioning "Adequacy" (Pt I) – Japan' (2017) 150 Privacy Laws & Business International Report 6-11 <https://ssrn.com/abstract=3096370> accessed 10 July 2023

—— 'Japan: EU Adequacy Discounted' (2018) 155 Privacy Laws & Business International Report 8 <https://ssrn.com/abstract=3276016> accessed 10 July 2023

—— 'Convention 108+ and the Data Protection Framework of the EU' (2018) UNSW Law & Justice Legal Studies Research Paper No 18-39 <https://papers.ssrn.com/sol3/papers.cfm?abstract_id=3202606> accessed 10 July 2023

—— 'Japan's Proposed EU Adequacy Assessment: Substantive Issues and Procedural Hurdles' (2018) UNSW Law Research Paper No 18-53 <https://ssrn.com/abstract=3219728> accessed 10 July 2023

—— 'Now 157 Countries: Twelve Data Privacy Laws in 2021/22' (2022) 176 Privacy Laws & Business International Report 3

Grindal K, 'Trade Regimes as a Tool for Cyber Policy' (2019) 21(1) Digital Policy, Regulation and Governance 19

Gulczyńska Z, 'A Certain Standard of Protection for International Transfers of Personal Data under the GDPR' (2021) 11(4) International Data Privacy Law 360

Gürses S and van Hoboken J, 'Privacy after the Agile Turn' in Selinger E, Polonetsky J, and Tene O, *The Cambridge Handbook of Consumer Privacy* (CUP 2018)

Hahn MJ, 'Vital Interests and the Law of GATT: An Analysis of GATT's Security Exception' (1991) 12(3) Michigan Journal of International Law 558

Hakimi M, 'The Integrative Effects of Global Legal Pluralism' in Berman PS (ed), *The Oxford Handbook of Global Legal Pluralism* (OUP 2020)

Hall W and Pesenti J, 'Growing the Artificial Intelligence Industry in the UK' Report for Government of the United Kingdom (2017) <https://www.gov.uk/government/publications/growing-the-artificial-intelligence-industry-in-the-uk> accessed 10 July 2023

Handley K and Limão N, 'Trade under T.R.U.M.P. Policies' in Bown CP (ed), *Economics and Policy in the Age of Trump* (CEPR Press 2017) <https://giovanniperi.ucdavis.edu/uploads/5/6/8/2/56826033/ageoftrump_june2017.pdf> accessed 10 July 2023

Hardinges J, 'What Is a Data Trust?' (*Open Data Institute*, 2018) <https://theodi.org/article/what-is-a-data-trust/> accessed 10 July 2023

Harrington J and McGabe R, 'What the U.S. Innovation and Competition Act Gets Right (and What It Gets Wrong)' (*Center for Strategic and International Studies*, 1 July 2021) <https://www.csis.org/analysis/what-us-innovation-and-competition-act-gets-right-and-what-it-gets-wrong> accessed 10 July 2023

Hathaway OA, 'Keeping the Wrong Secrets: How Washington Misses the Real Security Threat' (*Foreign Affairs*, 7 December 2021) <https://www.foreignaffairs.com/articles/united-states/2021-12-07/hacking-cybersecurity-keeping-wrong-secrets> accessed 10 July 2023

Häuselmann A, 'The ECJ's First Landmark Case on Automated Decision-Making: A Report from the Oral Hearing before the First Chamber' (*European Law Blog*, 20 February 2023 <The ECJ's First Landmark Case on Automated Decision-Making – a Report from the Oral Hearing before the First Chamber – European Law Blog> accessed 10 July 2023

Heath JB, 'The New National Security Challenge to the Economic Order' (2020) 129(4) The Yale Law Journal 1020

Helberger N, Zuiderveen Borgesius F, and Reyna A, 'The Perfect Match? A Closer Look at the Relationship between EU Consumer Law and Data Protection Law' (2017) 54(5) Common Market Law Review 1427

Herbert Smith Freehills LLP, 'Indonesia Proposes Amendments to Its Data Localisation Requirement' (*Lexology*, 11 December 2018) <https://www.lexology.com/library/detail.aspx?g=a116020b-cee3-433f-b62b-a5e988477d8e> accessed 10 July 2023

Hijmans H, 'The Transatlantic Trade and Investment Partnership and the Developments in the Area of Privacy and Data Protection' (2016) 43(4) Legal Issues of Economic Integration 385

Hilf M and Puth S, 'The Principle of Proportionality on Its Way into WTO/GATT Law' in Von Bogdandy A, Mavroidis PC, and Mény Y (eds), *European Integration and International Co-Ordination* (Wolters Kluwer 2002)

Hodson S, 'Applying WTO and FTA Disciplines to Data Localization Measures' (2019) 18(4) World Trade Review 579

Hoeffnagel W, 'Consumentenbond en DPS Starten Opnieuw Rechtszaak Tegen Facebook' (*Dutch IT Channel*, 16 March 2023) <https://www.dutchitchannel.nl/news/221853/consumentenbond-en-dps-starten-opnieuw-rechtszaak-tegen-facebook> accessed 10 July 2023

Hon WK and Millard C, 'Data Export in Cloud Computing—How Can Personal Data Be Transferred outside the EEA? The Cloud of Unknowing, Part 4' (2012) 9(1) SCRIPTed <http://script-ed.org/wp-content/uploads/2012/04/hon.pdf> accessed 10 July 2023

Hoofnagle CJ, van der Sloot B, and Zuiderveen Borgesius F, 'The European Union General Data Protection Regulation: What It Is and What It Means' (2019) 28(1) Information & Communications Technology Law 65

Horn H and Mavroidis PC, 'Economic and Legal Aspects of the Most Favoured Nation Clause' (2001) 17 European Journal of Political Economy 223

House of Representatives, Hearing before the Subcommittee on Commerce, Trade and Consumer Protection of the Committee on Energy and Commerce (The EU Data Protection Directive: Publications for the U.S. Privacy Debate 2001) <https://books.google.nl/books?printsec=frontcover&vid=ISBN0160658942&redir_esc=y#v=onepage&q&f=false> accessed 10 July 2023

Howse R, 'From Politics to Technocracy--And Back Again: The Fate of the Multilateral Trading Regime' (2002) 96 American Journal of International Law 94

—— *The WTO System: Law, Politics & Legitimacy* (Cameron May Limited 2007)

—— 'Regulatory Measures' in Narlikar A, Daunton M, and Stern RM (eds), *The Oxford Handbook on the World Trade Organisation* (Oxford Handbooks Online 2012)

—— 'The World Trade Organization 20 Years On: Global Governance by Judiciary' (2016) 27(1) European Journal of International Law 9

—— and Langille J, 'Permitting Pluralism: The Seal Products Dispute and Why the WTO Should Permit Trade Restrictions Justified by Noninstrumental Moral Values' (2012) 37 Yale Journal of International Law 368

—— Langille J, and Sykes K, 'Pluralism in Practice: Moral Legislation and the Law of the WTO after Seal Products' (2015) 48 The George Washington International Law Review 81

—— and Langille J, 'Continuity and Change in the World Trade Organization: Pluralism Past, Present, and Future' (2023) 117(1) The American Journal of International Law 1

—— and Nicolaïdis K, 'Legitimacy and Global Governance: Why Constitutionalizing the WTO Is a Step Too Far' in Porter RB and others (eds), *Efficiency, Equity, and Legitimacy: The Multilateral Trading System at the Millennium* (Brookings Institution Press 2001)

—— and Nicolaidis K, 'Enhancing WTO Legitimacy: Constitutionalization or Global Subsidiarity?' (2003) 16(1) Governance: An International Journal of Policy, Administration, and Institutions 73

—— and Trebilcock MJ, 'The Fair Trade – Free Trade Debate: Trade, Labor, and the Environment' (1996) 16(1) International Review of Law and Economics 61

Huberman BA, Adar E, and Fine LR, 'Valuating Privacy: The Value of Privacy' (2005) IEEE Security & Privacy <http://www.cond.org/deviance.pdf> accessed 10 July 2023

Hudec RE, 'GATT/WTO Constraints on National Regulation: Requiem for an Aim and Effects Test' (1998) 32(3) The International Lawyer 619

—— *The GATT Legal System and World Trade Diplomacy* (2nd edn, Butterworths 1990)

Hunt M, 'Trudeau Outlines Canadian Data Privacy Reforms' (*Global Government Forum*, 26 December 2019) <https://www.globalgovernmentforum.com/trudeau-outlines-canadian-data-privacy-reforms/> accessed 10 July 2023

IAPP-EY Annual Privacy Governance Report (*IAPP*, 2019) <ttps://f.hubspotusercontent20.net/hubfs/525875/IAPP_EY_Governance_Report_2019.pdf> accessed 10 July 2023

IAPP-FTI Consulting Annual Privacy Governance Report 2020 <https://static2.ftitechnology.com/docs/IAPP-FTI+Consulting+-+2020+Privacy+Governance+Report.pdf> accessed 10 July 2023

'Indo-Pacific Strategy of The United States' (*The White House*, February 2022) <https://www.whitehouse.gov/wp-content/uploads/2022/02/U.S.-Indo-Pacific-Strategy.pdf> accessed 10 July 2023

Irion K, 'A Special Regard: The Court of Justice and the Fundamental Rights to Privacy and Data Protection' (2016) Amsterdam Law School Legal Studies Research Paper No 2016-35, Institute for Information Law Research Paper No 2016-04 <https://ssrn.com/abstract=2836910> accessed 10 July 2023

—— 'Schrems II and Surveillance: Third Countries' National Security Powers in the Purview of EU Law' (*European Law Blog*, 24 July 2020) <https://europeanlawblog.eu/2020/07/24/schrems-ii-and-surveillance-third-countries-national-security-powers-in-the-purview-of-eu-law/> accessed 10 July 2023

—— 'Panta Rhei: A European Perspective on Ensuring a High-Level of Protection of Digital Human Rights in a World in Which Everything Flows' in Burri M (ed), *Big Data and Global Trade Law* (CUP 2021)

—— and Burri M, '§ 16 Digitaler Handel' in Gesa Kübek, Christian J Tams, and Jörg Philipp Terhechte (Hrsg), *Handels- und Kooperationsvertrag EU/GB Handbuch* (Nomos 2022)

—— Kaminski ME, and Yakovleva S, 'Privacy Peg, Trade Hole: Why We (Still) Shouldn't Put Data Privacy in Trade Law' (2023) The University of Chicago Law Review Online <https://lawreviewblog.uchicago.edu/2023/03/27/irion-kaminski-yakovleva/> accessed 10 July 2023

—— Yakovleva S, and Bartl M, 'Trade and Privacy: Complicated Bedfellows? How to Achieve Data Protection-Proof Free Trade Agreements' (2016) Independent study commissioned by BEUC and others <https://www.ivir.nl/publicaties/download/trade_and_privacy.pdf> accessed 10 July 2023

Irwin DA, *Against the Tide: An Intellectual History of Free Trade* (Princeton UP 1996)

Irwin DA, Mavroidis PC, and Sykes AO, *The Genesis of the GATT* (CUP 2008)

Jackson JH, *World Trade Organization and the Law of GATT* (Bobbs-Merrill 1969)

—— 'The World Trading System: Law and Policy of International Economic Relations' (MIT 1989) 205

—— *The World Trade Organization: Constitution and Jurisprudence* (The Royal Institute of International Affairs 1998)

Jarreau JS, 'Interpreting the General Agreement on Trade in Services and the WTO Instruments Relevant to the International Trade of Financial Services: A Lawyer's Perspective' (1999) 25(1) North Carolina Journal of International Law and Commercial Regulation 1

Järvinen H, 'BEUC and EDRi Urge the EU Commission Not to Undermine Citizens' Privacy in Trade Agreements' (*EDRi*, 13 June 2016) <https://edri.org/our-work/beuc-edri-urge-eu-commission-not-undermine-citizens-privacy-trade-agreements/> accessed on 10 July 2023

Jentzsch N, Preibusch S, and Harasser A, 'Study on Monetising Privacy: An Economic Model for Pricing Personal Information' (2012) ENISA <https://www.enisa.europa.eu/publications/monetising-privacy> accessed 10 July 2023.

Joinson AN and others, 'Privacy, Trust, and Self-Disclosure Online' (2010) 25(1) Human–Computer Interaction 1

Jordan P, 'Notes from the IAPP Europe Managing Director, 17 November 2017' (*IAPP*, 16 November 2017) <https://iapp.org/news/a/notes-from-the-iapp-europe-managing-director-17-november-2017/> accessed 10 July 2023

Juliussen BA and others, 'The Third Country Problem under the GDPR: Enhancing Protection of Data Transfers with Technology' (2023) International Data Privacy Law 1 <https://doi.org/10.1093/idpl/ipad013> accessed 1 August 2023

Jungkind V and Koch S, 'The Risk-Based Approach in the GDPR: Restating the Obvious and Reinstating a Guiding Principle' (2022) ZD 656

Jurcys P and others, 'The Future of International Data Transfers: Managing Legal Risk With a 'User-Held' Data Model' (2022) 46 Computer Law & Security Review 2

Kanetake M and de Vries S, 'EU-Japan Economic Partnership Agreement: Data Protection in the Era of Digital Trade and Economy' (*Renforce Blog*, 18 December 2018), on file with author

Kaplow L and Shavell S, 'Fairness versus Welfare' (2001) 114(4) Harvard Law Review 961

Ke X and others, 'Analyzing China's PIPL and How It Compares to the EU's GDPR' (*IAPP*, 24 August 2021) <https://iapp.org/news/a/analyzing-chinas-pipl-and-how-it-compares-to-the-eus-gdpr/> accessed 10 July 2023

Keller P, *European and International Media Law: Liberal Democracy, Trade and New Media* (OUP 2011)

Kerber W, 'Digital Markets, Data, and Privacy: Competition Law, Consumer Law and Data Protection' (2016) 11(11) Journal of Intellectual Property Law & Practice 856

Kerkmeester H, 'Methodology: General' in Bouckaert B and De Geest G (eds), *Encyclopedia of Law and Economics Volume I: The History and Methodology of Law and Economics* (Edward Elgar Publishing 2020)

Kerry CF, 'Breaking Down Proposals for Privacy Legislation: How Do They Regulate?' (*Brookings Institute*, March 8 2019) <https://www.brookings.edu/research/breaking-down-proposals-for-privacy-legislation-how-do-they-regulate/> accessed 10 July 2023

Key SJ, *The Doha Round and Financial Services Negotiations* (American Enterprise Institute Press 2003)

Kiss A, 'Abuse of Rights' in *Max Planck Encyclopedia of Public International Law* (Oxford Public International Law 2006)

Kokott J and Sobotta C, 'The Kadi Case – Constitutional Core Values and International Law: Finding the Balance?' (2012) 23(4) European Journal of International Law 1015

Komaitis K, 'The 'Wicked Problem' of Data Localisation' (2017) 2(3) Journal of Cyber Policy 355

Kondor D and others, 'Towards Matching User Mobility Traces in Large-Scale Datasets' (2018) IEEE Transactions on Big Data https://arxi.org/pdf/1709.05772.pdf> accessed 10 July 2023

Koops B-J, 'The Trouble with European Data Protection Law' (2014) 4(4) International Data Privacy Law 250

Korff D, 'Update on the Opinion on the Future of Personal Data Transfers from the EU/EEA to Israel & the Occupied Territories' (25 March 2022) <http://dx.doi.org/10.2139/ssrn.4066476> accessed 10 July 2023

Koskenniemi M, 'Fragmentation of International Law – The Function and Scope of the Lex Specialis Rule and the Question of "self-Contained Regimes": An Outline' (2009) <https://legal.un.org/ilc/sessions/55/pdfs/fragmentation_outline.pdf.> accessed 10 July 2023

Kotzur M, 'Good Faith (Bona Fide)' in *Max Planck Encyclopedias of International Law* (Oxford Public International Law 2009)

Krisch N, *Beyond Constitutionalism: The Pluralist Structure of Postnational Law* (OUP 2012)

Kritsiotis D, 'The Power of International Law as a Language' (1998) 34(2) California Western Law Review 397

Kudo F, 'World Economic Forum, We Must Enhance Cross-Border Data Flows: Here's Why' (*World Economic Forum*, 16 January 2023) <https://www.weforum.org/agenda/2023/01/data-flows-cross-border-wef23/> accessed 10 July 2023

Kudo F, Sakaki R, and Soble J, 'Every Country Has Its Own Digital Laws: How Can We Get Data Flowing Freely between Them?' (*World Economic Forum*, 20 May 2022) <https://www.weforum.org/agenda/2022/05/cross-border-data-regulation-dfft/> accessed 10 July 2023

Kummer M and Schulte P, 'When Private Information Settles the Bill: Money and Privacy in Google's Market for Smartphone Applications' (2019) 65(8) Management Science 3470

Kuner C, *European Data Protection Law: Corporate Compliance and Regulation* (OUP 2007)

—— 'Developing an Adequate Legal Framework for International Data Transfers' in Gutwirth S and others (eds), *Reinventing Data Protection?* (Springer 2009) <https://ssrn.com/abstract=1464323> accessed 10 July 2023

—— 'Data Nationalism and Its Discontents' (2015) 64 Emory Law Journal 2089

—— 'Regulation of Transborder Data Flows under Data Protection and Privacy Law: Past, Present, and Future' (2010) TILT Law & Technology Working Paper 016/2010 19 <https://papers.ssrn.com/sol3/papers.cfm?abstract_id=1689483> accessed 13 July 2023

—— 'Regulation of Transborder Data Flows under Data Protection and Privacy Law: Past, Present, and Future' (2011) OECD Digital Economy Papers No 187 <https://www.oecd-ilibrary.org/science-and-technology/regulation-of-transborder-data-flows-under-data-protection-and-privacy-law_5kg0s2fk315f-en> accessed 10 July 2023

—— *Transborder Data Flows and Data Privacy Law* (OUP 2013)

—— 'Extraterritoriality and Regulation of International Data Transfers in EU Data Protection Law' (2015) 5(4) International Data Privacy Law 235

—— 'Reality and Illusion in EU Data Transfer Regulation Post Schrems' (2017) 18(4) German Law Journal 881

—— 'International Agreements, Data Protection, and EU Fundamental Rights on the International Stage: Opinion 1/15, EU-Canada PNR' (2018) 55(3) Common Market Law Review 857

—— 'The Internet and the Global Reach of EU Law' in Cremona M and Scott J (eds), *EU Law beyond EU Borders: The Extraterritorial Reach of EU Law* (OUP 2019)

—— 'Data Crossing borders: Data Sharing and Protection in Times of Coronavirus' (*Information and Policy Center Blog*, 27 April 2020) <https://infolawcentre.blogs.sas.

ac.uk/2020/04/27/data-crossing-borders-data-sharing-and-protection-in-times-of-coronavirus-christopher-kuner/> accessed 10 July 2023

—— 'Article 44 GDPR: General Principles for Transfers' in Kuner C and others (eds), *The EU General Data Protection Regulation (GDPR): A Commentary* (OUP 2020)

—— 'Article 49: Derogations for Specific Situations' in Kuner C and others (eds), *The EU General Data Protection Regulation: A Commentary/Update of Selected Articles* (4 May 2021) 203 <http://dx.doi.org/10.2139/ssrn.3839645> accessed 10 July 2023

—— 'Article 49: Derogations for Specific Situations' in Kuner C and others (eds), *The EU General Data Protection Regulation (GDPR): A Commentary* (OUP 2020)

—— 'Schrems II Re-Examined' (*Verfassungsblog*, 25 August 2020) <https://verfassungsblog.de/schrems-ii-re-examined/> accessed on 10 July 2023

—— 'The GDPR and International Organizations' (2020) 114 AJIL Unbound 15

—— 'The Schrems II Judgment of the Court of Justice and the Future of Data Transfer Regulation' (*European Law Blog*, 17 July 2020) <https://europeanlawblog.eu/2020/07/17/the-schrems-ii-judgment-of-the-court-of-justice-and-the-future-of-data-transfer-regulation/> accessed 10 July 2023

—— 'Exploring the Awkward Secret of Data Transfer Regulation: The EDPB Guidelines on Article 3 and Chapter V GDPR' (*European Law Blog*, 13 December 2021) <https://europeanlawblog.eu/2021/12/13/exploring-the-awkward-secret-of-data-transfer-regulation-the-edpb-guidelines-on-article-3-and-chapter-v-gdpr/> accessed 10 July 2023

—— 'Protecting EU Data outside EU Borders under the GDPR' (2023) 60 Common Market Law Review 77

—— 'Op-Ed: "International Data Transfers after Five Years of the GDPR: Postmodern Anxieties' (2023) EU Law Live <https://eulawlive.com/op-ed-international-data-transfers-after-five-years-of-the-gdpr-postmodern-anxieties-by-christopher-kuner/> accessed 10 July 2023

—— and others, 'PRISM and Privacy: Will This Change Everything?' (2013) 3(4) International Data Privacy Law 217

Kurtz J, *The WTO and International Investment Law: Converging Systems* (CUP 2016)

LaCasse A, 'In Wake of Global Data Transfer Complexity, Need for Multilateral Treaty Grows' (*IAPP*, 25 April 2023) <https://iapp.org/news/a/schrems-3-transborder-data-flows-become-hot-button-topic-at-iapp-gps-2023/> accessed 10 July 2023

Lamp N, 'How Some Countries Became 'Special': Developing Countries and the Construction of Difference in Multilateral Trade Lawmaking (2015) 18(4) Journal of International Economic Law 743

Lancieri FM, 'Digital Protectionism? Antitrust, Data Protection, and the EU/US Transatlantic Rift (2019) 7(1) Journal of Antitrust Enforcement 27

Lang A, 'Reflecting on Linkage: Cognitive and Institutional Change in the International Trading System' 2007 70(4) Modern Law Review 523

—— *World Trade Law after Neoliberalism* (OUP Online 2011)

—— 'Protectionism's Many Faces' (2019) 44 The Yale Journal of International Law Online 1 <https://cpb-us-w2.wpmucdn.com/campuspress.yale.edu/dist/8/1581/files/2018/12/Lang_YJIL-Symposium_Protectionisms-Many-Faces_12.08.18-qedo7n.pdf> accessed 10 July 2023

Lauterpacht H, *The Development of International Law by the International Court* (Stevens & Sons 1958)

Lauw S and Stokols E, 'G7 vs. China: US, Europe Unite in Tough Messaging against Beijing' Politico (20 May 2023) <https://www.politico.eu/article/g7-vs-china-us-europe-unite-tough-message-summit-statement/> accessed 10 July 2023

Le Roux G, 'TTIP Negotiations, Policy Convergence, and the Transatlantic Digital Economy' (2017) 19(4) Business and Politics 709

Leblond P, 'CETA and Financial Services: What to Expect?' (2016) CIGI Papers No 91 <https://www.cigionline.org/sites/default/files/cigi_paper_no.91_web.pdf> accessed 10 July 2023

Leblond P and Aaronson SA, 'A Plurilateral "Single Data Area" Is the Solution to Canada's Data Trilemma' (2019) CIGI Papers No 226 <https://www.cigionline.org/static/documents/documents/no.226.pdf> accessed 10 July 2023

Lee A and others, 'Seven Major Changes in China's Finalized Personal Information Protection Law' (*DIGIChina Stanford*, 15 September 2021) <https://digichina.stanford.edu/work/seven-major-changes-in-chinas-finalized-personal-information-protection-law/> accessed 10 July 2023

Lee E, 'Globalization and Labour Standards: A Review of Issues' (1997) 136(2) International Labour Review 173

Lee PSN, 'The Rise of China and Its Contest for Discursive Power' (2016) 1(1–2) Global Media and China 102

Leff AA, 'Economic Analysis of Law: Some Realism about Nominalism' (1974) 60(3) Virginia Law Review 451

Lenaerts K, 'Exploring the Limits of the EU Charter of Fundamental Rights' (2012) 8(3) European Constitutional Law Review 375

—— 'Limits on Limitations: The Essence of Fundamental Rights in the EU' (2019) 20 German Law Journal 779

Leonard M and Shapiro J, 'Empowering EU Member States with Strategic Sovereignty' European Council on Foreign Relations (June 2019) <https://ecfr.eu/wp-content/uploads/1_Empowering_EU_member_states_with_strategic_sovereignty.pdf> accessed 10 July 2023

Leroux EH, 'Trade in Financial Services under the World Trade Organization' (2002) 36(3) Journal of World Trade 413

LeSieur F, 'Regulating Cross-Border Data Flows and Privacy in the Networked Digital Environment and Global Knowledge Economy' (2012) 2(2) International Data Privacy Law 93

Lesser I, 'Discursive Struggles within Social Welfare: Restaging Teen Motherhood' (2006) 36(2) The British Journal of Social Work 283

Lessig L, *Code and Other Laws of Cyberspace* (Basic Books 1999)

Lippman D, 'Trump Says He Plans to Ban TikTok in the U.S.' (*Politico*, 31 July 2020) <https://www.politico.com/news/2020/07/31/trump-plans-to-ban-tiktok-389956> accessed 10 July 2023

Lomas N, 'Ireland Probes Tiktok's Handling of Kids' Data and Transfers to China' (*Techcrunch*, 15 September 2021) <https://techcrunch.com/2021/09/15/ireland-probes-tiktoks-handling-of-kids-data-and-transfers-to-china/> accessed 10 July 2023

—— 'As Its Data Flows Woes Grow, Google Lobbies for Quickie Fix to EU-US Transfers' (*TechCrunch*, 19 January 2022) <https://techcrunch.com/2022/01/19/google-lobbies-for-new-privacy-shield/?guccounter=1&guce_referrer=aHR0cHM6Ly93d3cuZ29vZ2xlLmNvbS8&guce_referrer_sig=AQAAADTAUg1eK7FULgT-t9SdWOaCU-iAWRomypXA3JgmgXL0foL7DuWJTlSUr85ahiwuK8EbHVw1iG-sYj9WlkbiuRD4Hrj7RN3uAfaIEPB2ismpcHtRWScyKCjsyQ4A1IJRP4Mr0TKbwj7LUUqobS4snXkaCQ84FFnQ3aiG7laPBlHZ> accessed 10 July 2023

—— 'TikTok Privacy Update in Europe Confirms China Staff Access to Data as GDPR Probe Continues' *TechCrunch* (3 November 2022) <https://techcrunch.com/2022/11/03/tiktok-privacy-policy-update-china/> accessed 10 July 2023

—— 'Italy orders ChatGPT blocked citing data protection concerns' (31 March 2023) <https://techcrunch.com/2023/03/31/chatgpt-blocked-italy/?guccounter=1> accessed 10 July 2023

Luo Y, Yu Z, and Liu V, 'The Future of Data Localization and Cross-Border Transfer in China: A Unified Framework or a Patchwork of Requirements?' (*IAPP*, 22 June 2021) <https://iapp.org/news/a/the-future-of-data-localization-and-cross-border-transfer-in-china-a-unified-framework-or-a-patchwork-of-requirements/> accessed 10 July 2023

Lynskey O, 'From Market-Making Tool to Fundamental Right: The Role of the Court of Justice in Data Protection's Identity Crisis' in Gutwirth S and others (eds), *European Data Protection: Coming of Age* (Springer 2013)

—— 'Deconstructing Data Protection: The "Added-Value" of a Right to Data Protection in the EU Legal Order' (2014) 63 International and Comparative Law Quarterly 569

—— *The Foundations of EU Data Protection Law* (OUP 2015)

—— 'General Report Topic 2: The New EU Data Protection Regime' in Rijpma J (ed), *The New EU Data Protection Regime. Setting Global Standards for the Right to Personal Data Protection. The XXIX FIDE Congress in the Hague* (Congress Publications 2020, Vol 2)

Macaskill W and Dance G, 'NSA Files: Decoded' (*The Guardian*, 1 November 2013) <https://www.theguardian.com/world/interactive/2013/nov/01/snowden-nsa-files-surveillance-revelations-decoded#section/1> accessed 10 July 2023

MacDonald DA and Streatfeild CM, 'Personal Data Privacy and the WTO' (2014) 36(3) Houston Journal of International Law 625

Macenaite M, 'The "Riskification" of European Data Protection Law through a Two-Fold Shift'(2017) 8(3) European Journal of Risk Regulation 506

Madiega T, 'Digital Sovereignty for Europe', EPRS Ideas Paper Towards a More Resilient EU (2020) 1 <https://www.europarl.europa.eu/RegData/etudes/BRIE/2020/651992/EPRS_BRI(2020)651992_EN.pdf> accessed 10 July 2023

Mahieu R and others, 'Has the European General Data Protection Regulation Influenced the Data Protection Rights of Canadian Citizens?' (2021) 11 Journal of Information Policy 301

Maldoff G, 'Top 10 Operational Impacts of the GDPR: Part 8 – Pseudonymization' (*IAPP*, 12 February 2016) <https://iapp.org/news/a/top-10-operational-impacts-of-the-gdpr-part-8-pseudonymization/> accessed 10 July 2023

Manak I, 'U.S. WTO E-Commerce Proposal Reads Like USMCA' (*International Economic Law and Policy Blog*, 8 May 2019) <https://worldtradelaw.typepad.com/ielpblog/2019/05/us-wto-e-commerce-proposal-reads-like-usmca.html> accessed 10 July 2023

Manancourt V, 'The EU Court Ruling That Could Blow Up Digital Trade' (*Politico*, 13 July 2020) <https://www.politico.eu/article/us-china-data-flows-at-risk-in-top-eu-court-ruling/> accessed 10 July 2023

Manokha I, 'Foucault's Concept of Power and the Global Discourse of Human Rights' (2009) 23(4) Global Society 429

Manyika J and others, 'Digital Globalisation: The New Era of Global Flows' (2016) McKinsey Global Institute <https://www.mckinsey.com/~/media/McKinsey/Business%20Functions/McKinsey%20Digital/Our%20Insights/Digital%20globalization%20The%20new%20era%20of%20global%20flows/MGI-Digital-globalization-Full-report.pdf> accessed 10 July 2023

Marceau G and Trachtman JP, 'The Technical Barriers to Trade Agreement, the Sanitary and Phytosanitary Measures Agreement, and the General Agreement on Tariffs and Trade: A Map of the World Trade Organization Law of Domestic Regulation of Goods' (2002) 36(5) Journal of World Trade 811

—— 'A Map of the World Trade Organization Law of Domestic Regulation of Goods: The Technical Barriers to Trade Agreement, the Sanitary and Phytosanitary Measures Agreement, and the General Agreement on Tariffs and Trade' (2014) 48(2) Journal of World Trade 351

Marchetti JA, 'The GATS Prudential Carve-Out' in Delimatsis P and Herger N (eds), *Financial Regulation at the Crossroads: Implications for Supervision, Institutional Design and Trade* (Kluwer Law International 2011)

Marr B, 'Here's Why Data Is Not the New Oil' (*Forbes*, 5 March 2018) <https://www.forbes.com/sites/bernardmarr/2018/03/05/heres-why-data-is-not-the-new-oil/> accessed 10 July 2023

Marthews A and Tucker C, 'Government Surveillance and Internet Search Behavior' (2017) <https://ssrn.com/abstract=2412564> accessed 10 July 2023

Martines F, 'Direct Effect of International Agreements of the European Union' (2014) 25(1) European Journal of International Law 129

Matsushita M and others, *The World Trade Organization: Law, Practice, and Policy* (OUP 2015)

Mattoo A and Meltzer JP, 'International Data Flows and Privacy: The Conflict and Its Resolution' (2018) World Bank Policy Research Working Paper 8431 <http://documents.worldbank.org/curated/en/751621525705087132/pdf/WPS8431.pdf> accessed 10 July 2023

—— 'International Data Flows and Privacy: The Conflict and Its Resolution' (2018) 21(4) Journal of International Economic Law 769

Maurer T and others, 'Technological Sovereignty: Missing the Point?' in Maybaum M, Osula A-M, and Lindström L (eds), *7th International Conference on Cyber Conflict: Architectures in Cyberspace* (NATO CCD COE Publications 2015) <https://www.ccdcoe.org/uploads/2018/10/Art-04-Technological-Sovereignity-Missing-the-Point.pdf> accessed 10 July 2023

Mavroidis PC, 'Driftin' Too Far from Shore: Why the Test for Compliance With the TBT Agreement Developed by the WTO Appellate Body Is Wrong, and What Should the AB Have Done Instead' (2013) 12(3) World Trade Review 509

—— 'Sealed with a Doubt: EU, Seals, and the WTO' (2015) 3 European Journal of Risk Regulation, Symposium on the EU-Seal Product Case 388

Mayer FC, 'The Force Awakens: The Schrems Case from a German perspective' (*Verfassunsblog*, 16 October 2015) <https://verfassungsblog.de/the-force-awakens-the-schrems-case-from-a-german-perspective-2/> accessed 10 July 2023

McCabe D and Kang C, 'U.S. Pushes for TikTok Sale to Resolve National Security Concerns' (*The New York Times*, 15 March 2023) <https://www.nytimes.com/2023/03/15/technology/tiktok-biden-pushes-sale.html> accessed 10 July 2023

McCabe D and Satariano A, 'The Era of Borderless Data Is Ending' (*The New York Times*, 23 May 2022) <https://www.nytimes.com/2022/05/23/technology/data-privacy-laws.html> accessed 10 July 2023

McCallum S, 'TikTok under Investigation by Canadian Privacy Authorities' (*BBC News*, 24 February 2023) <https://www.bbc.com/news/technology-64759365> accessed 10 July 2023

McCreanor N, 'Pseudonymisation Is the GDPR's "Escape Hatch"' (*IT Governance Blog*, 14 May 2018) <https://www.itgovernance.eu/blog/en/pseudonymisation-is-the-gdprs-escape-hatch> accessed 10 July 2023

McGrady B, 'Necessity Exceptions in WTO Law: Retreated Tyres, Regulatory Purpose and Cumulative Regulatory Measures' (2009) 12(1) Journal of International Economic Law 153

McRae D, 'GATT Article XX and the WTO Appellate Body' in Bronckers M and Quick R, (eds), *New Directions in International Economic Law, Essays in Honour of John H. Jackson* (Kluwer Law International 2000)

Meddin E, 'The Cost of Ensuring Privacy: How the General Data Protection Regulation Acts as a Barrier to Trade in Violation of Articles XVI and XVII of the General Agreement on Trade in Services' (2020) 35 American University International Law Review 997

Mehra SK, 'Algorithmic Competition, Trade and Investment: The CFIUS as Privacy Regulator' (2020) 16 University of Pennsylvania Asian Law Review 8

Messerlin PA, 'The Political Economy of Protectionism: The Bureaucratic Case' (1981) 117 Weltwirtschaftliches Archiv 469

Meyer D, 'In the Wake of GDPR, Will the U.S. Embrace Data Privacy?' (*Fortune*, 29 November 2018) <https://fortune.com/2018/11/29/federal-data-privacy-law/> accessed 10 July 2023

Meyer T, 'The Political Economy of WTO Exceptions' (2022) 99 Washington University Law Review 1299

Miadzvetskaya Y, 'What Are the Pros and Cons of the Adequacy Decision on Japan?' (*KU Leuven CiTiP Blog*, 4 April 2019) <https://www.law.kuleuven.be/citip/blog/what-are-the-pros-and-cons-of-the-adequacy-decision-on-japan/> accessed 10 July 2023

Micallef JA, 'Digital Trade in EU FTAs: Are EU FTAs Allowing Cross Border Digital Trade to Reach Its Full Potential?' (2019) 53(5) Journal of World Trade 855

Milberg SJ, Smith HJ, and Burke SJ, 'Information Privacy: Corporate Management and National Regulation' (2000) 11(1) Organization Science 35

Miles T, 'EU and Canada Settle Cattle Battle at the WTO' *Reuters* (3 October 2017) <www.reuters.com/article/us-canada-eu-wto-meat-idUSKCN1C81HY> accessed 10 July 2023

Miller S, 'Foucault on Discourse and Power' (1990) 76 Theoria: A Journal of Social and Political Theory 115

Milliken J, 'The Study of Discourse in International Relations: A Critique of Research and Methods' (1999) 5(2) European Journal of International Relations 225

Mishra N, 'Data Localization Laws in a Digital World: Data Protection or Data Protectionism?' (2016) 4(1) The Public Sphere: Journal of Public Policy 135

—— 'Building Bridges: International Trade Law, Internet Governance, and the Regulation of Data Flows' (2019) 52(2) Vanderbilt Journal of Transnational Law 463

—— 'Privacy, Cybersecurity, and GATS Article XIV: A New Frontier for Trade and Internet Regulation?' (2020) 19(3) World Trade Review 341

Mitchell AD and Henckels C 'Necessity Testing' in Andrew D Mitchell and Elizabeth Sheargold, *Principles of International Trade and Investment Law* (Edgaronline 2021)

Mitchell AD and Hepburn J, 'Don't Fence Me In: Reforming Trade and Investment Law to Better Facilitate Cross-Border Data Transfer' (2017) 19(1) Yale Journal of Law and Technology 182

Mitchell AD and Mishra N, 'Data at the Docks: Modernizing International Trade Law for the Digital Economy' (2018) 20(4) Vanderbilt Journal of Entertainment & Technology 1073

Mitchell AD and Sheargold E, 'Reasonableness' in Mitchell AD and Sheargold E (eds), *Principles of International Trade and Investment Law* (Edgaronline 2021)

Mitchell AD, Hawkins JK, and Mishra N, 'Dear Prudence: Allowances under International Trade and Investment Law for Prudential Regulation in the Financial Services Sector' (2016) 19(4) Journal of International Economic Law 787

Moerel L, 'EU Data Protection Laws Are Flawed: They Undermine the Very Autonomy of the Individuals They Set Out to Protect' (*IAPP*, May 2020) <https://iapp.org/resources/article/gdpr-at-two-expert-perspectives/> accessed 10 July 2023

—— 'What Happened to the Risk Based Approach to Data Transfers? How the EDPB Is Rewriting the GDPR' (*FPF Blog*, 27 September 2022) <https://fpf.org/wp-content/uploads/2022/09/FPF-Guest-Blog-What-Happened-to-the-Risk-Based-Approach-of-Data-Transfers.doc.pdf> accessed 10 July 2023

Morozov E, 'What Happens When Policy Is Made by Corporations? Your Privacy Is Seen as a Barrier to Economic Growth' (*The Guardian*, 12 July 2015) <https://www.theguardian.com/commentisfree/2015/jul/12/ttip-your-data-privacy-is-a-barrier-to-economic-growth?CMP=Share_iOSApp_Other> accessed 10 July 2023

Muelas G, 'EU: Non-personal Data Transfers under the DGA and the Data Act' (*OneTrust Data Guidance*, July 2022) <https://www.dataguidance.com/opinion/eu-non-personal-data-transfers-under-dga-and-data> accessed 10 July 2023

Mueller M and Grindal K, 'Data Flows and the Digital Economy: Information as a Mobile Factor of Production' (2019) 21(1) Digital Policy, Regulation and Governance 71

Muir E, 'The Fundamental Rights Implications of EU Legislation: Some Constitutional Challenges' (2014) 51(1) Common Market Law Review 219

Murad A, Robinson D, and Waters R, 'Obama Attacks Europe over Technology Protectionism' (*Financial Times*, 16 February 2015) https://www.ft.com/content/41d968d6-b5d2-11e4-b58d-00144feab7de accessed 10 July 2023

Naef T, *Data Protection without Data Protectionism: The Right to Protection of Personal Data and Data Transfers in EU Law and International Trade Law* (Springer Cham 2023)

Nagy CI, 'Clash of Trade and National Public Interest in WTO Law: The Illusion of "Weighing and Balancing" and the Theory of Reservation' (2020) 23(1) Journal of International Economic Law 143

Nedzel NE, 'Rule of Law v. Legal State: Where Have We Come from, Where Are We Going To?' in Silkennat JR, Hickey Jr, JE, and Barenboim PD (eds), *The Legal Doctrines of the Rule of Law and the Legal State (Rechtsstaat)* (Springer International Publishing 2016)

Neeraj RS, 'Trade Rules for the Digital Economy: Charting New Waters at the WTO' (2019) 18(S1) World Trade Review s121

Newman AL, *Protectors of Privacy: Regulating Personal Data in the Global Economy* (Cornell UP 2018)

Newman M, 'Meta Lodges Appeal against EDPB Data-Transfers Decision at EU Courts' (*MLex Market Insight*, 15 June 2023) <https://content.mlex.com/#/content/1478542/meta-lodges-appeal-against-edpb-data-transfers-decision-at-eu-courts> accessed 10 July 2023

Newton M, 'Russian Data Localization Laws: Enriching "Security" & the Economy' (*The Henry M. Jackson School of International Studies, University of Washington*, 28 February 2018) <https://jsis.washington.edu/news/russian-data-localization-enriching-security-economy/> accessed 10 July 2023

Noyb, 'Is the DPC Actually Stopping Facebook's EU-US Data Transfers?! ..maybe half-way!' (*noyb*, 9 September 2020) <https://noyb.eu/en/dpc-actually-stopping-facebooks-eu-us-data-transfers-maybe-half-way> accessed 10 July 2023

—— '101 Complaints on EU-US transfers filed' (17 August 2020) <https://noyb.eu/en/101-complaints-eu-us-transfers-filed> accessed 10 July 2023

OECD, 'Emerging Privacy Enhancing Technologies: Current Regulatory and Policy Approaches' (2023) OECD Digital Economy Papers No 351 <https://www.oecd.org/publications/emerging-privacy-enhancing-technologies-bf121be4-en.htm> accessed 10 July 2023

Ogus A, *Regulation: Legal Form and Economic Theory* (3rd edn, Clarendon Press 1994)

Ohm P, 'Broken Promises of Privacy: Responding to the Surprising Failure of Anonymization' (2010) 57 UCLA Law Review 1701

Ojanen T, 'Making the Essence of Fundamental Rights Real: The Court of Justice of the European Union Clarifies the Structure of Fundamental Rights under the Charter: ECJ 6 October 2015, Case C-362/14, Maximillian Schrems v Data Protection Commissioner' (2016) 12(2) European Constitutional Law Review 318

Okonjo-Iweala N, 'The WTO's Contribution to the Challenges of Global Commons' (2023) 26(1) Journal of International Economic Law 12

—— 'The Case for Reimagining – Not Abandoning – Globalization' (*Foreign Affairs*, 8 June 2023) <https://www.foreignaffairs.com/world/why-world-still-needs-trade> accessed 10 July 2023

Oostveen M and Irion K, 'The Golden Age of Personal Data: How to Regulate an Enabling Fundamental Right?' in Bakhoum M and others (eds), *Personal Data in Competition, Consumer Protection and Intellectual Property Law: Towards a Holistic Approach?* (Springer 2017)

Orbie J and De Ville F, 'A Boost to Our Economies That Doesn't Cost a Cent: EU Trade Policy Discourse since the Crisis' in Carta C and Morin J-F (eds), *EU Foreign Policy through the Lens of Discourse Analysis: Making Sense of Diversity* (Routledge 2014)

Overbeek J, *Free Trade versus Protectionism* (Edward Elgar Publishing 1999)

Panizzon M, *Good Faith in the Jurisprudence of the WTO: The Protection of Legitimate Expectations, Good Faith Interpretation and Fair Dispute Settlement* (Hart Publishing 2006)

Paolini AJ, 'Foucault, Realism and the Power Discourse in International Relations' (1993) 28(1) Australian Journal of Political Science 98

Papaconstantinou GA, 'The GATS and Financial Regulation: Time to Clear-House?' (2020) 19 World Trade Review 379

Parisi F, 'Positive, Normative and Functional Schools in Law and Economics' (2004) 18 European Journal of Law and Economics 259

Pato, A, 'The Collective Private Enforcement of Data Protection Rights in the EU' (2019) MPI-IAPL Summer School, 3rd edn <https://ssrn.com/abstract=3303228> accessed 10 July 2023

—— 'The National Adaptation of Article 80 GDPR, Towards the Effective Private Enforcement of Collective Data Protection Rights' in McCullagh K, Tambou O, and Bourton S (eds), *National Adaptations of the GDPR* (Collection Open Access Book 2019) <https://wp.me/p6OBGR-3dP> accessed 10 July 2023

Pauwelyn J, 'The WTO in Crisis: Five Fundamentals Reconsidered' (*WTO*, 2012) <https://www.wto.org/english/forums_e/public_forum12_e/art_pf12_e/art9.htm#:~:text=WTO%20%7C%20The%20WTO%20in%20Crisis%3A%20Five%20Fundamentals%20Reconsidered&text=In%20times%20of%20severe%20crisis,so%20as%20to%20provoke%20discussion> accessed 10 July 2023

Peloquin D and others, 'Disruptive and Avoidable: GDPR Challenges to Secondary Research Uses of Data' (2020) 28 European Journal of Human Genetics 697

PEN America, 'Chilling Effects: NSA Surveillance Drives U.S. Writers to Self-Censor' (2013) Report <https://pen.org/wp-content/uploads/2022/08/2014-08-01_Full-Report_Chilling-Effects-w-Color-cover-UPDATED.pdf> accessed 10 July 2023

Peng S, 'Cybersecurity Threats and the WTO National Security Exceptions' (2015) 18(2) Journal of International Economic Law 449

Penney JW, 'Chilling Effects: Online Surveillance and Wikipedia Use' (2016) 31(1) Berkeley Technology Law Journal 117

Perju VF, 'On Uses and Misuses of Human Rights in European Constitutionalism' in Vöneky S and Neumann GL (eds), *Human Rights, Democracy, and Legitimacy in a World in Disorder* (CUP 2017)

Petersmann E-U, 'Human Rights and International Economic Law in the 21st Century' (2001) 4(1) Journal of International Economic Law 3

Petkova B, 'Towards an Internal Hierarchy of Values in the EU Legal Order: Balancing the Freedom of Speech and Data Privacy' (2016) 23(3) Maastricht Journal of European and Comparative Law 421

—— 'Privacy as Europe's First Amendment ' (2019) 25(2) European Law Journal 140

Pinchis-Paulsen M, 'Let's Agree to Disagree: A Strategy for Trade-Security' (2022) 25 Journal of International Economic Law 527

Pinchis-Paulsen M, 'Trade Multilateralism and U.S. National Security: The Making of the GATT Security Exceptions' (2020) 41(1) Michigan Journal of International Law 109

Polčák R and Svantesson DJB, *Information Sovereignty: Data Privacy, Sovereign Powers and the Rule of Law* (Edward Elgar 2017)

Pollicino O and Bassini M, 'Bridge Is Down, Data Truck Can't Get Through... A Critical View of the Schrems Judgment in the Context of European Constitutionalism' in Ziccardi Capaldo G (eds), *The Global Community Yearbook of International Law and Jurisprudence* (OUP 2017)

Porcedda MG, 'On Boundaries: Finding the Essence of the Right to the Protection of Personal Data' in Leenes R and others (eds), *Privacy and Data Protection: The Internet of Bodies* (Hart Publishing 2018)

Posner RA, 'Wealth Maximization Revisited' (1985) 2 Notre Dame Journal of Law, Ethics and Public Policy 85

—— *Economic Analysis of Law* (9th edn, Wolters Kluwer Law 2014)

Potjewijd G and others, 'Mass Damage Claims for GDPR Infringements: A Multi-Jurisdictional Perspective' (2021) 1 Mass Claims 5

Propp K and Swire P, 'After Schrems II: A Proposal to Meet the Individual Redress Challenge' (*Lawfare Blog*, 13 August 2020) <https://www.lawfareblog.com/after-schrems-ii-proposal-meet-individual-redress-challenge> accessed 10 July 2023

—— 'The EU's Proposed Data Act: Regulating International Flows of Non-Personal Data' (*Cross-Border Data Forum*, 11 May 2022) <https://www.crossborderdataforum.org/the-eus-proposed-data-act-regulating-international-flows-of-non-personal-data/> accessed 10 July 2023

—— 'Cultivating Europe's Data Garden' (*Lawfare Blog*, 4 March 2022) <https://www.lawfareblog.com/cultivating-europes-data-garden> accessed 10 July 2023

—— 'More than Adequate: New Directions in International Data Transfer Governance' (2023) Atlantic Council <https://www.atlanticcouncil.org/wp-content/uploads/2023/06/More-than-Adequate-New-Directions-in-International-Data-Transfer-Governance_-_FINAL.pdf> accessed 10 July 2023

Purtova N, 'The Law of Everything: Broad Concept of Personal Data and Future of EU Data Protection Law' (2018) 10(1) Law, Innovation and Technology 40

Quelle C, 'Does the Risk-Based Approach to Data Protection Conflict with the Protection of Fundamental Rights on a Conceptual Level?' (2015) <https://ssrn.com/abstract=2726073> accessed 10 July 2023

—— 'Privacy, Proceduralism and Self-Regulation in Data Protection Law' (2017) Teoria Critica della Regolazione Sociale <https://ssrn.com/abstract=3139901> accessed 10 July 2023

—— 'The "Risk Revolution" in EU Data Protection Law: We Can't Have Our Cake and Eat It, Too' (2017) Tilburg Law School Legal Studies Research Paper Series No 17/2017 <http://ssrn.com/abstract=3000382> accessed 10 July 2023

—— 'Enhancing Compliance under the General Data Protection Regulation: The Risky Upshot of the Accountability and Risk-based Approach' (2018) 9(3) European Journal of Risk Regulation 502

Rangel D, 'WTO General Exceptions: Trade Law's Faulty Ivory Tower. Only Two of 48 Attempts to Use the World Trade Organization's GATT Article XX/GATS Article XIV "General Exceptions" Have Ever Succeeded' (2022) Public Citizen's Global Trade Watch <https://www.citizen.org/wp-content/uploads/WTO-General-Exceptions-Paper_-1.pdf> accessed 10 July 2023

Regan DH, 'The Meaning of 'Necessary' in GATT Article XX and GATS Article XIV: The Myth of Cost-Benefit Balancing' (2007) 6(3) World Trade Review 347

Regan PM, *Legislating Privacy: Technology, Social Values, and Public Policy* (The University of North Carolina Press 1995)

Reid E, *Balancing Human Rights, Environmental Protection and International Trade: Lessons from the EU Experience* (Hart Publishing 2015)

Reidenberg JR, 'Lex Informatica: The Formulation of Information Policy Rules through Technology' (1998) 76 Texas Law Review 553

—— 'Resolving Conflicting International Data Privacy Rules in Cyberspace' (2000) 52 Stanford Law Review 1315

—— 'E-Commerce and Trans-Atlantic Privacy' (2001) 38 Houston Law Review 717

Reyes CL, 'WTO-Compliant Protection of Fundamental Rights: Lessons from the EU Privacy Directive' (2011) 12 Melbourne Journal of International Law 1 <https://law.unimelb.edu.au/__data/assets/pdf_file/0010/1686934/Reyes.pdf> accessed 10 July 2023

Richards NM and Hartzog W, 'Taking Trust Seriously in Privacy Law' (2016) 19 Stanford Technology Law Review 431

—— 'Privacy's Trust Gap: A Review ' (2017) 126(4) The Yale Law Journal 1180

Riffel C, 'The Chapeau: Stringent Threshold or Good Faith Requirement' (2018) 45(2) Legal Issues of Economic Integration 141

Riis N, 'Shaping the field of EU Data Law' (2023) 14(1) JIPITEC 54

Roberts A, Moraes HC, and Ferguson V, 'Toward a Geoeconomic Order in International Trade and Investment' (2019) 22(4) Journal of International Economic Law 655

Roberts H and others, 'Safeguarding European Values with Digital Sovereignty: An Analysis of Statements and Policies' (2021) 10(3) Internet Policy Review 1

Robinson J, 'What Are the Questions?' (1977) 15(4) Journal of Economic Literature 1318

Rockwell K, 'Recent WTO Ruling against the United States Highlights Challenges in Dispute Resolution' (*Wilson Center*, 15 December 2022) <https://www.wilsoncenter.org/blog-post/recent-wto-ruling-against-united-states-highlights-challenges-dispute-resolution> accessed 10 July 2023

Rodotà S, 'Data Protection as a Fundamental Right' in Gutwirth S and others (eds), *Reinventing Data Protection?* (Springer 2009)

Rodrik D, *The Globalization Paradox: Democracy and the Future of the World Economy* (W. W. Norton & Company 2011)

—— 'What Do Trade Agreements Really Do?' (2018) 32(2) The Journal of Economic Perspectives 73

Romer P, 'The Dismal Kingdom: Do Economists Have Too Much Power?' (*Foreign Affairs*, 11 February 2020) <https://www.foreignaffairs.com/reviews/dismal-kingdom> accessed 10 July 2023

Roth P, 'Adequate Level of Data Protection in Third Countries Post-Schrems and under the General Data Protection Regulation' (2017) 25(1) Journal of Law, Information and Science 49

Rouvroy A and Poullet Y, 'The Right to Informational Self-Determination and the Value of Self-Development: Reassessing the Importance of Privacy for Democracy' in Gutwirth S and others (eds), *Reinventing Data Protection?* (Springer 2009)

Ruggie JG, 'International Regimes, Transactions, and Change: Embedded Liberalism in the Postwar Economic Order (1982) 36(2) International Organization 379

Saez C, 'E-Commerce: Some Developing Countries Push Back on Idea of New WTO Rules' (*Tralac*, 2 October 2017) <https://www.tralac.org/news/article/12207-e-commerce-some-developing-countries-push-back-on-idea-of-new-wto-rules.html> accessed 10 July 2023

Salvatore D, 'Protectionism and World Welfare: Introduction' in Salvatore D (ed) *Protectionism and World Welfare* (CUP 1993)

Satariano A and Stevis-Gridneff M, 'Big Tech Turns Its Lobbyists Loose on Europe, Alarming Regulators' (*The New York Times*, 14 December 2020) <https://www.nytimes.com/2020/12/14/technology/big-tech-lobbying-europe.html> accessed 10 July 2023

Scarcello O, 'Preserving the 'Essence' of Fundamental Rights under Article 52(1) of the Charter: A Sisyphean Task?' (2020) 16(4) European Constitutional Law Review 647

Schäfer H-B and Ott C, *The Economic Analysis of Civil Law* (1st edn, Edward Elgar Publishing 2004)

Schill S and Vidigal G, 'National Security, Private Actors, and Political Risk: Judicial and Non-Judicial Responses – An Introduction' (2021) 22 Journal of World Investment and Trade 503

Schloemann HL and Ohlhoff S, '"Constitutionalization" and Dispute Settlement in the WTO: National Security as an Issue of Competence' (1999) 93(2) American Journal of International Law 424

Schmidtz D, 'Adam Smith on the Dark Side of Capitalism' (2013) 11 Georgetown Journal of Law & Public Policy 371

Schulhofer SJ, 'An International Right to Privacy? Be Careful What You Wish For' (2016) 14(1) International Journal of Constitutional Law 238

Schütte L and Dijkstra H, 'The Show Must Go On: The EU's Quest to Sustain Multilateral Institutions since 2016' (2023) 61(5) Journal of Common Market Studies 1–19

Schwartz PM, 'Privacy and Democracy in Cyberspace' (1999) 52 Vanderbilt Law Review 1609

—— 'Property, Privacy, and Personal Data' (2004) 117 Harvard Law Review 2056

—— 'Managing Global Data Privacy: Cross-Border Information Flows in a Networked Environment' (2009) Report from the Privacy Projects <https://paulschwartz.net/wp-content/uploads/2019/01/Global_Data_Flows.pdf> accessed 13 July 2023

—— 'The EU-U.S. Privacy Collision: A Turn to Institutions and Procedures' (2013) 126 Harvard Law Review 1966

—— 'Global Data Privacy: The EU Way' (2019) 94(4) New York University Law Review 771

—— and Solove DJ, 'The PII Problem: Privacy and a New Concept of Personally Identifiable Information' (2011) 86 New York University Law Review 1814
—— and Solove DJ, 'Reconciling Personal Information in the United States and European Union' (2014) 102(4) California Law Review 877
—— and Peifer K-N, 'Transatlantic Data Privacy Law' (2017) 106 Georgetown Law Journal 115
Selby J, 'Data Localization Laws: Trade Barriers or Legitimate Responses to Cybersecurity Risks, or Both?' (2017) 25(3) International Journal of Law and Information Technology 213
Semertzi A, 'The Preclusion of Direct Effect in the Recently Concluded EU Free Trade Agreements' (2014) 51(4) Common Market Law Review 1125
Semmel B, *The Rise of Free Trade Imperialism: Classical Political Economy, the Empire of Free Trade and Imperialism* (CUP 1970)
Sen N, 'Understanding the Role of the WTO in International Data Flows: Taking the Liberalization or the Regulatory Autonomy Path?' (2018) 21(2) Journal of International Economic Law 323
Seubert S and Becker C, 'The Democratic Impact of Strengthening European Fundamental Rights in the Digital Age: The Example of Privacy Protection' (2021) German Law Journal 22(1) 31
Shaffer G, 'Globalization and Social Protection: The Impact of EU and International Rules in the Ratcheting Up of U.S. Privacy Standards' (2000) 25 Yale Journal of International Law 1
—— 'A Structural Theory of WTO Dispute Settlement: Why Institutional Choice Lies at the Center of the GMO Case' (2008) 41 JILP 1
Shambaugh D, 'China's Soft-Power Push: The Search for Respect' (2015) 94(4) Foreign Affairs 99
Shavell S, *Foundations of Economic Analysis of Law* (Belknap Press 2004)
Sherman J, 'New Bill Proposes Banning TikTok in the U.S.' (*Lawfare*, 28 December 2022) <https://www.lawfareblog.com/new-bill-proposes-banning-tiktok-us> accessed 10 July 2023
Siles-Brügge G, 'Resisting Protectionism after the Crisis: Strategic Economic Discourse and the EU–Korea Free Trade Agreement' (2011) 16(5) New Political Economy 627
—— 'The Power of Economic Ideas: A Constructivist Political Economy of EU Trade Policy' (2013) 9(4) Journal of Contemporary European Research 597
Simchak S, 'Financial Services International Trade Jurisprudence: Revisiting the Prudential Exception and Its Implications for Indonesia' (2022) 25 Currents: Journal of International Economic Law 42
Singh P, 'Aadhaar and Data Privacy: Biometric Identification and Anxieties of Recognition in India' (2021) 24(7) Information, Communication & Society 978
Smith A, 'Of the Balance of Trade' in Edwin Cannan (ed), *Lectures on Justice, Police, Revenue and Arms* (Clarendon Press 1869)
—— 'Of the Opinion That No Expense at Home Can Be Hurtful' in Edwin Cannan (ed), *Lectures on Justice, Police, Revenue and Arms* (Clarendon Press 1869)
Smits JM, The Mind and Method of the Legal Academic (Edward Elgar 2012)
Spiekermann-Hoff S and others, 'The Challenges of Personal Data Markets and Privacy' (2015) 25 (2) Electronic Markets 161
Stigler GJ, 'The Theory of Economic Regulation' (1971) 2(1) The Bell Journal of Economics and Management Science 3
Stiglitz JE, *Globalization and Its Discontents Revisited* (W.W. Norton & Company 2018)
Strange S, 'Protectionism and World Politics' (1985) 39(2) International Organization 233

Streinz T, 'International Economic Law's Regulation of Data as a Resource for the Artificial Intelligence Economy' in Peng Lin, S-F, and Streinz T (eds), *Artificial Intelligence and International Economic Law* (CUP 2021)

Stupp C, 'Lawmakers Rebuke US 'Digital Protectionism' Charges' (*Euractiv*, 24 September 2015) <https://www.euractiv.com/section/digital/news/lawmakers-rebuke-us-digital-protectionism-charges/> accessed 10 July 2023

—— 'Commission Conducting Review of All Foreign Data Transfer Deals' (*Euractiv*, 9 November 2017)<https://www.euractiv.com/section/data-protection/news/commission-conducting-review-of-all-foreign-data-transfer-deals/> accessed 10 July 2023

Sugimoto T, Kawashima A, and Aaron T, 'A New Era for Japanese Data Protection: 2020 Amendments to the APPI' (*Future of Privacy Forum*, 13 April 2021) <https://fpf.org/blog/a-new-era-for-japanese-data-protection-2020-amendments-to-the-appi/> accessed 10 July 2023

Sunstein C, *After the Rights Revolution: Reconceiving the Regulatory State* (Harvard UP 1993)

Svantesson DJB, 'Privacy, Internet and Transborder Data Flows: An Australian Perspective' (2010) 4(1) Masaryk University Journal of Law and Technology 1

—— 'The Regulation of Cross-Border Data Flows' (2011) 1(3) International Data Privacy Law 180

Swire P, 'The Data Protection Commissioner and Facebook Ireland Limited and Maximillian Schrems. Affidavit of Peter Swire' (2016) 18-2 Georgia Tech Scheller College of Business Research Paper <https://ssrn.com/abstract=3097444> accessed on 23 July 2023

—— 'Schrems II' Backs the European Legal Regime into a Corner: How Can It Get Out?' (*International Association of Privacy Professionals*, 16 July 2020) <https://iapp.org/news/a/schrems-ii-backs-the-european-legal-regime-into-a-corner-how-can-it-get-out/> accessed 10 July 2023

—— and Litan RE, *None of Your Business: World Data Flows, Electronic Commerce, and the European Privacy Directive* (Brookings Institution Press 1988)

Sykes AO, 'Regulatory Protection and the Law of International Trade' (1999) 66(1) The University of Chicago Law Review 1

—— 'Economic 'Necessity' in International Law' (2015) 109(2) American Journal of International Law 296

Syrpis P, 'The Relationship between Primary and Secondary Law in the EU' (2019) 52(2) Common Market Law Review 461

Tarullo DK, 'Logic, Myth, and the International Economic Order' (1985) 26 Harvard Law Review 533

—— 'Beyond Normalcy in the Regulation of International Trade' (1987) 100(3) Harvard Law Review 546

Taylor L, 'What Is Data Justice: The Case for Connecting Digital Rights and Freedoms Globally' (2017) 4(2) Big Data and Society 1

Tene O and Polonetsky J, 'Big Data for All: Privacy and User Control in the Age of Analytics' (2013) 11(5) Northwestern Journal of Technology and Intellectual Property 239

Thang VN, 'Applicability of GATS Prudential Exception to Insurance Services: Some Interpretative Issues' (2007) 4(2) Manchester Journal of International Economic Law 88

The White House, 'Consumer Data Privacy in a Networked World: Framework for Protecting Privacy and Promoting Innovation in the Global Digital Economy' (*The White House*, February 2012) <https://www.hsdl.org/?view&did=700959> accessed 10 July 2023

Thrush G and Maheshwari S, 'Justice Dept. Investigating TikTok's Owner over Possible Spying on Journalists' (*The New York Times*, 17 March 2023) <https://www.nytimes.com/2023/03/17/us/politics/tik-tok-spying-justice-dept.html> accessed 10 July 2023

Tielemans J, Cooper D, and Maldoff G, 'EDPB's Data Transfer Recommendations Adopt a Risk-Based Approach With Teeth' (*IAPP*, 22 June 2021) <https://iapp.org/news/a/edpbs-data-transfer-recommendations-adopt-a-risk-based-approach-with-teeth/> accessed 10 July 2023

Tranberg CB, 'Proportionality and Data Protection in the Case Law of the European Court of Justice' (2011) 1(4) International Data Privacy Law 239

Trebilcock MJ, Howse R, and Eliason A, *The Regulation of International Trade* (4th edn, Routledge 2013)

Tsai JY and others, 'The Effect of Online Privacy Information on Purchasing Behavior: An Experimental Study' (2011) 22(2) Information Systems Research 254

Tucker CE, 'Social Networks, Personalized Advertising, and Privacy Controls' (2014) 51(5) Journal of Marketing Research 546

Tumlir J, *Protectionism: Trade Policy in Democratic Societies* (American Enterprise Institute for Public Policy Research 1985)

Turner J, *Robot Rules: Regulating Artificial Intelligence* (Palgrave Macmillan 2019)

Twining W, 'Normative and Legal Pluralism: A Global Perspective' (2010) 20(3) Duke Journal of Comparative and International Law 473

Tzanou M, *The Fundamental Right to Data Protection, Normative Value in the Context of Counter-Terrorism Surveillance* (Hart Publishing 2017)

Tzanou M and Vogiatzoglou P, 'In Search of Legal Certainty Regarding 'Effective Redress' in International Data Transfers: Unpacking the Conceptual Complexities and Clarifying the Substantive Requirements' (2023) 16(1) Review of European Administrative Law Review 11

UNCTAD, 'World Investment Report: Investment and the Digital Economy' (2017) UNCTAD/WIR/2017 <https://unctad.org/system/files/official-document/wir2017_en.pdf> accessed 10 July 2023

—— 'Digital Economy Report 2019: Value Creation and Capture: Implications for Developing Countries' (2019) UNCTAD/DER/2019 <https://unctad.org/en/PublicationsLibrary/der2019_en.pdf> accessed 10 July 2023

—— 'Digital Economy Report. Cross-border Data Flows and Development: For Whom the Data Flow' (2021) <https://unctad.org/system/files/official-document/der2021_en.pdf> accessed 10 July 2023

Van den Bossche P and Zdouc W, *The Law and Policy of the World Trade Organization: Text, Cases, and Materials* (3rd edn, CUP 2013)

Van Dijk TA, 'Ideology and Discourse Analysis' (2007) 11(2) Journal of Political Ideologies 115

Van Eijk N, Hoofnagle C, and Kannekens E, 'Unfair Commercial Practices: A Complementary Approach to Privacy Protection' (2017) 3(3) European Data Protection Law Review 325

van Eijk R and Zanfir-Fortuna G, 'Schrems II: Article 49 GDPR Derogations May Not Be so Narrow and Restrictive after All?' (*FPF Blog*, 4 February 2021) <https://fpf.org/blog/schrems-ii-article-49-gdpr-derogations-may-not-be-so-narrow-and-restrictive-after-all/> accessed 10 July 2023

Van Elsuwege P, 'Judicial Review and the Common Foreign and Security Policy: Limits to the Gap-Filling Role of the Court of Justice' (2021) 58(6) Common Market Law Review 1731

Van Gestel R, Micklitz H-W, and Maduro MP, 'Methodology in the New Legal World' (2012) EUI Working Papers LAW No 2012/13 <https://ssrn.com/abstract=2069872> accessed 10 July 2023

Van Hoboken J, 'The European Approach to Privacy' (TPRC Conference, Schertz, August 2014) <https://ssrn.com/abstract=2418636> accessed 13 July 2023

—— 'Case Note, CJEU 13 May 2014, C-131/12 (Google Spain)' (2014) EHRC <https://ssrn.com/abstract=2495580> accessed 10 July 2023

— Arnbak A, and van Eijk NANM, 'Obscured by Clouds or How to Address Governmental Access to Cloud Data from Abroad' (Privacy Law Scholars Conference, Berkeley, 2013) 28 <https://ssrn.com/abstract=2276103> accessed 13 July 2023

Vedaschi A, 'Privacy and Data Protection versus National Security in Transnational Flights: The EU–Canada PNR Agreement' (2018) 8(2) International Data Privacy Law 124

Velli F, 'The Issue of Data Protection in EU Trade Commitments: Cross-Border Data Transfers in GATS and Bilateral Free Trade Agreements' (2019) 4(3) European Papers 881

Venzke I, 'Making General Exceptions: The Spell of Precedents in Developing Art XX GATT into Standards for Domestic Regulatory Policy' (2011) 12(5) German Law Journal 1111

—— *How Interpretation Makes International Law: On Semantic Change and Normative Twists* (OUP 2012)

—— 'International Law and the Spectre of Inequality' (2019) Inaugural Lecture no. 607 University of Amsterdam < https://dare.uva.nl/search?identifier=a4b88a14-4772-4974-8123-346689262258> accessed 10 July 2023

Verhoosel G, *National Treatment and WTO Dispute Settlement: Adjudicating the Boundaries of Regulatory Autonomy* (Hart Publishing 2002)

Vermeule A, 'Connecting Positive and Normative Legal Theory' (2007) 10 University of Pennsylvania Journal of Constitutional Law 387

Vermulst E and Driessen B, 'An Overview of the WTO Dispute Settlement System and Its Relationship with the Uruguay Round Agreements' (1995) 29(2) Journal of World Trade 131

Vidigal G, 'WTO Adjudication and the Security Exception: Something Old, Something New, Something Borrowed – Something Blue?' (2019) 46(3) Legal Issues of Economic Integration 203

Von Bogdandy A, 'The Past and Promise of Doctrinal Constructivism: A Strategy for Responding to the Challenges Facing Constitutional Scholarship in Europe' (2009) 7(3) International Journal of Constitutional Law 364

—— and Windsor J, 'Annex on Financial Services' in Wolfrum R, Stoll P-T, and Feinäugle C (eds), *WTO – Trade in Services – Max Planck Commentaries on World Trade Law* (Martinus Nijhoff Publishers 2008)

—— and others, 'Reverse Solange: Protecting the Essence of Fundamental Rights against EU Member States' (2012) 49(2) Common Market Law Review 489

—— and Venzke I, *In Whose Name? A Public Law Theory of International Adjudication* (OUP 2014)

Wagener T, 'Scholars Identify Costs from EU Digital Agenda' (*Disruptive Competition Project*, 15 December 2022) <https://www.project-disco.org/european-union/121522early-alert-for-eu-digital-protectionism/> accessed 10 July 2023

Wai R, 'Countering, Branding, Dealing: Using Economic and social Rights in and around the International Trade Regime' (2003) 14(1) European Journal of International Law 35

Waldman AE, *Industry Unbound: The Inside Story of Privacy, Data, and Corporate Power* (CUP 2021)

Walker K, 'The Costs of Privacy' (2001) 25(1) Harvard Journal of Law & Public Policy 87, 102

Wang C, 'Invocation of National Security Exceptions under GATT Article XXI: Jurisdiction to Review and Standard of Review' (2019) 18(3) Chinese Journal of International Law 695

Wang E, 'China's Kunlun Tech Agrees to U.S. Demand to Sell Grindr Gay Dating App' (*Reuters*, 13 May 2019) <https://www.reuters.com/article/us-grindr-m-a-beijingkunlun-idUSKCN1SJ28N> accessed 10 July 2023

Wang H, 'Contextualising China's Call for Disclosure Power in International Politics' (2015) 13(3) China: An International Journal 172

Wasastjerna MC, 'The Role of Big Data and Digital Privacy in Merger Review' (2018) 2(3) European Competition Journal 417

Wathieu L and Friedman A, 'An Empirical Approach to Understanding Privacy Valuation' (2007) Harvard Business School Working Paper No 07-075 <https://www.hbs.edu/faculty/Publication%20Files/07-075.pdf> accessed 10 July 2023

Weber RH, 'Regulatory Autonomy and Privacy Standards under the GATS' (2012) 7(1) Asian Journal of WTO & International Health Law & Policy 25

—— and Staiger D, *Transatlantic Data Protection in Practice* (Springer 2017)

Weiler JHH, 'The Rule of Lawyers and the Ethos of Diplomats: Reflections on the Internal and External Legitimacy of WTO Dispute Settlement' (2001) 35(2) Journal of World Trade 191

—— 'Law, Culture, and Values in the WTO: Gazing into the Crystal Ball' in Bethlehem D and others (eds), *The Oxford Handbook of International Trade Law* (OUP 2009)

—— 'Dialogical Epilogue' in Weiler J and De Búrca G (eds) *The Worlds of European Constitutionalism* (CUP 2012)

Weinrib J, 'The Essence of Rights and the Limits of Proportionality. The Promise of Legality: Critical Reflections upon the Work of TRS Allan' (2023) (forthcoming) <https://ssrn.com/abstract=4321570> accessed 10 July 2023

Weiß W, 'Delegation to Treaty Bodies in EU Agreements: Constitutional Constraints and Proposals for Strengthening the European Parliament' (2018) 14 European Constitutional Law Review 532

Westin RA, *Environmental Tax Initiatives and Multilateral Trade Agreements: Dangerous Collisions* (Kluwer Law International 1997)

Wethington OL, *Financial Market Liberalization: The Nafta Framework* (Sheppard's McGraw Hill 1994)

White M, 'Preaching to the Choir: A response to Kaplow and Shavell's Fairness versus Welfare' (2004) 16(4) Review of Political Economy 507

Whitman JQ, 'The Two Western Cultures of Privacy: Dignity versus Liberty' (2004) 113(6) Yale Law Journal 1151

Whitt RS, 'The Politics of Procedure: An Examination of the GATT Dispute Settlement Panel and the Article XX Defense in the Context of the U.S. Embargo of Nicaragua' (1987) 19(3) Law & Policy in International Business 603

Willemyns I, 'Agreement Forthcoming? A Comparison of EU, US, and Chinese RTAs in Times of Plurilateral E-Commerce Negotiations' (2020) 23 Journal of International Economic Law 221

—— *Digital Services in International Trade Law* (CUP 2021)

Williams RD, 'In the Balance: The Future of America's National Security and Innovation Ecosystem' (*Lawfare Blog*, 30 November 2018) <https://www.lawfareblog.com/balance-future-americas-national-security-and-innovation-ecosystem> accessed 10 July 2023

—— 'Reflections on TikTok and Data Privacy as National Security' (*Lawfare Blog*, 15 November 2019) https://www.lawfareblog.com/reflections-tiktok-and-data-privacy-national-security> accessed 10 July 2023
Wolf C, 'Delusions of Adequacy? Examining the Case for Finding the United States Adequate for Cross-Border EU-U.S. Data Transfers' (2014) 43 Washington University Journal of Law & Policy 227
Wolfe R, 'Learning about Digital Trade: Privacy and E-commerce in CETA and TPP' (2019) 18(S1) World Trade Review s63
World Economic Forum, 'Rethinking Personal Data: A New Lens for Strengthening Trust' (May 2014) Industry Agenda <http://www3.weforum.org/docs/WEF_RethinkingPersonalData_ANewLens_Report_2014.pdf> accessed 10 July 2023
Wunsch-Vincent S, 'The Digital Trade Agenda of the U.S.: Parallel Tracks of Bilateral, Regional and Multilateral Liberalization' (2003) 58(1) Aussenwirtschaft 7 <https://dx.doi.org/10.2139/ssrn.393961> accessed 10 July 2023
Yakovleva S, 'Should Fundamental Rights to Privacy and Data Protection Be a Part of the EU's International Trade "Deals"?' (2018) 17(3) World Trade Review 477
—— 'GDPR Transfer Rules vs Rules on Territorial Scope: A Critical Reflection on Recent EDPB Guidelines from both EU and International Trade Law Perspectives' (*European Law Blog*, 9 December 2021) <https://europeanlawblog.eu/2021/12/09/gdpr-transfer-rules-vs-rules-on-territorial-scope-a-critical-reflection-on-recent-edpb-guidelines-from-both-eu-and-international-trade-law-perspectives/> accessed 10 July 2023
—— 'On Digital Sovereignty, New European Data Rules, and the Future of Free Data Flows' (2022) 49(4) Legal Issues of Economic Integration 339
—— 'The EU's Trade Policy on Cross-Border Data Flows in the Global Landscape: Navigating the Thin Line between Liberalizing Digital Trade, "Digital Sovereignty" and Multilateralism' in Fahey E and Mancini I (eds), *Understanding the EU as a Good Global Actor* (Edward Elgar 2022)
—— 'Meet the Author Event: Territorial Scope and Data Transfer Rules in the GDPR' (*YouTube*, 20 January 2022) at 17:30 <https://youtu.be/OlxQLE4lnrM> accessed 10 July 2023
—— 'Testing Restrictions on Onward Transfers of EU Personal Data against Free Data Flow Obligations in the CPTPP and US-Japan Digital Trade Agreement' (2022) Amsterdam Law School Research Paper No 2023-20, Institute for Information Law Research Paper No 2023-05 <https://ssrn.com/abstract=4423959> accessed 10 July 2023
—— and Irion K, 'The Best of Both Worlds? Free Trade in Services and EU Law on Privacy and Data Protection' (2016) 2 European Data Protection Law Review 191
Yang AYP, 'The Evolving Prudential Exceptions in Regional Trade Agreements' (2018) 13(2) Asian Journal of WTO & International Health Law and Policy 395
Yokoi-Arai M, '"GATS" Prudential Carve Out in Financial Services and Its Relation with Prudential Regulation' (2008) 57(3) International & Comparative Law Quarterly 613
Yoo JY and Ahn D, 'Security Exceptions in the WTO System: Bridge or Bottle-Neck for Trade and Security?' (2016) 19(2) Journal of International Economic Law 417
Young AR and Peterson J, *Parochial Global Europe: 21st Century Trade Politics* (OUP 2014)
Zalnieriute M, 'Big Brother Watch and Others v. the United Kingdom (Case Review)' (2022) 116(3) American Journal of International Law 585
Zang D, 'Divided by Common Language: "Capture" Theories in GATT/WTO and the Communicative Impasse' (2009) 32(2) Hastings International and Comparative Law Review 423

Zedalis RJ, 'A Commentary on US 'National Security' Import Restraints: The Situation with Crude Oil' (2019) 53(1) Journal of World Trade 83

Ziegler AR and Baumgartner J, 'Good Faith as a General Principle of (International) Law' in Mitchell AD, Sornarajah M, and Voon T (eds), *Good Faith and International Economic Law* (OUP 2015)

Zuboff S, 'Big Other: Surveillance Capitalism and the Prospects of an Information Civilization' (2015) 30(1) Journal of Information Technology 75

—— *The Age of Surveillance Capitalism: The Fight for a Human Future at the New Frontier of Power* (Public Affairs 2019)

Index

For the benefit of digital users, indexed terms that span two pages (e.g., 52–53) may, on occasion, appear on only one of those pages.

Tables and figures are indicated by *t* and *f* following the page number